ESSENTIALS OF LEARNING

ROBERT M. W. TRAVERS

Western Michigan University

ESSENTIALS OF LEARNING

FOURTH EDITION

Macmillan Publishing Co., Inc.
NEW YORK

Collier Macmillan Publishers
LONDON

Macmillan Publishing Co., Inc.
866 Third Avenue, New York, New York 10022

Collier Macmillan Canada, Ltd.

Library of Congress Cataloging in Publication Data

Travers, Robert Morris William, (date)
  Essentials of learning.

  Bibliography: p.
  Includes indexes.
  1. Learning, Psychology of. I. Title.
LB1051.T68   1977   370.15'2   76–4962
ISBN 0–02–421350–0

Printing: 2 3 4 5 6 7 8   Year: 8 9 0 1 2 3

PREFACE

The fourth edition of this book reflects new trends in thought related to human learning. During the last few years the new ideas related to Piaget and his associates at Geneva have had a spectacular rise to prominence. Although Piaget has long had a pre-eminent position among European psychologists, his impact on American thought and practice has been relatively recent. His influence on American psychology, as well as American education, has now reached a level that justifies assigning a substantial section of this book to his discoveries. Indeed, Piaget may well become the dominant influence on American education during the next decade. The slowness of his impact in America is largely due to the profound and scholarly style of his writing and to his lack of interest in promoting his work.

Another important reason why Piaget's work was so slow in becoming accepted here is that behavioral research has always been an extremely parochial enterprise. Psychologists in one country rarely embrace the ideas of psychologists in other countries, partly because of the language barrier and partly because the psychology of a particular country is so often closely tied to its political and philosophical position. Thus Russian psychologists have fitted the work of Pavlov into a Marxian framework, and the work of Skinner and his followers fits a capitalistic society, in which money reinforcements are believed to be all-important in controlling behavior. Piaget comes from a still different tradition, which must be identified with the work of Rousseau and Pestalozzi, and the other great Genevese thinkers.

The liberal tradition of education, found in the work of Piaget, has an important point of contact with American traditions in the American belief that the individual is a free-thinking rational agent with enormous capacities for inventing solutions to problems. It is this aspect of Piaget that makes him culturally acceptable to Americans and enables American educators to see him as part of the great tradition of Horace Mann, John Dewey, and the progressive education movement of the 1930s.

When the first edition of this book appeared in 1963, interest was focused on operant psychology, which at that time promised to produce a revolution in every phase of applied psychology. But though operant psychology has left its mark on the history of psychology, its impact has been far less than its original proponents expected. Perhaps the weakness of the approach of operant psychologists has been that they promised so much and, in terms of their original claims, delivered relatively little. But perhaps only operant psychologists are disappointed. Other psychologists, who take a broader view, are more likely to be impressed with the permanent contribution of operant psychology to the growing body of knowledge about behavior. They will also see operant psychology as having contributed substantial knowledge, particularly to experimental techniques for the study of behavior. Indeed, much research undertaken with infants today could not be undertaken but for the development of operant techniques, though oddly enough such research rarely uses operant ideas concerning the nature of learning. Perhaps the most damaging blows to operant psychology have come through unsuccessful attempts to commercialize it, and by such endeavors as the performance-contracting enterprises in schools in the early 1970s. These enterprises, perhaps because they involved attempts at applying psychology beyond the state of the science, were doomed to failure. Likewise, a large-scale attempt to apply operant psychology to the treatment and rehabilitation of criminals, in the Patuxent project, failed. Such massive failures are likely to produce an unreasonable rejection of all operant research and ideas. For these reasons, a substantial section of this book must still be devoted to operant psychology and the legacy it has left. One cannot present the views of operant psychologists with the same positive optimism with which they were presented in the first edition of this book, but many positive achievements still stand.

The renewed emphasis on cognitive psychology has brought with it an interest in cognitive aspects of motivation and values, conceived of as products of intellectual development. Cognitive psychology has also brought with it a certain skepticism concerning the usefulness of deriving behavioral principles from the behavior of lower animals, and then using them to attempt to understand human behavior. A new generation of psychologists is beginning to view human behavior as distinctively different from that of lower animals, and some of these psychologists believe that only in trivial respects can the behavior of lower animals be compared with that of human beings. Studies across species have become progressively more a means of showing the distinctiveness of the behavior of particular species than a means of discovering general laws valid for describing the behavior of all species.

An emerging new area of the application of psychology, one which merited the inclusion of a new chapter in this edition, is the area of the control of physiological processes by psychological means. This area is not yet well-structured in terms of psychological theory, in that many different approaches to the problem have produced positive results. Classical and operant conditioning and various meditative techniques, some odd bedfellows, have all shown some capacity for producing control over physiological processes. Despite the incongruity of these various approaches, they have here been brought together in a single chapter. The area is far too fascinating to be neglected. In that chapter some attempt has been made to separate what is known from the claims of promoters who sell equipment and courses of instruction. In this area, as in so many others of applied psychology, these promoters have done much to becloud the issues.

With each new edition of this book, the author becomes more overwhelmed with the difficulty of maintaining contact with an ever-expanding body of related research. The search of the literature between editions now involves some time every day. Of course, as much as 90 per cent of the articles reviewed never find a place in the next edition, but they have to be read and studied. Computerized reviews of the literature have been tried by the author, but this approach fails to determine the significance of a contribution and is therefore unsatisfactory. Actually, identifying the major articles and books is a quite simple matter for one who spends time regularly scanning the literature. Most of the time spent in preparing to write a chapter is devoted to evaluating and not locating the literature.

Rejection of an article for inclusion is rarely for technical inadequacy, but generally because it does not contribute to some significant theme that has been selected for inclusion in the book. This criterion may sometimes exclude important contributions. However, the limitations of book length require that the author exercise some judgment in selection of the content, and such decisions are always subject to honest differences in opinion.

R. M. W. T.

CONTENTS

LIST OF FIGURES

PART I

INTRODUCTION

Chapter 1

Basic Issues in the Study of Learning

The one area of science that has long been considered to hold the key to the improvement of education is the psychology of learning. The hope has been that with the development of a science of learning, children would be able to learn more in less time than was ever possible in the past. Some of the more optimistic predictions about the impact of a science of learning have come from psychologists. These predictions promised that the new science of learning would produce a dramatic revolution in education, but the resulting changes in education have not, in fact, been of this character. They have been slow and continuous, though highly significant, over the last half century. Neither scientist nor layman need be disappointed, however, that the emerging psychology of learning has not produced an educational revolution, for the slow evolution of education that it has produced has been of great importance.

The gradualness of the change in education through the impact of the psychology of learning has made it difficult for a single generation to recognize the changes that have taken place, but excellent descriptions exist of the way schools were run at the turn of the century, and these descriptions make it clear that the intervening years have produced far-reaching changes. When John Dewey founded his experimental school at the University of Chicago in 1896, he had great difficulty in purchasing movable furniture for the classrooms. Today, it would be difficult, if not impossible, to buy the traditional school furniture that was bolted to the floor. The change in the fixtures is one recognition of the fact that flexibility in the physical arrangements of the classroom provides flexiblity in planning instruction. The changes in the appearance of the classroom are but symptomatic of other aspects of the evolution of teaching skill. The child who fails to learn is no longer treated as one who fails because of lack of moral fortitude. Today an effort is made to determine the reasons for the lack of progress of the child who does not learn. It is hard to believe that most teachers at the turn of the century viewed acedemic failure as moral failure— a failure to try hard enough. The instructional materials to which the modern school child is exposed have been carefully designed in terms of what is known about learning, and the level of difficulty of the reading matter has been checked by the application of a readability formula. The subjects that are taught in the modern school have been selected on some basis other than tradition, and none of the subjects are there because of some vague hope that they may discipline the mind. Research undertaken as early as the turn of the century showed that school subjects, believed to provide a magic formula for disciplining the mind, not only had no magic to them, but often antagonized the student to all learning in school. Schools have changed, and much of the change can be attributed to research undertaken on the psychology of learning.

The extraordinary developments in schools that have taken place during the last three quarters of a century have remained unnoticed by most of the public, and research has been given little credit for the educational reform it has brought about. One reason for this is that the young adult, just a few years out of school, is quite unaware of what schools were like two or three generations ago. His limited knowledge makes him concur easily with those who mistakenly, but with a loud voice, claim that the schools are not of the quality they used to be. Another reason for the common failure to recognize progress is that the problems that still remain to be attacked are overwhelmingly great compared with those that have already been solved. Some of the knowledge presented in this volume may suggest solutions to a few of these problems.

There is also another very subtle way in which knowledge of a discipline such as psychology has influenced teaching in the classroom and the entire organization of the school. J. W. Getzels has pointed out on a number of occasions that psychology and the other behavioral sciences develop a conception of man and it is this conception of man that molds the way in which the young are raised. If man is viewed as a creature completely controlled by the circumstances to which he is exposed, then an educational plan must focus on the control of pupil behavior in such a way that appropriate development occurs. Within such a plan there can be no place for decision making on the part of the pupil, because the pupil is not considered to be a system that makes choices for himself. On the other hand, if the pupil is viewed as a system that initiates activity, makes choices and decisions, shows initiative, and is capable of taking responsibility for his own development, the resulting educational program has to be one in which the pupil has freedom to engage in these activities and control by the teacher or the program is minimal. Both conceptions of man can be found in contemporary psychology, and corresponding programs of education can be found across the United States that reflect these points of view.

There are schools in which there is a high degree of planned control over every phase of pupils' activity, and there are also schools in which pupils can exercise choice and decide what they are going to learn at a particular time.

HOW A SCIENCE OF LEARNING IMPROVES EDUCATION

Looking back on nearly three quarters of a century during which a science of psychology has had an impact on schools, one can begin to see how a basic science of behavior exerts its influence. Surprisingly little change can be attributed to direct attempts of psychologists to do research in school settings. Indeed, the three psychologists who have produced the greatest impact on schools—Edward L. Thorndike, B. F. Skinner, and Jean Piaget—never undertook any research in classrooms. Rather their approach was that of developing knowledge in the laboratory. The laboratory knowledge derived by Thorndike was applied to the design of school readers and dictionaries; to the modification of literary works to make them readable for young children; and to the design of procedures for the teaching of arithmetic and algebra, the design of curricula and of testing procedures. The most notable applications of the discoveries of Skinner have been in the development of improved methods of organizing subject matter, the concept of programmed learning, and in reinforcing in skill learning. Piaget's knowledge has had impact on the design of early education programs and science and mathematics programs at higher levels. The very substantial impacts of these psychologists has been possible not because they set out to investigate school problems in school settings, but because they were able to develop fundamental knowledge of learning phenomena through basic research studies conducted in the laboratory. One can contrast their success with the dismal failure of those who, in recent years, have advocated a direct head-on attack on school problems through conducting investigations in school settings. The hundreds of millions of dollars spent on ventures of the latter type have produced far less change in schools than the investigations of a few laboratory scientists, whose work has brought about most of the significant advances during the present century. A crude direct attack on educational problems, massive though it has been, could hardly be expected to produce the kind of revolution in school practice that has already begun to result from skilled laboratory investigation.

Too often the educational practitioner expects that the laboratory scientist will produce prescriptions for effective education that can be readily followed. This is not the case. The early physicists, from Isaac Newton on, did not provide prescriptions that engineers designing bridges could follow on a rule-of-thumb basis, but the knowledge they provided made bridge building a much more systematic and effective procedure than it had been in previous centuries. No longer did the bridge designer have to guess where the main stresses in bridges would occur; these could be determined by applying the principles of physics. The physicists provided the engineers with ways of thinking about bridge design and with some general problem-solving techniques. Physics also provided the engineer with a technical langauge that he could use to describe precisely what happens when a load is applied to a bridge. The bridge builder no longer had to use the vague and fuzzy language of tradition, but was armed with precise ways of describing specifications. Nevertheless, bridge building did not undergo any sudden revolution; the changes in these structures were subtle, more readily noticed by the expert than by the ordinary man.

The impact of a laboratory science of learning has also been slow and subtle, but it has permeated both the curriculum and the entire teaching act. There has been a steady alteration in the approach taken to educational problems. This is partly because the technical language of the laboratory can be used to describe, with infinitely greater precision than was possible in the past, the nature of the difficulties that are being encountered. Unless one can describe precisely what the problems are, one cannot hope to find solutions to them. Problem identification is always a first step toward progress. Although the lay public is not always impressed by the fact that the problems have been identified, for the public wants nothing short of solutions, there is great progress inherent in being able to identify problems clearly and precisely.

One must readily admit that the development of a science of learning has not produced solutions to many of the most pressing educational problems, though research with implications for education has been moving ahead. Twenty-five years ago medicine had reached the point of establishing that some diseases were due to viruses, but our ability to treat virus infections is still extremely limited. Before anything could be done about virus diseases, the discovery had to be made that virus structures existed. The study of the way in which viruses are produced led to an understanding of how the body manages to cope with virus diseases. This knowledge, in turn, has led to some techniques of prevention and, in a few cases, cure after a virus infection has become established. In the same way, educators and scientists together are slowly identifying the causes of educational failure and the keys to educational success, but new practices that will prevent failure and maximize success are in many cases still far off. Progress in education cannot be measured by changes in school alone; rather one must look at the subtle undercurrents where the new tides of educational ideas are formed.

WHAT IS LEARNING?

Although nearly everyone believes that he knows intuitively what is meant by learning, psychologists have long had difficulty in formulating an acceptable definition. A common definition of learning is that it involves a relatively permanent change in behavior as a result of exposure to conditions in the environment. Some psychologists prefer to convey essentially the same idea by saying that learning involves a relatively permanent change in a response R as a result of exposure to stimuli S. The terms *stimulus* and *response* seem to be easily defined, but they are quite slippery terms and difficult to pin down.

This definition of learning places emphasis on observable events, such as responses and situations in the environment, but the actual mechanism of learning lies within the learner, largely within the central nervous system. The mechanism of learning cannot be observed directly, but the evidence that learning has taken place can. One can find out for sure whether a child can undertake long division by giving him a problem that calls for that operation and seeing whether he can carry it out successfuly. If he can, one knows that he has learned the operation of long division, but one may know little about how he learned it. It is quite easy to study the modification of behavior that occurs during learning, but very difficult to find out what goes on inside the learner. Indeed, some psychologists have been so impressed with the difficulties of studying the internal processes of the learner that they have abondoned the attempt. Others believe that only trivial knowledge can be acquired by considering only that which is directly observable and that the underlying mechanism of learning has to be studied.

Learning can be positive or negative. One can learn or unlearn. Positive learning is commonly referred to as acquisition. Negative learning is sometimes referred to as extinction.

The psychologist views the term *learning* as embracing a wider range of phenomena than does the layman, who thinks of it largely in terms of school learning. Let us consider an example that illustrates the broad scope of the psychologist's concept of the term. A person stops his car at a traffic light and, a few seconds later, his car is hit in the rear with almost explosive violence by a truck. The person in the car is badly shaken by the impact and is taken to the hospital in a state of shock, but he recovers from the accident. Two weeks later he stops again at the same intersection and a funny thing happens. He turns white, his heart beats wildly, and he breaks out in a cold sweat. During the next year the same thing happens whenever he comes to the place of his original accident. The psychologist would say that he had *learned* all of these responses at the time when his car was hit by the truck. One can learn visceral and emotional responses just as one can learn academic skills. Such learning is a matter of particular interest to clinical psychologists, who often encounter patients who have acquired unwanted emotional responses and wish to learn to gain control over them.

Learning can occur in slow and subtle ways, and the learner may be quite unaware of it. A person who visits Japan for the first time begins by thinking that all Japanese look alike, but as time goes by he becomes more and more capable of differentiating one Japanese from another. The skill he has acquired is referred to as a perceptual skill and the learning involved perceptual learning. Although the experience of our traveler to Japan is a common one, neither he nor other travelers who have had a similar experience can describe how they learn to differentiate faces in the Orient. However, psychologists engaged in the experimental study of perceptual learning are beginning to understand something about the processes involved.

The definition of learning we have been considering excludes changes produced by fatigue or other transitory conditions, but there are borderline phenomena that may cause one difficulty in deciding whether they should or should not be classified as learning. Let us consider a few of these.

One of the borderline phenomena is known as habituation. A person buys a grandfather clock with a loud tick. The first night he is kept awake by the ticking of the clock. The second night he is less aware of it, and after a few nights he never notices the ticking either by day or by night. He has become habituated. Presumably, this habituation involves a change in the nervous system that blocks the signals from reaching the higher centers. Also, the change is relatively permanent, for he can go away on a vacation and when he returns be able to sleep the first night back and not have lost his habituation. Habituation falls within the commonly accepted definition of learning, but many psychologists refer to it as habituation rather than as learning. This is a matter of custom rather than of any profound knowledge concerning the difference between habituation and other learning phenomena. Habituation is commonly distinguished from more complex forms of learning by referring to the latter as conditioning, but this, in turn, produces difficulties, for some forms of quite complicated perceptual learning also cannot be classified as conditioning.

A second phenomenon that falls on the borderline of the definition of learning is sensitization. Let us illustrate this phenomenon by considering a dog brought to the laboratory for experimentation. The dog is placed in a harness and an experiment is begun that calls for the dog to make a response every time a faint light goes on, but the dog gives no indication that it is capable of responding to the light at all. The experimenter then gives the dog a strong electric shock, and from that point onward the animal shows responsiveness to the light. The shock has had a sensitizing effect, making the animal more responsive to all stimuli in its environment. The effect may be quite permanent in that when the dog is brought back to the laboratory a year later it may still show the same heightened sensitivity to the light. The sensitization is also likely to be specific to the situation in which it has occurred. The dog will not show the same heightened sensitivity in situations outside the laboratory.

Sentitization falls within the definition of learning given here, although, as in the case of habituation, psychologists typically make a distinction between sensitization and more complex forms of learning.

Transitory modifications of behavior are not generally regarded as representing learning. A person who takes a drink at a party and who becomes highly sociable for the duration of the effect of the alcohol is not considered to have learned sociable behavior. The transitory change in his behavior is explained in terms of the temporary removal of inhibitions that ordinarily interfere with his social life. On the other hand, consider the case of a person who has many sessions with a psychological counselor and as a result of the therapy is able to develop a more satisfactory social life, which he continues to pursue long after therapy ceases. Most psychologists would say that such a person had learned more effective social behavior through his contacts with the counselor. The change in behavior is clearly classified as learning.

Although the last two examples provide a fairly clear distinction between a situation in which there is no learning and one in which learning occurs, many situations cannot be so easily classified. Consider the case of a parent who observes that his child hardly ever opens a book and who decides to correct this situation.

He offers his child fifty cents for each book read and tells him that the money will not be given unless he can answer some questions about the book. The scheme works beautifully and during the next two months the child reads ten books, in comparison with zero books during the previous two months. The parent then decides that his child must by now have discovered the inherent rewards of reading and that he can stop offering him money to read. Accordingly, he stops, but during the next two months the child does not read any books at all. The incentive provided by offering money produced a change in performance, but no permanent change was produced in the child's behavior— as is evident from the results of withdrawing the reward. Some psychologists define learning in such a way that the temporary changed performance of the child would be classified as learning. Other psychologists, who define learning as it was earlier defined in the chapter, might say that performance had been temporarily changed but that the child learned from the experiment only that adults sometimes offer rewards and that the same adults are likely to withdraw the rewards arbitrarily. There was certainly no increase in the frequency of reading behavior other than that which was reward-dependent. No permanent change in behavior was evident. Rewards may produce quite transitory or quite permanent changes in behavior depending on the conditions under which they are applied.

Performance is very readily changed by offering money or other rewards, but the production of more permanent changes in behavior is a more difficult matter. In the case of our anecdote, the parent might have done a little better by changing from a condition in which the child was rewarded for every book he read to a condition in which there was only an occasional and unpredictable reward. Even then, one cannot be sure that book reading would have been continued.

THE TWO APPROACHES TO THE SCIENCE OF LEARNING

Most vigorously developing scientific areas are characterized by a multiplicity of approaches to the problems involved. Different approaches often involve different theoretical viewpoints concerning the nature of the phenomena being studied. Only rarely is there only one promising approach, though individual scientists sometime take the position that their particular approach is the only worthwhile one. Scientists, like other human beings, tend to be prejudiced in favor of their own ideas.

The developing science of learning manifests two main approaches at the present time. One approach involves an attempt to discover simple basic forms of learning that, some scientists hope, will constitute the elements of all learning including the most elaborate and sophisticated. The anticipation underlying such an approach is that complex learning, such as is involved in the making of a great discovery, can be reduced to these basic learning elements. Thus psychologists interested in problems of conditioning have long hoped that the learning of even very high-level problem-solving skills could be understood by viewing the process as the learning of perhaps a large number of conditioned responses. This is the *reductionist* position. It attempts to reduce the complex to the simple. The approach is very similar to that of chemists, who have developed their science by first discovering the nature of the chemical elements and then showing how the combination of these elements produces all kinds of substances. The argument is that an approach that has been so successful in the physical sciences should surely have equal success when applied to the study of behavior. Such an argument has persuaded a generation of American psychologists to adopt the reductionist approach and to search for basic elements of behavior.

Other psychologists argue that an approach that may be productive in developing a science of chemistry may not be appropriate for the development of a science of behavior. Piaget (1971, pp. 38–39), for example, has long argued that psychologists have made two major blunders in the development of their science. One was a blunder of the last century involving attempts to interpret the behavior of lower organisms in terms of human behavior. Dogs were assumed to have thinking processes similar to those of human beings and were believed to solve problems by the logical processes that adults use. Birds that mated for life were believed to have all the marital experiences of the human marriage. Such interpretations of animal behavior may seem ridiculous today, but they did not seem to be so a century ago. Virtually all psychologists today avoid the error of interpreting behavior at simple levels in terms of what is known about behavior at complex levels.

Piaget also holds the view that psychologists of the present century make a different but equally serious error that damages their research—that of attempting to interpret complex behavior in terms of simple behavior elements. Piaget argues that it is just as misleading to attempt to interpret complex behavior in terms of the simple as it is to interpret the simple in terms of the complex.

The point can be better understood by looking at an example from outside the field of behavior that illustrates the difficulty of understanding the complex in terms of the simple. There are difficulties in attempting to explain the complex in terms of the simple not only in the behavioral sciences but even in many simpler, mechanical areas. For example, a computer is made up largely of small transistors that are the essential working elements in the system; but a person who wanted to understand how to use a computer to perform particular operations or who wanted to understand the logic of computers would not study transistors. Indeed, experts in the field of computer operation, who can devise ways of making computers perform operations that have never been performed before, may know nothing about the way in which transistors operate. The crucial factor in the operation of computers is the complex interrelationship of the transistors that make possible the performance of elaborate logical and mathematical operations. Understanding the computer in terms of the lawfulness and orderliness of the operations it can perform does not require an understanding of the physics of the transistor. A similar argument in the case of human behavior is that the understanding of complex behavior is not aided by an understanding of simple responses. Complex behavior can conceivably be controlled and predicted without knowing anything about simple behavioral processes such as conditioned reflexes. The latter may be a simple form of learning, but complex learning, it may be argued, cannot be understood in terms of these simple elements. Complex behavior has to be understood in terms of the laws of complex behavior. From this viewpoint, complex behavior, such as that involved in problem solving, can be understood only in terms of laws of behavior related to problem solving. It cannot be reduced to simple conditioning processes. This is the *nonreductionist* position.

In addition, this position holds the view that at each stage of development structures develop that permit the performance of certain logical or semilogical operations. These structures are analogous to the subroutines of the computer that perform such operations as those of calculating a square root or calculating the logarithm of a number. The computer's subroutines are special programs of operations that are permanently stored in the computer and that can be immediately put to work at any time. Human beings store similar routines, which permit them to perform such acts as calculate percentages. The storage of these routines is to some degree cumulative in that the routine to calculate a percentage is dependent on the routine to multiply or divide. Mathematical operations are not the only operations stored by the developing child, who also learns and stores routines to perform such tasks as that of classifying objects, drawing true inferences from data, and making predictions about where moving objects will be at a given time from now. In the intellectual sphere, these structures or programs appear to be cumulative in what they permit the individual to do. For example, a child cannot learn to classify unless he has already learned to discriminate such attributes of objects as color, shape, texture, weight, and potential use. The structures in his intelligence that permit him to discriminate the attributes have to function when he classifies them into classes. The task of classification involves more than being able to identify object attributes. The classification activity calls for a particular structure that permits classificatory behavior to occur.

The way in which such structures develop, and the conditions under which they will or will not develop, will be considered later in this volume. This position has much to say about the orderly development of structures related to intelligence that permit the individual to manifest certain competencies, much as the presence of a particular subroutine in a computer's storage permits the computer to perform certain mathematical operations.

Let us now consider some of the basic features involved in the reductionist and nonreductionist approaches to research on learning.

REDUCTIONIST APPROACHES TO A SCIENCE OF LEARNING

Psychologists have by now discovered some of the elementary learning processes and can demonstrate them in the laboratory. They can also demonstrate that these processes play a significant part in the lives of both human and nonhuman learners, but they have been much less successful at demonstrating that all learning involves these processes and only these processes. Some psychologists have dedicated much of their lives to producing credible arguments that all complex forms of learning are merely combinations of more fundamental forms, but these arguments, though credible, are a far cry from proof. The fundamental forms of learning considered in the remainder of this chapter are presented because they have significance in molding our lives, but no claim is made that they represent a comprehensive inventory of all learning processes.

There is far from complete agreement concerning the processes that should be regarded as the fundamental categories of learning. Of the four basic processes considered here, the first two are found in most recent classification systems. Let us first consider these two categories together. In the one category a new stimulus comes to produce a response that it did not previously initiate. In the other category, a subject makes a response that, in turn, produces a new stimulus situation. One can think of these learning situations rather loosely as learning involving $S \to R$ in the first case and $R \to S$ learning in the second. The arrow can be replaced by the words *leads to*, and thus one can say that *S leads to R* or that *R leads to S*. The reader must note that there are also two other possible combinations of S and R that could form categories in such a system, namely, $R \to R$ and $S \to S$. Let us now consider the kinds of phenomena that fall into these four categories.

Learning Involving New $S \to R$ Relationships

Classical conditioning experiments reflect learning involving new $S \to R$ relationships. Russian physiologists, who first initiated systematic research in this area, typically focused their research on the learning of some familiar response such as salivation, which can be measured easily and quantitatively in terms of the number of drops of saliva produced, or the response involved in the withdrawal of a limb from a noxious stimulus, a response that can be measured in terms of speed of withdrawal. In a typical Pavlovian experiment a dog learns to salivate in the presence of a new stimulus, such as a light or a bell or a tone, which ordinarily does not make a dog salivate. Salivation is produced by food, but if a bell is sounded each time food is presented, the dog eventually comes to salivate whenever the bell sounds. The animal learns the response of salivation to the presence of the stimulus bell, and thus a stimulus that did not trigger the particular response before the experiment began comes to trigger it through the conditioning procedure involved in the experiment.

The essential feature of this kind of learning is that a stimulus occurs in the presence of a response that it does not ordinarily elicit and acquires the property of eliciting the response. Of particular interest is the fact that responses, such as salivation, that are not ordinarily considered to be under voluntary control can be conditioned. The classical conditioning case of learning, or the classical conditioning paradigm, as it is called, is probably a very significant case of learning. Consider the case previously cited of the person involved in an automobile accident. At the time of the accident the person experiences intense fear involving many reflexes including those of the viscera, which produce that well-known sinking feeling in the stomach. Many months later, when that same person is driving past the corner where the accident occurred, he experiences exactly the same sinking feeling in the stomach. What has happened is that the stomach and intestinal responses occurring at the time of the accident became conditioned to the stimuli present at that time. Later, when the person was again exposed to these stimuli, they again triggered the responses. At the time of involvement in the accident the person was conditioned to produce these responses in the presence of these stimuli.

Although classically conditioned emotional responses may be a plague in the life of civilized people, such responses may have been immensely valuable when people were living in a primitive state. Consider, for example, a man living in a primitive society who goes on a hunting expedition and encounters a new animal that has migrated from another region. Our primitive man attempts to capture the animal but discovers that it has extraordinary strength. In the process, he has strong emotional reactions that help his body perform at the peak of strength and perhaps save his life. He also experiences the bodily responses associated with fear. All of these responses become conditioned to the sight of the new species of animal. Several days later, our same primitive man is out again on a hunting expedition and sees the same animal again. Immediately, emotional responses associated with combat and fear are triggered in his system. These prepare him for combat with the creature or for rapid flight—an avoidance response that may this time save his life. These classically conditioned responses were of great survival value to primitive people, though they are a plague to people living in a civilized community, who do not have to respond to most situations with gut reactions; indeed, such reactions are a disadvantage in that they often interfere with the ability to think calmly about a situation.

In most studies of the classical conditiong type, the scientist must use a response that he can readily elicit. For this reason a reflex is commonly employed. One can very readily elicit a response such as salivation in any animal, including a human being. The experimenter also has no difficulty in eliciting a response such as the raising of a leg when a shock is applied to the floor on which the foot rests. Such situations have an advantage in that the experimenter can be sure of eliciting the response that he wishes to condition to a new stimulus.

Many psychologists have assumed that any stimulus that occurs at the same time as a particular response acquires some capacity to elicit that response, and the response does not have to be a reflex for it to be conditioned to a new stimulus. Although American psychologists have confined their studies of classical conditioning to studies of eliciting reflexes with new stimuli, Russian psychologists have long been interested in conditioning other forms of response (see Cole and Maltzman, 1969). One technique for doing this is for the child involved in the experiment to first learn to press a key whenever a light goes on. This is accomplished by giving the child instructions to do so. Then another stimulus such as a buzzer, is introduced that always precedes the light. After a few trials involving both the buzzer and the light, the buzzer is sounded alone and the child presses the key. The demonstration, suggests that the essential condition for a new stimulus to acquire the property of eliciting a response is for it to occur at about the time when the response is made, and that the response does not have to be a reflex. This kind of conditioning is particularly striking in very young children, but few adults show any conditioning of this type. However, the adult does show classical conditioning of many reflexes, notably those reflexes that are described as emotional responses.

Because learning of the $S \rightarrow R$ type has typically been studied through situations involving reflexes, the learning phenomenon is commonly referred to as the conditioned reflex. Reflexes are innate forms of behavior triggered by a particular stimulus, which is referred to as the unconditioned stumulus. The new stimulus that comes to trigger the response, after learning, is referred to as the conditioned stimulus.

Although one may speak of classical conditioning as if it were a simple phenomenon, it is in fact quite complex. It is a fairly clearcut form of learning in many laboratory animals and clean experiments can be undertaken with it—that is, experiments in which the results show clear evidences of learning and which can be reproduced, with the same results, in another laboratory. Great care has to be taken in carrying out such experiments if they are to provide clear results. Pavlov found in the early days of his studies that an animal might not learn a conditioned reponse if some slight distraction were accidentally introduced, such as the sound of footsteps outside the laboratory.

Human learning has sometimes been studied through the conditioned reflex paradigm. The late Kenneth Spence, for example, conducted most of his research on human learning through the study of the conditioned eye-blink response. The advantage of studying learning in such a simple situation is that the important factors related to learning can be readily measured and controlled. One can measure the strength of the puff of air that produces the eye blink. One can measure the delay between the puff-of-air stimulus and the eye-blink response, and one can measure the amplitude and strength of the eye blink. Nevertheless, when the classical conditioning paradigm is applied to human subjects, other factors tend to be introduced that make the phenomenon more complicated than it is with laboratory animals, and also more variable from person to person. This was brought home to this writer some time ago when he was interested in conditioning to the sound of a tone, a response that takes place when a person is administered an electric shock. One result of brief electric shock is a response known as the galvanic skin response, which is a marked change in the electrical conductivity of the skin of the hand. When an electric shock is given, and a tone is sounded simultaneously, the galvanic skin response may become conditioned to the tone. In one such experiment several of the subjects showed no conditioning of the response to the tone. When they were questioned after the experimental session, they volunteered the information that they had seen no connection between the tone and the electric shock and did not realize that the tone had anything to do with the experiment. The conditioning of the galvanic skin response obviously called for something more than the mere response to the shock and the mere response to the tone. The same experiment also demonstrated some other phenomena indicating the complexity of classical conditioning in human subjects. After the conditioning procedure had been followed, most subjects showed well-established responses to the sound of the tone, but the conditioned response would fail to appear on trials on which the subject was told that he definitely would not receive an electric shock. In other words, if the subject did not expect the tone to be followed by a shock, he showed no galvanic skin response. Many classically conditioned responses can be made to appear or not to appear depending upon what the experimenter tells the person involved.

The classical conditioning paradigm for experimentation with learning has involved many different responses. Some of these, such as changes in heart rate, or changes in respiration, are of obvious significance but some such as the knee-jerk reflex or the eyelid reflex do not have the same evident importance for daily living. However, the assumption is commonly made that what is learned about the learning process through the study of one reflex will be similar to what can be learned through the study of conditioning another reflex. Research has generally given support to this assumption, although there are some exceptions. For example, studies of the response of the pupil of the eye to light, known as the pupillary reflex, have shown it to be an extraordinarily difficult reflex on which to produce conditioning, a finding that suggests that in order for conditioning or learning to take place the response involved must be under at least indirect control from the higher centers of the brain. The pupillary reflex does not seem to be under such control.

Although the assumption has commonly been made that classical conditioning begins at birth and forms an important mechanism in the development of early behavior, Sameroff (1972) concludes that there is no acceptable evidence that classical conditioning can take place at birth or in early infancy. Indeed, he concludes from his review of the research that classical conditioning is not possible in early infancy because the infant is as yet unable to associate together two stimuli. Only later does the nervous system develop to the point where this is possible.

Most psychologists would take the position that many typical unwanted emotional responses have been acquired through classical conditioning in the laboratory of life. Emotional responses are, of course, basically unlearned responses that have value to living organisms. An animal that is frightened shows an increase in blood pressure, a raised blood-sugar level, rapid breathing, and a high pulse rate. All of these emotional responses are of value in placing the body in a state where great physical effort can be exerted either to provide a defense or to lead to an escape. The animal displaying these responses can fight with greater vigor or flee more effectively and rapidly than a relaxed animal.

Human beings show emotional responses very similar to those shown by higher animals, but we also manifest many inappropriate emotional responses that can plague our lives and prevent us from being effective members of society. For example, although we have reason to be fearful on many occasions, there are also occasions in the lives of most of us when fear responses occur even though we know that the situation should not really be feared. One person experiences fear responses when he has to pass close to a deep lake or river. He knows that these responses are irrational and that he has them because as a boy he nearly drowned. The psychologist would say that during the drowning episode, when he had every reason to respond with the deepest fear, his emotional responses related to fear became conditioned to the stimuli associated with the presence of deep water. Later, when he found himself near to a body of water, the fear responses would become immediately triggered. In this way an irrational and unreasonable emotional response would have been acquired through a mechanism closely similar to that of classical conditioning. The assumption is that most irrational and inappropriate emotional responses are acquired through classical conditioning in naturally occurring situations. The emotional responses first occur on some appropriate occasion, but they subsequently occur also in the presence of other irrelevant stimuli. Later these irrelevant stimuli show the property of eliciting the emotional responses with which they have become associated.

If psychologists are correct in assuming that many of the unwanted emotional responses are acquired through classical conditioning, the study of this type of learning may be expected to lead to the discovery of ways of getting rid of these responses. Because much of the work of psychiatrists and clinical psychologists is occupied with helping patients rid themselves of bothersome emotional responses, the study of classical conditioning can be considered to be an approach through which some parts of psychotherapy can be given a scientific foundation. Indeed, a type of therapy known as desensitization is based largely on what has been discovered in the laboratory about classical conditioning.

Learning Involving New $R \rightarrow S$ Relationships

In learning involving new $R \rightarrow S$ relationships the human or animal subject learns to make a response that produces events or states of affairs of a kind that are much sought after by the organism. Thus a hungry rat can learn to press a bar which, in turn, delivers a small amount of food into a trough, and a hungry pigeon can learn to peck a small white button on the wall which, in turn, brings the result of a food trough being raised into a postition that permits the pigeon to retrieve some grain from it. Although one can designate this type of learning in a simple form as $R \rightarrow S$ learning, the process is more complex than this simple designation would indicate.

When the response of the hungry rat has been learned, one can say that the response has been brought under the control of the prevailing conditions, or that it is under stimulus control, that is, the animal is very likely to make these responses under these conditions. Classes of responses that are under stimulus control are referred to by Skinner (1938) as *operants*. Sometimes the behavior involved is referred at as *instrumental behavior*. This term introduces an additional concept, namely, that the behavior involved is instrumental in producing a particular state of affairs—in this case a situation involving food. The implication is that the behavior is the instrument through which a highly preferred situation is produced. An operant may also be instrumental in avoiding particular kinds of situations collectively described as aversive.

The learning of operants may take place along two quite distinct lines. Place a rat in a box that contains only a bar and a trough into which pellets of food can be delivered. The rat will explore the box and eventually place its front feet up on the bar in such a way that the bar is pressed down. The rat eventually learns to press the bar down and thus to obtain food, and although at the beginning of the training session this is a rather infrequent form of behavior, once the animal is well trained, bar pressing becomes a very frequent form of behavior. The animal learns to press the bar to obtain delivery of food. Learning involves a change in the frequency with which the animal presses the bar. In technical terms one would say that learning produces a change in response probability, that is to say a change in the frequency with which a response may be expected to occur.

Similar increases in response frequency as a result of its consequences can be observed early in the life of the human infant. Give a hungry baby a few drops of milk every time he kicks a leg, and leg kicking shows an increased frequency of occurrence. The kick of the leg has become an operant. Give a child ten extra points every time his homework is neat and clean, and neat and clean homework is more likely to occur.

Sometimes instrumental learning involves far more than a change in the frequency of occurrence of a response. One may train a rat to obtain food by pulling a string suspended from the ceiling of the cage. Although a rat may occasionally push down a bar placed in its environment, rats do not pull pieces of string suspended from the ceiling. Rats may sniff the string, but one might wait through the lifetime of a rat and it would never pull a piece of string. Sometimes in instrumental learning an animal, such as a rat, can be trained in gradual steps to perform such a fundamentally new act as that of pulling the string and thereby obtaining the delivery of food. In such a case the response probability is initially at zero, for the animal does not make the response at all. Training produces a mode of response that did not occur previously.

Parallel cases of learning in young children are easy to find. When an infant is first given a spoon, he clenches the handle of the spoon so that the spoon is held upright and can retain no food. One may help the child by putting the spoon into the food, but the food falls off the spoon as soon as it is left in his unguided hand and the reinforcement of receiving food in the mouth through his own activity does not take place. A better procedure is to give the infant a baby spoon with the handle so bent that, when he naturally grips the spoon, the spoon remains horizontal and the food stays on it. He is then readily able to bring food from the plate to his mouth. One can then slowly adjust the shape of the handle of the spoon until he learns to use a normal spoon. A thoughtful arrangement of the learning conditions permits the child to acquire this important instrumental response.

Changes in behavior produced through instrumental learning are referred to as the *shaping of behavior*, a term introduced by Skinner some years ago and now widely used. It is applied both to the case in which a response is increased or reduced in frequency and to the case in which a fundamentally new response is learned. Those who apply what is known about the shaping of behavior to practical situations are often said to be engaged in *behavior modification*, though this term is applied to any technique that has established effectiveness in changing behavior.

Instrumental learning must be considered to be of some significance in the acquisition of human behavior. Skinner (1957) has taken the extreme position that most significant adult behavior and all verbal is a form of instrumental behavior, but only a few psychologists today would agree with him in this respect.

Within this category fall components of the learnings commonly encountered in schools, though any school task one can name also has components from the other categories of learning considered here, and perhaps also aspects of learning not well described by the basic categories. Thus children in the first grade in school have to learn to make responses to printed words that will bring praise from the teacher or that will provide them with some piece of information they need to have. The acquisition of appropriate new responses in school often produces the highly sought-after state of affairs known as good grades, which, in turn, results in social approval. Teachers generally attempt to control the responses that will or will not be acquired by the pupils. The teacher does this by dispensing sought-after situations such as good grades, praise, and special privileges.

Techniques for the experimental study of what we have called here $R \rightarrow S$ learning are numerous. The situation S, resulting from the instrumental behavior R, has to be some kind of preferred situation, that is, a situation that the learner seeks out and chooses in preference to other situations. In the case of preschool children, the preferred situations in experiments related to this kind of learning have commonly involved the delivery of such choice consumables as an M & M candy or a small marshmallow. Sometimes the situation for these young children has involved praise and occasionally opportunity to play with some special toy.

Psychologists have had some success in demonstrating that operant conditioning does account quite satisfactorily for learning in some situations and with some classes of individuals. Since much of the original research on operant conditioning was undertaken with animals, one can be hardly surprised that the results can be generalized best to human beings operating at relatively simple levels; including young children, patients in mental hospitals, and the mentally retarded. Furthermore, recent work by Miller (1969) and DiCarra (1970) has shown that visceral functions, such as heart rate and blood pressure, can be changed by operant conditioning, thus providing a potential technique that physicians might use to change these functions. Research workers have also demonstrated that operant conditioning, unlike classical conditioning, can take place shortly after birth. However, Sameroff (1972) takes the position that despite the demonstration of operant conditioning in the newborn, this process does not seem to account for the development of the infant's understanding of space. Sameroff takes the position that the parsimonious model of operant conditioning is inappropriate and prefers an organismic model in which the organism's own activity produces learning within the organism. Like most scientific models, the operant model has limitations and few will any longer take the position that it is the only worthwhile model. Nevertheless it still has substantial utility.

Certain important differences must be pointed out between $S \rightarrow R$ learning and $R \rightarrow S$ learning. In the one case learning begins with a response easily produced in the experimental situation, but in the other case the experimenter is interested in a response that is either very infrequent or nonoccurring. For this reason it has commonly been said that classical conditioning learning involves only the learning of a new stimulus that comes to trigger old behavior, while in instrumental learning a new response is learned. For this reason, the one is commonly called stimulus learning and the other is called response learning. In the one a new significance becomes attached to a stimulus, and in the other a new response acquires significance or an old response acquires new instrumental value. The terms stimulus learning and response learning are convenient because they focus on important central characteristics of what is learned.

Although one can make clear distinctions on paper between $S \to R$ learning and $R \to S$ learning, most significant learning involves both categories. Even when the scientist tries to produce pure forms of one or the other kinds of learning in the laboratory, both kinds of processes are generally involved. Liu (1964) has pointed out that when a rat performs the instrumental response of running through a maze to reach the food in the goal compartment, many reflexes related to eating take place along the way and these become conditioned to the stimuli provided by the maze. Thus, while the rat is learning the instrumental response of reaching the food, it is also acquiring classically conditioned responses to the maze. When a rat learns to press a bar to deliver a food pellet, the bar-pressing activity comes to trigger all kinds of reflexes related to the intake and digestion of food and these become classically conditioned to the stimuli provided by the box, bar, and food-delivery mechanism. At the human level the child may learn to place a coin in a slot machine to obtain delivery of a candy bar, but soon the mere sight of the coin-operated machine will produce the reflex of salivation, showing that not only did instrumental learning take place but, in addition, the classical conditioning of the salivary reflex took place at the same time. When a business executive makes an important decision, with either damaging or gratifying consequences, the emotional responses that accompany the decision-making process become conditioned to many features of the decision-making situation. A case of pure instrumental conditioning hardly seems to exist, and pure cases of classical conditioning are difficult or impossible to find. A person shows an eye-blink reflex if a slight puff of air strikes the eyeball and this response has been used in many laboratory studies of classical conditioning in human beings, but in such experiments results are often confused by the voluntary eye-blinks of subjects who try to anticipate the occurrence of the puff of air. These anticipatory responses must be considered to be instrumental responses. Incidentally, the puff of air does not have to be noxious to produce the normal reflex or to provide a situation in which conditioning will readily take place. Indeed, conditioning of the response to a light or tone takes place most readily with very mild puffs of air that are no stronger than those of a mild breeze on a pleasant day.

Learning Involving New $R \to R$ Relationships

Learning involving new $R \to R$ relationships pertains to the learning of chains of responses that are rapidly run off, as when a child learns to write a word or whistle a melody. A distinction must be made between making a slow sequence of responses in which the performance of one act provides the stimuli that initiate the performance of the next act in the sequence, and chains of acts that are run off too rapidly for any one response to produce new stimuli that set off the next response. An example of the former is knot tying. In the early stages of learning to tie a knot each stage of tying the knot is followed by a pause, the situation is examined by the person undertaking the task, and then the next step is initiated. After extensive practice, the knot-tying task may take place at great speed and the dependence of the process on chains of responses in which each component response produces stimuli that initiate new responses becomes much less obvious. In the case of motor skills that are undertaken at great speed, as in the case of playing a fast passage on a musical instrument, it is physically impossible for there to be such a simple chain of stimuli and responses for, as Hebb (1958) long ago pointed out, there would not be time enough for each response to produce stimuli that would initiate the next response. Remember that a musician may play notes at rates of up to five hundred per minute, and under such conditions the stimuli provided by the playing of one note would not have time to set off the next response. The alternative explanation is that the musician's brain sends out a sequence of correct signals to the muscles and that the total performance is monitored only in a very general way. The brain seems capable of running off whole sequences of commands to the muscles without waiting to see what happens to each. This phenomenon becomes particularly evident when one studies motor skills, as Keele (1968) has shown. Even subhuman brains, very remote from man in the evolutionary scale, seem capable of doing this. Consider the flapping of the wings of the hummingbird, which may occur as fast as ninety times per second. In order for this to happen, the brain of the bird would have to emit the proper sequence of commands to the muscles at this enormous speed.

Thus, learning to emit rapid sequences of responses seems to be somewhat different from learning to produce the component responses, or learning to make each response in a sequence in which each component response is triggered by the previous response. Learning, called here $R \rightarrow R$ learning, refers to the production of sequences of responses of the former rather than the latter kind.

Learning Involving New $S \rightarrow S$ Relationships

One way of demonstrating learning involving new $S \rightarrow R$ relationships is to undertake an experiment involving three stages. In the first step, two stimuli, such as a light and a tone, are presented together a large number of times. Then a response is conditioned to one of these stimuli. In the third step the other stimulus is presented and is found to elicit the conditioned response in the same way as the stimulus to which it was originally conditioned. If a dog were first exposed to the light and the tone for, say, one hundred trials, and the dog were then conditioned to salivate in the presence of the tone, then, later, the light would also be found to have the property of eliciting salivation. This phenomenon is known as sensory preconditioning. An eye blink conditioned in a human subject to occur when a tone is sounded will also be triggered by a light if the subject has been exposed to a pairing of the light and the tone prior to the experiment. In common language, one would say that the tone and the light had become associated. The essential condition for this kind of learning is that the two stimuli enter the perceptual sytem at the same time. The learning involved is generally described as perceptual learning in order to distinguish it from learning centered on the formation of new responses. This kind of associative learning represents only one form of learning in the perceptual category and there are others that will be considered in the chapter on perception.

There has long been dispute concerning the learning that should be considered to belong in the $S \rightarrow S$ category and the learning that should not. Pure cases cannot be found. For example, learning the names of different trees would be considered by most psychologists to be primarily a perceptual task involving the identification of the significant characteristics of each tree and the association of the cluster of characteristics that identify a tree with the corresponding name. Nevertheless, some psychologists would prefer to argue that this learning should be placed primarily in the $S \rightarrow R$ class, in that the person learns to say a particular name when he encounters a particular tree. Although the latter is a common outcome of such learning, there are strong reasons for believing that an idividual can learn to associate the appearance of a tree with the sound of the name of the tree or with the printed name of the tree without ever saying the name to himself through slight movements of his vocal cords. We do know that such learning can take place after the muscles involved in speech have been paralyzed—a fact that gives strong support to the idea that the learning involved is essentially perceptual and in the $S \rightarrow S$ category.

The learning discussed in the $S \rightarrow S$ category represents perceptual learning at a very simple level. More complex perceptual learning involves not just the associating together of two items of information, but such complex matters as the extracting of information from a very complex environment, the organizing of information, and the systematic storing of information in memory. Although there is ample evidence that a simple associative type of learning takes place and plays a significant role in the development of the individual, it does not mean that this is the only important perceptual operation involved in learning. Other perceptual learning processes can be demonstrated and there is considerable doubt whether these can be reduced to this category or to the other categories of learning discussed here.

Internal Processes in Reductionist Psychology

Most psychologists take the position that a science of behavior cannot limit itself to a discussion of observable responses, for responses take place within the organism that cannot be readily observed. These internal responses may also be conditioned responses. They are internal sequences of behavior and are referred to as mediating responses. Thus, when the stimulus is some internal response that confronts us, internal problem-solving processes take place before the solution is produced. These internal processes are the mediating processes involved in solving the problem. They mediate between the presentation of the problem S, and the production of the solution R.

A few psychologists, mainly associated with the operant school, believe that there is little use in being concerned with such internal responses, preferring to stay close to observables. A strong argument against the position of the operant psychologists, in this respect, is that the most sophisticated developments in science have involved concepts that referred to unobservable factors. No scientist has ever seen a neutron, and yet the concept of a neutron is fundamental to understanding the process of atomic fission. A science that limited itself to a discussion of only the observable would contain a very naive body of knowledge.

Some Overall Comments on the Reductionist Position

The reductionist postion is very attractive to many psychologists, some of whom make the dubious claim that it is the only scientific position to take. During the present century, American and Russian psychologists have allowed their work to be guided by a search for simple, basic processes that would account for all behavior. The approach has had positive outcomes that have had some practical impli- cations. The most successful applications have been in clinical psychology and in the broad area of behavior control. The results of research have not had notable success in their attempted applications to the area of intellectual development or achievement. The success of the approach in relation to problems of emotional development and control may well be a result of the fact that, in this area, quite primitive forms of behavior are involved. A man who has an overwhelming fear of flying has an emotional problem not very different from that of a dog terrified of the sound of a whistle. Both responses probably represent the same kind of basic, elemental behavior processes. On the other hand, a man who solves a diffi- cult scientific problem is exhibiting behavior in an entirely different category from that of a dog who has learned the trick of obtaining food by standing on its hind legs. The scientist's behavior and the dog's behavior probably cannot be reduced to the same elemental components.

NONREDUCTIONIST APPROACHES TO A SCIENCE OF LEARNING

The central idea underlying the nonreductionist appoach to the development of a science of learning is that the learning of complex forms of behavior, such as the ability to reason, cannot be understood in terms of simple processes such as con- ditioning. The chief proponent of this position has been Jean Piaget, the Swiss-born scientist, who does not view himself as a psychologist but prefers to be called a *genetic epistemologist*. Epistemology is the branch of philosophy that deals with the nature of knowledge. The term *genetic* implies that Piaget is concerned with development of knowledge in the human being. Piaget's concern is actually broader than this, for he has had a long and abiding interest in the development of reasoning and thinking processes that are central to intelligent behavior.

The position of Piaget, similar to that of others who take a nonreductionist pos- ition, is that intellectual behavior at each level of development involves processes that do not take place at lower levels. Processes taking place at lower levels only lay a foundation for the development of more sophisticated processes at more advanced stages. The processes that occur at each level cannot be understood completely in terms of the processes that occur at lower levels. Thus the ability of the 8-year-old to develop a systematic classification of a number of objects given him cannot be understood completely in terms of his earlier developed abilities that permit him to see similarities and differences between objects. The 5-year-old may recognize that two objects differ in shape and that the one is round and the other square, but he does not understand that the round object belongs to a *class* of round objects and the other belongs to a *class* of square objects. The 5-year-old does not understand what it means to place objects together so that they form a class, though he may form rough groupings of objects. The development of the concept of a class will occur at a time when the structures in the nervous system become capable of acquiring that concept and when the environment presents problems that call for the development of that concept in order for them to be solved.

The nonreductionist position stresses that little can be learned about the nature of mature human intelligence from the study of animals. One persuasive argument is that human beings have structures in the brain that simply do not exist in lower organisms, and not even in the nearest primate relatives of man, which are still distant relatives. There are, of course, brain structures common to man and lower organisms, but these are not the structures that involve what are called higher mental processes. The structures of the human brain that deal with such processes as motor coordination, some aspects of perception, and those that control the visceral and vegetative functions may well be very similar in human and nonhuman higher forms of animal life. There may be some legitimacy in generalizing conservatively, cautiously, and with qualifications from studies on animals to man when one is dealing with functions based on anatomical structures that are the same in both.

The argument presented by the nonreductionist is that there is *discontinuity* between different stages of development, that is, that the behavior occurring at one stage of development cannot be understood completely in terms of behaviors taking place at earlier stages. These earlier behaviors have to take place as a part of a necessary developmental sequence and they lead to behavior that represents a break with them. Thus, when a child begins to be able to reason abstractly, this represents a break with his earlier limited capacity to reason in relation to concrete objects. Once he can reason abstractly, he can perform in a way that is fundamentally different from his previous capacity to perform.

There is a tendency today to emphasize not only the discontinuity between one stage of development and the next, but also the discontinuity between the behavior of different species. Earlier psychologists believed that the simple learning processes studied in rats and in other infrahuman species could lead to substantial understanding of human learning. Such a position tends now to be viewed with skepticism. Indeed, there is tendency to place emphasis on the distinctiveness of the behavior of each species rather than to look for similarities across species. There has been a growing realization that each species evolved over a long period and developed both physical features and behavior adaptive to the circumstances under which the animal lived. Also different species developed different forms of adaptive behavior. Thus each species acquired distinct behavioral characteristics.

The nonreductionist argues, on the basis of extensive data, that the human species has certain quite distinct behavioral characteristics that set the species apart from others. Particularly impressive is the human capability for responding to objects that are not immediately present. Even the most developed primates, other than the human being, are not able to search for objects to be used as tools for solving particular problems, though they may use objects that are immediately present for the same purpose. These primates do not seem able to use internal representations of absent objects as though the objects were present. The human being can solve a problem, either internally or on paper, and then search for the tools needed to execute the solution. Lower animals show no ability to do this. The human being also has the related ability to be able to represent the future. Lower animals show anticipations of events in their immediate futures, but such behaviors are trivial in comparison with the human ability. The unique ability of the human being to represent that which is absent, including the remote future, seem also to be related to his ability to use language. Although our closest relative, the chimpanzee, shows some ability to use sign systems, which the animals learn, tediously, after immense amounts of training, we seem to have enormous capacity to acquire language through merely being exposed to it and the ability to use language for purposes far different from those for which it is used by the best-trained chimpanzee. Much of human language has to do with using language for manipulating situations that are not immediately present and particularly future situations.

The human ability to consider that which is not present, and to represent it behaviorally in symbols inscribed in stone or books, is made possible by developments in the human brain that took place a million or more years ago—not a very long time ago in terms of biological history. The human brain developed unique structures in the brain cortex that have permitted these forms of behavior. The development of new brain structures has resulted in the emergence of new forms of behavior that are not mere elaborations of more primitive forms of behavior, but distinctively human forms of behavior, manifesting a lawfulness different from the lawfulness of simpler forms.

Even in the physical sciences, it has long been conceded that the laws of complex systems are of a different character from the laws of the simple elements of which they are composed. For this reason, physical scientists of the late 1900s invented the science of thermodynamics, which dealt with the laws of complex systems. Thermodynamics became a science of the laws of complex systems, just as nuclear physics became a science of very simple systems. The physical scientist has long recognized that a science of complex systems is different from a science of simple systems. The nonreductionist argues that the same is true of behavior. Complex forms of behavior are characterized by their own laws, which are different from the laws of simple behavior.

An interesting point is that research on the psychology of language and language acquisition has been successful insofar as it has been based on the assumption that it cannot be understood in terms of simple conditioning procedures. Much of the unproductive psychological research on language development up to the 1960s was based on the premise that language could be understood in terms of simple learning mechanisms. This assumption had a stultifying effect on what was done and seems to have resulted in a failure of research workers to identify what are now known to be the important problems. More recent research has abandoned this attempt to explain the complex in terms of the very simple and, largely through the influence of linguists rather than psychologists, has gone forth into productive new avenues. A discussion of this new line of research forms an important component of this book.

Another point of contrast must be made between the conception of learning previously considered and that of the nonreductionist we are now considering. The two approaches view human beings as involving different kinds of psychological *systems*. (The term *system* is used here in a technical sense.) The human being, like all other organisms, is a physical system characterized by such attributes as wholeness, organization, interacting parts, and ability to interact with other systems (Bertalanffy, 1968). Systems can be either *closed* or *open*. A closed system is capable of a certain kind of repetitive activity. For example, if a plane is flying on automatic pilot, each time it drifts off course it will be brought back on course by the servo mechanism built for that purpose; the plane is operating as a closed system. Human behavior is given an analogous interpretation by those psychologists of the operant school who take the postion that organisms adjust their behavior to receive the maximum number of reinforcements. The latter adjustment is analogous to the plane being kept on course by the servo mechanism and represents a closed system. Such systems are limited in what they can do and function in repetitive cycles.

In contrast, open systems are not so restricted in what they can do. The human being can be considered to be an open system in that he shows such behaviors as inventiveness and creativity. He is capable, through his own internal workings, of inventing symbolic systems that, in turn, enhance greatly the ingenious uses that he can find for objects in the environment. Open systems have potential for redesigning themselves and thus producing entirely different systems from the one with which they started. The human being can be regarded as a system that engages in a continuous process of redesigning his behavior as he lives and experiences. It is not just the human being who can have this possibility, for computer experts have long considered it possible to design a computer that will redesign itself and show some ability to operate as an open system.

In the nonreductionist approach, the development of complex behavior is analogous to the construction of a building. First the foundation has to be laid. The form of the foundation has much to do with the kind of building that can be constructed on it; a round building cannot be readily erected on a square foundation. The size and strength of the foundation has much to do with the structure that can be built. The walls of the building determine the kind of roof that can be used to crown the structure. The human intellect is built by an analogous process. The foundation has to be laid in infancy, and on that foundation more and more complex and lofty intellectual processes are built. The intellectual processes of the preschool child are built on the primitive processes developed in infancy; they differ from them, yet they could not be built without a proper foundation. The foundation processes that the nonreductionists discuss are not simple conditioning processes. Just what the foundation blocks for human behavior are still remains a matter of controversy, but a picture of the nature of the foundation, laid in infancy, is beginning to emerge.

Conditioning approaches to the study of the newborn conducted early in the century gave the impression that the infant had relatively little capacity to learn. Psychologists evolved the picture of a newborn developing in terms of his genetic constitution, but having to develop far before much learning could take place. However, evidence has been forthcoming (see Stone, Smith, and Murphy, 1973) that the infant has extensive capacity for learning, though not in terms of conditioning models of behavior. The data suggest that the classical and operant conditioning descriptions of learning do not describe well the learning of the infant. There is ample evidence that the infant has enormous capacity to learn and that he takes in a great amount of information about his world. The processes appear to be mainly those involved in the infant's perceptions of the effects of his own activities. The knowledge he thus acquires from his interactions with his environment form the foundation on which all further knowledge of the world and ways of handling it are based. This action-based knowledge lays the foundation for more complex forms of behavior with their own forms of lawfulness. Such is the nonreductionist position.

The Nonreductionist View of Mediating Processes and Psychological Structures

The nonreductionist view of internal aspects of behavior uses extensively the concept of structure. In order to explain this concept, let us return briefly to the analogy between human behavior and the computer. The computer has a built-in capacity to perform such calculations as that involved in a square root because the computer's transistors are arranged in a *structure* that permits the computer to perform the necessary sequence of arithmetic operations. One can also view the computer as providing a structured sequence of arithmetic operations when it calculates a square root. The latter structure is referred to as a program by the people who operate computers. A similar conception of structure can be used in describing the intellect. For example, a child is able to develop a system for classifying objects—say, leaves from trees. The classification system that he develops shows structure and the intellectual operations that produce the classification also show structure. A person oriented toward the computer might say that the child had a built-in program that permitted him to develop a classification system for leaves. If the products of the intellect have structure, the intellect itself must have structures, that is, the structures necessary to perform a set of intellectual operations much as a computer has a program to perform a set of arithmetical operations. The nonreductionist position typically assumes that intellectual structures develop at particular ages, provided that the individual has been exposed to an appropriate sequence of experiences. It is the interaction of the intellect with the problems posed by the environment that produce intellectual structures. Thus a child of 4 cannot sort objects into classes in any way that makes sense to the adult; he does not have the concept of a class of objects. A child of 7 has this concept and can arrange objects into classes in an acceptable way; he has developed the intellectual structures for doing this.

It must be evident to the reader by this time that the internal events used to account for learning by the reductionist are very different from those used by the nonreductionist, partly because these two groups of psychologists are concerned with different forms of behavior. The nonreductionist, with his interest in high-level intellectual operations, is concerned with internal structures that make intelligent behavior possible. On the other hand, the reductionist is concerned with simple basic processes and the mediating conditions that facilitate those processes.

THE ADVANTAGES OF A DIVERSITY OF APPROACHES

The history of psychology has been characterized by the development of what have been referred to as *schools*. A school of psychology has consisted generally of a group of scientists who pursued the development of a science of behavior from a particular viewpoint. Unfortunately, each individual school of psychology has all too commonly taken the parochial position that its particular approach, and no other, represents a true science of behavior. Such was the position of the early behaviorists under the leadership of J. B. Watson and also of the later Gestalt school. In recent times, this form of parochialism has been particularly evident in the operant school of psychology, many of whose proponents have taken the extreme position that they alone should be considered to be the builders of a science of behavior. Others have not been convinced.

When schools of psychology are seen in historical perspective, it becomes quite evident that none can claim an exclusive monopoly of scientific advance. Different schools studied different problems and made contributions to different areas of the behavioral sciences. The Watson school of behaviorism was concerned largely with simple associative learning. The Gestalt psychologists worked on problems of perception. Kurt Lewin and his associates will long be remembered for their contribution to the psychology of group behavior. Operant psychologists have made notable contributions to what they refer to as the impact of reinforcers on behavior. The Piaget school has made significant contributions to our understanding of the complex intellect of human beings. Each school has made contributions in the areas it has studied, but most schools have also typically attempted to generalize discoveries to all of behavior. Thus limited findings have been discussed by writers and promoters of particular viewpoints as though they represented a complete science of behavior.

History has shown all too clearly that what psychologists of one era thought was a complete science of behavior turned out later to be only a set of very limited findings. We are probably at this time far from having a core of knowledge representing an enduring basic science. We have some knowledge, and some important findings, but not a unified science, in the sense in which there is a unified science of physics. Research has made important contributions to our knowledge of behavior, and the discoveries made to this time have been sufficient to inspire the next generation to pursue research in the future. Nevertheless, we are still only at the beginning of developing behavioral science.

Just as each school of psychology in the past made its unique contribution, so today each approach can claim that it is having its own specialized impact. This book will attempt to cover the main approaches to the study of learning and show the contributions and limitations of each approach.

The reader must also recognize that the impact of both major approaches to research on learning discussed in this chapter are combined in some areas of inquiry. For example, research on perception and perceptual learning shows approaches, in some of its aspects, that are combinations of the reductionist and the nonreductionist techniques. The two modern schools of psychology described here have both widespread and interwoven influences on the research of most psychologists.

The Source of Control of Behavior in the Two Approaches

A major difference between the reductionist and the nonreductionist approaches lies in the assumptions made concerning the control of behavior. For those psychologists who attempt to reduce all behavior to conditioned responses, behavior is completely controlled by events in the environment. That has been the position of Skinner and his followers. The position is plausible in view of the fact that, in the simple forms of behavior studied, experimenters are able to control the behavior of those on whom they do experiments merely by manipulating the experimental conditions. Thus, the subject's choice of which button he is going to push when the light goes on can be controlled by providing reinforcements for the pushing of one button rather than another. What the individual, acting as subject of the experiment, thinks about the situation has little to do with what he does. Such behavior is controlled by where the rewards lie, and by little else. Given such data from numerous similar experiments, psychologists have been tempted to generalize and conclude that all behavior is under control of events in the environment. Such a conclusion involves the fallacy of generalizing from the simple to the complex. What happens in simple situations may not be characteristic at all of what happens in complex ones and to assume such similarity is wholly unjustified.

Nonreductionist psychologists take the position that conclusions drawn from simple experiments concerning the control of behavior have little implication for what happens under complex conditions. These psychologists typically take the position that the human being is endowed with an internal decision-making system that controls behavior. This does not mean that external events play no part in determining what a person does, but the internal decision-making system may disregard certain aspects of immediate events. Piaget writes as though even the infant were a decision-making system.

This leads to the difficult question of whether the decision-making system within the individual can be considered to be " free." All too often psychologists have taken the position that such freedom is an unscientific concept, or that the existence of such freedom of choice would deny the possibility that a science of behavior could ever be built. A person can, of course, arrive at decisions on a completely arbitrary basis, as when he tosses a coin. Many decisions in life are arbitrary, and free, in the sense that they cannot be predicted because they involve something as arbitrary as the toss of a coin. Other forms of freedom of choice may also exist. The position taken here on such matters follows a statement of Tyler (1973), in which she said that neither the hypothesis of freedom of choice, nor its reverse, has been demonstrated as true. Tyler goes on to state that she thinks we are better off if we opt for the assumption that the individual has at least limited freedom to choose his own course of action.

Although some psychologists write as though a scientist was necessarily committed to the assumption that there is no such thing as freedom of choice, there is nothing in scientific method and theory that commits him to make such an assumption. Such an assumption, if it is made, is made strictly for convenience, and for no other reason.

SUMMARY

1. Although many research workers in the early part of the present century believed that the development of a psychology of learning would soon produce a revolution in education, the change it has produced has been gradual and subtle, but nevertheless pervasive and, after nearly three quarters of a century, impressive.

2. Not only has the appearance of classrooms changed, but there has also been a complete reorientation of the teacher toward the pupil and toward the problems of providing instruction. Research has produced a problem-solving attitude on the part of the teacher in handling the difficulties of the pupil, and what has been learned about learning has had considerable impact on the design of the curriculum. Although critics of the schools have often taken a position that there has been little change over the last few generations, nothing could be farther from the truth.

3. Little of the change in schools can be attributed to the work of those who chose to conduct their research in the schools themselves. On the contrary, most of the change has come from the ideas of academicians who gave the appearance of working alone in ivory towers. Men such as Thorndike, Skinner, and Piaget stand out as giants, who worked quietly in their laboratories to produce ideas that changed the course of education. The impact of such ideas is to be contrasted with the lack of impact of much recent research, which represents crash programs supposedly designed to solve critical problems. Such programs have typically had only the impact of a drop of a pin.

4. Learning is far from being the clearly defined phenomenon that it is commonly thought to be. There is a central area of well-defined phenomena, but there is a gray area around the edge where there are phenomena that some would classify as learning and others would not. Habituation and sensitization are two such borderline phenomena.

5. Definitions of learning differ sufficiently that there is often disagreement concerning whether a particular modification in behavior can or cannot be regarded as learning.

6. Two dominant positions are readily discernible among scientists studying learning. The traditional position has been that of the reductionist, who takes the position that all complex behavioral phenomena can be reduced to the simple. American reductionists have typically attempted to reduce all learning to component conditioned responses. On the other hand, nonreductionist psychologists do not believe that the complex can be reduced to the simple, but that phenomena at a particular level of complexity must be studied at that level of complexity. Piaget is the main proponent of the nonreductionist position.

7. The reductionist psychology of learning has tended to formulate its problems and findings in the traditional language of physiology, though this language is used with less precision. Although the terms *stimulus* and *response* may have quite precise meanings in a physiological context, they often lack this precision in the writings of psychologists. The corresponding symbols S and R generally represent quite complex sets of events and conditions. A stimulus is commonly a conglomerate of conditions to which a learner is exposed and the response is an intricate complexity of muscular and glandular activities. In most studies only a small component of the total response to the learning situation is studied.

8. Psychologists have long sought to find classifications of learning phenomena, but none that have evolved up to this time have shown themselves to be entirely satisfactory. The classification presented in this chapter serves primarily the purpose of showing the range of learning phenomena. It is also a crude classification, in that pure forms of learning in the various categories probably do not exist.

9. The first category of the fourfold classification represents classical conditioning. The essential feature of learning in this category is that a stimulus comes to produce a response that it did not produce in the first place. The essential condition of this kind of learning is that a response occurs in the presence of a stimulus that does not ordinarily elicit it. After some repetitions of the response in the presence of the stimulus, the stimulus then acquires the property of eliciting the response. Research on learning in this category typically involves a readily controlled response such as a reflex, but the response probably does not *have* to be a reflex. This category of learning is considered to be of significance in that it may encompass the learning that takes place during the acquisition of unwanted emotional responses, There can be no doubt that many emotional responses come to be triggered by all kinds of stimuli through learning as one passes through life, and the necessary condition for such learning may be that the emotional response occurs in the presence of the particular stimulus that comes to trigger it. Such learning had value when human beings were living under primitive conditions, but its value in a civilized society seems to be largely negative.

10. A second category of learning is the acquisition of responses that lead to the production of a new stimulus situation, which can be described as a preferred situation. Such learning is generally accomplished by presenting the preferred situation after the particular response, which then becomes a more and more frequently occurring response. This kind of learning situation has become known as operant

conditioning, to distinguish it from classical conditioning. It is also referred to as instrumental conditioning, because the response is an instrument for producing the preferred situation that follows it. Instrumental learning may involve more than a mere change in the frequency with which a particular response occurs and may result in the slow emergence of new responses. Behavior may be slowly shaped to produce behavior different in character from any shown by the learning organism prior to training. Although one would like to think of classical conditioning and instrumental conditioning as involving two entirely distinct categories of learning, this is not the case. Instrumental learning always has included in it some classically conditioned components. Classically conditioned responses also include some instrumentally conditioned elements. The two categories are closely interwoven in practice.

11. A third category of learning is that in which a response becomes part of a sequence of responses. Such learning produces a chain of responses. The learning of chains of activities is essential for the performance of most complex skills. Such chains are different from sequences of responses in which the stimuli produced by one response initiate the next response, for well-learned chains of responses run off so quickly that such a chain of S's and R's would not have time to occur.

12. A fourth category of learning was commonly referred to in the past as perceptual learning. It involves associating together two stimuli that enter the perceptual system at approximately the same time. Sensory preconditioning is one example of this category of learning. Many psychologists today would regard paired-associate learning as falling mainly within this category. The latter technique has become one of the most important tools for the study of verbal learning.

13. The reductionist position has been successful mainly in dealing with simpler aspects of behavior, particularly those that have to do with the responses of the young and the mentally and emotionally disturbed. Human intellectual activity has not been successfully reduced to systems of small learnable components.

14. The nonreductionist position has been developed, in recent years, largely by Jean Piaget. Piaget takes the position that overwhelming evidence exists, in all sciences, that complex phenomena have only limited capability of being reduced to simple elements. Processes at lower levels merely lay the groundwork for processes at higher levels. Piaget takes the position that although some aspects of behavior can be successfully studied through studies on lower organisms, human intelligence cannot. The study of lower organisms is useful insofar as these organisms share with the human being common structures in their anatomy. Piaget believes that the human cortex of the brain is fundamentally different in the way it works from the cortex of lower organisms. Piaget believes that there is discontinuity between the behavior of lower animals and human behavior. The nonreductionist takes the position that the human being is a different kind of system from that represented by any other type of organism. The enormous capacity of the infant to learn hardly seems to be accounted for by whatever operant and classical conditioning can offer.

15. The nonreductionist position of Piaget emphasizes the development of *structures* in the developing intellect that permit it to perform intellectual operations.

16. In the present primitive state of development of the behavioral sciences there are advantages in different scientists pursuing different approaches. One approach may produce useful knowledge in one area, but not in another.

17. An important issue in the matter of applying laboratory results to the solution of practical human problems is whether animal and human learning can be considered to represent a continuity, with the one differing from the other only in complexity. Many psychologists take the position that there is a lack of continuity between animals and human learning and that the human capacity to use language represents a function different from any found in subhuman species.

PART II

THE REDUCTIONIST POSITION

Chapter 2

Operant Psychology:
A Reductionist Approach to Learning

The reductionist position has had a long history of support in the United States and has been sponsored often by individuals who had a flamboyant zeal for promoting their cause. Not the least of these was the colorful John B. Watson, who shocked much of the book-reading public with the publication in 1924, of *Behaviorism*. The book was an instant success. It had sufficient impact to cause the *New York Times* to comment in an editorial on its radical views concerning behavior. Watson brought the American public a version of Pavlov's classical conditioning psychology, which had great influence on the subsequent development of American psychology.

The thesis of *Behaviorism* was that all behavior could be reduced to a set of conditioned responses. Watson rejected the notion that mental processes or any inner processes influenced behavior. Indeed, he took the position that mental processes did not have to be studied because they had nothing to do with the ongoing flow of behavior. All one had to do to understand behavior was to tease out the various components, which, he claimed, were nothing more than conditioned responses. The volume presented an elaborate attempt to describe the anatomy of the nervous system to support his contention that the body including the nervous system, were pieces of equipment that manifested only one form of learned behavior—conditioned behavior. Watson wrote with the forcefulness and conviction of a religious leader, but he had little taste for using data. Indeed, *Behaviorism* is almost wholly lacking in data to support his contention that the classically conditioned response is the basic elementary component of even the most complex of human behaviors. Watson himself went on to undertake a very successful career in the advertising field, for which he had great natural aptitude, and he died a very wealthy man. His impact on both American psychology and the public at large was far greater than should have been produced by such a volume. A part of his success must be attributed to the fact that he had managed to coin a word, *behavoirism*, that became a part of the English language. Later psychologists took it to be the descriptor of scientific psychology. It is an odd fact of history that although Watson preached that behaviorism should focus on data and facts, he himself felt free to write a completely speculative psychology and offered no apologies for the absence of data. Watson was more of a frontier preacher than a scientist, even extending his discusssions of behavior to issues of ethics. Like most frontier preachers, his case did not seem to be diminished by the fact that he failed to practice what he preached.

Although Russian psychologists have throughout this century attempted to reduce all behavior to chains of classically conditioned responses, Watson's popularization of Pavlov's classic work was a first major attempt by an American to promote this same approach. The Russians have been quite cautious in the generalizations they draw from their work, and one wonders how they would have responded to Watson's high-powered Madison Avenue approach to the popularization of Pavlovian principles.

Whatever Watson lacked in zeal for collecting facts was made up for by a generation of young American scientists in the late 1920s and 1930s who sought to expand greatly what was known about classical conditioning. The most notable of these new students of classical conditioning was Clark L. Hull, who was not only a great laboratory experimenter, but also a genius for bringing together data from diverse sources for the purpose of developing what he believed to be a comprehensive theory of behavior. This appeared in several versions, of which the 1943 and 1952 are the most famous.

Hull was a scientist and had no interest in following Watson's quest for notoriety. His work was extremely meticulous, mathematical, and logically precise. Some of his work is the most difficult to read of any that psychologists have ever written, but the difficulty is not due to obscurity of style but to the tightly woven logic of the arguments and the attempt to state all the major propositions of the system in mathematical terms. Although Hull's writing gives the impression that he was attempting to develop a comprehensive theory of behavior that would apply to human beings as well as to the laboratory animals on which it was based, he wrote with caution, *never* implying that his contribution could be readily applied to the solution of the practical problems of human living.

Hull's work was a notable scientific venture, but its contribution, more than anything else, lay in the difficulty that Hull encountered in reducing complex skills into simple, basic components. His work also demonstrated the immense difficulties involved in reducing statements about behavior to mathematical terms. Although Hull's work was carried on for a time by his student Kenneth Spence, even before midcentury American interest in classical conditioning as a model for human behavior had declined. One reason for this decline was that classical conditioning did not seem to provide a model of learning that had immediate applications, though the Russians had never viewed the model as being of only theoretical interest and had long considered it to be the one model that had implications for the improvement of everything from school learning to psychotherapy. Another reason for the decline was the emergence of a new, and later very popular, model of learning, which took the position that classical conditioning pertained only to quite trivial aspects of behavior. This new model attempted to reduce all complex behavior not to classically conditioned responses, but to a different form of conditioned response known as the instrumentally conditioned response. This new reductionist theory of learning and behavior was the lifework of B. F. Skinner.

SKINNER'S OPERANT PSYCHOLOGY

In the previous chapter, a major category of learning was described as that in which the organism learns to make a response R that produces a particular state of affairs S. The state of affairs S is always a preferred state of affairs, that is, one that has a high probability of being selected when the learner has an opportunity of choosing between this and other situations. A hungry rat readily learns to press a bar when the action is followed by such a preferred situation as the presence of food. A child learns to say "Please" to obtain a cookie. Learning in this category is commonly discussed in a language that has evolved in the writings of Skinner, and that is now used by psychologists who identify themselves as operant conditioning psychologists or behavior modification psychologists.

Skinner made an important break with tradition when he published in 1938 his classic work, *The Behavior of Organisms.* Older conceptions of learning regarded it as a matter of building up connections between stimuli and responses. In such theories all behavior was considered to be a response to some stimulus, and often because no external stimulus could be found to account for the behavior, an internal stimulus was thought to exist that might produce such behavior. This point of view made many scientists feel uncomfortable, for it really amounts to imagining the existence of stimuli in order to make a behavior theory acceptable. Skinner took the position that only some behavior is the result of specific and identifiable stimuli and that there is other behavior that simply does not stem from any such identifiable source. This was an important step forward.

As a matter of historical interest, one may note that Skinner classified behavior either as respondent or emitted behavior. Respondent behavior is behavior that follows some identifiable stimulus and is a result of it. A reflex such as an eye blink, which occurs in response either to a loud noise or to a puff of air on the eyeball, is an example of respondent behavior. Indeed, all reflexes, because they are triggered by specific stimuli, would be classified in the respondent class. Emitted behaviors occur initially without any identifiable stimuli initiating them. A class of emitted behavior such as foot lifting or saying a particular word is referred to as an *operant.* Some operants acquire a complex relationship to stimuli as the individual develops and learns. Let us consider an example of the development of such a relationship.

Anyone who has observed young children knows that vocal behavior in a 1-year old takes place in a great variety of situations. The infant will spend a part of the day babbling, regardless of where he is or what is happening in his surroundings. The same is not true of the 8-year-old, who is likely to be highly vocal in the presence of other human beings, but relatively silent when he is by himself. The presence of other people is the situation that comes to elicit talking behavior. The relationship of the presence of others to talking behavior is complex in that the young child, placed in a group of children, may often just talk to himself. The precise situation does not determine exactly what he says in the same way that, say, a tap below the kneecap produces the invariable reflex in the leg. The relationship of the social condition to the amount of talking behavior emitted is very complex. In this example, talking behavior is an operant that acquires a high probability of occurring in a social situation.

When an operant appears only in the presence of a certain stimulus, it is said to be a discriminative operant and the stimulus is said to be a discriminative stimulus. If particular stimuli are most likely to elicit a particular form of behavior, then it is said that the behavior is under the control of that stimulus.

The distinction between emitted and respondent behavior is not so clear as it might seem at first glance. When Skinner writes about a behavior that has an identifiable stimulus, he is referring to behavior very closely tied to a particular stimulus. The response of the leg to a tap below the knee satisfies the definition of respondent behavior. Reflexes fall into the classification of respondent behavior, but few other behaviors do. A pupil who pays attention to the teacher and takes occasional notes is not manifesting respondent behavior, and neither is a pupil who applauds at the end of a lecture. Skinner would not classify most of such behavior in the respondent class, for he would say that the relationship of the stimulus to the response is complex and not of the direct nature found in respondent behavior.

In the initial stages of learning based on emitted behavior, the learner shows a very low frequency of occurrence of the behavior to be learned. The child learning to use the expression "Give me" to obtain objects has almost certainly already used the words. Let us not go into the matter of how he has learned to say "Give me," but before he learns to use these words on appropriate occasions he will probably have been heard to say them while he is lying in his crib or on other occasions when the words have little relevance. Learning to use the words appropriately involves an increase in the probability that they will be used on occasions when the child is reaching for some desired object and a decline in probability that the words will be enunciated on occasions when they have no relevance. Learning involves changes in response probabilities in particular situations. When a response is brought under stimulus control it means that the situation determines whether the response will or will not occur. When I meet a friend as I leave for work and say "Good morning," the behavior has a 100 per cent chance of occurring under these conditions, that is to say it is under a high degree of stimulus control, and the response has a high probability of occurring.

Skinner and many of his followers have taken the postion that learning during childhood slowly brings behavior under stimulus control, that is to say, behavior, through learning, becomes more and more appropriate to the situation in which it occurs. These psychologists view the behavior of the young infant as largely random emitted behavior, such as arm and leg waving, babbling, and movements of the eyes. Such random behaviors are emitted in considerable quantity, but other psychologists, notably Jean Piaget, have pointed out that much of the behavior of the infant is highly controlled by stimuli provided by the environment. Skinner, of course, would classify these behaviors as respondents and tend to de-emphasize their significance, but Piaget would regard them as the very foundation of all future behavior. One can say, for sure, that the infant has a large repertoire of behavior under stimulus control. The infant in the early weeks of life sucks when any part of its face is stimulated, fixates a bright light and follows the light when it moves, shows a turning movement of the head in the direction of a sound, cries when hungry, goes to sleep when rhythmically patted, and so forth. Whether one regards the behavior of the infant as being largely random emitted behavior or behavior under stumulus control depends on what behavior one happens to observe. Skinner has tended to emphasize emitted behavior as the foundation of learned patterns of responses, and some learned behavior may well find its roots in the emitted behavior of the young infant. However, throughout the discussion the reader must keep in mind that learned behavior may be much more deeply rooted in the great variety of respondent behaviors shown at birth than the followers of Skinner have generally considered it to be.

Up to this point the assumption has been made that learning occurs and that behavior becomes more and more appropriate to the situations in which it occurs, but nothing has been said about the conditions that have to exist in order for learning to occur. A science of learning is concerned to a great extent with the discovery of the conditions under which learning occurs. Until one knows what those conditions are, one can do little to facilitate learning because one does not know what conditions to provide. Most of the remainder of this chapter is concerned with discussing what is known about particular conditions that bring operants under control. The major condition that will be discussed is the occurrence of events known as reinforcers.

REINFORCEMENT OF OPERANTS

Generations of psychologists have made the observation that certain kinds of events that follow particular behaviors increase the probability that the behaviors will occur. If a hungry rat is placed in a box equipped with a lever, the depression of which releases a pellet of food, the animal will soon learn to press the lever. The event that follows the pressing of the lever, namely, the release of food, is an event that increases the probability that the rat will press the lever. Other behaviors that occur in the box and that are not followed by this particular event will decrease in the frequency with which they occur. The delivery of the food is described as a reinforcing event or as a reinforcer. The behavior of the rat in the box is shaped by the reinforcing event, and soon the hungry rat directs most of its energies to the pressing of the lever to the exclusion of other forms of behavior. Many other events besides the delivery of food have been demonstrated to reinforce the behavior of the laboratory rat.

In the case of human behavior a large number of different events can be identified as having reinforcing properties. Skinner has pointed out that one of the most common reinforcers used in civilized societies is money, but not all members of such a society are reinforced by money. Young children are not generally reinforced with money and other events are generally found to have better reinforcing properties. The preschool child is typically reinforced for appropriate behavior with adult approval. Adolescent behaviour is highly reinforced by the approval shown by other adolescents.

The term *reinforcer* is used here rather than the older term *reward*, though an examination of the research literature shows that the two terms are used as if they were interchangeable. The term *reward* generally carries with it the implication that the event is pleasurable, and the term reinforcer is neutral and is used to indicate only that the event increases the probability of occurrence of the behavior it follows.

Learning is typically produced in animals through the control of reinforcing events. Rats will learn a maze by being deprived of food for twenty-two hours before being placed in the starting box of the maze. They then rapidly learn to find the goal box that contains, on each trial, a small amount of food. Hungry pigeons will learn a number of skills through the manipulation of reinforcing events involving the delivery of food. Although consumables represent the core element of reinforcing events used to produce learning in laboratory animals, human learning can be produced and controlled through the manipulation of a great range of other events, including money, approval, and the occurrence of words such as *right*. The teacher who has knowledge of the events that reinforce may be able to exercise control over what pupils do.

There is considerable question whether food should be used as a reinforcing event in the case of the young child, as it is when the mother says, "You have been very good, here is a piece of candy." The main argument against such practices is the belief of many physicians that overeating in the adult can sometimes be attributed to the fact that the reward system of the individual was originally tied to food during his childhood. When such a food-rewarded individual reaches adulthood, he may continue to reward himself with food to the point where he grossly overeats.

The impressive part that reinforcing events play in the control of learning in laboratory situations has led some psychologists to take the position that all learning involves reinforcing events and that, conversely, no learning will take place without the occurrence of reinforcing events. Such a generalization extends far beyond the limited laboratory data on which it is based. There is also an increasing body of experimental research supporting the position that learning can and does take place without the occurrence of reinforcers.

Those who maintain that all learning is dependent on the occurrence of rein-forcers refer to this generalization as the *law of reinforcement* or as the *law of effect*. The position taken here is that reinforcing events play an important role in learning, but there is no advantage in taking the extreme position that reinforcement is a necessary condition for learning.

A fact to be kept in mind in evaluating the literature on the manipulation of behavior through the control of reinforcements is that it is based largely on a few species, that is, rats, pigeons, monkeys, and, to a lesser extent, human beings. One can certainly point to other species in which the role of obvious reinforcers in the shaping of behavior is much less impressive. For example, one does not teach a parrot to speak by carefully regulating the reinforcements and reinforcing any speech activity that approximates what is desired. On the contrary, two factors seem to be important in teaching a parrot or parakeet to speak. One is that the bird has to be exposed to endless repetitions of the desired phrase. The second is that there must not be any other objects or events that compete for the bird's attention. Birds that are caged with other birds do not learn to speak, and the best procedure seems to be to take the bird from the cage and to perch it on a finger. The bird is unlikely to speak while perched on the finger, but after a large number of repetitions of a particular phrase, the bird will sometime later produce the phrase while it is in the cage. Again, although a dog's behavior is often readily shaped by means of reinforcements, there are also aspects of behavior that are more easily learned by other means. For example, a common way of teaching a dog to shake hands is to take the dog's paw in one's hand and to say "Shake." This is done a number of times and at the end of the session a scrap of food is given, though what is supposed to be reinforced by the scrap of food is not clear. After this routine has been per-formed a number of times, the dog will raise his paw and shake hands when the signal is given. The training does not involve the dog performing some action, for it is the trainer, and not the dog, who raises his paw.

Reinforcement theory generally assumes that certain conditions or events have the inherent property of acting as reinforcers. Thus food and water given to a hungry and thirsty animal may be assumed to function as reinforcers. Other stimuli may presumably have the same effect. Such stimuli might include, in the case of a child, a soft touch on the skin, a bright and shiny object, and moving objects.

A wide range of other phenomena may function as reinforcers. For a child, the process of exploring his environment may, in itself, reinforce the activity. Explora-tion whets the appetite for exploration. Money represents a generalized reinforcer for most people, although there are some whose behavior would not be reinforced by the offering of money. The commonest and most effective reinforcer in a learning situation is the knowledge that the response made was the correct one. There are also some children who may be much more concerned with obtaining the social approval of their classmates than with knowing that their response is in some way approved by society.

Some books assume that the reinforcers of behavior are known and can be identified. One common statement is that *all* children need social approval, implying that social approval is a major reinforcement. There is little or no evidence to support this point of view, though the behavior of some children under some conditions can be effectively reinforced through social events. Another common statement is that the experience of accomplishment is of particular importance because it will, in and of itself, promote development. In some it may, but here again there is little or no evidence to support this statement as a generalization.

When a reinforcement follows a particular response, rather than other responses, one says that the reinforcement is contingent on the particular response. When one speaks of the reinforcement contingencies in an experiment, one is speaking about the particular forms of behavior that are followed by reinforcements.

Primary and Secondary Reinforcers

A distinction is commonly made between primary and secondary reinforcers. The point has already been made that certain conditions appear to function as reinforcers without any learning taking place. Food will reinforce the behavior of any hungry animal, and from the earliest age. Every professional animal trainer, as well as the amateur training his dog, knows that food can be used to produce learning. Water will do the same for a thirsty animal, and so will any condition that satisfies a basic physiological need. Such a reinforcer is known as a primary reinforcer.

Secondary reinforcers are stimuli that did not originally reinforce behavior but that have acquired this property by having been associated with primary reinforcers. A stimulus that was not originally a reinforcing one can become so through being associated with one that *is* reinforcing.

If a pigeon is fed at ten-second intervals and if a buzzer is sounded before each presentation of the food, the buzzer comes to acquire the same reinforcing properties as the food. It is then possible to use the buzzer as a reinforcer—that is, the buzzer can be used to provide some modifications in the pigeon's behavior. If each time the pigeon stands on one leg the buzzer sounds, the pigeon will more and more frequently stand on one leg. In technical language it may be said that the sound of the buzzer has become a secondary reinforcer for the particular pigeon, a property that the sound ordinarily does not possess. A secondary reinforcer may lose its power after it has been used for some time without being paired with the original reinforcer through which it acquired its reinforcing properties. It is possible that some conditions of reinforcement may result in much greater permanence of secondary reinforcing properties than is ordinarily found in typical laboratory experiments. The failure of secondary reinforcers to continue to function as such is one of the difficulties encountered in using this type of mechanism to account for the fact that many different kinds of objects come to have reinforcing properties that remain stable over long periods of time. Money comes to have the property of being a rather general reinforcer, and even small amounts of money, too small to be of real economic significance to the individual, may still reinforce behavior.

Another example of the development of a secondary reinforcer is provided in a classic study by Wolfe (1936), who trained chimpanzees to work for chips which they were then able to insert into a slot machine in order to obtain grapes. After some training, the chips acquire some properties as secondary reinforcers.

They remain weak and transitory reinforcers and do not retain this property without reconditioning. The chimpanzees would even show some hoarding behavior, but difficulty was experienced in arranging conditions so that the animals would hoard as many as twenty chips. Nothing comparable to the extraordinary power that money acquires as a shaper of behavior for many human beings is seen in the property that the chips acquire for the chimpanzees.

Although numerous experiments have been conducted that involve the use of reinforcing procedures with children, nobody has been able to prepare a complete list of what might be considered the primary reinforcers of human behavior. There is no doubt that food will reinforce a hungry child and that water will reinforce a child who is thirsty, but a great range of other events will also reinforce the behavior of children. A child will learn to press a button on the wall with increasing frequency when the only reinforcement provided is a light that goes on each time the button is pushed. Should the light be regarded as a primary or a secondary reinforcing event? One cannot readily see how the light could have acquired secondary reinforcing properties but, unlike most primary reinforcers, it has no obvious relationship to the physiological needs of the child. The light functioning as a reinforcer fits the general rule that any mild and novel event is likely to have positive reinforcing properties.

Just as one can identify fairly clearly some events (such as food and water) that are primary reinforcers in their origin, so, too, can one identify some events that are essentially secondary reinforcers. The giving of money is one of the most universally effective of secondary reinforcing events. However, just as tastes for particular foods are often acquired, and hence some foods under some conditions may function as secondary reinforcers, so, too, may money be valued by the adult partly because that same adult as a child liked to play with shiny coins, and the response to bright objects may be largely an unlearned response. So-called primary reinforcers may have learned components to them and so-called secondary reinforcers may have primary components. The distinction between primary and secondary reinforcers is not as clear as one would like it to be.

Information Value and Incentive Value of Reinforcements

The term *reinforcement* represents a general category of events, perhaps much too broad for thinking about educational problems. Some reinforcements are clearly related to quite basic needs of living creatures, as when a hungry rat is trained to run a maze by providing small quantities of food each time the animal reaches the goal box. Under such learning conditions, it is reasonable to assume that an object that can be used as a reinforcer has incentive value, that is, it has value in energizing behavior as well as in strengthening responses. The difference between the use of the term *incentive* and the use of the term *reinforcement* is not always clear in current psychological literature. Consider an experiment in which children are shown a series of ten English words and their French equivalents, pair by pair. After the presentation of the ten pairs, the children are then tested on their ability to give the French equivalent of each of the ten English words. Then the pairs are presented together in a new learning trial, and so forth. Now let us suppose that in one of the procedures used in the experiment, the child was given an M & M candy immediately after each correct response. It would be quite customary to refer to the M & M as the reinforcement for the response. Now let us consider another procedure in which each time the child made a correct response he was given a token, and in which he also knew that at the end of the session he would be able to turn in the tokens for M & Ms. In the latter case, the M & Ms would probably be referred to as the incentive. The tokens might or might not be referred to as the reinforcers, depending upon the particular experimenter. The terms incentive and reinforcer are sometimes used virtually interchangeably, a fact that brings out the close relationship between the two.

Consider a child learning to add single digit numbers who is told after each addition whether he is right or wrong. In the latter case, the primary function of the reinforcing event is that of providing information. One cannot entirely separate the incentive-giving and the information-giving aspects of reinforcement, for even in those tasks in which the reinforcement is designed to be strictly informative, it also has incentive value. Numerous studies have shown that even with dull and uninteresting tasks, such as that of drawing a line three inches long over and over again, a person will continue to perform the task over long periods of time and perhaps even without improvement, provided he is told after each trial how well he is doing. Knowing how one is doing will in itself maintain behavior as well as serve the function of improving performance. Hence, in such a situation, one can think of knowledge of results as having incentive value, that is, it is an event that serves to energize behavior. In the training of animals, the reinforcements are designed largely around the incentives that have to be introduced in order to maintain particular kinds of behavior. In developing a circus act, a lion trainer has the problem of enticing a lion to sit up on its hindquarters on a stool. Now any lion is able to climb on a stool and to sit on its hindquarters, but the problem of the trainer is to introduce incentives so that the lion will do both when a particluar signal is given. The reinforcement that he uses in training the lion does this. On the other hand, in teaching a child arithmetic, the child neither knows nor understands the operations to be performed, and considerable information must be given to him in order that learning may take place.

In addition to providing information and incentive related to the task at hand, reinforcements also provide a message concerning the agent from whom they are derived. Bringle, Lehtinen, and Steiner (1973) have worked on this problem and have concluded that the pattern of rewards and punishments tells the learner something about the reinforcing agent, such as whether he is rigid, or arbitrary, or subject to some degree of control by the learner. This information may lead to the establishment of a particular form of relationship between learner and teacher that, in turn, may facilitate or interfere with learning.

Knowledge of Results—The Information Factor in the Guidance of Learning

If a person were to perform, but never knew how well he was doing, he would have no basis for improving his performance. It is difficult in daily life to find a task that a person can perform without receiving some information about how he is doing. In the laboratory such tasks can be readily devised. Over half a century ago Thorndike devised one such task in which human subjects were asked to draw a three-inch long line again and again on separate sheets of paper. The subjects were never told whether their line was too short or too long; hence they had no basis for improving their performance, and they did not improve. After practice they tended to draw lines of more uniform length, but they were not able to make adjustments in the length of the line so that it approximated more closely the required three inches in length. If, on the other hand, the subjects had been able to check the length of each line or had been told in some way how well they were doing, then improvement would have taken place.

The information the learner obtains about the usefulness, or effectiveness, or appropriateness of his response is called *knowledge of results* or *informative feedback*. Sometimes the term *feedback* alone is used. This information falls into the class of events known as reinforcers, because it modifies the probability that a particular behavior will be repeated or inhibited on subsequent occasions. Although knowledge of results can be classified as a reinforcer, placing it in the same category as food given to a hungry animal may obscure the problems involved in designing situations in which knowledge of results is effectively provided.

Although some psychologists include informative feedback and simple forms of reward, such as M & Ms, in the single category of reinforcers, they function in rather different ways. If my task is to draw 3-inch lines and I draw a line that I believe to be 3 inches, suppose I am reinforced with an M & M. The reinforcer increases the probability that I will draw a line of similar length on the next trial. However, if I am reinforced with the words " Your line was 3.2 inches long," I may be pleased that I was able to draw a line that came so close to 3 inches, but I will try and make it slightly shorter on the next occasion. Informative feedback does not necessarily just increase the probability that the same response will occur more often, but provides an information guide concerning how the response should be modified. The M & M provides minimal information to guide the next response.

Any ongoing activity requires informative feedback for the activity to be pursued successfully, even when no learning occurs. A very simple activity such as that involved in walking down the street requires a very complicated system of feedback for it to occur smoothly and effectively. The brain has to know where the person's legs are so that movements can be coordinated. In the normal individual, sensory information comes from the muscles and joints, giving him information and permitting him to walk in a coordinated manner. However, when a disease of the spinal cord, known as tabes dorsalis, occurs, the tracts of the spinal cord that carry this information are destroyed and the information from the muscles and joints can no longer reach the brain. The person then has difficulty in walking, though he can manage to do so by directing his eyes downward and watching his legs. In this way he manages to keep track of the position of his limbs; in the dark, however, when he cannot see his limbs, he is unable to walk and will fall to the ground when he attempts to do so. One takes this self-monitoring of ongoing activity so much for granted as to be unaware of its importance, but it is vital for the continuing flow of behavior. One of the more dramatic demonstrations of what happens when this feedback is disrupted is shown in the delayed feedback of speech. A person ordinarily hears his speech as it occurs, but it is possible to record a person's speech and then play it back to him through earphones as he speaks after a second or two delay. The effect of providing this unusual delayed feedback of his own speech is to disrupt the speech mechanism. A person thus receiving delayed informative feedback may stutter and become disorganized. A similar disruption occurs when a person is given a manual task to do with his hands hidden from view, but is allowed to see the image of his hands on a television screen delayed several seconds. Under such conditions he also becomes confused and fumbles the task.

The kind of feedback that has just been discussed is necessary for the production of most long sequences of behavior, and it must take place whether learning is or is not taking place. But for learning to occur, another kind of feedback is also necessary. This is the feedback provided by information concerning the extent to which new behavior is appropriate or correct. This feedback is generally what is meant by knowledge of results.

Knowledge of results may be provided in many different ways and under many different conditions. For example, a person learning to drive a car receives feedback as he drives down the street and sees whether he does or does not stay in his own lane. This is a continuous kind of feedback provided as the task is undertaken. Sometimes it is called concurrent feedback. Then, at the end of the driving lesson another kind of feedback takes place when the instructor tells the pupil the extent to which his performance has been adequate and the errors that he has to correct on the next lesson. The latter may be described as terminal feedback to distinguish it from concurrent feedback. The advantage of concurrent feedback over terminal feedback is obvious. The person receiving information about his performance while he is in action can take immediate steps to remedy deficiencies, whereas when he is given terminal feedback he must wait until the next trial or lesson before he can correct his performance, and by that time he may have forgotten what there was to correct. A person driving a car is likely to learn more by concurrent feedback than by the terminal feedback provided at the end of the lesson. However, one cannot be sure in every case that concurrent feedback will be superior to terminal feedback because there are some laboratory experiments in which the reverse has been the case. There are unquestionably certain situations in which concurrent feedback is less efficient than terminal feedback. This can be illustrated at an anecdotal level by the case of a man who learns to travel by jeep between two desert outposts one hundred miles apart. This he does once a week and he keeps track of his position by noting the hills and other landmarks as he goes along. These provide him with concurrent feedback, and arrival at his distination provides terminal feedback. Soon he learns to make the journey without error, but then, one day, he has to make the journey in the dark, and he loses his way because his learned performance was highly dependent on concurrent feedback, which was absent in the darkness. The point to note is that if he had trained himself to make the journey without concurrent feedback, that is to say, in the dark, then he would have been well prepared to make it under any conditions. The use of concurrent feedback is of limited value when the final performance, for whatever reason, is to exclude it.

The identification of the sources of feedback used by learners in a task is not the easy matter that it is commonly believed to be. A lesson in the difficulties involved is provided by research that has been done on the feedback involved in using a typewriter. Expert typists and teachers of typing have long claimed that highly qualified typists watch neither the keyboard nor the material coming out of the typewriter and that their eyes are fixated steadily on the copy they are typing. They also claim that they can identify errors they make because to type a word wrong "feels" wrong. When West (1967) studied the performance of some expert typists in a situation in which they could see neither the typewriter nor the typewriter roller, they showed a sustantial increase in errors. It seems that the expert does depend on visual cues to check his performance and his product and when deprived of those cues shows a decline in performance. It seems, though, that he must be unaware of the extent to which he uses vision for him to take the position in teaching typing that the learner should not use visual cues at all. The later procedure probably adds immensely to the frustrations of the beginner and is likely to be a hindrance rather than a help.

Holding (1965) has provided a quite elaborate classification of the different conditions under which feedback may be given, and part of the discussion here is based on his analysis. One distinction he brings out is the difference between intrinsic and artificial feedback. When a person learns to solve a problem and arrives at a solution, the feedback is his knowledge that the problem has been solved. In such a case the feedback is inherent in the solution of the problem and is referred to as intrinsic feedback or intrinsic knowledge of results. This intrinsic feedback is to be contrasted with what Holding calls artificial feedback, as would occur when a person is given a grade for his performance or is given a prize if he has performed particularly well. The most desirable kind of feedback is quite obviously intrinsic feedback because it is highly task-related and tells the person what was good or bad about his performance. Artificial feedback to be of maximum use has to be much more closely tied to the task than it usually is.

An example of the effective use of artificial feedback is found in an old World War I procedure for training men to fire a rifle. One of the main difficulties in instructing men in this skill is that of teaching them to fire the rifle by squeezing the trigger and butt with the thumb and first finger. Most men tend to *pull* the trigger, which is a wrong procedure. A simple device can be attached to the gun so that when the soldier squeezes properly a buzzer is turned on (or off). The buzzer provides artificial feedback for the purpose of drawing the attention of the trainee to the cues related to squeezing the trigger. That is, the buzzer alerts the individual to what is happening in his hand and how his hand should feel when it is correctly tensed against the butt and trigger. Holding also cites another example in which air-to-air gunners were trained in a simulator in which a buzzer was sounded whenever the gunner had the correct range adjustment. Trainees who learned with such a device made more rapid progress than those who had only more conventional forms of feedback.

Another example of the use of artificial feedback is found in the various devices designed to train children to stop bedwetting. A typical device for this purpose is described by Van Wagenen and Murdock (1966). The essential feature of this device is a buzzer that sounds as soon as the first drops of urine come into contact with the diaper. The buzzer would appear to serve the purpose of drawing the child's attention to how his body feels when urination is about to occur. If he is sleeping at the time, then the buzzer wakes him and permits him to attend to what is happening. Learning to recognize the cues that precede and accompany urination takes place rapidly with the use of such a device in the case of normal children who have passed the age when bladder control ordinarily occurs.

The Effect of Informative Feedback in Open and Closed Tasks

Until recently, the assumption was commonly made that informative feedback, such as saying "right" or "wrong," would be reinforcing under most conditions, but Nuttin and Greenwald (1968) have found that they are effective as reinforcers only when certain conditions exist. They refer to these kinds of reinforcing events as rewards and punishments, as did Thorndike fifty years earlier, but the modern trend would be to use the term informative feedback. Nuttin and Greenwald have undertaken experiments to show that this kind of informative feedback is most effective on what they call open tasks and that it is quite ineffective on closed tasks. An open task is one that the person undertakes knowing that he will later have to use the responses learned. A closed task is a one-time task, undertaken by a person on a particular occasion and with the knowledge that he is not going to have to perform the same tasks or similar tasks in the future. The person views the open task as a part of an ongoing activity that extends into the future. This is related to the notion, long stressed by educators, that learning will take place most effectively when it is related to the goals and needs of a child. The findings of Nuttin and Greenwald have been confirmed by research undertaken by Longstreth (1970), who points out that it supports a belief long held by educators that a learner's intentions are crucial in determining how much is learned. Repetition, without expectation that the material will have future utility, produces little learning.

Correlated Reinforcement

Correlated reinforcement is widely used in teaching. This condition requires that the quantity of reinforcement be related in some way to performance. The asssignment of a grade so that the grade reflects the quality of performance is an example of correlated reinforcement. This phenomenon has not been widely studied by experimental psychologists, although it was mentioned by Skinner as long ago as 1938. More recently, it has been examined within a program of experimental studies by Logan (1960), who has conducted his research with rats in a maze-learning situation. The limited data related to this problem and the fact that studies have been restricted to a single species—the rat—means that few generalizations can be made that apply to the human learner. However, several potential advantages of correlated reinforcement can be pointed out.

First, correlated reinforcement provides the learner with considerably more information than can be supplied through a reinforcement that does not vary in magnitude. If the learner is provided with correlated reinforcement, he finds out not only that his response is generally in the right direction, but also the degree to which it is in the right direction. The reinforcement has more information embedded in it when it is correlated with performance than when it is not so correlated.

Second, the learner may modify his behavior and obtain definitive information concerning the value of the modification when the reinforcement is correlated with performance. Thus, correlated reinforcement enables the learner to have some degree of control over the learning situation, which he would not have with uncorrelated reinforcement.

Third, a numerical grading system provides one form of correlated reinforcement that may have advantages if the competitive aspects of the system are suppressed.

Self-reinforcing Activities

Those psychologists who regard reinforcement as a necessary condition for human learning have long had difficulty in accounting for the fact that some human learning occurs in the absence of observable reinforcers. Certainly, a person can read a book and learn much from the process, but where are the reinforcing events? Such apparent exceptions to the notion that reinforcement is necessary for learning permit two courses of action. One of these is to take the position that not all learning requires reinforcing events; the other is to assert that hidden reinforcers are operating. The second of these two positions has generally been preferred by researchers in the field of reinforcement phenomena, perhaps because they tend to think of reinforcement as representing a general principle underlying all learning. Thus an activity such as reading is said to involve reinforcing events internal to the reader and the activity is said to be self-reinforcing. The purpose of invoking such unobservable reinforcers is to sustain the belief that reinforcement is a necessary condition for all learning; but the possibility exists that some learning may take place without the occurrence of such events, in which case the scientist would be guilty of imagining events that had no real existence at all.

The safest position at the present time is to stay close to the facts. Because there are some learning tasks in which the acquisition of a skill is closely tied to the presence of reinforcers occurring at the appropriate time in relation to the response, one can say that reinforcement is sometimes a condition of learning; but to say that it is necessary for all learning goes far beyond the facts.

Whether learning can take place without the presence of reinforcing events has long been a focus of controversy. In order to settle the matter it would be necessary to design experiments in which learning occurred but in which all possibilities of reinforcement were excluded. Some studies have been designed that come close to meeting this requirement, and these have shown that learning occurs when reinforcements are either absent or minimally present.

EXTINCTION OF BEHAVIOR

Learning has two important aspects. On the one hand, it is a positive process that results in the acquisition and emergence of new behavior. On the other, learning may proceed by the elimination of undesirable and unwanted behavior. Both the positive and negative aspects of the formation of behavior involve learning.

Teachers often think of learning only in a positive sense, emphasizing the skills that are slowly acquired through contact with the school. They forget that an important problem in school learning is also the getting rid of undesirable behavior acquired elsewhere. The child who is a so-called disciplinary problem in school is one who displays certain unwanted aspects of behavior that interfere with positive learning. The pupil may show high needs to interact with other pupils in ways that are not particularly constructive and may devote little of his energies to the pursuit of learning. He may be hostile to the teacher. He may be a bully. He may be interested in affairs outside the school and absent himself frequently. All of these are well-learned habits of behaving that the teacher may wish to see eliminated and may have to eliminate before constructive learning within the school situation can take place. Every teacher knows that this is a difficult task, for attempts to eliminate well-established patterns of behavior are likely to be quite fruitless.

The mental-health worker is faced with even more serious problems of eliminating behavior. The person who comes to the clinic with serious neurotic disturbances is often one who has learned a whole host of worthless responses. Perhaps the problem of the individual who reports at the clinic is that he responds to most of life's situations with anxiety. In other words, he has learned inappropriate anxiety responses to life that the clinician must help him to unlearn; but unlearning is a difficult matter.

Psychologists do not refer to the unlearning of behavior, but use the term *extinction* instead. The latter term needs some explanation, partly because it is not used with any uniform meaning among psychologists. Most of those who work in the field of operant conditioning define it in this way: *A response that has been previously learned through reinforcement may be extinguished if it is permitted to occur repeatedly without reinforcement.* This definition has been widely used in the writings of Skinner (1938, 1953), although the concept itself was originally developed by Pavlov before the turn of the century. In Pavlov's original demonstration of the phenomenon, he showed that once a dog had learned to salivate at the sound of a bell, then salivation would occur to a lesser and lesser extent as the bell was repeatedly sounded but without any food being provided. After enough soundings of the bell, the animal would cease to salivate when the bell rang, for the response had been *extinguished.* Skinner showed a similar phenomenon in the case of operants. A rat that had learned to press a bar that delivered food would press the bar less and less frequently once the food mechanism was turned off. Eventually, the rat would just give the bar an occasional press, as a rat would do even if it had never learned to obtain food in that way. The latter slow rate of bar pressing is called the *base rate.* When behavior has reached the basic rate, the response is commonly referred to as having been extinguished.

Up to this point the term extinction is fairly clear in meaning, but confusion arises because some psychologists use the term to cover all phenomena that are commonly called "forgetting," although the evidence seems absolutely clear that much of human forgetting involves very different phenomena from the extinction phenomena that have just been discussed. Just as in current literature the term reinforcement refers to a multiplicity of phenomena, so, too, does the term extinction. For the purposes of this book, the term extinction will be reserved for those situations in which a response previously learned through reinforcement is permitted to occur without the contingent reinforcement and shows a decline in strength. Not all learned responses show extinction when they occur without reinforcement. The self-destructive behaviors of some children who hit themselves repeatedly or claw themselves until they bleed do not extinguish. Many such children have died from persistent self-inflicted injuries. There are also many behaviors that are assumed to be learned and that do not extinguish. Nail-biting behavior shows great persistence even when allowed to occur freely. The common interpretation is that nail biting reduces some kind of inner tension and that the tension reduction reinforces the nail biting. Also, the self-stimulation itself may be reinforcing. This is falling back on the idea that there are hidden reinforcers. Because one cannot provide the conditions necessary for the extinction of nail biting, other methods have to be adopted to eliminate the habit. One method is to make nail biting punishing by making the person bite his nails deliberately in front of a mirror or by painting the nails with a substance intensely unpleasant to the taste.

Extinction is not as widely used by parents and teachers as it should be, partly because their own impulses are often to do the reverse. If a child has a tantrum, the parent may ignore it for a time (extinction), but soon the parent can stand the crying and whining no longer and gives in to the child's demands (positive reinforcement). In this way a behavior that should be extinguished becomes positively reinforced. Mental health workers use extinction extensively. A man who visits a psychiatrist because he has an almost uncontrollable desire to shout obscene words may be asked by the psychiatrist to shout those words in the office and in this way slowly extinguish the tendency. Extinction represents one of the few moderately successful ways of eliminating problem behavior.

Because extinction offers so much promise for behavior control, it has been important to find out what kind of a process is involved. At first sight one might guess that it is merely a process of obliterating or washing out learned behavior—perhaps the opposite of learning—but this does not seem to be the case at all. A key to the understanding of extinction is found in a phenomenon known as *spontaneous recovery*. Let us suppose that a child has learned that a particular candy machine is not working properly and that it will occasionally deliver a ball of bubble gum if the lever on it is depressed. The child continues to depress the lever until the machine has been emptied. Next day, he returns to the machine, which has since been filled and fixed, and begins to press the lever, but after thirty depressions no candy has been delivered and his response becomes extinguished. On the following day, he comes to the machine again, and this time presses the lever ten times before his response is extinguished. Still, the following day he presses the lever six times, and from then one he gives the lever a couple of presses each time he passes by. The latter is now his base rate and represents what he does whenever he comes upon a similar kind of machine. One day he makes one of his occasional presses of the lever and the machine delivers candy. Immediately he begins to press the lever furiously. There has been a *spontaneous* recovery of the response. Now note that a single reinforcement produces a complete recovery of the response in full strength. Extinction has not caused the response tendency to vanish, but merely to be temporily inhibited. In fact, the overwhelming evidence indicates that extinction is a process of inhibiting a response and is not a process of eliminating the basic learned mechanism on which the response is based.

A second procedure for the extinction of behavior, previously learned through reinforcement, is to arrange the situation so that the behavior would ordinarily occur and then to prevent the response from occurring. In training a dog to sit and wait for a command before coming forward to take a piece of food, this kind of procedure is used. What is generally done is to show the dog the food while another person restrains the animal from advancing and the person with the food says " Hold it." Then the dog is released when the command " Come " is given. Soon the animal learns to inhibit the tendency to approach the food when he is told to "hold it," and no physical restraint is necessary. In such a situation the dog also learns ways of inhibiting the approach tendency. For example, the dog will commonly turn his head away from the food so that it cannot see it during the waiting period. A related procedure for blocking an undesirable response is found in Wolpe's desensitization technique (1958) used for helping patients eliminate anxiety responses. (See also Paul, 1966, for a description of the technique.)

Extinction procedures should not be applied blindly because they do not always work. The classic case of the failure of extinction is that of attempting to eliminate crying behavior in infants by ignoring them. The evidence indicates that the crying response not only does not extinguish, but becomes enhanced by being ignored. Extinction procedures have limited applicability. The difficulty is that one does not know, for sure, the limitations.

Other procedures for eliminating behavior learned under reinforcing conditions do not depend on response inhibition but on increasing the strength of other responses. If a child in a classroom responds positively to almost everything except the ongoing classroom work, the teacher may try to find ways of making the classwork more rewarding for that particular child. In doing this the teacher is attempting to increase the strength of the responses related to classwork so that they will compete favorably with the responses related to other stimuli.

Vicarious Extinction of Avoidance Behavior

The extinction of many undesirable avoidance responses is often best undertaken through indirect means. Teachers and parents have long known that children can be helped to overcome unreasonable fears through being brought into contact with other children who do not display these fears, but only recently has this phenomenon come under experimental investigation. Bandura, Grusec, and Menlove 1967) attempted to help children who were fearful of dogs to overcome this fear by confronting them with situations in which they saw other children behave positively and without fear toward dogs. The fearful children thus exposed to fearless behavior on the part of other children showed a significant reduction in their tendency to avoid approaching or contacting dogs. The crucial factor in the learning situation appears to be the behavior of the nonfearful child toward the dog. If the adult who is present engages in explaining that there is no reason to be fearful or that dogs are nice animals, little is accomplished in reducing the avoidance responses of the fearful child. What is not clear from such studies is whether it is avoidance responses alone that are reduced through the observation of the model or whether the internal anxiety associated with those responses is also reduced. A child could remain intensely anxious in the presence of dogs but after having seen another child approach a dog fearlessly might be shamed into doing the same thing, although he might do it under considerable stress. Learning to be brave is quite different from learning to be nonfearful. Perhaps it is more desirable to be brave but fearful than to remain fearful and cowardly.

The Shaping and Modification of Behavior

In training a pigeon to move in a circle when placed in a training box, the first step for the hungry pigeon to learn is that when a buzzer is sounded then a food trough will move up into a position where the food can easily be reached for a ten-second period. The buzzer becomes a secondary reinforcer. Once the pigeon has mastered this lesson, training can be commenced. The experimenter watches the pigeon carefully, while having in his hand a switch that controls the buzzer and food trough, which always work together. The experimenter watches the pigeon until he sees the pigeon make a slight turn in the desired direction. The moment this happens he presses the switch and the pigeon is reinforced both by the buzzer and the opportunity to reach the food. Ten seconds later the food trough moves out of reach and the pigeon begins to engage in what appear to be random movements. Once again the experimenter waits for the pigeon to begin to move in a circle and, with luck, the pigeon will this time make a larger move of a circular kind. This is reinforced by the buzzer/food combination, and so the procedure goes on until the pigeon readily makes a full circle each time. An important point to note in this procedure is that not only are the right moves reinforced but the wrong moves are extinguished through the nonreinforcement. Thus the shaping of behavior involves the strengthening of all behavior involving closer and closer approximations to the desired behavior and the extinction of all competing responses. In this way, behavior is slowly brought under control and the pigeon will immediately begin to walk in circles as soon as it is placed in the training box. Additional controls can then be introduced. For example, the pigeon may learn to walk in circles only when a light is turned on. The latter is relatively easy to teach a pigeon once it has acquired the habit of walking in a circle. From that point on, the pigeon receives reinforcement only when the light is turned on. In a single session the pigeon will learn to walk in circles when the light is on and in other ways when the light is off.

The shaping of the pigeon's behavior involves the use of reinforcements that are not intrinsic to, that is, a part of, the pigeon's task. The behavior is manipulated through food, a need-related object in a hungry pigeon, and, according to the interpretation of this aspect of reinforcement given here, the effect of the reinforcer is probably that of providing an incentive effect. The procedure is adopted for the training of the pigeon because it is not possible to produce the behavior by saying to the bird, "Just run in a circle and you will get fed." The operation of slowly shaping behavior by waiting for behavior in the desired direction to occur is pursued only because there is no more efficient alternative procedure available. The general technique does offer promise in the modification of behavior in similar situations involving human beings where there are difficulties in communicating. Examples of human beings whose behavior needs to be shaped, but with whom there is often no more communication possible than there is with a pigeon, are found in the cases of persons in mental hospitals, autistic children, and the seriously mentally retarded. In the past, the training of such individuals has been severely limited by the fact that there is virtually no effective means of communicating with them. Operant conditioning techniques have provided a means of improving the adequacy of the behavior of many such individuals who previously would have been considered to be completely untrainable.

Auto-shaping: One Form of Learning Without Reinforcement

Anyone who has ever trained animals to perform tricks knows that this is not done by slowly shaping the behavior that happens to be emitted. The lion trainer who wants to make a lion climb on a stool will hit the top of the stool with a stick. The lion's attention then becomes directed to the top of the stool and there is a good chance that it will climb up on it. If a trainer wants to teach a chimpanzee to pick up an object, then he is likely to try moving the object, and the chances are that the chimp will then go over to the object and begin to examine it and then pick it up. One may then offer the chimp some form of reinforcement for its action, through this may not be necessary, and it may continue to pick up the object whenever it is presented. The problem of the trainer is to get the animal to attend to the object to be lifted or otherwise manipulated.

The methods of animal trainers have not been viewed by most psychologists as throwing light on the nature of learning. The fact that animal trainers use a technique of attracting the attention of animals they train finds no place in operant psychology because it means that at least some learning can be produced, without reinforcement, by simply directing and redirecting the perceptual systems of the animal. Nevertheless, a few psychologists have become interested in this phenomenon and have named it auto-shaping, a rather misleading term in that it implies that it somehow fits the shaping model of the operant psychologist, which it does not.

In the original study of this phenomenon by Brown and Jenkins (1968), a pigeon was placed in an experimental box with a "key" mounted on the wall at about the level of the pigeon's head. The "key" is usually a small button-shaped object that can be depressed. The box also contained arrangements for the delivery of pellets of food. In the usual preliminaries to experimentation with this arrangement, a hungry pigeon is placed in the box. The pigeon is unlikely to peck the key that operates the food delivery system, but the behavior of the bird can be slowly shaped so that it will eventually learn to peck the key and, thereby, obtain food. The first step often involves just feeding the animal through the food delivery system. Brown and Jenkins short-circuited this shaping procedure by doing just what animal trainers do. They drew the attention of the animal to the key by illuminating it for 8-second periods. Pigeons that ordinarily would not have pecked the key without special training involving shaping pecked the key. Brown and Jenkins observed that the phenomenon is due to the tendency of pigeons to peck at the object they are looking at. They also noted that the pecking of the key has little to do with any reinforcement that followed. What they did not point out is that the phenomenon is virtually one of learning without reinforcement. They avoided this conclusion presumably because they were working within the framework of a theory holding that reinforcement is an essential condition of learning.

The phenomenon of auto-shaping seems now to be well established, and various researchers have demonstrated it with monkeys, fish, quail, rats, and human beings (see Smith and Smith, 1972, and Jenkins, 1973). Operant psychologists have found it a convenient way in which to establish an operant, but the significance of auto-shaping is that animals automatically learn to respond to objects to which their attention is called and that they engage in a kind of exploration of those objects that leads to the acquisition of information about them.

NEGATIVE REINFORCEMENT AND PUNISHMENT

Living creatures avoid some stimuli and engage in escape behavior if exposed to them. Thorndike referred to these stimuli as annoyers, but in recent times a more common practice has been to refer to them as *aversive* stimuli. Some of these are fairly universally aversive to organisms, particularly if they produce strong stimulation such as is produced by electric shock or hot objects. Some are quite specific to particular species. Many birds and monkeys show panic behavior when snakelike objects come into their field of vision. Young children 4 or 5 months old commonly show signs of distress when approached by persons other than their immediate family. At 18 months they show fear responses when placed alone in a room with an unfamiliar object.

Aversive stimuli have long been used to control behavior, though less so in modern times. A great range of aversive stimuli has been used in this connection. Pain-inflicting stimuli were commonly used in the past, but the trend in recent times has been to produce an aversive situation through the withholding of an expected reward. Teachers and parents commonly undertake the latter by taking away a child's privileges. Thus a child may be punished by not being allowed to go out to play. The withholding of a reward is generally believed to be an effective means of controlling behavior. An interesting point to note is that while the withholding of an expected reward is punishing, the withholding of an expected punishment has not been established to have a consistently rewarding effect.

All aversive stimuli that actually occur may have two effects. They may inhibit behavior at onset, that is, at the time when they are immediately applied, but when they stop, the cessation may have much of the effect of a reward. When one obtains relief from pain, the relief may have many of the consequences of positive reinforcement. Behaviors occurring at the time when an aversive stimulus ceases are strengthened. This is the phenomenon referred to as negative reinforcement. A *negative reinforcer is a stimulus the removal of which increases the strength of a response.*

In the presence of an aversive stimulus, the organism typically shows escape behavior. When an escape behavior is successful, it reduces or removes the aversive stimulus. When this happens, the effective response is reinforced by the reduction or removal of the stimulus. The reinforcement thus operating is negative reinforcement.

Negative reinforcement phenomena were first explored with classical conditioning. In the typical demonstration, a dog is placed in a harness, a bell is sounded, and, shortly after the bell, an electric shock is applied to one of his paws. The dog then raises his paw and escapes from the shock. After several repetitions of this sequence, the bell is sounded and the dog anticipates the shock by raising his paw. Avoidance behavior has taken the place of escape behavior. Learning has occurred, and the character of the learning is such that it is commonly called *avoidance learning*.

A small child may show behavior parallel to that just described. The child, exploring his neighborhood, meets a larger and very aggressive child who begins hitting him. The smaller child is able to escape from this aversive situation and runs home, but the escape behavior and the resulting removal of the aversive condition do more than just increase the tendency to escape on future such occasions. The escape behavior leads to avoidance behavior and the child simply learns to avoid the stronger aggressive child. Aversive stimuli, the reduction of which originally reinforced the escape behavior, come to reinforce avoidance behavior.

At this point, punishment must be distinguished from negative reinforcement. Punishment is used in society for the purpose of either weakening or obliterating a response. Negative reinforcement occurs when an aversive stimulus is turned off, but punishment has its effect when an aversive stimulus is turned on. A situation involving punishment is one in which an aversive stimulus either accompanies or follows a learned response. In practice punishment and positive reinforcement are used in combination: Consider a situation in which a parent is watching a child play in the front yard. Each time the child shows signs of moving out into the street, the parent voices some mild threat. The latter punishment is designed to inhibit the response of running out into the traffic. The child also discovers that as soon as he settles down again to play in the yard the threats of the parent are turned off. The cessation of threat, like the termination of any other aversive stimulus, has the effect of strengthening the response that accompanies it. In this case, the response associated with the turning off of the aversive stimulus is that of playing in the front yard and hence this response is strengthened by the negative reinforcement. Punishment is likely to be most effective when it leads to an alternative and more desirable response that is strengthened by the turning off of the punishment.

Mowrer (1960) distinguishes punishment learning from learning involving negative reinforcement in this way: " It is proposed that so-called punishment be termed passive avoidance learning (learning to avoid by not doing something) and that the contrasting form of avoidance learning (learning to do something as a means of avoidance) be termed active avoidance learning" (p. 28). The distinction is a convenient one.

Aversive stimuli are commonly administered in the anticipation that they will lead to and strengthen desirable forms of behavior. Teachers expect children to walk in the halls in school and not run. If a child runs, he is punished, sometimes by having to go back to the end of the hall and begin again. After a few incidents of this kind, walking behavior may become established and running behavior is avoided. The teacher may hope to accomplish two goals by making the running situation aversive. On the one hand, he may wish to weaken the tendency to run, and on the other, he may hope to strengthen the tendency to walk in the particular situation. A child might learn always to walk in this situation, not because the tendency to run is any less strong, but because the tendency to walk is relatively stronger.

Society does not always provide punishment under conditions in which there is some clear and feasible set of avoidance responses to the act punished. The person who is punished as a habitual criminal may have no other course open to him than a career of crime, for nobody will give him honest employment. A child who is punished for thumb sucking may have no other comparably satisfying alternative activity to indulge in when he feels threatened. In such cases, punishment is directed toward the very temporary suppression of behavior, but it cannot provide a negative reinforcement for more desirable behavior.

The assumption is commonly made that a threat of an aversive stimulus will have much the same effect as the aversive stimulus itself. This is likely to be the case when the threat has been followed on some occasions by actual punishment. When it has been thus coupled, it would be expected to acquire some of the properties of the aversive stimulus for the shaping and control of behavior. When a mother smacks a child on the rear and at the same time says " No," she can expect that the word " No" will eventually acquire many of the aversive qualities of the smack and will have much the same effects on the child's behavior. Only the idle threat that is never paired with an aversive stimulus fails to have an influence.

Research on the Effectiveness of Negative Reinforcement and Punishment

The effectiveness of negative reinforcement in producing learning has long been demonstrated and studied in the laboratory. Before the turn of the century, Bechterev had shown that dogs rapidly learned to raise a paw to avoid shock and that this simple situation could be used to study a wide range of learning phenomena. The effectiveness of negative reinforcement has never really been questioned and some experimentalists such as Dinsmoor (1968) take the position today that negative reinforcement produces just as effective learning as positive reinforcement and also provides some laboratory advantages. In the study of animal learning using small pellets of food as a positive reinforcer, the food consumed may slowly produce partial satiation of the hunger drive and a resulting change in behavior. On the other hand, if the animal is learning in a situation involving avoidance of electric shock no such satiation has been shown to occur, though some have speculated that living creatures may habituate slowly to aversive stimuli.

The early experiments by Thorndike (1932, 1935) on the effect of punishment on responses produced data suggesting, at first sight, that punishment did not weaken a response; later, when the data were reworked, the effect of punishment was shown to be roughly the opposite of reward. Controversy over the interpretation of the Thorndike data gave the impression that the effect of punishment had to be considered a matter subject to dispute. This impression was strengthened by research by Skinner (1938), who studied the effect of punishment on rats placed in a situation in which they had learned to obtain food by pressing a bar. In such a situation the mechanism that delivers food can be turned off and the rat will continue to depress the bar for some time, but will eventually stop pressing it. Skinner took rats that had learned to depress the bar and turned off the food mechanisms for all of them, but allowed them to continue depressing the bar. Half of the rats were then punished for depressing the bar by the mechanical application of a slap to the paw placed on the lever. Although the rats were slapped during the first ten bar presses the effect was only a temporary slowdown in their bar-pressing behavior. Skinner concluded that the effect of punishment was a temporary interference with the performance of the punished response and that the interference rapidly wore off when the punishment was withdrawn. Quite similar results were obtained by Estes (1944), who gave electric shock as a punishment for bar pressing. Estes did find more positive effects of punishment, though only when the punishment was either severe or prolonged, but the effects of punishment in his research could be described as being generally weak and certainly not dramatic. Later research, however, has shown dramatic effects of punishment in the control of behavior. Far from being the weak and unpredictable phenomenon that it appeared to be in early experiments, it has turned out to be one that can have a powerful effect on behavior when administered under particular conditions. Later research has done much to indicate the condition that must exist for punishment to be effective.

Solomon (1964), and Brush (1971) have summarized much of the later basic experimentation and succeeded in identifying the conditions under which punishment does or does not suppress behavior. The first class of situation that Solomon examined was that in which an aversive stimulus is used to suppress a response previously learned by means of reward or positive reinforcement. Many experiments have been undertaken on a wide range of species, but the results did not begin to fit together until research workers began to vary systematically the strength of the aversive stimulus administered. Solomon points out that when that is done, the effects of punishment fall into a clear pattern. Very mild punishment does no more than make the victim a little more alert. As the punishment becomes stronger, then it temporarily suppresses the response punished. Still stronger punishment produces a more marked suppression, and with some lasting effects. Very strong punishment produces a very complete and very permanent suppression of the response. For the punishment to be effective, it must occur very close in time to the response.

Much the same appears to be true of avoidance behavior. Mild aversive stimuli are likely to produce inconsistent and unreliable avoidance behavior, but strong stimuli may produce dramatic effects known as traumatic avoidance learning, a phenomenon reviewed by Solomon and Wynne (1954) and Turner and Solomon (1962). The usual method of demonstrating the phenomenon involves the use of a piece of equipment known as the Miller-Mowrer jumping box. The essence of the phenomenon is that an animal is placed on a grid that can be electrified and is then given a near-fatal electric shock just after a light is turned on. The animal shows avoidance behavior by jumping off the grid. Without ever receiving another shock, the animal will continue to show escape behavior by jumping off the grid for hundreds of consecutive trials every time the light goes on. Indeed, the behavior virtually does not extinguish.

The results of research on punishment are not without surprises. One would expect that behaviors related to survival would have a resistance to punishment that would not be evident in the case of trivial learned behaviors, which are readily suppressed if a suitable intensity of a punishing stimulus is used, but this is not what has been found. If animals are severely punished several times by means of electric shock for performing actions instrumental in obtaining food and the punishment is subsequently withdrawn, the animals may well starve to death rather than attempt to obtain food through the act that has been punished. In such experiments the animals can obtain food only by means of the punished act and no other. A limited amount of research has also been undertaken on the effect of punishment on other forms of behavior that are considered to be essentially innate. Solomon points out that research generally shows that such innate forms of response can be suppressed by means of punishment if this occurs concurrently with the response. For example, birds that are just hatched tend to follow a moving object, which under natural conditions is the mother, and punishment will suppress that response. Once again it must be pointed out that the fact that punishment will suppress even those responses vital to survival indicates the extraordinary power of punishment to modify and control behavior—a conclusion that is quite contrary to the conclusions drawn from earlier research.

The general findings of Solomon are that severe punishment is highly effective in suppressing behavior, but he also cautions the reader from overgeneralizing from limited laboratory data. He points out, for example, that punishment that is very effective in one situation may be quite ineffective if the punished response is followed closely by a rewarded response. An illustration of the latter would be if a child were smacked for running out in the street and then, a few seconds later, were rewarded

with candy for playing on the sidewalk. Under such conditions the punished reponse may increase in strength, perhaps because it has led to a rewarding situation.

An aversive condition can also be produced through the withdrawal of a positive
reinforcement. This is quite a complex state of affairs and difficult to study, in view
of the fact that when the experimenter withdraws an expected positive reinforcer
he is thereby extinguishing the responses that were previously tied to the reinforcer.
For this reason, the withdrawal of an expected reinforcer has complex outcomes
that often make the outcome difficult to interpret. These difficulties are apparent in
the review of such research by Coughlin (1972). The matter is of practical interest
because parents commonly punish their children by taking away some pleasure to
which the children had looked forward. Such a punishment may have the combined
effect of punishing the act for which a pleasure was withdrawn and at the same time
contributing to the extinction of activities for which the pleasure might have been a
reinforcement.

There have been two main types of theories concerning how punishment works
(see Dunham, 1971). One type of theory involves the idea that punishment simply
reduces the strength of the response that is punished. The second type of theory
takes the position that the strength of the punished response is unchanged by the
aversive events but that some alternative response is strengthened. Most of the
current theories are not quite as simple as these statements imply, but they are
essentially elaborations of the one or the other of these two positions.

The first type of theory, originally attributed to Thorndike, has not been held in
its simplest form for many years because most psychologists assume that a response
once learned is not lost. The response can be inhibited or suppressed but continues
to exist in a latent form, and removal of the source of suppression or inhibition
will result in the punished response reappearing. However, there are ingenious
variations in the response-weakening type of theory of punishment that overcome
this difficulty. One suggestion, for example, is that the emotional responses that
accompany the punishment become conditioned to the stimuli that initiated the
punished behavior. Thus, when the individual later encounters the stimulus that
elicits the punished response, these classically conditioned emotional responses
occur and disrupt the behavior that was previously punished. One version of this
second type of theory suggests that the cessation of punishment also strengthens
the response that happens to be occurring, and the response thus strengthened can
then compete with the punished response.

There have been seemingly endless elaborations of theories concerning the way in
which punishment operates, and some have involved complex combinations of
classical and instrumental conditioning. However, psychologists have been far more
clever in concocting theories of how punishment works than they have been in
finding out which form of theory is most tenable.

Taxonomies of Instrumental Conditioning

We have discussed various categories of instrument learning, such as avoidance
learning and reward learning. Attempts have been make to develop classifications

of different forms of instrumental conditioning. Such classifications, or taxonomies as they are called, have not as yet proven particularly useful, but the student curious to find out what they are is referred to an article by Woods (1974).

THE OPERANT POSITION:
PRESENT STATUS AND TRENDS FOR THE FUTURE

Let us pause to consider here operant psychology as a scientific position on human behavior. We will postpone until the next chapter a consideration of its practical accomplishments, for significant practical accomplishments may or may not have a scientific foundation.

The operant position on how a science of behavior should be developed is founded on a view of science that was widely held during the early part of the present century—that science should limit itself to observable facts. Watson was influenced by that point of view, and he rejected the idea that one should attempt to understand behavior by finding out what happens, psychologically, inside the individual. Watson, like Skinner after him, rejected the notion that the psychologists should attempt to explore the inner life of the individual, for inner life was a private matter that the scientist could not explore directly in another individual. The scientist, it was believed, should confine his work to that which can be observed. A psychologist should thus avoid theorizing about the underlying causes of behavior. Stick to facts! This advice was given by both Watson and Skinner and embraced with almost religious zeal by generations of followers. In its day, the advice had merit, in that psychologists had been all too prone to develop theories based on the flimsiest facts, but it represents an extreme position that contemporary experts on the nature of science would not find acceptable. However, Skinner has virtually not changed his position in thirty years (see Skinner, 1975).

Every science that has built a significant body of knowledge has done so by going beyond that which can be observed. The history of science seems to show quite clearly that the scientist's ability to make good guesses about underlying causes of observable events is crucial to the advancement of science. Chemistry made little progress until the guess was made that matter consisted of atoms and that different atoms constituted different elements. Nobody had ever seen an atom when such a guess was made, and only much later was there direct evidence that matter did truly have an atomic structure. If the early chemists had stuck to the advice given by Watson and Skinner and confined themselves to that which could be observed, a science of chemistry could not have evolved. The development of scientific knowledge involves going far beyond the facts that can be directly observed and acquiring an understanding of the underlying mechanism. The claim of many operant psychologists that their approach to the development of a science of behavior is the only productive approach finds no outside support.

Critics of the operant position point out that most of what is taught as operant psychology has remained unchanged for at least the last quarter of a century. The operant psychologists believe that the unchanging nature of what they claim to be their basic body of knowledge is a result of the fact that they have arrived at eternal and immutable truths. This claim is highly unlikely to be true, for even the mature sciences no longer make such a claim for their branches of knowledge. Skinner's well-known book, summarizing and popularizing his position, was given the title of *The Science of Behavior*; a more modest title might have been *A Science of Behavior*.

Since operant psychologists have taken the position that they have developed *the* science of behavior, they have felt that the knowledge they have derived mainly from the study of a few subhuman species could be generalized to other species, including man. In doing this they have repeated Watson's fundamental mistake of overgeneralizing from a little data. They would have done much better to follow their own advice and stick to the facts, viewing data on rats as pertaining primarily, if not entirely, to the behavior of rats. This is one of the most serious criticisms of operant psychologists, who have come to be viewed by many as having far more of a flair for marketing their wares than developing scientific knowledge.

There has also been considerable criticism of the law of positive reinforcement that stands at the core of the system. The law states that a reinforcer that follows a response strengthens that response, which leaves us with the problems of defining a reinforcer. The definition usually offered is that a reinforcer is an event that follows a response and strengthens that response. Thus a reinforcer is defined as a condition that produces learning and learning is defined as that which is produced by a reinforcer. The law of reinforcement is thus not a law at all, unless one can find a definition of a reinforcer independent of the law of reinforcement. This criticism amounts to saying that the law of reinforcement involves circular argument and operant psychologists have difficulty in escaping this criticism of circularity, though they have made some effort to escape by finding an independent definition of reinforcers.

The law of positive reinforcement has also run into difficulties. Later chapters of this book will refer to demonstrations of learning without reinforcement, which have led many psychologists to believe that reinforcement is not central to learning. The reinforcements offered may determine what a person learns rather than the actual learning itself. If somebody pays me a dollar each time I learn a new Russian word, I am likely to spend a substantial amount of time and effort learning Russian, but the dollar brings me to the learning situation and is not a part of the learning process. This interpretation of the data of operant psychology views the role of the reinforcement as that of an incentive. The dollar is the incentive that leads me to learn Russian. Operant psychologists do not like the concept of incentive, because it involves an interpretation that goes beyond the data. Their objection is basically a philosophical one, but a very strong argument can be made, as Bindra (1974) has, for the incentive interpretation of reinforcement.

The incentive theory of reinforcement data raises questions about what is learned. Bolles (1972) has discussed this matter and concludes that what is learned is an *expectancy*. The learner learns to expect certain kinds of reinforcements in a typical operant experiment. If, in such an experiment, a child learns to push a certain button to obtain candy, what he is learning is not to push a button, for he knows how to do that, but that the pushing of a certain button can be expected to deliver candy.

Here again, operant psychologists object to this interpretation on philosophical grounds. The concept of expectancy goes beyond the data, and they reject any reflective ideas that go beyond the data.

During the last decade, a major weakness of operant psychology has become more and more apparent—its inability to describe or investigate the higher levels of reflective logical behavior in man. Although operant psychologists proclaim that they have discovered universal laws that apply to all forms of behavior, these proclamations are typically made without facts and are acts of faith rather than the products of research. Strike (1974) has pointed out that most of the claims for the supposed universality of the laws of operant psychology are based on the philosophical position that whatever is derived from the objective study of behavior must be no less than a universal truth. This philosophical position is of dubious validity and does not relieve the operant psychologist from demonstrating that what he calls "principles" are, truly, universal principles. It is an extraordinary paradox that those psychologists who boast most about the need to stick to observable facts should rely so heavily for support on a philosophical position.

Strike also points out that the inability of operant behaviorists to provide an acceptable account of higher forms of problem solving in human beings is partly a result of the fact that the language of the operant behaviorist (which Strike describes as behaviorese) is a very limited language, capable of making only a very limited number of statements about behavior. The key words in the operant behaviorist's language are *operant, response, reinforcer, stimulus, discriminative stimulus, extinction, shaping* and *response emission*. With such a language one cannot say much about behavior. Operant psychologists show considerable ingenuity in attempting to describe a variety of behaviors in such terms, but with a resulting impoverishment of the description. Operant psychologists have not been able to convince most other psychologists that the terms can be used to describe more than a very small segment of human behavior. Indeed, some psychologists who only a few years ago were considered to represent the operant position quite completely now emphasize that operant psychology is only one small aspect of the total science of behavior (for example, see Bandura, 1974).

Skinner has attempted to show how his supposed universal laws of behavior have implications for society and how society governs itself. His most recent effort in this connection is *Beyond Freedom and Dignity*. Although the book claims to be a scientific treatise, any scientific data on which it is based are so remote from the topics discussed that their relevance is doubtful. However, the book does provide a philosophical view of some interest concerning the nature of man, and elaborates on the consequence of this view of man for government and social organization.

Whether man does or does not have freedom of choice has become an issue among psychologists in recent years, largely through the publication of Skinner's book. In that book Skinner objects to a naive conception of human freedom that no competent individual today would attempt to maintain. He never really defines what he means by freedom of decision, but leaves the reader the task of deciding what he has in mind. Skinner implies that the notion of freedom of choice has no place in science and that all choices, that is, all decisions, are predetermined by present and past environmental events. His position is that external events produce particular decisions, and not events inside the individual, other than information retained about past events. We choose one course of action rather than another, according to this position, because this is the way in which we have been conditioned. At the best, this is a grossly oversimplified version of how choices are made.

Skinner does not deny that people want to be free, but he considers that the state that they call "free" is only one in which aversive controls are absent. This leads to the dubious position that human beings would call themselves free if they lived under a benevolent dictatorship. The possibility of eliminating aversive controls also, probably, is an impossibility, for even if society were controlled by positive reinforcements, the mere fact of not obtaining an expected positive reinforcement, as would often happen, would constitute a negative reinforcement. One cannot conceive of a society in which all, or even most, aversive conditons have been removed. Also, those who take the position that man has freedom of choice would also take the position that in an aversively controlled society they may be free to choose among aversive consequences.

The great advantage in eliminating the possibility of free choice from behavior theory is that it appears to simplify the task of the scientist. If all behavior is determined by environmental events, one only has to find out how to control environmental events if one wishes to control the behavior of another. Expose the individual to the correct sequence of events and one can ensure that he will perform in a particular way. Such a conception of behavior control assume that the other person, the person whose behavior is being controlled, has no freedom in making his own choices, but it assumes that the scientist has a certain freedom in choosing the conditions to which the other person is exposed. The theory also assumes that the scientist can choose between truth and falsity and has freedom to reject a position that is false. Skinnerians counter this by saying that the facts of science are the environmental conditions that determine the behavior of the scientist and that these facts lead the scientist to take positions that are true.

Although operant psychologists on the surface deny freedom of choice, many behave as though such freedom were a fact. Indeed, at least one book, widely used by operant psychologists, advocates *self-reinforcement*. The latter is an odd position for such psychologists to take seeing that their system does not recognize the reality of a self that can choose. Yet the whole concept of self-reinforcement implies that there is a self that can choose to reinforce the individual or not to reinforce. The self is conceived of as an executive control system that has the power to make or not make decisions.

One cannot leave the theoretical position of operant psychology without reflecting on the fact that it has been a development peculiar to American culture. A possible reason for this is that the beliefs of operant psychologists are similar to the beliefs of those who embrace the philosophy of a traditional capitalist society. Both believe that a person is controlled mainly by the reward system. Where there is scarcity of workers, wages are raised to attract workers. Pay systems are arranged to improve productivity. The common saying that "every man has his price" is another way of saying that behavior can always be controlled if strong enough reinforcers are available. Operant psychology and traditional capitalist philosophy have much in common, but the traditional view of man incorporated in that philosophy is becoming progressively less acceptable as a basis for action, and the newer economists conceptualize man in different terms. Newer conceptions of human beings recognize the fact that individuals strongly react against a social system that attempts to exercise control by controlling the reward system.

Man has a need to feel that he is not controlled by others. Regardless of whether freedom is a reality, or an illusion, man reacts negatively against attempts to restrict his freedom. The infant yells when his mother restrains him, the adolescent sulks under parental restraint, and adults may engage in revolution when even benevolent governments impose restrictions on them. There is a story told about the great industrialist Hershey, who, in the last century, provided his workers with generous benefits, including company housing and company health plans. One day his workers rebelled because they wanted the benefits to be controlled by them, and not by the company. Hershey wept like a good father who has been rejected by his children. Skinner's idea that a community filled with positive reinforcements would necessarily be happy, or what men would call a free one, is nonsense.

Wicklund (1974) has conducted extensive research on this problem of how individuals react to restraint and refers to it as *reactance theory*. When a person's choices are restrained, so that he can no longer choose goal A, but only goal B, certain responses occur. One immediate consequence is that goal B becomes more attractive to him. A second consequence is that the individual sets up new goals, like A, but even more taboo. The worker who is not allowed to choose his own union may set up the goal of establishing a system in which he participates in every decision regarding the company. The restraint, with respect to the choice of a union, may convert him into a radical revolutionary. Another consequence of restriction of freedom is aggression. Still another response is a heightened liking for the activity that the restraint on freedom forbids or makes difficult.

SUMMARY

1. The reductionist position has long been established as a dominant position in American psychology. Watson's *Behaviorism* was the first widely read presentation of this point of view. Those psychologists who followed him attempted to provide a data base for the kind of science of behavior that Watson had envisaged. Watson's views were based largely on the work of Pavlov, which also became a guide for the work of other behavioristically oriented psychologists. The Pavlovian approach to psychology ultimately became displaced in American psychology by the approach that Skinner originated, which became known as operant psychology.

2. The language commonly used for discussing the learning of instrumental responses ($R \rightarrow S$ learning) has been derived largely from the work of Skinner, who

distinguishes between respondent and emitted behavior. The former appears as a result of a well-identified stimulus, but the latter cannot be considered to be produced by a particular stimulus.

3. As the child develops, behavior becomes more and more a set of organized sequences of behavior. This change in behavior through learning is referred to as the shaping of behavior. As behavior is shaped, it shows a linking of behavior with certain situations, that is, certain behavior tends to take place in certain situations. These situations are said to provide discriminative stimuli and the behaviors involved are referred to as discriminative operants.

4. A reinforcer is an event following behavior, which changes the probability that the behavior will occur again. The term *reinforcer*, unlike the term *reward*, does not carry with it the implication that the event involved is pleasant or unpleasant. For this reason many prefer to use the term reinforcer, though the term reward is still widely used in such eminently respectable scientific sources as the *Journal of Experimental Psychology*. Some psychologists have taken the position that all learning involves reinforcing events, but this is a position that is becoming more and more difficult to maintain. Much of the research on reinforcement has been undertaken with a few species in which reinforcement plays a very clear, central, and powerful role in learning. The animal psychologist is always in danger of choosing species that fit closely his theoretical position on behavior.

5. Some events acquire their reinforcing properties as a result of learning, whereas others have reinforcing properties because of the inherent nature of the organism. The former are referred to as secondary reinforcers and the latter as primary reinforcers. There is no agreement at this time concerning the number of different kinds of events that should be included in a complete list of primary reinforcers. If such a list could be made, it would differ from one species to another. Although some books on education assume that the reinforcers of the behavior of young children can be identified, this is far from the truth.

6. Secondary reinforcing events are those that did not originally have the power of reinforcing behavior. They acquired the property of reinforcement by being paired with events that have reinforcing properties. A whistle does not reinforce the behavior of a dolphin, but after the whistle has been blown every time the dolphin is fed, the whistle acquires much the same reinforcing properties as the food. The sound of the whistle has thus become a secondary reinforcer. However, if the whistle is thereafter never paired with food again, but is used to reinforce the behavior of the dolphin, it will rapidly lose its reinforcing properties.

7. Reinforcement is a complex phenomenon and the single term covers a very broad category of events. In the case of human learners, events that are reinforcing include those involving preferred consumables, such as M & Ms, and also events that are verbal and information-giving.

8. The most common reinforcing event in the school-age child's life is that provided by knowledge of results, or informative feedback, as it is commonly called. A chain of behaviors, if it is of any substantial length, requires that the person involved know how he is doing. This requires some kind of concurrent feedback.

One could not tie a complicated knot if one did not know the exact position of the cord and of one's hand at each stage. Some of the feedback with which one is concerned in formal training sessions is feedback provided from a source external to ourselves. Such feedback may be either concurrent or terminal, concurrent when it is provided while the task is being undertaken, and terminal when it is provided after completion of the task.

9. Both concurrent and terminal feedback may be either intrinsic or artificial. In educational situations, artificial feedback is often tied too remotely to the task to be of value. An overall grade for work performed during a semester is probably almost useless as a means of improving future performance. The most the person graded can derive from such a procedure is a review of his notion of how much time to spend on schoolwork in the future. However, if artificial feedback is tied closely to the task to be mastered, it can have high utility in producing learning.

10. A crucial factor in determining the extent to which the results of feedback are retained is the learner's knowledge that the information provided by feedback is or is not going to be used later.

11. Some psychologists have attempted to explain learning, in the absence of observable reinforcements, by proposing that internal reinforcements are operating. They may be, but it is much better to stay close to the facts and to assume, in such cases, that learning is taking place in the absence of reinforcements. The introduction of the concept of self-reinforcement is an effort to salvage reinforcement theory in areas where it does not seem to apply.

12. Just as reinforcement increases the probability of occurrence of the response on which the reinforcement is contingent, so does the withdrawal of the reinforcement decrease the probability of the occurrence of the response. This decline in response probability when reinforcement is withdrawn is referred to as extinction. Once a response has been completely extinguished, it will show a rapid recovery to the strength it had before extinction, if the reinforcing contingency is reintroduced. This well-established fact suggests that extinction is not an erasure process that simply eliminates the learning that has taken place, but that it is a process of inhibition.

13. A second procedure for eliminating a response is to arrange the conditions that ordinarily produce the response and then prevent the response from occurring. The latter mechanism is closely related to the desensitization procedure that has become widely used by psychotherapists. There is some evidence that the desensitization procedure is effective in controlling unwanted behavior, such as anxiety responses.

14. The term vicarious extinction has been used to describe cases in which a child's anxiety reponse has been eliminated through contact with nonanxious children.

15. The shaping of behavior occurs through the positive reinforcement of any trend in behavior in the desired direction and the extinction of any trend in the opposite direction.

16. Attempts to shape behavior through the manipulation of reinforcement and

extinction have been particularly successful in the cases of young children of pre-school age, the mentally handicapped, and certain categories of patients in mental institutions. A strict copy of the procedures used with animals is rarely used effectively with human beings for the reason that one can communicate with the human learner through language, and language may be a powerful modifier of behavior. Only in very rare instances is it necessary to resort to simple manipulations of reinforcements. Although these behavior modification procedures have had considerable success with human beings operating at rather simple levels, very little application of consequence has been reported in improving academic learning on the part of individuals who fall within what is called the normal range.

17. Animal trainers have typically used methods different from the traditional ones of operant psychologists for the shaping of behavior. These methods are now referred to as auto-shaping methods. Typically they involve directing the attention of the animal to the object to be manipulated. The phenomenon of auto-shaping does not fit into the operant theory of behavior in that it does not seem to involve reinforcement.

18. Stimuli that living creatures typically avoid are referred to as aversive stimuli. Aversive stimuli have an immediate effect of inhibiting behavior, but the removal of an aversive stimulus has much of the effect of a reward. A first response to an aversive stimulus is escape, but the animal may ultimately be able to learn to avoid encounters with aversive stimuli. Escape behavior gives way to avoidance behavior. Punishment is a special case of the use of avoidance behavior. Punishment is generally administered in the hope that it will inhibit a response.

19. Sometimes the effects of negative reinforcement may be dramatic and permanent, as in the case of traumatic avoidance learning, but effects of this kind can be produced only when extremely severe stimuli are involved. With milder stimuli, the learning produced by negative reinforcement is probably comparable to that achieved with the use of positive reinforcers. The effect of punishment on the suppression of a response is highly dependent on the strength of the punishing agent. Mild punishment may only make the subject punished more alert, but severe punishment may block a response permanently. Moderate punishment has an effect in between. Some quite dramatic effects have been found in the use of punishment to suppress self-destructive behavior in young children. The side effects of punishment are not clear at this time. Physical pain may produce aggression and, under some circumstances, may produce a complete disorganization of behavior. Parents who punish the most tend to have children with the greatest number of problems in the area of aggression. The main arguments against the use of punishment for the control of behavior are moral and ethical.

20. There have been many theories of how punishment produces its effect. One type of theory is that punishment reduces the strength of the punished response. Another type of theory is that punishment strengthens alternative responses to the response that is punished.

21. The operant position reflects a philosophical position concerning the nature of science that is no longer widely held. Although operant psychologists firmly be-

lieve that a science of behavior should deal only with observables, every other branch of science has had to introduce abstract terms that are only remotely related to data. Scientific systems of knowledge always go far beyond the immediately observable. Although accepting the discoveries of operant psychology, most psychologists today prefer to take a more traditional position concerning what should be the characteristics of a science of behavior. They would also agree that psychology has been hindered by much wild theorizing. Theory development in psychology is going to be more cautious in the future than it has been in the past as a result of the criticism of operant psychologists.

22. The law of positive reinforcement has run into many difficulties as a law of learning. Some would even argue that reinforcement has little to do with learning as such, but rather reinforcement determines what a person learns and how his attention is directed. Some psychologists with fewer inhibitions about using theoretical concepts than the operant psychologists prefer to think of learning as a matter of learning expectancies. Of course, expectancies cannot be directly observed and, hence, represent a concept that the operant psychologists will not use.

23. Operant psychology has been least effective in finding applications in the area of complex problem solving. Indeed, it has little useful to say about intellectual activity.

Chapter 3

Applications of Operant and Classical Conditioning: Behavior Modification

The previous chapter reviewed the overall scientific position of operant psychology as it has been developed by Skinner and his followers. As a scientific system it has remained quite static for the last quarter of a century, but there has been considerable effort to apply the concepts to the solution of practical problems. There are real difficulties in expanding the system scientifically and development of practical applications has seemed the path to take.

The applied work of operant psychology has slowly acquired the name of *behavior modification*. This term derives from the belief of operant psychologists that the scientist should be concerned only with observable behavior and that the control and change of behavior involves only the control and change of events that surround the individual whose behavior is to be changed. This set of beliefs leads the operant psychologists working in the clinical area to take the position that it is profitless to spend time trying to find out the inner causes of the disturbed person's behavior, and that effort should be concentrated on manipulating conditions in the environment that will produce behavioral change. Within this theory, the conditions that are going to produce behavioral change are the reinforcers and aversive conditions and the contingencies to be reinforced or punished. The manipulation of these conditions is believed by operant psychologists to be the only effective way of changing behavior. A similar approach in schools leads to the position that one does not try to find out why Jimmy misbehaves, but one does try to arrange conditions so that Jimmy's behavior will be shaped up into a form more acceptable to the teacher. There is, of course, nothing particularly new about this position, for Watson promoted it in the early 1920s. The position implies that thoughts, feelings, inner attitudes, and personal goals have nothing to do with how a person behaves and that the behavior of the individual is controlled by conditions in the world that surround the person.

The behavior modification position is extreme and is rarely followed with complete rigidity. For example, if a child cannot solve percentage problems, despite the fact that he has been drilled in the mechanics thereof, the teacher will almost certainly attempt to find out the misunderstandings and difficulties that prevent him from solving problems. Even the advocates of behavior modification techniques abandon them quickly when other techniques seem more successful. For example, although Stunkard (1974) sings the praises of behavior modification techniques for controlling obesity, he makes frequent reference to the effect of inner states on eating. He cites the case of one woman who " recognized that anger stimulated her eating." Now anger is an inner state and not the kind of thing that behavior modifiers are supposed to consider to be important. A part of Stunkard's technique requires the patient to keep a diary related to eating in which observations on inner states are recorded. Stunkard's use of the term *behavior modification* voids it of any of its basic meaning. Indeed, he places great reliance on the subjective observations of the patient. Strangely enough, Stunkard's glowing account of the merits of behavior modification, accompanied by the abandonment of the strict behavior modification position, is rather typical of the literature on the subject. The label seems to carry with it a certain prestige, and thus it is used widely.

Prior to the use of behavior modification techniques, insofar as they are actually used, the behavior modifier is supposed to undertake a detailed study of the conditions in the environment that produce the particular behavior to be modified. If the psychologist treating obesity made such a study of the habits of a patient, he might find that eating behavior was triggered by such conditions as the sight or smell of food, the absence of other individuals, and the lack of any absorbing task to undertake. In theory, with such data available, the psychologist might then help the obese person plan his life so that he avoided the smell and sight of food, managed to have others around him much of the time, and had many absorbing tasks to occupy him. In addition, the psychologist might also be able to arrange conditions so that reinforcements were provided for avoiding food or engaging in other activities. However, few psychologists helping a person to avoid eating would limit themselves to such simplistic data. Most, like Stunkard, would be willing to discard the strict philosophical position of behavior modification in order to obtain some data about what was troubling the obese person at the time when he ate compulsively and unnecessarily. The philosophical position that only the environmental conditions that trigger eating behavior should be studied is not particularly persuasive for most practical psychologists.

Behavior modification approaches have been most successful in producing behavior change in those instances in which there is a fairly obvious relationship between behavior and conditions in the environment. A child who has learned that sulking gets him what he wants will change if the sulking no longer produces results. In such a case the relationship of events to behavior is clear. In the case of most of the problems that the teacher encounters in the classroom, the relationship of behavior to immediate events is quite obscure.

The overwhelming difficulties of conducting behavior analysis under natural conditions has led some behavior modification workers to take the position that systematic behavior analysis is not generally a practical venture. Those who take that position also hold that common knowledge about reinforcers can still be used to change behavior by a slow shaping process. The position is reminiscent of that taken by Machiavelli, nearly 500 years ago, to the effect that the Prince, who controls the reward system, can control human behavior. However, the modern behavior modifier commonly takes the position that the behavior that is modified by the reward system will remain modified after the reward system is withdrawn. The Prince never made that assumption.

STUDIES USING BEHAVIOR MODIFICATION WITH THE RETARDED AND DELINQUENT

The most frequently published accounts of the application of operant conditioning techniques are in the treatment of the mentally retarded. The number of studies in this area probably runs in the hundreds. Many of them deal with the problem of toilet training, largely because many institutions for the mentally retarded have assumed that the children confined in them were not capable of mastering this basic skill. The application of operant conditioning techniques, involving the reinforcement of partial success at first, has shown that these institutionalized individuals are much more capable of being trained than was previously believed possible.

Many studies report that mentally retarded children as old as 14 who had never acquired the rudiments of toilet training were trained in a matter of weeks. The general nature of the procedure is simple. First, some attempt is made to determine the times at which urination or bowel movements occur. Then the person is persuaded to sit on the toilet at that time. Whenever success is achieved, some reinforcement, such as a piece of candy, is provided. In addition, any attempt by the individual to move toward the toilet on appropriate occasions is rewarded, even if he has an accident on the way. The essence of the technique lies in closely observing the person to be trained so that even minimal behavior in the right direction can be reinforced immediately.

Other areas in which some success has been achieved include helping autistic children to respond more to others so that learning can be more readily elicited (see, for example, Hewett, 1966). At least one study—Schwitzgebel (1967)—shows that delinquents who were positively reinforced by praise in interviews for making more desirable statements showed improvement in this respect both in subsequent statements made in interview situations and in statements made in natural settings. Nevertheless, universal success has not been achieved.

The idea of behavior analysis finds its origin in the theory that behavior consists of conditioned operants, triggered by particular discriminative stimuli in the environment. Analysis involves discovering the particular discriminative stimuli that control the production of the operants. This is, of course, not a proven theory of the nature of behavior, but a set of assumptions. The concept of *analysis*, as it is used in undertaking behavior analysis, represents a logical outgrowth of the reductionist view of behavior and learning. Just as the chemist analyzes complex compounds into their elements, so, too, does the psychologist supposedly analyze behavior into its elements and their causative agents in the environment. The analogy is a persuasive, if not seductive, one. But what if behavior does not fit this model except at the simplest levels?

The prescription for changing behavior is, on the surface, simple. Indeed, those who promote it commonly hold the view that anyone can learn the basic techniques. This viewpoint has led to the production of a number of manuals that attempt to train the amateur in behavior modification techniques. The manual by Becker, Thomas, and Carnine (1969) claims to help teachers to reduce behavior problems in the classroom, and other similar manuals have been developed in other areas. The implication of these manuals is that one only has to watch behavior to be able to identify the environmental circumstances that control it. The assumption is that the relationship between behavior and events in the surrounding world is simple. Many psychologists would take the point of view that the relationship is complex, rather than simple, and that if it were actually simple a sophisticated science of behavior would have emerged a long time ago.

Numerous studies of the retarded have used punishment to shape behavior. Some have produced positive results. What purports to be a more general article by Johnston (1972) on the use of punishment in the shaping of human behavior comes to sweeping conclusions on the usefulness of the practice. However, if one examines the references cited by Johnston, one finds that nearly all refer to cases of children classified as retarded, autistic, or severely disturbed. One may draw, perhaps, limited conclusions from the article, far more limited than its author draws, that punishment is sometimes successful with certain deviant populations. The article was severely criticized by Kazdin (1973), who points out that much of Johnston's case rests on unjustifiable generalization from experimental data on animals. Kazdin points out that even if one form of punishment is effective in a particular situation, one cannot infer that another form of punishment will be effective in the same situation.

There have also been cases documented, with data from human subjects, in which severe punishment did little to change behavior. The classic case is that of the Patuxent Institution for defective delinquents (see Reppucci and Saunders, 1974, and Trotter, 1975) where the punishments used were declared by a Maryland Court to be cruel and unusual. Indeed, they were reminiscent of the Dark Ages and involved such acts as tying an inmate to a board by ankles, wrists, neck, and chest and letting him lie in his own excrement for a few days. Although the institution spent $40 million over 16 years, less than 5 per cent of the inmates were ever considered rehabilitated. Punishment was administered in the name of behavior modification as a part of a program to provide intensive psychiatric aid!

Simple laboratory studies, on which studies in more natural settings of the punishment of the retarded and the deviant have been based, fail to take into account what may be crucial factors in institutional settings. Severe punishment of delinquents may produce in them, collectively, a resentment and hostility toward the institution that may defeat all attempts to rehabilitate the inmates. Also, the interactions between the punished inmate and other inmates may have important effects. In other settings where mild punishments have been used the presence of a companion has been shown to reduce the aversive effects of punishment, but this effect probably takes place only under conditions involving a sympathetic relationship between the punished individual and his companion (see Epley, 1974).

Thus, in summary, positive reinforcing procedures have been well demonstrated to produce at least a temporary change in the behavior of the retarded, and perhaps also the delinquent. The long-term effects of such behavior modification techniques are not well established, except in the case of such basic skills of living as toilet training. The use of punishments remains controversial, with highly variable results depending on numerous circumstances, the effects of which are not well understood.

BEHAVIOR MODIFICATION FOR THE HOSPITALIZED MENTAL PATIENT

A decade or more ago behavior modification was enthusiastically proposed as a means of treating seriously disturbed patients in mental hospitals. Numerous anecdotal records were published describing how the manipulation of reinforcements and aversive conditions could be used to improve patients. The typical case described was that of an unresponsive patient who was slowly made more responsive to other persons through the use of reinforcements. The behavior therapist first identified some object or event that the individual wanted, such as candy or chewing gum. That object was then made available only when the individual made some kind of social response. Through using the object as a reinforcer, the number of social responses could be increased. In the more extreme forms of this kind of therapy, the patient was placed in a situation lacking any kind of comfort, but he could obtain some luxuries or comforts through manifesting social responses. Almost no evidence was forthcoming that such a procedure led to a permanent improvement of the patient, though the suspicion was that improvement was confined to the situation in the ward where the reinforcements could be given or withheld.

Early reports on therapy techniques are rather like early reports on new drugs. Astonishing results are claimed, which can rarely be replicated in later studies. One suspects that these early accounts of success are a result of luck, that is, fortuitous circumstances that do not recur in later studies. There is little in the literature at the present time to suggest that behavior modification has had any striking impact on hospitalized mental patients, though it may well have helped some. The 1973

Annual Review of Behavior Therapy (Franks and Wilson, 1973) provides virtually no data to show that the straightforward application of behavior modification techniques for shaping behavior works effectively on hospital wards. This latter volume does discuss a particular aspect of the reinforcement-shaping process, referred to as the use of token economies, but none of the material provided has to do with the shaping of behavior in psychiatric hospitals.

The behavior modification approach to the rehabilitation of the mental patient may have its place in a total psychiatric program, but it can be only one of many approaches. Certainly, the problems of many patients derive from malfunctions in their body chemistry. Manic-depressive patients seem to be unable to retain in their body the trace element lithium, but small daily doses of lithium will restore their body chemistry to a normal condition and they will then act normally. Placing such individuals in a token economy or on another reinforcement procedure would be quite inappropriate. Many suspect that other serious forms of mental disease may be due to chemical problems in the body that have to be corrected by chemical means. Nevertheless, there are patients who can profit from appropriate reinforcement plans, but much may depend on how the plan is administered. Luborsky *et al.* (1971), who have reviewed the psychological factors that make for effective therapy, conclude that success calls for a combination of patient factors and therapist factors. On the patient side, it is vital that the patient be devoid of schizophrenic trends. The patient should also be motivated to improve and be intelligent. The intelligence factor turns up in study after study, suggesting that once a patient reaches the point where rehabilitation is possible, the ability to learn new adjustments is crucial. Therapists who are most successful are those who are most like the patients they treat, who are experienced, and who can show empathy for the patient and his problems. The factors that make for effective therapy are closely similar to those that make for effective teaching, but recovery from a severe mental illness is clearly far more than just learning new habits of behavior, as the behavior modification people have sometimes tried to make us believe.

Aversive conditoning techniques have been used extensively with alcoholics with some positive results (see Davidson, 1974). Numerous procedures have been used, from giving drugs that interact with alcohol to make the alcoholic deathly sick when he drinks to the procedure of giving him strong electric shocks in the presence of alcoholic beverages. However, Davidson points out that there are serious ethical questions raised by some of these procedures.

THE TOKEN ECONOMY AS A BEHAVIOR MODIFICATION SYSTEM

Schools have long used systems whereby students accumulated points for good behavior. These points could then be turned in for some material reward. Psychologists have taken over this idea but have preferred to award tokens rather than points. At least one advantage of tokens over points is that they can be used with chimps as well as with human beings and, hence, permit comparative studies. Indeed, the classic studies in this area were undertaken by Wolfe (1936), who rewarded chimps with tokens that could be later inserted in a slot machine to obtain a desired food. This system of reinforcements has been adapted to the shaping of the behavior of psychiatric patients by Allyon and Azrin (1969), who described the effects on patient behavior in glowing terms.

A ward run on a token economy system provides the patients with the bare necessities for survival, and anything more luxurious has to be earned. Patients are given tokens for showing improved behavior and the tokens can be used for the purchase of better living conditions. Without a token, a patient may have only a hard bench on which to sleep, but if he earns a token, he can use it to rent a real bed for a night. Although the basic diet provides all essential nutrients, if the patient wants a nice dessert, he must pay for it with a token. All small luxuries such as candy and cigarettes must be paid for with tokens. The more desirable recreations also have to be paid for with tokens.

There can be no doubt that within such a system the patients work hard for their privileges and do show higher levels of behavior than they would otherwise show. The early accounts of the token economy system provided glowing accounts of how patients improved. Indeed, ten years after the first such systems were instituted, highly favorable stories continue to be circulated, but such stories are not a substitute for hard data.

Token economies can be viewed as an attempt to introduce into a system the incentive system of a capitalist society. Operant psychologists view it in a rather different light but, for practical purposes, it can well be viewed as an adaptation of the virtues of capitalism to the control of patient behavior. Capitalism has virtues, but as a system it is not without problems, and all these problems appear when the system is used to run a psychiatric ward. Patients compete with one another and begin to show all the conflicts and bitterness that people show when competing in a money economy. Token economies have also been introduced into schools on an experimental basis to provide a reinforcement system, generally for the purpose of reducing the amount of disruptive behavior, but they also have problems.

When hard data are available, they tend to indicate that the phenomena involved in token economies are more complex than the simple reinforcement interpretation might imply. Allen (1970) conducted a study in which sixteen adult retarded mental patients already living in a token economy system had the system extended to personal grooming. Once each day the patients were checked against a list of desirable grooming points and the patient was given a token if she either achieved a criterion score or made an improvement over a previous day's score. The token could be used for meals, cigarettes, or candy. The patients did make an improvement in their appearance. However, almost as much improvement took place when the same check list was used and patients were given a token regardless of improvement. What appeared to be happening was that the checking procedure in itself produced improvement.

Despite the fact that token economies have been used in many mental hospitals, the long-term value of such reinforcement systems to the patients is not known. Even if token economies produce improvement in the behavior of the ward patients, it is no guarantee that the improvement will be maintained after the patients leave the hospital. The behavior-modification psychologists argue that on leaving the hospital the reinforcements provided by society will take over and maintain the improved patient behavior, but this is a hope rather than an established fact. The book by Azrin and Allyon is notably lacking in any evidence to show that their token economy was effective and that it achieved the goals set for it.

Although Franks and Wilson (1973) describe the use of token economies with hospitalized psychiatric patients as "one of behavior modification's crowning achievements," data to support this claim are lacking. Indeed, their entire book is virtually devoid of data to show that token economies produce any permanent improvement in patient behavior, though there is some soft data to show that behavior may improve so long as the token economy system is in operation. A study by Galbraith (1972) not included in the Franks and Wilson book did provide some evidence of patient improvement through a token economy. However, the study also showed that whatever improvement was achieved by the patients was not sufficient to improve their probability of discharge. The evidence of the study indicates very marginal improvement. Despite the glowing appraisal given by Franks and Wilson in their 1973 book, their corresponding book for 1974 provides one of the most damning indictments of token economies, as used psychiatric institutions. In the 1974 book, Wexler (1974) reviewed the studies made of token economies for therapy in hospitals and concludes that there is no evidence to support their use. Indeed, he concludes his review on the note that other approaches may be more successful. In addition, Wexler finds that the use of token economies typically violates the basic constitutional rights of the patients and that they are likely to become taboo in the near future. Only new and overwhelming evidence concerning their value and a demonstration of their superiority to other approaches could save them as a form of therapy. In view of the kind of evidence that has come to light in the past, such new and overwhelming evidence is unlikely to be forthcoming. The remainder of the papers in the book by Franks and Wilson has to do with token economies in classrooms for delinquent or disturbed children. One can hope that before the next edition of this book is produced a scientific study will have been made of the use of token economies in mental hospitals.

The major studies of token economies that have been undertaken have occurred in classrooms for disturbed or delinquent children. The literature is a little misleading even here in that the titles of many such studies carry the implication that an ordinary classroom for normal children was the site of the study. A review of such studies by O'Leary and Drabman (1971) is called "Token Reinforcement Programs in the Classroom: A Review." The programs reviewed pertain to such populations as seventeen emotionally disturbed children, seven disruptive children, six hyperactive children, fifteen retarded children, and six classrooms of emotionally disturbed children. Within such token economies children do seem to show changes in behavior that make them more acceptable to the teacher. There is less disruptive behavior, and the children show the rather dubious "improvement" of spending more time in their seats. It is odd that psychologists have been preoccupied with keeping children in their seats, whereas professional educators view this matter as a triviality. Throughout the studies reviewed by O'Leary and Drabman there is almost no evidence that the token economy resulted in any improvement in the academic learning of the students. Indeed, one of the interesting findings is that the token economy may have the effect of reducing the attention of the student to academic matters, perhaps because the student becomes preoccupied with the mechanics of winning tokens, rather than with the acquisition of what he is supposed to learn. Although behavior modification psychologists suggest that as behavior improves the token system can be phased out and the naturally occurring reinforcers can be expected to maintain behavior, there is virtually no evidence available that this happens or can be made to happen. There is little evidence that any improvement in behavior generalizes to other situations or becomes a part of the individual's performance.

A single study of consequence that dealt with the use of token economies in classrooms for normal children was located. This study by Kazdin (1973) was undertaken in six elementary school classes, and an attempt was made to distinquish between the effect of the program on typical children and on children who showed considerable amounts of disruptive behavior. Instead of tokens, the teacher punched a card on the pupil's desk as a reinforcement for appropriate bahavior. The punches could then be exchanged for material items such as books, toys, trinkets, and candies. Unfortunately, the experimenters were concerned with reinforcing behavior appropriate mainly in the worst kinds of traditional classrooms. Behaviors reinforced were paying attention, working quietly, sitting in seat, facing forward, and not playing with materials. The token economy did increase these forms of behavior. An interesting finding was that with normal children it made little difference whether the reinforcements followed the desired behavior or whether they were passed out at random. A rewarding atmosphere "improved" behavior. On the other hand, in the case of the disruptive children, improvement occurred only when the reinforcement followed the desired behavior.

The study suggests that the concepts underlying a token economy may have little application to the normal classroom, a view that experienced teachers have long held. However, the deviant child may show at least some temporary improvement from the token economy system. One hopes that further studies will be undertaken on the use of token economies with normal children in normal classrooms, but with the reinforcement of behaviors related to the running of an effective educational program. There is little use in finding out how to eliminate pupil behaviors that teachers find difficult to cope with when the real need is for studies to find methods of training teachers to handle and tolerate normal pupil activity.

The use of token systems and rewards that are not intrinsic to the task have also become suspect of producing highly undesirable side effects. Levine and Fasnacht (1974) have summarized some fascinating research showing that the use of such rewards and token systems have the important side effect of reducing the level of interest in the task. If given a set of problems to solve, not only human beings but also primates will continue in varying degrees to continue to solve these problems of their own accord. However, if solving the initial problems is accompanied by a reward not intrinsic to the task, they spend less time, later, solving the problems of their own initiative. This same review also cites studies in which persons performing problem solving tasks produced more creative solutions when no material incentives were offered for their performance. The Levine and Fasnacht article concludes with the warning, "Tokens do lead to powerful learning, but the learning may, in fact, be token" (p. 820).

THE TEACHER AS BEHAVIOR MODIFIER

A widely cited story that may well be apocryphal tells that Skinner once visited his small daughter's classroom in elementary school to find out about her program. He was shocked by the lack of systematic control and planning of the learning process. The immense contrast between the careful way in which he taught an animal a skill in his laboratory and the quite haphazard ways of school instruction horrified him. He went home convinced that something had to be done to systematize school learning and invented some teaching machines, not knowing that Pressey had already invented teaching machines many years before. Skinner, it is said, was particularly disturbed by the lack of reinforcing events, and the inability of the teacher to provide reinforcers. The teaching machine was going to provide proper and rapid reinforcements for learning.

Since that time, considerable interest has been shown by psychologists in training teachers in the use of reinforcing techniques and the use of these techniques for the control of behavior; and since the late 1960s a flood of literature has appeared designed to train teachers in behavior modification techniques. These manuals take the position that these techniques are readily learned, easy to apply, and come with a guarantee of success, all of which are assumptions of dubious validity. One of the first widely distributed manuals of this kind was that by Becker, Thomas, and Carnine (1969), produced under the auspices of the U.S. Office of Education. The manual, entitled *Reducing Behavior Problems: An Operant Conditioning Guide for Teachers*, deals largely with a behavior modification plan for keeping children from doing the kinds of things that irritate teachers. The manual assumes that if children will "behave better," they will learn more. This is a doubtful assumption, but one commonly taken by psychologists without data to support it. The manual has a number of anecdotal records, derived from various sources, which are used to show the teacher how to handle various problems by manipulating reinforcements and punishments. The references cited at the end of the manual, which are supposed to support the proposed practices, deal largely with retarded, delinquent, and problem populations. Even today, there is still little worthwhile research to show that behavior modification programs are effective in ordinary classrooms with normal children. The manual has almost nothing to say about how to improve academic achievement, except that "better behavior" produces better learning. More recent books, such as that by Swift and Spivack (1974), are equally lacking a substantive basis. Pitts's collection of essays on the use of behavior modification in classrooms (1971) provides massive amounts of largely anecdotal "evidence."

An article by Winett and Winkler (1974) brings out the extraordinary preoccupation of behavior modification psychologists with the matter of making children docile, quiet, and still. A reply to this article by O'Leary (1974) is far from convincing and uses the argument that children with "marked social and academic problems" do not fare well in an informal classroom. The latter is philosophical speculation rather than established fact. The Winett and Winkler review is of particular interest because it deals with behavior modification in fourteen ordinary classrooms, though the child whose behavior is to be modified is typically, though not always, a deviate. The total picture presented by the results shows a preoccupation with the trivia of the classroom rather than with significant aspects of intellectual development.

Manuals for the training of teachers in behavior modification techniques have become more presumptuous and more expensive over the years. A complete training kit for teachers by Brown and Presbie (1974) sells for over $300 and includes all kinds of materials and filmstrips. It does not seem to be based on any more substantial research than previous, simpler training devices.

About the strongest argument one can find for the use of such training procedures is that the evidence on token economies shows that they have some use with the retarded, delinquent, and disturbed child, hence, the same techniques may help the teacher handle the isolated case of the child whose bahavior is disruptive to other children.

Although behavior modification techniques have offered teachers the promise of turning their classrooms into a kind of teacher paradise, where pupils no longer frustrate teachers, a short cut to this paradise has been offered by pharmacology in the form of drugs that will also reduce behaviors of the kind on which teachers frown. The best known of these drugs for controlling classroom behavior has been distributed under the trade name of Ritalin. It is a form of amphetamine, and although amphetamines have an invigorating effect on the behavior of adults, they slow down the physical activity of children. The drug has been widely prescribed by pediatricians, often on the basis of the teacher's complaint that a child is hyperactive. The drug has been widely used for the modification of the behavior of thousands of children in schools all over the United States. The research on the effects of the drug has been reviewed by Bosco (1973) and Robin and Bosco (1973).

Although the drug has been widely praised by teachers, principals, parents, and even pediatricians, the research on its effects fails to provide a clear picture of what it does. When the judgments of teachers are used in research studies, the results strongly favor the drug. When an independent observer uses a check list to describe the behavior of the children administered the drug, the results are still positive, but less favorable. On the other hand, when one looks for evidence that the drug facilitated learning in the pupil, one finds no evidence. Some of the literature is even misleading by being published under such titles as *"Improvement in Conditions Related to Learning through Ritalin."* An examination of such articles usually reveals that the study demonstrated that the child given Ritalin spent more time in his seat. The assumption that spending more time sitting improves learning represents an extraordinarily naive view of education and learning.

Bosco has pointed out some of the important side effects of the use of Ritalin. A child who misbehaves may excuse himself to his teacher by saying that he forgot to take his Ritalin that morning. Thus the child learns to deny responsibility for his own behavior.

Most of the work on behavior modification considered up to this point has been based on the assumption that learning takes place best when every child is in his seat, looking at his book. Overwhelming evidence shows that these conditions have almost nothing to do with how much is learned. Studies of this problem were commonly undertaken in the past, but the results showed uniformly no difference between classrooms in which there was much pupil movement and classrooms in which there was little. Few, if any, additional studies have been undertaken in the last two decades. Wallen and Travers have reviewed much of the earlier work (1963). More recently McKinney *et al.* (1975) reported that attending behavior was unrelated to academic achievement.

Rosenshine and Furst (1972) have reviewed available studies that relate teacher behavior to pupil achievement, and these studies provide little support for the practices advocated by those interested in behavior modification. The studies do show the effective teacher to be a well-organized and businesslike person who can make himself clear to the pupils, but he also has to share their enthusiasm and be supportive which is quite different from reinforcing behavior. A teacher who says to a child, "You want to work on this project so go ahead. You will find the work hard at times, but you have the ability and knowledge to do a good job, so keep going if you find it a little difficult. If you really get stuck then come and talk it over with me." The teacher is being supportive, but has provided no reinforcements. Such supportive behavior may be much more critical than providing reinforcements after the work is done. Once the child has finished his project, the triumph of success will probably be a greater reward than any the teacher can pass out.

Studies of the frequency of reinforcing behavior on the part of teachers shows that behaviors in that category are relatively few. A study by Friedman (1973) shows that when teachers reinforce verbal interactions initiated by students, students increase their initiative in this respect. Such reinforcements indicate to the pupil acceptable forms of behavior. An interesting finding of Byalick and Bersoff (1974) is that white teachers direct most of their reinforcements to black children and black teachers reinforce white children. Also boys are more commonly reinforced than girls.

Finally, a timely warning on the blind use of behavior modification techniques in the ordinary classroom is provided by Kounin (1970), who states that simple rules of reinforcement blindly applied are not likely to be particularly effective. For example, he finds that a desist technique (stopping the pupil from doing something) administered with punitiveness has a very different effect from the same technique administered without the same punitive element. How the teacher exercises control is at least as important as the specific techniques that the teacher uses. Simple negative reinforcement techniques administered in a social milieu have effects that are absent when the same techniques are used with a single isolated pupil. In the broader social context, a desist technique may also have a disruptive effect on the behavior of other pupils.

INDIRECT INFLUENCES OF OPERANT PSYCHOLOGY ON THE CURRICULUM AND PERFORMANCE CONTRACTING

During the 1930s, Ralph Tyler popularized the idea that all educational objectives should be operationally defined in terms of the specific performances that could be expected of pupils in whom the objectives had been achieved. Tyler undoubtedly found support for his position in what were then the current popular views of many philosophers that all words in a scientific system should be defined in terms of observable events. Tyler wanted to see the objectives of education defined in terms of observable performances of pupils. By midcentury, most philosophers had abandoned such a rigid position, for it became obvious that many important terms used by scientists could not be so defined and many terms had to be defined extremely indirectly. For example, there are no simple operational definitions of such words as *after*, *before*, *probability*, or *why*, and yet these words appear in highly significant scientific works. Even a common term such as *neutron* cannot be given a simple operational definition. Nobody has ever seen a neutron and its existence is only inferred indirectly from several different lines of thought, all of which lead to the conclusion that neutrons are real components of matter.

The position that every term in a scientific system has to be defined in terms of some observable event would have died had it not been kept alive by operant psychologists who have clung to it as if it were a tenet of science. The position was quite justifiable in Skinner's writing of the late 1930s, but it is hardly justifiable today. In line with the belief that all terms in a behavioral science should be definable in terms of observable events, operant psychologists revived Tyler's position that all educational objectives should be defined in terms of observable performances of pupils. Enthusiasm for this enterprise came to permeate the entire system of public education and state departments of education initiated projects in which teachers wrote lists of thousands of behaviors defining outcomes of education. Supposedly curricula were then to be developed that would systematically build these behaviors, and evaluation procedures could be used to discover whether the pupils could actually perform in the way they were supposed to perform.

A point to note is that there is no particular scientific justification for the enterprise that derives from a philosophical theory concerning the nature of behavior. The overall behavior of the individual may or may not be a collection of small bits of behavior, each one of which has to be learned separately. The theory says nothing about how the bits of behavior become organized into coherent patterns of action, although behavior is obviously not a patchwork of pieces of behavior, but an organized sequence. Nevertheless, operant psychologists devoted considerable energy to the diffusion of their philosophical position throughout education during the late 1950s and 1960s.

The revival of the movement to write behavioral objectives quickly found two groups of allies. One group consisted of consulting firms concerned with providing services to education. Some of these firms had also caught the enthusiasm of operant psychologists for educational reform and saw operant techniques as a sure approach to improving education. So certain were they that operant approaches would produce vast improvements in education that they offered their services to school systems with the understanding that they should be paid only insofar as the pupils in the consultant's programs achieved the standards agreed on in advance. Operant psychologists were sure of the effectiveness of their procedures, and even before the results of their work in schools had been systematically evaluated television programs were used to describe the wonders of the new procedures. The evaluation studies were conducted and the day of reckoning came; the Office of Economic Opportunity issued its final reports (Office of Economic Opportunity, 1972a, 1972b). Despite the added expense of the new systematic applications of operant psychology teaching system, the evidence showed that it had contributed nothing to the learning of pupils. Even worse, there were suspicions of fraud in the manipulation of the tests and test results by those whose salary depended on the results, not in all systems that sponsored the educational experiment, but in at least some.

Operant psychologists needed to return to the drawing board and think through the weaknesses of the applications of their system, but no analyses appeared that purported to do this. The time would have been ripe for operant psychologists to have made a reappraisal of their programs in schools in order to understand their shortcomings, but their own techniques were not applied to discover their own shortcomings, though the resulting analysis would have been both interesting and worthwhile. In view of this lack of analysis of the causes of failure, the conclusion to be drawn from the work was that the time was not yet ripe for the application of operant psychology to the reform of school systems. There was also the open question of whether the time ever would be ripe. Learning in schools might not be the simple matter of planning that operant psychologists had believed it to be.

A second and related offshoot of the operant position was the development of programmed learning. Operant psychologists viewed the acquisition of any complex skill as calling for the learning of a set of component skills. The favored example of the learning of such a sequence, or hierarchy, of skills is that of learning arithmetic. Thus in order to learn long division, the student must have previously learned multiplication, but before he could learn multiplication he had to learn addition, and before he could understand addition he would have had to have learned the nature of a number system.

Armed with the concept that learning involves the acquisition of sequences of skills, psychologists attempted to apply this concept to all kinds of subject matter and to develop exercises for systematically learning the necessary sequences. These systematically ordered sequences of learning tasks, involving the communication of information followed by an exercise or test, were called programs, and the procedure became known as programmed learning. Such materials were widely advertised during the early 1960s as a medicine for all educational woes, but two serious flaws resulted in its rejection. One obvious problem was that most subject matter is not readily arranged into a simple, best sequence for teaching; numerous different sequences are possible. Another problem was that programmed materials did not provide the advantages they were supposed to provide. There was no clear superiority for them in terms of pupil learning, and they were much more expensive than traditional materials to produce and publish (see the summaries of research by Hartly, 1966, and Zoll, 1969). For these reasons, programmed materials began to disappear from the market.

There are difficulties inherent in comparing traditional instruction with programmed instruction. First, there is the problem of what one should compare. Should it be a mediocre traditional type of instruction, given without any special preparation, and a set of programmed materials on which substantial effort has been devoted? Obviously not, but the selection of procedures to be compared is a difficult problem in itself. Then there is the matter of how and when one should measure outcomes. The two systems may perhaps compare well in terms of immediate outcomes, but over a longer period the one may be superior to the other. Any comparison is always badly contaminated by other conditions. A popular instructor who wants to show that he can do better than "any damn mechanical system" may be at an advantage, but an instructor who "doesn't care" may swing the bias the other way. Because of these difficulties of making comparisons, the most one can say at this time is that the early claims for the superiority of programmed materials have not been substantiated, even when carefully prepared programmed materials have been used.

Programmed materials came into being in connection with Skinner's excursion into the field of teaching machines. The program was to be the set of materials to be fed into the machine, and the machine would provide immediate reinforcement, but the machine, like the program, did not justify itself in terms of performance. Indeed, much of what was claimed as a theoretical justification for the machine turned out to be false, a matter that will be discussed later in this chapter under the heading of delay in reinforcement.

Perhaps the last surviving element in the attempt of operant psychologists to produce curricula is the Bereiter–Engleman curriculum in so-called basic skills. This curriculum represents a highly regimented, drill-oriented program, designed along operant lines. In this program, the materials dictate not only exactly what the pupil will do, but exactly what the teachers will do, too. At each step the teacher's manual gives exact instructions concerning what the teacher must say to the pupils. The common complaint of teachers using the system is that they can show no initiative and end up being robots engaged in a dull learning grind, an attitude that is all too easily communicated to the pupils.

Much of the research related to the use of the Bereiter–Engleman materials has been summarized by Beller (1972). There can be no doubt that the curriculum is successful in teaching children to read and perform other basic skills, and on the surface sometimes even more successful than other curricula, but there is other evidence suggesting that the program may produce immediate gains at the expense of long-term losses. When children who have been exposed to the program are followed through subsequent years and compared with children who learned other programs, the children exposed to the Bereiter–Engleman program fall further and further behind. The reason for this is obvious. Children who learn to read through a regimented procedure probably learn at the same time to hate reading. The suspicion is that the Bereiter–Englemen type of program does just that. Reading teachers have long said that the first problem that has to be solved in teaching a child to read is to find a way of making him want to read. If he wants to learn to read, the chances are he will learn to read easily and will develop a progressively deeper enjoyment of reading. The Bereiter–Englemen program neglects this aspect of reading, which is of paramount importance.

Finally, the point should be made that operant programs in schools have had a Calvinistic atmosphere about them, neglecting everything that might add to the pupil's enjoyment of life, which is why they tend to be rejected, particularly by teachers who want to make teaching fun.

TRAINING PARENTS IN BEHAVIOR MODIFICATION

Despite the fact that there is very little evidence that parents can use behavior modification techniques in ways that will benefit their children, numerous kits and manuals are marketed designed to train parents in ways of controlling their children by means of these techniques. O'Dell (1974) has pointed out in his review that there is little evidence to support the use of such training. In addition, one can raise questions about whether behavior modification techniques represent appropriate relationships between parents and children. An improved understanding of what that relationship should be might well yield better results in reducing problem behavior with children than the procedure of providing parents with means designed to modify the children to fit the parents' needs. Just as behavior modification in the school has the effect of making the classroom more congenial for the teacher, parent training in behavior modification techniques may make the home a better place for parents, but children may not benefit and even be harmed. Far more needs to be known about the problem before one can justify the dissemination of such parent training materials.

SOME PRACTICAL ISSUES RELATED TO THE MANAGEMENT OF REINFORCERS

The topics considered here could have been reviewed in the previous chapter, but it seemed more useful to consider them in relation to practical issues. Although the effect of delaying a reinforcement, the effect of magnitude of reinforcement, and the general plan for administering reinforcements have all been widely discussed in a theoretical context, such discussions have not been particularly productive. Nevertheless, the data related to such issues have some practical implications.

Delay of Reinforcement

Skinner developed his teaching machines largely because he believed that classroom learning was inefficient because reinforcements were delayed too long or were absent. He had little, if any, data on human subjects to back up his belief, but the data on animals had shown uniformly that delay in reinforcement led to inefficient learning. Indeed, in teaching a pigeon a trick, a delay of a few seconds might disrupt the learning so much that the pigeon became incapable of learning whatever the psychologist had planned for the pigeon to learn. Such data from animals generalized to human beings without any check to determine whether generalization was justifiable led to the firm belief among operant psychologists that immediacy of reinforcement was a necessity for efficient learning in all living creatures.

There can be no doubt that studies of animals, reviewed by Renner (1964), and Tarpy and Sawabini (1974), demonstrate that delay in reinforcement is generally deleterious to learning. The skills involved in laboratory learning in rats could be described as motor skills typically involving maze learning. Bilodeau (1966) has shown that in motor skill learning in human beings, delay in reinforcement also results in a decrement in learning. So far there does seems to be a parallel between motor skill learning in rats and human beings. However, these data still leave unanswered the question of whether one can also generalize across tasks. Are the findings derived from motor skill learning in human beings applicable to conceptual or verbal learning? As a general rule one can say that the findings of research using one form of task are not generalizable to understanding behavior in other tasks. Indeed, evidence has slowly accumulated over the last decade that what is true about the effects of delay in reinforcement in motor skill learning does not apply to cognitive learning.

As soon as psychologists began to experiment with the effect of delay in reinforcement on human learning in tasks other than that involved in motor skill acquisition, evidence began to appear casting doubt on the view that immediate reinforcement was superior to delayed reinforcement. Rieber (1964) undertook a series of experiments involving perceptual discrimination tasks with children and found no consistent superiority. Then Hetherington and Ross (1966) hypothesized that retarded children should be particularly susceptible to delay in reinforcement, but could find no deleterious effect produced by delay. Later, Sassenrath and Yonge (1968) reviewed a series of experiments involving schoollike tasks and conducted one of their own; they came to the conclusion that with such tasks delayed reinforcement was superior to immediate reinforcement. Lintz (1968) produced similar findings. The data on this point seemed quite clear. Later Sturgis (1972) extended this studies to include delays of twenty-four hours and found with a vocabulary learning task that delays in knowledge of results up to as long as twenty-four hours produced a quite dramatic improvement in performance.

Sturgis's study is of particular interest in that teachers usually delay giving feedback for 24 hours, except in the lower grades. A child does not receive back his corrected work until the following day. Operant psychologists have criticized the delay in telling the student how well he did as a mark of inefficiency, but it is not. It actually improves learning.

An interesting additional finding, which turns up in most of the studies of delayed reinforcement in school children, is that the effect of delay is not apparent on an immediate test of retention, but if the test is delayed, the advantage of delayed reinforcement becomes apparent. This effect is not only apparent when visually presented learning materials are provided, but it also shows up with auditorially presented materials (see Lintz, 1968).

The reader should still remember that there are conditions that require rapid reinforcement for human learning and that delayed reinforcement is not always propitious. Most motor skills require immediate feedback. Weiss et al. (1971) also found that the encouragement of conversational behavior required rapid reinforcement and that any delay resulted in a decrement in the rate of change. In addition, in discrimination learning in children, delay has not generally shown itself to be an advantage. If a child has to judge which of two objects is the larger, he needs to know right away whether his judgment was right or wrong. If he is told only after the objects are removed, he has difficulty in remembering the basis for his decision. Studies in this area have been reviewed by Goldstein and Siegel (1972).

The favorable effect of delay in reinforcement on learning is certainly not a simple phenomenon. A delay of 10 seconds may facilitate learning, and so may a delay of 24 hours, but for different reasons. Atkinson (1966) conducted a clever study in which he showed that delay in feedback facilitated verbal learning provided the period of delay was not occupied by another task. If the child were free during the period of delay to think about the task to be learned, delay facilitated learning. What happened was that the delay provided more time for learning. When feedback is delayed for, say, twenty-four hours, the occasion for providing feedback is also an occasion for the individual to rehearse what he has learned. This amounts to an additional learning trial. This, in turn, consolidates the learning.

The effect of delay in punishment is also an interesting and practical problem. Punishment with children is typically delayed. Children are kept after school for misdeeds committed many hours before. "Wait until your father gets home!" signals delayed punishment. Very little is known about this problem, largely because psychologists do not like to administer punishment to human beings in prolonged situations. The data from animals provides no clear picture. A particularly interesting case of delayed punishment in animals is that of delayed food poisoning; animals that become sick many hours after eating a particular food develop an aversion for that food and will avoid it in the future. Myer (1971), who has summarized the work, describes cases in which animals became sick 7 hours after eating a particular food and thereafter showed a very marked distaste for the particular food. In the latter case the food itself was not poisoned, but irradiation of the animals with X rays immediately after the intake of the food produced the later sickness. Later research, summarized by Nachman and Jones (1974), brings out the fact that these learned food aversions are not forgotten by rats and that they persist without weakening. Psychologists do not understand how the eating behavior becomes linked to the punishment, but they do become associatively linked. In another experiment Myer (1968) found that shocking rats for killing mice reduced the mouse-killing behavior, even when the shock was delayed for 30 seconds.

If delayed punishment can be effective in animals, one may well suspect that it can be effective in human beings, particularly in view of the human ability to associate events that do not occur together.

Although animal studies show a considerable advantage for immediate in contrast with delayed reinforcement, the same conclusion cannot be drawn from human studies. The human learner may benefit from delays in reinforcement in many subtle ways. Delay may provide opportunity to rehearse the response and may also distribute learning over a greater span of time, also with an added advantage. One can no longer justify the use of teaching machines on the grounds that they provide immediate reinforcement, for the evidence generally favors delayed reinforcement, particularly when the criterion of learning is retention over some substantial interval of time.

Finally, the point must be stressed that while delay in reinforcement is often critical in the training of animals, there are much more critical problems of timing in the case of human learning. For example, Bourne and Bunderson (1963) found that in a concept-learning task, the most critical matter in the timing of the task was the amount of time allowed *after* feedback or reinforcement before the next problem was presented. What appears to happen is that the subject is given a problem; he attempts a solution; then he is told whether he is right or wrong. After he has received this information, he needs time to assimilate it and perhaps to think over why he was right or wrong. If he is not given time to do this, but is hurried on to the next problem, learning is retarded. In such tasks as Bourne and Bunderson used, the critical matter is not how quickly the reinforcement or feedback arrives, but whether there is a pause after reinforcement to permit the subject to use the information provided. A later study by Jones (1968) confirmed the finding of the importance of the post-feedback interval and also suggested that this interval was the period during which the information provided by feedback was used by the subject. Jones also found that the length of the post-feedback interval was a much more critical matter than the length of the delay in providing feedback. The conclusion to be drawn is that it is not enough to tell a child whether his solution to a problem is right or wrong. The child must also be given time to think about what makes his answer right or wrong. Too often the teacher provides the child with feedback and then rushes on to the next problem.

Magnitude of Reinforcement

An important and significant problem is the extent to which magnitude or quantity of the reinforcer is related to learning. Suppose a person could keep his job only if he learned to speak Spanish, a language important in his business contacts, and let us say that during the period of learning the foreign language, payment was related to how much he learned. Would he learn faster if he were given ten cents for each foreign word learned than if he were given only five cents? In most learning situations the assumption is made by the teacher that minor rewards, such as the pupil being told that he is doing well, are just as effective as lavish praise. If money or candy were used as reinforcers, then most teachers would bet that a small amount would be just as effective in producing learning as a large amount. Data on this problem have been largely lacking.

As with most problems on learning, the main attempts to find a solution have involved work with animals. The difficulties involved in experimenting in this area stem from the fact that for there to be any effect the animals have to be able to discriminate a large reward from a small reward. In the case of a child it is easy to say, "Today you will get a piece of candy for every ten answers correct," or "Today you can get twice as much candy as yesterday, for we will give you a piece for every five answers that are right." A rat might not show any signs of recognizing the difference between one pellet of food and two pellets. We can point out to a child that a reward is larger or smaller than previously, or the child may readily recognize differences in the magnitude of rewards even if they are not pointed out, but sub-human subjects are much less capable of making this discrimination. Special techniques have had to be evolved for the study of the effect of magnitude of reward on the learning of animals.

Much of the knowledge in the area derived from research with animals has been summarized in two reviews. The first of these, by Pubols (1960), summarizes the main well-established empirical findings. The second, by Black (1968), is much more theoretically oriented and does an excellent job of pointing up the theoretical issues.

Pubols (1960) finds substantial support for a number of propositions as a result of his review of studies of animal learning. The fact that the findings fit with common experience with human behavior suggests that Pubols' conclusions may well apply in the human field, but this is a conjecture that should be applied with caution. First, Pubols states that studies generally show that an increase or a decrease in incentives or reinforcements does not affect rate of learning. A major exception to this is that the reinforcements or incentives cannot be reduced to zero without a corresponding reduction in learning. Second, as the incentive or reinforcement is increased in quantity, the final level of performance reaches higher levels. Responses learned with larger reinforcements have the appearance of being more resistant to extinction, but this is only because they are learned to higher levels in the first place as a result of the larger reinforcement. When responses are learned to the same level of performance but with different magnitudes of reinforcements, the rate of extinction is the same.

Black (1968) has summarized some other findings of the relationship of reward magnitude to behavior in such situations. First, a reduction in the reward results in a decline in the vigor of the response. Reduce the amount of food at the end of a single-alley straight runway, and the rat runs less rapidly. Second, an increase in the reward increases the vigor of the response. The rat runs more rapidly as the reward is increased. Third, when the reward is reduced, the rat shows a reduced level of performance but it is reduced below the performance level of rats that are run continuously on the lower level of reward. The latter is known as the contrast effect. This effect is shown only when the level of reward is reduced. There is no corresponding effect when the level of reward is increased.

Black (1968) favors an explanation of the phenomenon very similar to that proposed much earlier by Spence (1956, 1960). The increase and decrease in vigor of the response is attributable to the change in incentive value but this in itself does not mean that a higher reward produces more learning, although it does produce greater vigor of response. The contrast effect is understood as a building up of inhibition that occurs when the level of reward is reduced. Thus a reduction of reward results not only in a reduction in incentive value, but also in a building up of inhibition that also reduces the vigor of response.

Most of the studies reviewed by Black (1968) are concerned with the effect of reward on the maintaining of behavior, rather than with the acquisition of new behavior. Similar results have been found in studies involving the maintenance of behavior in children. Nakamura and Boraczi (1965) cite a series of studies to which they have contributed showing that the persistence of children's responses is related to the magnitude of the reinforcement involved. They have also demonstrated that children respond more vigorously when the reinforcement is increased and less vigorously when it is reduced. Another study with adults by Toppen (1965) has shown that increasing the pay on a dull repetitive task increased the output, and Leventhal (1964) found that such an increase made the task appear more attractive. These findings, like those just reviewed, are hardly astounding. Although these studies are of some theoretical interest, their practical implications hardly go beyond what the nonpsychologist already knows. In laymen's terms they can be said to suggest what is obvious, namely, that a person jumps more rapidly to pick up a five-dollar bill lying on the floor than he does a one-dollar bill, and also that a person who occasionally finds a five-dollar bill will engage more in searching behavior than a person who finds only one-dollar bills. These studies do not tell us what, as teachers, we may want to know, namely, whether increasing the size of the reward will increase the rate of acquisition of a skill. This is a very different matter from the matter of maintaining behavior already acquired.

A few early studies (Thorndike, 1935) in the area did attack the problem of interest to teachers and others in education, with results that fit quite well those summarized by Pubols and Black. More recent research on the effect of varying the amount of reinforcement on human behavior has been reviewed by Atkinson and Wickens (1971) with some interesting conclusions. The research reviewed is mainly that of W. F. Harley, Jr., who has been concerned with tasks involving paired associate learning. Atkinson points out that the Harley studies, like many of those previously conducted, show that giving the same subject different rewards on different parts of a task results in difference in amount learned. On the other hand, when some subjects are given a large reward, say twenty-five cents, for each item learned, and other subjects are given no money for learning, there is no difference between the high-reward and the low-reward group. Atkinson suggests that under the condition in which some items are to be rewarded if they are learned by twenty-five cents and the others are not thus rewarded, the subject simply studies those associated with the reward and neglects the others. The low-reward and high-reward items are thus processed differently. In addition, Atkinson suggests that the high-reward items may be rehearsed, whereas the other items are neglected. The subject is likely to bring to the rewarded items all the learning strategies he has. In addition, Atkinson cites data from an unpublished study by Gibson that also suggest that the effect of introducing a reward for performance on a portion of a task results in the adoption of an effective strategy with that portion of the task, but to the neglect of other unrewarded portions of the task. The effects of varying the magnitude of reinforcement seem to be indirect (see also Pihl and Greenspoon, 1969).

The review of the studies that have been made of the effect of varying the magnitude of the reinforcer on the amount of learning suggests how this factor should and should not be used in practical teaching situations. The results fit well with the experience of those who have attempted to introduce a token system or a point for controlling learning and have found that children under such a system soon take the attitude that they will learn only those things for which they are paid in points or tokens. This behavior is much like those of the subjects in the experiments reviewed who learned only the high-reward items in a list of items. Another finding of interest is that the reinforcements operating in most laboratory tasks are sufficient to ensure learning and that any increment in them is likely to have little effect on learning. One is tempted to generalize from this finding and to suggest that any increment in the reinforcements provided by the classroom will probably have little effect. The latter needs to be investigated.

Material Incentives: A Focus of Controversy

The problem of whether material reinforcements, involving objects desired by the child, are less or more effective than praise or other forms of verbal reinforcement is a matter of both scientific and practical interest. Numerous laboratory studies, reviewed by Benowitz and Busse (1970), have shown that reinforcements involving small trinkets, toys, and other items wanted by children produce more learning than is produced by verbal reinforcements. Benowitz and Busse (1970) conducted a study in a classroom situation and found similar results. The fact that their subjects were black children from poor families may have played some part in their results, but the weight of the evidence leads one to expect that even with white children from prosperous families a similar effect would be expected. The findings of research have led psychologists to suggest that all learning in school might be expedited by the universal use of material rewards. Some have even gone so far to propose that children be paid to learn in school, much as adults are paid to work. The idea is radical and interesting, but any recommendations concerning its implementation will have to wait until more is known about the side effects of such a system.

Most teachers would take the position that learning activities can be made intrinsically interesting and that when this is done material reinforcers may add little. They also suggest that any small gains produced by material reinforcers may be counterbalanced by undesirable side effects. They argue in this connection that it is very important to make the learning activity so inherently interesting that the children want to engage in further learning for its own sake. They are fearful that the use of material reinforcers may result in some children never acquiring an inherent interest in learning and that such children will learn only the desire to accumulate possessions. Some of these points may be sound. The area needs careful investigation.

Partial Reinforcement and Schedules of Reinforcement

In natural settings, few very specific behaviors are followed 100 per cent of the time by reinforcement. A predatory animal visits a particular location where food is commonly found but perhaps finds food there on only 50 per cent of the occasions. Whether it finds food or not is largely a result of numerous chance factors operating. One might say that under such circumstances the schedule of reinforcement is random. In a sense one might argue that the hunting behavior of an animal is always reinforced on 100 per cent of the occasions, in that the search for food had to be successful or the animal dies.

Many learned human operants are not reinforced on most of the occasions on which they occur. The nursery-school child who plays gently with another may be complimented from time to time by the teacher. There may also be some rewards intrinsic to the gentle play situation that maintain this behavior, but this kind of play situation seems to be quite dependent on the incidence of suitable external reinforcement for it to be maintained over any great length of time. The acquisition of social skills, where only some successful performances are reinforced, is to be contrasted with the acquisition of academic knowledge, in which some kind of reinforcement or knowledge of results is provided after every performance.

What happens when the frequency of reinforcement is reduced from reinforcement on every trial to reinforcement on only some trials? The rate of learning goes down as the frequency of reinforcement is reduced, which is to be expected. However, another thing also happens. As the reinforcement is reduced, the behavior becomes less and less amenable to extinction. A favorite kind of experimental situation for the study of this phenomenon is the one-armed bandit, the Las Vegas type of slot machine. With such a device a person can be reinforced on every trial or on any percentage of trials that the experimenter may wish. In studies using this kind of equipment, the typical finding is that the most difficult response to extinquish is the one that has been reinforced on about 50 per cent of the occasions, though there are some exceptions to this rule. On the other hand, when the subject is reinforced on every trial and the reinforcements are then cut off, the response is readily extinguished. The phenomenon discussed here is known as the partial reinforcement effect. One hundred per cent reinforcement is most effective for rapid acquisition, but the response that is most stable and the most resistant to extinction is one that has been learned with a schedule of reinforcement of less than 100 per cent reinforcement.

Because there are many habits of behavior that one hopes will be permanent and that may be reinforced only rarely after they are acquired such habits should be learned on a schedule of less than 100 per cent reinforcement, or, if they are initially learned on a schedule of less than 100 per cent reinforcement, they should probably be maintained for a period following acquisition with a tapered-off frequency of reinforcement. Such a rule would appear to apply well in planning the learning of habitual modes of behaving, but there is no evidence that the acquisition of academic knowledge should be learned on this kind of basis. Indeed, most psychologists would unequivocally advocate that in the case of academic knowledge, the pupil be reinforced on every trial.

The partial reinforcement effect, commonly referred to as PRE, is of considerable theoretical interest, a fact that accounts for the continued large numbers of researches that appear on the topic. Excellent reviews of the massive literature published on the subject have been written by Jenkins and Stanley (1950) and by Lewis (1960). These reviews have been mainly directed toward an examination of the theoretical issues and the formulation of a theoretical interpretation of the phenomenon.

No theoretical explanation is entirely satisfactory at this time, and, indeed, there may be no single satisfactory explanation of the partial reinforcement effect. The nearest to a defensible explanation is the discrimination theory. This theory states that resistance to extinction is a function of the difference between stimuli present during acquistion and stimuli present during extinction. The theory argues that when acquisition is accompanied by 100 per cent reinforcement and then the reinforcement suddenly stops, the subject quickly discriminates between the original state of affairs and the new one. If, on the other hand, the subject is reinforced on only 25 per cent of the trials during the acquisition series and then reinforcements are stopped, the change is not as easily identified and behavior continues as though there had been no change in the situation. When reinforcements are provided on only 25 per cent of the trials, there will sometimes be quite long runs of trials without any reinforcement at all; and thus when the reinforcements are switched off, there are no very dramatic changes in the situation, but just a very long series of trials without any reinforcement. Most, but not all, of the experimental attempts to verify the discrimination theory experimentally have produced supporting evidence. There are also alternative explanations, all of which encounter as much, if not more, conflicting evidence in the studies designed to test them. These alternative explanations all tend to single out some special aspects of the behavior observed during partial reinforcement to account for the phenomenon. The so-called aftereffects theory, for example, is based on the fact that at the end of a nonreinforced trial in maze running in rats, the rat engages in behavior related to searching for food and behavior related to frustration. These behaviors produce stimuli inside the rat that become conditioned to the running response on the next trial. Hence, next time the animal engages in food-searching behavior in the goal box, the internal stimuli tend to produce running behavior as soon as the rat is placed back in the starting box. What the animals essentially learn, according to this theory, is to respond to the frustrations of not being rewarded by further running behavior on the next trial. If the rat is reinforced on every trial, it does not have the opportunity to learn to respond to the nonreinforcement situation.

There are a vast number of different ways in which reinforcements on less than a 100 per cent basis can be arranged. One may decide to reinforce every second or every third or every fourth instance of the behavior with which one is concerned. This is called a *fixed-ratio* schedule of reinforcement. After each reinforced response there are a number of nonreinforced responses before the next one is reinforced. Sometimes an abbreviation is used in discussing a fixed-ratio schedule. For example, if the sixth response and no other were to be reinforced, the term *FR-6* would be used to indicate that a fixed-ratio schedule was used and that every sixth response in the category of interest was reinforced.

A second schedule of reinforcement is the *variable-ratio* schedule. In setting up such a schedule, the experimenter may decide that 25 per cent of the behaviors are to be reinforced, but that the number of nonreinforced behaviors that lie between two reinforced behaviors may vary from zero to eight. The number of nonreinforced trials between successive reinforced trials may be determined by throwing dice or other means of obtaining a list of random numbers. The variable-ratio schedule under consideration would be denoted as *VR-4* to indicate that, *on the average*, one behavior in four is reinforced.

Schedules of reinforcement may be established not in terms of the number of consecutive behaviors that are nonreinforced following each one that is reinforced, but in terms of the time that elapses from one reinforcement to the next. One might decide, for example, to reinforce a child for the first occurrence of attentive behavior following the end of a five-minute period measured from the last attentive behavior that was reinforced. If one did this, the reinforcement schedule would be described as a *fixed interval* schedule or, in this case, a *FI-5* schedule. Finally, the interval of time between reinforcements may be varied and form a random pattern. When this is done, the interval is said to be a *variable-interval* schedule.

Numerous other schedules have also been used in rare experimental designs. For example, in one unusual type of schedule, reinforcements always occur in pairs with two successive behaviors being reinforced. There is no limit to the number of patterns or combination of patterns that can be devised.

The effect of these schedules of reinforcement on behavior has been extensively studied in the case of rats, pigeons, and a few other subhuman species, using mainly consumables as reinforcers. The applicability of the results of these studies to problems of learning and maintaining human behavior in natural situations is largely a matter of conjecture, although a few experiments with human beings using rather artificial laboratory tasks have produced fairly similar results. Thus many studies have found that a fixed-ratio schedule of reinforcement provided for a pigeon pecking a small disk on the wall of its training cage results in a uniform output of pecking behavior, but pecking stops almost immediately when the reinforcements are stopped. This is very much like a factory worker paid on a piece rate, who receives a dollar for every five pieces he makes. Industry has long found that such a payment plan produces a very uniform output of work. If one wishes to have the behavior continue after reinforcements are terminated, a variable-ratio schedule of reinforcement is to be commended, but it cannot be introduced in a factory, although it can be used in a school. The latter schedule produces the partial reinforcement effect previously discussed.

Fixed-interval schedules produce a very different effect. Animals reinforced on this basis tend to show a low output of the reinforced behavior except toward the end of the interval, when the reinforcement is about to occur. If a pigeon is reinforced for pecking at a disk on the wall for the first pecking response following the end of each minute, pecking behavior is likely to be absent during the first forty-five seconds of each minute and then become more frequent as the time arrives when reinforcement is due. The output of work is very variable under the fixed-interval schedule. When the variable interval is introduced, the performance becomes more steady and may even approach that of the variable-ratio schedule.

In the fixed-interval schedule of reinforcement, there are times when the subject can obtain no reinforcement. Such periods are commonly referred to as *time out from reinforcement*. Such time outs represent quite aversive kinds of situations.

Some Issues Related to the Use of Aversive Stimuli in the Control of Behavior

There can be no doubt that punishment can be extremely effective, under some circumstances, in facilitating learning but the effectiveness of aversive stimuli for this purpose does not necessarily justify their use. If changes in behavior can be brought about by pleasant means, the use of aversive stimuli should be avoided. Those who administer education have shown a trend toward reducing the aversive stimuli to which pupils are exposed and, as far as possible, they attempt to control learning by means of positive reinforcers. John Dewey long ago took the position in many of his writings that education cannot be regarded just as preparation for life. Education and childhood are a part of life and should provide experiences that are valued in themselves. Within the framework of such a philosophy, the adult has a questionable right to make life disagreeable for the child.

A real difficulty in arriving at practical educational policy in such matters is that one does not know the extent to which an individual can grow up to meet the demands of the real world without having some profitable experiences with aversive conditions. Painful experiences with hot objects and sharp objects appear to be quite important in enabling the individual to avoid being burned and injured. Animals that do not have these experiences during the growing period (see Hebb, 1958) show an extraordinary incapacity to avoid injury when they are mature. The person who loses sensitivity to pain has difficulty in preventing himself from being harmed. At a very basic level, the aversive stimuli produce learning that prevents injury. The real issue is whether aversive stimuli can be used effectively without undesirable side effects for promoting social and academic learning. If a child were never punished for hurting another child, would he learn not to hurt other children? If a person were never punished, or never saw another person punished for taking the property of another, would he learn to avoid stealing? The answers to these questions are highly controversial, and so the use of aversive stimuli and punishment in education remains highly controversial.

One argument commonly put forward against the use of aversive stimuli for the control of learning is that the use of such stimuli is believed to have unfortunate side effects. This argument is found in many of the early writings of Skinner and of others who wrote on the subject before midcentury. Whether there are or are not such side effects to punishment as it might be used in educational situations remains a matter for argument. Solomon's review of the problem (1964) takes the firm position that there is no evidence to support the idea that the use of punishment has bad side effects that outweigh the advantages to be achieved through its use. Nevertheless, one can point to studies that show clearly that painful aversive stimuli often produce serious consequences. Brady's primates (1958), which were periodically shocked at random intervals shortly after a given signal, developed stomach ulcers if conditions were arranged so that an alert animal could press a key to turn off the anticipated shock. Maier's rats (1949), which were confronted with an insoluble problem and, if they made an incorrect response, were physically punished by falling onto a hard surface, showed deep and prolonged disorganizations of behavior. Ulrich, Azrin, and Hutchinson (1965) reported that electric shock produces aggressive behavior in a wide variety of species. Sears, Maccoby, and Levin (1957) found that children who were punished most during early childhood showed at later ages the greatest frequency of behavior problems in the area of aggression. There is much evidence of this kind. The first three of the previous four references could perhaps be written off as irrelevant in that they used very strong aversive stimuli and the Brady and Maier studies involved noxious stimuli over many weeks. In educational situations, it is very unlikely that such intense aversive stimuli would be used for so long. The Ulrich et al. review covered experimental situations using a single electric shock but of extremely high intensity and representing a level of stimulation not used in the control of school learning. The Sears et al. study is not so easily dismissed. There is also evidence that anxiety builds up for a period of several hours after a punishing experience. This is known as the Kamin effect and has been demonstrated on a wide range of species. The review of the subject provided by Geller, Jarvik, and Robustelli (1970) indicates the generality of the phenomenon, though it still has to be demonstrated on human beings. Thornton and Jacobs (1971) also describe a phenomenon they call learned helplessness. When punishment is administered at random, and in a manner unrelated to what the individual does, responsiveness declines and a state of general apathy sets in. Thornton and Jacobs' study is particularly significant since it replicates with college students the phenomenon of learned helplessness already established with rats. The ill effects of punishment seem to this writer to be well established though other writers would take issue with him on this point.

Sometimes the disadvantages of punishment may be outweighed by the gains. One such case is found in the treatment of children hospitalized for self-destructive behavior. Such children may literally tear their bodies apart and have to be restrained. Oddly enough, the punishment these children inflict on themselves does not stop the behavior, but electric shock administered by the physician may inhibit the self-destructive actions, if the shock follows immediately the self-destructive behavior. Bucher et al. (1968) describe the successful treatment of such children through the use of punishing shock, which should be administered by several different persons in different situations. Similar success has been found in using electric shock to suppress pathological screaming behavior (see Hamilton and Standahl, 1969).

An additional consideration must be introduced in evaluating the use of aversive stimuli for promoting learning. Dinsmoor (1968) points out that one cannot reject the use of aversive stimuli merely because they may have bad side effects, because positive reinforcers also have side effects and these are not all desirable. The spoiled child is typically one whose life has been overwhelmed by an abundance of rewards. The excessive use of positive reinforcers may have effects just as unfortunate as the excessive use of negative reinforcements and punishments.

Much more needs to be discovered in this area before firm recommendations can be given to the teacher.

CLASSICAL CONDITIONING APPROACHES TO THE MODIFICATION OF BEHAVIOR

The material discussed in this chapter up to this point has focused on applications of operant psychology because American psychologists for the last few decades have had an overriding interest in that form of psychological inquiry. This interest has not been worldwide, for Russian psychologists still continue to be influenced in their thinking primarily by Pavlov. Skinner's influence comes, to a substantial degree, from his preoccupation with those factors believed to make a capitalist society function, namely, the reward system. Pavlov's influence derives from the belief of Russians that classical conditioning represents a psychology compatible with the basic beliefs of a communist state. In addition, Pavlov's prestige has long been enhanced by the fact that he was an early supporter of the Russian revolutionary movement, though he later protested the involvement of scientific organizations in Soviet politics. Even before Pavlov's death in 1936, considerable effort had been directed toward the application of his theories of behavior to the treatment of psychiatric cases in Russian hospitals. The research that accompanied these applications has not been available to American research workers, and, hence, it did not stimulate any corresponding applications of classical conditioning on this side of the world, much as operant psychology has had little impact on the work of Russian psychologists.

Although American applied psychology has been dominated by operant psychology, in the last two decades attempts to apply classical conditioning procedures to psychotherapy have taken place in the form of what are known as desensitization techniques. Desensitization was developed by Wolpe (1958), and the general procedure has been described by Paul (1966). The procedure finds some support in animal studies, according to Wilson and Davison (1971). The technique is applied to individuals who have deep anxieties and is designed to eliminate those anxieties. The technique is based on the extinction principle, which states that a response will become extinguished if the stimulus required to elicit the response is presented, but the response is prevented from occurring. In the case of the anxiety-ridden patient, the therapist can arouse an anxiety response by asking the patient to think of a particular situation known to make the patient anxious. The therapist then has to find a way of inhibiting the anxiety response, which he does by asking the patient to relax completely, for it is known that relaxation is incompatible with anxiety.

In the desensitization technique, the patient begins by making a list of all the situations that make him anxious and then arranging them in order, from those that produce the least anxiety to those that produce the most. The therapist then begins the desensitization by asking the patient to relax as completely as possible. When the patient is relaxed, the therapist asks him to think about the situation from those listed that produced the least amount of anxiety. If the patient is throughly relaxed, he will be able to think about the situation without feeling anxiety, since the anxiety will be incompatible with the relaxed state. What usually happens is that the patient will not be able to attain sufficient relaxation on his first trials, but slowly the therapist will help him reach the point where he can contemplate the anxiety-producing idea in a state of relaxation. Once he has accomplished this, he is on the road to being able to think of and encounter the anxiety-producing situation without it producing anxiety in him. The therapist will then help him to handle the second item on the list, and so forth. Thus the patient is desensitized to the ideas and events that produce anxiety in him.

The studies that followed the development of the technique were summarized by Rachman (1967) and generally leave a favorable impression of what it can accomplish. Rachman notes that although some psychologists and psychoanalysts had predicted unfavorable side effects of desensitization, none had been reported. In particular, the expectation that patients would substitute one symptom for another did not materialize. The more recent review of research by Franks and Wilson (1973) also evaluates the technique in hopeful terms.

Nevertheless, the technique has aroused some controversy. Wilkins (1971) reread some of the research related to it and came to the conclusion that some aspects of the technique were irrelevant to its success; in particular, Wilkins could find no evidence to support the contention that relaxation was significant. If he were correct, the theoretical basis for the procedure would be destroyed. Davison and Wilson (1972) questioned Wilkins' conclusions. Wilkins in a rebuttal pointed out that although the evidence might be weak, it was still more in favor of his position than the original Wolpe position on desensitization that he had criticized. Thus the present position in the matter is that although there is no question that the Wolpe desensitization technique produces favorable results, therapists are not sure what the essential features of the technique are. The theoretical basis of the technique is not yet on firm ground.

One aspect of the technique needs to be pointed out. Those who use the classical conditioning model feel quite free to concern themselves with inner processes. They do not believe as operant psychologists do that inner processes are irrelevant. Of course, when Watson first popularized classical conditioning as a model of all learning, he, too, propounded the philosophy that inner mental processes were irrelevant to the understanding of behavior, but true Pavlovians have never taken that position. Pavlov himself took the position that inner verbal processes played an important role in controlling human behavior. Indeed, Pavlov saw a basic difference in this respect between the behavior of animals and the behavior of other living creatures.

An alternative form of therapy to achieve the same goal is known as "flooding."

This technique floods the patient with anxiety-producing ideas. It has no theoretical basis in learning research and so far has a history of failure rather than success, commented on by Franks and Wilson and clearly evident in the critical review by Morganstern (1973).

BEHAVIOR MODIFICATION: PRESENT SHORTCOMINGS AND FUTURE POTENTIAL

A review of attempts to apply behavior modification procedures to the solution of practical problems leaves the reviewer with mixed feelings concerning how these attempts should be evaluated. The task of evaluating what has been acomplished is made doubly difficult by the trend toward using Madison Avenue techniques to promote the enterprise, just as Watson half a century earlier was able to use effective rhetoric to promote his ideas. Skinner has great skill in using arresting titles such as *Beyond Freedom and Dignity* to promote philosophical ideas that he presents as scientific concepts. The many films and slide shows developed by operant psychologists present more artistic than scientific skills, but they often convince audiences that psychologists are near to solving many of our most perplexing problems. The position of operant psychologists in the 1970s is very similar to that of the followers of Watson in the late 1920s. Watson and his followers claimed too much, announcing that they could condition any young child to perform satisfactorily in any occupation and with respect to any moral code. Such claims were excessive. Indeed, validated practical applications of Watson's behaviorism did not come until half a century later when Wolpe developed his desensitization technique. Even there, some doubts exist as to whether Wolpe's technique is a genuine application.

In the case of behavior modification, as developed by Skinner's followers, one can say that they have had some successes in the training of the mentally retarded. Less clear-cut are successes in the control of emotionally disturbed children. Evidence on the use of the techniques with hospitalized mental patients raises questions about the usefulness of the techniques. The conclusion that the patients on whom the techniques were used showed improvement but did not change their likelihood of discharge is not impressive. There are, of course, anecdotes that tell of dramatic changes in particular patients, but dramatic changes sometimes take place in untreated patients. Certainly the emphasis on how to design an environment for a mental patient so as to facilitate his recovery is a new and healthy emphasis, which may be more important than any real success achieved up to this time. One can probably expect far more genuine successes in the future, because the whole idea of building environments that will help problem children and problem adults is promising.

Behavior modification techniques have also had their greatest success when the behavior involved is a broad habit rather than a specific intellectual skill. There is no evidence to show that behavior modification can contribute to the intellectual development of children, except very indirectly. On the other hand, it can contribute to controlling the amount of time children in school spend in their seats, though one may question whether this is important to control. We live in a society in which much of our gross behavior is controlled by rewards, so it is hardly surprising that the behavior of children can also be controlled by rewards. This is not necessarily a good way to control behavior. The child is not likely to develop internal controls over his own behavior so long as adults exercise more than minimal external controls.

The emphasis of proponents of behavior modification on the systematic analysis of behavior before an attempt is made to change behavior is healthy. However, all too often behavior analysis becomes nothing more than armchair speculation. Examples of such speculation are "A Functional Analysis of Depression" (Ferster, 1973), an article that provides an operant analysis of depression without any data, and, "A Behavioral View of Sesame Street"(Ulrich, 1970). Where real behavior analysis begins and armchair speculation ends is far from clear.

The relationship of theory to practice in behavior modification is far from being as clear as it is supposed to be. Indeed, some writers, such as London (1972), have pointed out that little of what behavior modifiers do is related directly to psychological theory. Sometimes, in fact, the behavior modifiers, as when they refer to an individual reinforcing himself, contradict the basic premises of operant psychology. Much of behavior modification is a hit-or-miss type of technology, with virtually no scientific basis.

Finally, the point must be made that operant psychology has been vastly overgeneralized to areas where it almost certainly does not apply. Operant psychology is based on limited data, is limited in scope, and applies only to limited situations. Only insofar as it is conceived of in this way can it expect to have a significant future, filled with modest claims and modest successes.

SUMMARY

1. Operant psychology has remained a quite static scientific system that has shown little innovation over the last quarter of a century. However, there has been extensive effort to apply the concepts of operant psychology to the solution of practical problems. Much of this applied effort has come to be known as behavior modification.

2. Although the position of the proponents of behavior modification denies the significance of inner processes, practitioners make quite free reference to such processes when there is some evidence that they are relevant.

3. Behavior modification is supposed to be preceded by what is termed behavioral analysis, the process that logically follows from the reductionist position. If behavior can be reduced to simple components, such as simple operants or simple classically conditioned responses, behavioral analysis should involve the identification of such components in the behavior under investigation. Unfortunately, behavioral analysis does not have the well-defined techniques of analysis available in other scientific areas. There is nothing comparable in psychology to the analysis of compounds made by inorganic chemists. Much of behavioral analysis involves a subjective analysis of what the observed phenomenon involves. The claim is com-

monly made that behavioral analysis is simple and can be learned easily by individuals who have had little training. Behavior modification techniques have been most successful in situations in which there is a fairly obvious relationship between environmental events and the behavior to be changed. Sometimes behavior modification procedures may be used even when a detailed behavior analysis does not seem to be feasible.

4. One of the earliest areas of successful application of operant techniques was in the training of the mentally retarded. Punishment has been extensively used to shape behavior of delinquents, but the results are quite controversial. The use of what have been termed cruel and unusual punishments at the Patuxent Institution for certain classes of delinquents seems to have been a failure. The behavior modification techniques failed to take into account such subjective factors involved as the resentment and hostility to authority produced by these techniques. Behavior modification psychologists often unfortunately make the assumption that such consequences of punishment are unimportant.

5. Although the early literature on the use of behavior modification techniques with mental patients produced accounts of extraordinary success, there have been no well-replicated studies that suggest that this method of therapy has the power claimed for it. Behavior modification techniques probably have their place among other techniques for helping mental patients. One form of behavior modification technique in a mental hospital setting involves the use of token economies that represent, in many ways, a miniature form of our national economy. The use of token economies in a ward introduces most of the problems that are found in our own free economy outside of the hospital. Patients compete for the rewards and show bitterness toward one another. After more than a decade of using token economies, there is no hard evidence to show that they have the virtues claimed for them. Indeed, some recent reviewers of the evidence conclude that token economies may be less successful than other approaches to therapy. There is also the thorny problem that token economies may well violate the constitutional rights of patients who have been committed.

6. The application of the token economy form of behavior modification to education has been limited largely to classrooms for children who have serious problems. The use of the technique does seem to produce more behavior acceptable to the teacher, but this is different from producing more learning. There is also the problem that students in a token economy program may become more concerned with winning tokens than with learning. All the proponents of such a system claim that tokens can be phased out as behavior improves, but there is no solid evidence to suggest that this can be undertaken without loss in the gains already made. One effect of a token type of economy is that it may provide a rewarding atmosphere that may have desirable effects.

7. Many manuals have been produced that attempt to train the teacher in the use of behavior modification techniques. Most of these manuals have been written from a quite naive viewpoint about education and are designed to help the teacher produce a classroom in which the teacher can be happy. Evidence to support the

use of such procedures is largely lacking. Another approach to the control of pupil behavior has been the use of drugs such as Ritalin. There is virtually no convincing and replicable evidence that the use of such drugs is justified. There is also no evidence that the behaviors sought after by those who use such drugs have much to do with the amount of learning that takes place. In addition, slight changes in how behavior modification techniques are applied may produce great differences in the results achieved.

8. Operant psychologists have attempted to have an impact on curriculum design by reviving the procedures developed by Tyler in the early 1930s. These procedures involved the breaking down of objectives into small components, and of building tasks, arranged in a suitable sequence, through which these objectives could be achieved. The breakdown may be intó thousands of items. This "analysis" of the behavior involved in the achievement of important goals is basically an armchair process of analysis, undertaken without the collection of data and without the observation of children.

9. Ambitious school programs were built by operant psychologists during the 1960s, which were sold to schools on a payment-by-results basis. Although these programs cost more than those ordinarily used in schools, they produced no particular gains and were ultimately abandoned. Programmed learning, which became a part of the operant psychologist's package for schools, was also offered as a curriculum innovation, but failed to produce any notable gains in learning. The materials were more expensive to produce than ordinary materials, which meant that they would have had to produce substantial gains to justify the added expense. Regimented programs of learning also seem to present the problem that even though they may produce immediate results, they may do this at the expense of long-term results.

10. Skinner considered that delay in reinforcement was harmful to human learning and designed teaching machines that would provide immediate reinforcement. However, he did not recognize that although delay in reinforcement is deleterious to motor skill learning, it does not have the same effect on cognitive learning. Evidence has been produced that on cognitive learning tasks delay in reinforcement up to 24 hours may facilitate learning. The improvement produced by delay in reinforcement is not generally apparent on tests given immediately after learning, but it is apparent after an interval of days or weeks. A short delay in the presentation of feedback may facilitate learning for a different reason than from a long delay. Short delays may permit the learner to think about what he is learning. Longer delays have a different effect.

11. The effects of delayed punishment are far less clear than the effects of delayed rewards. Delayed punishment may well be effective under some circumstances.

12. The time allowed after feedback is provided may be a quite significant factor in cognitive learning. Time is required to assimilate the information provided by feedback.

13. The data on the effect of magnitude of reinforcement on learning is unsatisfactory. Increasing the magnitude seems to increase the vigor of response, but

this conclusion may not hold for cognitive learning. On the other hand, when some items are rewarded with money for being learned and others are not, subjects tend to learn only the rewarded items.

14. The use of material rewards is also controversial. They appear to be effective, but whether they also depress any inherent interest in the task still needs to be determined.

15. Reinforcement may occur on every trial or on only a certain percentage of trials. The pattern of the distribution of reinforcements is known as the schedule of reinforcements. The partial reinforcement effect is the name given to the condition occurring when the schedule of reinforcement is reduced below 100 per cent and is administered on a random basis. In the partial reinforcement condition the rate of learning decreases, but the rate at which the response is extinguished after the withdrawal of the reinforcement is also decreased. Various explanations have been offered for this phenomenon, but none are entirely satisfactory. Some of the common schedules of reinforcement have been given such names as fixed-ratio schedules and variable-ratio schedules.

16. The negative side effects of punishment still have not been well established. There appears to be a building up of anxiety after punishment. Also, when punishment has been administered at random, as it may often appear to be to children, a general state of apathy may result. Self-destructive children may be helped with punishment, but there the gains far outweigh the side effects. Rewards may have undesirable effects, if used in unreasonable amounts.

17. Classical conditioning has been extensively applied in clinical practice in the form of desensitization techniques designed to reduce anxiety. The techniques seem to be effective, but the reasons for their success are controversial.

Chapter 4

Acquisition of Motor Skills

Tasks that involve complex muscular responses, and particularly those that involve the use of equipment, are said to call upon the subject to perform what are termed *motor skills*. Driving a car involves a motor skill and so, too, does using a hammer, or engaging in the pole vault, or sewing by hand or by machine, or tight-rope walking, or flying a plane. All such activities require that complex responses be made in keeping with the requirements of the task and the nature of the equipment involved. The term motor skill is also used rather loosely to refer to some complex responses that do not involve equipment. For example, sometimes it is said that speech is partly a motor skill, in that it involves the precise control of musculature. On the other hand, nobody would be likely to refer to a handshake as a motor skill. Where the cutoff between simple muscular responses and motor skills should be made is a matter for judgment at this time.

Motor skills are sometimes referred to as psychomotor skills to indicate that more is involved than just movement and that the performance calls for complex psychological processes. Another term commonly used is perceptual-motor skills, which indicates that motor skills involve perceptual processes from which they cannot be readily separated. No uniform term or set of terms has emerged, so in this chapter reference will be made to motor skills rather than to the more elaborate terms that have evolved.

A motor skill, as defined here, is one in which a major component is muscular activity that has some direct impact on the environment. Driving a car clearly meets this requirement, for the mechanical manipulation of the controls has direct physical effect on the motion of the automobile. Most athletic activities fall into the motor skill category. Crafts and trades of a century ago would have involved mainly motor skills, but today the use of machine tools has largely eliminated the importance of fine muscular adjustments in their pursuit. Although Stradivarius shaped each piece of his violins by hand and the precision of the craftsmanship depended on his steadiness and control, only a few modern violinmakers follow the same procedure. Most manufacturers of violins today produce the parts through the use of jigs that guide the cutting tools, and motor skills play only a very minor part in the production of the instruments. Modern manufacturing operations require little skill or practiced motor control.

Motor skills can be regarded in many different ways. One of the modern ways is to view the human being and what he is doing as a system having a certain input and a certain output. In driving a car, there are inputs through the eyes and the ears concerning the location of the car in relation to the road and other objects, and there are outputs of the human operator that result in the car being driven properly through traffic. Much of the study of motor skills involves a study of the relationship of the inputs to the outputs. If the driver of a car does not manage to maintain a proper relationship between the inputs and the outputs, he is likely to land in the ditch. The inputs may be very simple, as they are when a car is driven along a monotonous interstate highway, or they may be very complex, as when a person is driving in heavy traffic through a city bedecked with numerous traffic signs and traffic lights, and with many lines of traffic entering and leaving the main flow. Outputs on motor tasks may also be simple or complex. The driver of a train produces simpler outputs than the driver of a vehicle that has to be guided. Still more complex is the output of the operator of a space vehicle, who has to guide the craft in three dimensions, rather than the two dimensions used by the driver of a ground vehicle.

MOTOR SKILL ACQUISITION AS SEEN IN HUMAN DEVELOPMENT

The development of motor skills has long been a subject of study of psychologists. The classic studies of Arnold Gesell and Myrtle McGraw earlier in the century laid the foundation for much of the work that has taken place since. The early studies were dominated by the idea that the key to understanding motor skills lay in close and detailed observation of their emergence and enormous effort was directed into doing just that. Both McGraw and Gesell developed the most detailed inventory of how the infant progresses from the prone to the upright position, with an emphasis on when maturational skill components emerge. Stewart (1974), has brought together these data with that provided by Piaget in his *Origins of Intelligence in Children*. She has been able to show that the data fit together well and show virtually no discrepancies, which leaves us with the question of whether there are principles of motor skill development underlying the development during infancy of all motor skills.

Stewart attempts to derive from Piaget (1963), Werner (1957), Bruner (1973), and

Bernstein (1967), a model for the description of the development of motor skills. She agrees with others who have worked in the area that motor acts find their origins in reflex behavior and that the original reflexes remain interwoven with the mature and fully developed form of the motor skills. Thus the infant shows reflexes related to supporting his weight against gravity long before he can walk and, in the early stages, will show alternating movements of the leg and feet if held in the upright position with the soles of the feet just touching the ground. These reflexes do not disappear as the infant grows and masters upright walking, but they become integrated into the total performance.

Stewart is impressed with the value of the concept of intent in understanding the development of motor skills and uses a concept of intent similar to that used by Jean Piaget in much of his writing. The development of motor skills is seen to involve the operation of an executive decision-making system within the infant that directs behavior toward certain goals. The infant's motor skills are not random movements, some of which happen to be reinforced and consolidated, but they are skills acquired in the achievement of certain goals—that is, the infant anticipates certain outcomes. Thus Piaget's own infant might first accidentally contact with his hand an object suspended from the top of the bassinet and then lose contact; but the infant struggles as if to restore that contact with the object and ultimately to be able to make that contact intentionally. In Stewart's conceptualization of motor skill development, the intention of the infant is related to the infant attempting to match what he is doing with an internal model of what he intends to do. Effort is then directed toward reducing this discrepancy. This concept is similar to Piaget's concept that much of the motor activity is an attempt to conserve an experience—to produce an action that reinstates a previous state. However, Piaget hedges in saying that the infant is capable of representing internally a goal state, though the idea that the infant is attempting to reinstate an experience implies such internal representation.

In Stewart's model, coordination involves the merging and integration of separate skilled motor acts that prior to coordination were disassociated. The process has three essential steps: precoordination, basic coordination, and refinement. In precoordination, focus swings back and forth between the components of the skilled motor acts that are to be integrated. With experience through feedback efficiency increases in the attempt to merge the skills into a unified sequence. With further incentive to continue and perfect the coordination, refinement occurs so that the right action is performed at the right time and coordination is marked by the ability to anticipate future actions.

Most observers of the acquisition of motor skills in infants have been impressed with the extreme concentration that infants show when attempting to master a skill. Infants, like adults, have limited capacity for handling information and easily become overloaded. In the early stages of mastering a motor skill, the infant may find that mastering the actions related to his balance and movements of the limbs is as much as he can handle, and often perhaps more than he can handle. Overload of information produces disorganization. One can understand this if one recalls one's first experiences in learning to ride a bicycle. Keeping oneself upright on the machine seems impossible because one must not only maintain balance, but keep track of the position of one's legs and arms at the same time, and the position of all the limbs is essential for the maintenance of balance. One's first impression in learning to ride a bicycle is that the task is enormously difficult.

When the immediate goals of the infant become too difficult to achieve, simpler goals may be sought. An infant unable to reach an object just outside his playpen and unable to master the task of reaching it with a stick may settle for playing with a toy that is more easily reached. An infant having difficulty in moving in an erect position may return to the crawling posture.

Stewart makes the interesting point, citing the work of Bernsten (1967), that many of the motor skills of the infant do not reach a full stage of coordination until adolescence. The act of walking is not fully mastered until that stage. The development of coordination is to some extent a matter of learning timing. Motor activities sometimes appear as sequences of acts separated by pauses, but the discrete acts slowly become fused into a single act. In learning to use a spoon the infant may begin by experimenting with holding it, then he may work on putting it in the food, and, finally, he has to master the problem of carrying the food to his mouth. These various aspects of the total activity may at first occur in any sequence, with pauses between each aspect. Thus the infant may manage to push some food on the spoon, and then become preoccupied with holding the spoon so that the food drops onto the floor; then he may place the empty spoon, upside down, in his mouth. The various components have to be coordinated, sequenced and built into a single smoothly performed complex act. Bruner (1973) has been impressed with the way in which component acts are built up into complex acts and has used the word *module* to describe the component. For Bruner, the main problem of producing coordinated motor skills is that of building up of modules into larger action systems. To Werner (1957), this represented hierarchical organization.

Stewart derives considerable support from many authorities that the development of motor skills in the infant require that the infant be encouraged to venture. Without such encouragement the infant may lack the boldness to acquire many motor skills at as early an age as they could be acquired.

Stewart finds that considerable controversy surrounds the issue of whether very young children should be given assistance in the performance of motor acts. The extreme view would take the position that responsibility for action should remain with the infant. In a program based on such a view, the infant should not be raised into the sitting position by the adult but he should be left to perform such an activity by himself at the time when he is capable of doing it without assistance. This does not mean that the infant should not be given encouragement in his efforts, but only that he should supply the initiative. Stewart was not able to find much evidence to support such a radical view of child rearing. Certainly, it runs against what mothers naturally do. One cannot discard lightly what 2 million years of evolution has produced in human mothering behavior even though the characteristics that have evolved are not always suited to modern times.

Classes of Motor Skill Tasks

Motor skills may involve the continuous adjustment to an external situation or the task may involve modules, each one of which has to be completed before the next module appears. A continuous adjustment motor task is illustrated by driving a car or riding a bicycle. Tasks that come in modules are those of throwing a basketball into the net, replacing an electrical switch in the house, or applying the emergency brake of the car. The motor skills of infant development fall into both classes. An infant may slowly master the task of grasping an object with his hand. The mastering of this motor skill begins with the infant fortuitously bringing his hand into contact with an object. He holds it for an instant and then loses his grasp of it; he waves his arm and hand around until he manages to grasp the object again. This activity is repeated from time to time over several days until the uncoordinated waving of the hand and arm becomes replaced by a smooth and coordinated effective grasping of the object. The motor skill has then been mastered.

The continuous type of motor skill has typically been studied through what are called pursuit tasks, to be considered later in the chapter. The discrete task type of motor skill has been studied through such simple tasks as that of moving a lever from a fixed position by a given amount. Thus the subject might be asked to move the lever 6 inches. After he has moved the lever what he believes to be 6 inches, he removes his hand from it and the lever is returned to the base position. The subject may be told the size of his error or be given some indication of how well he did. There are a great number of variations on this task, how it is administered, and how feedback is provided.

STAGES IN LEARNING PERCEPTUAL-MOTOR SKILLS

Fitts and Posner (1967) have attempted to describe the course of learning motor skills in relatively mature individuals in general terms. Their analysis provides a good introduction and a basis for more detailed discussion of some of the problems involved in motor-skill training. They suggest that motor-skill learning can be conveniently divided into three phases.

In the first phase, which Fitts and Posner describe as the early or cognitive phase, the emphasis is on learning to recognize the important cues that have to be attended to, which might be referred to as the perceptual phase of learning. In learning to operate a typewriter, the novice must first learn to recognize what the various controls will do, such as which key to press to write a particular letter or to back-space. All motor tasks involve this phase of learning, although in some it is undertaken under informal conditions. In the case of learning to drive a car, much of the perceptual phase of learning is undertaken through casual observation long before the young person ever sits in the driver's seat. By the time he is old enough to learn the skill, he knows where all the controls are and how they are operated. To a lesser extent this is true in the case of typing, but in the case of some skills the cognitive phase is learned through formal instruction. For example, most of those who learn to fly a plane are unfamiliar with the arrangement of the controls in the cockpit and have to begin by acquiring knowledge of the location of the controls and what they do. In addition, the novice has to learn about the various instruments in the cockpit and what their dials show. There is much to be learned about the task of flying long before the novice ever takes to the air. Perceptual familiarity with the controls and gadgetry in the cockpit is essential for learning to fly the plane.

In the cognitive stage, the pupil learns the responses that can be made but he does not yet learn to make the responses on appropriate occasions. In learning to typewrite, he will know at the end of this phase where the various keys and controls are. In a sense, he has all the responses necessary for typing, but this is not enough to make him a skilled typist.

In the second phase of learning a perceptual-motor skill, the responses become tied to the appropriate stimuli. This may be much more complex than it seems. In learning to type the word *man*, the student must not only see each one of the letters and type the appropriate letter, but the striking of each key must become the trigger that initiates the striking of the next key. This stage in the learning is not too different from a corresponding stage in many verbal tasks. For example, in learning a poem the student will begin by familiarizing himself with the general content of the piece of verse. Then, in this second stage, he must learn to say the various phrases in proper order, and the completion of one must trigger the initiation of saying the next.

In the second stage, wrong habits that are brought to the skill from past experience must be eliminated. The pilot must learn that one does not turn the plane by manipulating the hand controls, but through the foot pedals. As a car driver he learned to steer with his hands, but he must learn to abandon this habit as soon as he climbs into a plane. He must also learn not to feel for the gas pedal on the floor, for planes do not have such a pedal. In this phase, such inconsistent habits have to be extinguished.

In the final stage, the skill becomes more and more automatically performed as control is taken over by the lower centers of the brain. This is the stage where performance becomes so smooth and automatic that the person can engage in the skill while thinking about other things. Thus the automobile driver, after years of practice, can easily hold a conversation with a passenger while driving down the road.

Studies of the discrete type of laboratory task have provided some findings that support the view that the activity on each successive trial is guided by an internal representation of the activity engaged in on the previous trial. Adams (1971, 1972) has attempted to develop a theory of motor learning, which he calls a closed-loop theory, similar to that of Werner. Adams calls this internal representation a *trace*, which other psychologists might call an image. A task that Adams has used requires an individual to move a lever ten inches. He can do this either watching what he is doing or blindfolded. He can also perform the task with the lever easy to move or hard to move. Adams's theory is that each time the individual performs the task, the tensions in his muscles and the visual information leave a trace behind. He then learns whether he pushed the lever too far or not far enough. The trace, together with the knowledge of results, is what he brings to the next trial. If he moved the lever too far on the previous trial, he must now perform so that the new trace differs from the trace on the previous trial. Thus each trial is guided by the trace from the previous trial. Now one can increase the intensity of the experiences involved in moving the lever. The experiences are minimal when the eyes of the individual are blindfolded and the lever moves very easily. The experiences have greater intensity if the individual can watch himself move the lever and if the lever is hard to move. Adam's theory holds that the more intense experiences should leave a stronger trace, which should be a better guide than a weak trace on the next trial. This is exactly what Adams found. Increase the strength of the trace on each trial and learning is facilitated. A strong trace also helps in the retention of the skill.

Other important features of the acquisition and performance of motor skills have been studied through the use of what are known as *tracking tasks*. Motor skills have been studied in the laboratory in situations that resemble tasks commonly encountered during life but generally involve much greater simplicity. For example, driving a car along a winding road involves keeping the car in a fixed position with respect to the edge of the road or the center line, if there is one. This task is very much like many tasks, known as tracking tasks, that are used in the laboratory study of motor skills. In tracking tasks there has to be what is referred to as a target, which is simply a mark such as a spot of light on a screen. The movement of the target is controlled by the experimental equipment. In addition, there is also a marker, which may be another spot of light, but this is controlled by the subject in the experiment. The task of the subject is to watch the target and when it moves to move the marker to keep it directly over the target. The subject moves the marker by pushing or pulling a lever, by turning a crank, by pressing a brake pedal, or by some other mechanical device. The target may move in a regular pattern, or with complete irregularity, depending on the particular experiment. The rate of movement can also be fast or slow. Many common motor-skill tasks are tracking tasks. For example, learning to write in the first grade by copying letters and words written on the chalkboard or elsewhere is essentially a form of tracking behavior, and in performing this task the child is learning a form of motor skill.

The kind of laboratory tracking task considered up to this point is referred to as a *pursuit tracking task*, but other tracking tasks have also been invented. Another is compensatory tracking in which the target is fixed but the marker tends to drift away from the target, and the subject must bring it back onto the target through moving the controls.

Other devices that have been used for the study of motor skills include simulations of the cockpit of a plane equipped with both a joystick and pedals for rudder control. With these devices the flight pattern of a miniature plane in front of the cockpit can be controlled. Another simple device is the track-tracing apparatus in which the subject must move a metal stylus along a path without touching the boundaries of the path. Designed to study other aspects of motor skill is the apparatus for measuring steadiness, in which a stylus must be held in a small hole without the stylus touching the sides of the hole. Other equipment has long been used for the study of speed of reaction.

Of all the various techniques used for the study of motor skills in the laboratory, none has been used more widely, nor produced more information, than tracking tasks. These tasks seem to be peculiarly well suited to providing knowledge about motor behavior.

An excellent review of the literature on tracking behavior has been prepared by Poulton (1966). The literature is not readily summarized because tracking behavior may be very simple, as when the target moves at a uniform speed along a line, or very complex, as when the target moves in three dimensions in a pattern that never repeats itself. In addition, the target may move at a uniform speed or accelerate or decelerate. Thus tracking tasks may vary from very simple ones that involve a single control to complex ones involving three or more controls. The conclusions that can be drawn about learning simple tracking tasks cannot always be applied to the complex tasks.

Most of those who have ever undertaken a tracking task have the impression that it involves a continuous adjustment on the part of the operator of the equipment. The driver moving his car along a winding road has the impression that he keeps the car moving smoothly around the curves. In actual fact, he does not do this at all. What he does is to turn the steering wheel in a number of short and discrete adjustments. Each is a separate and distinct movement followed by a pause when he takes stock of the results of the previous adjustment. If the driving is difficult, he may make perhaps two adjustments of the steering wheel in a second, but normally he does not make more than one adjustment per second.

The Poulton article points out that there is considerable evidence that tracking behavior involves a series of decision-action sequences. The person performing a tracking task makes a decision to move in a certain direction and once the move has been initiated, the direction cannot be readily altered. It is estimated that it takes about a third of a second to make a new decision and to change the direction of action. Thus there is a delay of about a third of a second between the arrival of information at the performer's eyes and the initiation of action and then, if new information arrives, it may take about another third of a second to change the direction of the action again. These kinds of delays may be serious to a person landing a jet plane under conditions of poor visibility, when the plane may move one hundred feet before a pilot can change from the initiation of an incorrect decision to the making of a correct decision. However, in many tracking tasks, the lag in behavior is not serious in that the person can anticipate, in advance, what he has to do. Thus the driver of a car can watch the road as it winds into the distance and make decisions well in advance of the actions that have to be taken. It is under conditions where the equipment operator cannot anticipate what is going to happen that lags in decision-action sequences become of real importance.

Thus, in tracking tasks the equipment operator does not make continuous adjustments; rather, he makes a jumpy set of adjustments. He makes one adjustment and then remains stationary, and then he makes another adjustment. The task is continuous, but the adjustments of the operator are discontinuous. Furthermore, the operator can make only about two adjustments every second, at the most. This fact has important implications for equipment design. If a piece of equipment, involving a tracking task, requires the operator to make more than about two adjustments a second, then it may be impossible for the operator to keep on target. Of course, if the adjustments can be anticipated, then the tracking task is greatly simplified, and more than three adjustments per second can be made.

A key to training persons to perform in many tracking situations is to teach them to *anticipate* changes in the direction of the track. A person learning to drive a car often begins by concentrating on the immediate state of affairs, and in turning a corner he may fail to begin to turn the wheel in time. As a result, he overshoots the turn and swings far out from the side of the road where he should be. Learning to run and catch a baseball is largely a problem of learning to anticipate where the ball will be after a particular interval of time.

Performance on most tracking tasks can be improved if the person is given supplementary feedback concerning the size of his errors. For example, in a laboratory tracking task a buzzer may sound whenever the performer has been particularly accurate in keeping the marker on the target. An alternative procedure is for the buzzer to sound whenever a particularly large error has been made. Both of these procedures lead to more accurate performance than is otherwise achieved. One presumes that similar feedback would also be of value in learning to drive a car. Although the driver knows well whether he is or is not roughly in the correct position on the highway, the instructor will probably facilitate learning by indicating when he is doing particularly well or particularly poorly. Such supplementary information probably has quite complex functions, in that it serves to provide a standard by which the driver can judge whether he is doing well enough or whether he is not meeting the standards expected of him.

One of the problems that has been studied using tracking tasks is whether the learning of a motor skill is best undertaken through learning the components, piece by piece, before the total skill is attempted, or whether it is best to go about learning by attacking the total task in its entirety from the beginning. This kind of problem is encountered in planning training on any complex piece of equipment that requires simultaneous operation of several controls, such as, for example, a bulldozer, fork-lift truck, or crane. The question is whether practice should be given on each of the component control systems separately before the total task in its entirety is attempted. The answer to this problem cannot be stated in simple terms. If the controls really operate completely independently of each other, there seems to be some virtue in practicing the component skills first; but when, as is generally the case, there is some interaction between what is done with one control and what is done with the other, the complete skill should be practiced as an entirety. An example of where the component skills interact is found in the case of the operation of a stick-shift car. The clutch is one control and the foot brake another, but the two interact in that when the person wants to stop he must know that he depresses the brake first and then depresses the clutch slightly later. The brake and clutch skills have to be practiced together because they interact.

The most important single factor that has been identified in relation to the training of individuals in motor skills is the rate at which the initial task is increased in difficulty. There is some agreement that in the case of those skills where the task can be slowed down, as it can be in tracking tasks, initial training should be given at a slow rate. The rate should then be increased as rapidly as the learner can adapt to the new rate. Indeed, without such an increment in rate, the learner's performance may decline, for he seems to need the incentive of an increased rate from time to time in order to provide some challenge. If a training device is built to teach a particular skill as, for example, in the case of flying light aircraft, the trainer can be designed so that the difficulty of the task is always adjusted to the level of skill of the learner.

Some understanding of the reason for the need to adjust the task difficulty to the level of performance of the learner is found in the work of Fitts and Peterson (1964), who took the position that a crucial factor in the learning of a motor skill is the information capacity of the learner. When a task is adjusted so that it involves excessive speed, the learner has difficulty in coping with it because he cannot handle the information required to perform the task effectively. This conception of the main source of difficulty in the learning of motor skills interprets well the common experience of learning to ride a bicycle. The novice who first attempts this task finds himself confronted with an array of controls and a mass of visual, kinesthetic, and other sources of information that he does not yet know how to use effectively. He is clumsy, partly because he is flooded with all kinds of information that he cannot relate effectively to what he can do to maintain his balance. If the task can be slowed down, in the sense that he has less information to handle at any time, this will facilitate learning. In the case of learning to ride a bicycle, one can attach training wheels so that at first the learner need only attend to the problem of pedaling and steering. Once he has learned to handle these automatically, he can turn to the problem of balance. The training wheels can then be slowly raised so that the learner becomes more and more dependent on his own skill for the maintenance of balance.

Performance on tracking tasks is characterized by a quite rapid decline in performance, presumably caused by the building up of inhibitions. In popular language, one might say that the learner of the motor skill quickly becomes tense, with a resulting decrement in performance. For this reason, during the acquisition of a motor skill rather short sessions, interspersed with rest periods, are likely to provide a learning situation in which there is continuous improvement. There is some evidence that even though performance on a motor skill that is being learned shows a rapid decline during a particular learning session, learning still continues to occur. It is just that the learning is not manifest in immediate performance, although it may be evident in the level of performance at the next training session. A similar decrement in performance in a motor skill does not appear to happen when the skill is highly practiced. A skilled typist may show a small decline over the course of a morning, but it is a very small decline compared with that found in the learner.

When the level of performance on a motor skill has shown a decline toward the end of a training session, even a short rest period is likely to produce a remarkable increase in performance. This rise in performance is due to the dissipation of the inhibitory effects that had built up during practice.

RETENTION OF MOTOR SKILLS

Common experience tells us that the retention of motor skills is excellent over long periods. A person may not skate for a ten-year period, and when he takes to the ice he finds that he can skate almost as well as when he left off. Psychologists have found similar data in the laboratory. Studies of the long-term retention of motor skills have been undertaken by numerous research workers over the past half century and all with similar results. A study by Fleishman and Parker (1962) will be discussed briefly as a basis for opening up an understanding of the reasons for the lack of forgetting on such tasks.

Fleishman and Parker used a task that resembled, in some superficial respects, the manipulation of the controls on a plane. A joystick was held by the subject and could be moved forward or backward or to either side. The stick provided two dimensions of movement. The feet were used to control a rudder bar that could be moved like a seesaw about an axis. The stick had to be manipulated so that it maintained a dot of light on a cathode-ray tube in a central position. The dot tended to drift away from the central position and the stick could be used to return it. The foot controlled rudder bar was used to adjust a voltmeter placed just below the cathode-ray tube. Whenever the needle on the voltmeter strayed from the central position, the subject had to recenter it by moving the rudder bar with the feet. Thus the task was complex, involving both the observation of a dot of light and the observation of a needle on a voltmeter. The subject then had to adjust the position of the dot and the needle by manipulating the stick and the rudder with hands and feet. The task was not readily learned and required 50 practice sessions, each of 6 minutes' duration, in order for the subjects to achieve a level of learning that showed no improvement. The practice sessions were spread over 17 days. So much for the training part of the experiment. Then Parker and Fleishman tested their subjects for the retention of the skill, with one third of the subjects being retested after 9 months, one third after 12 months, and one third after 24 months. The 9-month and the 12-month group showed virtually no loss of the skill. The 24-month group showed a slight loss that was almost completely recovered after three 6-minute practice sessions. In other words, the data showed a high degree of retention over a 2-year period and the findings were consistent with everyday experience. Now let us consider why there is so little loss of motor skill, compared with a corresponding loss in verbal knowledge, over such a long period. One cannot be certain of the validity of the answers given here, but those answers are highly plausible and consistent with what is known.

Consider first one part of the task performed in the Fleishman and Parker study, namely, the adjustment of the voltmeter needle with the foot bar. This is essentially a highly repetitive task, for the subject must, again and again, bring back the needle to center by moving the foot bar. After 300 minutes of doing this, the subject must be considered to have had an extraordinarily large amount of practice. Perhaps a comparable task in the verbal field might be one in which the subject had to say "X" immediately, every time the experimenter said "P". Three hours of practice on such a task would bring it to the point where the response would be made immediately and without hesitation. The simplicity of the response and the extended amount of practice would almost certainly ensure that the learning would be highly permanent, for the reason that overlearned responses are less easily lost than are responses that have had little practice. The superior retention of most motor responses studied may be attributable not to the fact that they are motor reponses but to the fact that they are highly overlearned and rather simple in character.

A second factor is that such tasks are continuous tasks. If one were to design motor tasks so that they involved a number of separate and distinct responses, they might not be so well retained. The latter kind of tasks involve more distinct components than a simple tracking task, such as the Fleishman and Parker task, and in this respect might be more comparable to verbal tasks. Complex motor tasks involving discrete responses generally involve, like a game of checkers, a number of distinct moves that have to be made. These may each involve the throwing of a correct switch or the moving of an appropriate lever. Generally, some kind of complex signal is given, such as the turning on of a combination of lights. The signal indicates the switch to be pushed or the lever to be positioned. Once the subject has responded, the lights go off and the machine is reset for the next stimulus and the next response. On such tasks forgetting is extremely rapid and closely comparable to that found in verbal learning tasks.

A third factor that may help to account for the superiority of the retention of motor skills has to do with the fact that the laboratory tasks used are not similar to those used in daily life and for this reason the learned skill is not disrupted by subsequent activities with related motor skills. The retention of a verbal task is probably readily disrupted by similar verbal behavior undertaken day-in and day-out, for the laboratory task involves just the same elements as are undertaken in daily life. This argument is not particularly strong, in that we have no way of determining the extent to which laboratory motor tasks are similar or dissimilar to tasks involved in daily life.

There is still the possibility that motor skills are actually more readily retained than are verbal skills and verbal information. Motor skills are highly dependent for their retention on the cerebellum and lower brain centers, which have the capability of taking them over and making them quite automatic. These centers may have a greater capability of retaining the traces necessary for their performance than have the parts of the brain concerned with the retention of other skills and information.

The Retention of Motor Skills as the Retention of a Program

When a child first learns to tie his shoelaces, he tediously performs each component act step by step. After he has performed the first small part of the task, he is likely to stop and inspect what he has done and from the results figure out what the next step should be. Each step is guided by his visual inspection of the previous step. What a contrast the early performance of this skill is with the smooth, efficient, and quick performance of the older child!

The evidence now seems clear that the early performance of a complex motor skill is quite different from a mature performance. In the early stages of learning a complicated motor skill, the components are executed one at a time. The feedback provided by the accomplishments of one stage is used to trigger the next stage. If a stage has not been successfully completed, the next stage does not take place. In contrast, in the case of the well-practiced and expert performance, there is no clear division between the various stages, for behavior flows smoothly. Although the learner divides the execution of the skill into stages, the skilled performer shows a continuous flow of behavior until the goal is reached.

Keele (1969) points out that there is substantial evidence to show that although a motor skill may be learned in the first place component by component, the more advanced stages of the acquisition of the skill involve the development of an internal program that permits the complete performance to run off with very little feedback. The concept of a *program* is derived from the area of computers. A computer program involves a complete set of directions for performing a sequence of mathematical operations. One can, for example, have a computer program for working out the square root of a number. Once the program is set to work, it will carry through the entire process of deriving a square root. The square root program is a relatively short program, but some programs may involve many hundreds of steps.

Now consider how the analogy of the computer program applies to our understanding of the performance of a well-practiced motor skill. Just as the computer may store a program containing all the operations necessary to perform a particular computation, and may produce the operations one by one, so, too, may the brain store the entire program necessary for performing a complex motor skill and then send out the correct sequence of commands to the muscles to execute the skill. In the case of the program in the nervous system that controls a motor skill, the commands to the muscles go out in sequence, and with very little monitoring of the behavior involved. For example, the series of acts involved in bowling is run off as a smooth sequence. If one of the movements is not quite correctly performed in the latter stages of the bowling act, the bowler may not be able to stop the sequence in time and may throw a bad ball. He knows that the ball will be a bad one before it even leaves his hand, but the entire sequence of activities has been triggered and in order to halt the action the bowler must not only make the decision to stop it, but he must also take the necessary action to do so. This may take perhaps half a second and during that time the last step may have been taken and the ball thrown.

In the case of highly practiced skills, the program in the nervous system may run off with very little monitoring by the perceptual system. Thus one may open the door of the car, enter, sit down, put the key in the ignition, and start the car while thinking about other matters. Intervention in the sequence is likely to occur if something goes wrong, such as the lock of the car sticking in winter, but otherwise the program runs off quite automatically.

The learning of a motor skill, beyond the initial clumsy stages, involves the laying down of a program for the performance of the skill within the central nervous system. This program, when triggered, runs off smoothly and with each step in proper sequence. One presumes that the cerebellum has the function of assembling and coordinating such a program.

Rate of Learning and Degree of Retention

Studies have been undertaken in which the retention of slow and fast learners have been compared. The usual procedure involves training all subjects to the same initial degree of proficiency and then measuring retention of the material after some time interval. A point to note is that the fast learners inevitably take fewer trials than the slow learners, and the number of trials needed to reach some specified degree of proficiency may be ten times greater for the fast learners than for the slow. Melnick, Lersten, and Lockart (1972) have reviewed some of these studies as a preliminary to conducting a study of their own in the motor area.

The evidence generally indicates that fast learners retain information better than slow learners. The slow-but-sure maxim does not apply in this area. An explanation of these results is not easy to pin down.

One explanation is that the fast learners come to the experimental situation with the task partially mastered. Thus in a balancing task that requires a person to balance with one foot on each pan of a scales, some individuals may have managed to have already acquired balancing skills that the other subjects have not. They may well start out at a higher level of proficiency, which is why they may take only three trials to reach a criterion performance. Such subjects come to the experimental situation with a partially mastered skill that the practice trials quickly bring up to peak performance. Since they then have a well-practiced skill, it is easily retained until it is again measured an hour or a day later. The slow learners may well come to the experimental situation with little skill and although they reach criterion in perhaps twelve trials, they still have only a weakly learned skill that fades before its retention is measured.

ANALYSIS OF TYPEWRITING

One of the few analyses of a motor skill that have any deep significance for the educator is found in West's book (1969) on the analysis of typewriting skill. West's analysis is based on the broad understanding that psychologists have already achieved of the nature of motor-skill learning as well as on research on the learning of typing, at which time the learner has had only the common familiarity with the typewriter as it is seen by the nonuser. The learner knows that keys have to be struck in order to produce writing but that is about all, and his task is to strike keys denoted by the letters on the page of copy placed besides the machine. West points out that in the first phase of instruction (Fitts and Posner's second stage) the learner is involved in a long chain of internal activities that partly account for the slow pace of the skill during the initial stages. The chain of internal events involves (1) the perception of the letter to be copied and the vocalization of the letter, (2) the location of the key to be pressed, (3) the selection of the finger to be used in striking the key, (4) the vocalization again of the letter, and (5) the striking of the key. An important point to be noted is that the internal activity that triggers the striking of the key is that of the person saying to himself the letter in stage (4) of the sequence. After the letter is struck, the typed letter provides the feedback necessary for the learner to know whether his response has been correct. In the second phase, acquistion of speed in the performance of the skill involves first a reduction in the internal processes involved. When the learner has achieved a speed of about fifteen to twenty words per minute, he has reached the stage where he perceives a letter, and then says it to himself, and immediately strikes the right key. In addition, at this stage he has learned to take cognizance of the sensations in his muscles so that a stroke either feels right or feels wrong. As his level of skill is increased, he becomes more and more dependent on the information coming from the muscles within his body, which tells him where his fingers are and what they are doing. As the latter happens, he becomes less and less dependent on looking at what he has typed in order to check the accuracy of his work.

In a still later stage of learning the skill, the typist no longer has to vocalize each letter, but the stroke occurs in response to the perception of the letter. Then the perceptual-muscular behavioral unit ceases to be focused on individual letters; instead, groups of letters are read and the entire group typed as a unit. Although West implies that the typing of one letter produces sensations that become the stimuli for initiating the next letter, and thus a chain of behavior is established, it seems more likely that groups of letters are run off through sequences of messages being sent to the muscles from the brain. Indeed, the speed of typing at the level of the expert is such that no credence can be given to the theory that the sensations accompanying each stroke are the stimuli for initiating the next stroke. If this theory were correct, the maximum possible level of performance of the typist would be extremely slow. At a fast typing rate there is just not enough time for the stimuli produced by each stroke to initiate the next stroke.

The analysis of the learning of typing skill leads West to propose training methods that are in direct conflict with those that have been emphasized in the past. He points out that in the early stages of learning, the student should be concerned with learning the locations of the letters. In order to do this, he should use a typewriter that has the letters printed on the keys, and not the blank keyboard that has been preferred by teachers of the past. In order that the student may not have to shift his eyes back and forth from the copy to the keyboard, the teacher may read the letters to be typed. Later, of course, the habit of watching the keyboard has to be eliminated. As the student learns to type material presented beside the typewriter, and begins to strive for speed, he is forced into glancing at the keyboard less and less. Perhaps this is one of the reasons why the emphasis on speed rather than on accuracy produces the best learning condition during the early stages of acquiring the skill. The research evidence seems to be overwhelming that emphasis on speed rather than accuracy is extremely important for the effective acquisition of this particular skill.

The fact that this generalization emerges from research on typewriting does not mean that it is applicable to other motor skills. For example, it is extremely probable that the person studying a musical instrument should strive for accuracy rather than speed. It is the consensus of teachers of music that speed comes naturally if the pupil will just concentrate on accuracy but, unfortunately, most pupils want to strive for speed. Teachers of music could be wrong, as teachers in other fields have been demonstrated to be wrong, but the evidence still has to be collected.

Probably no generalizations can be made at this time in the matter of deciding whether speed or accuracy should be stressed in the learning of particular motor tasks except in cases such as typing, in which the matter has been closely studied. The problem is really quite complex. Striving for speed can give the learner the feeling of accomplishing something, even if he makes errors, but slow, deliberate, accurate typing may at first be at such a slow speed that the learner may give up, simply because he feels he can never master the task. On the other hand, emphasis on speed means that many errors will be practiced, and the practice of error always interferes with the learning of any task. In the case of typing, the advantages of speed seem to outweigh the negative effect of the increased practice of error. In the case of learning a musical instrument, the practice of errors probably has an overwhelming bad effect on ultimate level of performance.

West (1974) has brought together what he believes to be the most important implications of typing research for the training of the student. The essence of his conclusions are contained in the following statements:

1. Avoid concentrating on stroking skills. Special exercises for developing stroking, such as typing lists of words or particular combination of letters, is largely a waste of time.

2. Concentrate on production skills; that is, devote most time to typing realistic materials. Provide instruction at an early date in the layout and placement process.

3. Emphasize speed. Push the student to attempt to work at five words per minute faster than that at which he can produce satisfactory copy. Then let him test himself at a slower speed to determine his proficiency.

4. Since copy can now be rapidly corrected, the training problem is not so much that of eliminating stroking errors, but the recognition of errors so that they can be corrected. Little time is lost in the correction of an error, provided the typist is aware of having made an error.

5. Instruction in typing should be completely individualized with respect to speed and accuracy practice. Presumably some group instruction in such matters as layout can be given in a group form.

6. Production typing is a cognitive rather than a manipulative task. Since making decisions about layout and arrangement of the materials lies at the core of production typing, the student should be given extensive opportunity to make such decisions for himself, after brief initial instruction. Typing from unarranged materials, which the student must lay out, appears to be an essential exercise.

INDIRECT METHODS OF TEACHING MOTOR SKILLS:
MENTAL PRACTICE AND OBSERVATION

Instructors in physical education sometimes assume that improvement in a motor skill will take place through an internal rehearsal entitled mental practice, and through observation of a demonstration. The effectiveness of these techniques needs to be studied experimentally, more than it has been, but some evidence is available at this time.

Some rather weak evidence was found by Hammer and Natale (1964) that the initial stages of touch typing could be learned with greater accuracy, though not with increased speed, by a procedure involving mental practice rather than by a traditional procedure. Whether mental practice is or is not effective probably depends on the nature of the skill and the extent to which it involves high-level cognitive processes. If this is correct, one would not expect much effect from mental practice in the case of a skill in which cognitive processes did not play an essential role, but in which the person had to learn to use cues from his own muscles. Thus in the studies by Start (1964a, 1964b) on the effect of mental practice on performance of the single-leg upstart on the high bar, one would not expect much effect because what has to be learned is probably dependent on the lower centers of the nervous system and particularly on the cerebellum. Start could not find any effect of mental practice. However, in a rather similar study by Jones (1965) an effect was found. A much earlier study by Harby (1952) showed a slight but statistically significant effect of mental practice on the development of skill in the basketball free-throw. The greatest improvement was shown by the group that combined mental practice and physical practice.

An additional eleven studies on the effect of mental practice on the development of a motor skill have been reviewed by Richardson (1967). These studies involved such varied skills as the tennis forehand and backhand drive, dart throwing, muscular endurance, card sorting, and juggling. The overall evidence from these studies is difficult to interpret, often because no tests of significance were applied. Richardson concludes that the trend of the studies is to show that mental practice is associated with improved performance. As one would expect, a combination of both mental and physical practice generally gives the maximum improvement. Richardson points out that one of the crucial factors in determining the efficacy of mental practice is the familiarity of the learner with the task. A person can hardly be expected to undertake mental practice on a task he has not yet performed on any single occasion with any degree of success, for under such conditions all he can do is rehearse his inadequate performance. The studies reviewed by Richardson also produced some unexpected and perhaps inexplicable results. One of these is the tendency for mental practice to produce an improvement in tasks involving simply muscular endurance! Richardson also points out that at least two of the studies stress the difficulties that subjects experience in undertaking mental practice and that, if it is used at all, the periods of practice should be short. Indeed, there is even the suggestion that periods of mental practice that exceed only a few minutes may result in either boredom or frustration and lead to a lowered performance.

DELAY IN KNOWLEDGE OF RESULTS

Irion (1966) has reviewed the literature on the effect of delay in feedback or delay in knowledge of results on the acquisition and performance of motor skills. Much depends on the nature of the task. If it involves some continuous activity, as in tracking tasks or driving a car, the immediate knowledge of results is important for the guidance of behavior. On the other hand, if the motor skill involves discrete acts, as in drawing freehand a line of specified length or in throwing a ball over the shoulder at a target, the feedback on a particular trial may be delayed seconds, minutes, days, or even weeks without it losing its effectiveness. In such tasks a person may be able to use information about his performance, given after a long interval, to just the same extent as information given immediately after the act. This concept is used in the training of professional athletes in many fields, when their performance is filmed during contests or during practice and then the films are shown later for the purpose of correcting errors. In training programs of the latter kind, more time may be spent in the classroom studying films of practice than in the actual sessions themselves.

In the case of the question of the efficacy of teaching motor skills by demonstration, the problem is not whether they can or cannot be taught by this method, for obviously demonstration often has to play an important part. If one is training a person to tie a particular knot, a common problem in training Navy men, some kind of direct demonstration of what is involved is necessary. In the case of the knot-tying task, the minimum that the learner has to be given is an example of the knot as it is finally tied, but this final product is generally not a sufficient basis for learning. Additional information can be provided by showing the knot at various stages of being tied. A more complete version of the task can be provided through a film that presents the complete process of tying the knot. Whether the motion picture is superior as a teaching aid to the set of partly completed knots is a matter of conjecture. The advantage of the set of incomplete knots is that the learner can move both forward and backward and when he has difficulty at a particular stage, he can examine the corresponding stage as long as he wishes. On the other hand, the film is not so readily stopped and held and generally cannot be slowed up at a particular stage to help a particular learner. A finding of Rimland (1955), which has not been pursued further despite its intrinsic interest, is that a film demonstrating knot tying was most effective when it was shown twice without intervening practice, suggesting that practice is not effective until the learner's knowledge has developed beyond a certain critical point. Still earlier studies have also shown that in order for a demonstration to provide a useful, immediate guide to practice, the demonstration must proceed rather slowly (see, for example, the 1949 study of Roschal, the 1950 study of Jaspen, or the 1953 study of Ash and Jaspen). It seems that the learner becomes overloaded with information rather easily in the early stages of learning a motor skill and that when this happens learning may cease. For this reason, teachers would probably do well first to provide a complete and slow demonstration of the motor skill before permitting the learner to attempt to re-produce it. A difficulty in following this advice is that many motor skills often can-not be slowed up for the purposes of demonstration. The high jump in its entirety cannot be performed in slow motion and neither can the long pass in football.

THE LIMITS OF SKILL

Very little can be said about the limits of the improvability of motor skills. Much depends on the incentives provided for improvement and the amount of time de-voted to practice. Fitts and Posner (1967) have summarized some interesting findings concerning the improvement of skills that are practiced over extended durations. Several studies are presented in which the improvement in the perfor-mance of a motor skill continued over long periods. In such studies the patience of the experimenter often became exhausted before the subjects showed any decline in daily gains. Much more extended practice is found in some industrial studies in which the recorded performance of workers has been available over periods of years. In a well-known study by Crossman (1959) the production of cigar makers with varying amounts of experience was recorded. The data seemed to indicate that improvement in production occurred for at least the first four years and perhaps even longer. The data in the area suggest that improvement in motor skills takes place over long periods and that the achievement of any limit on the level of skill requires an immense amount of practice to attain. During the first year employees produce, on the average, 1 million cigars each. After the first few days, when they learn the job, they take about twelve hundreths of a minute to make a cigar. After a year, the time taken to make a cigar has declined to about ten hun-dreths. After two years the time is about nine hundreths. A slow increment in speed is still apparent after four years. One suspects also that, if added incentives had been provided gains in speed would have been made.

There is much evidence from the area of athletics to suggest that once a maxi-mum level is achieved, massive amounts of practice are necessary in order to main-tain that level of skill. Professional bowlers find it necessary to have their own private bowling alley in order to put in the practice required for maintaining their maxi-mum level of skill, and they may bowl twenty or more games a day. Musicians may have to practice eight or more hours a day to stay at their professional peaks. The professional pool player has to practice almost continuously to stay in champion-ship form. Years of practice seem to be required to reach a peak of performance, but to stay at that peak requires the same kind of practice that made it possible for the peak to be reached initially.

THE EFFECT OF STRESS ON PERFORMANCE

The effect of stress on the acquisition and maintenance of motor skills is of in-terest both to teachers and to the designers of equipment, but first let us consider a definition of stress. Fitts and Posner (1967) suggest that stress in a task be defined in much the same way that one might define stress in engineering. Stress is applied to a beam by providing it with an unusually high input. One can apply stress to a bridge by running a lot of traffic over it, or by piling sandbags along the roadway. One can apply stress to a person by giving him a task in which he has to handle a large amount of information.

When one asks a person to operate a piece of equipment with numerous gauges that must be kept in balanced conditions and with numerous controls that have to be adjusted, and when the task is such that it is far more complex than the skilled operator can handle, the person is unlikely to adopt the attitude that he can perform only part of the task and neglect the other part. He will almost certainly attempt the entire task and produce a confused and disorganized performance. An excessive input of information to the operator, a condition of high stress, produces poor performance. Now let us consider a situation in which there is very low stress, that is, a situation in which there is a low input of information. Such a situation is provided by tasks similar to those undertaken by operators of radar equipment, who must watch radarscopes for the appearance of small bright spots indicating the presence of an unknown flying object. Such tasks are known as vigilance tasks. They all involve watching for rare signals, and the information input to the human operator is at a very low level. These are by definition very low stress tasks. When an individual is faced with a very low stress task, he also becomes very ineffective. After he has performed a vigilance task for less than thirty minutes he begins to miss signals. His problem is that the input of information is so low that he finds it impossible to concentrate on the task. A certain amount of input is necessary in order for the operator to remain effective.

The picture resulting from such data is that performance on a perceptual-motor task is most likely to be effective when the conditions are somewhere between those of very low and very high stress. A moderate information input is necessary in order to keep the individual operating efficiently, but this level must not be raised beyond a certain level or behavior will become disorganized. This generalization holds true not just for motor tasks but also for many verbal tasks. When speech is speeded up to 300, 400, and 500 words per minute, the point is soon reached where the listener ceases to understand anything, despite the fact that the individual words are still intelligible. If speech is slow enough, say 40 words per minute, the thread of each sentence may be lost before it is finished, and behavior is also inefficient.

APTITUDES FOR MOTOR SKILL LEARNING

Pyschologists have long been interested in the identification of those persons most likely to be capable of learning motor skills successfully. The problem is one of great practical significance, for training in some motor skills can be an extremely expensive venture, as it is in the case of learning to fly a light airplane. In order to develop a successful means of identifying persons who learn motor skills easily, one has to know whether there is just a general motor ability that some individuals have more of and some less, or whether there are a number of separate and distinct aptitudes involved. For example, does a watchmaker who successfully dismantles, cleans, and reassembles watches have the same aptitudes as a person who uses his motor skills to assemble a frame building successfully? If different aptitudes are involved, one would choose people for training as watchmakers on a different basis from that one would use for selecting trainees who are to learn how to put together frame buildings. One activity involves fine manipulations of the fingers whereas the other involves gross movements of the limbs.

Tests of motor skills have had a long history, and their development preceded the developments of tests of intellectual skills. Some of the earliest were developed a century ago by Galton, who administered his battery to many thousands of subjects of all ages. By the turn of the century, American psychologists had become interested in the area; and most of the work undertaken was prompted by the idea that tests of simple motor skills could be used to predict performance in complex activities that involved these skills. Thus it might be assumed that tests of hand steadiness might predict rifle marksmanship, because steadiness is a component in the total skill of rifle marksmanship. Another example is the possibility that finger dexterity might be used to predict success in watch-repair work. Here again, the skill that is measured, finger dexterity, is a component of the total skill involved in repairing watches. Sometimes such predictions were found to work out rather well; sometimes, for unaccountable reasons, the expected relationships did not materialize.

The advancement of knowledge in this area has been handicapped greatly by the difficulties of undertaking research. Tests of motor skills generally require apparatus that is expensive to build and maintain. Unlike most paper-and-pencil tests of intellectual skills, students taking the tests show great improvement with practice; and the question has to be raised whether the most useful measure is a person's initial performance or his performance after he has had some practice. All these problems have added greatly to the difficulty of the task faced by the research worker interested in the area. Some meager knowledge is, however, available concerning the number of different motor skills that may be involved in complex tasks, and this must now be considered.

At the present time there appear to be a limited number of distinct abilities in the motor area. Measurement of these abilities may be used at a future time for the purpose of predicting the ability of individuals to learn skills that involve these motor abilities. The abilities as identified by Fleishman and Hempel (1956) are:

REACTION TIME. This is the speed with which an individual can make a response to a stimulus he is expecting. One measure of this ability is that of raising a finger at a predetermined signal, such as a click, or when a light is turned on.

TAPPING ABILITY. This skill is the speed with which an individual can perform a rapid movement, such as tapping a table top.

PSYCHOMOTOR COORDINATION. This ability is represented by such skills as require the coordination of the eye and the hand. It is involved in both fine and gross movements.

MANUAL DEXTERITY. This skill is a popular term with a technical meaning. It refers to the ability to make skillful, controlled arm or hand movements at a rapid rate. In one test of this ability, the subject must turn over blocks as rapidly as possible.

FINGER DEXTERITY. This skill involves the rapid manipulation of objects with the fingers. It does not include arm motion, as does manual dexterity. In one test of this ability, the subject is required to manipulate small pegs with tweezers.

PSYCHOMOTOR PRECISION. This ability, although very little is known about it, appears to involve speed as well as precision. It is similar to finger dexterity, but seems to involve more eye-hand coordination.

STEADINESS. Steadiness is measured by tests in which a steady hand yields a high test score.

MOTOR KINESTHESIS. This skill is measured by placing the individual in some unstable piece of equipment, such as the simulated cockpit of a plane. The cockpit is so arranged the it may tip to one side or the other, but can be righted by the movement of a rudder. The person must maintain the cockpit in an upright position by control of the rudder.

AIMING OR PSYCHOMOTOR SPEED. This is skill in performing at a high speed a simple task such as making dots in circles or making marks on standard answer sheets.

AMBIDEXTERITY. This skill is measured by asking right-handed subjects to perform simple tests, such as tapping tests, with the left hand, and vice versa.

Many of these abilities require equipment for their measurement, although some of the others can be measured through paper-and-pencil tests. There is little possibility that reaction time can be measured through a paper-and-pencil test, but such tests have been devised to measure tapping and aiming. The abilities identified by Fleishman are quite distinct from one another. A person who scores high on one of these does not necessarily score high on any of the others. The abilities are highly independent one from the other.

The motor skills that we have considered here do not represent, so far as is known, stable and enduring traits and should not be used, at least not at this time, for making any long-term predictions concerning what trade or skill a person can or cannot learn.

SUMMARY

1. Perceptual-motor skills are complex outputs of behavior involved in performing specified tasks. The performance of these skills generally requires that the individual take in information through his sense organs, and the motor skill represents adjustments to the intake of information.

2. Much of the study of motor skills involves the study of the relationship of human inputs to human outputs.

3. Several important attempts have been made to describe the development of motor skills. Although these vary in the language they use to describe the pattern of motor skill development, there is no basic disagreement among them. Motor acts appear to develop as a series of modules of behavior. Combinations of these modules then become coordinated to constitute more complex acts. Components of a complex act can become coordinated after the infant manifests extreme concentration on the activity. Most of those who describe the process imply that the

infant's behavior is characterized by intent. The infant has to be encouraged in these endeavors if they are to develop optimally.

4. Motor skills may involve a continuous activity, as in driving a car, or a series of trials, as in throwing a basketball into a basket. Several stages have been identified in the acquisition of motor skills. In the first phase the learner has to recognize the cues he will later use to guide his behavior and the general characteristic of the equipment used in the performance of the motor skill. Thus the initial phase is a perceptual phase. The second phase is an action phase in which responses come to be triggered by certain cues. Responses have to become tied to whatever external stimuli trigger them (as when one types a letter of the alphabet after seeing the letter on the printed page) and also have to become coordinated to some extent by the responses that preceded them. In the final stage, the responses become almost automatic and are taken over by the lower centers of the brain, and probably particularly those in the cerebellum.

5. Adams has developed a theory of how motor skills are learned. On each trial after the first the individual brings to the trial a trace of what he experienced on the previous trial and a knowledge of how he performed on that trial. He then strives on the new trial to produce a trace that differs from the previous trace in a particular way. Features of the situation that increase the strength of the trace may facilitate motor skill learning.

6. The laboratory tasks most commonly used for the study of motor skills are tracking tasks. Many of these tasks bear a considerable resemblance to tasks undertaken in daily life, such as driving a car or copying written material. Tracking tasks may be either pursuit tasks or compensatory tasks and may be varied systematically in difficulty, often by varying the number of dimensions involved and the number of controls that have to be manipulated. Tracking behavior involves a sequence of decisions followed by actions. In a task involving keeping a pointer in line with a moving dot, the subject will wait until the pointer and the dot become out of alignment and then make a movement to adjust the pointer. The dot and the pointer are kept approximately in line by such sequences of inactivity followed by an adjustment movement. About three such movements per second are commonly made in fast moving tracking tasks. Tracking behavior is undertaken in small jumps and not in a smooth continuous movement. Supplementary feedback may improve tracking behavior.

7. The remarkable way in which motor tasks are retained is probably a result of the large amount of practice involved when they are acquired and usually after they are acquired. It may well be that motor skills are better retained than verbal skills or cognitive skills, given equal amounts of training, but there is no evidence to support such a hypothesis. Motor skills are retained as complete programs within the cerebellum. Rapidly learned skills are generally the best retained.

8. One of the few motor skills taught in an educational setting that has been extensively studied is typewriting. The early phase of learning this skill takes place largely informally. Instruction usually begins in what Fitts and Posner refer to as the second stage. This stage, in the case of typing, is more complicated than that

described by these scientists, in that it involves also verbal behavior that forms an important part of the skill in the early stages of learning. In other words, the learner says to himself the letter he is going to type before he types it. At a later stage, the typing of sequences of letters takes place immediately and unhesitatingly in response to the perception of the copy being typed. The typist probably runs off sequences of letters emitting the proper behavior in sequence. It is doubtful, however, whether the response to one letter becomes the stimulus for the response to the next letter. West proposes that typing should be taught using typewriters on which the letters are printed on the keys, although emphasis should be on speed rather on accuracy.

9. Some motor skills can be learned to some degree through what has been termed mental practice. The extent to which a motor skill can be learned in this way depends upon the extent to which it involves mediating processes. If mental practice is used at all, it should be for very short periods.

10. In the learning of some perceptual-motor skills, knowledge of results or feedback may be delayed for considerable periods, even days, without any loss in the resulting learning. Demonstration has some utility in the learning of some skills The rate at which demonstrations are given is crucial in determining their success.

11. Skills may improve over long periods and there are instances where there have been increments of skill over several years. Even when the person has reached what he believes is his limit of skill, frequent practice is necessary in order for the person to stay at his peak.

12. Stress on the performer is defined as the extent to which he is overloaded with information from the task itself. Excessive inputs of information to the operator of a piece of equipment produce stress and generally also produce inefficiency. Very low inputs of information also produce inefficiency. Examples of the latter kinds of tasks are vigilance tasks. Perceptual-motor tasks are performed at the peak of efficiency, when the task provides neither a very low nor a very high input of information, but an input at the intermediate level.

13. Psychologists have long been interested in the aptitudes involved in the learning of motor skills. Motor ability appears to be fairly complex and involves a number of distinct components. Those that have been identified have been named reaction time, tapping ability, psychomotor coordination, manual dexterity, finger dexterity, psychomotor precision, steadiness, motor kinesthesis, aiming, and ambidexterity.

Chapter 5

Learning to Control Autonomic Functions and States of Consciousness

The previous chapter on behavior modification discussed methods of eliminating classically conditioned anxiety responses through desensitization techniques that also follow the theory of classical conditioning. The chapter did not discuss the use of operant conditioning for changing emotional responses or responses that are not under direct voluntary control. Skinner took the position in *The Science of Behavior* that reinforcement was not effective in changing glandular and emotional responses because the responses of the glands and of the smooth muscles in the viscera and skin are not under direct control of the higher centers of the brain, and such control seemed necessary for the reinforcement procedures of the operant psychologist to function in changing behavior. Nevertheless, in the 1950s evidence began to accumulate indicating that all kinds of bodily functions could be influenced by reinforcements. Kimmel (1974) has summarized the history of this research. For example, Russian research showed that human beings could learn to prevent the experimenter from giving them an electric shock by dilating the small blood vessels in the hand. A shock has the opposite effect, causing the vessels to contract. Elsewhere some research began to suggest that reinforcements could be used to change heart rate, though the effect of these early experiments were minimal. Changes in the electrical properties of the skin of the hand, known as the galvanic skin response, were also demonstrated to be modifiable by operant techniques. In some of these experiments the subjects did not know which response was being modified, making it all the more remarkable that in one such study heart rate was systematically changed by providing money as a reinforcer. Such data soon led to the suggestions that some disturbances of cardiac function could be remedied through the conditioning of new responses in the vascular system. Let us begin the study of this matter by taking a look at the component of the nervous system that has much to do with the control of vascular and visceral functions before considering the research on how individuals can learn to control such functions: the autonomic nervous system.

THE AUTONOMIC NERVOUS SYSTEM
AS AN INDEPENDENT SYSTEM

Traditional textbooks on the anatomy of the nervous system describe it as being divided into two relatively separate components, the central nervous system and the autonomic nervous system The autonomic system is a diffuse network of nerve fibres and groups of nerve cells known as ganglia that seem to coordinate the activity of the system. The autonomic network of nerves has a major distribution to the viscera, but it also supples the skin and blood vessels and exercises control over the blood supply to every organ of the body.

The autonomic system consists of two main components that produce opposite results: the sympathetic and the parasympathetic systems. The systems are said to be antagonistic, and yet in a sense they also work closely together to produce adaptive responses. The nerve cells in the system function through the production of chemicals that have quite specific effects on the receptors. Thus some neurons produce a chemical known as norepinephrine, which they store in quantities described as quanta. When a quanta of this substance is released at a particular location, it may have quite specific effects on particular muscle cells, which, in turn, may produce the contraction of a small blood vessel. In this way activity of the autonomic system may raise blood pressure, and activity on the part of the parasympathetic system may lower it. The autonomic system plays an important part in controlling blood pressure, heart rate, blood supply to particular organs, activity in the intestinal tract, the availability of glucose in the blood, and numerous other basic physiological processes. In addition, the system exercises control over those glands that secrete important hormones. For a more detailed description of autonomic function, read DiCara's article on the subject (1973).

Traditionally the autonomic system has been viewed as one that does not come under direct voluntary control; that is, the individual cannot do anything himself to control the functions controlled by the system. The traditional view has been that the individual can do virtually nothing to make his autonomic system lower his blood pressure, decrease his blood rate, calm down his intestines, or make his stomach produce less hydrochloric acid. Pavlov took this position but was able to demonstrate that these functions could be classically conditioned to almost any stimulus. Such learning was believed to be automatic and under the control of external circumstances and not under the control of the person whose responses were being conditioned.

Pavlov maintained that the controls associated with what he termed voluntary behavior were tied to a verbal system. This verbal system could exercise control over the skeletal muscles but did not control the muscles and glands that were ordinarily controlled by the autonomic system. Such was the theory widely espoused until recently and adopted virtually without change by operant psychologists.

Few scientists were disturbed by the lack of fit between the theory and the facts. Data on yogis run counter to the idea that autonomic responses cannot be controlled voluntarily, but a great amount of other data seems to indicate a close interaction between the individual's verbal system and autonomic responses. Physicians have long suspected that many psychosomatic diseases, including hypertension, are produced by the way in which the person wrestles with life's problems. This is tantamount to saying that autonomic functions can be influenced by higher mental processes. Some psychotherapists, notably Albert Ellis, take the position that there is a direct relationship and that, for example, the person who tells himself that he is calm will become calm and that the person who says to himself that he is afraid will show all of the visceral responses related to fear. Therapists of the Ellis school take a position almost directly contrary to that of the traditional learning theorists, and yet their position is compatible with common experience. Most people believe that it is possible to calm down an excited person by saying the right things to him. Most people also believe that it is possible to work up a mob into a frenzy of fear or rage, also by making particular statements. These kinds of beliefs are obviously sound and are almost certainly not mere superstitions.

A well-known case in which the human being has learned to control a function under the direct control of the autonomic system is the control of urination. As those concerned with child rearing know the acquisition of this control is difficult, and the difficulty may be a result of the fact that we are dealing with a function under autonomic control. Another function under autonomic control that can come under voluntary control is the production of tears. Children learn to control tears to some degree, but the most extraordinary control is evidenced by actors and actresses.

BASIC EXPERIMENTAL STUDIES OF THE CONTROL OF AUTONOMIC RESPONSES

Rigorous experimental approaches to the study of the control of autonomic responses through the action of the higher centers of the nervous system have been slow in coming. The main difficulty has been the development of a technique that would eliminate the indirect control that can be exercised through the action of the voluntary muscles. For example, one can slow down heart rate by breathing deeply. Such deep breathing washes out the carbon dioxide in the blood, which is one of the main stimulants of cardiac activity. Again, the skin can be flushed by holding the breath and raising the pressure inside the pulmonary cavity. There are all kinds of indirect controls through muscular activity that can be exercised over the functions ordinarily controlled by the autonomic nervous system. The problem is to find out whether some more direct form of control can be exercised over autonomic functions.

One way in which the effects of the muscles under voluntary control can be eliminated involves the injection of curare into the blood stream. Once the injection has been made, the substance injected sets up a block between the muscles under voluntary control and the nerves that supply these muscles. The result is that the muscles are paralyzed and no movement is possible. The drug does not interfere with the activity or innervation of the muscles controlled by the autonomic system. This technique of eliminating the effects of the voluntary muscles cannot be readily undertaken with human subjects, though it has been, since the curarized individual has to be kept alive with artificial respiration. According to Miller, this technique would permit studies of the control of autonomic functions by the central nervous system. His plan was to give curare to rats and then to determine whether changes in heart rate and blood pressure could be produced by means of ordinary reinforcement techniques, but this led to the problem of how to reinforce a rat that is paralyzed.

The solution to the reinforcement problem lies in the fact that electrical stimulation of certain regions of the brain, within what is termed the limbic system, has effects similar to that of a strong reinforcer. Electrical stimulation of this kind, produced by electrodes implanted in the brain, can be used to strengthen a response or shape behavior. The area stimulated has been referred to as the pleasure center. This kind of stimulation was first used by Miller and DiCara (1967) as a means of reinforcing the behavior of curarized rats. The essential part of the technique involved giving the rat curare, maintaining respiration through artificial means, recording a function such as heartbeat, and reinforcing changes in the function in a particular direction. Thus with one group of rats any increase in rate of heartbeat was reinforced. In another group any decline in rate of heartbeat was reinforced. The important finding was that reinforcement of a change in rate of heartbeat tended to strengthen that change. One group of rats ended the experiment with increased rates of heartbeat and the other group with decreased rates. Reinforcement seems to have much the same effect on autonomic functions as it has on activities of the skeletal muscles. The Miller and DiCara studies suggested that just as instrumental behavior might be shaped through reinforcement so, too, might blood pressure and heart rate and other visceral functions also be shaped. The effects were quite striking with changes of over 20 per cent during the experimental shaping. Oddly enough, later experimenters have been less successful at achieving as great an effect, and Miller (1973) has commented on the fact that there has been an extraordinary decline over the years in the magnitude of the effect reported by experimenters. Recent experimental effects are about half the size of those found in early experiments. Miller has been at a loss to explain this peculiar effect, but suggests that it might represent a change in the characteristics of laboratory animals.

Later research workers (Hahn and Slaughter, 1972) have shown that heart rate can be instrumentally conditioned in rats without the use of curare. An interesting finding is that without curare the effect is much less, a finding that provides a timely warning that the results of experiments undertaken under particular conditions should not be freely generalized to other conditions, let alone to other species.

The research findings have held out the tempting suggestion that individuals suffering from some forms of disturbed visceral functions might be able to have these functions restored to normal through instrumental conditioning. One must of course, be cautious in generalizing the results derived from curarized rats to individuals being treated for some visceral disturbance. Curare manages to block so many effects that may interfere with or strengthen the experimental effect. There is also the problem of what to provide as a reinforcement. Of particular interest in this connection is the possible control of some forms of high blood pressure.

Let us consider what is done in attempts to control high blood pressure through this kind of a technique. Some forms of hypertension — that is, high blood pressure — are not amenable to control through any kind of conditioning technique because they are a result of degenerative changes in the walls of the blood vessels. On the other hand, some individuals have high blood pressure because of the tensions produced by the situations in which they find themselves. As a matter of fact, a single stressful incident may raise blood pressure for as long as two days after the incident terminates. It is not surprising that after long periods of stress the individual may have what appears to be a permanent condition of hypertension. Such individuals whose hypertension derives from the situations in which they find themselves are those that have potential for reducing their hypertension by psychological means. Individuals who suffer from hypertension due to psychological causes are the best candidates for attempts to remedy the condition through instrumental conditioning.

The technique involves biofeedback, that is, feedback concerning how the particular biological condition is functioning. In the typical training session, the patient comes to the treatment center rather frequently and probably daily. He is placed in a relaxed position and is told that whenever his blood pressure declines a light will go on. Also, a meter accumulates the time during which he is successful at either lowering his blood pressure or in maintaining a lowered blood pressure. Shapiro and Schwartz (1973), who have reviewed the studies in this connection, report cases of lowering of systolic blood pressure by 16 to 34 mm. of mercury. Some of these patients had as many as 30 sessions of therapy. The technique seems to be useless in lowering the blood pressure of individuals whose high blood pressure has been caused by physical changes in the tissues.

A similar kind of procedure has been used for the treatment of tension headaches that are due primarily to muscle spasms in the involuntary muscles of the head or neck. In this case, feedback is provided by picking up the electrical activity in the muscles that are tensing, and this signal is turned into a high pitched tone. The patient during the therapy sessions tries to keep the tone as low as possible. The research on this problem indicates that the effect of the treatment will last only when it is followed by daily periods of relaxation.

In all of these forms of treatment with feedback, the therapist has to aim at making the patient less and less dependent on the equipment. There is some evidence that patients learn to pick up other cues. For example, some of those treated for tension headaches reported that they learned to take note of feelings that had to do with the building up of tensions in their muscles. Once they could pick up these slight cues. they could begin to take steps to curb the tension and produce relaxation.

Several points must be made about the learning involved in this kind of therapy. First, when the conditions are correctly arranged, the learning appears to take place automatically. What the individual thinks about may sometimes influence the effect. One can certainly raise one's own blood pressure by thinking of an embarrassing incident that happened to one recently. One could conceivably lower one's blood pressure by thinking of calming and relaxing situations. However, the essential element in such learning is not in the imagery produced. One cannot imagine a rat attempting to control blood pressure, heart rate, or intestinal activity by thinking the right thoughts, for obviously the rat does not know what is being controlled. The main reason for change in the circulatory functions in the human being must be assumed to be something other than the thoughts involved.

A second point to note is that the treatment probably does not remedy the basic condition that produced the undesirable autonomic response. One may be able to lower blood pressure in some individuals with hypertension, but the tendency to worry and be anxious, which produced the hypertension in the first place, is probably unchanged, and it may well produce increases in the blood pressure in the future.

There is also the fact that the treatment is expensive in that it involves many sessions that require the patient to report to the office of the therapist. Some attempt has been made to design and build equipment that can be used in the home, but there is little evidence that this is an effective form of therapy. Home equipment is generally less sophisticated than that used by the therapist.

Shapiro and Schwartz also point out that the symptoms that are eliminated through biofeedback may serve a purpose in the individual's life and removing the symptom may leave a vacuum that may be filled with other symptoms. A person who develops tension headaches may use them as a reason for escaping the work situation that produce them. What does this individual do if he does not have headaches to enable him to escape? Furthermore, as Kimmel has pointed out, the changes in blood pressure and heart functioning are typically minimal. In only a few studies have clinically useful changes been produced. (See Schwartz, 1973, and Blanchard and Young, 1973.)

Finally, the point must be made that very similar techniques were developed and used by Jacobson (1938) many years ago and that although these techniques have been used by physicians and physiotherapists for a long time, this method of treating hypertension has not spread outside the offices of a few. This is not to say that the treatment is ineffective, for many useful forms of therapy have remained rejected for a generation or longer.

STATES OF CONSCIOUSNESS, FEEDBACK, AND WELL-BEING

The problems discussed up to this point have pertained to correcting body functions that are malfunctioning as a result of the signals received from the autonomic nervous system. The central nervous system can apparently intervene and perhaps correct the malfunction. What has not been mentioned up to this point is the possibility that biofeedback may have potential for modifying what has now come to be called states of consciousness—of course, defined in terms of what the individual says about his feeling of well-being, relaxation, or lack of anxiety.

Behavior modification psychologists and operant psychologists do not mention this problem because the concept of consciousness does not enter their system of psychology. Of course, operant psychologists make statements beginning with "We know that . . .," which implies a conscious knower. Although they make this assumption of a conscious knower, they exclude the concept of consciousness from their system because they believe that the topic is not amenable to scientific study, at least not by the particular methods to which they limit themselves. However, other scientists disagree, and substantial research has been undertaken on the modification of states of consciousness.

This problem has long been studied using an entirely different approach from that considered up to this point. The great physiologist Hans Berger demonstrated nearly a century ago that the brain produced electrical rhythms that could be recorded on the surface of the skull. Later research workers demonstrated that different electrical rhythms appeared under different conditions. One of these, the occipital alpha rhythm, appeared in bursts when the individual was in a relaxed mental state, not concentrating on anything in particular, but not asleep.

Studies suggested that occipital alpha rhythms always accompany a "good" mental state and that one cannot have a "bad" mental state and at the same time have a strong alpha rhythm. Although a strong alpha rhythm is incompatible with feelings of tension and is generally accompanied by a feeling of well-being, it is also a state that occurs when the individual is not attending to anything closely with his eyes and when he is in a quiet and nonactive state. Although such a state of alpha rhythm activity accompanies a meditative state, one knows little about the long-term effects of meditation on the individual's well-being. Whether the feeling of well-being that accompanies a meditative state may be immediately beneficial, little is known about the persistence of the effect after the meditative state is terminated.

The technique used for attempting to produce increases in amounts of alpha rhythm involve giving the person being trained a signal to indicate when he is showing a good alpha rhythm in his brain (see Gaardner, 1972). Since the rhythm is disturbed by a visual signal, there would appear to be little point in providing a display of the actual alpha rhythm. The signal given is auditory such as the sound of a quiet hum. The task of the individual in training is to increase the amount of alpha rhythm that he produces. Presumably, if he can do this, he will have an enhanced feeling of well-being. In some studies, this has been facilitated by giving training in transcendental meditation. Such training is easily given and does have the effect of increasing the amount of alpha rhythm. Also quite brief training seems to be effective.

Unfortunately, the issues concerning the merits of alpha rhythm training have been clouded by the attempt of some manufacturing concerns to cash in on the commercial possibilities. Numerous devices now on the market are sold with the claim that they will promote alpha rhythm training. However, there is no evidence, as yet that training with feedback from such devices produces a greater ability to produce alpha that can be achieved without them. Most religious groups that engage in meditation of the kind that can be expected to enhance alpha rhythm seem to have little difficulty in falling into deep meditative states (see Wallace and Benson, 1973).

The various techniques that have been described for producing pleasant relaxed states are the opposite of those that are typically used in so-called civilized society for the production of pleasure. Modern technology produces an enormous volume of stimulation in an attempt to make life pleasurable. The nightclub with the loud band, the roar of the crowd at the football game, the deafening noise of the motor-bike, the raucous, insistent music in stores and shopping plazas are all examples of stimulation designed to produce pleasure, but they probably have very little effect because they are likely to lower alpha rhythm. Some balance is probably needed between high stimulation states and low stimulation states. Our present environment provides no such balance.

Finally, this section on altered states of consciousness has to give brief considera-tion to hypnosis, which has long been claimed to produce rapid learning, superior retrieval of information from memory, heightened perception, and so forth. In this area it is difficult to separate fact from fiction, particularly since the stage hyp-notist has often invoked a certain amount of trickery in order to dramatize his act.

There are two fundamentally different schools of thought on the nature of hypnosis. The one school views it as a fundamentally different state of conscious-ness from that ordinarily found in waking states, sleep, or meditation. The other school takes the position that most of the very exotic demonstrations of hypnosis are deceptions but that some of the more typical demonstrations are not essentially different from the phenomena that can be observed in common life situations.

The first of these two schools points to the long history of hypnosis as a clinical tool in the conduct of psychotherapy and points to the fact that clinicians have often been able to produce improvements in patients through the use of hypnosis that could not have been produced otherwise. Somewhat more convincing is the argument that some experimental studies of hypnosis produced by recognized scientists have been able to produce effects in their hypnotized subjects that they could not produce in their unhypnotized controls. An example is a study by Mas-lach, Marshall, and Zimbardo (1973) in which subjects were instructed to increase the temperature in one hand and decrease it in the other. These research workers were able to produce changes in temperature of 5°C in the hands. The hypnotized subjects in this experiment had been previously trained in hypnotic procedures and apparently readily fell into a hypnotic state in ten minutes. All subjects, both the hypnotized and the unhypnotized, were encouraged to use imagery, such as imagin-ing that one hand felt hot and the other felt cold or imagining an ice cube in one hand and a hot object in the other. The findings were that the hands of the hyp-notized subjects showed substantial changes in temperature that averaged about 4°C, but the subjects who were not hypnotized showed no consistent changes at all. The results are quite surprising in that one might have suspected that the un-hypnotized subjects might have been expected to produce small changes in temperature, for there are clear demonstrations that cognitive function can influence autonomic processes, of which temperature control is one.

Another major source of data suggesting that hypnosis is a special and distinct state comes from demonstrations of the suppression of pain under hypnotic suggestion. In the nineteenth century major surgery was reported as having been undertaken painlessly after the patient had been hypnotized and told that he could feel no pain. There are some similar phenomena related to the suppression of pain that do not involve hypnosis and that may indicate how the suppression can take place. A person deeply immersed in some ongoing activity, as is the case of a football player participating in a game, may have some quite severe injury and yet be quite unaware that it has taken place. During the game he feels no pain, but as soon as the game has ended, or he is out of the game, he may suffer to an agonizing degree. The reason for this phenomenon appears to be that one can attend to only so much at one time. If one is greatly preoccupied with the ongoing game, nerve impulses related to pain may never reach the higher centers of the brain. During a hypnotic session, the individual hypnotized may be so preoccupied with attending to the hypnotist that he may feel no pain from a hot object or a pin prick.

The trance theory of hypnotism holds that the special trance state is crucial to the supression of pain and that those persons who suppress pain at other times are in self-produced trances. Certainly, one has to concede that one cannot in the ordinary way control pain merely by wanting to control it. In this respect, the ordinary waking state does differ from the hypnotized state and a strong point is scored for those who hold that the hypnotic trance is a special state of consciousness.

In a series of papers, particularly those by Barber and DeMoor (1972) and Barber (1973), the alternative position has been forcefully stated. Barber and De-Moor take the position that the hypnotist simply arranges a situation in which the person "hypnotized" is highly likely to accept suggestions. He does this in a number of different ways, which Barber and DeMoor list as follows:

1. By labelling a situation hypnosis, the subject knows what is expected of him. A mass of research shows that, by and large, people perform in the way expected of them.

2. The hypnotist removes all fears from the situation so that the subject feels thoroughly secure in doing what he is asked to do.

3. The hypnotist either selects individuals who want to be hypnotized or who can be motivated to cooperate. The hypnotist may promise interesting experiences and that the tasks involved are not difficult to perform. (Barber and DeMoor cite some research indicating the importance of this factor.)

4. The hypnotist generally arranges for the subject to have his eyes closed during most of the session. Often the session begins with instructions, "You feel drowsy. Your eyelids feel heavy," etc. The closing of the eyes blocks out distractions and helps the subject to concentrate on what he is being told.

5. The repeated suggestions of relaxation, drowsiness, and sleep seem to enhance suggestibility. Hypnosis is not sleep, but a drowsy and relaxed state is readily accepted by subjects as a state of "hypnosis," and in a state of hypnosis one is expected to behave in certain ways. The situation involving the closing of the eyes, the relaxation, and the state of consciousness much like a mediatative state, give the person involved the impression of being in a new state, which he can think of as a trance.

6. Suggestions of body phenomena have to be built up slowly. The subject is not told simply that his right arm is becoming warm but that he feels a tingling sensation in the right arm, that the blood is now flowing more rapidly to the arm, that the skin is flushing. It seems that these more complex suggestions permit the individual to conjure up images that facilitate what is happening. In the previously cited research, in which hypnotized subjects produced temperature differences in the two limbs, the failure of the control subjects may well have been due to the distractions resulting from the eyes being open and the nonrelaxed state.

7. The trained hypnotist couples suggestions with naturally occurring events. Thus the hypnotist may tell the subject to concentrate on a spot of light held above the level of the eyes. Since the subject must strain his eyes upward in order to fixate the spot of light, it is not surprising that he soon begins to feel tired and wants to lower his eyes. When the hypnotist then tells him that his eyes are becoming heavy and he wants to close them, it reflects what is actually happening. Sometimes special devices are used to enhance suggestions. (Barber and DeMoor report on one hypnotist who would suggest to his subjects that "the room was becoming red" and would secretly light a small red electric bulb to give a faint red glow.)

8. The hypnotist, to be successful, must stimulate goal-directed imagery. If the subject is told that his clasped hands are locked together tight and that he cannot separate them, the suggestion is most likely to be successful if he imagines his hands glued together, held in a vise, or paralyzed and gripping each other. Barber and DeMoor cite evidence indicating that such imagery is of crucial importance for accepting suggestions. The imagery may function by calling for the response suggested and excluding all other responses. If I imagine vividly that my hands are firmly glued together, this imagery may be so incompatible with the response of separating the hands that I may be unable to undertake it. The response of producing the image is inconsistent with the response of separating the hands. Only one of the responses can occur, and since the hypnotist helps the individual to maintain the images related to the locking of the hands, the hands remained locked.

DeMoor and Barber also point out that hypnotists sometimes use physiological devices to produce their effects and that some of these are very dangerous. For example, some stage hypnotists produce a drowsy state by telling the subject to stretch his head back and to breathe deeply. The hypnotist then places his fingers over the carotid arteries of the neck and exerts mild pressure. The result is that the flow of the blood to the brain is reduced and the person may become dizzy and drop to the floor. The hypnotist takes advantage of this and commands the person to sleep at the moment when dizziness and loss of consciousness begin. The practice is, of course, extremely dangerous because depriving the brain of blood could, conceivably, produce brain damage.

In summary, there is little evidence that hypnosis is any more than a state of controlled attention and heightened suggestibility, which does produce certain consequences of interest. In such a state it is possible to block sensations of pain or, in a sense, just not attend to them. The main effect of this state on learning is that it facilitates retrieval of information from memory. This latter phenomenon has made hypnosis particularly useful in the history of psychotherapy, though therapists have also made use of the high level of suggestibility of the hypnotized subject. Although there have long been claims that hypnosis provides a state in which rapid learning takes place, such claims have never been substantiated. One would expect that learning under hypnosis would be about the same as learning under any state of concentrated attention.

Although there have been many statements made about the value of hypnosis in producing learning, genuine demonstrations in this respect have been few. There is previously cited evidence that hypnotized subjects can learn to produce localized changes in skin temperature, but there is little evidence that it is a good condition for learning to control heart rate and blood pressure. There is some evidence that hypnosis may facilitate recall, and particularly the recall of noxious events that may not be recallable at other times. Claims that hypnosis can be used to produce phenomenal increases in the rate of learning of information have no basis. Rate of learning seems to be controlled by factors other than those that the hypnotist can control. There is also not much evidence that hypnosis can be used to increase the amount of alpha rhythm or produce moderately lasting improvement in the individual's state of consciousness.

LEARNING TO CONTROL AUTONOMIC FUNCTIONS THROUGH THE CONTROL OF STATES OF CONSCIOUSNESS

The previous section considered the matter of learning to control states of consciousness and its potential for happy living. Research on this problem has turned up evidence to support the position that states of consciousness can also exert powerful influence on autonomic functions. Thus one may manipulate body processes to produce desirable states of consciousness in order to produce healthfully functioning body processes. The interaction has potential for working both ways.

Although DiCara and Miller had produced evidence that autonomic responses could be controlled by operant procedures, the finding did not imply that only operant procedures can control them. Another source of information suggests that other conditions, which are far from understood, may exercise even more powerful controls over autonomic functioning than those produced by reinforcers. A form of control is claimed by yogis, some of whom have stated that they can stop their heart beating at will, change their heart rate, and lower their consumption of oxygen to the point where breathing appears almost to stop. The viewpoint of yogis is at the opposite pole from that of behavior modification psychologists, and it is a strange paradox that the most vigorous competitor of behavior modification psychologists in this respect should be those concerned with states of consciousness, an area that behavior modification psychologists avoid.

Wallace and Benson (1973) have reviewed the studies that have been undertaken on what they collectively describe as yogis, a term used quite loosely in this connection. They point out that some of the effects claimed by the yogis are genuine but some are not. For example, early research workers reported that some religious meditators were able to stop their hearts since the cardiograph ceased to record heartbeats during meditation. It is now believed that this is due to what is known as the Valsalva maneuver, which is accomplished by holding one's breath and straining downward. The effect is to block the transmission of electrical impulses from the heart to the chest wall; these electrical impulses, when blocked, cannot then be recorded by the cardiograph, and the illusion is produced that the heart has stopped. Research workers have been able to show that the heart of the yogi does not stop but that the heartbeat continues though it becomes difficult to observe. Nevertheless there may be very pronounced changes in the rate of heartbeat and in the consumption of oxygen. There is a possibility that some yogis may be able to stop their hearts for short periods, since McClure (1973) has documented the case of a patient who was able to do this and in whom there was no Valsalva effect.

A major difficulty in the study of these phenomena is that different yogis use different methods of meditation, and the data do not relate particular activities in which the yogis engage to particular physiological effects. This difficulty has been overcome in recent research, which has concentrated on the study of a type of meditation, known as transcendental meditation, common in the United States that calls for the use of a particular method. Those who pursue transcendental meditation are given training in the method before they become independent meditators. Wallace and Benson (1973) studied the effects of such meditation on physiological processes. They found, as others studying meditative processes have found, that meditation produced a reduction in oxygen consumption, a decline in blood lactate, and a rise in skin resistance. They also found an interesting increase in blood flow in the forearm without an increase in blood pressure. The increased blood flow to the muscles may account for some of the beneficial effect ascribed to meditation by increasing the supply of oxygen and at the same time speeding the removal of waste products. The investigators did not find an immediate lowering of blood pressure, which one might perhaps have expected to find. A later study by Arne-Johnson (1974) showed that transcendental meditation produced a calming reaction to stress.

A special case of meditative activities having marked effects on body functions is found in what are known as autogenic exercises, developed by a group of German physicians. These exercises which, were first introduced into medical practice in Germany many years ago, involve developing a meditative mood, much like that developed in transcendental meditation, but the initial concentration is on some aspect of the body. Thus the person performing the exercises may concentrate on his breathing, on a sensation of coolness in his forehead, or on the apparent heaviness of a limb. The exercises are performed several times a day and are designed to produce a state of relaxation in the patient. There is no feedback and no direct attempt is made to modify directly such functions as blood pressure or heart rate. The central and most important part of the exercises is the production of a state of relaxation and the resulting feeling of well-being. Luthe and Schultz (1970) in their comprehensive multivolume work on the subject have reviewed some of the evidence concerning the effects of autogenic exercises on body functions. They provide evidence that in at least some cases of hypertension the exercises may result in substantial declines in blood pressure and an even more dramatic lowering of blood serum cholesterol. For a summary read Luthe (1972).

Two points need to be noted. First, the effect of the use of autogenic methods of training is not immediate but takes many months. For example, in one group of hypertensive patients the mean systolic blood pressure fell from 166 mm. Hg. to 132 mm. Hg. over a four-month period, but a large fraction of this drop occurred during the first month. Second, the autogenic techniques cannot be undertaken immediately with success. The techniques require some practice, particularly because they are disrupted in the early sessions by thoughts about distressing incidents, anxiety, and tension. In other words, a learning process has to take place. One is tempted to speculate that whatever the person does to produce a good meditative state is reinforced by the agreeable nature of effective meditation. A reinforcement interpretation of learned states of consciousness is something of an anomaly in view of the operant psychologists' preoccupation with observable behavior and rejection of all that cannot be observed directly.

The data collected through experiments on autogenic techniques provide quite convincing evidence that gross changes in bodily function can be produced through the altered states of consciousness produced by the autogenic physicians. Indeed, the changes seem to be much more substantial and clinically much more significant than those produced through operant techniques.

The kinds of data that have been discussed in the previous paragraphs suggest that civilization has produced states of consciousness that have very undesirable side effects on physical health. These are learned states, and autogenic training and related meditative states represent conditions that result in the learning of new states of consciousness that are more conducive to health. It is much easier to conjecture what the learning mechanism might be than it is to provide definitive tests related to that mechanism. Let us keep in mind that all such conjectures are strictly speculative.

The physiological changes that occur during meditative states are quite different from those found during sleep or during hypnosis. For example, during sleep there is an increase in the carbon dioxide content of the blood, but during meditation there is a decline. The electrical waves in the brain, recorded through an electroencephalogram, are also quite different in the two conditions.

The importance of these studies is that they demonstrate the influence of self-imposed meditative states on quite basic physiological processes. They suggest that it may be possible to control body functions, ordinarily considered to be beyond direct voluntary control. The early studies of meditative states, together with some more recent results, have led physiologists and psychologists to explore the possibility of developing these techniques for the direct psychological control of basic physiological processes.

The use of meditative states for the control of heart functioning probably suffers from the same overenthusiasm that characterized the use of biofeedback for the same purpose a few years ago. There has undoubtedly been a tendency for the promising data to be published and unpromising data to be filed. Nevertheless, the material that has appeared is quite tantalizing. The summary of the findings by Blanchard and Young (1973) takes the sober point of view that the effects of biofeedback and operant procedures have been minimal, and of questionable practical significance; the use of meditative states seems to offer more promise but promise is different from solid, reproducible findings.

Finally, reference must be made to an article by Smith (1975) that reviews the research on meditation and psychotherapy. Smith suggests that the main therapeutic effect of meditation may derive from the fact that the activity requires the individual to sit quietly for a short period each day. It may well be that the relaxation involved is the crucial factor. However, there is also a growing body of knowlege that a person's thoughts may control his emotions and that individuals can learn to control their thoughts (see Lazarus, 1975).

AN OVERVIEW

This chapter has raised some questions concerning the learning of control over body processes that have in the past been considered to be outside of the individual's ordinary control processes. The provision of some kind of feedback does seem to facilitate the acquisition of this kind of control, but in the case of the control of blood pressure and alpha wave production, the use of biofeedback seems to be less effective than the use of a meditative or relaxed state. More than mere relaxation appears to be involved because individuals actually have to learn the techniques used in meditation or relaxation therapy. Whether such relaxed or meditative states can be used to control autonomic functions other than cardiac functions and brain rhythms still has to be determined. A final point to note is that the quiet meditative state that seems to be conducive to good body functioning is the opposite of that which much of a modern technological society attempts to produce. In such a society individuals are kept continuously in a state of tension by being bombarded with stimuli designed to produce a high level of arousal—in stores music interspersed with commercials, usually transmitted through the public address system at such a high volume that they cannot be disregarded. Even the home is no longer the quiet place that it used to be, for hi-fi, television, and radio are likely to be turned on continuously. Even state parks, set up originally as places where individuals could commune with nature, are often bedlams of noise. The human body does not seem to be able to function well under such conditions, and the conditions produce unhealthy autonomic responses that, in turn, produce many of the typical diseases of modern man.

SUMMARY

1. Glandular and emotional responses have long been known to be modifiable through classical conditioning, but only recently has it been shown that these responses can be modified through operant conditioning.

2. The autonomic nervous system exercises control over glandular and emotional responses. It is a relatively independent part of the total nervous system and consists of two components, the sympathetic and the parasympathetic. The system controls blood pressure, the distribution of blood to the various organs and skin, activity of the intestinal tract, and all basic physiological processes. Some voluntary control can be exercised over these functions but such control is difficult to achieve. This difficulty is seen in the child's learning to control urinary function. Some recently developed viewpoints in psychology take the position that the individual can exercise direct control over some physiological functions by engaging in appropriate verbal behavior.

3. A basic problem has been to determine whether basic physiological processes can be controlled through activity other than that of the voluntary muscles. The injection of curare can eliminate the activity of the voluntary muscles. Animals injected with curare but kept alive by artificial respiration can be studied to determine whether autonomic responses can be controlled by operant conditioning. The animals are reinforced by means of direct stimulation of the limbic region of the brain. The evidence is that functions such as heart rate and blood pressure can be shaped through reinforcement. This form of conditioning can take place, even in lower animals, without the use of curare. In the case of human subjects, conditioning takes place through the use of biofeedback equipment, which indicates to the individual how his bodily functions are performing. The use of equipment provides a procedure for remedying some forms of psychosomatic disorders, but the changes thus produced are generally quite small, though cases of dramatic changes can be found. These biofeedback techniques look very similar to those developed by Jacobsen many years ago, which he referred to as progressive relaxation procedures.

4. The control of physiological functions also seems to take place, perhaps more effectively, through the control of states of consciousness. Conditions that produce pleasant mental states are typically the opposite of those provided by modern civilization, which bombards the individual with stimuli and produces, rather than reduces muscle tension.

5. Hypnosis represents an altered state of consciousness that is believed by many to be a condition that may facilitate the control of physiological processes. However, most hypnotic phenomena are very much like phenomena that occur in normal waking states. Hypnotists also use common and predictable phenomena to produce states of heightened suggestion in which the hypnotized subject is willing to cooperate with the hypnotist.

6. Studies indicate that yogis can produce altered physiological states by voluntary means, but the effects are not as dramatic as they are claimed to be. Attempts to stop the heart are probably not genuine in the case of most yogis who claim that

they can do so. The yogis themselves may well believe that they are able to stop their hearts from beating.

7. Meditational techniques have shown some ability to produce a state that results in the control of some physiological processes. Meditative techniques have been used extensively by physicians practicing autogenic medicine. Such techniques appear to produce more marked effects than are produced by biofeedback techniques. The effects are slow in becoming apparent and the meditative techniques seem to require practice before they can be used effectively. Meditative states seem to be quite different from those of either sleep or hypnosis. Nevertheless, their effect may be a result of learning the discipline of having a quiet time each day, away from the turmoil of the world of technology.

PART III

THE NONREDUCTIONIST POSITION

Chapter 6

Piaget's Approach to Learning and the Development of the Intellect

The previous chapters emphasized the reductionist position on learning, presenting those researches that attempt to demonstrate how learning can be reduced to simple operants, the shaping of operants, or the production and modification of classically conditioned responses. This view of learning assumes that the central processes of learning are those of reinforcement and extinction. The nonreductionist position is vastly more complex for it assumes that learning at very complex levels, such as that of learning mathematical problem solving, involves different learning processes from those involved in learning, for example, a simple conditioned avoidance response. Understanding learning at one level does little to help understand learning at another level. The nonreductionist position does not deny the existence of classical conditioning and operant conditioning as learning phenomena, but they are viewed as constituting very simple forms of learning that have little implication for more complex forms. From the point of view of learning intellectual skills, classical and operant conditioning are viewed as being of only marginal importance.

Although the reductionist position attempts to provide a few simple laws that are descriptive of all learning, the nonreductionist position has to provide a complex set of laws, arranged in a staircase, with those at the bottom describing the simple acquisitions of infancy and those at the top the learning of complex logical and rational behavior. Such a theory has to be tied to the development of the child, with each stage of development being dependent on the laws of learning of that particular level. Thus the position we now have to consider is closely tied to the development of the child. Indeed, one cannot discuss the nonreductionist position without discussing child development.

Just as the reductionist position in the last few decades has been dominated by the ideas of a single figure, Skinner, so, too, has the nonreductionist position been dominated by the concepts developed by the individual genius of Piaget. Although the major developments must be attributed to Piaget alone, others have made contributions. Notable among these is Gagné, who has attempted to evolve a theory of learning involving many different learning processes at different levels, yet building on the work of classical and operant conditioning. Gagné's work is not the radical departure represented by the work of Piaget, but it is a sufficiently distinct development to deserve discussion here, particularly in view of the fact that it has had impact on some aspects of curriculum design.

Gagné, like most other psychologists, takes the position that classical and operant conditioning offer only limited possibilities for understanding learning in childhood, but that these are nevertheless two important categories of learning. Gagné (1965, 1970) believes also that there are six other categories of learning. The eight categories of learning are the following:

1. Signal learning.
2. Stimulus-response learning.
3. Chaining-of-behavior learning.
4. Verbal association learning.
5. Multiple discrimination learning.
6. Concept learning.
7. Principle, or rule, learning.
8. Problem solving.

The first category corresponds roughly to classical conditioning, that is, learning that a particular signal has significance in terms of subsequent events, as when the infant learns that the appearance of the bottle signifies dinner time. The second category, which includes learning to make appropriate responses on particular occasions, includes the conditioned operant. The other categories largely explain themselves.

The categories have a special relationship to each other; for example, in order for an engineer to solve a problem concerning the amount of heat needed to heat a house in winter, he must be familiar with the related principles of physics. In order to understand the principles of physics, he must have previously learned certain concepts such as that of energy and calory. In order to learn concepts related to heat, the individual as a child had to learn to discriminate hot from cold objects and different degrees of heat. Thus the learnings at each stage demand that the individual has previously engaged in other simpler learnings. Prerequisites for complex learning find their roots in the simplest signal learnings of infancy. This is the essence of Gagné's theory of development: it requires the learning of a hierarchy of skills. The argument presented by Gagné is quite convincing, but it depends entirely on a logical analysis of the components of complex learning. The sequence of learning categories suggested by Gagné may well represent a useful system for organizing learning rather than a necessary sequence in the learning of complex behaviors.

The intuitive approach to the development of complex learning and complex behavior must necessarily remain suspect until it is backed up by experimental evidence. The system of categories has not as yet stimulated a large body of research as has the sequential learning system proposed by Piaget. In time, it may stimulate such research, but at present research workers interested in the Gagné system seem to have difficulty in beginning a program of systematic research related to it.

The Gagné type theory of development has done more to stimulate curriculum research than it has to provide a basis for the study of child development. It leads curriculum makers to ask questions concerning whether children have the prerequisites for particular learnings and suggests reasons that particular children may have difficulty in mastering particular materials. It implies that the mature intellect is a system that has mastered particular principles and can apply them to the solution of problems. No psychologist could seriously disagree with this, but it is not a very profound analysis of the nature of the mature intellect. A much more thorough analysis is provided by Piaget, who has spent a lifetime in the study of this problem, to which we now turn.

MAJOR FEATURES OF PIAGET'S CONCEPTUALIZATION OF THE NATURE OF INTELLIGENCE

Piaget begins with the belief that mature intelligence has already been well described in general terms by logicians. He believes that some of the details still have to be filled in by research, but he finds that descriptions provided by logicians to be adequate for him as a starting position. There are, of course, different schools of logic, and Piaget's affiliation in this respect is commonly described as neo-Aristotelian, a modern version of Aristotelian logic. Widely used textbooks on logic generally espouse this same position. Indeed, a good way to begin preparing oneself for reading Piaget's account of the relatively mature thinking of the adolescent is to read a good introductory textbook on logic.

Once the decision had been made that a good account already exists of the operations performed by the mature intellect, Piaget's next problem was to identify the previous sequence of states of the intellect that could account for the development of the mature intellect. Presumably there was a logic in the preadolescent period that permitted the individual to provide some rational solutions to problems at the adolescent level. This simpler and earlier form of logic he describes as the logic of concrete operations; it is similar to that of the mature intellect, but it is limited in the use of abstractions and in how many things can be taken into account at one time. The logic of concrete operations is a necessary prerequisite for the development of mature abstract logic; it has as an important component what Piaget terms the logic of classes. Until the child understands that some objects with similar properties can be assembled into a class, he cannot understand what is meant by a class of objects that float in water and a class of objects that sink, or how to assemble such classes by looking for some kind of common property that characterizes all members of each such class. Classificatory behavior, and the related behavior of arranging objects into a series, has to be mastered as a basis for all further logical development.

The logic of classes is preceded by a period from about age 2 until age 6 during which the child learns to master certain prerequisites of the logic of classes. He must, for example, be able to discriminate perceptually, shape, form, color, texture, and other attributes of objects before they can be sorted into classes. Children learn the attributes of objects and the way they can be grouped gradually through many years of playful activity related to the real world. This period is called the period of preoperations, or the period of preoperational thought.

This period of preoperational thought also has precursors during the two years of infancy that precede it. During these years the infant acquires an understanding of the fundamental properties of the world around him. The most basic of these properties are those of space, time, cause and effect, and the permanency of objects. At a more complex level are understandings of the orderliness of movement, the topological properties of space, and the interrelationship of different sensory inputs.

Thus, in summary, the infant begins by learning about the fundamental properties of the world around him through interacting with the objects presented by the infant environment. Then he learns more and more about the properties of objects and the way in which objects resemble one another or differ. Then he slowly masters the way in which objects can be classed in terms of their properties and the ways in which objects can be ordered, which lays the groundwork for performing simple logical operations about the problems of the concrete world that he encounters. Finally, he extends the logic of the concrete world to an abstract world.

Piaget does not observe children in the hope of coming up with ideas. A part of his genius lies in the fact that he knows what to look for before he starts looking. It seems to have been quite obvious to Piaget that the logic of classes has to be mastered before more complex logical processes can be undertaken. Suppose a child is given the problem of finding out why certain objects float in water and certain objects sink. The 5-year-old will settle for taking a few objects and saying that he thinks they will float and a few that he says will sink. When asked to put them in the water to find out whether they will actually sink or float, the 5-year-old may discover that some of the objects he said would float actually sink, but he may try to remedy this failure by holding the objects on the surface of the water. Such a child is quite unable to undertake the first necessary step in solving the problem, that of testing each object in the water and then dividing the objects into two classes, those that float and those that sink. The child may take this first necessary step at perhaps age 7 or even a little earlier. Even then, after he has divided the objects into those that float and those that sink, he may still be unable to give a good reason for why some float and some sink. A part of his difficulty stems from the fact that several factors have to be taken into account in predicting sinking or floating. The weight of the body is one, but size is another; it is the relationship of the body to its size that is crucial. The child of 8 or 9 may come near to this solution by dividing the objects into light and heavy classes and then subdividing each class into small and large. This brings him near to the solution, but the actual solution depends on the child understanding that whether an object sinks or floats depends on the relation of the weight of the object to the weight of an equal volume of water. This he cannot do until he is capable of handling abstract concepts for the notion of an *equal volume of water* is abstract, and not directly observable. In solving this problem, the accomplishments of each stage accumulate to make it possible to solve the problem at about age 12 to 14. There is continuity throughout the period of intellectual development and the accomplishments of each stage are essential for all later accomplishments.

Piaget views human intelligence as basically a logical system, but he expands this idea to say that intelligence is a logical mathematical system. His position in this respect derives from the fact that he views mathematics as an aspect of logic. Logic and mathematics are for Piaget, as they were for Bertrand Russell and Alfred North Whitehead, components of a unified discipline. This unity may not be evident to many adults who can think logically but who have little competence in mathematics. Piaget suggests that this lopsided development is a result of the way in which mathematics is taught in the elementary school. He believes that, with proper teaching, most individuals can acquire competence in mathematical thinking.

How did it happen that the human brain evolved so that the adult by his very nature is a mathematical-logical system? The answer is that human beings live in a universe that has logical-mathematical laws. In order to adapt to that universe, human beings and their hominid ancestors had to evolve a brain that could solve logical-mathematical problems. A brain that lacked such a capability would not permit its owner to acquire the kind of comprehension of his world that has permitted human beings to survive as a species; they lack other traits that have permitted other species to survive such as superior strength, great speed in predatory activities, or defenses against enemies such as are provided by the shell of the turtle or the thick hide of the rhinoceros. The key to survival has been the evolution of a brain that allowed human beings to gain understanding of a universe governed by mathematical-logical laws, which has permitted them to develop technologies that have been the keys to survival—at least up to this point in history.

PIAGET'S THEORY OF LEARNING AND DEVELOPMENT

There can be little doubt that Piaget has most influenced the theory of developmental psychology in recent years. This influence did not come suddenly, for Piaget, born before the turn of the century, was a prolific publisher of significant works on child development before most present-day American psychologists were born. The contributions of Piaget were ignored in the United States during most of Piaget's lifetime, and the reasons must now be considered briefly.

Piaget does not consider himself a psychologist, but refers to his own particular discipline as *genetic epistemology*. Since he is both the original developer of genetic epistemology and also its most distinguished student, one has to search for the meaning of the term in Piaget's own personal history. Two great influences seem to have played a part during his years in high school. He developed an early interest in biology and published his first short note in a journal at age 11, but a more notable contribution on mollusk biology at age 15 led him to be offered the post of curator of the mollusk collection of the Geneva natural history museum; he was not able to assume the position because of his schoolwork. Nevertheless, he continued to have a consuming interest in biology and published more than a score of papers on mollusks before age 21. Biology was his first love, but such narrow specialization at such a young age did not please his godfather with whom he spent a summer. His godfather decided to expand the young man's horizons by exposing him to philosophy and particularly to the works of Bergson.

It is clear that Piaget became enormously intrigued in the new areas of philosophy opened up to him but he developed a special interest in one area of philosophy, epistemology, which concerns itself with such matters as the nature of knowledge. This interest in the nature of knowledge became the keystone in his entire intellectual development.

Piaget refers to himself as a genetic epistemologist, by which he means that he is concerned with the central problem of how human beings acquire the knowledge they have. The term *genetic* simply emphasizes Piaget's concern with the genesis of human knowledge, or the processes through which knowledge is developed and acquired. The term knowledge is here broadly conceived. After reading Piaget's major works one would probably conclude that, in the language of American psychology, Piaget's central concern is with the nature of adult intelligence, the way in which it functions, and the conditions through which it is developed. Knowledge and intelligence are not clearly distinct entities. Piaget regards the development of intelligence as largely a biological problem, but he uses philosophy as a guide in developing his biological studies. This relationship Piaget has developed between philosophy and biology is difficult to grasp, particularly by those brought up in an American academic atmosphere in which philosophers and biologists scarcely ever interact. Let us look at this relationship, as perceived by Piaget.

Piaget derives his conception of the nature of adult intelligence from logic. He does not think that logicians invented logic, but rather that they describe in quite precise terms how the mature intelligence functions. At full intellectual development, intelligent behavior follows what may be described as the laws of logic, for this is what is meant by maturity in intelligence. Nevertheless, the adult who behaves logically is also a behaving organism with a particular history of particular experiences that have led to intellectual maturity. Piaget is interested in the discovery of the sequence of events in the life of an individual that result in the development of the highly logical performance of the mature intellect, beginning with the very earliest reponses of the newborn infant.

In order to understand Piaget's writing one has to become familiar with his language and the special terms he uses. Also, Piaget has certain fundamental objections to the terms and concepts used by most American and Russian behavioral scientists, particularly the concepts of the reflex and conditioning as a basis for understanding all behavior.

BASIC CONCEPTS IN PIAGET'S SYSTEM

Although Piaget's conception of child development departs substantially from the view that learning of the child can be understood in terms of elaborations of classical and operant conditioning, it still begins with descriptions of human development focusing on the simple behavior of the newborn infant. However, Piaget's description of the reflex is different from that found in standard textbooks on physiology. In the writings of Pavlov, as well as in the writings of more modern physiologists, the reflex is seen as a well-identified form of behavior produced by very specific, and also well-identified, stimuli. Some reflexes, such as the response of the pupil of the eye to light, are of this character and, because of their uniformity in these respects, have been favorite subjects for study. In contrast, reflexes that appear to form the very nucleus from which the infant acquires a knowledge of the environment show a quite striking plasticity and modifiability when they are first performed. Piaget, who observed the development of sucking in newborn infants noted that however well endowed with automatization a reflex may be (1952, p. 29), in order for the reflex to be used adaptively it must undergo modification. Piaget pointed out, as a result of observation on his own infants, that the reflex is set off initially by a number of environmental circumstances such as the hand accidentally striking the mouth or stimulation of the cheek. Sometimes the sucking reflex can be initiated in the newborn, followed by swallowing, by placing the nipple in the mouth, but some babies have to be coaxed into taking their first meal of colostrum. Sometimes the infant may not adapt at his first attempt. Furthermore, within the first few days of life, the touching of the mouth by any part of the breast begins to initiate not sucking but a form of searching behavior that brings the mouth in contact with the nipple, which, in turn, initiates sucking and swallowing. Piaget takes the position that the sucking reflex is not rigid and specific but plastic and modifiable.

Piaget prefers to avoid the term reflex in discussing these early organizations of behavior and uses the term *schema*. A schema (plural schemata) is an organization of behavior around which new behavior is developed. The schema has perceptual and action components and new components can be added to it. One can in a sense think of the schema as a nucleus around which primitive information about the environment is organized, but Piaget himself does not use the word *information* in this connection.

The concept of a schema has long been used in European psychology but Piaget uses it in his own distinctive way: a schema is a system around which behavior is organized. The early organizations of behavior are centered on reflexes and behavior becomes organized around these. The sucking response becomes the focus of exploratory behavior that leads to the finding of the nipple and the learning of which type of sucking to use on which occasion. (Sucking the fingers or tongue soon become different from the sucking involved in feeding.) Thus the behaviors associated with the original reflex expand and become related to a diversity of objects. These behaviors still show a certain unity that reflects the fact that they are organized within the same schema. Whereas other psychologists (such as Bartlett, 1932, and Head, 1920) had earlier viewed schemata as *organizations of ideas*, Piaget regards memory at this state of development as being primarily a retention of actions and their consequences. Memory is memory for action, and Piaget's schema is an organization of memories for action.

Piaget distinguishes between motor schemata and representational schemata (1952, p. 341). The schemata considered up to this point are motor schemata, for there is no evidence that the infant in the first months of life has any capacity to have internal representations of objects in the environment. The absence of such internal representations is highly limiting in what the infant and young child can do. Representational schemata develop later. The development of intelligence requires that there be internal representation of the environment and that there be internalizations of the operations that the individual can perform on the outside world. For example, the young child learns that when he takes two objects and adds another three objects, he ends up with five objects. At first he can perform this operation with actual objects, but later he will be able to represent internally the operations involved and perform these in his head.

New responses, or new information, if one prefers that term, can be added to a schema through two kinds of processes: *assimilation*, which is simply adding an action system that is consistent with those that are already organized within the schema; *accommodation*, which involves incorporating a new action in the schema, but at the same time modifying the schema to make it consistent with the new response.

The earliest examples of assimilation are what Piaget terms "generalizing assimilation" (1963, p. 42). By this he means that the child first discovers how to apply a particular response to a particular object (the sucking of the breast) and then later applies the response to a great range of other objects in the course of his exploratory activity. Piaget also states that assimilation is involved in three functions, which he refers to as the *recognitory*, the *reproductive*, and the *generalizing*. The latter has already been discussed. Recognitory assimilation means that assimilation leads to a recognition process. The infant exposed to the nipple of the breast comes to recognize it, which he shows by the emerging smooth and well-developed pattern of behavior that the nipple comes to elicit. The reproductive aspects of assimilation are illustrated by those that have to do with the infant finding the nipple more readily from the first feeding to subsequent feedings. The infant becomes capable of reproducing the situation that permits feeding. Assimilation by generalization is illustrated when the infant applies the sucking response to an object other than the breast.

New behaviors become incorporated within the hereditary reflex pattern. The first two of these behaviors involve the protrusion of the tongue, which is then sucked, and finger sucking. These involve the introduction of elements that were not in the original reflex pattern. Piaget makes in this connection a point that is crucial to his whole conception of development, namely, that they imply an active element. There is no innate basis for sucking the fingers or the thumb, but the baby is an active organism and through his activity the fingers are brought into contact with the mouth and sucking ensues. Slowly, the infant acquires the ability to reproduce this act, arrived at initially through random movement.

The accommodative aspects of the original sucking reflex are well brought out in more recent studies of the behavior by Bruner (1969), who has observed that by the fourth week sucking differs according to the situation. The infant adjusts his sucking according to whether the flow of milk is plentiful or meager. The behavior also varies according to the object sucked. The mother's nipple is gripped differently by the lips and gums from the way in which an artificial nipple is gripped. The sucking schema is not rigid, but very plastic.

In such cases the behavior is said to be accommodative because the behavior itself is modified in the process of adaptation to the environment. The accommodative aspects of the response have to be distinguished from what Piaget refers to as the assimilative aspects of behavior. As the infant grows the sucking reflex becomes the basis for exploring some of the environment. The blanket is sucked, the fist is chewed, and so forth. The sucking behavior is expanded to produce what has been called buccal exploration, a basic form of exploration of the environment. In broad terms one can say that in the infant accommodation involves a modification of behavior to meet new circumstances, but assimilation involves the extension of behavior without modification to new circumstances.

The concept of accommodation can be more easily understood by considering an example of behavoir at a more mature level than that of the infant. Suppose a person is strongly convinced that most welfare recipients are on welfare because they are too lazy to work. Such an individual hears a lecture in which data are presented to show that a substantial proportion of welfare recipients are women with several children, who have no other means of support and who have no place where they can leave their children if they were offered employment. The lecturer is a credible authority for our listener, which makes it difficult for him to reject what he hears. Since he cannot reject the facts presented, he modifies his position, now holding the view that, although many welfare recipients may be too lazy to work, there are also many who cannot accept employment because they cannot abandon their responsibilities to their children. The new position taken by the individual is an accommodative response to the lecture he has heard. He has assimilated the information provided by the lecture and accommodated his overall position to make it possible for him to integrate the new information with his general body of knowledge about welfare. Thus, the information provided the individual by the lecture results in both assimilation and accommodation.

The dual processes of assimilation and accommodation are always closely intertwined. There are no pure cases of the one or the other, but in a particular activity accommodation may be dominant or the dominance may be in terms of accommodative processes. Later, assimilation may play a primary role.

At this point the reader may well ask why Piaget does not discuss the development of the infant's sucking behavior in the simple terms provided by operant psychology. The operant psychologist is likely to say that the infant first sucks at various objects making random movements. These movements bring his lips in contact with the nipple and he is then reinforced for doing this by receiving colostrum and later milk. He is also reinforced for bringing objects to his mouth by the stimulation they provide the lips. This description provided by operant psychology of what is happening is moderately accurate, but it provides only a very limited description of events. Piaget and his associates fit their observations on infant sucking into a much larger theory of what is happening. They attempt to show that the infant is not just learning first to suck the breast, then to suck his comforter, and then his rattle, but that each of these activities progressively builds an organized repertoire of behavior that slowly comes to represent knowledge of the spatial organization of the world. The operant description is accurate as far as it goes but, compared with the description of infant behavior provided by Piaget, it is deficient in the large amount of information it neglects. One can accurately describe a penny as a small metal object, but the description would not be very informative to a person who had never seen a penny.

Many of the innate reflex responses or basic schemata of the infant serve in a similar way as foci for the acquisition of information and systems of responses. For example, the newborn infant also has a clutching reflex. Stimulate the palm of the hand of the newborn and the infant clutches his fist, grasping whatever is there. As the days pass, the infant has the experience of grasping all kinds of objects including perhaps, the bottle or breast, the quilt, a blanket, the mother's finger, and whatever is placed playfully in the infant's hand. The grasping activity slowly becomes extended so that objects grasped are brought to the mouth or held before the eyes. The infant also learns to grasp an object it sees, thus learning to coordinate the world of vision with the world of touch. All these activities and the information they bring are assimilated to the schema involving grasping. They become assimilated around a relatively simple reflex that forms the original focus of learning.

PIAGET'S CONCEPTION OF STAGES OF DEVELOPMENT

Piaget takes the position that there are distinct and identifiable stages of development; others view development as a continuous process. Let us consider briefly these contrasting views by considering language development. Those who view language development as a continuous process study such matters as growth in vocabulary, which can be plotted as a smooth and continuous curve. Similar smooth curves are shown by plotting such functions as the length of sentence used and the average number of syllables involved in the words used. Such data are consistent with the idea that intellectual development is a continuous process without breaks. Those who embrace a reinforcement theory of intellectual development expect to find such a slow and continuous process without breaks. On the other hand, much data on language development that has to do with language structures does not show this kind of continuous development. For example, if one examines the language forms used by children of different ages, one finds that at about age 3 children suddenly begin to use the question form in which sentences are initiated by such words as what, which, and who. Children quite suddenly reach a stage at which they become capable of handling the abstract concepts involved in wh--- words. Children do ask questions before they are able to use such words, but they do not ask them in the standard adult form.

Stage theory of development implies that each stage sees the development of structures of the intellect necessary for subsequent stages of development. The stages cannot take place in any order, no more than the construction of a building can be undertaken in any order. The foundation has to be built first, and the roof cannot be put in place until the walls have been built. Stage theory of the construction of the intellect implies that the mature intellect represents a structure that has to be built in a certain order.

The fundamental understandings that the child has to achieve are those related to knowing the nature of space, the nature of time, and the fact that the world is filled with objects that have a permanent existence. In addition, the young child has to acquire some understanding that certain events cause other events and that the person can be the cause of certain happenings. Much of the infant's intellectual development early in life has to do with the development of these fundamental understandings. This foundation is laid down in a series of stages. On this foundation the child is able to build a further understanding of the nature of objects.

Piaget does not state precisely the age limits of each stage of development. What he does is to indicate the age at which his three children could perform various acts related to a particular stage. The reader of Piaget's works has to infer the rough age limits of these stages. There is much spade work to be done by others to determine norms indicating ages at which children move from one stage to another. Piaget has provided a general map of a territory, but the surveyors that follow him must fill in the details. It is for this reason that the ages ascribed to particular stages of development in this chapter may not match exactly the ages given in other treatises on the subject.

Piaget has much to say about the conditions that facilitate stage transition. First, there has to be a problem that challenges the child, that is, the child must want to solve it. The child may have hit upon the problem himself or it may have been brought to his attention by an adult. Second, stage transition takes place when the child becomes dissatisfied with the solution he produces as a result of his present stage of intellectual development. This second condition is described by Piaget as a condition of disequilibrium. When the child finds a new solution to the problem at a higher level, equilibrium is restored. The process is described as that of equilibration. Ample data have been provided to show that when children reach a state of transition, from one stage to another, they begin to question the solutions to problems they have been giving. Such doubts have to precede the development of more sophisticated solutions. Also, until the children themselves display such doubts about the validity of their solution, they are unlikely to change the solutions they provide. Telling a child that his solution is "wrong" is likely to have no effect.

Equilibrium theory is rather different from homeostatic theory found in biology.

In homeostatic theory a disturbance of the state of an organism, such as is produced by hunger, results in activity and then feeding, which restores the chemical balance in the organism. This illustrates the essence of the homeostatic process; activities restore the internal chemical balance of the organism to its original state. The balance is always restored to its original state in homeostatic theory, but in equilibrium theory a state of disequilibrium leads to a restoration of balance at a higher intellectual level.

The data that support Piaget's equilibration theory come mainly from children beyond the 2-year age level, but he applies the theory to younger children. Let us consider the kind of data that Piaget uses as a basis for equilibration theory.

Consider the 5-year-old child who is given an assembly of geometrical shapes of different color and asked to put together all those that belong together. The child strings out a graphic collection consisting of a red square, a red triangle, a green triangle, another green triangle, a green circle, and so forth. The child is pleased and fully satisfied with what he has done. His state is one of equilibrium. Give the child a similar problem a year later and he may begin by going about it in the same way, but, after arranging a few of the objects in a line, he may stop and look at his solution and then perhaps return all the objects to the pool from which he has drawn them. His behavior shows doubt about the validity of what he is doing. Piaget describes this as a state of disequilibrium. The child may then try various ways of placing the objects together, reflecting his general disapproval of the solution he has previously applied. Ultimately, he manages to provide a classification of objects that not only meets his own approval but that demonstrates that he has at last mastered the concept of a class. Once he can group objects into classes he achieves a new stage of equilibrium.

An additional point to note is that the new type of solution that appears as the child moves from one stage to the next is constructed by the child. Telling the child what the "right" solution is accomplishes little. Learning, in equilibration theory, is produced by the child constructing new solutions for himself. This position has sometimes been interpreted incorrectly by American psychologists as indicating that the solutions are innate. Piaget is firm in his position that he assumes little to be innate and, indeed, later research on infancy indicates that Piaget has been overcautious in his estimate of what is innate. A solution is constructed by the child in much the same way that a computer may construct a proof of a theorem that it does not have stored in its memory. The computer has to be so designed that it can construct new proofs and then store them. Such computers have the potential of being able to construct proofs of theorems that mathematicians have not yet been able to construct. The artificial intelligence of computers that perform this kind of function are rough models of the human intellect, as envisaged by Piaget, but they are probably nearer to being flawless in their logic than are their human counterparts.

The problems that a child can logically solve at any level of development depends on his understanding of the world around him. Thus Piaget is concerned with specifying just what understandings the child has at each stage of development because these understandings limit the problems that can be solved and the logic that can be developed. The infant's explorations of space slowly bring him to the point where he can reach for and grasp objects easily and smoothly. Slowly he begins to understand the trajectories of objects and as he does so begins to be able to predict where moving bodies will be after they go behind a screen and emerge on the other side. Later, his knowledge of trajectories will enable him to catch a ball. These experiences with space slowly lead him to understand such concepts as speed and volume, more and less, and ultimately the idea of quantity and the use of numbers for measuring quantity. Such a development requires the construction of an understanding of the logic of measurement and the use of a series. Finally, the child acquires understanding of such abstract properties of objects as density, and these understandings expand greatly the range of problems that can be solved and the logic the child can invent to solve such problems. Intelligence for Piaget is inventive intelligence.

THE SENSORIMOTOR PERIOD: LEARNING FUNDAMENTAL PROPERTIES OF THE ENVIRONMENT

The experiences of the infant during the first two years of life establish a foundation for the development of a logical and inventive intellect. During these first two years the infant begins to learn about the fundamental properties of the world around him. The basic properties of the environment are conceived to be those of space, time, cause and effect, and the fact that objects have permanency and do not depend for their existence on the whims of the perceiver. Piaget acknowledges that he was influenced by the great philosopher Immanuel Kant in deciding that these were the basic areas in which the infant has to expand his knowledge in order to cope with his environment. However, he differs from Kant in believing that the infant has little native knowledge in this matter but that all knowledge related to the development of understanding in these areas is learned. As this chapter develops, and work other than Piaget's is discussed, it will become evident that Piaget has not recognized sufficiently the importance of inborn understandings of some aspects of the environment. Piaget emphasizes learning and not native capacities to cope with the environment.

The understandings of space, time, cause and effect, and the permanency of objects that take place during the first two years are merely the fundamentals of the developing intelligence, for the rest of the period of intellectual development is occupied in a further expansion of these understandings.

The text that follows discusses infant development within the framework of Piaget's general theory of learning and development, but there has been no attempt to restrict the discussion to his findings. Piaget's own work on infant development was undertaken with his three children and represents one of his earliest contributions to knowledge. It is not surprising that he was not always right in his conjectures, but it is remarkable how often he was right.

The Six Stages of Infant Development

Stage 1. The first stage involves approximately the first month of life. It is characterized by the use of schemata and the adaptation of what others have called reflexes to circumstances. The reflex-related schemata become the focus of initial learning and new responses become organized around them. Although the infant at birth cannot possibly have a concept of an external world nor of the existence of objects in that world, a number of objects become incorporated into the sucking pattern. When the infant is hungry, he will suck any object presented to him. The infant acquires what Piaget refers to as motor recognition, that is particular responses become tied to particular objects. The sucking reponse thus becomes exercised for its own sake and illustrates primitive forms of repetitive behavior that play an important role in the subsequent development. During the first month the process of assimilation is seen in the development of motor recognition, and especially in motor recognition of the nipple. The latter is closely tied to what Piaget refers to as the *mechanism of repetition*, which is a tendency to reproduce whatever experiences the infant may have. The repetition of experiences always involves assimilation for it involves the "incorporation of an actual fact into a given schemata" (1952, p. 43). Assimilation involves a growth of primitive forms of knowledge that are highly tied to responding and to motor recognition. The modification of the sucking pattern to adapt it to different objects represents the accommodation of sucking behavior.

Piaget has taken the cautious position that there is little innate in infant behavior, but as psychological research has become more sophisticated, more and more evidence of innate capacities has emerged. Bower (1974) has summarized evidence that the newborn has some capacity to localize sounds and tends to turn his eyes in the direction of the sounds. Thus there is not only the ability present to localize sounds but there is also some native coordination between hearing and vision.

Bower also reports considerable research indicating that infants in the first week after birth show an avoidance response when an object moves fairly rapidly toward the face, indicating some primitive understanding of space. In such studies the effect of air motion is avoided either by placing a plastic screen in front of the infant or by producing the illusion of movement by optical means.

Stage 2: 2 to 4 months. Stage 2 is characterized by what are primary circular reactions. Primary circular reactions are initiated by one part of the body touching another part. The infant then attempts to reproduce the experience. Thus in the first few weeks of life the infant may happen to place his fingers in his mouth, whereupon he begins sucking them. Then a movement of the arm removes the fingers from the mouth, and immediately the baby shows great activity of his arm until by chance the fingers are once more inserted in the mouth. After this has happened many times, the baby becomes able to insert his fingers into his mouth quite deliberately and without waste motion. These primary circular reactions all involve interaction between one part of the body and another part of the body. In addition, the reflex behaviors have superimposed on them some related responses. For example, the sucking reflex becomes tied to the circular reaction involved in finger sucking and the infant also shows a sucking behavior involving the tongue that sometimes involves placing the tongue between the lips. There is no finger sucking reflex or tongue sucking reflex as such, but these behaviors become extensions of the basic sucking response. They emerge through the gropings of the infant, which constitute a kind of primitive exploratory behavior. Furthermore, sucking is differentiated according to the object presented. Piaget noted differences in the sucking of his daughter Jacqueline at 4 months and 27 days according to whether a bottle or a spoon was offered. Toward the end of this period, the infant begins to show anticipations such as stopping crying when preparations are being made to offer her a meal. The infant also shows an emerging tendency to attend closely and for quite a prolonged period to objects that fall within its field of view. It will look at parts of the crib for long periods and its attention is also attracted to almost any object held within the field of gaze.

The explanation of behaviors related to sucking and grasping that occur in the first two months serve another important purpose. They all contribute to the infant's understanding of space. When the infant has learned to bring his fingers to to his mouth, he has also learned something about the spatial arrangement of his body. The first understanding of space involves a development of understanding of the relative locations of different parts of his body and how one part can be moved to bring it into relationship to other parts. Space comprehension begins with the body and only later becomes focused on the surrounding world.

Considerable doubt has been thrown on the view that the infant starts at almost no understanding in his comprehension of space. Bower (1971) has undertaken an ingenious series of experiments that indicate that infants, even shortly after birth, show a coordination of visual space and tactile space. Bower's clever technique was to produce the illusion of a solid object in front of the infant. When the infant's hand moved into a position that would contact the object, and there was no contact, the infants cried and showed other forms of extreme distress. However, when the same object was presented in real form and the infant could touch the actual object, no distress symptoms occurred. Thus when the tactile and visual cues came in normal relationship to each other, the infant behaved in an undisturbed fashion, but when the relationships were different from those that occur in a normal world, the result was upset. To behave in this way the infants must have some built-in understanding of what is a normal world and that tactile and visual space are related. Other interesting observations made by Bower are that infants at the age of 2 weeks will lift a hand to ward off an approaching object indicating again a coordination of tactile and visual space.

A key factor in Bower's studies is the observation that infants in the reclining position do not show these responses, perhaps because when they are prone they are in less of a waking state. Piaget's infants were all studied in their early months in a prone position and for this reason may not have shown their full capabilities in coping with space.

Although emphasis has been placed here on the sucking reflex, the grasping reflex, and the expansion and ultimate coordination of their associated schemata, behavior also develops around other reflexes. Responses related to vision and hearing also reflect the child's slowly emerging ability to cope with the world. Although the first responses of the eyes are merely those of fixating bright lights, the visual behavior becomes more and more that of an examination of objects accompanied by what appear to be carefully directed movements of the eyes. The child also learns to follow moving objects. The following of an object with the eyes represents a variety of circular reaction because it prolongs and conserves a particular experience. Sight and hearing show some coordination by the third month in that the infant of that age will move the head in the direction of a sound, showing a further step in space understanding.

During the first two stages of development, prehension—that is, the grasping reflex—changes from a state of being a pure reflex or a set of "impulsive movements" (p. 89) to that in which circular reactions are made related to the bringing of the hand to the mouth. Then at about 3 months coordination develops between prehension and sucking, that is, whatever is grasped is brought to the mouth. Although the child is able to bring to his mouth that which he grasps, and although he can see what he grasps, it does not mean that there is a coordination between vision and grasping. The infant can see objects and can hold objects, but the grasping at an object *seen* did not appear in Piaget's children until they were into their fourth month.

Visual space slowly becomes more coordinated with other aspects of space. Thus when Piaget's infant Laurent was almost 3 months he would hold one hand with the other examining it visually and also hold objects in front of his eyes. Such activities show the primitive beginnings of the coordination of visual space with the concept of space derived from movements (kinesthetic space). There is also the increased coordination of visual and auditory space as the infant learns to turn in the direction of a sound. All such activities and preoccupations indicate a slowly expanding concept of the nature of space. Piaget assumed little coordination of different aspects of space, but there may exist more than he assumed.

Another important acquisition at this stage is the appearance of imitative behavior in the vocal and auditory area. The infant begins to show anticipations. The infant sees the bottle and begins to make sucking movements. Piaget interprets imitation as an attempt on the part of the infant to conserve an experience that he did not initiate.

At this stage the infant shows through his behavior that he has no concept of objects having permanency. Piaget summarizes many sources of evidence to indicate that the child lacks such a concept in the early months of life. When an object is moved outside of the infant's immediate field of vision, the infant does not search for the missing object. The infant behaves as though objects existed only so long as he can sense them. Objects that cannot be perceived with the senses simply do not exist.

Bower (1971) has some evidence that he interprets to indicate that children develop a concept of object permanency at a much earlier age than Piaget suggests. The evidence has to do with the infant's ability to predict the trajectory of objects that move behind a screen and reappear, but various other interpretation of his evidence are possible. He also has unveiled the curious fact that when an object is first stationary and moves, the moving object is responded to as a different object from the stationary object.

The reason why infants have difficulty in developing the concept of object permanency is that they have little capacity for representing within themselves the objects they perceive. Out of sight is, literally, out of mind because there is no lingering representation they can bring to mind of the object perceived. Memory at the infant level is to a considerable degree only memory for the actions to be taken when confronted with an object. Piaget takes the extreme position that infant memory is completely limited to an action kind of memory. For him, an object out of sight does not elicit actions and, hence, there is no memory of the object. Piaget does have a considerable body of evidence to support his position, but there is also evidence indicating that the infant may have more extensive records in memory than Piaget credits him with. The strongest line of evidence contrary to Piaget comes from the classic studies of Fantz (1965), who was able to show that when very young infants were exposed to two designs, placed above their heads and in their line of vision, they directed their gaze to the one they had not seen before. This action implies a memory for the design that had been previously seen. This recognitory behavior on the part of the infant for a design previously seen appears shortly after birth.

Although the out-of-sight-out-of-mind conclusion of Piaget remains unchallenged and his experiments on this subject can be easily replicated, this conclusion does not mean that the infant has no record in his memory of the objects to which he has been exposed. The memory may record the existence of an object, but the memory of the object may not influence behavior when the object is not present. The concept of object permanency, as used by Piaget, implies that the memory of the absent object can influence behavior. The memory can be there but it may not influence behavior in the absence of the object. Bower (1974) has demonstrated that fact. Bower showed 8-week-old infants an object and then placed a screen in front of the object. When the screen was removed, the infants saw the object again on some occasions, but on other occasions the object was missing. When the object was missing, the infants showed a response they did not show when the object was present. Bower refers to the response as surprise, but it was measured by a slight change in the heart rate. The absence of the object involved a discrepancy with the infants' memory of the presence of the object. The infants continued to retain a memory of the object, but on Piagetian tasks they would show no signs of the concept of object permanency.

Many features of Piaget's model of early development are similar to those of contemporary American psychologists who have been engaged in the study of perception. From the point of view of such psychologists, for example, Gibson (1969), the perceptual system is primarily an information extracting and organizing system. According to this conception of higher organisms, the perceptual systems have the property of automatically extracting information from the events presented to them through the sensory systems, and the extracted information is internally organized as it is handled by the storage system. Studies of perception provide data demonstrating this information extracting and organizing function, just as Piaget's studies of the very young infant demonstrate the manner in which information and responding become organized around some of the original reflexes.

The early months provide the infant with the experience of being the cause of certain events and therein lie the seeds of the concept of causation. It cannot be said at this stage, nor at even later stages of the sensorimotor period, that the infant has a concept of causal relationships. What he has is the direct experience of being a causal agent.

Stage 3: 4 to 10 Months. The infant first discovers interesting things he can do with his own body, but sooner or later he discovers things to do with objects beyond himself. These he discovers by chance, as when random movements of his arm bring his hand into contact with a doll suspended above his crib. Having produced motion in the doll through such chance movements, he attempts to "conserve" what he had done. He then makes movements of various kinds until the doll is struck again. After much practice with similar experiences he learns to grasp objects. These attempts at the conservation of such an experience are referred to at this stage as *secondary circular reactions*. The reader should note that the *secondary* circular reactions begin in the *third* stage of development. (This is an example of one of the problems that readers of Piaget's original works encounter; the numbering of stages, reactions, and other phenomena do not correspond.)

Secondary circular reactions occur in relation to objects external to the human body, but primary circular reactions occur when one part of the body interacts with another part. In the early months of this stage the child learns to grasp objects he sees but will not seek to grasp at objects he has seen placed behind other objects. He shows no ability to respond to objects that are not immediately present.

The act of reaching and grasping has now been described in greater detail by the research workers at the Harvard Center for Cognitive Studies (see Bruner, 1973). It is now known that there is an area of good accommodation about seven inches from the young baby's eyes. When objects move into this area, the 12-week-old infant responds with a pumping activity of the arms, shoulders, and head. This is followed by a swiping movement. As the infant grows, such activity becomes less explosive, and the movement becomes slower and more controlled. The gaze becomes fixed on the object and does not move back and forth from hand to object. The hand is moved forward with the fingers open in a grasping posture. An interesting observation made is that when the task of reaching becomes difficult, the 7-month-old infant may at times close his eyes. This seems to be a way of reducing frustration by blocking out the complexities of the world and finding a simpler state of existence.

Just as in the first two stages of development everything that comes within the infant's universe is to be sucked, held, viewed, or listened to, so, too, in the third stage does every object come to be something to be grasped, shaken, hit, thrown, dropped, turned over, and so forth. Through these experiences the infant comes to learn that certain objects are the source of particular visual experiences, particular noises, particular tastes, and particular touch experiences.

The third stage of development shows the first forms of behavior indicating that the child is beginning to recognize intuitively *classes* of objects. For example, in the fourth month Piaget's infant Laurent strikes with his hand the toys hanging from his bassinet. Then he quite obviously varies the force with which he strikes the toys and spends time observing the results (1952, p. 185). This graduated behavior represents a recognition that striking-with-the-hand behaviors form a class and that they form a scale of how hard the object is struck A related and interesting phenomenon is observed at this stage. An infant who has learned that pulling a chain will produce movement in a doll may move his arms and legs when he sees the chain. The movement of the arms and legs is a substitute for pulling the chain and appears to be a way in which the infant recognizes the chain as an object to be pulled. Once again, this demonstration shows that primitive memory is at least partly an action-oriented system and that the first representations of the outside world are movement-related representations.

During this stage the child's comprehension of space expands rapidly. He learns to relate visual space to tactile space and thus can grasp objects he sees and can bring into the field of vision objects he touches but cannot yet see. Movements also begin to show properties similar to that of a mathematical group by which Piaget means that the infant shows in his behavior that movements have such properties as being additive, that for any movement there is an inverse that brings the limb back into its starting position, that there is a zero of movement, and that adding a large and a small movement produces the same result as adding a small and large movement. This statement represents only a crude presentation of the way in which Piaget adapts the mathematical concept of a group to the description of motor behavior, but in essence he describes the properties of coordinated movements as being analogous to those properties of a set of natural numbers or any other set that shows the mathematical properties of a group.

Throughout this stage the infant shows an increasing comprehension of object permanency, but this is a slow development. Toward the end of this stage the infant may search for an object hidden behind a screen if he were interacting with it at the time when it became hidden. In other words, his memory of the object is related to his actions, and not to any internal representation.

Piaget's focus on intellectual development has caused him to ignore social development in the infant, yet strides do take place in the latter respect even in the first few weeks of life. Smiling is the most readily recognized social response and it is essentially social in nature. By the age of 4 months the infant smiles more to a face that smiles than to one that does not smile. Eye contact has also been formed with the mother or caretaker. Bruner (1973) points out that eye contact permits the mother to anticipate the responses of the infant but that the infant also learns to anticipate the responses of the caretaker. Thus there develops a form of reciprocal anticipation of each others responses. Babies that spend the initial days or weeks in a hospital setting are slower in developing such social anticipations. The infant also learns in this context that he can produce certain effects on the caretaker, at first by producing very strong responses such as crying, but later these become reduced and he learns to produce the effect with minimal responding on his part. Thus gestures are slowly learned as a means of producing certain consequences in the adult. A 4-month-old infant may yell for an object he cannot reach. At 10 months he may reach for it and make a noise to attract the attention of an adult, and at 18 months he asks for it. The development from explosive behavior to language is continuous.

Stage 4: 10 to 12 Months. The third stage of development is dominated by the secondary circular reactions through which the infant learns how to produce certain effects on the environment. These secondary circular reactions develop organized forms of behavior with respect to particular kinds of actions directed toward the environment, and Piaget describes the situation by saying that they represent secondary schemata. The latter tend to represent independent areas of activity. Thus the child may learn to grasp objects, shake them, hold them up for visual examination, and he may also learn to move objects by pulling strings to which they are attached, place objects inside boxes, and so forth. In the fourth stage, these schemata, and their corresponding actions are related to one another. For example, an infant may have learned to grasp a desired object and to move an object by shaking a string to which an object is attached, but it is not until the fourth stage that the child will obtain an out-of-reach object by pulling a string attached to it. Another illustration given by Piaget is that of his own child, who knew how to move Piaget's hand to shake dolls and produce other effects, but did not learn until the fourth stage to remove Piaget's hand from in front of an object in order to grasp the object. This is what is meant by the coordination of the secondary schemata, and it is this coordination that constitutes the essence of the fourth stage and opens up a whole new range of activities that the child can now undertake.

This stage also shows precursors of what are called seriation concepts, that is, those concepts necessary for arranging objects in order in a series. An interesting demonstration of this is provided by Piaget on his 9-month-old Laurent. When he would say " papa ", the baby would say " papa " or " baba." When he said " papa papa," the baby would say " bababa." Thus the infant made a distinction between one and more than one. He also noted that the baby could also distinguish two repititions from three, or four, or five, but could not discriminate among the latter. It is as if the infant could discriminate one repetition, two repetitions, and more than two repetitions. The schemata represent at this stage primitive concepts. It is as if the child had acquired a concept of pulling, as distinct from the idea of pulling in a particular situation. Piaget uses the term *mobile schemata* to describe the organizations of behavior at this stage.

The mobility, or adaptability, of the schemata to new situations also makes it possible for the schemata to become interrelated. In obtaining an object hidden behind a screen by pushing aside the screen, there has to exist a relationship between schemata related to pulling and pushing and schemata related to object constancy. A coordination of pieces of knowledge that have previously functioned as

preted by Piaget as a process of accommodating existing schemata. The child has already learned to strike a distant object, but the schema involved must now be modified so that the striking is undertaken in such a way that it moves the object in the desired direction. The pursuit of the task also involves assimilation, for the accomodations could not occur if the child did not also acquire new information or new ways of acting. The child could not learn to obtain an object with a stick if he did not observe that striking it with a stick produced movement, and such an observation involves assimilation. The task also involves the *coordination* of different schemata. The schema of grasping an object has to be coordinated with the schema of striking an object. Piaget also refers to this accommodative aspect of the development of schemata as involving *differentiation*. By this he means that as the schemata develop through experience, they involve to a lesser extent gross activities and involve more specific acts related to particular activities.

The child's understanding of space has considerably expanded by this stage. He will search for missing objects, but he still shows some confusion in the process. For example, Wegg, Massar, and Nadolny (1972) found that when a game was played with 16-month-old infants, in which an object was hidden in different places, the infants showed some confusion. When the object was first hidden, the infants went to the correct place, but when they then saw the object hidden in another place, they searched for it in the first hiding place. There was a delay of up to fifteen seconds between the hiding of the object and the opportunity to search for it.

Search strategies are very primitive at this stage, partly because the child's concept of space is what Piaget refers to as topological rather than geometric. By this Piaget means that the infant has the concept that space involves different areas where different things happen. There is an area where one eats, another where one sleeps, another where one is bathed, and still others where various activities occur and where certain objects are found. Areas may have proximity to one another or they may be widely separated. The concept of space does not involve geometric shape or distance and locations are not precisely determined. Indeed, it is not until the child approaches the age of entering the elementary school that he begins to acquire the precise concepts of geometrical space.

In earlier stages the infant has shown some prevision of events. The crying baby stops crying when he hears the footsteps of his mother that signify feeding. In these earlier stages, the signs to which the infant responds are all closely tied with ongoing activity, but in stage 5 the child begins to note events that raise in him anticipations unrelated to what he is doing. For example, the year-old infant engaged in eating whimpers when his mother, seated next to him, moves as if to leave. The movement of his mother is not directly related to his ongoing activity of eating, but it is incidentally observed. At an earlier stage it would not have been observed and responded to, unless it had been closely related to the feeding activity.

Thus throughout this stage, as throughout the preceding stages, there is an increased ability to anticipate events. The child comes to recognize certain signs that presage a forthcoming event. At earlier stages he may anticipate events closely related to some ongoing activity; at this stage he is sensitive to events that are more remote from his immediate activity. His understanding of time has become expanded as has also his understanding of cause and effect.

In his discussion of this stage of development, Piaget takes stock of his overall concept of the nature of sensorimotor intelligence (pp. 321–322). He notes that intelligent behaviors at this level fall into two groups. In one group are those behaviors that spring primarily from environmental circumstances and have an immediate relationship to environmental events. Circular reactions fall into this category because they involve the repetition or variation of an interesting effect found by chance. Activities related to prevision and the interpretation of signs are of this character.

The second category of intelligent behavior involves (1) the discovery of new means through experimentation, (2) the invention of new means through internal activity, and (3) the invention of new means through what Piaget terms "mental combination" (p. 322), that is, an internalization of activity as when the child figures out in advance what will be the result of a particular action. The three categories represent a progressive gradation in terms of the extent to which the solution to a problem involves internal activity.

At this stage of development the capacity to represent objects internally is still very rudimentary. Such an internal representation is first seen in earlier stages in which the infant searches for a missing object and it is evident in this stage in prevision and the use of signs. However, the internal representation is crude and limits the activities that can be undertaken with these internal representations.

Stage 6: 18 to 24 Months. The main new behavior taking place at this stage is the ability to invent new means of solving problems not by experimenting with objects, but by internal activity. In the previous stages the solutions to problems are arrived at by slowly discovering new means for handling them. The child attempting to reach an object beyond its grasp first tries to reach it with its arm. Then the child gives up and picks up a stick. In the course of his activities with the stick, he strikes the object. Sooner or later, striking the object produces movement. finally, the movement of the object produced by the stick is understood to be a means of moving the object toward him. A sequence of slow discovery, through experimentation, is to be contrasted with the sudden inventions of new means that appear during the sixth stage. These inventions, though tied to previously acquired knowledge, are nevertheless novel uses of that knowledge.

This kind of invention through internalized activity cannot take place without internal representation of the objects and components of the problem that are involved. Piaget views these representations at this stage as being not images but the conglomerates of behavior represented by schemata. Objects are not just represented internally by the images of the objects, but by action systems that are object related. However, action systems can be tried out internally, and the child does not have to experiment directly with components of the problem in order to know what the outcome of a particular act will be. A component of the representation may be a word, as when Jacqueline, aged 18 months, who has misplaced a toy frog, searches for it while saying the name she has for the frog. Piaget insists that invention at this stage does not involve simple perceptual reorganizations, but rather is the combination of schemata for problem solving.

The inventions at this stage of development are so simple that they would ordinarily be overlooked as inventions. Piaget cites as an example (1952, p. 338) the case of Lucienne and her first experiences with a doll carriage at the age of 18 months. Lucienne first pushes the carriage across the room until it is against the wall. She then cannot move it any further. She pauses and then goes to other end of the doll carriage and pushes it away from the wall. Lucienne has had no previous experience with doll carriages and her action of reversing the end pushed is a simple invention produced without experimentation on her part.

Some American Interpretations of Piaget's Sensorimotor Period

The present interest in Piaget's work among Americans was initiated about two decades ago by Bruner's stay in Piaget's laboratory and his later reports to Americans on the work of Piaget. Certainly Bruner was enormously impressed with the research he saw in progress at Geneva and Bruner's own stature as a scientist gave weight to his judgments in the matter. In addition, Bruner was sufficiently impressed to initiate on his own campus a program of research along Piagetian lines. This research has focused on the early development of infants, but some effort has also been made to make use of findings from studies of development of other primates. Through the conduct of these studies Bruner has been able to evolve a language to describe early development that is far more intelligible to American psychologists and educators than is the language of Piaget, with its heavy loading on philosophical terms.

Bruner, like Piaget, is impressed with the fact that the early stages of behavior are marked by the attempt of the infant to reproduce deliberately actions and experiences that have occurred by chance. Bruner notes also that these actions are accompanied by the most concentrated attention, which indicates the heavy part played by perceptual learning in the acquisition of the simplest motor coordinations. Bruner takes the position that the infant learns small modules of behavior that are controlled by "programs" in the nervous system analogous to computer programs. More complex skills represent the combination of these modules. The modules are essentially the same as the basic schema described by Piaget, who also talks about the building up of more complex behaviors as involving the "coordination of schemata." which is essentially the same as Bruner's building up of complex behaviors out of modules.

Bruner is also impressed with the role that the contact with an adult has on the development of the skills of the infant. He points out that the infant learns much of his competence by imitating the behavior of the adult in playful types of interactions. However, Bruner realizes that the use of the term imitation in this connection does not mean a simple copying of the behavior of the adult. He has discussed extensively his research on this subject in two important papers (1972, 1973) and relates it to corresponding work on primates.

A particularly significant finding is that the human young, like the young of other primates, will imitate behavior only if the infant has already mastered the various component modules called for in the behavior to be imitated. For example, a chimpanzee reared without the opportunity of inserting sticks into holes will not imitate an adult chimpanzee that he sees doing this in order to catch termites that are later eaten. The modules out of which complex behavior is constructed have to be largely learned by the kind of process that Piaget describes. At this time there is also no inventory of basic modules, but one assumes they include such elements as those of extending the arm to touch an object, closing the hand to grasp, turning the hand to examine an object held in it, placing the hand or finger in a hole, and turning the head to give a better view of an object. Some of these become combined to form larger modules of behavior, as when the infant grasps a stick that he then examines. This grasping of the stick is likely to lead first to behaviors involving the hitting of everything within reach with the stick, but later other modules of behavior become related to it, as when the child uses the stick to retrieve out-of-reach objects or when he probes inside a narrow orifice. It is at the latter level of behavior where the model of the adult becomes particularly important. Psychologists have written much about the use of the child modeling the behavior of the adult, but Bruner has given some meaning to what the process involves. Modeling is not simply a matter of the child copying what he sees, but rather the child uses the cues provided to assemble from his repertoire a suitable sequence of behavior modules. The child observes what the adult is doing with great concentration and thereby identifies the nature of the task that is being performed. The child's task is to construct from his own resources behavior that will permit him to achieve the same goal. Through close contact with the mother, the infant is given cues concerning the modules of behavior to assemble together into larger programs of action.

Now it is important to note that modules do not become combined through the operation of a principle of reinforcement, but the new, more complex form of behavior is *constructed* by the child as a way of adapting to the situation that confronts him.

Bruner also assembles some evidence strongly suggesting that one of the effects of cultural deprivation is to deprive the child of many of the opportunities of useful modeling provided by parents in the middle-class home. The lower-income home is more likely to provide an environment filled with prohibitions and conflict between the purposes of the child and the purposes of the adult. The lower-income home is also more likely to be characterized by the adult commanding the child to perform or not to perform in a particular way. At later stages the middle-and lower-class homes are also differentiated in terms of the use of language as a source of guidance and a source of information.

Piaget has not given much attention to the role of the parent, nor particularly of the mother, in the intellectual development of the child—a factor that Bruner stresses. Perhaps the reason for this is that Piaget, in describing the behavior of his own children, has thought of himself as the experimenter. In his role as experimenter, he has not recognized the important role that he is also playing as parent. If he had watched other parents interacting with their children, he might have been far more impressed with the enormously important role that the parent plays in the development of the infant.

Bruner views play largely as the exercise of these modules of behavior and the entry of the modules into novel combinations. Much of play, he points out, has to have meaning in terms of the activities he sees the adult pursue. The playful imitation of the mother represents the beginnings of learning to be an adult and to function effectively in the adult world. Incidentally, Piaget's conception of play (1962) is much more limited in that he limits his concept of play to those activities already mastered that are repeated for the pleasure they provide. In this connection Bruner deplores the increasing distance of the activities of the adult from the activities of the child and the resulting lack of good play models. He also points out that much of adult activity is meaningless routine to the adult himself. Meaningless adult activities mean meaningless models for the child.

Most of what Bruner has to say supports the work of Piaget. Supportive also is the work of Fleisher et al. (1973), who have assembled considerable evidence showing the universality of the pattern of intellectual development described by Piaget and have added substantial data from their own study of Eskimos. The data generally support the position that the same sequence of stages is evident regardless of culture. Piaget would view such a finding as inevitable in that one step in development is logically necessary before the next step can be undertaken. Some differences may occur in rate of development, but not in order of development. It is also conceivable that the development of some individuals living under deprived conditions might be arrested before it can proceed to the stage of formal operations.

Much of the very extensive American research related to the problems considered in this chapter has been ably summarized in two volumes edited by Cohen and Salapatek (1975).

Finally, the point must be made that there have been numerous attempts to describe infant and child development in terms of operant psychology. Bijou (1975) cites much of this work. However, the fact is that it has had little impact on either educational programs or research.

Education at the Sensorimotor Stage

Infancy has long been regarded as a period when natural processes run their course and when the adult can do little more than see that the child is properly nourished and kept clean. Studies now clearly show that infancy is a period during which the infant has the task of mastering specific aspects of his environment and not all circumstances are favorable for this mastery. There have long been suspicions that such was the case. Nearly half a century ago the noted psychiatrist R. A. Spitz pointed out that infants raised in institutions in which the environment is a uniform white do not have enough to stimulate them to ensure adequate psychological development. Spitz described the infants raised in such an environment as listless, uninterested in the world around them, and backward and referred to the collection of symptoms as the *hospitalism syndrome*. When Spitz first made these observations he was not taken seriously, perhaps because nobody had a good theory concerning the specific learnings that the infant had to undertake as a foundation for further intellectual development. The dissemination of the work of Piaget brought this era of ignorance to an end. It became clear that the infant had to master the fundamental properties of his environment. One should perhaps note that there had been earlier attempts to inventory the competencies of infants, and the work of Arnold Gesell was of pioneer importance in this respect, but the studies undertaken in that framework were normative, that is, designed to describe the activities typical of particular age groups. Piaget, in contrast, has no interest in normative studies, but has been concerned only with the development of a comprehensive theory of intellectual development. For this reason his work has provided a basis for the development of infant training programs.

The focus of infant training programs has been on those segments of the population that have been viewed as providing unfavorable circumstances for infant development, namely, the lower socioeconomic groups. Notable among these programs is the pioneer effort of Gordon (1969, 1973) in the rural South. Gordon's program is based on the observation that infants in poor Southern rural homes have little interaction with adults. They are left to lie in a box, or crib, or on a mattress, receiving attention only at those times when they are fed. Often the mother must leave them for hours on end, but even more important is the fact that when the mother has time to interact with the infant, she does not know how to interact with him. Gordon trained paraprofessionals, who visited the homes of such mothers and began to give them instruction in how to interact with the infants. Mothers were taught very specific skills such as that of holding an object above a 4-month-old infant, for the infant to grasp it, or providing a suspended object that the infant might either grasp, strike, or just observe. Tasks were related to the development of the infant's understanding of the basic characteristics of the world around him, namely, those of space, time, cause-and-effect, and the permanency of objects. A description of the tasks is provided by Gordon (1970). In addition, the mothers were trained to talk to their infants in ways that would help them develop and to avoid a monolgue of reprimands, which was the typical verbal behavior pattern in the untrained mothers. Of interest is the fact that the mothers were so eager to learn to interact with their infants, reflecting the fact that they recognized their own inadequacies in this respect.

Gordon (1973) was able to follow through and study the effects of early training on the later competencies of children, up to the time they entered elementary school. The effects of the early training were marked, and a particularly important finding was that the earlier training was started the better it was in long-term effects. Gains in intelligence quotient were striking, of the order of 8 to 9 points. The training techniques and materials used on the 3-to-12-month infants appeared to be particularly significant for subsequent intellectual development. The data leave little doubt that much has to be done in infancy to build the intellect. Similar positive effects of training in infancy have been found by Karnes et al. (1970).

The point must be made that different cultures may encourage different forms of infant precocity, and this may have a long-term effect of the nature of cultures. There has been some evidence provided that African native children are precocious in motor skills, though this has been doubted by Warren (1972). Other cultures may well produce verbal precocity. What is the effect of these precocities in the long run, if they are real, still needs to be studied.

Effective transfer of previously acquired knowledge to new situations requires a certain plasticity of behavior. What is transferred cannot usually be applied without some modification or adaptation of the knowledge to be used. The extent to which children show this plasticity at different ages does not present an entirely clear picture. The typical situation in which this problem has been studied involves a choice discrimination. Two objects belonging to different classes are presented and the child has to learn which class represents " right " objects and which " wrong." In one series, round objects might be right and square ones wrong. Having learned which class is right and which is wrong, the experiment than reverses the classes so that what was previously right is now wrong. Typical studies have reported that 5- and 6-year-old children have substantial difficulty in making the shift, but that children in the middle elementary grades do not. Such data are interpreted as indicating that the 5- and 6-year-olds have to extinguish the response first learned before they can learn the reverse response, but that older children are able to formulate and apply a new rule to guide their behavior when the rules are changed. The only difficulty with this theory is that an old study by Ling (reported by Gibson, 1973) was able to show that infants, aged 6 to 12 months, were able to handle reversal problems quickly and with great plasticity. The infants were shown two objects; one was fixed and the other could be grasped and moved. The movable object had a sweet substance on it that the infants liked to suck. Ling's experiment needs to be repeated; if the data still hold, they will be very hard to explain. Apparently, infancy is a time of great plasticity in learning.

Preoperations and Operations: Ages 2 to 11

Although memory has been largely memory for action throughout the six stages of infancy, the later stages show a transition to new forms through the establishment of representational memory. Memory for action does not seem to permit the infant to recall that which he has experienced in the absence of the objects and events that produced the original experience. For there to be recall in the absence of the object to be recalled, there has to be an internal representation of the object. The beginnings of such internal representations are seen in the case of a child attempting to insert an object into a slit in a box who opens his mouth to represent the slit. There is no clear line of demarcation between such figurative representation and symbolic representation. Consider another case of a 5-year-old who has been shown a rod six-inches long and is then asked to draw what he has seen. He draws a line 1-inch long. The line is in a sense a portrayal of the rod, but also in a sense a symbol for the rod.

From ages 2 to 5 or 6, known as the period of preoperations, the child shows an enormous growth in his ability to represent objects and events symbolically. Much of this growth is in language. The typical uninhibited talk of the child to himself reflects his use of language in thinking about objects that are not actually present. Language is not the only means through which this is accomplished. Another important avenue for doing this is imagery. Piaget and Inhelder (1971) have made extensive studies of imagery in young children and the functions they have in relation to thought. They regard images as events and objects and make no distinction between a child who imagines an object he has seen and a child who shapes his hand to represent that object. Both would be regarded as images, and both would have the function of representing an object that was not present. Both represent an imitation of that object. Just as language expands during the period of preoperations to permit an ever increasing capacity to think about that which is not present, so, too, does the child's capacity to use images also expand. At the age of 5 the child has little capacity to change or modify an image of an object, but by age 7 he can manipulate images to represent objects in positions in which he has never seen them, and he can even concoct images of objects he has never seen. These changes increase his capacity for thinking about the world and effects to be expected from actions on that world.

During the preoperations period other important developments occur. The child begins to acquire a large fund of information about such characteristics of objects as color, shape, and size. The infant seems to have little understanding of the geometrical properties of objects. He has a topological understanding of space, recognizing that space is divided into certain areas in which certain things happen, or where certain objects are located, but he has no comprehension of what is termed Euclidean space, that is, space that forms geometrical shapes. Without such an understanding the child cannot possibly learn to discriminate the shapes of letters of the alphabet and other common uses of geometrical shape. He also has to acquire such concepts as larger and smaller and more and less. The acquisition of such concepts represents an expansion of his understanding of space.

During the preoperations period a similar development occurs in relation to other attributes of objects. The child becomes more sensitive to differences in colors, recognizing progressively more subtle hues and differences in saturation. A parallel expansion takes place in his understanding of time. He learns the use of such concepts as before and after and acquires a primitive understanding of the concept of speed. The child expands his ability to discriminate one object from another and also to recognize the identity of two objects. Although his vocabulary has grown and enables him to describe the ways in which objects are similar or different, the recognition of these similarities and identities precedes the use of words to describe them.

The preoperations child expands his knowledge of the world around him but in doing so he is a complete realist, often interpreting what he sees in ways that are entirely different from the adult. Thus such a child walking down the street in the evening notes that the moon is always to his right and, however far he walks, the moon never moves behind him. He concludes that the moon is following him. The preoperations child is also an animist in interpreting natural phenomena, attributing to objects qualities he sees in himself. The 4-year-old child may say that a piece of wood floats because it " wants " to float and that another object sinks because it " wants " to sink.

Piaget also claims that the preoperations child interprets the world in an egocentric manner. Thus the child says that the sun shines to make him warm, his mother exists to take care of him, the milkman is there to bring him milk, and the grass grows for him to play on. Russian psychologists criticize Piaget's views in this matter, claiming that the egocentric behavior of the children in Western culture may be due to the bourgeois society in which they are raised. Thus such children are told from their earliest days that the things they use belong to them and are for their personal use, and the life of the child is central in the life of the family. In contrast, the Russian child, raised in a nursery, plays with toys that belong to the collective, and each toy is too large to permit a single child to play with it, so that the children have to cooperate to play with the toys. The issue is interesting, but there are no hard data to show that Russian children are less egocentric than Western children.

The preoperations child is not yet able to perform operations, the basic elements in thinking rationally about the world around him. A brief consideration of the nature of an operation is in order because it is a central concept in Piaget's description of the intellect. An operation is defined as the transformation of one state to another state by means of a logical transformation. Consider a simple example:

$$5 = 3 + 2.$$

In this case the number 5 is converted to the sum of two numbers, 3 and 2. The transformation involves the splitting of a whole into its parts. Both sides of the equation are numerically equal, but they are expressed in different forms. The person performing the operation, if he really understands it has not learned it by rote memory, knows that the numerical value of both sides of the equation are equal. The preoperations child is incapable of understanding this. If he is shown a group of 5 counters, uniformly spaced in a line, and then two groups of 3 and 2 counters, he will say that the two small groups have more counters in them than the large group. He cannot move from the 5 counters to the $3 + 2$ counters and understand that the transformation does not change the number of counters. In fact, he cannot perform an operation. He may be able to say that "three added to two makes five," but he will not know what is meant by this. He may be able to count, but even after he has counted the 5 counters and the $3 + 2$ counters and agreed that each comes out at 5, he will still insist that there are more counters in the $3 + 2$ arrangement than in the single group of 5 counters. He can count, but does not understand numbers because he cannot yet perform logical operations with numbers.

Logical operations also have the property of being reversible. The 5-year-old who has learned that "three plus two makes five" may be able to say this by heart, but when he is asked what he can divide five things into, he will not be able to give an answer. Even the 6-year-old who has learned to write $3 + 2 = 5$ may not solve the problem $5 = 3 + ?$. He cannot do this because his thinking has not acquired reversibility. It will not acquire reversibility until age 6 or 7 and until it does he will not be able to perform logical operations.

The preoperations period prepares the child intellectually for the time when he will learn to perform operations. He will have to master two main forms of operations in order to be able ultimately to think logically. These two forms are those of classification and seriation, which play a crucial role in intellectual development It is to the development of these operations that we must now turn.

From Preoperations to Operations

The development of classificatory behavior and seriation behavior during the preoperations period has been described by Inhelder and Piaget in *The Early Growth of Logic in the Child* (1964). The book includes massive amounts of data, some of it in the form of case descriptions of children of different ages solving particular problems, and some of it involving normative data, showing the ages at which particular transitions occur. Although the normative data must have called for massive amounts of work, they do not provide the data of central importance, —descriptions of how the children solve the problems presented to them.

Classificatory behavior has already established roots in the sensorimotor period when all objects of a certain class come to elicit the same action. Thus small objects are things to be sucked, strings and tapes and ribbons are things to be pulled, and so forth. The schemata of the sensorimotor stage classify objects crudely in terms of the actions that can be performed with them. The world for the infant is filled with things to be sucked, pulled, looked at or followed with the eyes, thrown on the floor, and so forth. Classifications of objects in terms of the actions that can be performed on them are more primitive than classifications of objects in terms of their attributes such as shape or size or function.

Development of Classificatory Behavior. Several kinds of materials are used for studying the development of classificatory behavior. Many of the original experiments were conducted with cardboard geometrical shapes differing in color or with pictures of flowers and other objects. Other sets of materials involved beads of different colors and colored letters of the alphabet. A child is given the materials and given directions such as " Put together those that go together." After the child has done what he wants to do on the tasks, he is asked why he has put together certain objects, or whether there are other ways of sorting the objects. The same results are achieved with pictures of meaningful objects as with geometric shapes.

Classificatory behavior goes through a number of different stages of development described.

STAGE 1A: GRAPHIC COLLECTIONS. The first classifications of objects in terms of their properties (in contrast with classifying things in terms of what one does with them) are reported for children about $2\frac{1}{2}$ years old. The classifications of these children are what are referred to as graphic collections. One set of the materials used by Inhelder and Piaget (1964) for this purpose was a collection of triangles, squares, and semicircles colored in different ways. The child is given this collection of colored shapes and is asked to "Put together things that are alike." The child below $5\frac{1}{2}$ years old confronted with this task goes about it in a characteristic way. His typical performance is to make a line of some of the objects. He may take a few squares and line them up. He may then be satisfied with what he has done and neglect the rest of the objects, or he may continue the line by adding perhaps a few triangles or a mixed collection of objects. Sometimes a child will take a square, than add another square, which happens to be red. Then he notices the redness of the square and adds to the collection a red triangle. Then he adds another triangle. It is as if he examined each object, noted some property of it, and then sought another object with a similar property. In this activity there is no conception that a whole group of objects should include only members having common properties that distinguish them from nonmembers of the class. As the child moves along his line of objects, he forgets what the last criterion was for adding a new member and selects a new criterion at each choice point. In the more advanced stage of the linear arrangement, some effort is made by the child to keep together in the same part of the line the objects that are more similar.

The basic difficulty of the young child in attempting to divide collections of items into classes is that he can comprehend only two objects at a time. He is unable to consider *all* of the objects at once. This same limitation of the thinking of the young child is also found in the way in which he interprets pictures (see Travers, 1973). The child looking at a picture of, say, the inside of a busy store states that he sees a particular object, such as a lady in a red dress, but he is unable to describe the total scene. He fails to comprehend *all* of the picture as a totality. He is guided by what he immediately perceives, and what he immediately perceives is all he perceives.

STAGE 1B: COLLECTIVE OBJECTS. At a slightly more advanced stage the child may depart from the linear arangement of the shapes and may build them into a collective objective. He may, for example, begin by taking a square; then he places a triangle first on one side of the square and then on another side. The collective object is in more than one dimension and represents a departure from the linear arrangements shown earlier. The collective objects may show an understanding of a symmetrical relationship, as when two circles are placed on either side of a rectangle.

STAGE 2: NONGRAPHIC COLLECTIONS In this intermediate stage of nongraphic collections the child begins to show some understanding of what it means for objects to belong to a group, but classificatory thinking is still limited. At this stage the child is likely to take the materials he has been asked to arrange and may begin by building some kind of complex object with it. If pictures of common objects are used, instead of geometrical shapes, a child may begin by arranging a picture of a baby with all the things used to feed and take care of the baby. However, if pressed to arrange the materials in a different way, the child may make groups that have common shapes (all the squares) or all the objects that have common attributes (all the animals or all the pictures of furniture). The child may use the word "all" in connection with his classification but still has little idea that in classifying a group of objects by placing some in category A, this category is now set off against *all* the other objects that are not in the A class. In a true classification system, the establishment of a category of *squares*, implies that all other objects fall into the category of nonsquares. Essentially, the child at this stage achieves a classification by a kind of trial and error. He shows little ability to anticipate a basis for classification after scanning the objects. Since the child does not understand this characteristic of the classification process, he usually ends up with some objects that do not fit into his system. He understands that the expression "all of the squares" refers to his collection of squares, that is, he has some understanding of exclusion relationships. What he does not understand is inclusion relationships through which characteristics of the group are related to the characteristics of other groups of objects. He still has some difficulties with relations of exclusion, as when he is shown a group of red circles and red squares. He then has difficulty in understanding that *all the circles are red*. He is confused because some of the squares are also red. Inhelder and Piaget describe the difficulties of classification of children of this age as a failure to coordinate relationships of exclusion to relationships of inclusion. The child does not understand that relationships within a group of objects that make the objects constitute a group (with subgroups) are also involved in the relationships of the group to other groups.

At this second stage, the child may begin the classification task assigned to him by making small collections of objects each having some kind of common property and then building these into larger collections. On the other hand, he may start by building large collections and then breaking the collections down into smaller collections. The child does not seem able to combine these two methods, working first in one direction and then in another until a satisfactory classification is achieved. The more mature person is able to do this, experimenting with the arrangement of the materials in different ways until a satisfactory classification is achieved. The suggestion is that the younger child is not able to do this because he cannot anticipate the results of this or that way of attempting to arrange materials.

STAGE 3. A striking change takes place in classificatory behavior about age 6 at which time true logical classifications of objects are first undertaken. At this stage the child has a genuine understanding of what is meant by some and all in such statements as "Some of the squares are blue" and "All of the circles are red." Thus the child can understand that "All the blue squares together with all the blue circles form the class of blue objects," but he also understands that "If all the blue circles are taken away from the blue objects, only all the blue squares remain." The second of these statements is the inverse of the first, and to understand the meaning of these two statements the child has to be able to move backward and forward conceptually, first adding blue squares to blue circles and then taking them away again. Inhelder and Piaget describe this ability to move forward and backward in thinking as *reversibility*. The acquisition of reversibility, at about age 6, constitutes an important new step in the child's ability to think. Through the acquisition of the ability to perform this operation, the child's thinking comes closer to being strictly logical, and Piaget takes the position that maturity of intelligence is reflected in thought approaching more and more the model of good thinking proposed by logicians and mathematicians.

Once the child has achieved the kind of reversibility of thinking just described, he becomes capable of performing not only true classifications, but also quite complex forms of classification, such as hierarchical classification; for example, if a child were given a collection of red and blue circles and squares and first divided them into blue and red objects before breaking down each color category into squares and circles, he would be engaged in hierachical classification.

Although the basic understanding of the logic of classification is achieved at about age 6, some concepts related to classification cannot be achieved until later. The child does not understand until age 7 or 8 that a single object can constitute a class. The concept of a singular class is difficult to acquire. Even more difficult is the concept of a null class, that is, a class into which no objects can be placed. This concept is apparently not found in children much before age 10 or 11. This is the stage in which true classification appears. Inhelder and Piaget provide very precise criteria to determine whether the child has or has not mastered the operation of classification. Merely making some piles of similar objects does not mean that the child has reached the stage of concrete operations and can perform classification as an operation. The criteria are as follows (see Inhelder and Piaget, 1964, p. 48):

1. All elements must be classified.

2. There are no isolated classes that do not belong in the system. If there is a class A characterized by a, than there is a complimentary class A' that is characterized by not having the characteristic a.

3. A class A includes all the objects having the property a.

4. A class A includes only objects having the property a.

5. This criteria involves the idea of the *rank* of a class. Suppose a child divides some geometrical shapes into squares and circles, and then divides each geometrical shape into the red ones and the blue ones. The total collection of objects represents Rank 1. The division into squares and circles represents Rank 2, and the further subdivision by color represents Rank 3. An object cannot belong in two different categories at the same rank in an acceptable classification system.

6. If objects are divided into a category A, characterized by a, then the complimentary class A' is also characterized by some attribute of its own.

7. A class at one rank is included in all classes of higher rank. Thus, in our example, the class of blue squares is included in the higher class of squares of different colors.

8. The system must have simplicity. If each object were placed by the child into a separate pile, he would not have produced a classification system.

9. Classes at the same rank are distinguished by similar criteria. Thus, in our example, shape distinguishes the classes at Rank 2 and color at Rank 3.

10. The system of classes must represent a symmetrical subdivision.

One should note that none of these properties are seen in stage 1, even though children may, to some degree, group together similar objects. At stage 2 more of these conditions are satisfied, although criterion 3 is rarely met, for children typically have some objects left over that do not fit any group of objects. Only at stage 3 are classification systems produced by children that meet all of the criteria.

Certain aspects of classification remain difficult for children to grasp even at age 8 or 9. Not until about age 11 do children begin to be able to grasp the idea of setting up a class that contains no cases. Suppose that there are red and blue triangles and circles, but only red squares. A comprehensive classification system would leave a place for blue squares, even though there are none. Such a class is referred to as a null class. The difficulty of the 10-year-old in grasping the idea of a null class derives from the fact that such a child is limited in his thinking by that with which he can have direct physical contact. A null class is an abstraction and refers to something that is not present to the senses. Such a child cannot grasp such an abstraction. Finally, the point must be made that mature classification behavior involves a strategy. A child who has reached a skillful stage of classification will look over the objects to be classified and will then settle on a strategy and classify the objects. The younger child who is in a stage of transition, and near to being able to classify objects, will go about the task with a certain amount of trial and error, arriving at a classification system by successive approximations.

Seriation and the Concept of Number. The operation of seriation represents the capability of arranging objects in a series, which is fundamental to all mathematics. It finds its roots in the early behavior of infancy in which the infant shows some ability to recognize that two events occur in a certain order and that the occurrence of one event can be taken to signify the subsequent occurrence of another event, as when the sound of opening the refrigerator door is taken to signify the forthcoming feeding. Primitive precursors of seriation are also seen during the sensorimotor period, as whan a child piles boxes of different sizes one on top of the other. He may not place them completely in order of size, but he does a little better than chance in this respect. The development of the operation of seriation involves the development of the concept of quantity. Basic research related to this aspect of learning is provided in Piaget's *The Child's Conception of Number* (1965).

Piaget's studies began with investigations of the development of the concept of quantity. Number has *cardinal* as well as *ordinal* properties. A number may indicate a quantity, its cardinal property, or a position in a series, its ordinal property. The development of the cardinal concept of quantity goes through a number of stages as follows:

STAGE 1. The child thinks that the quantity of a substance changes as it changes form. He believes that when a liquid is poured into a tall, thin vessel from a short, wide one it becomes more. There is a perceptual illusion of more liquid, and the illusion dominates the thinking of a child. Also, when the liquid in a glass is subdivided into smaller glasses, the young child also believes there is more.

STAGE 2. This is a transitional stage. When the liquid is poured into another container it is recognized as the same quantity of liquid, but when it is subdivided it is considered to change in quantity.

STAGE 3. At about age 6 or 7 the child has developed a concept of quantity and understands the idea of the conservation of quantity.

Similar phenomena can be observed with discontinuous quantities, such as beads. The younger child sees the beads as changing in quantity as they are poured into different vessels, or as a pile of them is spread out on a table.

Related to the development of conservation of quantity is the development of what Piaget calls one-to-one correspondence. One set of materials used to study this phenomenon is a set of small water jugs or bottles and a set of glasses. The child is asked to take just enough glasses so that there is one for each bottle. The development of one-to-one correspondence goes through a number of stages.

STAGE 1. The child may be able to pair some of the glasses and bottles but ends up with an extra glass at one end of the row or an extra glass at the other end.

STAGE 2. The child may succeed in arranging the bottles and glasses in pairs, but when the glasses are spread out he insists that there are more glasses. So long as the objects are arranged close together in pairs, he can understand the correspondence perceptually, but he has not grasped the concept of one-to-one correspondence, for the spreading out of one row destroys the physical image of pairings and he no longer understands the problem. When one row is spread out, even counting does not lead him to believe that there are the same number of bottles as glasses.

STAGE 3. The children understand correspondence and do not need the visual presentation to comprehend it.

An important point to note is that although children in the first two stages may count the bottles or glasses, they do not have a concept of number. Counting has been learned by a mechanical routine. The understanding of one-to-one correspondence is a step in the development of the understanding of number. Clearly, the child can have no understanding of the concept of number in counting objects if he does not understand the one-to-one correspondence between the numbers he says aloud and the objects that are counted. The young child does not understand that correspondence and, hence, does not understand number.

One-to-one correspondence has hidden in it another process necessary for its effective execution, that is, seriation, the arranging of elements in order. The one-to-one correspondence involved in counting can be undertaken successfully only if the child understands that the objects have to be counted in order that all objects are counted, and that no object is omitted from being counted. A 5-year-old who can say his numbers and who is asked to count a set of objects typically does not count some objects and counts other objects twice. This is because he has not been able to incorporate the concept of seriation into his activity. Piaget views numbers as seriated classes. Children ages 3 to 6 may still have crude concepts of number. Gelman (1972) has shown that such children show surprise when small numbers are increased or decreased.

The materials commonly used for the study of seriation involve such objects as cardboard dolls of varying size and cardboard umbrellas of varying size. Tasks may involve arranging one of these sets in order, or finding the umbrella that goes with the particular doll, or double seriation involving the arranging of both sets in corresponding orders. Children can handle aspects of this task perceptually before they can handle the task conceptually. That is, they can sometimes shuffle the objects around until they are in order, without yet being able to conceptualize a series and proceed with a plan. The more mature child proceeds with a plan, perhaps starting with the longest and then the next longest, and so forth.

One basic task used in the study of seriation with young children has involved a set of about 10 rods varying in length from about 4 to 7 inches. The difference in the size of the rods is easy to see, being about one-third of an inch. Inhelder and Piaget (1964) elaborated on this procedure by helping the children to understand what was required by showing them four dolls arranged in order of size. In addition, they painted the rods different colors and asked the children to draw with colored crayons the arrangement of the rods when placed in order. The latter and more complex form of the task made it easier to explore the thinking of the children.

In arranging the rods in order or in copying the rods with crayon, children necessarily have to anticipate what the final arrangement is going to look like. The task is necessarily anticipatory and, if the children cannot conceive in advance what the final product is going to be like, they cannot perform the task. Thus, the children have to be able to represent the final product internally before they can work effectively on the task. The task was administered to children ages 4 to 9.

At the lowest age levels, the children showed little conception of what the task involved. Piaget had shown this earlier (1952). The 5-year-old may arrange two or even three of the rods in a correct order, but he is unable to grasp what has to be done with *all* of the rods. He lacks the global conception of what a series involves and is unable to focus attention on the entire collection of rods. In the task involving the colored drawings of the colored rods, the 4- and 5-year-olds generally show no understanding of what seriation involves. They draw some rods but the rods in these drawings do not represent a series and the colors show no relationship to the size of the rods of corresponding color.

In the second stage, mostly at the 6- and 7-year level, the child shows an ability to draw a series of different lengths. He shows no signs of being able to anticipate what the final outcome of his work is going to be. Oddly enough, after he has made the drawing that shows a series, the child is typically unable to order the rods themselves. Also, if he uses colors for drawing the series, the colors of the drawn lines do not correspond to the colors of the rods. He is unable to take into account both color and shape.

The reason given for this ability to draw a series, although the child cannot arrange a set of objects in order at this stage is that the objects call for a strategy that the drawing of the lines does not. A strategy for arranging the rods in order is to take the smallest, and then the next smallest, and then the next smallest, and so forth. In the case of each choice, in arranging the real objects the child has to look at all the remaining objects. In the case of drawing the next line, the child has to look at only the last line and draw a larger line. The strategy involved in the latter case is much simpler.

In the third stage, the child is able to arrange objects into a series. He can anticipate what this involves and what the product has to be. He can do more than just compare one stick with another stick and note differences, but has the strategy of looking first for the shortest or the longest stick. His activity shows a plan and is more than a series of trial-and-error moves.

In order to perform the operation of seriation effectively, the child must be able to view the objects to be seriated as a class of objects. At age 5 he cannot do this. He can only take one object and compare it with another object and recognize that one object is larger than the other. This may lead to two or three objects being placed in order of size, but it will not result in the proper arrangement of the entire series. The arrangement of the entire series cannot take place until the child can grasp the group of objects as a group and understand that a certain kind of order can be introduced into that group.

The operation of seriation implies reversibility. The child has to be able to understand that if one element is longer than another, it is also shorter than still another. The child has to be able to work forward from smallest to largest, and backward from largest to smallest.

The basic studies of seriation all involved seriation in terms of size, that is, space relations. Events can also be arranged temporally. Mandler and Anderson (1971) found that temporal ordering precedes spatial ordering. Temporal ordering is probably more primitive in character, for the anticipations of the infant represent a basic intuitive comprehension of time ordering.

Conservation: A Basic Element in Classification and Seriation

Current discussions of the work of Piaget often focus on a phenomenon known as *conservation* because it is an interesting and easily demonstrable phenomenon. It was first described by Piaget in *The Child's Conception of Number* and has since formed the basis for literally hundreds of studies. In the original experiment Piaget asked children to pour orangeade from a beaker into a tall glass funnel. They were then asked whether they then had more, less, or the same amount of liquid as they had before. At age 5, children uniformly said that there was now more liquid. When the liquid was poured back into the original vessel, there was then said to be less again. Piaget thought that this response of the children might be due to the fact that they might have some idea that the nature of liquid changed through being transferred to another vessel. For this reason he repeated the experiment using beads in the same glassware. When the beads were poured from the beaker into the tall tube, the 5-year-olds insisted that there were then more beads. When Piaget pressed the children on this point and asked whether the beads would now make a longer or shorter necklace, the children insisted that the beads would now make a longer necklace. Even after the children counted out the same number of beads into the beaker and into the tall glass tube, they insisted that the beads in the tall glass tube would make the longer necklace. What appears to happen is that children concentrate on the single dimension of the height of the column and judge number or quantity in terms of it. This concentration is so complete that they fail to take into account either the width of the tube or the fact that they themselves have counted out the beads.

Children who have reached age 7 behave very differently with respect to such problems. By that age they have acquired the understanding that the quantity of material is unchanged by changing its form and understand that the dimension on which they have been focusing is irrelevant to the problem. This understanding of conservation is essentially an extension of the understanding they have acquired in the area of classification: they have learned by age 7 that dividing a category into components does not change the basic amount of materials involved. The mastery of classification problems is critical to the development of the concept of conservation.

Until the concept of conservation has been achieved, the child cannot understand the nature of addition and subtraction. He can, of course, learn by rote memory to say certain additive and subtractive statements, as when he says "two added to three is five." Such statements have to be differentiated from understanding the nature of the additive relationship. A 5-year-old able to make such a statement will still insist that there are more objects when a group of 5 is divided into subgroups. In a similar way the understanding of subtractive relationships is dependent upon an understanding of the nature of conservation. The understanding of numerical relationships is dependent upon the development of logical thinking. In addition, the concept of measurement cannot be developed without these underlying and necessary concepts of logic.

The interesting point has been demonstrated (Macready and Macready, 1974) that at least some aspects of conservation are learned first in relation to the child's own body. For example, children have been demonstrated to conserve their own weight and another person's weight before they conserve the weight of nonhuman objects.

Some confusion is introduced into the picture by claims that very young children can "conserve" very small quantities of two or three objects (see Winer, 1974). However, from Piaget's point of view this is a precursor of conservation and a matter of being able to make perceptual discriminations. A child can recognize quantities as being the same or different on a perceptual basis long before he understands the constancy of quantity regardless of form or shape.

The transition from preoperations to operations involves not only the development of logical structures, but also changes in the way in which perceptual data are handled. The child of 5 who watches a glass of lemonade being poured into a tall, thin vessel and who sees the liquid rise is entranced by the extension of the liquid over the vertical dimension. He is so preoccupied with the height of the liquid, and the resulting illusory increase in the quantity of the liquid, that he cannot take anything else into account. Melnick has shown that the amount of perceptual distortion is related to whether children will or will not conserve when they are in a transitional stage.

The Effects of Training in Accelerating Conservation
and Other Aspects of Operations

Piaget has not had a central interest in education, though he has made important contributions to educational activities, including UNESCO. He has written about educational problems, but not in detail nor at length. Many of the concerns of educational technologists, such as those involving the acceleration of education, he regards as trivial. In view of his stated position in this regard, one can surmise what his reaction would be to the hundreds of studies undertaken in America that have been concerned with the acceleration of the development of operations in children, mainly of elementary-school age. Piaget is not concerned with accelerating intellectual development in childhood, despite the fact that he was a child prodigy— perhaps the source of his lack of interest.

Most of those who have undertaken attempts to accelerate the learning of conservation have been doctoral students, and few have had the benefit of the guidance of a professor well read in Piaget's massive contributions. The students who conducted the studies have not had any prolonged contact with Piaget's thinking, at least not judging by their research. A review of the studies up to 1971 has been supplied by Brainerd and Allen (1971), but their conclusions may be questioned. They conclude that conservation can be accelerated by amounts that are statistically significant. The successful methods tend to be those that stress reversibility in an object-bound setting. In addition, there appears to be some transfer of what has been learned to related situations. Now let us look at these conclusions.

In the typical experiment, children near the age at which they may be expected to show a particular form of conservation are first divided into those who conserve and those who do not. Then the nonconservers are given training. The choice of children is such that many of them may be expected to construct the idea of conservation for themselves, given the appropriate experience. The experimenter gives them the appropriate experience and, of course, they learn to conserve. Within Piaget's model some degree of trainability is to be expected, but for a child living in an environment rich with experiences one might expect him to learn to conserve anyway. The accelerating effect of providing conservation training merely gives him a lesson that common experience will give him. In the case of grossly underprivileged children, the environment may be slow in providing the experiences that will cause the child to construct the idea of constancy in number, weight, volume, and whatever else. For such children there may be advantages in providing the critical experiences.

In many of the experiments one really does not know what is learned, for children may be drilled in saying that two quantities are equal, and few experimenters probe to find out what the child has learned other than a verbal response. What he says may be merely an empty word routine, but even then some transfer of that routine may be expected in similar, but not identical, situations. Again, some research workers have tried to " extinguish " the response of conservation and claim success. Piaget would expect that the children involved in such " extinction " studies would be either extinguishing an empty verbal response or performing in ways that they thought pleased an experimenter.

Many of the findings of research in this area provide foregone conclusions. Brainerd (1974) found that it was easier to train for conservation than for classification. This is not surprising, for conservation is a prerequiste of classification; indeed, classification is not possible without conservation.

One cannot be impressed with research showing that 6-year-olds who do not conserve can be helped to conserve by being provided with appropriate experiences. The learning of conservation requires appropriate experiences. If one actually could demonstrate that 4-year-olds could be taught to conserve quantity as a reversible operation, one would have a valuable finding. But the research undertaken in this field is trivial and has added confusion, rather than clarification.

Perhaps the most careful and well-thought-out study of the effect of training in this area was undertaken by Inhelder, Sinclair, and Bovet (1974). They found that training had impact when the child was in a transitional state and was on the verge of being able to perform the operation. In other words, training has impact when it occurs in the child's life at the teachable moment.

Finally, research has shown that the underprivileged achieve classificatory and conservation skills at a later age than the middle class (see Wei, Lavatelli, and Jones, 1971). The reasons for this are obscure.

Classification, Seriation, and Mathematical Development

Throughout his works Piaget takes the position that as thinking matures it takes on a mathematical and logical form. One is, therefore, not surprised that Piaget regards the development of classification and seriation as necessary for the development of mathematical understanding, as well as providing a foundation for all logical problem solving. A simple mathematical problem such as subtracting 6 from 9 to produce 3 requires the child to understand that a collection of objects can be divided up into components and that the sum of the component must equal the total aggregate from which they are derived. This understanding is basic for the solution of all classification problems, namely, that aggregates can be broken down into subaggregates.

Children can learn by rote that $9 - 6 = 3$, but there is the world of difference between being able to make this statement and knowing what it means. The rote version of learning does not involve the performance of a logical operation as does the solution of the same problem after the child has developed classification skills at the logical level. The child who has learned this subtraction by rote has no basis for solving problems for which he has not learned a rote solution. The child who has developed logical thinking related to classification is able to solve a great range of such problems by the application of logic and counting.

There is a place for the rote learning of number combinations in both addition and multiplication, but one must not confuse the acquisition of such rote skills with mathematical knowledge. There is a difference between "knowing how" and "knowing that." A child may know that $9 - 6 = 3$, but he may not know how a group of 9 objects can be divided into two groups of 6 and 3 objects and that the groups of 6 and 3 objects can then be recombined to form a group of 9 objects. Until the child has acquired the ability to reverse operations and to move backward and forward on problems, he cannot move from $9 - 6 = 3$ to knowing that $6 + 3 = 9$.

Piaget and his associate Inhelder have developed a number of ingenious situations for studying problem solving involving classification and seriation in children during the school years (1958). Let us consider one of these situations in order to obtain some understanding concerning the way in which logical thinking develops during these years.

A simple apparatus, like a pinball machine with a plunger-type mechanism that can be used to fire the ball against the side of the table and from which it can rebound, is used. The ball rebounds well from the side, much as a billiard ball rebounds from the cushion along the side of the table. The child playing the game puts a ball in the plunger and then tries to hit a target with the ball after the ball has rebounded from the cushion. The child can vary the angle at which the ball is shot at the cushion and can, hence, adjust his aim to hit the target. An advantage of this particular device is that very young children can have fun playing with it and yet the problem becomes a challenge to older children. A number of stages take place in the solution of this problem.

STAGE 1 : BEFORE 7 YEARS. Children 5 years old and some younger children hold the view that the ball goes in a curve from the plunger that fires it to the target. They have no idea that there is a relationship between the angle of the firing mechanism and the trajectory of the ball; they just fire and hope for the best. Perhaps the concept of a variable angle is too difficult for these young children to master. As the children approach age 7 they become aware that the ball goes in a straight line toward the cushion and then rebounds in a straight line. They have noticed the rectilinear nature of the trajectory. At this stage there is no internal conceptualization of what is happening, only a preoccupation with the actual data. Their behavior is completely preoccupied with achieving the goal and they are not concerned with why they succeed or fail. They are unable to use the facts presented before their eyes to develop any kind of generalization about why they sometimes succeed and sometimes fail. The children at this stage have not reached the point of performing concrete operations, that is, operations internal to themselves.

STAGE 2A: AGES 7 TO 8. Beginning about age 7 children begin to make generalizations based on the data derived from shooting the ball. At this stage they may make some primitive generalizations—for example, the more you move the plunger to the left the more the ball will go to the left. This is a primitive application of seriation. Children no longer just fire and hope to hit the target but are able to adjust their aim to make the ball go where they want it to go. They understand that shots can be classed as successes and failures and begin to search for conditions that distinguish the two classes.

STAGE 2B: AGES 9 TO 11. At about age 9 children have discovered that the angle at which the ball hits the cushion is crucial. They believe that for any particular angle at which the ball hits the cushion there is a corresponding angle at which the ball bounces off. They view the data as a rank ordering of angles of arrival and a rank ordering of angles of departure from the cushion, which they can do because they understand seriation. The children at this stage do not attempt to explain the facts thay have observed, but they stick closely to the facts—a striking characteristic of problem solving at the stage of concrete operations.

At this stage children have not reached the most mature level of thinking, which Piaget calls the stage of formal operations, to be described later in this chapter.

Let us now consider another example of problem solving at the concrete operations stage involving classificatory behavior. The problem involves presenting the child with a number of objects and a tank of water. He is asked why some objects float and others do not and is encouraged to experiment with the materials provided. The objects are large, small, flat, rounded, thin, or thick. At the preoperational level the child may make a classification of the objects into those that float and those that do not, but his explanations are contradictory. He will say that one object floats because it is large and another because it is small. One object is said to float because it is thin and another because it is thick. The child is not in any way concerned about the inadequacy of his explanations and neither is he with his contradictions. For each object the child has an explanation that does not fit other objects. When the child reaches the 7-to-9-year-old level he becomes concerned with these contradictions. He then begins to understand that he has to set up two classes of objects, objects that float and objects that do not float and identify a property that distinguishes the two. At this stage the child may set up subsets of objects, for example, by dividing those that float into those that float because they are light and those that float because they are small. Toward the end of stage 2 he begins to make the discovery that not all small objects are light and not all large objects are heavy. He is not able at this stage to relate weight to volume, which he has to do to find a solution to the problem, but he can obtain an approximation to this solution by first dividing objects into the light and heavy and then subdividing them into the large and the small.

The ultimate solution to the problem involves understanding that the crucial factor is the relation of the weight of the object to the weight of the water displaced, but during the stage of concrete operations the child does not grasp this fact. He tends to think that the total amount of water in the tank is of importance but he is unlikely to come to grips with the central problem involved. A stumbling block for him is that he has difficulty in conceptualizing the *quantity of water displaced* because this cannot be observed directly and represents an abstract concept. The child at stage 2 can undertake operations that pertain to concrete observable elements, but is unable to handle such abstractions.

The Mature Intellect: Formal Operations

In the previous section problem solving was discussed, but there are fundamental differences between problem solving at the stage of concrete operations and at the later stage of formal operations. Piaget and his associates are far from being as clear as one would like them to be concerning the difference between the two stages, but some of this lack of clarity is due to the fact that their research has been concentrated at the younger levels of development and research on the mature intellect has had a relatively low priority.

Let us point out that the difference between the level of concrete operations is *not* that one involves what is *commonly* called abstract thinking and the other does not. The child of 10 engages in abstract thought when during a classification task he leaves a place for a class of green triangles, even though there are no green triangles. The null class, as it is called, is an abstract concept. In ordering objects in a series, the child of the same age has to have the idea of the nature of a series before he starts out on the task. This is an abstract concept. The child does use abstractions before he reaches the stage of formal operations.

Nevertheless, there are certain forms of abstraction that appear at the formal operations level that are not evident at lower levels. Consider the child with the pinball machine problem. At the level of concrete operations, the child sticks closely to the data. He sees that this kind of aim produces that kind of result. He may even conclude from his data that the bigger one angle is the bigger is the other angle. The older child tries to formulate generalizations. He may see that there is a relation between the angle the ball strikes the side and angle it bounces off. He will probably conclude that the two angles are equal and they will be so *under all conditions*. If he arrives at this conclusion it is because he is not bound by the facts given him but can expand his thought to all possible trajectories of the ball, whether he has seen them or not.

This capacity to generalize appears to be reached by stages. At first the child solving the problem will see that there is some relationship between the angle the ball strikes the edge and the angle it leaves. Once the child is sure there is some relationship, he may well try to find out what it is and arrive at the conclusion that the two angles are equal. In doing this, the child capable of formal operations will set up hypotheses, which are theories concerning what is possible. At the stage of concrete operations, the child does not formulate hypotheses and seems quite unable to pursue such a line of abstract thought because he is so data bound. Piaget says that the child at the stage of concrete operations is very objective, in that he deals with the facts at hand, but it is this matter of being tied to the facts that limits his thinking. Infinitely greater power is available to him when thought is no longer tied to the immediate. In the stage of formal operations he can do this and, no longer tied to the facts, great intellectual power is open to him.

In the case of the problem involving floating bodies another factor becomes evident. The floating bodies problem involves many different factors including size, shape, and weight. The child has to try to vary one factor and hold the others constant if he is to achieve a solution, and this means that he is making use of the concept " other things being equal." This concept is extremely important in much empirical investigation and plays a central role in what is called hypothetico-deductive thinking.

Another problem studied by Inhelder and Piaget (1958) brings out an additional feature of thinking at the formal operations stage. A number of rods are provided that vary in thickness, cross-sectional shape, and material. The rods can be mounted so that when a weight is attached to one end, the rod will bend. This problem involves many variables and the child has to find out the factors that contribute to flexibility of rods.

The child at the concrete operations level approaches the problem in a helter-skelter manner, comparing first one pair of rods and then another. The child who is at the formal operations stage behaves entirely differently. He compares two rods with a purpose in mind. In other words, he formulates hypotheses before he carries out an experiment. He assumes that a particular factor is capable of producing a particular effect and goes about discovering whether that is so.

A still further factor in the thinking of children at the formal operations level is that it can take into account the interaction of factors. For example, the child may conclude that the flexibility of a rod depends on length, with long rods being flexible. Then he finds that a certain long rod has little flexibility and attributes that to the thickness of the rod. He then sees that the flexibility of a long rod may be negated by the rod being thick. The child at the concrete operations level is quite unable to formulate such a hypothesis or even to comprehend how such factors can interact. He cannot understand that length is a factor only if other things are equal, but the child at the formal operations level can.

The flexibility-of-rods problem shows how children acquire the ability to separate the many variables in a problem and how the ability to perform formal operations is necessary to do this. Another type of problem calls for the ability to separate relevant from nonrelevant variables. An example is the pendulum; the child is provided with a string and a set of weights and is asked to find out what makes a pendulum go fast or slow. Some of the factors to be considered are those of the length of the string, the weight attached to the string, the amplitude of the swing, and the push given the pendulum in starting it. The child has to exclude all except the first of these. At the concrete operations stage children may discover that the length of the string is significant but are not likely to exclude the other factors. At the formal operations stage, children are able to exclude factors by experimenting with them separately and holding all other factors constant. Such an approach is beyond the comprehension of children at the concrete operations level.

Piaget takes the position that at each stage psychological structures develop permitting the performance of logical operations that could not be performed previously. These structures are not innate but emerge through an interaction between the individual and his environment. The structures result in the ability to perform certain intellectual operations. Just as Piaget is quite specific concerning the intellectual operations that the child of 7 can perform, including seriation and conservation of quantity, so, too, does he have specific suggestions concerning the operations that characterize the adolescent engaged in formal logical problem solving. His inventory of these operations cannot be considered to be comprehensive, for it is only a beginning. Let us consider some of these operations of the formal stage of thought. (See Inhelder and Piaget, 1958.)

1. COMBINATORIAL OPERATIONS. In broad terms Piaget means by combinatorial operations that the child reaching the formal operations stage is able to handle combinations of propositions. For example, in the pendulum problem situation the child may have such hypotheses as

The length of the pendulum is important and the weight of the bob is important, too.

Either the length of the pendulum is important or the weight of the bob is important.

The length of the pendulum is not important and neither is the weight of the bob.

These propositions have been written out in such a way as to indicate to the reader that each statement involves two propositions that have been combined. Various combinations of statements can be made about the pendulum in formulating hypotheses concerning the factor or factors that are related to the frequency of swing. The child may formulate hypotheses combining together many propositions. If he succeeds in solving the problem, he will conclude with a complex proposition such as "Only the length of the pendulum is significant. Other factors explored such as the weight of the bob, the amplitude of the swing, and the force applied to make the pendulum swing are not significant factors." Such a conclusion shows a capacity to consider many factors simultaneously, an ability that younger children at the concrete operations level do not have. Piaget has developed a systematic way of classifying pairs of propositions that are logically related in some way, and the classification involves sixteen categories (referred to as Piaget's sixteen binary propositions).

2. PROPORTIONS. Piaget cites evidence indicating that children at the concrete operations level do not understand proportion, namely, the equality of two ratios $x/y = a/b$. Of course, children ages 7 to 11 do manage to learn to solve problems involving ratios and they learn to do this by rule-of-thumb methods. The inability to understand and use proportions at the concrete operations level has been studied by Piaget in a variety of problems involving probability, space, and speed. An important form of the proportion is found in the analogy. There appear to be certain forms of thought that precede the use of numerical proportions that also involve the analogy. When a child learns that the feathers of birds have analogous functions to the hairs of mammals, he is learning the relationship *feathers are to birds as hairs are to mammals*. An understanding of such equivalencies is a step in the direction of understanding proportion.

3. THE COORDINATION OF TWO SYSTEMS OF REFERENCE. The original data for the study of the coordination of two systems of reference came from Piaget's studies of the development of the understanding of speed and motion. In one of the problems used for this study, a snail shell was placed on a board and the "snail" could be given either a forward or backward motion. The board could also be moved forward or backward. When both the board and the snail were in motion, then the motion of the snail with respect to a fixed point on the table would be the sum of the two motions of the snail and the board. Children at the stage of concrete operations are unable to solve this problem because they are not able to take into account simultaneously the two frames of reference (one is the relation of the snail to the board and the other is the relation of the board to the table). Children who reach the stage of formal operations are able to take account of both frames of reference at once and can then make predictions concerning where the moving object will be after a given amount of time. Much of the process of development described by Piaget involves growth in the number of events or relations that can be taken into account at the same time. Thus, the 5-year-old can compare two objects simultaneously, but he cannot consider several objects at the same time and find out why they constitute a class.

4. THE PROCESS OF MECHANICAL EQUILIBRIUM. At the stage of concrete operations children will understand mechanical equilibrium when direct perceptual evidence of equilibrium is available. Thus children ages 8 to 11 can readily grasp the nature of the equilibrium of a balance where an object on one pan and a set of weights in the other pan keep the beam in a horizontal position. However, when the forces at work are hidden, or not so obvious, the same children are not able to understand the equilibrium involved. In the case of the pressure exerted by a piston on the fluid in a system, such children have difficulty in understanding that the pressure is exerted against every part of the cylinder wall and that the cylinder wall exerts an equal pressure against the fluid. There is a similar difficulty in understanding that the downward weight of the table top is exactly counterbalanced by an upward thrust from the legs. Indeed, the latter kind of statement seems like so much nonsense to children at the level of concrete operations. They are not able to understand such matters of equilibrium since it requires understanding that goes beyond that which they can observe.

5. THE CONCEPT OF PROBABILITY. Piaget believes that the concept of probability requires a comprehension that goes beyond what is immediately perceived and real. Probability is a difficult concept to master because it involves such abstract notions as that events in a series can be completely independent. At the concrete operations stage a child may think that because an ordinary penny comes down heads four times in a row it is more likely to come down tails on the next trial. At the level of concrete operations events appear to influence one another because they come in sequence, and sequence is mistaken for cause and effect. The child has to be able to separate himself from such apparent relationships in the immediate data before he can comprehend the nature of probability.

6. THE CONCEPT OF CORRELATION. At the stage of formal operations the child can examine two sets of measurements and conclude that there is a correlation between them and that increases in the one are related to changes in the other. At the concrete operations level the child may have an intuitive idea that there is some kind of relationship, but he has not grasped the concept of the covariation of two variables. Of course, even at the stage of formal operations he has not acquired the statistician's concept of correlation and he does not have formulae for calculating a relationship, but he does have nevertheless an intellectual grasp of the idea that two measures can vary with one other and that the relationship does not have to be perfect to be there. The development of this form of understanding is related to the development of an understanding of proportion. If an increase in one measure involves an increase in the other measure, the increases imply a proportionality in the two measures.

7. THE CONCEPT OF MULTIPLICATIVE COMPENSATION. The basic idea involved in the concept of multiplicative compensation is that a decrease in one dimension can be compensated for by an increase in another dimension. Although at an earlier age the child has learned that the volume of liquid is unchanged when it is poured from a wide beaker into a narrow, tall funnel, he has not yet realized that a reduction of one dimension (width) can be compensated for by an increase in another

dimension (height). In the same way he comes to realize that the weight of a person is related to both his height and thinness and that an increase in height can be compensated for by an increase in thinness to keep the total weight constant. Inhelder and Piaget point out that children arrive at this concept, just as they arrive at the concept of correlation, without any mathematical reasoning and without realizing that they involve the concept of proportion.

8. CONCEPTS OF CONSERVATION THAT GO BEYOND OBSERVABLE CASES. An important development at the stage of concrete operations has been the emergence of schemata that provide an understanding of conservation. However, this understanding has to do with observable cases of conservation that can be verified experimentally. Several important scientific concepts involve the idea of conservation in situations that cannot be readily observed. For example, the concept of the conservation of momentum implies that a body will remain in uniform motion unless acted on by a force. Now in actual experience bodies do not remain in uniform motion, but they all tend to slow down and stop. Also, the forces that stop them are not particularly observable. The concept of the conservation of momentum is derived very indirectly from data. Hence, because of its level of abstraction, such a concept is difficult to acquire. For this same reason the scientific concept of the conservation of momentum was developed only rather late in history.

This review of the capacities that can emerge at the formal operations level, provided by Inhelder and Piaget, is not claimed to be an exhaustive inventory of all the thinking skills that the adolescent can show. It is the beginning of such an inventory and includes the schemata that Inhelder and Piaget have observed most frequently in their research on the adolescent.

Inhelder and Piaget have some very interesting comments on the effect of the acquisition of formal operations on the entire thinking process of adolescents. They point out that the central feature of the adolescent's thinking is that he is no longer confined to thinking about that which he can concretely experience. He can think in terms of the possible as well as in terms of actuality. Armed with this new capability he no longer is constrained in thinking about society as it is, but can think about other possible forms of society that he has never experienced. Once he can do the latter he can think of building a society to his own liking and the path is opened for him to become a social reformer. It is not surprising that adolescents are caught up in social reform movements, for not only is their thinking no longer tied to immediate reality but they can imagine possible worlds that would solve most of the problems that they anticipate in life. Up to that point in life, the adolescent has had to adapt himself to the world as it is, but now he sees that perhaps he does not have to adapt but can adapt the world to his needs.

Inhelder and Piaget attempt to reduce the entire logical process of problem solving to four fundamental transformations or thinking operations that are designated as identity, negation, reciprocity, and correlativity (designated by the letters INRC). The explanation of what these involve requires a much more extended discussion than can be presented here. The interested reader is referred to Inhelder and Piaget (1958) and to Flavell (1963).

The stage of formal operations is also characterized by a rational conception of cause and effect that emerges after having undergone a long process of development during childhood. During the preoperations stage, the child conceives of everything as having been made by God or other human beings and that objects behave in the way they do because they were created to behave in that way. The child also has ideas that through his actions he can force objects to do certain things. and may mistake associations of events for causal relations. For example, a child watching a steamship sees smoke coming out from the stack. When asked what makes the ship move he says that it is the smoke. He might have said that it was the waves that made it move. If he sees any two things as occurring together, he may conclude that one causes the other.

Somewhat later, animistic notions are introduced. The ball bounces because that is what it wants to do. Children in the concrete operations stage also begin to introduce the notion that objects behave as they do because they have some inner unseen force that makes them behave in the way they do. This concept of inner forces in objects tends to replace animism and is a more advanced concept than the concept that all objects have a consciousness of their own and can make decisions for themselves.

The first genuinely physical explanation of events in the world is referred to by Piaget as *explanation by reaction of the surrounding medium* (1969, p. 263). In this kind of physical explanation, children commonly say that the clouds set the air in motion and the moving air keeps the clouds in flight. This type of explanation is applied to all kinds of objects including projectiles, moving boats, and balls flying through the air. It is a logically more advanced type of explanation than that which involves either the notion that objects have consciousness and wills of their own or that they are moved by the wills of human beings. It does recognize that physical objects act on other physical objects to produce particular effects, but it reflects little understanding of the actual nature of this interaction. As the child acquires knowledge of the nature of physical phenomena, this type of explanation leads to a more sophisticated attempt to explain the mechanical effects of one event on another. When that stage of development is reached, the child is able to explain the mechanics of the clouds being carried along by the wind. However, before completely rational explanations of mechanical phenomena are developed, the child manages to concoct some quite extraordinary fantasies concerning how physical events are caused. Children for example, may display the idea that just as all human beings are born from other human beings, so are bodies like the sun and earth born from other heavenly bodies.

From about the tenth year onward the child's explanations of physical events become more and more rational and based on the knowledge he has acquired. The ultimate step in his understanding of causality is when he arrives at explanations by logical deduction. At this stage, for example, a child can deduce that a balloon will or will not rise in the air depending on the mean density of the balloon in relation to the density of air. By such a logical deduction he can not only predict the behavior of a balloon but he can also account for the effect of updrafts and downdrafts on balloons.

Before leaving this discussion, some emphasis must be given to the fact that the research of Piaget and his associates is far less complete at the formal operations level than it is at earlier levels. For example, there are clear criteria to be applied to determine whether a child has or has not mastered classification operations, but there are virtually no criteria that can be rigidly applied to determine whether the adolescent is or is not able to perform formal operations. Ennis (1975) has written at length on this problem.

TRADITIONAL APPROACHES TO THE STUDY OF CHILD DEVELOPMENT

The work of Piaget and his associates has been the central concern of much of this chapter because of the impact it is having on the entire area of child development and learning. As a grand plan of research it is to be contrasted with the more limited approaches to research on child development that have characterized American research. Many American research workers would even doubt whether the time has come when an effective grand plan can be produced. In the meantime, it is argued, research that fits smaller plans will continue to be important. Some of this research will be considered in the next chapter.

Perhaps the previous paragraph has not indicated the full significance of traditional research approaches, which have produced results of great importance, despite the fact that they do not fit a grand plan. Another point to be made is that much of traditional research on child development investigates problems that are not included within Piaget's horizons. For example, Piaget has virtually nothing to say about the acquisition of such personality characteristics as security and aggression. Piaget's discussion of language is minimal, though he did write a book on the subject in his early years. He has little to say about the effects of various forms of intellectual and social deprivation on subsequent development. His is a model of human beings, insofar as they can be considered to be rational.

MEASUREMENT OF INTELLIGENCE WITHIN A PIAGET FRAMEWORK

Piaget originally became involved in building a model of learning and intelligence when he was in his early twenties. An important experience in his life was a two-year period spent in the laboratory originally founded by Binet and run in later years by Simon. His experience there led him to believe that the Binet model of intelligence left much to be desired. Binet, for example, assumed that at each age level the child could undertake tasks that differed only in difficulty from the tasks at higher and lower levels. Thus on the Binet test the child's vocabulary is measured at each level, with the words becoming progressively harder. Memory is measured by a series of tasks involving increasing memory span, and so forth. The test includes a few exceptions to this kind of procedure, which Piaget viewed as being fundamentally unsound.

In contrast to Binet's conceptualization of intelligence, Piaget viewed intelligence as involving fundamentally different processes at each level. The child at the formal operations level performs operations that are fundamentally different from those at the concrete operations level; the child at this level in turn can perform intellectual operations that are of a quite different character from those that the pre-operations child can perform. Although Piaget has not been interested in developing a test of intelligence, others, particularly Americans, have been. Graded series of Piaget tasks have been developed. These tasks, as Kaufman and Kaufman (1972) have shown, predict school achievement about as well as the more typical intelligence test. Piaget type tests measure a somewhat different variable from that measured by more typical intelligence tests. The predictions that can be made from them need to be more carefully studied.

SUMMARY

1. The nonreductionist position is vastly more complex than the reductionist position, for it calls for the discovery of laws at each level of complexity of behavior. These laws are arranged in a hierarchy. Thus in the development of the child, new laws appear at each level of development. The study of child development becomes the means of discovering laws at different levels. Although most of the work on the nonreductionist position has come from Piaget and his collaborators, Gagné has made some contributions to the nonreductionist position in the United States.

2. Gagné has proposed that learning can be viewed as involving a number of different levels of complexity, ranging from classical conditioning to problem solving. At each level, learning can be undertaken provided that relevant learnings at lower levels have already been undertaken. The system of categories is not based on any experimental evidence, and not on any sophisticated overall theory of behavior, but seems to be intuitively based.

3. Piaget's basic assumption is that logicians have already provided an accurate description of how the mature intellect operates. His central problem is that of discovering how the mature intellect is built, step by step, from infancy. Mature logic can be shown to call for simpler forms of logic Piaget believes he has demonstrated in the behavior of children. The logic of concrete operations is a necessary prerequisite for the logic of formal operations. A central portion of the logic of concrete operations is the logic of classificatory behavior, of which both classification and seriation are components. The period of concrete operations is preceded by a period in which the infant engages in prelogical operations and learns about the characteristics of the world.

4. Piaget does not observe children in the hope of turning up some useful observation; he is looking for particular characteristics. He views the adult as a logical-mathematical system, and mathematics is viewed as an extension of logic. Piaget sees only one way in which a logical-mathematical conception of the universe can be developed, and he studies the behavior of children to find evidence of the developmental pattern he postulates. The human intellect is a logical-mathematical system because the universe is a logical-mathematical universe that can be understood only by such an intellect. A logical-mathematical brain evolved in man as a means of mastering the complex world around him.

5. Piaget's theory of the nature of the intellect is founded both on the basis of

biology and on the basis of logic and epistemology. Although epistemology and logic are different branches of philosophy, they both contribute to our understanding of the nature of the intellect, which Piaget does not separate from the problem of the nature of man's knowledge.

6. For Piaget, the very foundations of intelligent behavior begins with the reflexes to the newborn. The reflex is viewed not as a rigid form of behavior, but quite plastic in the case of those reflexes that form the foundations of intelligence. The term schema is used to describe simple organized forms of behavior that may be modified as the infant explores his universe. Schemata have both perceptual and response components. The early schemata are referred to as motor schemata. They have no capacity for representing ideas or concepts. Later representational schemata develop. Through interactions with the environment, the basic schemata are added to or changed through the processes known as assimilation and accommodation. Assimilation has three basic functions referred to as the recognitory, the reproductive, and the generalizing. Schemata are expanded through the infant's capacity to explore the world and his capacity to invent new responses. Accommodation is shown even in the earliest behaviors involving sucking. Assimilation and accommodation are always intertwined. Through new assimilations and accommodations, the infant learns about the fundamental properties of the universe, namely, space, time, causation, and the permanence of objects.

7. Stage theory of development implies that at each stage structures develop in the intellect that permit the individual to undertake tasks that he could not undertake at an earlier stage. The stages cannot take place in any order, for the development of a logical system requires that the prerequisites of logical thinking appear in a logical order. Stage transition takes place at a time when there is disequilibrium in the intellectual system and the child has to invent new means of solving problems. The most common sign of disequilibrium is a state of doubt. Disequilibrium theory is different from homeostatic theory in that the restoration of equilibrium results in a state different from that which originally existed. The new solutions to problems that appear at each stage are not learned by reinforcement in an operant sense, but are inventions of the child. Logic is not innate, but is constructed by the developing child. This construction process can be simulated on computers.

8. The child experiments with all the fundamental properties of the universe. Thus his experiments with space lead him to learn about such matters as the trajectories of objects, falling objects, and the movements of objects in motion.

9. Piaget refers to the period of infancy as the sensorimotor period of development. Particularly important during the first year are the repetitive reactions known as circular reactions. These involve the conservation of particular experiences and the systematic attempt to produce particular experiences. Children seem to start with an intuitive understanding of space on which systematic knowledge has to be built. The extent of this basic understanding has not yet been fully determined. Visual space and auditory space and touch and movement space have to become coordinated as a single system of space.

10. The development of the concept of the permanency of objects is not entirely

clear. However, infants do have difficulties in comprehending object permanency because they do not have a means of representing objects internally and are not able to recall those representations. Memory at the infant level is memory for actions in particular situations. The experiments of Fantz show that the infant may have extensive records of experience stored within him, but this does not mean that he has the capacity to recall an object when the object is not present. Infants do recognize objects they have been exposed to before and this recognitory ability appears shortly after birth, if not at birth. Piaget seems to be correct in his belief that for the infant out of sight is out of mind. Piaget's model views the nervous system and the perceptual systems as information extracting systems. Information extraction is completely automatic.

11. Infants have the experience of being the cause of certain events, and therein lies the basis of the infant's concept of causation in the wider world.

12. Action slowly comes to be related to the prehension of objects, but at first this is limited to objects in the field of view. Only much later will the infant reach for hidden objects. Prehension has a clear pattern of development and the pattern corresponds to the development of space comprehension, of which it forms a part.

13. In the third stage of development, the infant begins to show evidence of recognizing intuitively classes of objects. Concepts are intuitive classes of objects, defined at a crude level. At the same level also primitive concepts of seriation are formed. Movements show the properties of a mathematical group, a concept that Piaget introduces at numerous different points in his system.

14. Eye contact is another important aspect of behavior that slowly develops and permits the infant and the caretaker to have a reciprocal relationship of anticipating each other's behavior.

15. Schemata become interrelated as the schemata become adapted for a variety of uses. Flexibility of schemata is essential for different schemata to be interrelated. So long as they are rigidly used, in particular situations, they cannot be interrelated.

16. The development of the concept of the permanency of objects slowly emerges over the first year of life. Probably the concept is first developed in relation to the mother or caretaker. The development of a general concept of object permanency seems to be related to the quality of the relationship of the infant to his mother.

17. The concept of time is shown in the first few months of life when the infant begins to understand that certain events signal feeding. The concept of time as an ordered series slowly emerges over the first year of life.

18. The beginning of the second year of life is notably characterized by attempts of the infant to produce novel effects, which he then studies closely. Through the effects the child produces he is able to expand his knowledge of causation.

19. In the second year of life the child provides evidence of an expanding concept of space. He understands that objects continue to have locations, even when he cannot see them. He understands that space includes different areas where different activities are undertaken. The concept of space is not of geometrical space. Search strategies show an expanded understanding of space, but his ability to search

for objects shows very limited search strategies. In the second year, the infant also develops an expanded concept of time, noting sequences of events other than those in which he is engaged.

20. In the second year one can first begin to observe discovery and experimentation, which constitute the very core of intelligent behavior. This development is possible partly because the infant has acquired some capacity to represent objects and events inside of himself in such a way that the representations can be used in the absence of the object. However, one should note that the inventions of this stage are so simple that they would not ordinarily be thought of as inventions by adults.

21. Some American psychologists have attempted to translate the unfamiliar concepts used by Piaget into concepts familiar to American psychologists. Bruner, for example, does not talk about schema, but prefers to use the more familiar concept of modules of behavior. Attempts have also been made to relate the modeling of behavior to Piagetian concepts. American psychologists have been particularly critical of Piaget's lack of recognition of the role played by the caretaker or parent in the development of behavior. Some attempt has been made to extend Piaget's concept of development by introducing social factors into it. Much of the research undertaken by Americans does support the ideas developed by Piaget.

22. Some circumstances seem to be much more favorable than others for the development of the infant. Under very unfavorable circumstances the infant's behavior manifests what has been termed the hospitalism sydrome. Efforts have been made to improve the environment of infants living under particularly unfavorable circumstances. The typical program has involved first teaching the mother how to interact with and talk to the infant. Then tasks are provided through which the infant learns to master space, time, causation, and permanence. The earlier training is started the more effective it is. Different cultures may well produce precocity in different areas, but this is not well established.

23. In the preoperations period the infant shows a transition from a memory system that is a memory for action to a representational memory system. The growth of representational memory also involves a growth in the ability to use symbols. He learns to use language for talking about objects that are not present. Images also become means of representing that which is not immediately available to the senses. The use of images becomes greatly expanded about age 7 when the child acquires some capacity to concoct images of objects he has never seen. During the preoperations period the child also acquires an immense amount of information about the characteristics of objects in the world around him. He also acquires a new concept of space as he begins to understand geometrical forms. The child at this stage interprets the world around him in a completely realistic manner, and his interpretation of the world is often different from that of the adult. He is also animistic in his interpretations of events. Piaget claims that the young child is completely egocentric but this view is disputed by Russian psychologists, who claim that Piaget's children are egocentric because they are raised in an egocentric environment.

24. The preoperations child is preparing himself for the point when he will be able to perform intellectual operations. All operations represent a transformation,

but there is also some aspect of the transformed entities that remain unchanged, that is, invariant. Thus when a ball of clay is rolled into a sausage shape the total quantity of clay remains unchanged by the operation. The preoperational child does not understand that such operations involve the unchanged nature of the quantity of clay. They also do not understand that such operations are reversible and can be made in either direction without changing the quantity involved. The child's thinking does not acquire reversibility until about age 6 or 7.

25. An important set of operations is that related to classification. The development of classificatory behavior goes through a number of stages during the preoperations period. The first stage involves the production of groups of objects strung out along a line. As the child constructs his line of objects he changes the criterion used for adding new objects. He seems unable to keep a single criterion in mind and does not have an overall plan. At a more advanced stage he builds collective objects. Unity is provided by the total meaning of the object. Still later he begins to show some understanding of the overall task of classification, but he fails to include within a category all the instances that should be placed there. He also completes the task with some objects left over that do not belong in any category. He has particular difficulty in understanding the distinction between *some* and *all*. His behavior is manipulative and fails to show evidence of a preconceived plan of action. Finally, true classificatory behavior appears.

26. Once the child has achieved classificatory behavior, he proceeds on a classification task with an overall plan. Very precise criteria can be applied to determine whether a child has mastered the basic logic of classification. Certain aspects of classification are not mastered until as late as age 10 or 11. One of the most difficult is that of the null class, a class in which there are no instances available.

27. Seriation represents an important operation closely related to that of classification and developing parallel to it. Primitive seriation, like primitive classification, is seen during the sensorimotor period. The development of number goes through a set of stages during the time of preoperations. The concept of number involves the development of a concept of quantity, invariant with respect to form, and also a concept of one-to-one relationships, which is the basis of seriation. Children learn to count before they understand the concept of number and, hence, counting is undertaken before it can be a meaningful task. Before true seriation is achieved, the child will shuffle around objects and place them in order, but the activity shows no plan or strategy. In true classification, the task is anticipatory, that is, the child anticipates the final result and goes about systematically achieving it. Children can draw a series before they are able to arrange objects in a series. The operation of seriation, like all other operations, involves reversibility. Temporal ordering is more primitive than spatial ordering and appears at an earlier stage.

28. Conservation is a component of all operations, but it has attracted widespread interest because its presence or absence can be easily demonstrated. Common arithmetical operations cannot be performed meaningfully until the child understands conservation.

29. American psychologists have been intrigued with investigating whether the

development of the ability to perform concrete operations can be accelerated by suitable training. Piaget views this as an unimportant matter, for he sees childhood as a time to be enjoyed rather than hurried through. There is some evidence that experiences provided at a time when a child is in a state of transition from one stage to the next may facilitate growth to the new stage. This is what Piaget would have expected to happen.

30. Much of the interest in classification and seriation has been related to a concern for the development of a mathematics curriculum. Piaget suspects that much of the difficulty experienced by so many children in the acquisition of mathematics is a result of the fact that they are taught computation before they understand the underlying logic of it.

31. The mature intellect shows a capacity to undertake problem solving at a formal logical level. In order to do this the child must be able to conceptualize conditions that cannot be directly observed. He must be able to set up hypotheses or theories of what is possible and then test for their validity. He must also understand the concept of being able to undertake an experiment involving the variation in a particular condition while holding other conditions constant. At the formal operations level, the child undertakes an experiment with a clear purpose in mind, and he shows a capacity to separate one variable from another. At the latter level, the child is also able to handle combinations of propositions in a systematic way. In addition, he can handle such concepts as those of proportion, equilibrium, probability, and correlation.

32. At the level of formal operations the child becomes able to handle concepts of conservation that go beyond the observable facts. The conservation of energy and the conservation of matter are concepts in this class.

33. Inhelder and Piaget have attempted to reduce all problem-solving operations at the mature level to a simple logical model involving four transformations.

34. The stage of formal operations is also characterized by the development of a mature concept of causation. The child abandons animistic interpretations of physical events, and he seeks rational explantaions of what he observes.

Chapter 7
Further Studies of Development and Learning

LANGUAGE DEVELOPMENT

The previous chapter focused on Piaget's model of the development of the intellect, emphasizing that the mature logic of the adult has to be learned through a sequence of prerequisite acquisitions. Learning to perform logical operations is acquired largely through an interaction with problems calling for those operations. A child invents classification operations by undertaking tasks that call for classification, and not by discussing classification with a teacher. The operations of logic are learned by interacting with the concrete world and are generally learned in a nonverbal context. The child learns to perform the logical operation first and only later is able to discuss it in verbal terms. Language follows the development of the various stages of the development of the logical intellect and does not precede them. Yet language plays an important part in human learning. The preschool child intuitively knows this and floods the adult with questions, not all of which reflect a thirst for knowledge. Often the child will ask a long series of "Whys" merely to prolong his contact with the adult. But aside from the occasions when the child has ulterior motives in asking questions, his questioning is an important avenue through which he accumulates information.

Thus the process of language acquisition is significant for the study of human learning, partly because language is an important tool through which learning is accomplished and partly because language itself is one of the major learning accomplishments of the child.

Although language development has long been considered to lie at the very heart of the development of intelligence, research workers have not succeeded, until recently, in discovering productive approaches to the study of this aspect of development. Early studies tended to concentrate on such matters as the growth of vocabulary or the age at which particular speech forms develop. Much of the latter research was closely tied to the study of intelligence tests in that most such tests were built around the idea that intelligence could be measured through the study of the child's verbal behavior, and particularly that component of verbal behavior which is related to problem solving. The thousands of studies that were undertaken in the first half of the century within that context have been reviewed and summarized by McCarthy (1954). The reader of this review comes away with the impression that the strictly descriptive and normative approach to language development has yielded very little despite the immense amount of effort that has been invested in it.

Since midcentury new approaches have become evident and these have come from two main sources. First, operant psychologists have attempted to formulate a conceptualization of how language is learned by the child. Second, linguists and psycholinguists who have long studied related problems have come to have impact on psychological research. Particulary notable in this respect has been the work of Chomsky (1967, 1969), not an experimentalist himself but a person who has undertaken the kind of thinking that has to be pursued before research can be conducted efficiently. From the point of view of the psychologist, the work of Chomsky is new, but he brings to his work a long tradition of the thinking of linguists with which psychologists have been largely unacquainted.

The Operant Point of View

Skinner's book on verbal learning (1957) was hailed by psychologists in its time as a prime attempt to provide a psychological conceptualization of how language is learned. The book had transitory impact but did little to stimulate research. It also received devastating criticism at the hands of linguists, notably Chomsky (1959), whose review has become the classic criticism of the operant position. Skinner's position has not been successful as a stimulant for research, as is evident from the fact that his name is rarely mentioned in modern books covering research on the learning of the native language. Nevertheless, Skinner's attempt to conceptualize the way in which language is learned continues to be revived in modified forms and the reader should be aware of the approach and of the difficulties it involves.

Skinner writes about language development with conviction, charm, and wit. These characteristics gave his book far greater acceptance than it should have had when it was first published. The work has virtually no research foundation directly related to language development, but is an attempt to explain language development in terms of operant conditioning. Language behavior is claimed to obey the same laws as any other forms of behavior. Indeed, according to the operant position, the behavior of creatures that do not have language, such as pigeons, is believed to follow precisely the same laws as are involved in the behavior of linguistically oriented human beings.

The essential position of Skinner is that speech is an instrumental form of behavior, that is, a form of behavior that is used as an instrument for achieving goals and manipulating the environment. Behaviors that are instrumental in achieving goals are referred to as operants. Verbal behaviors are referred to as verbal operants. Having taken this position, Skinner (1957) then attempts to describe the development of language in the same terms as he describes the development of any other skill.

Skinner's interpretation of verbal behavior is that it is a form of instrumental, behavior that results in the manipulation of the environment. It is shaped, he claims by the same laws of learning that shape all other forms of instrumental behavior. The child who learns to say "please" to obtain a cookie has learned an instrumental act that has been promptly reinforced in the past by his being given the desired cookie. Skinner does not introduce the notion that the word *please* has meaning for the child; rather, it is an effective form of goal-directed behavior. The word *please*, then, is a verbal operant. A thirsty 2-year-old who says "water" expects that this word will produce the desired substance and, according to Skinner, is functioning in much the same way as a rat that presses a lever in order to obtain food. That the environment is rich in the reinforcements it provides for the linguistic efforts of the child cannot be denied. Within limits, a reinforcement concept of the development of language has high plausibility, particularly in the early stages.

Skinner classifies usage of speech not in terms of categories used by grammarians, such as nouns and adjectives, but into categories representing the behavioral function that the particular usage serves. A brief discussion of two of the major categories of speech introduced by Skinner will serve to illustrate the kind of analysis of language he is attempting to make. These two categories he names the *mand* and the *tact*.

The term *mand* is derived from such words as *demand* or *command* and represents a form of speech designed to produce a change in the environment. A young child who says to his mother, "Come," is using a mand that may have the effect of bringing his mother closer to him. *Give it to me, Take it away*, and *Put that down* are all mands. Sometimes the mand may be quite subtle in the way in which it manipulates the behavior of others. The student who comes to the counselor and says, "I am just no good at anything." is probably fishing for the answer, "But that is not true; you are good at quite a few things." In this case the behavior of the student would be wrongly interpreted if the bare meanings of the words were taken at their face value. The student is almost certainly not attempting to inform the counselor of his incompetence. His statement is, rather, a verbal operant likely to produce a reassuring response from the counselor.

The *tact* is another major category of behavior within Skinner's classification system. The tact is a verbal behavior that directs attention toward an object in the environment. *What is this? What is happening here? I wonder how this works? Could this be fixed if this part were replaced?* are all tacts. The term *tact* is derived from the word *contact* and refers to a contact with the environment.

More complex forms of verbal behavior can be explained within the system by the proposal that the child can also be taught, through reinforcement, to copy behavior and to echo the speech of the adult. Such imitative verbal behavior is called *echoic* behavior. Children may thus learn to produce complex chains of words.

Skinner also assumes that there are a number of classes of subvocal behavior controlled by external stimuli. He assumes, for example, that a person reading a book makes subvocal responses that correspond to the words of the text. Skinner refers to these as *textual responses*. He makes a similar assumption about the behavior of the person who is listening to a lecture and implies that there is some internal echo of the words that are heard. Some readers do make such subvocal responses, but the evidence is clear that such responses are quite unnecessary for understanding either printed or spoken verbal material. Also, the evidence suggests that the muscular responses involved in reading silently are quite different from those involved in talking aloud.

Skinner's book on verbal behavior is filled with delightful anecdotes told in a style that reflects his own habits of thinking. He has done little to follow up on any of his speculations with research, although a little work has been undertaken by others.

A very similar, but more recent, attempt to describe the learning of language in terms similar to those of Skinner is found in a book by Staats (1968). Although this appeared more than a decade after the Skinner book, it adds no evidence to back up the speculative analysis. The Staats version also does not have the persuasive charm that characterizes the writings of Skinner and it offers an unconvincing attempt to describe the development of language in terms of instrumental and classical conditioning.

Experimentation on language change and language development from the Skinner point of view has not been forthcoming except in a very limited area. One approach to the testing of his position has been to determine whether language habits can be changed by means of reinforcements. If, for example, an individual is reinforced for beginning his sentences with "I," does he then slowly increase his usage of the word *I?* A considerable experimental literature has developed related to this problem, but the results are not entirely clear. A grunt of approval from a listener whenever a person uses the singular personal pronoun has, in most such studies produced an increase in frequency in its use, but not all studies show such an increase. The effect is generally a rather weak one, which partly accounts for the fact that it sometimes appears and sometimes does not. Those mainly interested in such studies have been clinical psychologists who, through such research, have been alerted to the fact that their grunts, smiles, and other gestures may be reinforcing aspects of the way in which the client talks about himself. An extensive research literature has developed around the problem of whether it makes a difference whether the person whose behavior is being modified is or is not aware of the significance of the reinforcing events, the ambiguities of which have been pointed out by Rosenfeld and Baer (1969). Such research has not yielded very useful results, in that research workers have encountered difficulties in identifying and defining what is meant by a subject's being aware of a reinforcer.

The Skinner position on the development of language lacked any direct experimental foundation and since the time when it was first published, it has gathered little additional support. Indeed, much of the evidence that has accumulated in recent years has led psycholinguists to take the position that instrumental conditioning and classical conditioning have almost nothing to offer in the matter of understanding the nature of behavior involving language.

The Psycholinguistic Point of View

An alternative to the operant point of view, which has come to the forefront in the last two decades, is labeled here the *psycholinguistic approach*. As an approach it draws on many fields including those of linguistics, psychology, sociology, and anthropology. It rejects completely the view that there is some simple key to the understanding of language development and the nature of language. Unlike Skinner's approach, it is thoroughly experimental and has been supported by experiments and research on language development in children. Developers are not satisfied to speculate that some quite remote principles derived mainly from the study of animals can be used to "explain" the growth of language in children. It represents a body of knowledge that has been summarized in such works as those of Deese (1970), McNeill (1970), Dale (1972), and Brown (1972, 1973).

The early babbling of infants has long intrigued psychologists but the data derived from observing babbling behavior has been difficult to fit into a theory of speech development. Operant psychologists proposed the theory that sounds are randomly emitted by the infant and that these are slowly shaped through reinforcement and extinction into words. However, the data do not fit such a theory at all. McNeill (1970), who has summarized the research on the babbling of infants, finds that it shows a definite pattern of development, but that the pattern can hardly be viewed as having been produced by reinforcement. For example, back-of-the-mouth consonants are produced first (*ge*, *koo*, *ha*) and are followed by front-of-the-mouth consonants, but the vowels follow the opposite pattern of development (front vowels *i* and *u* and later back vowels *a* and *o*). Also, during the first year, the child is able to make sounds quite easily that he has difficulty making later. For example, many 6-month-old children can roll an *r* (uvular *r*), but when they come to use language in the second year of life, they may be quite unable to use the *r* or the rolled *r* sound at all.

Early speech is a combination of front consonants and back vowels, of which the word *mama* is an example. Speech in probably all languages shows the same development in the babbling stage, and it is not surprising that the common babbles emitted by most children at about the first year become the first words. Thus, *mama* is said by children in such diverse cultures and linguistic backgrounds as the English and the Japanese. This word sound simply appears at about the time when the child is ready to use words, and it becomes tied to the mother and related figures. It is certainly not slowly shaped from related sounds.

The pattern of sound development in babbling infants appears to be fairly universal. Sounds that appear in only certain languages (such as the *th* in *th*ing) appear far later than the babbling period. Also, inflections that are of vital importance in some languages do not enter speech until relatively advanced stages. Russian, for example, is a language in which inflection is important for meaning, but Russian children do not show inflections either in their babbling or in their early stages of talking.

How children start using their first words is something of a mystery. Words may appear suddenly and be said with complete correctness. There is no evidence that shaping is a part of the process of learning these words. Children also invent words of their own for particular purposes. A word may be *expressive* as when a young child says " No!" to express disapproval. A word may state a want, as when a child says " cookie." A word may also refer to an object or action that is observed. Verbs are largely missing at this stage and speech consists almost entirely of nouns.

Comprehension has to come before acquisition, so speech acquisition cannot possibly begin by the child making the appropriate word sound in the presence of the corresponding object and then being reinforced for the performance. Since comprehension precedes the ability to produce speech one is forced to assume that children through exposure to speech manage to slowly decipher the speech code. Words then come to be understood as the code for thoughts and ideas that preceded the speech itself. This is the position of Piaget, who was one of the first to point out that thought processes typically precede the development of corresponding linguistic processes.

A theory of early language acquisition dependent on the notion of thought processes that precede verbal processes has been advanced by MacNamara (1972). The theory is that the infant begins language comprehension by determining the intent of the person speaking to him and then, by analysis, works out the relationship between the meaning of the situation and the expression that he has heard. MacNamara helps to make his point clear by comparing the task of the baby with that of a linguist attempting to decipher a language he has never before heard. The linguist would probably attempt to relate meanings he already possesses to words said by the person speaking the strange language. If the speaker of the strange language offered the linguist some eggs to eat, and then said a word, the linguist might presume that the word meant either egg or eat. Later experiences would have to determine which one was the meaning. The linguist's approach to deciphering of an unknown language always has to begin with familiar meanings. Indeed, there seems to be no other way of deciphering a language.

The infant, like the linguist, begins his analysis of an unknown language by first learning a vocabulary of nouns. In order to do this he must have some capacity to analyze sounds into components, so that he can differentiate one word from another. He must also understand that a word relates to an object, and not a property of an object. If he sees an apple and then hears the word "apple," the infant will link the word to the global entity of the apple, and not just to its roundness, color or flavor. The basic meanings of objects are apparently the objects as entireties. Particular characteristics of objects are recognized only later. The general order of language development is from words that denote objects (egg), to actions related to those objects (eat the egg), to attributes of the objects (the egg is yellow).

The young child also has to learn the essential syntax of the language. For example, he has to learn that word order is essential for understanding. Broad rules of word order are understood at a very young age. An infant of 15 months who has lost his ball may say "Ball gone," but he almost certainly will not say "Gone ball." In some languages, word order is not important so the infant, in learning such a language, does not have to learn rules related to word order. Of course, the infant does not learn rules in the sense that the linguist learns the rules of a language he is studying, for the infant cannot state the rules. Nevertheless, the rules must be entered in code somewhere in his nervous system for his behavior soon shows that it is governed by such rules.

Luria and Yudovich (1971) report an interesting case history that throws considerable light on the development of some of the social aspects of language. These investigators had come across the fact that twins sometimes show an abnormal pattern of speech development as a result of their close association, sometimes to the exclusion of other social relationships. In the particular set of twins studied, the children seem to have been left largely to their own devices. At age 2 they virtually had no language. At age 4, they made sounds that they used to communicate with one another in play situations. At age 5, they used some common words largely for communicating with adults; most of their own exchanges were in terms of words they had invented, but they were used quite sparsely. They seemed to have quite a normal understanding of the language of adults, even though they had little ability to use that language. Their play was very primitive and did not involve the making of constructions with whatever was available. When they went to kindergarten, they played together and ignored the other children.

The language of the twins, even when it involved common words, was extremely imprecise, even for children of that age. The same word might be used for many objects. The only words that had any stable meaning were those related to their activities. The primitive nature of the play activities of the twins was suspected to be a result of their primitive language skills. They were also unable to hold a conversation with an adult, partly because they were virtually unable to produce sentences and partly because they had never learned to attend closely to the speech of another. During storytelling time in kindergarten they showed no capacity to listen to a story. They had some difficulty in understanding sentences, simply because they had never been exposed to sentences.

When the twins were separated during most of the day and one of them was forced to interact with adults, the twin that interacted made great strides in her capacity to use conventional language. The speech also became more disconnected from immediate action and began to involve anticipations. The improvement was not due to speech training as such, but was due to the direct speech communication between the adult and the child. The child was also able to formulate plans and goals and could, hence, engage in much more complicated play activities than it had undertaken before. Such interaction is of central importance in speech development.

The speech of the child aged 12 to 18 months is often described as holophrastic, that is, a single word of the child represents what the adult would say in a complete sentence. For example, an infant may say the word "door" to indicate that he wants to have the door opened or that he was just hit by the door. The adult will know the meaning of the child's one-word sentence by noting the situation.

The child learns certain rules concerning which sounds can be put together into words and which cannot, but these rules are only slowly learned. While we are not aware that we have such built-in rules we can, for example, look at a word and tell whether it is an English or a foreign word, even if we do not know the word. *Tampion* might be an English word but *zuschlagschein* is not. The first of the two words includes groups of phonemes (sounds) that are common in the English language, but the latter word includes sound combinations more common to German. The fact that we can recognize the difference between words that sound like English and words that sound like another language indicates that we have a knowledge of the rules concerning sounds and sound combinations that characterize the English language. Such rules are learned over a period of many years during childhood.

The child in his second year begins to put together words into sentences. The way in which words are put together is not random but involves what is referred to as grammar. This is not grammar as the teacher of English may think of grammar but the words of the young child are strung in a way that shows rules are involved. Psycholinguists also use the term generative grammar to describe the rules concerning which sentences can be produced and which cannot in a particular language.

The speech of the child in his second year does show a certain orderliness, that is, it shows a certain kind of grammar, but it is not like adult grammar. Just a few years ago a popular theory was that children in this age bracket would compose two-word sentences consisting of a *pivot* word and an *open* word. Pivot words were believed to be few in numbers and could be combined with many different *open* words. Thus a child will make such statements as "John coat," "John egg," "John toy." According to the pivot grammar hypothesis the word John is a pivot word and the other words are open words. Brown (1973), who has reviewed the data related to this problem, concludes that no such distinction is justified. He does think that a legitimate distinction can be made between words that enter into many combinations with other words and those that enter into few combinations. Brown, however, says that the language of young children does have what he calls a pivot look to it. He point out that words ordinarily described as pivot words come from three classes as follows:

1. Words used to designate objects such as *it*, *this*, *that*, and *there*.

2. Words used to indicate that something is no more such as *all gone*, *no more*, and *'way*.

3. Words indicating recurrence such as *more* and *again*.

Words in these three classes can be combined with numerous other words and hence give the appearance that the language of the child is conforming to a pivot-open-word type of structure. The classes of words are not unique to children learning English but corresponding words have similar frequencies in the speech of children in other languages.

Another important characteristic of speech in the early stages is commonly described by saying that it is telegraphic. By this is meant that the child says perhaps only in two words what an adult would say in many words. The language of the child is much like that used by an adult in sending a telegram in which as much as possible is said with few words. For example, a child says " Ball dere." The meaning of this statement cannot be interpreted from the words alone. If the child says the words while extending his hand toward the ball, the adult will interpret the statement as " I want the ball over there " or " Give me the ball over there." On the other hand, if the child does not extend his hand and the ball belongs to another child who is playing with it, the statement is likely to be interpreted by the adult as " There is a ball over there." Psycholinguists generally take the view that there is some evidence (see Brown 1973) that such "rich" interpretations are justified. For example, in the illustration just cited, the child whose behavior is interpreted as being that of wanting the ball is likely to kick up a fuss if the adult does not make an effort to bring the child a ball. On the other hand, the child who is merely pointing out the ball will not remonstrate if he does not get it. The rich interpretation of the short sentences of the child seems to be justified in terms of the rich behavior related to the production of these sentences.

Brown (1973) considers that the first strictly grammatical feature that the child begins to acquire is word order, but to understand this point some comments on the role of word order must be made. In the English language word order is of crucial importance in showing the role that each word plays in an utterance. In many other languages word order is not of great importance. In English it makes a difference whether one says " The man moved toward the car " or " The car moved toward the man." In a language such as Latin the order of the words is immaterial to the meaning because the ending of each word indicates the role it is to have in the sentence. In contrast, the child learning English has to master the rules related to word order before he can make meaningful statements. Even when the child is making statements involving only two words, the order of the words is likely to correspond to the order that adults would place them. This does not mean that the child masters all the rules of word order as soon as he begins to string together two words. The full ability to place words in correct order is not acquired for many years. The 1-to-2-year-old child applies such simple rules as that in agent-action utterances, the agent is said before the action.

Now let us return to the discussion of telegraphic speech. This description of the young child's language is at the best crude. Brown (1973, p. 173) provides a more extended description of the meaningful two-unit utterances of the young child listing eight different classes of such statements. These are given with examples as follows:

1. Agent and action: Bill eat.
2. Action and object: Hit ball.
3. Agent and object: Billy milk.
4. Action and locative: Eat dat.
5. Entity and locative: Milk dere.
6. Possessor and possession: Billy socks.
7. Entity and attributive: Ball big.
8. Demonstrative and entity: Dat dog.

The examples given would be examples only if the situation were appropriate for all capable of other interpretations. Brown believes that these eight sets of relations between words in two-word utterances are found in all languages and cites some data to support his position. Brown also has some other rarely occurring categories of relations found in the young child's language that will not be considered further here.

Brown makes the interesting observation that the child in the early stages of learning his native language treats all components of an utterance as though they were optional and the child is not concerned with leaving out one or another component on different occasions. He behaves as though he expects to be understood, which is a realistic view for he is understood most of the time. Certain classes of words he does not use at all when he is at the two-word stage of language development. The words he does use are described by Brown as being *contentives*, that is, mainly nouns, verbs, and adjectives. He does not use *functors*, that is, prepositions, articles and auxiliaries, and the verb *to be*. Brown also points out that the 1-to-2-year-old child uses speech very much as one would expect it to be used in the sensorimotor stage with a high emphasis on action.

How the child moves from the one meaningful unit (linguists use the term *morphene* for the meaningful unit) utterance to the two-unit utterance is not at all clear. It does seem clear that the child has some comprehension of the way in which words can be put together before he first puts them together. The child does not start by combining words at random and then proceeding to retain the pairs that are reinforced. Operant psychologists have long held to the latter view but it is inconsistent with the data. Also, at more advanced levels children are not slowly reinforced for correct word arrangements. Indeed, as Dale (1972, p. 112) points out, children are consistently reinforced by their parents for incorrect forms but still manage to acquire correct speech.

A much more plausible hypothesis is that children have an innate capacity for the analysis of language that permits them to acquire some comprehension of speech before they produce much in the way of speech themselves. Certainly, the child's comprehension of speech advances much more rapidly than his ability to produce speech and speech comprehension probably has to precede speech production. What appears to be assimilated as a result of exposure to speech is not only vocabulary, but also a set of rules concerning how words are assembled into utterances.

The theory of generative grammar takes the position that the growing child discovers rules in adult speech that permit him to produce statements that conform more and more closely to those of the adult world. The idea that the nervous system is a mechanism for inventing rules and order is not unique to the area of knowledge developed by the psycholinguists, for a similar assumption is commonly made by those engaged in research on perception.

A generative grammar underlying speech is not much like the traditional grammar that has been taught in schools for generations. It is also not a set of rules taught to the child, but a set of rules he invents. He does not know the rules in the sense in which an adult knows the rules of the highway and can describe them to a foreigner. They are rules that govern the behavior of the child and represent lawfulness of his behavior. A sentence that is perfectly correct from the point of view of traditional English grammar may be quite unacceptable in terms of the underlying generative grammar. Chomsky (1969) cites such a sentence: "For him to understand this sentence is difficult" (p. 410). The nature of the underlying generative grammar has not been worked out at this time, though many of its characteristics at different stages of development have been determined.

Chomsky implies that before a sentence is enunciated, a complete program for its production is internally formulated. A sentence is not produced by each word being the stimulus for the next word, as traditional learning theorists would want us to believe. A sentence is produced much as a complex motor skill act is produced, as a whole, and not as a chain of elements with each element in the act triggering the next element.

The main issues of controversy related to the development of language are also the central issues in other areas of psychology: they pertain to the nature of human beings. To what extent are human beings to be regarded as passive creatures whose behavior is molded by circumstances in the environment and to what extent are they active organizers of and experimenters in the use of the information that the environment provides. Human beings to some extent are probably both of these, but psychologists of the past have almost certainly grossly underestimated the extent to which they are active organizing agents.

In the second stage of language development described by Brown, the mean length of the utterance is extended to within the range of 2.00 to 2.50 morphemes. Brown does not tie this stage to an age range since children differ in the age at which particular forms of speech are used, but the implication is that this stage takes place mainly in the 2-year-old. The speech that develops is tied to the child's expanding comprehension of the world and fits well with what Piaget has to say about conceptual development. For example, the child's conception of time has expanded from what it was at the sensorimotor stage and, hence, one finds an expanded use of time concepts in the child's language. In this second stage of speech development the child begins to use the past tense and the present progressive (Man coming in). The use of articles indicates a distinction between the specific and the nonspecific that is also made at this stage. A point of interest to note is that, although children learning English as their mother tongue learn to make a distinction between the use of *a* and *the* by the end of the third year, Japanese adults acquiring English rarely learn to make the distinction even after many years of experience. The Japanese language, of course, does not use articles.

Brown lists fourteen forms of speech that come to be used at the second stage. Again, one cannot attribute learning to reinforcement because of the well-established fact that parents reinforce the more primitive forms of speech the child uses and show no signs of shaping the speech of the child.

The difference in sentence length at different ages is of interest. An important factor in limiting the length of a sentence is the span of attention. Young children cannot generate very long utterances because they do not have the capacity of remembering the first part of the utterance while speaking the last part. For this reason, the utterance of the 2-year-old generally involves only one or two words. Adults also limit the length of their utterances. One could build a grammatical sentence using a thousand words, but it would be quite unintelligible. One simply cannot keep track of the information in such a long utterance. Before all the dependent clauses have been said, the listener or speaker has forgotten what they were dependent on. For this reason, intelligible speech generally involves quite short sentences.

The study of the acquisition of language has focused on the first five years of life, but language development is not completed during that time. Palermo and Molfese (1972) have pointed out that many important aspects of language are not fully developed until much later. Phonological development—that is, the correct production of speech sounds—continues until about age 8. Younger children do not seem able to analyze the sound components of words and thus cannot reconstruct in their own speech the sounds they have heard. Accurate perception has to develop before accurate articulation of speech can occur. In addition, some syntactical features cannot occur early because the child lacks the necessary intellectual development to understand what the features mean. For example, the use of the connective *or* implies that the user understands that if he makes two statements connected by the word *or* if one is true then the other will be false and vice versa. A child who says "I left my ball in the house or in the car" understands that the ball cannot be both in the car and in the house and that if it is in the house it is not in the car. The use of this syntactical form has an intellectual prerequisite, as Piaget implies. Again, the use of the plural form requires that the child have at least a primitive concept of number. The use of sentences beginning with "If" imply that the user can think in terms of hypothetical situations and a form of thought wholly absent in the case of the 4-year-old.

The increasing complexity of rules used to generate utterances as language develops is also accompanied by another change in language, in which Piaget has been particularly interested. This is the change from the use of language to refer to highly concrete and immediate situations to the use of language to refer to situations not immediately present or to abstract situations. Deese point out that language does not always show the complete development from the simple descriptive language of the young child to the complex abstract statements of the adult. Deese (1970) points to evidence, that others question, indicating that those brought up in underprivileged conditions may continue throughout their lives to speak a dialect resembling more the language of the child than that of the educated adult.

American psychologists have commonly taken the position that human intellectual development is closely tied to language development. Piaget has taken issue with this position because he finds that logical reasoning always seems to precede the ability to explain verbally how a problem is solved. Piaget recognizes that the language-deficient child may be penalized within most educational systems, but, since the development of the logic of thought has little to do with formal education, the child's development in the logical sphere should not be hindered. Of course, Piaget does contend that the stage of formal operations involves to a great degree verbal reasoning and at that level of development the language deficient child may have difficulty in undertaking some logical operations that are highly dependent on verbal processes.

This relationship of logical thought to verbal development has been studied through investigations of deaf children. Such children have in most cases only minimal understanding of language and even less ability to use it. In school they fall behind their classmates and quickly become severely educationally retarded. Although they obviously cannot acquire the information and skills that normal children acquire, the question remains whether they have the same capacity as normal children to think logically. Furth (1971, 1973) has worked extensively in this area, conducting studies of his own and bringing together the information gathered by others. Although he finds that deaf children are severely retarded in linguistic skills, their retardation on reasoning tasks is slight and no more than can be accounted for by the difficulty of administering a test. Bornstein and Roy (1973) took issue with Furth's thesis, claiming that there is no solid evidence that deaf children are language deficient, but Furth (1973) attempted to refute their argument. Furth's position is probably fairly solid, for those who work with the deaf agree that language deficiency is not so slight that it could be a matter of opinion, but overwhelming. This writer takes the position that the evidence from deaf children generally supports Piaget's position that thinking up to and through the concrete operations period is not dependent on verbal processes.

Nevertheless, language factors play an important role in learning in areas involving the reasoning operation described by Piaget. One may well learn the nature of seriation without recourse to verbalization, but many of the applications of seriation involve language. The typical word problem in grade school mathematics requires that the child be able to read and understand language. The problem is communicated through a verbal medium and proficiency in that medium is essential for understanding the problem. Primitive man may well have been able to solve problems of seriation without recourse to verbalization. He may have been able, for example, to arrange his arrows according to weight so that he could readily pick the arrow most suitable for killing the game he was stalking. This is a very different matter from reading a problem in a book and then writing out the solution. The evidence summarized by Aiken (1972) shows quite clearly the enormously important part that verbal transactions play in typical problem-solving activities in school. Aiken brings together substantial evidence that reading skill is related in a vital way to the learning of mathematics in school. Furthermore, vocabulary plays a role. Some writers take the position that the vocabulary and syntax of mathematics texts are unnecessarily complicated and that the progress of many children is retarded by this heavy emphasis on the verbal factor. There is evidence that training in the vocabulary and the syntax of mathematical statements helps some children. The English of mathematics is different from the English of other school subjects.

Mathematics teaching probably does not have to be loaded with a language factor. The trend toward teaching mathematics through handling concrete problems logically is a trend supported by the work of Piaget. There is no reason why mathematics should be a tongue-twisting exercise. A part of the problem of the oververbalization of mathematics seems to stem from the verbosity of mathematics teachers (see Aiken, 1972).

These issues related to the teaching of mathematics are important because the evidence indicates that children are introduced to mathematical terms before they are capable of understanding the underlying concepts. The result is that children learn at an early stage that mathematics is something they do not understand. Once they are set in this attitude, they are on the way to becoming academic failures in this area.

LANGUAGE ACQUISITION AND THE ENVIRONMENT

The general description of language development given to this point leaves much to be desired, particularly in view of the fact that it tells little about the conditions of learning that facilitate or retard acquisition. Only certain broad facts have been established in this regard. For example, there can be no doubt that children from a poor background have poorer mastery of English, as it is used in education, than children from higher socioeconomic levels. Foster and Newman (1971) point out that ghetto children not only have a smaller vocabulary than children from more prosperous areas but they also use words with special meanings in their dialect. Whether the language skills of the ghetto children are actually inferior, or just different, is a matter of controversy. Some argue that the matter is a difference of language, and not a difference in the ability to use language. However, Baldwin et al. (1971) found that ghetto children had more difficulty in communicating a task to another child than did the suburban children.

A single study by Quay (1972) showed that when the Stanford-Binet test was administered to one group of black children in standard English and to another in black dialect, there were no significant differences in mean performance. The impression is that the black children understand standard English, even though they do not use it. The study also suggests that black dialect is a suitable language for test administration, without indicating what the limitations of the dialect are.

Research in this area is very limited and quite inconclusive. Many dialects are not very useful for particular purposes. For example, Pidgin English, an English dialect spoken through much of the world, is a very limited language both in vocabulary and in grammatical form. It evolved as a kind of international language for handling common day-to-day situations that do not require a high degree of precision. Many dialects evolve for a specific purpose. The language of the bureaucrats in Washington is a kind of dialect particularly suited to the handling of government business. It has its own vocabulary and a grammar borrowed mostly from the field of law. Bureaucratese is hardly suitable for discussing scientific and technical matters, but within the area in which it has developed it is valuable. Presumably, black English, like all other dialects, has its virtues and its limitations.

There is also a difference in the verbal behavior of mothers in different social classes. At higher socioeconomic levels mothers talk more to their children and expand the utterances that children make. Such a mother who hears her child say " Go " meaning to go for a walk will say to the child " Go for a walk." The mother has expanded the single-word utterance of her child. Dale (1971) points out that such mothers expand as many as 30 per cent of the utterances of their children. Although one suspects that the expansion of the utterances of children may facilitate language development, there is little *direct* evidence to indicate that this is an important factor.

There is no doubt that mothers modify their speech in talking to their infants (Snow, 1972) and in ways that are generally favorable for the infant. The mother's speech in relation to her infant is simpler, more redundant, and less confusing than when she is talking to adults.

LANGUAGE LEARNING—SOME KEY ISSUES

The acquisition of the first language represents the development of one of the most important tools for learning, but the learning of the language represents a learning problem in itself. No one would claim that a full account can be given concerning how language is acquired in the human being. On the one hand, there are those who believe that language learning can be described in terms of the simple reinforcement principle, though evidence is almost wholly absent from studies of children. The only evidence to support the reinforcement interpretation of language learning comes from teaching chimpanzees sign language. The chimpanzees do learn a simple language through reinforcement, but only after an interminable amount of work with them. Compared with the child, the chimpanzee is a very slow learner of language and demonstrates none of the spontaneous learning shown by the young child. It is all too easy to watch the films of chimpanzee language usage and believe that one is watching a performance similar to that of the young child, but there is still a place for some skepticism, as Brown brings out (1973). Some would even express the opinion that the talking of the chimpanzees is no more genuine than the ability of the famous horse, Glücke Hans, who gave public performances demonstrating his ability to solve mathematical problems. Glücke Hans was clever, but what he had learned was to respond to slight cues given him by his master. Undoubtedly the talking chimpanzees' performance is to some degree contaminated by such an artifact, but their performance is more than an artifact. They do learn to make signs, and perhaps even to give very short strings of signs. They also learn to do this by a reinforcement procedure.

In contrast to the chimpanzee, the speech of children is acquired with great rapidity and there is no evidence that reinforcement plays more than a trivial role. In the child, the understanding of speech precedes the use of speech, but the chimpanzee learns to understand language through his own performance. The language of the child seems to be learned largely through the child's native ability to analyze the sound patterns he hears and to search for meaning related to them. Exposure to speech seems to be the essential factor in learning to understand speech, and a child may acquire very substantial understanding of speech from mere exposure. There can be no doubt that the brain is an information-analyzing mechanism, as will become evident in a later chapter on perception. One of the basic tasks of the information analysis capacity of the brain is to analyze speech sounds and to relate them to actions.

The concept of information analysis is not enough to account for language development in the child. Whenever one undertakes information analysis it is always in terms of a plan or system. A chemist analyzes an unknown compound in terms of the established system of elements. A physicist analyzes changes in motion in terms of forces and directions. A child has to analyze the speech sounds he hears in terms of some system. Two views are held concerning the nature of that system. One view proposed by Chomsky is that all children throughout the world are endowed with a system of analyzing speech sounds, which he terms a universal grammar. All languages have some similarity of structure and such similarity can be ascribed to the existence of a universal grammar allegedly built into every child.

A great amount of evidence has been brought together by Lenneberg (1969), showing that the general pattern of speech development is surprisingly little affected in its *early stages* by gross deprivations. The speech development of children of deaf parents who do not speak, for example, is remarkably similar to that of children raised under more normal circumstances. Lenneberg also points out that children in an institution in which their main exposure to speech was a television set that was on all day showed, again, a typical pattern of development. Lenneberg argues that it is mere exposure to the language rather than the reinforcements provided by the adult world that stimulates the early stages of speech development. The language the children are exposed to determines the language they will speak, but he argues that they are endowed with a nervous system that permits them to analyze the language they hear, to find structures in it, and to experiment with structures of their own. Such a theory goes far beyond the facts.

An alternative is suggested by Piaget, who rejects the notion of a universal grammar. Piaget suggests that the child constructs a structure for language, much as he constructs logical structures, discovering for himself classification systems and other logical operations.

Any theory of language has to account for the enormous amount of language that a child learns in a relatively short span of time and with, often, virtually no formal instruction. Other complex skills requiring the assimilation of enormous amounts of information call for prolonged and systematic training and an immense amount of organized practice. For example, the learning of the Morse code requires a year's full-time training on the part of the adult, with long hours of daily practice at graduated speeds, for the acquisition of even minimal skills. Yet the child in his second year of life learns to use speech and acquires a vocabulary of hundreds of words without any formal training or systematic practice. The child has extraordinary capacity for learning language, perhaps more extraordinary than any other capacity.

LEARNING CONDITIONS IN THE HOME

Intellectual Outcomes

The most significant studies in intellectual outcomes involve the long-term follow-up of infants and very young children whose parents have been studied. Such studies require that the behavior of the children be systematically followed over several decades since the effects of parental behavior on child behavior are often not immediately apparent. Three important longitudinal studies have been undertaken in this century, and the procedures involved in these studies have been summarized by Eichorn (1973).

Nancy Bailey initiated the Berkeley Growth Study in 1928 with 61 infants ranging from birth to 15 months of age. Close track has been kept of these infants who have been studied through their thirty-sixth year and who will be studied further in the future. In 1929, Jean McFarlane began a study, known as the Guidance Study, of 248 children born in the first half of 1928. The third study, the Oakland Growth Study, also known as the Adolescent Growth Study, was initiated by Harold Jones and Herbert Stolz in 1931 and involved the follow-up of 212 children in the fifth and sixth grades. In all of these studies a strong effort has been made to keep track of the original children and to collect data on them as they move through life. Data are still being collected on all those survivors of the original sample who can be located. Freeberg and Payne (1967) have summarized the more important findings through the 1960s and a more recent review by Eichorn (1973) systematically compares the three studies on the basis of the most recent data available. Much of the information provided has to do with relating conditions in the home to subsequent intellectual development, that is, with the matter of the conditions under which children become effective learners and problem solvers.

The long-term data from these studies has focused on factors related to intellectual development, measured by intelligence tests, and achievement and success, measured in a variety of ways. A first question to be answered in the interpretation of such data is the extent to which intelligence tests measure a stable variable over the life span. The answer to this question is not simple. Infant intelligence scales show an overall low prediction of later scores on later tests, with one exception. Measures of a vocalization factor in infancy taken at about the last half of the first year were highly predictive for girls even to the age of 26. The relationships are less when predictions are made of childhood intelligence quotients. A verbal factor is the most predictive and consistent aspect of behavior when one compares performance in the preschool years with later performance, even though there is considerable instability in the intelligence quotient during the childhood years. Eichorn, summarizing the changes reported in intelligence quotients during childhood found in the three studies, comes up with some startling figures. In the Bayley study, the mean change in intelligence quotient from ages 6 to 9 was 12 points, with a fourth of the children changing 17 points or more. The McFarlane data provided even more striking changes with 35 per cent of the children changing 20 or more points from ages 6 to 18. Some children showed a steady increase and others a steady decline; also, some children showed an abrupt change and others were essentially stable. However, as adolescence approaches the intelligence quotient tends to stabilize but continues to show some increase into the thirties.

Conditions in the home play an important role in determining the level of the intelligence quotient, but studies have come up with the interesting finding that the effects become progressively more apparent as the child grows older. A relationship between a characteristic of the home and the level of development of the child may be negligible at age 2, but substantial at age 26. For example, the extent to which the home has play facilities when the infant is 21 months shows little relationship to early childhood intelligence quotients, but the relationship becomes increasingly positive through preadolescence and continues to be substantial in adulthood. Although the better educated parents provide better play facilities than the less educated, a part of the relationship is a result of the play facilities themselves. The data suggest that the sponteneous interaction of the children with the toys and facilities is an important factor in intellectual development. The finding is important, particularly in view of the attitudes of so many parents that toys are merely devices for keeping the child occupied.

A particularly important characteristic of the home is upward mobility. Gain in intelligence quotient is related to socioeconomic status, but the gain is greatest in the case of upwardly mobile families.

Gains in intelligence quotient are associated with amount and quality of schooling. Those attending kindergarten showed gains in intelligence quotient, but the gains were immediate and seem to have been relatively transitory. Generally, those adults who had had the most education showed the greatest gains in intelligence quotient, and attendance at high-ranking universities rather than junior colleges was particularly favorable to gain.

Perhaps no study has shown more dramatically the effects of schooling on measures of intelligence than that conducted on the children in the Prince Edward County, Virginia, school district where the schools were closed for several years (see Green et al., 1964). After a few years without school, children of elementary-school age were unable to hold a pencil to write and could not follow simple directions. These children had intelligence quotients 15 to 30 points lower than similar children in neighboring counties. The schools do have great impact on the development of intelligence as it is defined by tests. Although an educated middle class might be able to make some provision for the education of their children in the home, a group of uneducated economically disadvantaged parents might be quite unable to help their children in this respect. The children in Prince Edward County probably obtained little educational help from their homes.

Even exposure to nursery school seems to produce significant increments in intelligence quotients. Goulet, Williams, and Hay (1974) report one such study and cite others. Those who write in this area seem unaware of the fact that similar studies were conducted during the 1930s with similar results. The earlier studies, when they were first published, were brushed aside or even ridiculed because they violated what was then viewed as the sanctity of the intelligence quotient.

Parental personality makes a contribution to the development of the intellect, particularly in the case of boys. After age 4, loving behavior, in contrast to hostile behavior, is related to intellectual development in the case of boys. Girls do not show such a consistent relationship. During the school years, concern for achievement on the part of the mother is related to boys' intelligence quotients, but the relationship disappears after sons reach age 36. The sons' intelligence quotients were higher in those cases where there was a close mother-son relationship but the daughters' test scores were more related to the friendliness of the relationship to their fathers. There seem to be sex differences in the parental relationships that are important, but able, concerned parents make their contribution to intellectual development. An active and stimulating mother has a particularly significant role.

Many relationships were found that could not have been readily predicted. Mothers who were worrisome, tense, and unstable had sons who showed superior mental development. One of the most striking relationships was found between the mother's level of energy and the children's mental test scores. Honzik (1967) points out that this finding suggests that the energetic mothers are those who stimulate their children early in infancy and that such stimulation has been found in subhuman species to foster the development of the higher levels of the nervous system. In contrast, the father's energy level was negatively related to the intellectual level in the case of both boys and girls. Perhaps fathers may tend to direct their energies to activities outside the home, from which the children do not directly benefit. Mothers who worry and are concerned are also probably those who stimulate their children intellectually through frequent attention to them.

Unrelated to the boys' intellectual development are such factors as the father's irritability, his reaction to conflict, and his energy level. The father probably does not have sufficient contact with his children for his energy level to have the same effect as that of the mother. Daughters are affected little intellectually by the father's energy level, and they are also unaffected by the father's stability, worrisomeness and self-confidence.

A particularly important finding is that the mother's concern for educational achievement is considerably related to the intelligence test scores of both boys and girls and particularly the boys. Of interest is the fact that concern for achievement on the part of the parent of the opposite sex is of greater importance than the concern of the parent of the same sex. The parent-child relationship expressed by these findings is probably complex. Other evidence, reviewed in the chapter on motivation, suggests that it has to do with the acquisition of motives. The father's satisfaction with his work situation seems to have some effect on the test scores of his son. This is also probably a motivating effect. The father who feels he is getting nowhere may well have a son who believes that striving to achieve is hardly worthwhile.

Relationships involving affection within the home are correlated with intelligence test scores, and, in fact, provide some of the highest correlations found. The closeness of the mother to the son is of particular importance and has a striking effect on the development of verbal intelligence. This finding fits well with data derived from earlier studies. The girl's mental development does not seem to be influenced in the same way and seems to be more related to the extent to which the parents have a compatible relationship. Close mother-daughter relationships, over the long haul of the growing period, make for a lowered rather than a raised level of intellectual development.

Honzik attempts to put together a picture of the environment that produces the most favorable condition for intellectual and academic achievement. Her conclusion is that it is of paramount importance for the boy to have a warm and close relationship with the mother and then, later, opportunity to identify with a father who is both successful and concerned about his son's success. In the case of the girl, optimum conditions are found when the father has a friendly relationship with his daughter and a compatible relationship to the mother. Parental agreement and lack of conflict about discipline and cultural standards is also important. The early environmental conditions that accelerate development are less clear in the case of girls than they are in the case of boys.

The findings of studies concerned with the development of intelligence cannot be readily translated into what is known about learning. The effect of vigorous and concerned interaction of the mother in the early years of life may be to provide many reinforcements for a boy's attempts to master his environment, but this is unlikely to be the whole story. At least as important a factor is that this interaction constantly brings the child into contact with new aspects of his environment, and this interaction can have two effects. One effect is the development of the perceptual system, as Hebb (1972) has postulated in his theory of early learning. Hebb implies that mere frequent exposure to numerous aspects of the environment will result in the development of mechanisms in the child's brain that permit accurate perception of his environment. Stimulation also has another consequence. It has an energizing effect on behavior. There is certainly much evidence that children raised in bleak environments, with little to stimulate them, show retarded development. The mother who is concerned with the achievement of her child and who interacts warmly with him provides just the reverse kind of environment.

The Honzik study is of particular interest because it is concerned with intellectual development as it is measured by the broad objective measures provided by intelligence tests. There are also other behaviors that can be considered to represent competencies in dealing with the environment. Some of these were studied in a research by Baumrind and Black (1967). Examples of such characteristics are independence, assertiveness, cooperaiveness, and friendliness. Baumrind and Black studied the relationship of the characteristics of the family to the development of these and other characteristics in 107 preschool children. Because the average age of these children was only 47 months and because relationship's between children's characteristics have not fully emerged by that age, it is quite surprising that some relationships were found.

Warmth was not found to be an important factor in predicting the aspects of competence studied, although there was a weak relationship between the warmth of the parental behavior and the degree of independence shown by the boys. This fits with the data provided by Honzik. An interesting finding is that punitiveness on the part of the parents was not found to be associated with fearful and compliant behavior. Oddly enough, punitive behavior on the part of the father was associated with domineering behavior in the girls. In the case of the boys, punitive behavior of the parents was associated with the child's being described as unlikeable.

Baumrind and Black found that consistent paternal discipline was associated with independence and assertiveness in boys and with affiliativeness in girls. When the children were studied in a school setting, consistent discipline in the home was associated with what they describe as "constructive nonconformity" in the boys and with "well-socialized, friendly, and dependable" behavior in the girls. Parental willingness to be reasonable and to listen to the child was also associated with independence in the boys and stability in the girls.

Finally, the study showed that restrictiveness on the part of the parent and an inability to permit independent behavior was accompanied by lack of imaginative behavior in the child and also a tendency to be stereotyped in thinking.

This study, like the Honzik study, brings out the fact that intellectual skills are developed or restricted by the characteristics of the home in which the child is raised. Even in the homes of above average middleclass children, the characteristics of the home can make very large differences in the extent to which children develop competence in handling the problems of their environment.

Personality Outcomes

In the last decade some information has been accumulated concerning the relationship of child-rearing practices and certain aspects of social learning. The outstanding study in this area is one conducted by Sears, Maccoby, and Levin (1957), which involved the child-rearing practices of 379 mothers. Child-rearing practices are defined as dimensions of maternal behavior.

In the Sears et al. study, the mothers carefully studied came from two suburban towns in a large metropolitan area of New England. The group was derived from a complete range of social classes, and in this respect must be considered highly representative of a New England population of mothers. The median age of the group was 33.6 years. Both ends of the education continuum were well represented, with 22 per cent having completed college and 14 per cent never having completed high school. The group also represented a wide range of income.

Data were collected concerning the child-rearing practices of this group of mothers by means of extended interviews that had been carefully planned. The aspects of the mothers' behavior studied were those considered to be most influential with respect to the child. For this reason, careful inquiries were made into such matters as disciplinary measures, permissiveness, severity of training, temperamental qualities of the mother, and attempts to develop more mature behavior. Much of the study is descriptive and provides a record of the child-rearing practices of a group of New England mothers at midcentury. Studies of child-rearing practices conducted fifty years from now will undoubtedly compare the data with that collected by Sears et al. The strictly descriptive aspects of this study are not related to the topic at hand, and therefore will not be reviewed here. We are concerned here with the ways in which these characteristics group themselves and the relationship of these groups of behavior to aspects of the learning process.

Sears et al. subjected their data to a factor analysis in order to determine the way in which the characteristics of child-rearing practices grouped themselves. Five major groupings were found, which are described as follows:

PERMISSIVENESS-STRICTNESS. The permissiveness-strictness characteristic emerged from the study as the most all-pervasive of those studied. At one end of the scale are mothers who imposed strong restrictions on children with respect to play in the house and showed high demands for good table manners, quietness, orderliness, and neatness, low permissiveness with respect to aggression toward parents, siblings, and other children, as well as low permissiveness with respect to sex behavior. The relationship of this aspect of parental behavior to the behavior of the child brings out the interesting finding that permissiveness concerning aggression results in a high level of aggressive behavior on the part of the child. The implication is that such behavior is not learned by reinforcement but has to be controlled by some degree of suppression. This fits well the findings of Lebo and Lebo (1957), who found that children who expressed most aggression in their classrooms also expressed the most in a free-play situation conducted by a therapist. They did *not* find that those who failed to express aggression in daily life tended to show aggression in play therapy. Aggression, it appears, can be either generally expressed or generally absent. The same effect is not evidenced in the case of dependency relationships. A permissive attitude toward dependency does not seem to encourage dependency.

GENERAL FAMILY ADJUSTMENT. The general family adjustment characteristic is the extent to which the mother manifested such attributes as high esteem for herself and her spouse, was happy about becoming pregnant, enjoyed interaction with her baby, and was satisfied with her present life situation. Although this has commonly been considered to represent one of the most important conditions related to the development of desirable attributes of personality, the study provides virtually no data concerning its relationship to the later characteristics of the child.

WARMTH OF MOTHER-CHILD RELATIONSHIP. The warmth of the mother-child relationship appeared to have an all-pervasive effect on the behavior of the child. Maternal coldness was associated with difficulties related to the negative functions such as feeding and bladder control, and emotional difficulties related to these functions. In addition, maternal coldness was associated with slowness in the development of a conscience. The authors of the study suggest that the warm mother offers more reinforcements than the cold mother, and hence provides a more favorable condition for many of the learnings that must take place in the first few years of childhood.

RESPONSIBLE CHILD-TRAINING ORIENTATION. The high end of the responsible child-training orientation scale describes a mother who takes her child-rearing duties with great seriousness and feels the weight of her responsibilities. Little information is given concerning the relationship of this factor to child behavior.

AGGRESSIVENESS AND PUNITIVENESS. The mother who is high in aggressiveness and punitiveness expects the child to be aggressive toward other children, but administers severe punishment if the child should show aggression against the parent. The high end of this scale identifies a mother who has a high level of aggression, but who will not tolerate aggression toward herself. The researchers concluded that a high level of punitiveness is quite ineffective in training, a conclusion that is consistent with data reported in other parts of this book. They also point out that their data support the position that punishment does little to eliminate undesirable behavior. Severe physical punishment was associated with feeding problems and with aggression in the home. Nevertheless, some caution is necessary in drawing conclusions from this aspect of the study. Sears and his associates conclude that under certain conditions punishment may be effective, but the nature of these conditions has not yet been determined.

A follow-up of the Sears et al. study was conducted years later by Sears (1970), who administered a series of self-concept scales to 84 girls and 75 boys whose mothers had been interviewed. Good self-concepts were found to be associated with both maternal and paternal warmth. Also those with the most desirable self-concepts came from the smaller families and tended to have an early position in the order of birth. Some differences were found between the relationships of boys and girls to their home background. In the case of boys *only*, a good self-concept was associated with low father dominance in the father-mother relationship.

Other cultures provide different contrasts in child-rearing practices that may add to an understanding of early training conditions to adult personality. A particularly striking contrast is presented in Israel, where the child-rearing practices with children raised in the kibbutz can be contrasted with those of the more typical family situation. Rabin (1965) compared the behavior of children and young adults who had been raised in each of these two situations.

Each kibbutz is a voluntary organization of individuals who have come together to pool their energies and resources, to live in a state of economic collectivism, and to delegate to the group as a whole the main responsibilities of child-rearing. In such a collective, the mother has continuous contact with the infant only during the first four months; after that, the contacts are steadily reduced until daily contacts between parent and child are restricted to one or two hours, when the parents visit the child raising houses and interact with the child. The typical child-rearing practices of the parents are taken over by the *metapelet*, translated as "one who takes care of." Thus in infancy and early childhood, those raised in the kibbutz come into contact with many adults who are responsible for their welfare, including the biological mother, the metapelet, the people who relieve the metapelet at various times during the day, the night watchman, and perhaps others, too; and the child must compete with many other children of similar age for the services and attention of these adults. The kibbutz child-rearing situation appears to provide a socially more complex environment than does the typical family situation; and in the early years the kibbutz situation may be intellectually more deprived. There are also lessened opportunities for intense identification with single adult figures.

The complexity of the early environment in the kibbutz appears to have a retarding effect during the first few years. The children are not only less intellectually developed than are the family-reared children, but they also show a greater frequency of emotional problems such as are reflected in tantrums. Nevertheless, such problems are short-lived, for the difficulties of early life are soon overcome and a benign educational environment produces effective educational development. The kibbutz child with his relationships to many adults shows few strong attachments and also fewer conflicts with adult figures, particularly during adolescence. The conflicts of the teen-age period are largely absent because the youngster does not have to struggle for independence and for personal identity—he has already gained these at a much earlier age.

The study suggests that early emotional problems do not necessarily forewarn of subsequent emotional problems at a later age. Apparently they do not represent learned patterns of responding, but rather they reflect states of disorganization, which are replaced later by more adequate patterns of responding. The data also suggest that an intellectually barren infancy does not do irreparable damage that a stimulating environment in the later years cannot remedy.

A striking feature of the outcome of the child-rearing practices of the kibbutz is that the children develop almost no intellectual aspirations. Few ever go on to college, although such a possibility is open to them. Indeed, the kibbutz may often have to bring in from the outside some of the technical skills needed because their own youth have little interest in higher education. The kibbutz-reared child may fail to develop any drive to achieve because he lacks a close relationship to a mother deeply concerned about her child's achievement, or a relationship to a father who is enjoying success. The lack of such relationships removes from the kibbutz child's environment some of the most important sources of achievement motivation. Thus the children develop in a manner that makes for good social adjustment in a static and nonprogressive society.

LONG-TERM EFFECTS OF DEPRIVED AND ENRICHED ENVIRONMENTS ON INTELLECTUAL GROWTH AND LEARNING

A problem of great interest is the extent to which various forms of deprivation during infancy result in later intellectual deficits. Studies in this area have a long history, beginning with studies in the 1950s of deprivation in animals, and the classic observations made by Spitz on foundling home babies made a few years years earlier. Spitz (1945) described a collection of behavioral symptoms in found-ling home infants. He named these symptoms collectively *hospitalism*. The infants were observed to be passive and nonresponsive and as they developed became progressively more backward in perceptual and motor skills. Spitz claimed that the failure of the infants' behavior to be either adequately energized or developed resulted from the confinement of these infants to cots, which he saw as resembling the cells of penal institutions. He believed that a major factor in the lack of develop-ment of the infants was the lack of human contacts, and particularly the lack of a partner in the form of a mother. As infants developed they began to show behavior characteristic of patients in psychiatric institutions. Normal play behavior seemed to be lacking, an absence supposedly attributable to the fact that play generally develops in the context of the mother-infant relationship. The significance of Spitz's observations were not appreciated for at least a decade after they were made. Indeed, not until experiments had been undertaken on depriving infant primates of their normal environment were the Spitz findings recognized as important.

Classic research on this problem with subhuman primates was began in the mid-1940s with significant results. A long series of studies by Harlow and Harlow (cited by Rutter) show that isolation-reared rhesus monkeys show a total inability to relate to their species in adulthood, even to the point of being unable to engage in so basic a form of behavior as reproductive activity. Such animals also show a sitting-and-rocking form of behavior very much like that manifested by many institutionalized mental patients. However, even with animals whose conditions of rearing can be carefully controlled, there are often questions raised concerning the conditions that produce particular effects. A monkey raised in social isolation is also in a less intellectually stimulating environment than one raised under con-ditions that permit the animal to observe the activities of other monkeys manipu-lating objects. In addition, particularly striking were the studies showing that absence of social stimulation during the infancy of primates produced irreparable harm in both the intellectual and social spheres of development. Stone, Smith, and Murphy (1973b), who have reviewed these studies, point out that the evidence of extensive behavioral damage is overwhelming. They also point out that although the damage in primates produced by social isolation is irreversible after 6 to 12 months, human beings may have greater capacity for compensating for social deprivations. Even though human beings deprived of mothering relationships may suffer from such deprivation, there is the possibility that relationships with other children may become the vehicle for learning what they failed to learn in a mother-infant relationship. Most psychologists have learned to be extremely cautious in generalizing from what is found with one species to another species. However, there is some parallel between what has been found in deprivation studies with subhuman primates and what has been reported with human babies. The result of maternal deprivation in both cases is a reduced level of responding to any form of stimulation, a dependency of behavior on familiar settings, and a withdrawal from those situations that involve novelty. The monkeys thus deprived tend to be ex-extremely fearful.

There is little doubt that the mothering relationship is important for providing support for the young in learning to explore the world. The mother is not only a guide for that exploration, but also helps bring the young into contact with suitable and significant situations. The role of the mother in this respect is partly intellectual and partly emotional and motivational.

Animal studies have shown the importance of exposing young animals, notably rats and mice, to perceptually elaborate environments, for the brain weight is thereby significantly increased (see Rosenzweig, Bennett, and Diamond, 1972). Such studies may not be as significant as they may seem for two reasons. One reason is that the laboratory rat is typically raised in a highly deprived environment consisting of a barren cage. Whatever is done to improve the environment might improve development. Indeed, there is evidence that the ordinary laboratory rat is an extra-ordinary stupid animal compared with his wild ancestors. Some psychologists have even insinuated that the laboratory rat has been bred to provide an extraordinarily stupid creature that will behave highly consistently in the psychologist's experiments. Whoever doubts this statement should read Kavanau's accounts (1964) of the remarkably complex learning engaged in by wild strains of rat, learning that would be far beyond the capability of the ordinary laboratory strains.

A second reason for doubting the significance of studies of brain weight in relation to stimulation in rats is that one knows little about the significance of brain weight. Certainly, in the human species size of brain has little to do with intellectual power.

Nevertheless, a long history of research has shown that depriving the growing organism from sensory stimulation and opportunities for perceptual activity may produce deep and lasting effects on the later capacity to use the sensory and perceptual systems. (See Zubek, 1969, for much of the classic research in this area.)

Extensive research has been undertaken on the effect of depriving animals of the use of a particular sensory system. Deprivation of vision has most commonly been used because of the ease with which an animal can be raised in the dark, although other means of preventing the use of vision have also been used. Such studies also make it possible to study what happens when the animal is later given the opportunity to use vision, and physiological studies can be undertaken to determine whether deprivation of the use of a sensory system results in deterioration of that system. The evidence indicates that sensory deprivation, if extreme and if prolonged enough, may produce permanent damage to the sensory system. However, when von Senden (1960) studied patients who acquired vision in adulthood through corneal grafts, he found that after prolonged training most of them, but not all, managed to learn to use the visual system. It may well be that physiological deterioration did not occur in the case of the von Senden patients because all of them had eyes that were exposed during the day to light. Light stimulation, even when filtered through a clouded cornea, may be sufficient to prevent physiological deterioration from taking place. In subhuman subjects deterioration has generally been noted in the optic tracts of animals that have been confined in total darkness during the period of growth. In summary, sensory deprivation can result in permanent damage, but this kind of deprivation is rare in human beings, except for the occasional child raised in a darkened or semidarkened environment. Such children are generally illegitimate and have been hidden away because the mother is ashamed of having given birth. Of much greater relevance to the study of human development are those studies in which the effect of a psychologically enriched versus an impoverished environment has been studied. Enrichment may involve introducing any element of variation and change. With animals, this has often involved no more than handling them occasionally rather than leaving them in a cage.

We have pointed out the significance of mothering relationships in the intellectual and motivational spheres, but there is still another factor involved in this relationship. About a quarter of a century ago Weininger (1953) showed that handling of young rats and stroking them, a procedure called gentling, produced adult animals that handled stress better than littermates raised without handling. Later research workers shows that the same effect could be produced by handling the animals roughly or by giving them electric shocks. What appeared to be needed was a situation at an early age that would invoke a stress response in the young animal. Even the gentling treatment seemed to be a mild stress situation. Much of this work has been summarized by Salama and Hunt (1964). Recent work (Levine, 1971) suggests that the effect of handling the young animals may be to produce glandular development, particularly with respect to the adrenals, and this superior glandular development results in an adult that behaves effectively under stressful conditions.

Research on human beings in this field has been far from as thorough and extensive as the importance of the subject demands, but the meager knowledge available has been widely distributed and often used as a basis for making important decisions. Particularly influential have been Bowlby's monograph for the World Health Organization (1969) and his later book on the bond between an infant and his mother and the effect of the loss of this attachment (1969). The influence of such writings was to question the value of day-care centers for working mothers and to emphasize the need for keeping mother and child together in the early years of life. More recent work has led to a questioning of many of the inferences made on the basis of this early work.

The excellent summary of the effects of early deprivation, and particularly maternal deprivation, has been prepared by Rutter (1972). This book points out that the previously reported effects of maternal deprivation, based largely on studies of foundling children, involve far more than the mere loss of an attachment relationship on the part of the child. Mothers influence the kind of environment to which a child is exposed in many different ways. For example, the mother makes most of the decisions concerning the choice of objects that the infant has the opportunity to grasp and manipulate. She also chooses the diet of the infant, and her behavior determines the language usage to which the child is first exposed. The mother is in control of the main sources of the infant's intellectual development. All too often when a child is left without a mother, he is placed in an institution that makes no provision for the intellectual development of the child and often only poor provision for taking care of his physical needs. The value of the mother-child relationship is far more than a simple matter of mother love. The fact that the role of the mother is at least partly intellectual suggests that other sources of intellectual stimulation may be as effective in producing cognitive growth.

Rutter concludes in his review that the longer such infants stay in such foundling institutions the greater is the intellectual deficit. Some of the earlier writers suggested that the deficit was due to lack of stimulation ordinarily provided by maternal handling, but data show that infants removed from the hands of mentally retarded parents and placed in more stimulating environments tend to show intellectual improvement. Children in underprivileged homes also tend to show a decline in IQ with age.

Some data also suggest that the opportunities that infants have to form bonds with adults may be quite crucial to the later development of attachments to other individuals. The lack of bonds of affection in infancy is likely to lead to an attitude of detachment from society and an absence of ties of affection. The previously cited experiments with animals demonstrate the disastrous consequences that social isolation during infancy may have on subsequent social behavior.

A most dramatic form of deprivation is sudden separation from the mother or the father or of both parents. Popular belief holds that children deprived of typical parent-child relationships grow up to be emotionally unstable. Such beliefs must be treated with skepticism since the nuclear family is honored in our society as being almost a sacred institution; other societies do not so honor the nuclear family. Some societies raise children in extended families of thirty or more persons, and others assign the responsibility of child rearing to the community. There is certainly no evidence that these other forms of child rearing are inferior to our own. Nevertheless, each one of these alternative forms of society provides a situation in which the child can form strong attachments and receive the same kind of mothering behavior that children receive in the home in our own society. The question raised by Weininger is not whether a child deprived of parent-child relationships shows developmental problems but rather whether difficulties occur when not only the parents are absent but no effective substitutes are offered for them. Weininger (1972) has reviewed studies in which such an absence of parental relationships or their substitutes have been related to subsequent personality characteristics. In American society the loss of one or more parents is rarely compensated for by the provision of effective alternatives. For example, an infant who does not have parents is typically placed in an institution that provides little more than custodial care. The child is fed and kept clean but lacks affection and security-giving support and does not receive the kind of intellectual and verbal stimulation so necessary for adequate development. Thus in our society loss of one or both parents usually results in serious deprivation that may be expected to interfere with the entire development pattern of the child.

Weininger concludes that the parent-child relationship is vital for normal physiological and perceptual development if adequate substitutes are not provided. The relationship to the mother is also important in helping the child to differentiate between himself and other objects and between himself and other people. Weininger believes that real attachments are not observed until the third quarter of the first year and these cannot be developed until the child can clearly differentiate himself from others. There is little evidence that brief separations from the parents, such as are involved in hospitalization, have any marked effect on subsequent development. Separation has to be sudden and long to have impact. Separations of six months or more seems to have quite marked effects. At least, adult psychotics show a high incidence of such separations in their backgrounds. Dissolution of the maternal bond in early childhood is reported to result in a deterioration of speech habits, motor skills, and social behavior. When there is a permanent separation from the parents the effect may be much more dramatic. For example, in one study reviewed by Weininger it was found that 64 per cent of suicide attempts by children come from broken homes in which the break was produced by the death of a parent. Such associations have also been found in the case of drug addiction and alcoholism. Psychopathic personality also seems to be associated with maternal deprivation. Weinberger also conducted some studies of his own and concluded from the entire mass of evidence that children deprived of their parents show later in life depression, suicidal tendencies, and tendencies to withdraw from the world. Such individuals, as adults, seem to have the greatest difficulty in forming bonds of affection with others. Weinberger also takes the position that the immediate and key effect of parental deprivation is that it deprives the infant or child of appropriate perceptual motor experiences.

The effects of early deprivation in human beings are difficult to study because many sources of deprivation are usually combined. One of the more identifiable sources of deprivation in the United States is malnutrition. Green et al. (1973) have summarized much of the available knowledge about this factor though the quality of this research has been criticized by Warren (1973). A first point to note is that generations of students of human development have made the assumption that the embryo will never be deprived of essentials because it supposedly will have priority over the mother in obtaining essential nutrients from the mother's blood. This assumption appears to be quite unsound and a malnourished mother may not provide the child she is carrying with enough of the nutrients needed to build his body properly. The nervous system of the infant suffers in two ways from malnutrition of the mother. First, the child may be born with a smaller brain than he would otherwise have. One can now demonstrate that such newborn infants have brains that do not fill the skull cavity properly. Second, malnutrition results in high incidence of premature births and prematurity is an important cause of mental retardation. When a child comes into the world prematurely, the nervous system does not develop as it should. The reasons for this are not clear. One suggestion is that the infant in the hospital incubator is not moved enough and certainly not moved around as he would be in the uterus. Such lack of stimulation, reminiscent of the gentling experiments, may well hold back development.

The evidence is now striking that one effect of poverty is to produce a newborn infant whose nervous system is either poorly developed or defective, and this effect of malnutrition takes place before birth. This same child now has to face the same malnutrition of which his mother was a victim. The inadequacy of the diet is brought out particularly by studies that have shown that dietary supplements may result in striking gains in intellectual development. Even a simple measure of adequacy of nutrition such as birth weight is correlated with school achievement (National Institute of Education, 1974).

The Green *et al.* article paints the dismal picture of each generation of poor producing a new generation with basic defects in the nervous system, which, in turn, has difficulty in competing in society and is condemned to poverty. The data suggest that the poverty cycle is thus institutionalized and that it may be possible to break the cycle by providing proper diets to expectant mothers and young children. Certainly, compensatory eduction is not enough. The area calls for more and better research than that which has been undertaken. The excellent analysis of the difficulties of doing research has been made by Kaplan (1972), who believes that the conclusions of research undertaken need to be reexamined.

Little is known about the reversibility of the deficits produced by early deprivations of various kinds. Those that derive from inadequate and inappropriate intellectual stimulation may well be far more remediable than those that derive from poor nutrition. Children who come from homes that do little to favor intellectual growth move ahead when placed in a more favorable environment. Actual brain damage may well be irreversible, though there are ways in which a person may be able to steer a course around some of his difficulties, much as those who are blind may learn to compensate to some degree for their blindness.

Deprivation generally means an absence of conditions typically provided. Deprived children are those who do not have the favorable conditions for growth, development, and learning that the majority of the middle class enjoys. This leads to the question of whether the effects of long periods of deprivation can be counteracted by subsequent periods when a more favorable environment is provided. This more favorable environment is generally referred to as an *enriched* environment. There is also the related question of whether an environment superior to that of a typical middle-class child will produce gains in development beyond that which the average middle-class child shows.

Although one has to be extremely cautious in generalizing from studies on animals, let us consider some of the studies that have relevance to the problem at hand. The previously considered studies of the effect of stimulating young animals by handling them suggest the importance of vigorous adult behavior, perhaps the opposite of that seen in foundling homes to which Spitz raised such strong objections. Certainly the evidence is overwhelming that a stimulating environment, including such a feature as a vigorous mother or a vigorous caretaker, is important for intellectual development.

Some of the now quite old studies undertaken by Hebb (1966) are relevant. In these studies, some puppies were raised in the house of an experimenter while littermates were raised in cages in which they had minimal contact with human beings or with manipulable objects. The home-reared puppies were generally superior in their ability to solve problems and also showed marked personality differences compared with those raised in cages. One difference of interest was the social spontaneity toward visitors shown by the pups raised in cages. The pups raised in the home were sophisticated enough to know that visitors to the laboratory were not worth paying attention to. Particularly interesting is the behavior of dogs in the McGill laboratory, who were raised under circumstances that deprived them from experiencing pain through contact with hard or pointed objects or from falling off high places. Such animals showed an extraordinary inability to respond effectively to pain when released to more normal circumstances. One such animal repeatedly knocked its head on a low pipe and, although it behaved like an animal that had hurt itself, showed almost no ability to learn to avoid the object (Hebb, 1966).

The implication from the Hebb type of study is that the effects of extreme perceptual deprivation are irreversible, and they may well be in the case of the animals studied. Generalization of the conclusion to human beings is dangerous, for they are much more flexible creatures and capable of adjustments that simpler creatures cannot make. The effects of deprivation are undoubtedly difficult to overcome, even for human beings. However, a review by Hunt (1966) has focused on the problem of the effect of cultural deprivation on adolescence and points out the mounting belief that the effects of deprivation may be largely irreversible. Although educators should not give up all hope that the culturally deprived child has not been damaged beyond repair, the chances at this time are not good that educational intervention can make up for a prolonged inadequate background.

More dramatic evidence of the effects of impoverished or enriched environments on human intellectual development comes from much earlier studies undertaken on identical twins raised apart. Identical twins are rarities—roughly one in three hundred births at the time when the studies were taken, but they occur more frequently today. Even more rare are those identical twins who are raised separately in different environments, and still more rare are those that are raised in fundamentally different environments in terms of the enrichment-impoverishment dimension. Nevertheless, Newman, Freeman, and Holzinger (1937) were able to find nineteen pairs of twins reared separately and, in the case of a few of these pairs, the environments are about as different as one might expect to find in the United States. In the case of such twins reared apart, the maximum difference in the intelligence quotients of the twins thus separated was 24 points—the difference between a person of limited educability and a person of average intelligence. Such a difference is large.

The nineteen pairs of twins reared apart were classified according to the differences in the education to which each member of a pair had been exposed. The most pronounced differences were seen in three pairs in which members of a pair differed on an Intelligence Quotient Scale by 24, 19, and 12 points, respectively. The greatest of these three differences was between a pair of twins known as Gladys and Helen. Gladys had received only three years of grade school, while Helen had received a college degree and had become a teacher. The intelligence quotients of these two youngsters were 92 and 116, respectively. The pair whose intelligence quotient differed by 19 points were James and Reece, whose measured intelligence quotients were 96 and 77, respectively. James had lived with a good small-town family and had completed high school; Reece had lived with a primitive mountain family and had gone to school part-time through the eighth grade. The third pair, Eleanore and Georgiana, had intelligence quotients of 66 and 78. Eleanore had gone through five grades of schooling; her sister had received a full high-school education and an additional three years of normal school.

Much of the more recent evidence of the effect of cultural conditions on the development of the intellect comes from studies other than those involving identical twins. Stein and Susser (1970) have reviewed data from numerous different sources that all point in the same direction. For example, they show that the socially disadvantaged tend to manifest a decline in intelligence quotient as they grow older. Children in institutional settings have depressed intelligence quotients, which tend to be raised after they are moved into homes. Enduring gains and losses appear to follow marked changes in the social and economic environment. However, there is even some evidence that a decline in the frequency of mental retardation accompanies improved social and educational conditions. Stein and Susser also point out that the level of the intelligence quotient is not determined solely by social and economic conditions, but there is a mounting body of data showing that it is also related to quality of schooling.

COMPENSATORY EDUCATION

The most ambitious social program that has attempted to compensate for intellectual deprivation is the Head Start program for underprivileged and its related Follow-Through program. These programs embody the concept of compensatory education, that is, that intellectual deficit produced by poor socioeconomic conditions can be compensated for by providing educational facilities specifically designed for that purpose. The idea was new to America in the 1960s, but a similar idea had been developed in the late 1940s in Israel, where the government was faced with the problem of educating for a technological society children who were being raised in such a simple environment that they were not familiar with common objects such as a spoon and fork. Israel attempted to expand the knowledge and intellectual horizons of these underprivileged children by providing them with special preschool programs designed to provide them with the knowledge that more privileged children ordinarily acquire in their homes.

The development of programs of compensatory education was accompanied by unreasonable expectations. Indeed, they were established by Congress in an atmosphere that encouraged the thought that years of impoverishment that produced intellectual, social, and physiological deficits could be remedied in a few weeks of remedial education. The studies that were undertaken of the children who passed through such programs did show that they made substantial progress as a result of such enterprises. The gap between them and the more privileged was reduced.

Abelson, Zigler, and DeBlasi (1974) have summarized such studies. Although the early outcomes seemed promising, the gains made by the Head Start children were not always maintained (see Jacobson and Greeson, 1972). Critics of the program urged its abolition, demonstrating how a little misinterpreted data can do massive harm. The fact is that such programs could be considered to be only a minuscule attack on the problem of breaking the poverty cycle. The children in the Head Start programs at the end of the school day returned to a poverty-stricken environment where little sleep could be had because of crowded conditions and where the diet had debilitating effects on their bodies. At the end of the program, these children could be expected to slip back, for their homes contained none of the educational advantages provided by middle-class homes.

Although the mood of many legislators was to abolish the program, together with most of the other War on Poverty programs, a more reasonable approach was followed. A program was established to provide some continued facilities for the Head Start children. The Follow Through program came into being for this purpose, and studies were undertaken of the effect of such programs. In one of the first studies to be published, Abelson, Zigler, and DeBlasi (1974) found that the children in Follow Through were superior to non-Follow Through children in both achievement and social-motivational levels. In addition they maintained the increase in intelligence quotients produced by the Head Start program. The data support what is quite obvious, namely, that the impact of an impoverished environment continues to exert a depressing effect unless strong steps are taken to combat it. In other efforts in which the disadvantaged have been given continued help, promising results have also been achieved (see Gray and Klaus, 1970).

There are still further implications of what is known about the problem of combating the effects of an impoverished background on poverty. The effects of poverty on the child do not end at the third grade, where the Follow Through program is terminated, but continue until adulthood. Additional help needs to be provided for the children of the poor, for many years and perhaps through high school. Even that may not be enough. Cyril Burt (personal communication) has described a simple experiment he undertook early in the century in the poor East End of London. The school authorities were concerned about the low mathematics scores achieved by children in a particular school. Burt established a program in which half the children were given an additional hour of mathematics instruction each day and the other half were moved to facilities where they could sleep. At the end of the semester, the children who had been given the opportunity to sleep had made more progress in mathematics than the children who had had the additional mathematics instruction. The crowded and noisy environment of the London slums did not allow the children enough rest to profit from their school work.

This leads us to consider the problem of desegregation in schools. Although busing and desegregation are thought of largely as a race problem, it does mix together different socioeconomic groups. Some evidence concerning the effects of such mixing has been reviewed by Weinberg (1970). There seems to be little doubt that the disadvantaged gain academically through their contacts with the privileged.

Also, the privileged do not lose academically through their contacts with the disadvantaged. The data on academic achievement seems to largely support busing as a means of achieving some degree of equal educational opportunity.

SUMMARY

1. The study of language acquistion is important for understanding learning because it becomes the tool for learning, particularly during adolescence. Most of the early studies of the development of language were normative and descriptive and were tied to the idea that intelligence can be measured through verbal behavior. Such studies were largely unproductive.

2. The operant point of view concerning the development of language is mainly of historical interest. Skinner views language as an instrumental form of behavior learned, like other instrumental forms of behavior, through reinforcement. Skinner has his own categories of word forms, such as the *mand* and the *tact*, which fit his viewpoint on language function. Skinner presents his case with charm, wit, and personal conviction, but lacks a data base on which to rest his case. The operant theory of language learning, through reinforcement, has not stimulated a body of research, so it remains much as it started as an interesting set of conjectures. Research on the reinforcement of particular aspects of verbal behavior has not produced any clearly reproducible pieces of knowledge.

3. The psycholinguistic approach in the last decade has become thoroughly experimental. The pattern of speech-sound development in the infant has now been well described. The babbling of infants appears to be universal, regardless of the language that the children will ultimately learn to speak. Language characteristics that are peculiar to only certain languages appear relatively late in the speech development pattern. How the first words are made, apart from naturally occurring words such as *mama*, is somewhat of a mystery. Words often appear suddenly and may be said on the first occasion with complete correctness. There is no gradual shaping of many first words or expressions.

4. Comprehension has to precede the production of speech. Through exposure to speech children manage to find structure in it and, slowly, meaning. In order to find meaning the infant may have to determine the intent of the speaker. The infant begins by learning a vocabulary of nouns. In order to do this, he must understand that some words relate to objects. The young child also has to figure out the essential syntax of language. In English, this first involves learning the significance of word order, which children learn at a very early age. Children raised in environments in which there are extreme language deficits, such as that of Luria's twins, may develop very primitive forms of language. These primitive forms of language limit the sophistication that can be introduced into play activities. The young child also learns which sounds can be put together into words in his native language and invents words of his own. At about age 2 the child begins to put together words into sentences. The idea of a pivot grammar has been widely held, but the evidence for it is not strong. Nevertheless, one authority does concede that the language of the 2-year-old does have a pivot look to it. The telegraphic character of the language

of the young child is on firmer ground. The adult is able to interpret the rich meaning of the two-word sentence since he knows the needs of the child and uses this knowledge to interpret what the child says. The child expects to be understood and generally is. Telegraphic speech can be classified into a number of different statment forms. At the two-word stage the child is selective in the words he uses, most of these being contentives. Functors are rarely used. The child has some understanding of grammar before he uses the two-word sentence. He does not put together words in random order and slowly accept correction.

5. The child slowly invents a generative grammar that permits him ultimately to generate an infinite number of different sentences. A widely held hypothesis is that the child has an innate ability to analyze speech and to invent a grammar that permits him to produce appropriate expressions. The child is not aware of the rules and cannot state them. His behavior shows that his speech is governed by such a set of rules. The precise characteristics of a generative grammar have not yet been worked out. A sentence is produced as speech only after a complete program has been worked out for its production.

6. After the two-word sentence stage, language becomes expanded because the child's conception of time has grown and he becomes able to use the past tense as well as the present progressive. The length of the utterance is also limited by the memory factor, A child would not emit a sentence of such length that he would forget the first part before the last part had been said.

7. Many aspects of language cannot develop for several years because the child does not have the understanding necessary to master them. In addition, some phonological aspects of language occur late because the child does not seem able to make the necessary sound analysis to understand them. Age also is related to the use of progressively more abstract forms of speech. The use of either-or constructions depends on an understanding of logical forms of thought.

8. The relationship of speech to thinking has been investigated, mainly through the study of deaf children, who perform in ways comparable to children with hearing on tests of concrete operations; but there is some controversy concerning the extent to which deaf children have an understanding of language. Piaget has taken the position that speech is not necessary for thinking at the concrete operations stage. Thinking in mathematics may be obstructed by the complexity of the language used in the area. Mathematics does not have to be verbally complicated.

9. Many questions with respect to the use of dialects remain unanswered. Dialects generally develop for particular purposes of communication. This does not make them suitable for purposes other than that for which they were developed. Mothers in different social classes give different verbal responses to their children. Mothers modify their speech to make it easier for the infant.

10. The acquisition of the first language has been intensively studied in recent years. There appears to be a fundamental difference between the acquisition of speech by the chimpanzee and by the child. The study of one may not help us to understand the speech of the other. Children have enormous capacity for spontaneous learning in which reinforcement seems to play no part. Chomsky proposes that all children have the innate capacity to analyze speech and that all languages

have the same basic structure. Speech development seems to be uninfluenced by a wide range of circumstances that might be thought to influence its development. Piaget suggests that the child's mastery of language is related to the child's inventive capacity. He believes that children invent grammar, much as they invent logic.

11. Studies relating child-rearing conditions to later development have now followed up children from infancy to middle life. These studies show marked changes in intelligence quotients from one period to another in a child's life. Conditions in the home also seem to be important in determining level of intelligence; toys and related facilities seem to be an important factor. Gain in intelligence quotient is related to amount and quality of schooling. Without schooling and with poor learning facilities in the home, children would grow up with little intellectual competence. Even exposure to nursery school seems to produce an increment in measured intelligence. Loving behavior also seems to be important, especially for boys. There appear to be important sex differences in children related to what makes for an intellectually stimulating home.

12. The mother's level of energy, and the general concern of the mother, is important for intellectual development, as is the mother's concern for educational achievement. Lack of conflict between parents is also a significant factor. Numerous other factors make a contribution.

13. Permissiveness related to aggression is related to child aggressiveness later, but a permissive attitude related to dependent behavior on the part of the child does not produce dependency. General family adjustment seems to be unrelated to the adjustment made by the child. Warmth of mother-child relationships represents an important condition related to personality development over a broad front.

14. Studies of the kibbutzim have provided important information related to personality development. Early emotional difficulties seem to have little effect on later adjustment. Although the kibbutzim provide many favorable conditions related to personality development, they do not seem to encourage intellectual aspirations.

15. The effect of impoverishment of the environment on development has been studied in primates, after observations on human beings indicated that early deprivation might produce long-term intellectual damage. The primate studies show that social deprivation early in infancy produces irreparable harm and probably irreversible harm. The typical response to such deprivation is withdrawal and a reduced level of responding. The deprived animals are also extremely fearful. The mother has an important relationship as a base from which the world is explored. Sensory stimulation is important for producing good development. Sensory deprivation also has prolonged effects, some of which may be reversible, as was evident in some of von Senden's patients after corneal grafts. Handling and movement appears also to be an important condition for good development. There are probably good substitutes for the mother as far as intellectual and emotional development are concerned. In American society there is rarely any compensation for the loss of the mother. Brief separations from the parents are probably not important, but a sudden and lasting separation may have profound effects.

16. The effects of malnutrition may contribute to intellectual deficit in the child.

The data are indicative of these relationships but are not as satisfactory as they should be. The data do suggest that malnutrition of the fetus and young child may be one of the ways in which the poverty cycle is perpetuated from generation to generation. Little is known about whether the deficits thus produced can be reversed. Studies of the effect of enrichment of the environment early in life generally indicate positive effects.

17. The most dramatic effects of enrichment or impoverishment on the human intellect come from studies of identical twins raised apart and under widely varying conditions. These studies have shown how environmental differences can produce large differences in intelligence test scores.

18. The results of attempts to compensate for an underprivileged background through special educational programs are not very clear. What is clear is that a disadvantaged background continues to exert its harmful effect right through school. There is no quick and simple way of overcoming cultural disadvantage. Studies of school desegregation indicate that the disadvantaged gain by coming into contact with the privileged, but the privileged are not harmed.

PART IV
STUDIES OF BASIC COMPONENTS OF LEARNING INVOLVING MIXED APPROACHES

Chapter 8

Some Acquisition and Retention Phenomena

A learning curve is a way of representing the progress of learning. A beginner at bowling may keep a careful record of his score, week by week, and may plot his scores on a graph to show his progress. The graph is a learning curve. A quite typical learning curve for the acquisition of a motor skill is shown in Figure 8-1. The performance of the skill shows a typical rapid increase during the early stages of practice and much less progress during the later periods. For a long time psychologists thought that the type of curve represented by Figure 8-1 was the typical learning curve and, indeed, similar curves were produced in experiments that involved a whole range of tasks including verbal tasks.

Questions have been raised about whether the typical learning curve of the kind that has just been discussed can be regarded as representing the overall course of learning. Learning of most tasks does not start from scratch. The person who bowls for the first time brings to his performance extensive practice with the task of throwing balls and other objects. Although bowling is new to him, it is only new with respect to certain aspects of the task. The ball is likely to be larger than any he has thrown or rolled in the past and also considerably heavier. The targets at which he throws the ball are different. The surroundings are different from those in which he has manipulated balls in the past, for he has been used to throwing and rolling balls in out-of-door situations. Despite these differences, he brings to the situation a range of previously developed skills that permit him to score perhaps as high as eighty the very first time he bowls. He is not so much learning a new skill as trans-

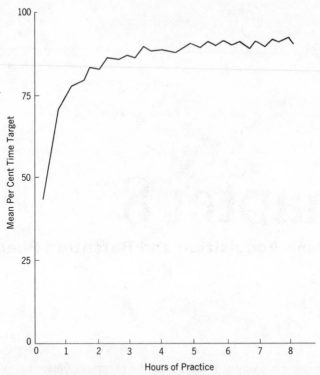

Figure 8-1. Curve representing learning of the skill involved in the control of the performance of a miniature plane, the movements of which are manipulated by means of a set of controls similar to those used in an aircraft. Data from Ammons, et al., 1958. (*Reproduced by permission of the American Psychological Association.*)

ferring the skills he has acquired to a new situation. His learning curve for bowling is a curve reflecting his ability to transfer to the bowling situation the skills he has already learned.

What kind of a learning curve would be produced in the acquisition of a skill for which the individual came to the learning situation without any previously acquired related skills? Such situations are difficult to find. One source of such learning curves is the learning that takes place in infancy and early childhood. An example of such a curve is presented in Figure 8-2, which shows the vocabulary acquired by a child during his first six years. This curve represents only the lower portion of the complex learning curve which, would continue to rise but at a decreasing rate and eventually would become horizontal. Even by the age of six some tendency for the curve to bend toward the horizontal position is already apparent. If data had been available for ages above 6, the complete curve would have had the appearance of an extended S, with learning very slow at first, then becoming more rapid, and finally slowing down again. A good question to ask is why learning

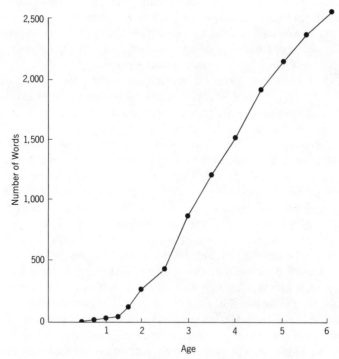

Figure 8-2. Relations of size of vocabulary to age. (*Graph drawn from data by M. E. Smith, 1926.*)

is slow at first. The answer to this is provided by Gibson (1969), who points out that before language is spoken the child must first engage in extended perceptual learning. The child must first be able to discriminate perceptually one word from another and be able also to differentiate the distinctive features of particular words. The perceptual skills must, almost certainly, precede the actual production of speech. Only as these skills slowly develop can the child begin to produce and use words. The development of these prerequisites makes it inevitable that the early production of speech will be very slow. Once these perceptual skills have been developed, the acquisition of speech can take place at the rapid rate with which it proceeds, after about the age of 18 months.

The learning vocabulary will flatten out in the teens, when it will have reached what is called a crude limit of learning. The fact that a person may cease to add to his vocabulary after he leaves high school does not mean that he is incapable of making additions. He may have reached the limit of the vocabulary that he needs for performing in life and have no incentive for additional vocabulary learning. The crude limit of learning simply represents the limit occurring under particular conditions; it does not represent any maximum level that cannot be exceeded.

Another source of data that may shed light on the shape of the learning curve is found in animal studies. In both classical conditioning and instrumental conditioning studies one can find cases in which the learning task involved is so novel that the animal cannot be expected to bring to the learning situation any previously mastered skills. The classical conditioning of an eyelid response might be such a case, but few studies of this kind are available because psychologists have been more interested in the factors that modify learning than in the pure form of the learning curve. However, Hilgard and Marquis (1936, p. 190) have provided the learning curves for three monkeys in a classical conditioning eyelid experiment and show curves that are approximately S-shaped. Spence, who became interested in this problem many years later (1956), came to the conclusion that, at least for instrumental conditioning, the shape of the complete learning curve was S-shaped. Some interesting data have been provided in this connection by Harlow (1959), who trained chimpanzees to solve very extended series of problems and demonstrated the development of problem-solving skills. The procedure involved presenting an animal with two dishes, upside down and different in some way. The animal had to find out which dish covered a small amount of food. In the first set of trials it might always be the square dish, and not the round one. In the second set it might always be the black dish, and not the white dish. In the third series, the large one and not the small one was correct, and so forth. With each problem, the animal had six trials. On the first trial of each series, he could only guess, but within eight trials he would make considerable progress in solving the problem. In the early learning series, the chimps would be likely to be responding correctly 70 per cent of the time by the ninth attempt at a problem, but after solving thirty to forty such problems, with six attempts on every problem, the chimps would solve a problem 90 per cent correct after a single trial. Learning curves provided by Harlow, shown in Figure 8-3, make it possible to see how the shape of the learning curve changes from the initial problem, where the problem is highly novel for the particular animal to the case where a problem is solved after much previous practice with other problems. The learning of the first problem provides a curve resembling a long drawn-out S, but the learning curves for problems late in the series look more and more like the typical learning curves produced by human beings on tasks to which they bring many component skills.

The evidence generally points in the direction of suggesting that a learning curve, involving a task that starts the learner off from scratch and does not draw upon what he has learned previously, is S-shaped. The learning curve that shows a sudden rise from the beginning belongs to a task that involves many skills that the person has previously learned. Although the S-shaped curve is simple, it is a product of complex circumstances. A very young child, or an animal, placed in a novel learning situation, may have difficulty initially in differentiating the stimuli to which he must respond. He may also be distracted by novel aspects of his environment. Learning in an unfamiliar world makes for slow learning, but the slowness is likely to be a result of a combination of factors. Once the initial difficulties have been surmounted, learning then proceeds at a much more rapid pace. Finally, a crude limit of learning is reached when incentives no longer exist for further learning.

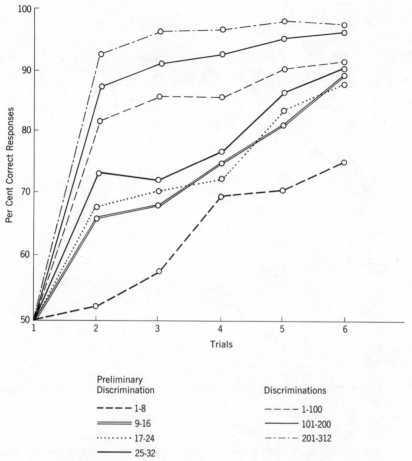

Figure 8-3. Family of learning curves showing the development of a learning set. (*From "Learning Set and Error Factor Theory," by H. F. Harlow, in* Psychology: A Study of a Science, *Vol. 2, edited by S. Koch [copyright 1959 by McGraw-Hill Book Company, Inc.] Used with permission of McGraw-Hill Book Company, Inc.*)

Some learning curves have been described as showing portions where learning is slowed down, followed by a period when learning takes place rapidly again. Such phenomena were first reported by Bryan and Harter (1897) in their classic study of learning Morse code. Figure 8-4 reproduces some of the curves from the Bryan and Harter study. The slowed-up portion of the learning curve, seen only in the curves for the receiving code, was referred to by Bryan and Harter as a plateau, but the evidence for the existence of such plateaus was not striking. If the reader will scrutinize the curves in Figure 8-4, he may well have difficulty in finding anything that looks like a plateau at all. Because the graphs were plotted to show daily per-

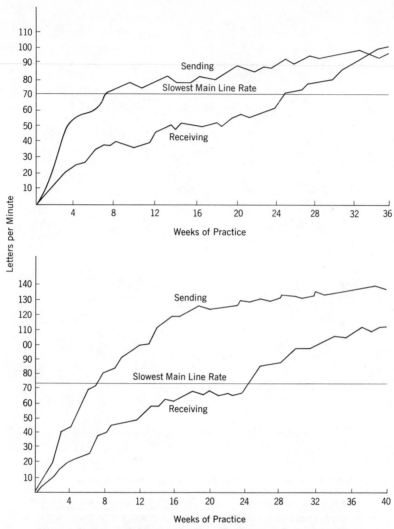

Figure 8-4. Curves for the learning of Morse code for individual subjects showing plateaus on the receiving curves. (*From Bryan and Harter, 1897, p. 49.*)

formance over a period of forty weeks, it is quite possible that any slight slow-up in the rate of learning during one-part of the forty-week training period might be due to short periods of ill-health, difficulties in attending to the task caused by worry, or perhaps even lack of sleep, which may have prolonged effects upon performance. Many writers have attributed to whatever plateaus they could see a much deeper significance. It is claimed, for example, that in learning to type the pupil first learns to hunt and peck letter by letter. When he becomes skilled in striking individual letters, his performance reaches a maximum and learning seems to stop for a time. Then he begins to type by groups of letters and the resulting learning curve begins to go up again. This is a convincing argument, but this writer has been unable to find learning curves that provide convincing evidence that such plateaus exist at all except as artifacts.

MATHEMATICAL MODELS AND LEARNING CURVES

During the last two decades, considerable interest has been shown in attempts to derive a learning curve by mathematical methods from assumptions made about the learning process. For example, if the assumption is made that equal amounts of practice produce equal increments in the number of correct responses, learning would be represented by a straight line on a graph that related the percentage of correct responses to the amount of practice. Such an assumption would not be valid and would not produce a learning curve that corresponded, to any extent, with that produced by real data. The problem is to make assumptions that lead to curves that correspond closely with those produced through the analysis of real data. If a set of assumptions can be made about learning from which mathematical procedures can derive a learning curve that fits closely that derived from real data, one can then say that the mathematical model has validity. This procedure is roughly that followed by scientists in the physical sciences who frequently make assumptions concerning the nature of the phenomena they are studying and derive mathematical equations from those assumptions. The next step is to find out whether experimental data fit the mathematical functions that have been thus derived. Elaborate computers are often used to calculate the results expected in terms of theory, which are later compared with those from actual data.

Psychologists have attempted to produce theoretical learning curves, starting with many different assumptions about the learning process. Some of the curves thus produced have shown a remarkable degree of correspondence with actual data. An example of such a theoretically derived curve is shown in Figure 8-5. In

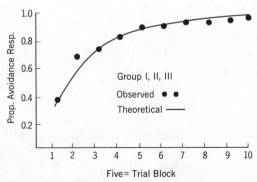

Figure 8-5. Graph showing the fit of actual data to a theoretical learning curve. (*After Brody, 1957, p. 243. Reproduced by permission of the American Psychological Association.*)

this figure the circles represent the points on the curve derived from experimental data. The continuous curve represents a theoretical curve. The data in this case fits well the theoretical learning curve. Indeed, the fit is exceptional. Other cases could be presented in which a much poorer fit was obtained. The Brody (1957) data are presented here to indicate that this approach may well have a future.

RETENTION

A discussion of recording the progress of learning is appropriately followed by a discussion of the related problem of recording the retention of what has been learned. Just as the learning curve is a record of only one aspect of learning measured in a particular way, so, too, is a curve of retention a record of a product of learning as it is measured at various intervals of time after the learning conditions have ceased to operate. Because retention can be measured in a number of different ways, a graph representing the degree of retention can be drawn for each way in which retention is measured.

Different measures of what has been retained are dependent on different internal processes. Each involves its own skills. Let us consider the various methods, beginning with what is generally considered to be the least sensitive.

The Free Recall Method. The free recall method is the method most frequently used by teachers. The student studies the French equivalents of a number of English words and then must show that he can write out the French words when the English words are presented. Although the term *free recall* is commonly used to describe such a situation, the person making the recall has to have some cues in order to know which French words to produce. In the minimum cue situation, the student is simply told to write out all the English words and their French equivalents from the list he has been studying. Generally, the teacher will provide more cues and he will typically provide a list of the English words against which the student must enter the French equivalents. Still more cues can be provided by measuring retention through a situation in which the French word has to be entered in a blank space in an incomplete French sentence. An essay test approximates a free recall situation, but often in such tests the student is not given sufficient cues to tell him what he is supposed to be able to recall. When the recall method is used, the person involved must retrieve information stored in memory, but not all information stored can be demonstrated to be stored. In order that he can demonstrate what is stored, he must be able to provide an output related to it. In the case of memory for verbal material this is easy, for he can demonstrate either through speech or writing that he knows the particular words. In the case of the retention of crude visual data, such as what a neighbor looks like, the person may have no means of demonstrating in a free recall situation that he has this information unless he has the artistic skills necessary for making a sketch. The same is true of memory for music. Unless a person can hum a tune or write it out in musical notation, he cannot demonstrate through a free recall method that he has stored information about the tune.

The Recognition Method. The recognition method probably involves different internal processes from the free recall method. In the case of learning French vocabulary, a recognition test might involve the presentation of the English words, each followed by a number of French words. The task of the person taking the recognition test is that of selecting the correct French word from the alternatives provided. The person taking this test has certain options. Under some circumstances he may have to do no more than read the several words that follow the English word and determine which word was the one he recently saw during the study period. To do this, he may only have to identify certain attributes of the word. For example, he may note that one of the French words from which he has to choose begins with *w* and is long, and he may also remember that one of the French words he studied began with *w* and was long. Therefore, he chooses that word. In such a case the test merely shows that he has remembered some characteristics of the French word, and not that he can recall the actual word. Recognition measures of memory involve a perceptual analysis of what is presented and then some matching of the results of that analysis with information stored about previous experiences. Recognition may be based on very fragmentary information. Recall requires that very detailed information must have been stored internally. For this reason, it is generally a more difficult process than that of recognition and is dependent on more complete retention.

The Relearning, or Saving, Method. Some sensitive techniques have been developed that can demonstrate that there has been retention even though all of the ordinary tests of retention used in schools indicate that there has been none. A very sensitive technique widely used in laboratories is known as the saving method. In this method the subject learns the material to a certain standard of proficiency. If he is learning a list of words, he may learn them to the point where he can repeat the list back perfectly on three *successive* trials. This is generally done by presenting him with the list of words, permitting him to read it through once, and then asking him to recall the list he has read. This is repeated time after time until he reproduces the list perfectly on three successive occasions. After a period of time, the degree to which he has retained the list is measured by determining how much more learning must take place in order to relearn the list to the point where, once again, it can be repeated perfectly on another three successive occasions. If twenty-five repetitions were required in the original learning series to reach the point of perfect recall, only five repetitions might be required at a later time to reach the same point of learning. And because, on relearning, five instead of twenty-five repetitions were required, one might say that on relearning there was a "saving" of 80 per cent. This is how the method acquired its name. In some studies it has been the only method so far developed that is sensitive enough to provide evidence that there has been some retention of the original information learned.

Curves of Retention

Retention is the continued capacity to behave in a particular way that has been learned. Forgetting is the gradual or rapid loss of a response in the repertoire of the individual. When a child forgets a poem, it means that he has lost the ability to recall the poem—that is, he has lost the capacity for making the responses involved in the recitation of the poem. The word *forgetting* is used here loosely. Although the pupil has forgotten the poem insofar as recitation is concerned, he has not forgotten everything about the poem. He would probably still recognize the poem as one he had learned previously. Even if he had so far forgotten the poem that he did not recognize it, he might still find it unusually easy to learn.

Forgetting is a normal everyday event and a constant reminder of our limitations. There are also certain kinds of forgetting that the clinician tries to produce in individuals in order to help them with their problems. To a great extent, the treatment of behavioral disorders is an attempt to rid the person of certain unwanted aspects of behavior. These unwanted aspects of behavior may vary from minor twitches of the muscles of the face to deep-seated anxiety responses that torture the soul. That such responses are generally very difficult to eliminate is attested to by the fact that therapy is a long and rather unsatisfactory process. Behavior is not eliminated easily. Sometimes there seems to be no method through which unwanted behavior can be eliminated. It seems that the things we want to retain most, such as intellectual knowledge, are not easily retained, but neurotic behavior of which we would like to rid ourselves remains remarkably persistent.

A typical curve of retention is shown in Figure 8-6. Although the curve is derived from data from this century of Cain and Willey (1939), the general form of the curve was known to Ebbinghaus and to other psychologists of the last century. The reader must realize that only in general features does the curve remain the same from one batch of data to another, the most notable of these features being the rapid decline in the information or skill retained during the period that immediately follows

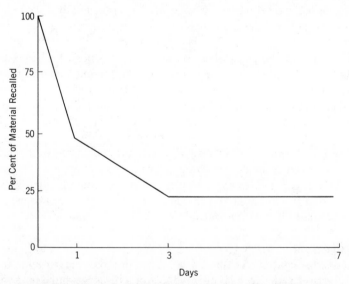

Figure 8-6. Curve of retention for nonsense syllables. (*After Cain and Willey, 1939, p. 211. Reproduced by permission of the American Psychological Association.*)

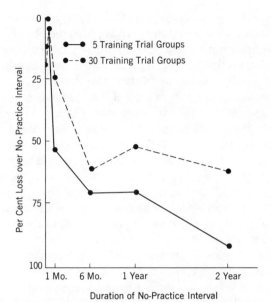

Figure 8-7. Loss of performance on sequential task over a period of no practice up to two years. The loss is shown for two groups, one of which had five training trials while the other had thirty training trials. (*From Ammons, et al., 1958, p. 322. Reproduced by permission of the American Psychological Association.*)

learning, and then a declining loss as time progresses. Many different conditions determine the extent to which there is an initial rapid loss in what has been learned.

Ammons et al. (1958) studied long-term retention of two skills. One skill was referred to as a procedural skill. It involved the manipulation of a set of controls in the correct sequence by following a chart on the wall. The other task involved the control of the performance of a miniature plane by operating a set of controls similar to that found in an aircraft. Figure 8-7 shows the loss in skill in the procedural task over a period of two years. The two lines on the graph are for the subjects who had five training trials and those who had thirty training trails. The difference in the percentage of the acquired skill lost is markedly less for the group that had the most training. However, there is a sense in which this graph overestimates the loss, for a large part of the losses tend to be rapidly regained once practice trials are given. The greater the time interval during which no practice took place, the greater was the amount of retraining required to regain the original skill.

MEMORY SYSTEMS

Although the belief is commonly held that there is a single memory system, scientific evidence points to a number of distinct memory mechanisms, each one of which has special characteristics and unique functions. The evidence for this has been well reviewed by Adams (1967) and in Howe's very readable brief book (1970) on the subject.

Psychologists have long suspected that most higher organisms are able to retain for a short time a trace of the signals they receive from their environments. Evidence for this transitory retention mechanism comes from a number of sources. One of these is the fact that one can readily condition an animal to salivate to the sound of a bell by exposing the animal to the sequence *bell-food* repeated a number of times, but conditioning does not take place if there is too long a delay between the sound of the bell and the presentation of the food. The experience of experimenters is that if there is a delay much greater than about three seconds, the animal never learns to associate the sound of the bell with the presentation of food. In most such experiments, delays up to two or three seconds can take place and still permit conditioning to occur. The usual explanation is that what becomes hooked up, in the conditioning process, is an internal memory or trace of the bell and the appearance of the food. If the delay is prolonged much beyond about three seconds, the memory trace of the bell has faded to the point where it cannot be linked with the appearance of the new stimulus.

A similar kind of trace is also provided as an inherent part of the human memory system. Broadbent (1958) refers to this as a short-term memory system, although the latter term is now reserved by most writers for a memory system of longer duration. Broadbent has shown in a series of studies that the trace fades in a matter of a few seconds, and also that the trace has great significance for many common activities of everyday life. For example, a person reads a telephone number in the directory and remembers it just long enough to reach the telephone, then usually has to repeat it to himself before dialing. By repeating back the number to himself, he is able to put it back into the trace system. If he has to walk to another room before dialing the number, he may have to keep on repeating the number to himself as he goes for, if he does not, the trace is likely to have faded into oblivion before the telephone is reached. Broadbent's experiments are much more systematic than this discussion implies, but our purpose here is only to give the gist of his concept of a rapidly fading memory trace that characterizes all experience. The trace described by Broadbent is similar to the trace discussed by those who have experimented with conditioning in animals. The transitory trace is a memory mechanism particularly important for understanding human perception. Sperling (1960) has demonstrated experimentally the existence of a brief trace-memory system.

The second and third memory systems to be considered here are now widely referred to as the short-term memory system and the long-term memory system. In much of the current literature the abbreviations of STM and LTM are used. Of these two concepts the short-term memory is the one least well defined, although much of our knowledge about it comes from an area of rigorous experimentation, namely, the area of verbal learning. In typical verbal learning studies, the subject has to learn to associate together pairs of words or nonsense syllables. After learning such a series of paired associates the subject learns, for example, to respond with the syllable *wub* whenever the syllable *zer* is presented, or to respond with the syllable *jex* whenever the syllable *gur* is seen. A list of ten such paired associates may have to be run through ten or more times before the subject can respond correctly to each of the ten syllables presented as stimuli. Retention of such a task is generally rather short and within twenty or thirty minutes after the end of the experiment, the subject has forgotten the set of correct responses.

Long-term memory is a permanent memory system reserved for information that has high utility and, in particular, high future utility. The language a person acquires in childhood represents one of the sets of learnings that become placed in permanent memory.

Short-Term and Long-Term Memory—Two Systems or One?

There has long been controversy concerning whether there are two distinct memory systems—short-term and long-term—or a single system. Adams (1967) has provided a readable account of the arguments for proposing two systems, which is not very different from the later more technical account given by Wickelgren (1973). The issue is whether there are two distinct records, or traces, of the information retained: one that fades within perhaps 30 minutes and one that is relatively permanent. The most convincing evidence comes from cases of brain injury in which memory functions are disturbed. The most dramatic case is that known as H. M. (see Pines, 1974), in which a patient after brain surgery showed dramatic evidence that there were two recording systems. After surgery, H. M. was able to remember satisfactorily events that occurred sometime previous to surgery, but was not able to add to that store of events. Thus he could not remember what he did the day before and could even read the same story day after day as though it were completely new to him. He was able to read a story because not only were his perceptual systems intact but his short-term memory was also intact and he was able to remember the beginning of the story before he reached the end. The memory of the story then faded, and soon after he could read the story again as though it were a new story. H. M.'s short-term memory was intact, as was his long-term memory, but there was no way in which information could be transferred from the one system to the other.

A second source of evidence is that the information seems to follow a different decay function in the two cases, that is, the curve representing retention is quite different in the two memory systems and the curves have different mathematical properties. Also, some conditions that facilitate short-term memory interfere with long-term retention and the reverse. Some years ago Kleinsmith and Kaplan (1963) conducted a study of learning to associate together pairs of words. Such a learning situation is commonly studied in the laboratory, but these research workers introduced a novel element into the experiment. They measured what is known as the galvanic skin response to each pair of words. This response is a changed resistance across the skin of the hand that occurs when a person is presented with an emotion-arousing situation, and it is commonly taken to indicate the extent to which the person is aroused by the situation presented. Kleinsmith and Kaplan found that when a pair of words produced a strong galvanic skin response, indicating arousal, the retention of the association between the words was reduced for short-term memory but improved for long-term memory. If a condition that improves long-term memory depresses short-term memory, and if a condition that improves short-term memory depresses long-term memory, the two memory systems would appear to be quite distinct.

A further source of evidence of the distinctiveness of short-term and long-term memory is that the errors of recall in many kinds of experiments are different for short-term and long-term memory. There is a marked tendency for errors of short-term memory to be what are called acoustic errors. In such an error the person substitutes a similar sounding word for the correct word, as when the correct word to be recalled is *dark* and he recalls *bark*. On the other hand, in recalling information held in long-term memory, the tendency is to provide similar meanings. Again, if the word to be recalled was *dark*, the person might recall the word *night*. The fact that the errors of recall are different for short-term and long-term memory suggests that two separate systems are at work.

Another argument is that the short-term memory system appears to have a rather small capacity whereas the capacity of the long-term memory system is relatively large.

Capacity of the Memory Systems

Although there has been an enormous amount of reflective thinking and research concerning the capacities of the various memory systems, no clear-cut answers can be given on this matter. The initial trace appears to be a large capacity system though Holding (1975) disputes this claim. The trace of a visual experience certainly contains a large amount of information, most of which cannot be retrieved for further use. The decay of the trace during the few seconds of its existence is so rapid that only a small fraction of the information present can be snatched for further use. What is snatched from a single brief exposure to the environment is a very limited amount of information. This amount is commonly referred to as the *span of attention* or *memory span*, and it is generally limited in quantity to about seven digits, seven letters, seven words, or seven chunks of information. This is not the capacity of the short-term memory system, however; it represents only the amount of information that can be obtained and used from a single brief viewing of the environment.

The capacity of the short-term memory system is controversial. Writers of a decade or more ago were inclined to view the system as having a quite small capacity, but a number of studies have suggested that the capacity may be much larger than was previously estimated. One such study is that by Shepard (1967). In the first part of the Shepard study two groups of 270 words each were selected, one group representing common words and the other group rare words. These words were shown in random order, one after the other, to the subjects, who were then tested to determine whether they could remember the words they had seen. The test consisted of presenting the subjects with pairs of words, one of which belonged to the list they had seen and one of which was new. In the test, the subjects had to identify the word they had seen. The new words that were paired with the words they had already seen had similar characteristics to the words in the original list, that is, they belonged to the same difficulty level and were derived from the same general source. The surprising finding of the study was that after the subjects had been through the list of 540 words once, they were able to identify with an 88.4 per cent accuracy the words they had seen. They were slightly better at identifying the rare words than the common words, but the difference was only a matter of a few percentage points. Shepard then went on to perform the same demonstration with approximately the same number of short sentences and, in a third study, he employed a procedure that used pictures. For sentences, the retention was about the same as for words, but the immediate retention rate for pictures went up to 96.7 per cent. The test for retention of pictures was also given after seven days and then again after 120. Different subjects were used for each of the delayed recognition conditions from those used for the immediate recognition condition. The surprising finding was that even after seven days the percentage recognition of pictures was 87.0 per cent. After 120 days the percentage recognition was 57.7, but this is not as high as it may seem to be, in that, by guessing alone, the subject would be expected to achieve a score of 50 per cent.

These results are unexpected and quite puzzling, for it is as if a transitory contact with materials led to the transfer of these materials to long-term memory. The general conditions of the experiment are those used in the study of short-term memory and one would have expected that the evidence of the experience would have vanished within a few hours, at the most. Instead, the record of recognition even seven days later indicated that permanent memory had taken place. The fact that little evidence was left after 120 days suggests only that subsequent exposure to words, sentences, and pictures may have interfered with the memory. Also, one commonly makes the assumption that when information is transferred to the long-term memory system it becomes organized in the process. The very large quantity of information to which subjects were exposed in the Shepard experiment appears to have left a record, but there is no indication that the information was in any way organized as it was taken in or after it was taken in. The experiment clearly brings out the fact that there is much we do not know about the human memory system.

The capacity of the long-term system has been a matter of controversy for many years. Many well-known scientists have believed that the human information storage system has a vast capacity. An argument commonly introduced to support the position of an almost limitless memory is the well-established fact that there are billions of nerve cells in the central nervous-system. This argument is not as impressive as it might appear to be on the surface because nobody knows how many of these nerve cells are actually concerned with the storage of information. Many of the cells have other functions, including those of the conduction of information in and out of the system, the analysis of information, and the control of the general level of activity. The storage system may well involve only a small fraction of the total number of cells in the brain. Even if all the cells were involved in storage, there is doubt whether the system would be sufficient to record all the information provided by the sensory system at any given instant.

The concept of a permanent memory of vast capacity has been claimed to find support in the work of Penfield (1951), a neurosurgeon who started out with an interest in the control of epilepsy by the surgical removal of parts of the brain. Penfield's technique involves the removal of part of the cranium and the exposure of large sections of the cortex, and this is done with the use of local anesthetics only. The patient experiences no pain and is fully conscious during the entire operation. Although the operation is performed for the purpose of removing a small section that seems to be the seat of the epilepsy problem, Penfield has also been able to explore with his patient the effect of stimulating electrically various portions of the exposed cortex. When Penfield stimulates a particular area of the cortex, the patient reports what he experiences. The so-called sensory projection areas, such as the visual cortex and the auditory cortex, do not produce meaningful experiences when stimulated, although they do produce experiences related to the particular sensory system involved. Stimulation of the visual cortex produces flashes of light of different colors, but never a picture, and stimulation of the auditory cortex produces ringing and other sounds, but never a melody. Other areas, when stimulated, do produce the most vivid images of past events and it is the study of these that are of the greatest interest in research on memory.

Several facts are significant about Penfield's observations. One is that the experiences reported when the temporal lobes are stimulated are not single static memories, such as might be represented by a single frame on a motion picture film, but rather, they are like the sequences of events as they were orginally experienced. The person being stimulated does not see the image of a friend, like a portrait, but rather the friend walking toward him and meeting him. Penfield claims that the experiences are so lifelike and vivid that the patient can pick out details which he did not notice at the original time. Often the material recalled represents events that the patient believed he had long forgotten. On the surface, the research gives the impression of providing evidence that whatever is experienced is recorded in memory in the greatest of detail, but there are certain weaknesses in the data that leave doubts about this conclusion.

The data are greatly limited by the fact that Penfield was an explorer rather than a systematic experimentalist. Penfield did not expose his patients to particular materials, such as a sheet of newspaper, and then try to revive an image of the experience through his surgical technique. If he had done this kind of thing, and could show that the patient could later report the content of printed sections of the sheet of newspaper not observed at the time of the original esposure, he would have a strong case for claiming that memory is like a photographic process providing a permanent record of detail, regardless of whether such details were or were not noted at the time. Because Penfield was not an experimentalist in this sense, he caught what data he could, but the significance of the data is not clear. Suppose a patient has one of his temporal lobes stimulated and reports that he sees an old friend of twenty years ago walking toward him. He reports that the friend is wearing a blue pin-striped suit, has a red handkerchief protruding from his pocket, and that the suit is single-breasted, with two buttons on the front. Given such data, one cannot tell whether the "memory" genuinely represents what was originally seen, or whether it represents a plausible reconstruction, with perhaps the addition of details that were never really there. There is substantial evidence from the literature of experimental psychology that human beings have a great capacity for making constructions of what they believe happened, but these constructions may have little relationship to what actually happened. This is a major reason for conflicts of evidence in courts of law, when two witnesses provide entirely different accounts of what happened and each swears that his account is the correct one. The phenomena reported by Penfield may be artifacts of a person's capacity to make constructions that he believes represent events in the past.

Another problem is also presented by the Penfield findings. Suppose that the stimulation of a particular area results in the patient's recalling and reexperiencing a dinner he had with a friend. Now if this area is surgically removed, the patient does not lose all memory of the dinner with the friend. Indeed, the particular memory is not likely to be disturbed at all, indicating that the site stimulated, which produces the particular memory, is not the site where the memory is stored. The site stimulated may represent an area of the brain where the visual memory is *reconstructed*.

An entirely different view is presented by those who take the position that much evidence supports the position that the permanent memory system has a very limited capacity. First of all, it takes work to place an item in relatively permanent storage. We all know what a struggle it is to learn a foreign language, and this is because of the immense amount of work necessary to memorize the large vocabulary required for obtaining command of a new language. If information is slow to enter the long-term memory system, it surely is extremely probable that a very limited amount of information can be placed there. Life would be too short to store, piece by piece, a *vast* quantity of information.

A second argument is that the human system appears to be designed so that a minimum of information is stored for long-term purposes. Both a perceptual trace and a short-term memory are available for holding information for brief periods, and much of our daily life is made possible by these systems that hold information long enough for it to be used and then discarded. If an engineer were designing a memory system, he would introduce such short-term memory mechanisms in order to prevent the long-term memory from becoming cluttered with details that are of only transitory interest. The system for retaining information is designed *as-if* the long-term system had to be protected from being over whelmed with unnecessary detail.

Finally, an additional factor will be discussed further in the section on the theory of forgetting, which has considerable implications for estimating the capacity of the memory system. This is the fact that every item of information introduced into the memory system tends to disrupt information that is already there. The addition of a new piece of information to the system does not produce that much gain in the information stored, for the amount added is partly balanced by a certain amount of information that is taken away from the system by the addition. This is the major reason why a review of what we know from time to time is important to strengthen the storage of it in the memory system. Review is necessary largely because the store of information is being constantly eroded as new information is stored. This in itself limits the amount of information that can be placed in the system.

Retention in Terms of Chunks

In free recall tasks, the number of units that can be presented and later recalled has little to do with whether the units are fairly large units or small units. For example, Bower (1969) undertook a study in which he compared performance in a free recall task in which subjects were either exposed to a list of nouns or a list of three-word expressions such as *fair-weather friend*, *good old days*, and *Happy New Year*. He found that the ability to retain and recall, in terms of the number of units involved, was the same for the single nouns as for the three-word expressions; that is, if the average recall performance was twelve nouns, the average recall for three-word expressions would be twelve three-word expressions. The material is said to be learned in *chunks*, and the hypothesis tested in the Bower experiment is known as the *chunking hypothesis*.

A point to note in this connection is that the task of the student is not that of learning the nouns or expressions, for these are already familiar to him and all of them have been previously stored in his long-term memory system. What he is learning is, so to speak, to tag these nouns and expressions already in his permanent storage system as the particular ones now presented to him. The task is like pulling off a library shelf those books mentioned in a review. This is an entirely different task from placing the books on the shelf when they are first purchased. Thus the studies of chunking show that information already stored can be tagged as easily in large chunks as in small chunks. One is tempted to generalize and suggest that information in the long-term memory system is stored in chunks, but too much evidence points in another direction.

The Structure of Long-Term Memory

The fact that one can retrieve, almost instantly, much of the information stored in long-term memory implies that the memory system is organized. An unorganized system of knowledge does not permit rapid retrieval. If encyclopedia articles were arranged in random order, one would have to spend countless hours in locating a single item of information, but the encyclopedia articles are arranged in terms of alphabetically organized key concepts and, hence, retrieval from the system is relatively fast. Retrieval from the encyclopedia is not as fast as retrieval from one's own memory, but it is quite rapid because the knowledge in the encyclopedia is well organized. One can retrieve knowledge rapidly from the memory system, because the memory system is well organized. There is no other acceptable explanation. The difficulty is in finding out how the memory is organized, for one has no way of looking into one's memory to see how the items there are arranged. All one knows is that there is a great source of information collected in life and that one can generally pull out needed items of information.

One can make statements about how the knowledge is not organized. It certainly is not organized alphabetically. It is not simply a system like a photograph album. It is much more complicated than the kind of organization of knowledge found in a library where all books on the same topic are placed on the same shelf. Procedures for retrieving knowledge from a library are relatively slow and primitive compared with those involved in the recovery of information from the brain. Another important point to make is that no computer system so far devised has the storage or retrieval capacity of the human brain. Rapid retrieval of the stored information is a feature that provided man with survival capability, for it often permitted quick action.

Many theories have been produced concerning the way in which long-term memory is organized. The classical theory, which goes back to Aristotle, is that memory is a system of ideas with associations linking together the ideas in a complex network. This concept of memory has persisted into modern times, as the hundreds of modern studies of word association testify. Up to a point the associationistic model of memory is convenient and within certain narrow limits one can consider the memory to be structured in this kind of way.

A second kind of model for the structure of long-term memory is the hierarchical model, which proposes that memory is structured with specific ideas categorized under more general ideas. Thus the concepts of a robin and a sparrow are categorized under birds, and birds are categorized under animals. This theory has also had a long history of exploration by philosophers, but every ten years or so an experimental psychologist proposes this structure as though it were a brand new idea. One can find some support for this concept of memory structure, which is not surprising, since learning in many academic areas takes place in a hierachical structure. We learn that sparrows and robins are birds and that birds are animals.

A third model, proposed by Kintsch and Keenan (1974) and Kintsch (1974, 1975), proposes that long-term semantic memory is structured in terms of propositions. These propositions are not precise records of the language we use, but a kind of shorthand containing the essential meaning, and from which a statement can be constructed that contains the essential meaning. Kintsch and Keenan talk about the surface structure of a statement, that is, the statement as it is actually said or written. Then there is the base structure, which is the meaning of the statement as it is recorded in memory. Kintsch has shown in ingenious experiments that if two sentences convey the same meaning but one uses a much more complex structure than the other, the more complex one takes longer to comprehend than the simpler one. However, when the person is asked to retrieve the meaning, there is no difference in the time taken. The data suggest that both the simple and the complex sentences are recorded with the same base structure. Kintsch and Keenan take the position that the base structure propositions are ordered in a hierarchy, with some propositions being subordinate to others. Comprehension involves constructing a base structure for the proposition as it is heard. The surface structure of propositions is remembered for only a short time and is rapidly lost in the short-term memory system. In addition, Kintsch and Keenan have evidence to show that access to a particular proposition stored in memory appears to involve a search process. One cannot go directly to a particular proposition, but only to a block of propositions and then one can search that block.

Kintsch's approach is interesting and refreshing. Its main weakness lies in the fact that it seems to be a model of adult verbal memory. The memory of children almost certainly functions differently, for there is substantial evidence that children can perform logical operations before they can verbalize these operations. The memory of children does not seem to have this propositional character at all.

Kintsch and Keenan (1974) propose that the content of short-term memory determines how an item is stored in long-term memory. Thus I hear some information about a *big wheel*. The content of short-term memory gives me the context and tells me whether to store the information in relation to what I know about my boss or what I know about round objects that rotate on an axis. The short-term memory has implicit in it a code that is used for coding all incoming information.

Another recent proposal concerning the gross structure of long-term memory comes from Tulving (1972), who suggests that long-term memory is organized two major ways, referred to as the episodic and semantic memory systems. The Tulving proposal is highly controversial at the present time (see Watkins and Tulving, 1975; Light, Kimble, and Pellegrino, 1975; and Watkins and Tulving, 1975), but it is such an interesting one that it cannot be passed over.

Episodic memory refers to a record of incidents that happen to the individual. Included in my episodic memory are such incidents as a record of the lady in the red hat who sat next to me yesterday on the bus, the drive to work through this morning's snowstorm, a flight to London in 1970, a moment in a high pass in the Medicine Bow National Forest, and the telegram announcing my mother's death. All of these are personal events that happened to me at a particular time and in a particular place, and a part of the memory is the time and place when they occurred. They are also, in a sense, autobiographical and are stored in the order in which they have occurred. They are analogous to a card file of some of the happenings of one's life stored in chronological order.

The semantic memory, on the other hand, stores a very different class of information. In the semantic memory are stored such pieces of information as that the circumference of a circle is equal to $2\pi r$, that a mixture of blue and yellow pigments produces a green pigment, that the temperature of a furnace for firing pottery is as high as 2,000°F, that a nitrogen deficiency in a lawn results in a yellowish green color, and that insulin controls sugar metabolism. An important point to note is that none of these items of information is tied to a particular situation or episode in life. Their main characteristic is that they are a part of an organized system of knowledge. They are components of an overall cognitive system that can be called upon to solve a great range of problems. One cannot remember when or how one learned each item except in a few special cases in which the memory is also recorded in the episodic memory system.

The episodic memory records information very largely as it happens. The record of the lady in the red hat whom I encountered yesterday is printed in the episodic memory system pretty much as it happened. On the other hand, the newspaper article I have just read on the environment will be remembered, but in a different way. If somebody were to ask me about the article tomorrow, I would be able to tell him the gist of the information it contained. The words I would use would be largely different from those that appeared in the article, and the sentence structure would be different, but the essential information contained in the original article would still be communicated. The information from the newspaper article would have been organized prior to storage. I would have thought through what I was reading and have extracted the central ideas and these I would have placed in the permanent memory system. In the case of the semantic memory system, much work is undertaken on the information to be stored prior to storage, but information is placed in the episodic system pretty much as it arrives.

In contrast to episodic memory organized in a time sequence, semantic memory is organized in terms of the many ways in which knowledge is organized. Some knowledge, such as mathematics, is organized within a logical structure. Knowledge of geography may be organized partly in terms of space relations on the surface of the earth. Knowledge of physics may be organized largely in terms of the laws of physics, though the different aspects of physics may also have a subject-matter organization. Most subject-matter fields have multiple systems of organization. Historical knowledge is organized partly in terms of time and partly in terms of geographical location, economic concepts, theories of historical process, and so forth. Semantic systems of memory have complex forms of organization.

Tulving also notes certain important differences related to taking information out of the two systems. When an episode is taken out of the episodic system, the record of the event is likely to be changed. For example, each time that the witness of an accident attempts to report what happened, he is likely to change his story slightly. It is not that he is motivated to change his story, but the telling of the story changes the information stored in memory. In contrast, information can be taken out of the semantic system again and again without the stored information being changed. However, many times I may explain to children that the circumference of a circle is $2\pi r$, I still continue to store the information that the circumference of a circle is equal to $2\pi r$. The information held in the semantic system is held in a highly stable form.

If this conception of the dual function of long-term memory holds up as more research is undertaken, it will be found to have considerable potential for understanding educational phenomena. For example, suppose that children are shown a film about the Swiss Alps and the people who live there. Two days later an attempt is made to find out what they can recall. The main facts they remember were the green of the valley, the bright peasant costumes, the impressiveness of the mountains silhouetted against the blue sky, and the goats on the hillsides. These are essentially items in episodic memory and form an unstable and transitory form of knowledge, but that is not what one hopes to achieve through the use of audiovisual materials.

The information from the film on the Alps entered the episodic system but this did not have to be the case. Instead of recording the vague image of goats, the pupil might have learned that goats are raised because these are mountain animals that thrive on the mountainsides and help to complete the dietary requirements of the Swiss by providing not only meat but also milk and cheese. Such information can become a part of the organized information of the child and a part of the semantic memory system.

Kintsch and Keenan (1974) suggest that there is always a close relationship between semantic and episodic memory. For example, the word *chisel* has a place in semantic memory where it has relations to other words denoting tools and operations performed on wood. The word *chisel* is also related to certain experiences I have had, such as the occasion when I had a chisel stolen, and the occasion when, as a boy, I used a chisel as a screwdriver and ruined the edge. The episodic memory gives meaning to words, in terms of specific and concrete events. These records in memory can be considered to be *like* a set of propositions such as:

A chisel is a tool
A chisel has a cutting edge
A chisel cuts wood
A chisel was ruined by using it as a screw driver
A chisel was stolen on a certain occasion.

This does not mean that these items are stored as sentences, but rather that they are stored in a form that makes it possible to produce a sentence.

Piaget and his associate Inhelder have made a unique contribution to our understanding of long-term memory (Piaget and Inhelder, 1973). Unlike American research workers, Piaget and Inhelder examine memory on a developmental basis and reject the assumption that memory is the same from birth to death. In contrast to Tulving, who has been interested primarily in sophisticated memory systems, Piaget and Inhelder have been concerned with developing a comprehensive picture of long-term memory at all levels of functioning. For them, the most primitive memory system of all is that involved in the antibody system that "conserves" a record of the organism's fight with diseases. This memory system provides a permanent record of aspects of the organism's history.

At the next higher level memory involves the conservation, that is, preservation of the sensorimotor schemata and the recognition of signs that the schemata can be successfully used. Memory, at this level, is a memory of action systems and the signals in the environment that trigger them. Thus the 5-month-old infant may learn to recognize a rattle as something to be sucked, shaken, and looked at. When presented with the rattle, the sight, touch, or noise of the rattle will evoke one of the action schemata and the infant performs one or more of his routines in relation to the rattle. This does not mean that the infant has any internal representation of the rattle or can think about the rattle when the rattle is not present. Indeed, the infant behaves toward the rattle as though out of sight were out of mind. Memory at this level does not include capacity to recall an object not present, to think about it in its absence, or to think of things to do with it the next time the object appears. Infants have recognitory memory, in the sense that previous experiences with objects modify their future behavior with the same or similar objects, but they do not have representational memory, which permits the recall of a representation of an absent object. Early recognition processes are fundamentally different from later recall.

Primitive memory is memory for habit. It is the basic mechanism used throughout life that results in the elicitation of the correct motor skill on the correct occasion. Driving a car would seem to involve this kind of memory. Signals such as red lights elicit appropriate responses, and without any thought on the part of the driver. It is true, of course, that we have the capacity to think about our driving skills in the absence of the car and, hence, our memory for those skills is in this respect at a more advanced stage than is that of the infant. Nevertheless the storage and memory of them is at a similar level.

The third level or memory, in terms of the theory of Piaget and Inhelder, involves recognition and recall with strict reference to the past. The infant responds to the rattle in a way that shows his familiarity with the object does not have such reference. Although the object is familiar to him, he probably does not recall having seen it before. Memory at the third level has a reference to events in the past. We recognize a visitor to our office because we ran into him a week earlier at a party. We may even recognize a visitor as someone we had previously met somewhere before, but cannot quite remember where. In both cases there is a clear reference to the past, even though in the latter example the reference to the past is not specific with respect to time and place.

We take for granted the fact that remembering in adult life always has a past reference and that it is difficult to conceive of the possibility of remembering without such past reference. Yet such is the memory of the infant, and probably the memory of most subhuman creatures. The experiments that Piaget and Inhelder report in their more recent research on memory pertain to this third type of memory with a past reference.

Let us consider a typical experiment. A child is shown a series of rods arranged in order of size:

The child is asked to take a good look, at the rods and to remember what he has seen. About a week later, he is asked to tell about what he has seen, first by running his finger over the table top, and then he is asked to make a drawing.

The 4-year-old draws a number of lines that are about equal in size. He shows no recognition of the fact that the original lines varied in size, nor that there were a particular number. Children at that age have no comprehension of the nature of a series, but they do recognize straight objects as straight objects. Piaget and Inhelder say that there is no schema involving seriation to which the child can assimilate the memory of the graded series of rods, so he assimilates it to a much simpler schema, namely, that of a set of straight objects.

At a slightly more advanced stage of development the child may produce drawings such as the following:

Here there is recognition of differences in length, but no concept of ordered differences in length. Somewhat more mature representations are the following:

What Piaget calls stage 2 development occurred in children ranging in age from 4 years and 5 months to 5 years and 8 months. They show typical drawings such as the following:

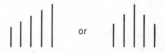

The stage 3 child reproduces an ordered series with the bases all on a single line as they were in the original.

The important point to note is that the child recalls from memory only that which he can structure in terms of the schema available to him. If he has not acquired the schema of seriation, and has no comprehension of the nature of a series, he will be unable to reproduce an image of a series. His reproduction represents the structures he possesses for assimilating knowledge. The knowledge he cannot assimilate will not appear in his reproductions.

A still more interesting finding is reported by Piaget and Inhelder. About eight months later they asked those of the children whom they could still locate to reproduce what they had seen. They found that the reproductions were superior, in terms of level of development, to the reproductions made immediately after seeing the rods. Some children who had not been able to reproduce a series when they had originally attempted to make a picture of the rods were now able to do so. The change in their representations was related to the change in their intellectual state of development.

The results of the delayed memory study raises a number of issues. They suggest that the memory contains the essential information of the original material presented, but that the intelligence of the younger children is too limited to permit them to use the information. As their intellect grows, the children become progressively more able to use the information in storage, and the reproductions of the original situation become more accurate.

The study using the series of rods was reproduced with other materials and generally yielded similar results. However, in one of the more complex situations no long-term improvement was found. Piaget and Inhelder have an explanation for this exception, but it cannot be presented here for reasons of space (see Piaget and Inhelder, 1973, pp. 74–97).

The Piaget and Inhelder research on memory in relation to logical structures brings out the distinction between what is memorized and what can be retrieved from memory. Their research shows that the process of remembering is a reconstructive process, and not a process analogous to that of pulling an item of information from a card file. Memories are reconstructions. If they involve logical constructions, they are limited to the logical constructions and operations that the individual is capable of undertaking.

This leads us to a consideration of another attempt to introduce the categories of iconic memory and symbolic memory into long-term memory. Those who make the distinction commonly believe that iconic memory is characterized by a recall of images that may be in terms of any one of the perceptual systems. Thus one has visual images of past scenes, images of the sound of music, and images of particular bodily experiences. The assumption is generally made that iconic memory does not consist of a set of images. In other words, visual iconic memory is not in terms of a set of internal pictures, analogous to a set of pictures in a photographic album, but rather that it represents a set of material out of which images are created. The image is a creation of the retrieval process, which is why one may have images of events that did not happen. The witness in court swears that he saw a large blue Cadillac, driven by a man, but the fact was that it was a small green Chevy driven by a woman. The witness's image may be brilliant and clear, even though it was an image of that which was not there. The image is a creation of material stored in memory.

Iconic memory is typically contrasted with symbolic memory, and the form of symbolic memory most frequently studied is that of verbal memory. There is some evidence that much of the information is transformed into verbal information for storage. Such a transformation is referred to as a process of coding. The human memory system seems to be particularly adept at storing symbolic material and providing accurate retrieval. The retrieval of information from the iconic system yields generally rather inadequate information and the images are not only poor in detail but often grossly incorrect. In contrast, a person may remember and recall the entire set of words and music from a major role in an opera. Shakespearean actors recall their lines with flawless accuracy. Such observations have suggested that iconic memory is a much more primitive form of memorizing than is the symbolic system.

Although images are quite deficient in detailed information, recognition memory for scenes previously observed may be highly accurate. Indeed, Entwistle and Huggins (1973) found that first-grade children could recognize accurately pictures they had previously viewed and performed better with these visual materials than with materials that consisted of verbal descriptions of the scenes. Entwistle and Huggins cite data from other sources leading to the conclusion that iconic memory reaches its peak of efficiency at the third-grade level.

There has long been a controversy over whether memory for visually presented objects is generally better than memory for verbally presented ideas. Murdock (1974) has reviewed the evidence and comes to the conclusion that the question is not answerable because there are too many factors that cannot be controlled. Consider, first, the selection of materials to be compared. In terms of retention, a comparison of a picture of an object such as a shoe with the word *shoe* is just one comparison one might make. Under such conditions, the picture probably produces a greater amount of retention. But what happens when the presentation of the shoe is compared with a verbal description of the shoe giving all the detail that the picture provides. When the two presentations are equated for amount of detail provided, differences in the two forms of memory disappear. The crucial factor seems to be not so much whether the presentation is pictorial or verbal, but the number of attributes that are presented.

There is a parallel between the distinction between iconic and symbolic memory and the distinction between episodic and semantic memory. Episodic memory is presumably mainly iconic, and semantic memory mainly symbolic. Each of these distinctions is quite crude, but it may be the same distinction.

Most of the matters discussed in this section have pertained to gross categories of memory phenomena. The studies discussed present theories concerning the general nature of retention phenomena. Only a few psychologists have considered the actual nature of storage. If storage is in terms of specific pieces of information, held at the level of the nerve synapse, it should be possible to identify the nature of these small pieces of information held.

Underwood (1969) has suggested that what is stored in the memory system is primarily a set of attributes, that is, characteristics of experiences. In the chapter on perception, the point is made that recognition processes are possible because the person making the recognition can analyze whatever he experiences into its attributes, and from the attributes thus analyzed is able to recognize what is before him. Underwood expands on this concept in describing the memory system. The memory for most common objects would almost certainly involve an immense number of different attributes as well as other components. For example, my memory of the car I drive involves the retention of many action systems related to driving it. When I enter the car, I perform a sequence of acts related to starting the car and leaving the garage, and these take place quite automatically. In addition, I have stored information related to the attributes of the car such as whiteness, year of model, the noise made by the engine, the sound of a bad rear bearing and numerous other characteristics. Some of these attributes are probably stored in a form closely related to auditory language, but some, such as the sound of the rear bearing, have not been coded into words. It is the total sum of the retained attributes and action systems that form what might be called the memory of the particular car.

Evidence that information in the memory system is stored piecemeal comes from many sources. An interesting approach is in the story of what is called the tip-of-the-tongue phenomenon, in which one is attempting to recall a word but can recall only words similar in form or meaning. Brown and McNeill (1966) initiated work in this area and came up with some interesting findings. Their technique involved the preparation of the definitions of a list of rare words such as *ambergris, nepotism,* and *cloaca,* which occur less often than once in a million times in English written materials. Each definition was read to the subjects. After the definition was read, some subjects said they knew the word and others said they did not know it. These subjects indicated their knowledge or lack of knowledge on a sheet of paper and had nothing more to do. The others were those who felt that the answer was on the tip of their tongues but it would take them a little time to retrieve the word from their memory. These subjects were asked to indicate some of the characteristics of the word they were searching to find by indicating how many syllables they thought it was, what was its initial letter, what other words were similar in sound to it, and what words might be similar to it in meaning. The word sought is referred to as the target word.

A very significant finding from this study is that subjects in the tip-of-the-tongue state were able to identify significant aspects of the words they were trying to recall, even though they could not recall the actual words. They had considerable success in identifying the number of syllables in the target word, if the words were of one, two, or three syllables in length. Longer words tended to be identified as three-syllable words. In addition, subjects were able to guess with better than chance accuracy the first letter of the word sought and also the syllable that was stressed when the word was spoken. In the case of the words similar in sound that they wrote down, there was a tendency for the first and last letters to be matched correctly. There was also a tendency for subjects to be able to identify correctly suffixes involved in the target word.

Another finding is that the subject is able to judge which one of two words most resembles the target word. This is also a familiar experience. When we are seeking to retrieve a person's name, one can often say " It is a name like Black and not like the name Cross you have suggested." Furthermore, when we are told the correct name, we know immediately that the name suggested is correct. Now in both of these cases we take in information and are able to compare it with information already stored. Somebody suggests that the missing name may be " Black " and we behave as if we were able to compare this suggestion with the name stored within us and say that it is close, but that it is not an exact match. When the name " Stack " is suggested, we know that we have found what we were looking for. Again, we behave as though we received the suggested name, compared it with the stored name, and concluded that there was an exact match. The odd thing about the entire process is that one can compare incoming information with information already stored while having no direct knowledge of the stored information.

Brown and McNeill have a more complicated explanation of the phenomenon, suggesting that we do not store whole words but perhaps only critical components. The critical components of the input are then checked against the critical components of the stored word. This does not explain how one can recognize that a word is not the correct one even when it varies in some quite minor way from the correct word that is stored. It is much simpler and probably as satisfactory to assume that the entire word is stored, perhaps in an auditory form, than to assume an attribute storage.

Many studies have been undertaken purporting to demonstrate that words are processed as a set of features. For example, Nelson, Brooks, and Fosselman (1972) showed that words were recognized in terms of particular features, of which the first and last letters were quite crucial. Words that had been remembered were easily confused with other words that had the same letters in the same positions. Visually presented words do not seem to be relegated to memory as total units, but as a set of distinctive features, of which the individual letters seem to be important. A study by Ellis and Daniel (1971), using randomly designed shapes, indicated that the individual stored in his memory not representations of the shapes as units, but a record of their distinctive features.

Attribute theory of memory has had a long history and the evidence generally supports it. Murdock (1974), starting with an information-processing model of recognition and memory, also comes to the conclusion that memory is in terms of a set of attrubites. Attribute theory of memory will continue to be rediscovered for a long time to come.

Tulving and Watkins (1975) have also produced a theory of memory as the retention of a set of attributes, suggesting that such attributes are stored in an organized form. The form of organization depends on how the information is to be retrieved. Thus if a person expects later to have to describe what is meant by a parallelogram, he will store the information about parallelograms in the form of a description that he can later communicate to another.

Short-Term Memory—Primary Memory

Short-term memory is sometimes referred to as primary memory, which carries the implication that all information must primarily enter the short-term system before it can be transferred to the long-term system. The broad characteristics of short-term memory, despite the extensive research related to it, still remain in doubt. An article by Watkins (1974) summarizes three ways in which short-term memory is conceptualized. Watkins defines primary memory in a more restricted sense than it is considered in this book, but let us move on to the three ways in which he sees that primary memory can be conceptualized.

1. SHORT-TERM MEMORY AS A STORE FROM WHICH INFORMATION IS SELECTED FOR TRANSFER TO LONG-TERM MEMORY. The first theory states that information can enter the long-term memory system only after it has first entered the primary memory system; that information has to be kept some length of time in the short-term system before it becomes transferred to the long term; and that the transfer is accomplished through rehearsal. By repeating the line of poetry we are trying to learn, the material is kept in the primary memory system and if it is kept there long enough, it will be transferred to a more permanent form of memory system. Thus long-term memory is slowly built up through information entering, and being maintained in, the primary memory system. The model fits well our common understand-

ing of how we memorize, for it implies that the longer we rehearse the better will be the retention in long-term memory.

2. PRIMARY MEMORY AS CONSCIOUSNESS. A second conception of short-term memory or primary memory is that it is the conscious element in memory. Since consciousness does not exist as such, and only *consciousness of something*, one has to reinterpret this concept of memory as consciousness of information. The short-term memory represents that part of our store of information of which we are conscious. This interpretation of short-term or primary memory does not exclude the one previously considered. This concept of short-term memory makes no real distinction between short-term and long-term except insofar as some information is in the conscious field and some is not.

3. SHORT-TERM MEMORY AS A RETRIEVAL PROCESS. The third conception links short-term memory with perception. In short-term memory are all immediate perceptions; thus it includes not only inputs through the sensory systems, but the interpretation of these inputs through the use of information stored in memory. Confronted with another individual, one is able to identify him and give one's perception of him meaning by using information stored in memory, which tells one that the individual has a particular name, that one has seen him before in such and such a place, and so forth. In addition, the short-term memory may include information drawn from the long-term system. I may sit back in a chair with my eyes closed and reminisce about past events. Clearly, the function of the short-term memory is closely related to the process of retrieving information from the long term system.

All three conceptualizations of short-term memory can be incorporated into a single concept. The short-term memory system may incorporate the features of all three conceptualizations. Most models of short-term memory also include other features. Typically it is conceived to be the locus where information is organized prior to memorization. There is certainly overwhelming evidence that such organizing activities are vital for retention. Organizing strategies appear to be vital in preparing material for long-term retention. This is such an important feature of short-term memory that it will have to be considered separately.

There seems to be little uniformity in the rate at which different pieces of information decay in the system. Paivio and Bleasdale (1974) have reviewed the numerous studies that have attempted to find the decay rate of information in short-term memory and have come to the conclusion that more than just decay is involved. Information in the system may become temporarily inaccessible. When this happens it may appear to have shown complete decay, but then the information may return. There seem to be many different conditions that influence actual decay time, so it is not possible to draw a simple curve showing rate of decay of information.

The Short-Term Memory as an Organizing System

The long-term memory is an organized system of information, but the organizing of the information stored there seems to take place in the short-term memory. A good place to start a consideration of this problem is the work of Ausubel.

For Ausubel (1963), information can be most readily stored if it is related to a pivotal idea, referred to as an *organizer*. An organizer is a key concept that may form a basis for understanding a great many happenings. One can point to concepts in physics, such as density, which are of crucial importance in organizing knowledge. The concept of density organizes such information as why ships float, why divers have to wear weights, why smoke rises in the atmosphere except on a hot and muggy day, and numerous other common events.

The problem of how memory is organized has also been attacked by experimental psychologists, using special materials developed for experimentation. An early experiment on the organizing functions of memorizing and retention is illustrated by a study conducted by Underwood (1964), who presented to his subjects lists of words that could be organized into groups. For example, one list consisted of four names of countries, four birds, four diseases, and four elements, which were presented in a jumbled order so that words in the different categories were likely to be separated. Other lists presented sets of words that did not fall into obvious categories. At the end of the reading of each list, the subjects were asked to write down all the words they could remember. Although the lists containing groups of words had the individual words presented in random order, the words were recalled by the subjects in groups. That is, the learner tended, after hearing the words, to recall all the diseases together, all the countries together, all the birds together, and all the elements together. He didn't just remember the list as it was presented, but organized the list into categories. In addition, the lists that included categories of objects were remembered more easily than were lists that did not include obvious categories.

A series of related studies by Bousefield and his associates have also been conducted on the organization of material in the memory system. The technique adopted for the study of this problem is that of free recall. The learner is presented with a list of words one at a time, and then after the entire list has been read must recall all the words he can remember. Shuell (1969) and Tulving (1967, 1968) have summarized the results of these studies. The recalled items do not generally appear in the order in which they were presented. If the experimenter has selected the words so that they are easily categorized, the learner is likely to use the organization into which the words readily fit. However, if the words have been selected by the experimenter at random, the learner imposes his own organization on the material. For example, if the list of words includes the items—*house, stamp, envelope, tree, street, office*—the subject might repeat back the words in two groups, (1) *house, tree, street,* and (2) *stamp, envelope, office.* He might also use other groupings, such as placing *office* and *street* together. The subjective organization imposed by the learner is not always apparent from examining the list of words in the order in which they are reproduced by the learner, but some organization is always there. Organization appears to be crucial in the transfer of information from the short-term to the long-term memory system. Indeed, one suspects that one of the major differences between the mentally handicapped individual and the normal individual lies in the incapacity of the former to organize information for transfer to the long-term memory system. The mentally handicapped often show excellent performance on short-term memory tasks, but on tasks that call for organized stored information they experience difficulty. Shuell also cites evidence that young children show less capability to develop subjective organizations in free recall tasks than do adults, a fact that points up the conclusion that the strategies involved in organizing information are learned.

The reader can now see one reason why it is that well-organized material is better retained than poorly organized material. If the learner is left to organize material as it enters the short-term memory system, some of the information is lost in the process. Organizing the material before it is presented to the learner saves him this step, and perhaps makes it possible for the information to enter directly into the long-term memory system.

The data suggests that a primary fact remembered is the category to which objects belonged. Thus a person reading the Underwood list remembers that there were four birds. In the case of the particular list, he would only have to remember that it included four *common* birds to have most of the answers in this category correct, but subjects also remembered enough about the specific birds mentioned to be able to identify them, for very few errors were made on recall. The fact that errors of memory of material stored in the long-term system tend to involve the recall of the wrong item in the right category suggests that items to be remembered are tagged with a category and that one starts with the category when one wants to retrieve the item. The category is generally more readily retrieved than is the actual item itself. Thus we may recall having gone to a lecture some years previously on thetopic of poetry, but we may not remember which particular poems were discussed.

Numerous experiments have been conducted showing that the more readily a list of words is structured, the easier it is for the learner to remember. However, Bower et al. (1969), who have reviewed these studies, point out that the gains produced by word lists including words that are readily organized have been what they describe as " disheartening." They then proceeded to conduct a study in which they were able to show that under some conditions organized material might be learned two or three times as quickly as the same material presented in a disorganized order. Bower et al. prepared a list of words that could be presented with varying degrees of structure. The material involved the following words and categories in which they belonged:

Minerals

	METALS			STONES	
Rare	*Common*	*Alloys*	*Precious*	*Masonry*
Platinum	Aluminum	Bronze	Sapphire	Limestone
Silver	Copper	Steel	Emerald	Granite
Gold	Lead	Brass	Diamond	Marble
	Iron		Ruby	Slate

Such material can be presented in many different ways. Earlier experiments had generally compared the presentation of the words, one by one, either keeping together words in particular categories or arranging the words in random order. A comparison of the learning under these two conditions generally showed that the organized list was learned a little better than the random list.

Bowers et al. point out that the method of presenting words one by one does not help the subject utilize the organizational structure in the material. In one condition in their experiments they presented the entire body of material at the same time; either they showed the words within a structure, as in the case of the structure of minerals, or the words were assigned at random to groups and the set of groups of words was shown at one time. Under the former condition, the learner could make the most use of the structure of the words. He could see the various categories and learn the words as groups in terms of the categories to which they belonged. Under the random condition he would have to study the words and find some structure into which he could arrange them. Under these conditions, the categorized words were learned about three times as effectively as the randomly presented words.

Bowers et al. conducted a series of experiments related to this problem, and its explanation and their data are very consistent. The real problem is why the organized material is more readily learned than the random material. They conclude that if the learner can discover a simple rule that can be used to characterize and group the items in a list of words, then he uses that rule in carrying out a retrieval plan that permits him to reconstruct the list from memory. If he remembers, for example, that four of the words refer to the four commonest precious stones, then he can easily reconstruct the list of words that includes sapphire, emerald, diamond, and ruby. It is much easier to generate a set of words using a principle or rule than it is to recall a set of words unrelated to one another. For example, a person may not be able to remember the names of all the shops on Main Street, although he has seen the names many times, but it is easy to remember all the shop numbers if he knows that they start at 1 and go up to 218. Organized information calls upon the memory system to remember less information than when the information has no inherent organization. When one recalls a list of words by using a rule to generate the list, the errors that occur are called intrusion errors. They result from the rule's failing to discriminate between the words that should be produced and other words. However, in applying a rule such as that the names of rare metals are to be given, a person may recognize a name of a metal as not belonging on the basis of the knowledge that he knows he has not seen that word in print recently. Words are tagged, so to speak, with a recency label. One knows whether he has or has not seen a particular word recently. The recency and time of an experience is recorded as a part of the memory of that experience.

The way in which the plan of organization of the material is presented to the learner may be quite crucial. Nelson and Smith (1972) found that a chart showing the plan of organization was superior to a mere listing of the relationships involved between the elements. The latter fits common experience. Competent lecturers know the value of a chart showing the general plan of the materials being discussed.

Teachers of special education have long recognized that the retarded have special difficulties in memorizing. Early workers assumed that the memory difficulties of the retarded were due to a defect in the memory system and that the retarded rapidly forgot what they had learned. This is not so. For example, Shuell and Keppel (1970) have shown that if material is learned equally well by both slow and rapid learners, it is remembered about equally well after 24-hour and 48-hour intervals, a finding that suggests that the differences in the two groups do not lie in their memory systems, once information is stored there.

The difficulty of a majority of the retarded seems to lie in their inability to organize information in the short-term memory system. In addition, they do not use tricks that normal people ordinarily use in order to keep information in the short-term system. A study by Butterfield, Wamboldt, and Belmont (1973) illustrates this point. These research workers devised a simple memory task that would permit the study of the strategies involved in memorizing. The task involved a line of slots in a screen that could be opened one by one to expose a single letter. The learner pressed a button to open the first slot and expose the letter. Then he pressed the button again, which closed the first slot and opened the second slot. The learner thus opened each slot in turn by pressing the button and set his own pace for learning the letter in each slot. After he had opened and closed each slot successively, his final press of the button exposed a test letter. He had to indicate in which slot the letter had been previously exposed. Normal adults go about this task with a characteristic strategy. They expose the first three letters fairly quickly and stop to rehearse them. The next three letters are exposed and followed by another pause. The last three letters are exposed and immediately the test letter is called for. There is no pause after the last three letters, indicating that the learner is going to rely on immediate memory to retain this last group of letters.

Retarded learners show no such strategy. They expose the letters in the slots one after another, but never pause to rehearse the letters they have seen. They can be taught to rehearse but after learning this simple strategy do not manage to use the strategy at the right time. They seem quite capable of learning the strategies involved in this memory task, but have difficulty in calling up these strategies when they can be used to greatest advantage. The use of the strategies for facilitating memory seem to require a super strategy related to when they can be appropriately used. The retarded do not seem able to acquire this super strategy.

The retarded seem to lack even the simplest strategies of being able to rehearse material long enough for it to be transferred to long-term memory. Brown et al. (1973) established quite clearly this inability of the retarded to make use of rehearsal.

Forgetting

Forgetting in Short-Term Memory. There is agreement among psychologists that forgetting in short-term memory is a decay process, that is, the information fades from the system. One can prevent decay by rehearsing the information, as when one repeats a zip code number to keep it in mind long enough to address an envelope. One can accomplish the same goal by visualizing the number and keeping it before one's mind's eye. One of the functions of the short-term memory seems to be to keep the long-term system from becoming cluttered up with detail, and to do this a rapid decay of the information in short-term memory seems necessary. Since the individual can control the extent to which there is decay in short-term memory, research workers have had difficulty in producing graphs that might show the basic decay function of information.

Forgetting in Long-Term Memory. The popular, but wholly inadequate idea of how we forget material in long-term storage is decay theory, derived from our experience with short-term memory. Research provides the much more tenable theory that forgetting in this system is due to one piece of information interfering with the retention of another piece of information. Before considering interference theories at greater length, let us consider some findings that show that, in the absence of such interference there may be very little forgetting. In order to investigate this problem one has to find areas of information quite unrelated to new information acquired subsequently, in which one can follow the retention of such information over years. One such area is the retention of the names of one's fellow high school graduates, which was studied by Bahrick, Bahrick and Wittlinger (1975). These research workers were able to obtain from high school yearbooks the names and pictures of graduating classes. They gave these names and pictures to individuals who had graduated anywhere from 3 months to 50 years previously. The data show a surprisingly small decline in memory. After 15 years the graduates were able to perform the task with 90 per cent accuracy, and with 60 per cent accuracy even after 48 years. The graphs show relatively little decline in the extent to which this information was retained until about 40 years after graduation, at which time a rapid decline begins to set in. One suspects that after about the 60th year there is a decline in brain functions owing to physiological deterioration. Of course, on free recall there was a much greater decline beginning at a much earlier age. One suspects that the latter involves a difficulty in retrieving the information rather than a decay in the trace.

The follow-up studies of high school graduates show dramatically the extent to which information is stored permanently in the long-term memory system. There is little new information coming into memory that is likely to disrupt this particular memory trace. However, if we were members of a graduating class for each year, through life, we would undoubtedly confuse the names and faces of one graduating class with those of another. That would be the kind of interference that produces most forgetting in the long-term system.

Interference that produces forgetting occurs in two forms. First, there are retroactive effects, that is, learning may have a depressing effect on the retention of material previously learned. Second, there is a proactive effect, that is, learning taking place at a particular time may have a depressing effect on the retention of material subsequently learned.

Most of the research undertaken to date has been on the retroaction effect, which can be clearly demonstrated in the laboratory. The usual demonstration involves the learning of a set of paired associates, referred to as the *A-B* series, in which the learner has to learn to make a response with the word designated here as *B* whenever he sees the word designated as *A*. After learning this series, he is then required to learn a new paired associate series designated as the *A-C* series. In this series the stimulus words are the same as in the original series, but the responses learned to the stimulus words are different. Thus the first two words in the first list might be *chair-car*, and the first pair of words in the second list are *chair-box*. In doing this, the experimenter has taught the subject one habit, namely, to say *car* whenever the stimulus word *chair* is presented, and then the subject is taught a second and inconsistent habit, namely, that of responding to the same stimulus word *chair* with the word *box*. One can then demonstrate that the learning of the second of these associations disrupts the retention of the first set of associations. This is the retroactive inhibition phenomenon. It is a well-established phenomenon and is presumed to account for some of the forgetting that occurs in daily life. It is not specific to the learning of verbal associations, but is also found in the retention of motor skills involving the manual manipulation of the environment (and other physical manipulations as well). It will be referred to again in the chapter on transfer of training, where it will be viewed as a case of negative transfer.

The second interference effect, known as proactive inhibition, has not been investigated to the same extent, but the effect is clear, and generally somewhat stronger than that of retroactive inhibition. The common procedure for demonstrating this effect is that of the subject learning, first, the paired associate list *A-B*. He then learns the list *A-C*, and it can be demonstrated that the previous acquisition of the list *A-B* interferes with the learning and retention of the list *A-C*. The proactive effect, as with the retroactive effect, occurs not only in the case of verbal learning, but also with motor skills.

There is much theoretical speculation about how retroactive and proactive inhibition exert their disruptive effects. One proposed explanation of the retroaction effect is that the learning of the one response tends to extinguish the other response that has been learned. Up to this time, no experiment has been designed that can clearly demonstrate whether the extinction hypothesis is an acceptable explanation. Regardless of the value of particular explanations, interference theory is still the most influential theory of forgetting.

A strong argument for the interference theory of forgetting is that research has tended to indicate that very little forgetting occurs during sleep. The classic study by Jenkins and Dallenbach (1924) demonstrated this phenomenon, and the results have been replicated in later experiments. A decay theory of forgetting in long-term memory would lead one to expect that the memory for particular events would continue to decay during sleep. An interference theory would lead one to expect very little forgetting during sleep when presumably psychological activity is at a very low ebb. Yaroush, Sullivan and Ekstrand (1971) found this to be true for the first 4 hours of sleep, but not for the second 4 hours, and they have argued that an interference theory of forgetting should require as little forgetting during the second 4 hours as during the first. However, one can also argue that more psychological activity may well take place during the second 4 hours and produce as much forgetting as would a waking state.

Finally, we must consider a problem that has intrigued research workers in recent years; the effect of giving the learner instructions to forget. In some studies this problem is described as the effect of intent to learn in contrast to the intent to forget. The basic study in this area was conducted by Bjork (1970), who presented a paired associate learning task to subjects and signaled that certain items were not to be remembered. He was able to show that the to-be-forgotten items are not retained as well as the to-be-remembered items. In subsequent studies, Bjork and Woodward (1973) and Spector, Laughery, and Finkelman (1973) showed that the learners do not rehearse the words that are to be forgotten; they read them and work on remembering the words to be remembered. At the end of the list they will review in their minds the words to be remembered, but not the words to be forgotten. There is also an additional factor: The items to-be-forgotten are not organized in short-term memory in the way in which items have to be organized if they are to be retained over any length of time. There is not an effort to forget, but rather there is an effort to ignore and to avoid doing things that have to be done to retain the items. Martin and Kelley (1974) provided evidence for this view by showing that when individuals had to perform another task while learning the list of words they worked better on the other task following words to be forgotten. Work on the other task became a way of *not* working on the to-be-forgotten words. Macleod (1975) has shown that the difference in recall between the to-be-remembered items and the to-be-forgotten items remained after a 2-week interval.

These studies raise an issue that plagues all research on memory. Is the difficulty of recalling the to-be-forgotten items a result of the fact that they were not properly stored in memory or was it that the information was stored, but there was difficulty in retrieving the items? Epstein, Wilder, and Robertson (1975) found evidence to suggest that the difficulty was one of retrieving the items.

The Retrieval System

For several decades the literature on memory has stated that the memory system includes a separate retrieval mechanism, believed to be fundamentally different from the mechanism involved in placing information in long-term memory. This line of thinking has been stimulated by the design of computer systems, which include a mechanism for storing information and another for retrieving information from the memory system. However, in contemporary research literature on memory the term *retrieval* is used in several different meanings.

In the broad meaning of the term retrieval from memory refers to any process by which information is pulled out of the long-term memory system. The narrow meaning refers to a search process. In a search process a number of items are inspected successively to determine whether any one of them is the item of information needed. This raises the question of whether one can conceive of a retrieval process that does not involve a search. Some psychologists think that one can. In order to illustrate this point, consider the way in which one may want to retrieve a piece of information from the page of a book. Suppose one wishes to identify the date of a reference by Wickelgren. All one has to do is to look at the page of the book and out pops the printed words *Wickelgren* (*1965*). One does not have to search the page to do this, but the page as a whole can be examined with almost immediate location of the information. This process does not seem to involve a systematic search of the page. In the narrow meaning of the expression *retrieval from memory*, this immediate identification of what is sought is not referred to as a retrieval process. In most current literature the expression retrieval from memory is used in the narrower sense to cover a systematic search process.

McCormack (1972) has provided an excellent review concerning the use of the term retrieval in the narrower sense and the conditions under which such retrieval occurs. He concludes that most experimental psychologists take the position that information can be obtained from long-term memory either by an immediate identification process or by a search process. The opinion of these psychologists is that recognition memory involves the first of these, but that recall involves a search as well as a recognition process. Anderson and Bower (1972) have provided a detailed description of what they believe to be the retrieval process involved in recall, and they also take the position that recognition is a much simpler process.

A refreshingly new position has been taken by Tulving as a result of research over a decade. Tulving originated the distinction between episodic and semantic memory. He takes the position that most research on memory in the laboratory involves episodic memory, that is, the person learns a list of words, and the words and the conditions surrounding them become stored as a unit in episodic memory. The essential condition for the recall of those words is providing cues that were present during the learning of the words. The way in which information is stored determines the cues that are necessary to recall the information. Tulving (1973) states clearly and explicitly that he can find no basis distinguishing the process of recognition and recall and that both involve identical processes. Suppose I am shown a list of pairs of words, such as *black-CHAIR*, and receive the instructions to read both words but to learn only the words printed in capital letters. Later I am asked to recall the list of words. I may do this haltingly, but when I am presented the words in small letters (*black*, etc.) they help me to recall the words in capital letters. The words printed in small letters represent a retrieval cue. I could also be presented with the words in capital letters and be asked whether they were the words I had seen. Tulving would say that in the latter situation involving recognition, there were simply better cues involved than in the recall form of the task. For him, recognition and recall differ only in the cues provided, and both involve identical processes in obtaining information from memory. This theme has been expanded in a later paper by Watkins and Tulving (1975).

The Tulving position is that the cues for recalling information from episodic memory are the events that accompanied the original episode. I recall the man with the dog on the bus when somebody provides me with a recall cue by saying, "Whom did you see on the bus yesterday?" Another cue might be "Whom did you see on your trip downtown yesterday?" On the other hand, if an item of information is entered in semantic memory, the most effective cue for recall is likely to be a semantic one. If asked the question, "Are there other streets in your neighborhood named after English counties?" I could immediately give the names "Sussex" and "Devonshire." These names are a part of my organized knowledge concerning English counties. The cue provided by the question is not some accidental relationship, as between the bus and the man with dog, but the cue refers to an organization of knowledge. In both cases recall is cued, but the relationship of the cue to the item recalled is different. Tulving concludes that the circumstances involved in placing information into long-term memory are crucial in determining the conditions that will produce recall.

Thus the area of retrieval from memory is one in which there is a very active program of research, but the research has led to controversy rather than the settling of issues.

Controversy surrounds not only the theoretical issues but also some practical issues. Psychologists have long been interested in the fact that older individuals have memory difficulties, and the theory has been proposed that older individuals have difficulty not so much with the memory system itself, but with the retrieval of information from that system. The theory is that the functioning of the retrieval system deteriorates with age. The older person may be able to learn as well as the younger person, but he has difficulty in recovering from memory that which he has learned. Drachman and Leavitt (1972) have reviewed much of the research related to this problem, which suggests that the deficit of the older individual is in his retrieval system. However, Drachman and Leavitt provide some evidence that the deficit may be in the memory system itself rather than in the retrieval system. Of course, the deficit may be both and more in one than in the other depending on the nature of the learning task. The issue cannot be settled at this time.

There is now quite overwhelming evidence that the effectiveness of both recognition and recall depends on the context. Many readers may find this so obvious a matter that it would seem scarcely worth mentioning. A young man recognizes his former elementary school teacher when he sees her in the old school building, but may pass her by on the street. A celebrity can walk around a town on vacation without being recognized. In daily life, our recognitions, or lack of them, depend on the context. The problem, however, has deeper significance if one asks such questions as, "Does the child who has learned Archimedes' principle in the classroom think of applying it to the design of a boat he is building?" Teachers assume that he will, but the general evidence indicates that the child will be much more likely to apply the principle in the classroom situation than elsewhere.

Numerous studies have been undertaken on the effect of context on recall and recognition (see Murdock, 1974). The message of these studies seems clear. Change the context from the one occurring during learning and the chances of recall are reduced; so, too, is recognition reduced. What this means in terms of teaching is that learning should take place in a variety of contexts. Archimedes' principle may be first learned in the classroom, but on the next field trip the teacher would do well to point out that the smoke rising in the factory chimney illustrates Archimedes' principle. A big cloud billowing up to great heights is also another example. The principle should be discussed in many contexts, so that the child begins to look for examples himself. All too often what is learned in classrooms becomes class-room-bound. Ellis, Parente, and Walker (1974) were interested in the problem of the effect of presenting material in different contexts, or only in a single context, and then later measuring the recall or recognition of the material. Teachers have long believed the use of multiple contexts facilitates learning and retention. Ellis, Parente, and Walker found that the use of multiple contexts facilitated recall, but was not favorable for recognition. The results are difficult to understand, but should caution us that whatever may facilitate one aspect of learning may not facilitate another.

Reminiscence

The first discussion of reminiscence comes from a paper by Ballard (1913), which became famous. Ballard worked for the London County Council school system and visited classrooms as an inspector for the system. On one such occasion he observed the children in a class memorizing a poem he had assigned to them. At the end of the class period he asked them to write out as much of the poem as they could remember, and he then collected and scored the papers. What the children did not know was that he was to return to the same class on the following day, when he asked the same children to write out again all that they could recall of the poem. Much to his surprise, he found that the children remembered more of the poem on the following day than they had immediately after learning. The additional learning that apparently occurred after the end of the learning period was referred to as *reminiscence*. The same pattern of study was repeated with a variety of other materials, which ranged from nonsense syllables to meaningful material, and similar results were achieved. The curve of retention did not show a decline beginning immediately after learning, but rather, it first showed a rise before the typical fall began. For nearly half a century students of education were taught about the reminiscence phenomenon, until an experiment was undertaken that indicated that in all likelihood the phenomenon was nothing more than an artifact of the experimental situation. Perhaps one lesson to be learned from this is that the mere repetition of an experiment is not enough to demonstrate the soundness of the conclusions.

The demonstration that the phenomenon of reminiscence with verbal material is probably an artifact of experimentation and not a genuine phenomenon provides a worthwhile lesson in the problems of experimenting with learning. For this reason we may spend a little more time in discussing the matter than it would otherwise merit. Let us consider first the classical design that has been used in the supposed demonstration of reminiscence. In this design the following steps were taken:

1. A learning period.
2. A test of retention.
3. A period of unrelated activity.
4. A test of retention.

Ammons and Irion (1954) saw that there was a basic defect in this design. It is conceivable that the measurement of retention that occurs immediately after the learning period may function as an additional learning period and produce learning that does not show up until the next time retention is measured. Reminiscence may be nothing more than the learning produced by the situation in which learning is measured. What Ammons and Irion did was to test this hypothesis by the following experimental design, which used two groups rather than the one that had been typically used in previous experimentation:

Group A	Group B
1. A learning period.	1. A learning period.
2. A test of retention.	2. A period of unrelated activity.
3. A period of unrelated activity.	3. A test of retention.
4. A test of retention.	

The only difference in the treatment of the two groups lies in the omission from group B of the test of retention immediately after the learning period. The results of this experiment are interesting. What happens is that in group A the final test of retention shows a rise in comparison with the test of retention given immediately after learning. However, group B, on the final test of retention, shows a performance similar to that of group A immediately after learning. In other words, group B does not show the reminiscence phenomenon, though it should if the phenomenon is a genuine one. Only group A shows the reminiscence phenomenon, and only group A had the advantage of the test of retention immediately after learning and the possibility of benefiting from the practice that this test of retention may have provided. The data strongly suggest that the reminiscence effect with verbal material is due to the practice provided by the test of retention given immediately after learning.

The reminiscence phenomenon and the way in which it is produced reflect some of the difficulties that are encountered in collecting data for plotting a curve of retention. One cannot plot a curve of retention by the simple procedure of measuring from time to time the amount retained; for each time one does this, additional learning opportunities are afforded. What one generally has to do is train a large group to a given point of proficiency and divide the large group into a number of subgroups, which are then tested, each at a separate and distinct interval of time. Thus subgroup 1 might be tested after one day, subgroup 2 after two days, and so forth. Each person would be tested only once after the end of the learning period.

Although the Ballard type of reminiscence phenomenon appears to be an artifact of the experimental situation, there is a related phenomenon that is genuine. Reminiscence over a short period of time, of the order of several minutes, takes place with a task involving muscular coordination. This phenomenon has commonly been demonstrated with what are called *pursuit tasks*. In these tasks, the subject is required to turn or move levers in order to keep a movable sight on a moving target. The target moves and has to be followed by the sight through the appropriate manipulation of the levers or cranks. When practice is given on such a task, the level of skill continues to improve after practice has stopped. This has been shown by many research workers, including Bourne and Archer (1956), Ray (1959), and Eysenck (1956).

The interpretation generally given to this short-term type of reminiscence is that during the period of practice an inhibition process develops that has the effect of interfering with the performance of the skill. When the period of practice ends, the state of inhibition slowly dissipates and the level of skill improves.

There has been considerable controversy concerning whether there are individual differences in reminiscence on motor skills. Some research workers have suggested that such differences might be related to the individual's physiology. However, a review of the evidence by Peters (1973) leads to the conclusion that there are no such significant individual differences and that the phenomenon is basic and inherent to the human organism. However, Huang and Payne (1973) have shown that some individuals, on some tasks may show unusual amounts of reminiscence. Individual and sex differences are task specific. Boswell and Spatz (1975) provide supporting data.

Meaningfulness and Retention

The opinion is commonly held that meaningful material is more easily retained than nonsense material. The early students of learning phenomena, such as Ebbinghaus, who conducted his classic experiments in the last century, were impressed with this difference in retainability, which appeared to be dramatized by the results of their experiments. However, the experimental results are not as clear-cut as they appear to be on the surface, for this happens to be a difficult area for experimentation.

Consider, for example, the problem of obtaining meaningful and meaningless material for the conduct of a study of retention. Suppose a poem is to be compared for retainability with a list of nonsense syllables. Immediately one is confronted with the problem that any poem is meaningful, because it has already entered into past learning. A child who is learning the lines

Listen my children and you shall hear
Of the midnight ride of Paul Revere

is not learning completely novel material. He is already familiar with the name of Paul Revere and the story associated with him. He has also learned something about the typical order in which words appear. When he encounters the word *you* in the first line, he knows that it is almost certainly followed by a verb. Thus many of the associations between words that the learning of the poem requires have already been to some extent made. Meaningful material, because it is meaningful, is material that has already entered into some learning. To conclude, then, that meaningful material is more easily retained than meaningless material would be merely to conclude the obvious—that the material already partially learned is the more readily retained.

Verbal Mediators in Learning Association

Experimenters have noted that when a person is asked to learn a paired-associate task (such as associating bus-house, bird-auto, or lamb-china), the subject often introduces words that link up the two terms to be associated. In the case of the pairs of words just cited he may say to himself, "The bus stops at the house," "The bird was killed by the auto," and "The lamb was made of china." The words introduced are verbal mediators, and the learner introduces them to facilitate retention. Similar mediators are commonly introduced in daily life, as when we say to ourselves, "Mr. Green is as young and green as his name denotes," thereby linking the name of Green to the person designated by it.

Montague, Adams, and Kiess (1966) have reviewed a number of studies showing that associations learned that involve verbal mediators are better recalled later than are associations that do not involve them. In their own study, the task used was a paired-associate task in which pairs of nonsense syllables were presented and in which the subject had to learn to give the second syllable when presented with the first. In learning such a task, subjects commonly use verbal mediators. A subject, in reading the pair of syllables *san-lub* may transform it into something like *santa-club*, or *santa is lubly*. These research workers found, when they tested the subjects twenty-four hours later, that retention was substantial for those pairs in which the subjects had reported using verbal mediators in learning, but negligible for those pairs of syllables on which no verbal mediators had been reported as being introduced. The evidence suggests that the use of verbal mediators makes it possible to transfer the information from short-term memory to long-term memory, but that in the absence of such mediators the information is more likely to be lost.

Why such mediators are effective in promoting attention is not at all clear. One suggestion has to do with the fact that the introduction of a mediator introduces an association that is already strongly established and that this helps to establish a link. In the case of the syllable *san-lub*, which the subject encounters for the first time, there is probably virtually no association. Then the subject introduces the mediator *santa-club*, representing a strong and well-established association. The strength of the latter association may transfer to the association between *san* and *lub*. This is very speculative. Another possibility is, of course, that it is not the mediating, verbal behavior that produces the improvement. When there is verbal mediation, the subject may spend a longer time dwelling on the materials to be associated, and this, in turn, may produce more effective learning. This is generally a less attractive hypothesis than the one previously cited because there is substantial evidence that retention is closely associated with the fitting of the new incoming knowledge into the previously stored system of knowledge.

Another interesting finding of the Montague et al. study was that exposing the syllables for a longer time during learning resulted in the more frequent formation of verbal mediators and, hence, superior retention. This finding may well account partly for the fact that the amount of learning taking place is commonly related to the amount of time provided for each trial. In addition, these research workers also found that the more the syllables resembled meaningful words the more verbal mediators tended to be introduced and the more learning and retention took place.

This study, once again, brings out an important distinction between short-term and long-term memory. In the former, information is taken in as is, but in the latter there is a linking with previous knowledge. In the one system information is stored, much as books are stored higgledy-piggledy in a closet when they first arrive at a library, but in the long-term storage system ideas are stored within an ordered system, much as catalogued books are stored within an ordered system.

What is said here does not imply that information lacking a high degree of organization cannot enter the long-term memory system, for obviously it can. Children learn such isolated associations as capital cities and the states in which they are found, but such information is difficult and time-consuming to learn because there is only the weakest link between the knowledge involved and knowledge already acquired.

Overlearning and Retention

Material may be learned to the point where immediate recall is just possible, or it may be learned beyond this point. If practice occurs beyond the point where immediate and complete recall is first possible, then overlearning is said to have occurred. Typically in schools, learning is organized so that considerable overlearning is scheduled. There is little merit in a child's learning to spell only to the point where he can spell the particular words immediately after practice but is unable to recall the spelling at a later date. Teachers for centuries have been familiar with the fact that the best single way of preventing subsequent forgetting is to provide for overlearning.

Overlearning does not have to take the form of drill or rote learning. For example, once a child has acquired some minimal mastery of the number products used in multiplication, the utilization of these products in the solution of daily problems both within and outside the classroom will provide extensive overlearning, so that the skill is ultimately retained for a lifetime. Similar overlearning occurs in reading, though many of the illiterates identified at induction stations during World War II had once learned to read but had not retained the skill.

Many skills are characteristically learned to the point where they are retained for life through extensive overlearning. Few persons ever forget how to ride a bicycle once they have learned, for there is extensive opportunity for overlearning. Much the same applies to skating; people who have learned to skate may spend years away from the sport and yet return to it with little loss of skill. Secretaries who leave the office for marriage do not forget how to type. Later, if they have to return to an office job, they regain their old skill in a matter of hours. Overlearning is generally a sound investment of the pupil's time, particularly if it is coupled with a meaningful activity, as when the pupil overlearns his multiplication tables by solving mathematical problems of consequence to him.

One cannot always count on unplanned opportunity to provide the needed overlearning. An interesting example of this is found in the teaching of music, where the learner must acquire technique before he can perform a composition adequately. Simple pieces of music have been found to be of limited value in developing technique, because they do not provide opportunity to practice particular skills that must be mastered. For this reason the great teachers of music have developed exercises, commonly known as études, which provide such practice. In learning the violin, the student will work on études whatever the level of his development. In the earlier stages he may work on études that provide him with extensive practice in such matters as rhythm, scales, and so forth. Later he will work on études by Paganini, which provide some of the most difficult aspects of violin performance. In violin playing there is an exercise to provide practice for whatever aspect of technique the person may be deficient in. Such exercises are the products of great teachers who had an intuitive understanding of the problems of learning we are now considering. In other areas of learning there has been much less done to provide such specialized opportunities to learn specific aspects of the skill involved. Although many teachers have worked on this problem, few of them leave behind a record of their experience or of the techniques of learning they have used. Musicians, in contrast, have handed down their systematic teaching skills.

An interesting instance of overlearning is found in the case of a person who has spent time reading and rereading material in order to memorize it, then continues to repeat it to himself after he has put the printed version aside. These additional repetitions add to learning or overlearning, which is of theoretical interest in that it appears to be a case of learning occurring without any identifiable reinforcement. While the reader has the material in front of him, one might postulate that he spends much of his time trying to repeat it without looking at the page, and then a glance at the page would indicate the part he has right, which in itself provides some kind of reinforcement. This is perhaps plausible, but when the learner repeats the material to himself, these kinds of reinforcements are absent.

Learning and Retention as a Function of the Time Schedule

Almost every educational program is planned so that it fits some kind of time schedule that is believed to be efficient for the purpose at hand. Often, of course, such time schedules have to fit into a system prescribed by the administration of an educational institution, as when particular courses at a university are planned to fit the quarter system. Most educators also acknowledge the fact that some schedules are more efficient than others for learning particular aspects of subject matter. Difficult mathematics courses are always spread out over a considerable time, never compressed into short periods of one or two weeks as are some language courses given by universities during the summer.

When learning is scheduled on a concentrated basis with a single long period of practice that is extended until the material to be learned has been learned, it is said that the practice is *massed*. When learning takes place in a number of learning periods separated either by other activities or by periods of rest, the practice is said to be *distributed*, or *spaced*. The relative merits of spaced versus unspaced practice was one of the earliest problems studied by psychologists interested in the systematic investigation of problems of learning. Ebbinghaus (1885), who is regarded as the father of modern learning psychology, published a classic work describing a series of experiments that he had conducted in the field of learning, and laying the foundation for the future experimental development of the scientific study of learning. In particular, he was the first to realize that the study of learning could not easily be undertaken through the learning of meaningful materials, because some people would come to these materials with more previous experience than would others. In order to eliminate this source of difficulty, Ebbinghaus asked his subjects to learn nonsense syllables, such as *gub, zac, ref,* and *kes.* These nonsense syllables have the advantage of being fairly unfamiliar, and hence all learners start at roughly the same point in their learning. But some initial differences may exist in familiarity with these materials, for at least some of them will be recognized as parts of words familiar to some of the subjects; and the person who is familiar with the greatest number of words is most likely to have the most familiarity with these syllables.

With such materials, Ebbinghaus was able to conduct experiments with massed and distributed practice. His conclusion, which has been well substantiated by other studies, is that distributed practice has a considerable advantage over massed practice—that is, it takes less time to learn material if learning is distributed over several spaced sessions than if all the work is done at a single session. At one time the advantage of distributed practice was ascribed to the effect of reminiscence, but this explanation does not hold today. A more likely explanation is that, with massed practice, inhibition builds up that interferes with learning. Spaced learning provides opportunity for the inhibition to dissipate. What is commonly referred to as mental fatigue is an inhibitory process similar to the one considered here.

Another possibility comes from the fact that the processes involved in retaining information continue after formal learning has ended. These processes involved in the consolidation of what has been learned may continue to take place for twenty or more minutes after the material to be learned has been put aside or the person ceases to practice. A pause after a learning trial may take advantage of this continuation of the learning process. Distributed practice takes advantage of this continuation of the learning process, which extends beyond the student's immediate efforts.

It would be useful if we could now state how long a learning period should be and how far apart the periods of practice should be spaced. But although there have been many studies undertaken of the relative efficiency of learning when the intervals between trials are varied, there is no consistency in the results they have produced. The results of such studies are conflicting because the kind of task to be learned probably makes a difference. For example, in an early study by Warden (1923), subjects were required to learn to find a path through a maze. Different groups were given practice at intervals of six hours, twelve hours, and one- three-, and five-day intervals. In this study the twelve-hour interval produced the most efficient learning. In another study by Lorge (1930), rather different results were obtained. Lorge used three tasks as follows:

1. Mirror drawing. In this task the subject was required to draw a line around a given pattern, being guided by what he could see in a mirror.
2. Mirror reading. The subject had to read printed material appearing in a mirror.

3. Code substitution. The subject was required to substitute letters in printed material with new letters, according to a code given him.

In the Lorge study, the tasks were learned under three conditions. One of these was massed practice; the second was distributed practice, with one-minute intervals between trials; the third was distributed practice, with twenty-four hour-intervals between trials. With every task, the subjects performed more efficiently when practice was distributed than when it was massed. Surprisingly small differences were found between the distributed practice with one-minute rest intervals and twenty-four-hour intervals.

What are the practical implications of the work on distributed versus massed practice? The most obvious one has already been put into effect—namely, that the work in school should be divided into rather short sessions covering particular areas of content. The fact that distributed practice is generally (but not always) more efficient than massed practice may raise some problems about the efficiency of a core curriculum as it is commonly run. The breaking down of subject-matter lines and the assignment of rather long blocks of time to combinations of subjects such as English and social studies, which are not then taught as separate subjects, may sometimes tend to make for massed practice, but this does not have to be so. The forced division of time into periods has certain advantages in this respect. It does require the teachers to change regularly the learning activities involved.

There is probably the least application of the principle of distributed practice when the pupil studies in his own home. Such study tends to represent massed learning and is consequently much less efficient than it should be. The high-school pupil who has to learn a speech from Julius Caesar is likely to sit down and attempt to learn it at a single session; and this practice is indirectly encouraged by teachers who give occasional large assignments of this kind and ask that they be completed in too short a time (or too long a time, which results in procrastination, with similar effects). In such an assignment the pupil should probably start by reading through the speech to be learned a few times, concentrating on the meaning and looking up any words that he does not understand. He should then plan several short learning sessions distributed over several days. There are also some advantages in planning these sessions for just before going to bed, so that the learning period is not followed by any activity that could interfere with the learning of the speech.

The educational psychologist can never be content just to know that one method of learning requires a shorter total time than does some other method. Quite as important as the matter of speed of learning is the extent to which material is retained. What would be the use of a speedy method of learning if it were found that retention was poor? Our immediate question is whether learning by distributed practice produces as satisfactory retention as does learning by massed practice. Numerous studies have been designed to answer this with a great range of different materials.

Cain and Willey (1939), who compared retention curves of massed and distributed practice for meaningless material, found that after seven days those who had had distributed practice retained almost three times as much material as those who had had massed practice. Much the same results hold for meaningful material, although the results are not always quite so dramatic. The results hold for a variety of materials. In a study by Cook (1936), the finding was that the solutions to puzzles were retained better over a considerable period when the problems had been solved by distributed-practice sessions than by massed-practice sessions. The nature of the materials learned is also a factor in determining what is retained.

Nearly all of the research on distributed versus massed practice has been undertaken with materials that do not much resemble the kinds used in schools, but a study by Leith, Biran, and Opollot (1970) used materials related to the teaching of physics in a classroom setting. They found a quite clear advantage of spaced practice over massed practice. The result is not only significant in terms of classroom practice, but it also shows how laboratory results can, sometimes at least, be generalized to the classroom situation.

Total Time Hypothesis

Bugelski (1962) suggested what has become known as the total time hypothesis. The essence of this hypothesis is that in a learning task, such as that involved in learning a list of words, the most important condition of learning is the total amount of time devoted to the task. Thus time between each successive presentation of the list is as important as the time spent in presenting the list. Time spent in attempting to reproduce the list is a part of the total time involved in learning, and, indeed, Tulving (1967) has shown that the time spent in writing out the words one can recall from a list of words produces about as much learning as a reading of the original list. Although the hypothesis and the experiments on which it is based have been criticized, Bugelski and McMahon (1971) have successfully answered the criticisms. Other research by psychologists skeptical of the hypothesis (King, 1974, and Koffman and Weinstock, 1974) generally confirms the hypothesis. Tversky and Sherman (1975) demonstrated the total time hypothesis with picture material.

Total time seems to be important for two main reasons. First, the more time available, the greater is the opportunity the individual has for rehearsal. Second, the greater the amount of total time, the greater is the opportunity for processes related to the consolidation of learning to occur. The nature of these processes is not known at the present time.

Imagery and the Retention of Information

From the time of Francis Galton in the last century until the last two decades, psychologists avoided the study of imagery. Studies of this phenomenon would have been frowned upon as involving subjective phenomena incapable of objective definition. Traditional conceptions of imagery involved such ideas as "what one can see in one's mind's eye" and seemed scarcely to have a place in a science of behavior. The logical difficulties involved in utilizing such a concept of imagery have been explored by Pylyshyn (1973), who points out that much more sophisticated concepts of imagery could be used in research in the field than are typically used. Let us begin this discussion by turning to a series of studies involving a sophisticated conception of imagery, found in Piaget and Inhelder's *Mental Imagery and the Child* (1971).

The traditional view of imagery has been that it represents a form in which information is stored. Thus a particular visual scene was considered to be stored in the form of a visual image of that scene. This is a kind of photographic theory of visual storage though the images, at best, represent faded and unclear records of the original information. Piaget and Inhelder (1971, 1973) have taken an entirely different position with respect to this matter. They view the image as constructed from information stored in memory, though the form cannot be identified at this time. The view that the image is a construction is supported by the variability in the image shown from occasion to occasion, and also by the intrusion into the image of items that were not in the original scene. The image also has plasticity except in the young child. One can conjure up an image, change items in it, and add and subtract items. One can also perform all these operations without being aware of doing them. Lawyers have long been aware of the unreliability of this kind of recall and with the fact that much recall is a reconstructive activity.

In the Piaget and Inhelder studies the image is not viewed as a representation of an object seen in the mind's eye. Consider the case of a child given the task of drawing a two-inch line. Piaget and Inhelder argue that in order for the child to do this, he must have some internal representation of a 2-inch line. The argument is logical. There is simply no way in which the child can begin to draw a 2-inch line unless he is able to represent, internally, a 2-inch line. Piaget and Inhelder make no claims concerning the way in which that representation is made. Never do they say that the child sees a 2-inch line inside himself. They say only that there must be some form of representation that they refer to as an image. They do not even claim that the child is aware of such an image. Indeed, the representation may be outside his field of consciousness. They assert only that such a representation is logically necessary for the child to know what he is doing and to guide him in attempting to draw a 2-inch line. Consider another example. Suppose that we show a child sitting opposite us an arrangement of a few toys. We then ask him how the toys would look if they were viewed from our side of the table. We may obtain his response by showing him various pictures showing how the toys might look from our side of the table and ask him to pick the one which is a correct view. In order for the child to do this task he must have some internal representation of the objects and be able to manipulate that internal representation called an image. We do not know what that internal representation is in a 5-year-old, but Piaget and Inhelder point out that to perform the task the child must be able to manipulate that internal representation, that is, turn it around and find out what it would be like if viewed from the other side. The 5-year-old cannot perform that task because he cannot manipulate the internal representation. The 8-year-old can perform the task. Inhelder and Piaget argue that the task can be performed only if the internal representation can be manipulated to arrive at the answer, which they consider to be a logical necessity. Although they use the term *mental image* as a label for this form of internal representation, they do not imply that the individual is conscious of the representation, and neither do they imply that the representation is some form of mental picture.

Furthermore, Piaget and Inhelder take the position that the image is never some kind of stored picture, which traditional literature in psychology implies. They avoid this naive view and refer to the image as an internal construction, based sometimes on immediate experience, sometimes on information stored in memory, and sometimes on a combination of these two sources. The image is a creation, which may sometimes be described as so clear that the individual regards it as a reproduction of reality that has been stored in memory, but it is not a stored representation. The image is a construction derived from stored information, and not merely a piece of stored information. For this reason the image may mislead, for it may be a false reconstruction.

Although a sophisticated conception of imagery is possible, the experimental psychologist may often have to discuss imagery in quite naive terms in giving directions to individuals in experiments. For this reason, much of the literature of experimental psychologists gives the appearance of representing a naive approach.

Paivio (1969) has conducted a series of investigations on the role of imagery in retention. He finds that just as mediating verbal associations may help tie ideas together in memory, so, too, may images provide mediating processes that also facilitate memory.

Some of his research derives from the old parlor trick that starts with memorizing a list of numbers and concrete nouns such as *one-bun, two-glue, three-tree, four-door.* The person first masters this list, which may include one hundred or more items. The person is then in a condition to master quickly another list of concrete nouns, which are read to him in a numbered list. If the first word in the new list is *car*, he imagines a car inside a bun. If the second word is *ham*, he imagines a piece of ham, covered with glue. At the end of the reading of the list, he is asked, for example "What was the fourth word?" The fourth word was hamburger, and when that word was originally presented, he imagined a hamburger tacked to the door. In recalling the fourth word, he conjures up the image of the door and sees a hamburger tacked to it. In this way he can readily recall any word in the list by referring to the images he created when the word was presented. Such images appear to have the property of fixing information in memory and can be as powerful in this respect as verbal associations used for a similar purpose.

The findings suggest that groups of words that produce imagery should be more readily remembered than groups of abstract words. This is exactly what Paivio and Rowe (1970) found. Research of this kind tempts one to jump to the conclusion that, in the teaching of a foreign language, vocabulary should first be built with words that evoke images, for the new words can then be attached to the images and be readily learned. Such plausible applications of studies of imagery jump too far ahead of knowledge, however, for, as Palermo (1970) has pointed out, the facilitating effect of imagery is only for short-term memory. There is as yet no evidence that imagery facilitates long-term memory. Any effect it may have on long-term memory is probably very weak, if it exists at all, in comparison with its effect on immediate memory.

One can classify words, sentences, and paragraphs as having high potential or low potential for imagery. A word, sentence, or paragraph has high imagery potential if it is capable of concrete representation. Research has shown that high imagery words (Bugelski, 1974), sentences (Sasson and Fraisse, 1972), and paragraphs (Sasson and Carter, 1973) are all easier to remember over a short period than are low imagery materials. The meaning of this is not entirely clear. Does it mean merely that the material with a concrete reference is more readily remembered than material with an abstract reference? Some research suggests that imagery itself is a crucial factor. For example, Robbins et al. (1974) have shown that the form of imagery is quite crucial in how much is remembered. If one is trying to remember a link between, say, a person's name and the street in which he lives, imagery can be introduced into the operation in different ways. Let us suppose that the friend's name is George and he lives on Utah Avenue. In trying to remember the connection, I can picture George, and I can picture the mountains of Utah. I can also develop what has been called an interactive image. I can picture George climbing the mountains of Utah. Experiments indicate that the interactive image has greater power to facilitate memory than the separate images (see Robbins et al., 1974).

THE EXTERNAL AND INTERNAL STORAGE OF INFORMATION

There has long been a controversy among educators concerning the extent to which the pupil should be expected to store information internally and how far he should become dependent on the use of reference works, such as encyclopedias, for the storage of information. This is a complicated problem. In order to take sides on the issues one would have to know the storage capacity of the human being and also something about the time it takes to store particular bodies of information. If the human being has a limited-capacity storage system, it is clear that he must learn to use reference sources, where information is stored external to himself, for he would have no other choice. On the other hand, if his storage capacity is very large, there are advantages in storing internally as much information as possible— unless disproportionately large amounts of time are needed to acquire and store the information.

The practices that have evolved in our society place emphasis on systems of storing knowledge external to the individual. Thus a machinist operating a lathe must have available a handbook that stores all the information he needs for setting up the tool. He consults the handbook to determine the cutting speed he should use on a particular piece of metal. He does not have to store within his brain the equivalent of several pages of detailed specifications for cutting speeds; all he has to store is the knowledge that the information can be found in the handbook. If he were to commit the material to memory, he would have to spend many hours of study distributed over several weeks. Even after devoting this much effort to the task, he would still not be able to reproduce the data from memory with the same accuracy with which he could find it in the handbook.

The occupation of the machinist is not unique in this respect. Workers in almost every occupation use extensive bodies of information stored externally. Most professional people have at hand a library of important sources of information they can consult. Even a source of twenty or thirty books can contain large quantities of information. Salesmen do not have to remember the names of all of their customers; they have a file containing such information with the data placed in some order, such as alphabetical order, from which information can be readily retrieved. Modern civilization is highly dependent on the existence of information storage systems that vastly increase the human capability of using available knowledge.

Although human beings have long used storage systems external to themselves, in the form of scrolls and tablets and, later, books, no entirely satisfactory system has been devised for enabling them to obtain access to the information thus stored. The index to a book, the table of contents, the library catalogue, and related devices are all designed to assist the individual to gain access to stored knowledge; but none of these is completely satisfactory, as any user knows. Extensive research is now being undertaken on this problem, mainly by people involved in information science.

The assumption generally made is that whatever is learned in elementary school should be stored internally so that the performance of the skills involved can take place without referring to a book or other source of information. At the secondary school level, there are clear advantages in being able to add and multiply without having to consult a table. The same can be said for the learning of a foreign language. Unless a person can store internally the vocabulary and general rules of syntax of a foreign language, it is of little practical use to him. On the other hand, the fine details of geography might as well remain stored in a book, though the pupil should undoubtedly retain a broad general knowledge of the subject. Perhaps it is important to know that Paris is in France, but it is much less important to know exactly where in that country the city is located or on what river it is to be found. However, the pupil should know just where to find these details.

SUMMARY

1. The progress of learning is commonly represented by a graph known as a learning curve. Such a curve represents only one aspect of learning. Each one of a number of separate curves may represent several distinct aspects of the learning involved in the acquisition of a complex skill.

2. Learning curves may have many different shapes, depending on the conditions of learning and the degree to which the skill or component skills have been previously mastered. Although the typical form of learning curve that has been presented in textbooks of educational psychology for the last fifty years shows a rapid early rise followed by a period of less rapid learning, such a curve is not necessarily found. Many learning curves are found that are shaped approximately like an S.

Such curves are found in cases in which the skill is learned right from the beginning. They are found in both classical conditioning and in instrumental learning. Typical school learning may be considered to represent the upper portion of such a curve.

3. Families of curves produced in studies of learning sets may show progressive changes in the shape of the learning curve as the learner becomes more sophisticated In the illustration given, the learning curves showed a progressive change from a S-shaped curve to the typical learning curves that have long been given in textbooks.

4. Some curves representing learning show a flattened-out portion followed by a rise. Such a flattened-out portion is referred to as a plateau. The conditions under which such plateaus occur are obscure, and there is even some doubt whether they are genuine phenomena. There is the possibility that they may be produced by some uncontrolled factor in the learning situation and would not occur if such a factor were controlled. If plateaus are genuine phenomena, many explanations may be offered for their existence.

5. The typical flattening-out of the learning curve represents a crude limit of learning. This is not the absolute limit of learning but the limit under the particular conditions operating. If conditions are changed, the learner may achieve higher levels of skill.

6. Attempts have been made to derive theoretical learning curves from assumptions about the nature of learning. This represents a new avenue to the study of the learning process, one that offers considerable promise.

7. The degree to which acquired skills are retained can be studied by many different techniques. Some are much more sensitive than others for indicating that some skill has been retained.

8. Methods for measuring retention differ in the extent to which they provide cues that can elicit the skill originally learned. The recall method provides the fewest cues; the recognition method provides a greater number. The most sensitive of all methods is the relearning, or saving, method, which may measure retention even when the recognition method fails to do so. The saving method has been widely used because it is extremely sensitive and capable of showing very slight residuals of learning. It is well adapted for use with verbal materials.

9. The curve representing retention generally shows a sharp decline after training ceases. This is followed by a much less marked decline as additional time passes by. The development of any theory of forgetting is handicapped by the lack of knowledge concerning the mechanism involved in the retention process.

10. Several distinct memory systems exist in the human being. First, there is a transitory trace that lasts for only a few seconds. Such a trace can be demonstrated in animals as well as in human beings. Second, there is a short-term memory. In view of the fact that it may take as long as thirty minutes to transfer information from a short-term memory to a long-term memory, the short-term memory system would appear to be necessary to hold information long enough to make the transfer possible. Third, there is a long-term memory system. Although short-term and long-term memory systems share many common properties they also have their own

distinctive properties that make it necessary to consider that there are two distinct systems. Particularly compelling evidence is found in cases of individuals who, through brain damage, have good short-term memories but are unable to transfer the information to the long-term system. In addition, the two systems produce different errors of recall; also, a high level of arousal facilitates long-term memory but disrupts short-term memory.

11. There is strong evidence that a short-term memory is a real entity. Particularly impressive evidence is provided by the case of H. M., who had a short-term memory, but was unable to transfer information from it to long-term memory. In addition, conditions that facilitate short-term memory may interfere with long-term memory. Errors of recall are also different in the two systems, which differ in information capacity.

12. The capacity of the memory systems is not known, but the evidence generally points to a long-term memory system that does not have the vast capacity suggested by the number of nerve cells in the nervous system. The short-term memory system is of more limited capacity.

13. The observations of Penfield are interesting, but their interpretation is controversial. They can hardly be taken to support the idea that the memory system makes a permanent record of all that happens. Penfield may have demonstrated the brain's capacity to reconstruct past experiences, but the reconstructions may not be accurate.

14. Long-term memory represents an organized system, for only from an organized system is rapid retrieval possible. A simple model of memory is the associationist. A more complex and more plausible model assumes that knowledge is organized in a hierarchy of items. A third model proposes that memory is in terms of propositions that form an organized system. Another proposal is that long-term memory is structured in two forms. One of these is the episodic form. In this form, memories are entered in the sequence in which they occur, much as pictures are entered in sequence in a snapshot album. The second proposed structure of memory is the semantic system, which represents an organized body of knowledge. Most subject matter fields are probably organized in several different ways within the semantic memory system. Tulving proposes that each time information is retrieved from the episodic system, the information stored is changed, but retrieval from the semantic system does not change the information stored. Tulving's conception of memory has important implications for education.

15. Piaget and his associates have also provided important conceptualizations of the nature of memory. For them, the most primitive level of memory involves retention of antibodies, which are records of conflicts with diseases and foreign substances. At the next higher level, there is a memory for action systems that are conserved through the sensorimotor schemata. At the highest level, memory involves internal representation and the ability to recall events in the past. Piaget and Inhelder have shown that information in memory becomes organized in terms of the structures of logical thought as soon as these develop.

16. A distinction has also been made between iconic and symbolic memory. There is no strong evidence that retention is better in the one form than in the other. Images are reconstructions from memory, and not information as it is stored in memory. Whatever may be the general form of a memory system, the evidence indicates that information is stored in quite small components within it. The tip-of-the-tongue phenomenon is one form of evidence showing how a word could be stored as a series of components. Evidence generally supports an attribute theory of memory.

17. Short-term memory is sometimes called primary memory. It is commonly viewed as a store of information, with a brief life, from which information is selected for transfer to long-term memory. The concept of short-term memory also commonly relates it to consciousness, for it is a memory of events of which one is immediately conscious. The short-term memory is also closely related to perception, and perception involves the retrieval of information from long-term storage. In addition, the short-term memory is commonly considered to be a location in which information becomes organized before it is transferred to long-term memory. The information from the short-term system is lost through decay. Research has tended to focus on the short-term memory as a device that results in the organization of information. Teachers can facilitate learning by providing some degree of organization of the material to be learned. The retarded seem to have difficulty in organizing information in the short-term system; they also have a poor repertoire of strategies for organizing material and may not comprehend the structure that may be inherent in material to be learned. They can learn strategies, but they have the difficulty of identifying the correct strategy to use on particular occasions. In addition, they are not able to make use of rehearsal.

18. Forgetting in long-term memory appears to be a result of one piece of information interfering with another. In the absence of such interference, there is very little forgetting, even over periods as long as forty years. Interference occurs in two forms: the retroactive effect and the proactive effect. The evidence for the interference of forgetting is substantial, including such intriguing items as that little forgetting occurs during sleep when interference is at a minimum. Instructing individuals to forget material that is to be read results in poor retention, largely because such material is not rehearsed and is not thought about and organized in the short-term memory system.

19. The retrieval mechanism appears to be a mechanism distinct from that involved in placing information in memory. Information may be in memory, yet one may be unable to retrieve it. Recall requires that there be cues in the recall situation indicating where to search in the memory system. The cues present when the information was originally placed in memory appear to be the important cues for retrieving from episodic memory. The difficulty that older individuals have in recall may be a result of the declining efficacy of the retrieval system or it may be a result of defects in the storage system itself. Since context is important for recall, children should learn concepts for later application in relation to many different contexts.

20. The classical demonstration of what was believed to be reminiscence produced an artifact. There is no demonstrable reminiscence effect for verbal materials over a period of hours or days. However, there is a short-term effect on motor tasks in which inhibitory processes build up during practice and interfere with the performance of the task. As these dissipate, after practice on the task has stopped, the individual shows an improvement in performance.

21. Mediating processes facilitate learning by providing links between the elements.

22. Although meaningful material appears to be more readily learned than relatively meaningless material, this effect is due to the fact that the meaningful material is already partially learned.

23. Overlearning is necessary if information is to be retained over a long period. Overlearning seems to prevent information from being disrupted.

24. Information distributed over time is more efficiently learned than information learned in a concentrated session. Even an interval between trials as short as a minute may facilitate learning. The advantage of spaced learning has been demonstrated not only in the laboratory but in the school situation.

25. The most important condition related to the amount of learning taking place is total time. This is the total time hypothesis.

26. Imagery facilitates learning. The most acceptable view of imagery is that it represents a reconstruction from information stored in memory. The unreliability of imagery as a representation of the past is well established.

27. Information may be stored either internally or externally to the human nervous system. External storing of information takes place in books and libraries. These permit the individual to have large quantities of information available without going through the process of transferring the information to memory. The individual has to have access to externally stored information by understanding the key concepts involved in the classification of knowledge.

Chapter 9

Perception and Perceptual Learning

THEORETICAL CONSIDERATIONS

Although psychology has long been influenced by the language of physiology, many take the position that such a language has very little utility for developing a science of behavior. In recent times, some psychologists have taken the position that more is achieved by viewing the human being not as an organism making stimulus-related responses, but as a system concerned with the handling of information. One can view the human being as a creature living in an information-filled environment, from which some information is taken in and utilized in one or more of a number of different ways.

In this chapter we are concerned with human information analysis and reception. Some of the knowledge possessed about this process has been derived from the physiological study of the nervous system and will be reviewed in a later chapter on this subject. The knowledge presented in this chapter has been derived from studies of how man handles the information presented to him. The general plan of these studies is to present subjects with some source of information, that is, to provide some inputs of information and then to study some outputs, along with the processes through which information is utilized, transformed into different forms, and stored. Discrepancies between inputs and outputs provide knowledge of how the information has been handled.

[298]

The Collectors of Information

The nervous system collects information both from sources in the external environment and from sources within the body. The basic collectors of information, the sense organs, are extensions of the nervous system that are particularly sensitive to changes in their surroundings. This statement can be better understood by knowing that in the developing human embryo the eye begins as a bud that grows out of the primitive nervous system and consists at first of cells that are much like any other nerve cells. As the eye grows, and as the cells multiply within it, they become progressively more specialized in the function they perform, but they still are essentially a part of the brain structure. Much the same story can be told about the other systems of sensitive cells that handle the reception of information.

The sensitive cells that receive information are organized into five main systems, as Gibson (1966) has pointed out. Within any one of the systems, many different kinds of sensitive cells may be involved. The sensitive cells, called receptors, are not arranged so that one kind of cell, and only one kind of cell, is found in only one of the systems. Generations of thinkers since the time of Aristotle have become involved in arguments about how many different senses there are, and in recent times much of this argument has revolved around the question of how many different sense cells there are. The question is not important and it diverts attention away from the fact that the receptors are only components of information-gathering systems. Indeed, it is not very meaningful to talk of the senses, for a much more meaningful concept is that of an information system or a perceptual system, as some prefer to say.

Gibson takes the position that there are five major information systems related to the human being's orientation to his external environment. These systems are the visual, the auditory, the haptic, the taste-smell, and the basic orienting system. Each of these five systems consists of far more than a collection of receptors that wait passively to receive information from the environment. They are active systems for the collection of information.

Let us consider further the concept that each one of the five systems is an active information-gathering system. The visual system, for example, is not just a retina on which a picture of the outside world imprints itself. It is an extremely active system, for the eyes are designed to rotate in their sockets and continuously scan the world, first in one direction and then in the other. Watch the eyes of a person walking down the street. They are not fixed in a position looking directly ahead of him; they scan fairly large sections of the environment. When the eyes are viewing a newspaper, they stop at various points across a page, and sometimes they move along a line, stopping at perhaps two or three points. The eyes form a part of a scanning system. The scanning of the environment by the visual system is also aided by the fact that the head and body can turn so that more can be taken in than would be possible if the system were static. The eyes do not just wait for information to arrive; they are involved in an active search for information. Thus the visual system must be considered to include not only a set of light-sensitive cells in the retina and the general structure of the eye, but also a very complex muscular component and the nervous network that coordinates the muscles.

The auditory system has much less capacity for scanning the environment for information than has the visual system, and this capacity is notably less in man than in other higher animals. A dog has the capacity of turning its ears and will typically move them in order to pick up particular sounds. Man has negligible capacity for orienting his ears, but he does turn his head in order to adjust the strength of incoming signals.

The haptic system is a highly complex and active exploratory system involving touch receptors in the skin and also an extensive system of receptors in the joints and muscles. This system has related to it a musculature that makes it possible for the person to actively explore the world through the touch system. Watch a person in a department store pick up a china ornament that he wishes to explore further. He will handle it, run his fingers over its general contour, and gently feel the texture of its highly polished surface. The examination of the object is an active, not a passive process. The exploratory process involves much more than the mere stimulation of the receptors in the skin by the surface of the object handled. Movement is involved, which provides information about shape, and this information is picked up by the receptors in the muscles and joints through which the movement is executed. The adult learns to acquire a great amount of information about shape and texture by the visual inspection of objects, but the need to explore through the haptic system still remains strong, a fact which is evident from the "Please do not touch" signs so prevalent in department stores, museums, zoos, art collections, and flower shows.

The taste-smell system represents a single basic system relatively underdeveloped in man. The receptors are cells that are highly sensitive to certain chemical substances and, indeed, as a detection system, the taste-smell system is often comparable in sensitivity to many micro-chemical techniques. The system permits a limited amount of exploration when substances are placed in the mouth. Watch a young child who is given a new food. He will roll the food around in his mouth to bring it into contact with the various sensitive membranes. He may also fill his mouth until it is stuffed, as if to stimulate as many taste buds as possible. Exploration by the taste-smell system is also facilitated through the hand, which, in the case of the young child, tends to bring to the mouth every object grasped as if to explore it more fully. Although the muscles of the tongue are those that form the essential component of the taste-smell system, the muscles of the arm and hand, and other muscles too, may function as components of the system. Objects must be brought to the mouth before they can be explored by the mouth.

The main organs of the basic orienting system are two sets of three canals, one on each side of the head in the inner ear. These organs are not a part of the hearing mechanism, although they are located close to it. The main function of these organs is to respond to sudden movements of rotation, such as occur when there is a loss of balance. The information provided by this system brings into play righting reflexes, which then keep the individual right side up to the world and restore his balance. The orienting system has relatively little relevance to the topics discussed in this volume.

Most of our concern here is with the first three of the perceptual systems considered here, for they are the systems through which most teaching and organized learning occur. One can refer to these and the other two systems as the perceptual systems or, if one prefers, as the information systems. Through them arrives all the information used in learning and in adjusting to the environment.

Pain as a System and Its Relation to Anxiety

In the previous analysis of the perceptual systems, no mention was made of pain, although pain shares with the perceptual systems such features as peripheral stimulation and transmission to the higher centers. Sternbach (1968) has made an excellent review of the problem of pain. Although it is agreed that pain typically results from the impact of injurious or potentially injurious stimuli, there is no clear evidence concerning the nature of the receptors that transmit information about this injury or threat of serious injury to the higher centers. Some physiologists have accepted the idea that pain is produced by the stimulation of bare nerve endings that are present in all parts of the body, but some of these nerve endings are known to transmit the experience of touch. Within the spinal cord, and through to the midbrain, there appear to by particular pathways that transmit pain, which suggests that these might have impulses fed to them by particular receptors. The picture of the nature of pain is very much clouded by the fact that pain and anxiety are intimately related, although anxiety is fundamentally different from pain and involves anticipation of noxious circumstances. Pain is also particularly puzzling in that it commonly occurs in the absence of any stimulation that might produce it. Thus a person may experience intense pain from the skin on the back of the hand and yet there may be no signs that the skin is being stimulated in any unusual way.

Pain has the peculiarity that when it occurs in a particular situation, the stimuli present in the situation may acquire the property of eliciting pain. Thus one may experience pain at the sound of a dental drill or on hearing an impact between two cars. Also, any increase in the level of anxiety is likely to enhance pain and a reduction in anxiety to reduce pain. Pain is a part of the individual's total response in coping with a situation that contains noxious stimuli or potentially noxious stimuli. Almost any sensory input can interfere with that pattern and, hence, lower pain. Strong tactual stimulation and loud sounds have been shown to reduce pain. An additional finding from research is that those who complain of chronic pain have an underlying condition of depression, which may be a response to the loss of a loved one or a response to unexpressed anger. The person complaining of chronic pain may be unaware of the condition of depression from which it arises. Psychiatric treatment that relieves the depression may also relieve the pain. Through such treatment the individual may learn to express sadness and anger in appropriate ways and the pain is thereby relieved. Oddly enough, it does not seem to matter how the condition of depression is treated. Almost any treatment for depression may help to relieve the pain.

The reduction of pain through the reduction of anxiety or depression seems to be particularly effective when the cause of the pain is a physical stimulus. Hypnosis may well work through producing a state incompatible with the experience of pain. Relaxation itself may result in the reduction of pain.

Pain avoidance and anxiety avoidance are so intimately related to learning that an understanding of the nature of pain will be of the greatest value in providing an understanding of this aspect of motivation for learning.

Of particular interest at the present time is the control of pain by acupuncture. Considerable research has been undertaken on the nature of acupuncture. When stories of the use of acupuncture by the Chinese for the control of pain first came to America in the 1960s, the immediate response of psychologists was that it involved some form of hypnotic suggestion. Doubts were thrown on this explanation when it was learned that acupuncture was used by the Chinese to control pain in animals. Some research was then undertaken to determine whether the control of pain by acupuncture could be considered to be merely a result of suggestion or hypnosis. One such study by Anderson, Jamieson, and Man (1974) showed quite clearly that the pain produced by immersing the hand in ice water could be reduced by acupuncture. In such experiments those who receive genuine acupuncture are compared with those who also have needles inserted in them at places in the body where no pain reduction is expected. There seems little doubt that acupuncture is a genuine physiological phenomenon in which perception is modified through stimulating tissues in appropriate places.

Information Available to the Perceptual System

The amount of information available to the perceptual systems is always very large. Indeed, it has been said that all the information that can be provided by a single glance at a scene of the countryside is so large that it could not be recorded by the human memory system or in any artificial memory system so far developed. Such a scene would include an immense amount of detail about the exact position of each leaf on each tree, the location of each blade of grass, as well as the gross features of the scene. The quantity of information at the detailed level presented each instant to the visual system is enormous. It is not only quite clear that the amount of information available to the visual system is vast, but it is also clear that only a very small quantity of this information is ever used. A parallel situation exists in the case of the auditory system. A very large amount of auditory information available to the perceptual system is never used. A person listening to the conversation of another is unlikely to be able to record the precise intonation of each word, the syllables that were slurred over, the pitch of the speaker's voice, the breathing noises that accompany speech, the numerous other sources of sound that occur in almost any environment, and so forth. The perceptual systems are almost continuously flooded with information. What the systems have to do is to abstract essential information from the mass of detail and interpret that information. The perceptual systems are continuously engaged in information analysis, a process that must now be considered.

Information Analysis at the Sense Organ Level

Perception is taken so much for granted that it is difficult for the layman to understand that there is any problem to be investigated in the matter of how persons acquire the information they do acquire. The difficulty of the task of perception becomes more apparent if one considers the problem of designing a machine that will undertake some kind of perceptual task, such as that of recognizing a word printed on a piece of paper. This is a relatively straightforward perceptual task that one might design a machine to do, particularly if there are spaces between the letters. The machine would have to be able to discriminate black from white, identify the spatial location of the various sections of the black marks, and it might be designed to recognize each letter by comparing the shape of each of the printed letters with some stored shapes. The machine would have to be quite complicated even though the perceptual task involved is really quite simple. Indeed, the design of such a machine might well tax the ingenuity even of competent engineers. If the task set for the machine were the more complicated one of recognizing a particular portrait, the design of the information-processing equipment involved might well be beyond the capability of modern engineers. Yet this same recognition task is undertaken readily by creatures at a much simpler level than man. Pets recognize their owners, though perhaps not through the contours of the human features. Pigeons are able to perform the enormously complicated task of distinguishing between pictures that include the form of a human being and those that do not (see Herrenstein and Loveland, 1964). Such a task is performed by the perceptual system of the pigeon, although the total weight of the pigeon's brain is less than an ounce. How the perceptual system or systems take in the information available sort out that which is necessary for the solution of the problem at hand, and analyze the information in order to arrive at some decision is the very difficult problem we must now consider. Some knowledge is available concerning how this is accomplished, but our information about it is far from complete.

The analysis of information begins at the sense-organ level. The eye, for example, can analyze incoming light into different colors. The retina can also locate the position of particular points of light. When one is looking straight ahead, a point of light from a source to the right will strike a different part of the retina from a point of light coming from the left. The arrangement of light sources in front of us corresponds to the arrangement of light in the corresponding image on the retina.

The ear is a mechanical analyzer of sound. The sound-sensitive receptors are activated by vibrations of a membrane known as the basilar membrane, but different parts of this membrane vibrate most vigorously to sounds of particular pitch. The basilar membrane can take a sound to bits and analyze it in terms of its components, much as the retina takes light apart and analyzes it into color components.

The haptic system also has a complex system of analyzers. The system can analyze various aspects of touch into such components as temperature, roughness, and shape. One knows that an object is both hot and rough because when it is touched, heat-sensitive cells in the skin are activated in it and so also are touch-sensitive cells intermittently activated to indicate roughness. All the details of how the information provided by an object in contact with the skin is analyzed are not yet clear, but there is no doubt that the receptor system does undertake an extensive analysis of the incoming information that is then passed on to the higher centers of the nervous system.

Other analyzing mechanisms occur in both the taste-smell system and in the basic orienting system, but we will not consider these at this time.

The kinds of analyzer mechanisms mentioned here are characteristic of the human being, but other analyzer mechanisms exist at the level of the sense organs in other living creatures. In the chapter on the nervous system, it is pointed out that the retina and optic nerve of the frog have analyzer mechanisms that permit it to identify certain kinds of objects having food value. The human being probably does not have such mechanisms at the sense organ level.

Coding at the Receptors

Information arrives from the environment at the receptors as light waves, sound waves, mechanical pressure, and in various other forms. The receptors function as devices that engineers call transducers, that is, devices that change energy from one form into another form. The energies from the outside world, if they have sufficient impact on the receptors, result in the production of nerve impulses that then travel up the sensory nerves toward the central nervous system. The change in the form of energy that occurs at the receptors is also sometimes referred to as a coding process, for the pattern of nerve impulses produced represents, in some way, the pattern of impact of the energies of the outside world on the receptors. As the reader will find in the chapter on the nervous system, the nerve impulses are generally all or none and along any nerve fiber are of uniform strength.

Nerve impulses cannot vary in size in any particular nerve, they can only vary in frequency. In the case of most receptors, the stronger the stimulation, the greater is the frequency of the impulses that pass up the nerve fiber leading from it. In other words, the intensity of a stimulus is coded into frequency of nerve impulse. The exception to this general rule is found in the auditory nerve in which the intensity of the stimulus does not produce any change in the frequency of impulses along the particular fiber that leads from a particular receptor. A stronger sound stimulates more nerve fibers.

This is not the entire story of the coding of information by the receptors. Indeed, physiological coding is much more complicated, and several factors of great psychological importance have been identified. One is that the higher centers of the brain can depress the sensitivity of the receptors. Thus a receptor may not react and code information because it has been inhibited from doing so by the higher centers.

The nervous system does not give quite the true-to-life picture of the world that one assumes it does. Indeed, the nervous system is so built that it can emphasize aspects of the environment that are of particular importance in adapting to one's surroundings. For example, the retina of the eye functions in such a way that it emphasizes boundaries of objects. This is accomplished through a process known as lateral inhibition. The biological advantage of emphasizing the boundaries of objects is obvious: in order to move around the world we need to know them. Thus in order to go through a door we need to know only the boundaries of the door frame. All other information about the door frame is irrelevant to the task of going through the opening. Lateral inhibition in the retina and optic nerve results in this emphasizing effect (see Abramov and Gordon, 1973).

Although this effect of the accentuation of boundaries of objects has been discussed here as a physiological effect produced by lateral inhibition, it does have its psychological parallel. Visual materials developed for instruction are commonly produced in such a way that they present only boundaries. The typical black and white sketches used for illustrating textbooks are of this character. They are highly informative because they accentuate the characteristics of objects that are the most significant, namely, the edges and boundaries.

Information-processing Time

Considerable attention has been paid by research workers to the problem of information-processing time. If one could find out just how long it takes to process a particular amount of information, one could determine the rate at which the human being can process information. Information can be measured in terms of a unit called the *bit*. If one could measure information-processing rate, one would know how many bits per second the individual could handle. Studies related to this problem have been undertaken mainly with visual stimuli. Some evidence shows that there is a steadily increasing rate at which information can be processed during the growing period (see Bosco, 1972, and Wickens, 1974). It is clear that when the individual is provided with more information than he can process, he is likely to become disorganized, even to the point of being unable to process any information at all. Every teacher knows that the child who is told too much too quickly may learn nothing.

Visual and auditory information have different features that influence how information is processed. The visual system can provide an immense amount of information in less than a hundredth of a second. Auditory information has to enter the system piece by piece—in the case of language, word by word. Auditory language has to be processed in terms of quite large chunks. One may have to wait until an entire sentence has arrived before one can extract information from it. A sentence which begins "He was fired . . ." can mean many things depending whether "He was fired for incompetence" or "He was fired by devotion to his cause." Single words cannot be processed until the entire communication has arrived through the ear. Sentences also have to be processed both at the level of word meaning and the level of sentence structure. Massuro (1972) has provided an analysis of auditory information processing.

Studies of speech that has been speeded up, by a method that does not raise the pitch, show that information of the order of complexity of ordinary conversation can be processed at a rate far exceeding the typical rate of the spoken word, that is, about 150 words per minute. Such materials can be understood without any difficulty at least at double the rate, and some individuals can understand speech at nearly 500 words per minute. The typical academic lecture provides information at a quite inefficient rate. (For studies of this problem see the handbook edited by Duker, 1974.)

Central Coding and Classification of Inputs

When the inputs arrive at central locations of the nervous system, they undergo a complex process of coding related to recognition and interpretation. Garner (1974) has done much to help clarify the general nature of the central response to sensory inputs. He begins by pointing out, as others have done before him, that inputs influence behavior through two different properties. First, they may influence behavior because they have certain energizing properties; if one touches a hot object, the immediate withdrawal response is a result of the energizing properties of the input. Second, they provide information. One sees a roadside sign that says "Steep grade"; the sign gives information to the person who reads it. Sometimes information is provided in a much more subtle form, as when the color of the leaves of a tree tell that fall is approaching. The study of perception has to do with the informational properties of inputs and how that information is used, stored, and interpreted.

Garner takes the position that much of what we respond to in the external world has structure and that perception involves the recognition of that structure. It is not just the beholder who imposes structure on what he sees, though that may sometimes happen. Consider the following arrangement of dots:

$$\bullet \ \bullet \ \bullet \quad \bullet \ \bullet \ \bullet \quad \bullet \ \bullet \ \bullet$$

In such an arrangement the dots are physically structured in three groups of three dots. The structure is a part of the physical world. On the other hand, other stimuli have little structure, or the structure is extremely ambiguous. An ink blot is such a case of low physical structure, or ambiguous structure. When presented with such a stimulus, the person looking at it decides "what it looks like" to him and that is the structure he sees in it. In such a case the structure is largely a product of the viewer's own imagination, and it is not a result of unambigous structure. There is often considerable difficulty in finding out what is in the head of the perceiver and what is in the environment.

Garner also makes the important point that when a single input is examined and interpreted, the activity always implies that the element perceived is classified as a member of a *set* of elements. Consider the following representation of a card containing a mark:

A

Ask a person what he sees when he is shown the card and he will say "a letter
A." During his life he has seen many letter As, some small, some large, some lower
and some upper case, some with serifs and some without, and so forth. When he
says he sees "a letter A," he is not specifying which particular member of the class
he is seeing, only that he sees a member of that class. The statement that he sees
"a letter A" implies that here is a member of a set to which the letter belongs.

Now show the same subject a card printed as follows:

Ask the same person what he sees and he will now say, "I can see a small letter
a" or perhaps "I see a lower case a." The presentation of the second card results
in him focusing on features of the input that he did not notice with the first card.
By doing this he is limiting his identification of the letter a to a subset that includes
only lower case letters. If a third card were given him, with a very large lower
case a printed on it, he might then say that he saw "a large small a." This again
limits his identification to a smaller subset, namely, that which includes large lower
case as.

Thus recognition involves assigning an element perceived to a set or class of
elements to which it belongs. The more precise the identification of the object,
the smaller the subset to which it is assigned. There is some evidence provided by
Ingling (1972) that recognition may involve the assignment of the object perceived
to a class without the object specifically being identified. Thus the witness says,
"I saw a man enter the bank," but he is unable to say anything about the characteristics of the man. The man was identified as one of a class of men, but with no
specific attributes that might distinguish him from other members of that class.
The advantage of such nonspecific identification is that it is economical and produces more rapid identification than would be possible if specific attributes also had
to be identified.

Information may also be recoded into a different form at the higher levels of the
nervous system. Much visual information is converted into a verbal form, as when
I look at the sky and say to myself "What a lovely day!" Freides (1974) also points
out that information is typically recoded into the perceptual system that handles
the information most effectively. Thus when somebody gives me a verbal description
of a piece of furniture, which he gives through the auditory channel, I may find
myself visualizing the piece of furniture. What I have done is to recode the auditory
information into visual information.

Figure and Ground

Although a vast amount of information arrives at the perceptual system and is
picked up by the receptor system, only a small part of that information becomes
available for use. Sperling (1960) has stated this fact in an interesting way by saying
that we recognize only a small part of what we see. Much the same fact was

presented in entirely different words half a century ago by the Gestalt psychologists who said that the perceptual field was always separated into a figure and ground. David Rubin is credited with first having made the figure-ground distinction in 1915 (see Kennedy, 1974). The part of the perceptual field called the figure was a part that appeared highly structured and that the person recognized as the object of his attention, and the ground was the undifferentiated background of vague detail against which the figure was contrasted. In viewing a particular object, one sees it as standing out against an undifferentiated and quite amorphous background.

What is structured in the visual field changes from time to time. One looks at one object and then looks at another. The visual environment is continuously scanned and different objects become figure against the ground.

The structuring and recognition of some object as figure in the perceptual field is sometimes referred to as the development of a percept. It is not an instantaneous process at all, even though with familiar objects, the structuring is rapid. This statement might suggest that a brief viewing of some object, say for one tenth of a second, would not permit a full perception of the object to occur, but it actually does. A brief glance at a scene for one tenth of a second permits one to recognize many objects, even though object recognition may sometimes take as long as half a second. This perception and recognition is possible because although the sensory impression is brief, it leaves behind a trace from which information can be read. Evidence for the existence of such a trace is discussed in the chapter on memory. In a sense, the trace is a very short-term memory that holds information for not more than about two seconds. The existence of such a sensory trace has long been recognized by psychologists and has to be introduced for understanding many phenomena related to perception.

Some structuring takes place without learning, but the structuring is primitive and is almost devoid of meaning. This was demonstrated a long time ago by the German ophthalmologist von Senden (1960), who became interested in the psychological problems of patients who gained vision for the first time as adults, as a result of a corneal graft. These patients all had had opacities in the cornea virtually since birth and gained vision when their own opaque cornea was replaced by that of another human eye. Von Senden was particularly impressed with the fact that when these patients recovered from surgery, with optically perfect eyes, they were still unable to use vision. Indeed, some of them never did, but continued to live as if they were blind people. Others found the impact of the visual world so bewildering and frightening that they would avoid opening their eyes when the scene was complex, as it is on a crowded street, but would venture to use visual information only in the security of their own homes. From the point of view of the present discussion, a very important point brought out by von Senden was that one of the few positive things the recovered patient could do was to be able to say that there was an object in front of him. He could be shown a simple object, such as a piece of board cut into a square, and the patient could say that he saw an object in front of him, but he could not say that it was a square. The data indicate that the visual world can be structured in some kind of way even before the individual has learned to identify the details of what he sees. Newborn infants show some evidence of being able to structure their visual world, even though they clearly cannot respond to the details or discriminate shapes. For example, an infant as young as a few days will fixate a bright source of light but it cannot discriminate a square source of light from a round source

The structuring of particular objects as figures takes place so rapidly that only in the last fifty years have psychologists come to recognize that a process is involved and that the process takes time. Several different techniques have been developed to order to slow up the process of perceptual structuring and make it amenable to study. One procedure developed has been to show a person an object or scene for a very short time and ask him what he sees. Then the object or scene is shown again and he is again asked what he sees. This is done again and again until a clear perception is achieved. In this way the development of a percept can be studied. The technique is not quite as straightforward as it may seem, for even after a person has had a brief glimpse of an object he still retains a representation of it in what we call his mind's eye. Conditions have to be arranged so that the effect of this delayed internal representation of the object is minimal. The device used for making such short presentations is called a tachistoscope. Such devices are generally designed to provide very short presentations of material of the order of one thousandth of a second or less.

An illustration of research on the development of perception utilizing this device is found in the work of Haber (1969), who exposed words, one word at a time, for a duration of only a few milliseconds. The subjects were told that a single word would appear for a very short interval and that they were to try to see the word and all the letters of which it consisted. On the first exposure the viewers would generally report that they saw nothing. Then the same word was flashed on the screen again and again repeatedly. After a few repetitions, the subjects would report seeing parts of letters. Then one or more complete letters might be seen. Oddly enough, a person might report seeing a particular letter, clearly and un-equivocally, on one exposure, and yet on the next exposure the letter could not be seen at all. Finally, the entire word would be seen. In that final stage the subjects would report that they could see the entire word very clearly together with all the letters. If all the exposure times are added together to the point where the word is clearly seen, the total exposure time is only about fifty milliseconds. Presumably, the recognition of common and familiar objects takes place at about this speed, which gives the perceiver the impression that perception is instantaneous. However, the data of Haber indicate that perception takes place through a piece-by-piece analysis of whatever is presented to the senses.

Another and older method for slowing up the perception is to provide material that is difficult to structure, such as an ink blot, and then study the slow emergence of the percept or percepts that gradually emerge. Allport (1955), who has made a classic review of the historical literature on the subject, and more recent writers, too, take the position that the structuring of all inputs to the perceptual systems is preceded and accompanied by a state of expectancy. Solley and Murphy (1960) have elaborated on this idea. Each individual is characterized by a host of expectancies of what he is going to perceive at a particular place and a particular time. We awake in the morning and expect the alarm clock to go off, we expect that the sun will be just above the horizon, we expect to hear the sounds of breakfast being prepared, and we expect to hear a chatter of voices from the family preparing themselves for the day. The ordinary control of behavior involves matching expectancies with actual inputs to the perceptual systems. If we awoke and the sun was shining, but a deathly silence devoid of the rumble of traffic met our ears, we would be immediately aroused into action to determine why there was a discrepancy between expectancy and perception. This continuous matching of expectancies with inputs is only one function of expectancy, for expectancy also determines to some degree how the perceptual inputs are structured. One tends to see what one expects to see rather than the unexpected. Indeed, when highly unexpected events occur, one may comment afterward, "I did not believe my eyes." What this means is that the percept had a certain unreality about it because it did not conform to expectation. Also, under such circumstances, the percept may have been difficult to structure. A percept is more readily structured in terms of expectancies and may be very difficult to structure otherwise. A midwestern American may have to look several times, and give several long looks, before he will actually see the escaped tiger in his back yard. He has no expectancy of seeing a tiger under such conditions and has difficulty in structuring the information that his visual perceptual system presents.

The perceptual systems do not necessarily structure the incoming information in a way that provides correct information about the environment. When the incoming information is structured in such a way that it leads to adaptive behavior, one says that the percepts are veridical, a word that implies that the perceptions have a certain truthfulness to them. Under conditions when the expectancies do not correspond to the inputs of the perceptual systems, there is difficulty in achieving veridical perceptions. The midwesterner into whose back yard an escaped tiger has wandered may perceive it first as a patch of brown in the flower bed, or even as a pile of fabric. Only after every attempt has been made unsuccessfully to perceive it as a common and expected object will a veridical percept be achieved, and he will see it as a tiger. Similar situations can be simulated in the laboratory in which words are flashed on a screen. The situation is arranged so that the viewer expects to see certain words, such as state captials. Under such conditions he sees ATBAUY as ALBANY, and insists that he has seen the word ALBANY. Only after several brief exposures to the word is he able to read it for what it is.

There is considerable evidence that children's perceptions are less veridical than those of adults. One reason for this is that children have had much less experience than adults on which to build their expectancies and, in the absence of a useful system of expectancies, nonveridical perceptions are most likely to occur. Children also have difficulty in distinguishing between what happens inside them and what happens outside them. In addition, they lack sophistication in checking on the percepts they form to determine whether these percepts are veridical or should be restructured to provide a more realistic perception of the world.

At least in the relatively mature individual, the formation of a percept is commonly followed by some kind of check on its veridicality. The hunter thinks he sees a deer, but is not sure. He waits until the brown object moves so that he can see more of it. As he sees more of it, it begins to look less deerlike. For one thing, it is too large, and when he has realized this, it no longer looks as much like a deer as it did. It begins to look like a cow, but then its head appears above the brush and it is seen for what it is, an elk. At least some perceptions involve a sequence of the formation of a percept, the checking of the percept against further information, the formation of a new percept, and perhaps then a further check. This is particularly likely to occur when the information available is fragmentary or in some way partially obscured. This process may sometimes occur with such great rapidity that it is not recognized.

In the case of perception in common situations, such a process of arriving at a final verdical perception by trial and error probably does not occur. In reading a page of print, perceptions of sections of the printed material are rapidly perceived and recognized, with considerable help from the fact that what has already been read provides expectations of what is going to be read and these expectations guide the perceptual process efficiently and smoothly. Sometimes the expectations lead one astray and cause one to perceive words other than those that are there. This is shown in proofreader's errors, in which the proofreader sees the correct word in print and not the incorrect word that is actually printed.

When there are virtually no expectations concerning what one is going to perceive, the process of developing a structured percept is slow. This happens when a person is shown an ink blot and is asked what he sees in it. The person viewing such a blot may look at it for several seconds before he says that he sees it as a butterfly or as some other object, but he does slowly manage to find some structure there, a structure that he virtually imposes on it. In order for an ink blot to be seen as a butterfly, it is necessary that the individual structure his perception with minimum help from the blot itself. This is the reason why a person's perceptions of such an unstructured visual display may throw light on other aspects of his behavior, for it reflects propensities to structure sensory information in particular ways.

A person viewing one of the ink blots develops a perception slowly but does not typically arrive at the development of a stable percept. He tends to produce one perceptual hypothesis after another, first seeing this object, and then that object, and then still another object in the blot. The unstructured nature of the blot makes it impossible for him to achieve a final stable and veridical perception of what is there.

Although some primitive structuring occurs without learning, most structuring of perception is almost certainly learned. That such learning is necessary can be made evident by pointing to some common experiences. Listen to a completely unfamiliar language, such as Mandarin Chinese, which few Americans have heard spoken. When one first hears this language, it seems to be nothing but a jumble of noise. If one wishes to learn the language, he must begin by familiarizing himself with some of the commonly recurring sounds and groups of sounds. When one has had some experience at recognizing the common sound components, that is, the phonemes, he can begin to pick these out from the flow of sound produced by the speaker of Mandarin. At this stage, one has acquired the ability to structure perceptually some of the sound components of the spoken language, but they may as yet have little meaning. One may be able, then, to copy a sound pattern that has been spoken, an act that he could not do at first because of not being able to structure perceptually the vocalizations of speakers.

When the information provided by the environment is clear and unambiguous, veridical perceptions are most likely to occur, but when the cues are not clear, then distortions in perception are common. The perceptual process manifests a characteristic tendency to supply missing details, so that the perceiver reports that he sees a complete object even though the entire object is not presented to his senses. A simple demonstration of this is to present a small circle with a broken boundary through a tachistoscope, thus ◡. The presentation has to be for a very short exposure, perhaps no more than a few hundredths of a second. Under such conditions, the person perceives not a circle with a break in the contour, but a complete circle. At a more complex level, the brief presentation of a display such as *Wxshxxxton, D.C.*, will almost certainly be read as "Washington, D.C." and the person will insist that that is what he saw. These kinds of phenomena demonstrate that perception is not just an interpretation process but an active process of constructing a representation of the environment.

One of the mysteries of the perceptual process is that the eye provides the brain with a quite "dirty" picture of the world, much like a bad television picture. Nevertheless, the brain has a means of cleaning up this picture so that one has the impression of seeing a "clean" picture of the world. There are, of course, ways of cleaning up a "dirty" television picture by filtering out the noisy part of the picture. There are also ways of cleaning up all kinds of other pictures. For example, the pictures taken of Mars by the spaceship were cleaned up to improve the definition. Presumably, the brain can perform a similar cleaning up operation and does.

One of the most important and elemental tasks in acquiring perceptual skill is that of learning to identify those aspects of form and structure that have constancy in the world in which we live. Let us now turn to that aspect of perceptual learning.

Learning the Perceptual Constancies

A child raised in a particular environment has to learn the perceptual constancies in his environment. These are the features of his environment that are of significance in his life. They are also features to which he must give a uniform interpretation regardless of the condition under which they are perceived. He must learn, for example, that the dish from which he eats must be recognized as a dish and be perceived as the same dish regardless of whether the dish is near or far away, whether it is seen from above so that it projects a circular image on the retina, or whether it is seen obliquely and projects an eliptical image. The child has to learn to see the dish as the round dish it is, regardless of the size or shape of the image that it projects. He must learn that despite variation in the sensory input, the meaning must always be the same. Constancies related to size and shape are of the greatest importance for transacting his business with the world around him, but he has to master many other constancies. One of these pertains to the matter of the whiteness of a surface. A piece of black cloth placed in the sun is, in terms of the amount of light reflected, whiter than a piece of white paper placed in the shade, but even a pre-school child will call the piece of cloth in the sun black and the other piece white. He has learned that the whiteness of an object has to be judged in terms of circumstances and the amount of light reflected by other objects in the surroundings.

The constancies of speech have to be understood before spoken language can be interpreted. The child has to learn that it is not the pitch of the sound that matters in order to understand a word, but the inflections and changes in pitch as the word is enunciated. Once he has mastered this feature of interpreting speech, he has some potentiality for differentiating words. He must also understand that the loudness of a sound is not usually a critical element in speech interpretation.

Although emphasis has been placed here on the learning of the environmental constancies, all may not be learned. An earlier chapter pointed out that depth perception may have innate components to it. In addition to the studies previously cited, we must add the studies that have been done on the visual cliff phenomenon. The apparatus used in demonstrating this phenomenon involves a flat surface at the edge of which there is a sharp drop of several feet that is typically covered with a transparent sheet of glass. Very young animals placed on the flat surface will avoid the edge by the drop, called the cliff, and they cannot be coaxed across the glass. Animals that can locomote as soon as they are born will avoid the cliff from birth. Infants will avoid the cliff as soon as they can locomote. At least in lower animals, learning does not seem to be involved. The suspicion is that infants avoid the cliff because of an innate avoidance response, which represents a primitive understanding of space and distance.

Perception and Memory

Gibson (1966) has long emphasized that perception and memory are intimately connected. This is demonstrated by the fact that perception is highly dependent on a system of anticipations, called expectancies, and these expectancies are residues of past experience and can exist only insofar as a memory system exists. Another illustration of how the perceptual and the memory systems are intimately related is that the little bit of the world we see in front of us is assumed to be a part of a total visual world that includes also everything we cannot see at any particular instant, including the world behind our backs. The immediate perception of the world has a continuity with the rest of the world and also a continuity with the past, which one cannot know in the immediate present except through one's memory. The memory systems and the perceptual systems are not two distinct sets of systems, but are highly dependent on one another.

The Identification of the Structured Figure

Let us consider the basic problem of how an object perceived as figure against a ground may be identified as a meaningful object. The various theories of how objects that have been perceptually structured can be identified have been reviewed by Neisser (1967), who points out that the oldest theory is what he calls the template matching theory. According to this theory, one may structure a tree as a figure against the background of its surroundings and then attempt to identify it by trying to match it with other representations of trees stored in memory. The representations of trees stored in memory are the templates, and if a reasonable match with one of these is achieved, the object is identified as a tree.

Template matching theories sometime make the assumption that each previous experience is stored separately and that the new experience is matched with the record of previous experience that best fits. This is very implausible, because it assumes that the capacity of the nervous system to store information is vast. Most evidence suggests that the nervous system does not have a vast capacity for information storage. There is, however, another brand of template matching theory that does not make such extraordinary demands on the nervous system. The alternative template matching theory is that the traces of previous experience are not stored separately, but are somehow consolidated into a composite trace. An analogy to this is a composite photograph of a group of people, which is produced by photographing each person separately and then making a print by exposing the photographic paper to each one of the negatives separately for a short time. Such composite photographs bring out differences in appearance between groups of people, such as northerners and southerners or vegetarians and meat eaters. There is a possibility that an analogous kind of consolidation may take place in memory and may result in the formation of a limited number of templates. This form of template theory has plausibility and has appealed to many psychologists including Bartlett (1932), who made use of this concept in his theory of memory. This form of template theory places much less strain on the memory than would the alternative, which involves storing each experience separately, but there are difficulties associated with it. One major difficulty, which virtually eliminates it as a plausible hypothesis, is that perception takes place too rapidly to permit a process of rummaging through a large inventory of templates to determine which one matched best the immediate input. Recognition of an object is described by the human observer as being almost immediate. Although the nervous system functions with great rapidity, it could not function rapidly enough to make this form of template theory tenable. Although this may not be the common way in which recognition takes place, there is still the possibility that perception may *sometimes* involve this kind of a matching process.

A second theory, which is by far the most plausible theory of recognition, is that an object is recognized by a two-step process. The first step involves the identification of the distinctive features of the object to be recognized, and the second step requires that the particular combination of the features is used to identify the object. At first sight, this theory would appear to involve as much time as would the template theory, but this is not the case. Devices have been developed that will do this at very high speeds. For example, a device has been developed to enable blind people to read printed material. The device makes an analysis of the features of each printed letter, and feeds the information into an analyzer, which immediately triggers a device that says the letter aloud. The entire process takes place at very high speeds. Also, the device does not have to store vast quantities of information, for only some of the information about each letter has to be stored. This theory of recognition is supported by a great amount of experimental evidence. We know, for example, that children learning to read recognize particular words by identifying such distinctive features as double letters, particular letters in particular locations, and features such as the length of a word. An animal seen in a fleeting glimpse in a forest may be identified only by its color and size, to name one common experience of recognition and identification by feature analysis. The laboratory provides much more solid evidence that recognition takes place by this kind of process. One can briefly expose pictures by means of a tachistoscope and study how the recognition of an object slowly develops. Show a child a picture of an elephant in this way for one tenth of a second. He is likely to say after this single short exposure that it must be an animal because he saw four legs. After a second exposure, he may say it has to be an elephant because it not only has four legs but it also has tusks. Thus the attributes of the object are identified and, once this has been accomplished, the nature of the object can be guessed or readily identified.

If this analysis of recognition is correct, one can readily understand how misinterpretations occur. One sees a distant figure on a street and recognizes it as that of a friend one is meeting. All one sees is an upright oblong object, but the few features identified are sufficient to reach the conclusion that it is the friend and not anyone else. Recognition is a conclusion drawn from limited fact, but the perceiver generally manages to glean enough information from the situation confronting him to jump to right conclusions. Occasionally he does not, and then he experiences a misperception. Such misperceptions are most likely to occur when only fleeting glimpses of a situation are obtained. The glimpses of an automobile accident that one catches in the fraction of a second that the accident takes to happen are typical of a situation that results in misperception. That is why witnesses so often disagree about what happened in an accident, even though they were present. They just did not pick up enough information to reach a sound conclusion, and correct perception is a matter of reaching a sound conclusion on the basis of fragmentary information. There are some cases of misperception that are not so easily handled by this theory of recognition still to be considered.

The chapter on the nervous system provides important additional evidence supporting the attribute analysis theory of recognition. In that chapter substantial evidence is cited showing that many creatures have built-in mechanisms for recognizing particular features of the environment.

An interesting question is whether the mechanisms that analyze the features of an object all operate simultaneously or whether they work one after another in a step-wise fashion. Perceptual recognition would be a very slow process in the case of recognizing objects where many attributes had to be identified, if recognition took place through attributes being identified one at a time. However, it also seems unlikely that all analyzing mechanisms operate simultaneously. Work by Dick and Dick (1970), for example, has provided evidence that in a task involving letter recognition, the position of a letter in the visual field is recognized before the features of the letter related to its identity are analyzed. This does not mean that all the analyzing mechanisms operate one after the other, but only that some operate sequentially in this way. The total data suggest that some of the analyzers operate simultaneously, but that some operate one after another.

An extension of feature analysis is what Sutherland (1973) calls structural description. One may recognize a face merely on the basis of the unusually blue eyes, in which case recognition is based on a single feature. On the other hand, one might recognize the face on the basis of not only the eyes but also the straight nose, the bushy eyebrows sloping upward and outward, the low forehead, and so forth. Such an identification based on both multiple features and their interrelationships is referred to as identification by *structural description*. Although recognition does occur on the basis of simple feature identification, much recognition is better described as involving structural description.

Corcoran (1971) has both reviewed the evidence and conducted some of his own experiments on how information is extracted. He concludes that on the initial inspection of a visual display information is extracted from the picture by a serial process. The person scans the display, taking in the information piece by piece. However, when a familiar picture is seen it may not be scanned but may be taken in as a whole. The latter is possible because some kind of representation of the picture is stored internally and only a limited amount of information about the picture need be received through the senses in order for the person to "know" the picture that confronts him. This means that any material presented to the pupil for the first time on film has to provide the time necessary for the pupil to engage in a serial strategy. Once he has pursued the strategy with that particular visual display, he is ready from then on to handle the display by a different, parallel strategy when it is subsequently presented. The serial examination of the display, one suspects, permits the individual to form an overall impression of the total display. One also suspects that the soundtrack that accompanies such a visual display could assist the pupil in undertaking a serial scanning strategy by indicating the parts of the display to be examined in turn.

The problem of serial versus parallel processing of information is widely discussed in the research literature. One popular hypothesis has been that the viewer of a picture uses parallel processing and the viewer of a word uses sequential processing. Snodgrass and Antone's research (1974) seems to indicate that there is little validity to such a simplistic model. Das and Molloy (1975) have reviewed literature indicating that children have to learn when serial strategies of perception should be used and when the simultaneous strategy is likely to be most successful.

A third theory of recognition, which is really two theories, is referred to as the analysis-by-synthesis theory. This theory was evolved originally by scientists working on problems of speech, where some attractive evidence can be found to support it. The essential nature of the theory is that when the perceptual system is confronted with some problem of recognition, an attempt is made to build, inside the nervous system, a representation similar to the image of the object presented by the perceptual system. Thus if one heard a word, recognition of the word would be achieved through an internal attempt to build a word to be matched with the word presented. This may seem to be a roundabout way of recognizing the objects of the real world, but not entirely as unrealistic a suggestion as it may seem. Neisser (1967), who finds the suggestion to be a very plausible explanation of recognition, points out that this is exactly the kind of process used by a machine developed by the U.S. Post Office to recognize the written name of the state to which letters are addressed. The device attempts to synthesize a written address until it comes up with one that closely matches the one written on the envelope. In the case of the Post Office machine, this procedure for recognizing addresses seems to be more feasible than that of feature or attribute analysis, or template matching. The computer that performs this process of matching does it at tremendous speeds, far in excess of those of which the nervous system is capable.

The two theories of speech recognition through analysis by synthesis have been referred to as the active model and the passive model. The active model proposes that speech is recognized through the listener actively synthesizing speech with his vocal cords. The synthesized speech must match the trace of the speech coming from the outside. This theory, like motor theories of thinking, does not fit the facts very well. Speech recognition takes place much too rapidly for it to have to depend on silent speech of the listener. Also, speech recognition takes place quite well when the vocal cords are fully occupied by translating the heard speech into a different language, as in the case of United Nations interpreters, who hear in one language and speak in another at the same time. But perhaps one should not be too quick in discarding such a theory, for young children often repeat back a sentence immediately after hearing it, as if the saying of it was necessary for comprehension. Recognition and understanding may perhaps sometimes assume this form, but adults almost certainly do not use vocal or subvocal echoes of what they hear as a basis for understanding.

The latter theory of recognition through analysis by synthesis is known as the Haskins model because it was developed at the Haskins laboratories. It is to be contrasted with the Halle and Stevens model (1962), which is sometimes called the passive model. An essential difference between the two models is that in the Haskins model muscular activity is essential for recognition, but in the Halle and Stevens model the attempts to synthesize what is heard take place entirely within the nervous system. The Halle and Stevens model is much more complicated than is implied here and suggests very specific mechanisms of analysis and synthesis.

Analysis-by-synthesis theories of recognition find support in one very interesting phenomenon known as the verbal transformation effect. Warren (1968) has summarized the research on this effect. A typical way of demonstrating it is by playing the same word again and again on a loop of tape. The listener first hears the word correctly, but then suddenly he begins to hear a different word and in a few minutes he may report that he has heard several different words played back to him. When the word *tress* was played over and over again in one study, the listener reported hearing a variety of words such as *stress, dress, Jewish, Joyce, florist,* and *purse.* It is not that the word presented sounds like the various words reported. The words reported are heard and are like vivid hallucinations that the person cannot differentiate from reality. The transformation effect does suggest that, under some circumstances, the person does synthesize internally a representation of what he hears, but this does not necessarily imply that all recognition involves a synthesis process.

Object Orientation and Perception

The orientation of an object is an important factor in perceptual recognition which one can easily demonstrate by turning this page upside down and then trying to read it. Reading becomes extremely difficult when the orientation of the book is reversed. Those who try to read from the upside-down page usually report that they look at each word or letter and then try to imagine what the word or letter would look like right side up. The result is extreme slowness in deciphering the printed code. Rock (1973) has made some interesting studies of this phenomenon. Object orientation is learned as a factor that has to be taken into account in visual recognition, which involves not only an orientation of up-down, but also an orientation of left-right. The absence of such an orientation in many 5-to-6-year-old children results in them writing from right to left or left to right indiscriminately. These same children in learning to read have difficulty in discriminating letters that are mirror images of one another, as, for example, *b* and *d*. The young child learning to read may hold his book upside down and stumble along from word to word with about the same amount of difficulty as he has in reading with the book right side up. His stumbling skill is quite similar to that of the adult who holds the book upside down or who tries to read the words in a mirror. To do this, great attention has to be paid to the details of print and the cues they provide.

In the mature individual a visual input through the eye appears to be first assigned to coordinates of up-down and right-left. Once the spatial orientation of the object has been identified, the individual is in a position to interpret what he sees. By doing this there is no longer any confusion between *b* or *d* because the spatial coordinates tell him which way to read the letter. Inverting a page of print destroys this frame of reference for the mature reader and causes him great difficulty. The young child who does not have such a rigid frame of reference has much less difficulty with the task.

Stimulus Sampling

Visual perception appears to involve what is referred to as *stimulus sampling.* The general conception of stimulus sampling, as presented by Neimark and Estes (1967), is that all situations can be regarded as being comprised of a large number of stimulus elements, which are collectively called a population of stimulus elements. The person responding to the situation does not respond to all of the stimulus elements simultaneously, but only to a sample of them. Some research workers have speculated that the person viewing a situation samples the stimulus elements at random, while others have preferred to assume that each stimulus element has a certain probability of its own of being included in the sample. Certainly one responds much more readily to some elements in the environment than to others, and the latter position seems to be the more justifiable. Stimulus sampling theory always makes the legitimate assumption that the perceptual system is a limited capacity system that can take in and process only a limited amount of the information provided by the environment. It is assumed that the perceptual system draws a sample from the information available. If the sample does not provide a basis for action another sample is drawn.

Stimulus sampling theory helps one to explain some common experiences that teachers encounter. A teacher shows a travelogue film to children, giving them a rapid tour of Stockholm. After presenting the film, the teacher asks the children what the town hall was like. A brief glimpse of the building had been included in the film. One child says the town hall had high brick walls. What else did he see? Well, he didn't see much else. Another child then says he noticed that the town hall had battlements on top. Did the building have any windows? He didn't notice that, but another child noticed that the building had tall and narrow windows. Different children sampled the information differently. Some obtained a sample that included information about the brick walls, and other students obtained other information. As the teacher goes over the film, it becomes apparent that each child obtained a rather different sample of information from every other child. That is one of the reasons why it is desirable to discuss in advance of showing a film the features that should be noticed. The discussion exercises some control over the sample of information that the children are going to obtain from the film. The procedure does not provide complete control over the sample of information that each child will obtain, but it provides some control. Also, some children will obtain a larger sample of information from a film presentation than will others.

There is evidence beyond question that the development of a perception of a complex scene requires successive stimulus sampling. If a picture of a common scene is presented by means of a tachistoscope, so that it can be seen for only a short interval of one fourth second at a time, the individual will see little the first time the scene is exposed. On the second exposure, he will pick up a few more features and, after perhaps ten brief exposures, will have a good idea of what the picture presents. What is shown in this demonstration is that on each successive exposure the individual is able to obtain an additional sample of information. The total sample needed to provide a comprehensive description of the picture cannot be obtained in any one brief viewing of the picture.

Travers (1969) undertook a study using the technique described with children of ages 4 to 12 and found some interesting differences in the way in which the children of different ages sampled information. The older children behaved very much in the way already described. In contrast, the younger children failed to obtain new samples of information on successive exposures of the picture, but tended to report the same items on each successive exposure. It would seem that the young children had not yet learned to obtain new samples of information from each successive exposure to a scene. The children would have recognized most of the elements in most of the pictures at all of the ages studied, so it was not just that the younger children latched onto the few objects they recognized. They simply failed to sample widely the information presented. The study also led the investigator to suspect that even the more mature individuals, in the group of children studied, often failed to sample information effectively, suggesting that training in sampling skills might possibly have value.

Trabasco and Bower (1968) have provided some interesting data that show how stimulus sampling is related to learning. In their studies they have used a learning task of the type in which the subject has to learn to put diagrams including red circles into class A and those that include a blue square into class B. The point to note is that subjects can learn this task in a number of different ways. They may learn to classify in terms of shape (square or triangle), in terms of color (red or blue), or in terms of both shape and color. It is also conceivable, but probably rare, that a person might put those with triangles in one category and those that were blue in another. It seems that subjects generally either sample for shape or sample for color. An outcome of considerable interest is that those who solve the problem on the basis of shape rarely note that color could also be used to solve the problem, and that those who solve it in terms of color do not notice that shape could also be used to solve the problem. When a sample of information is found to be successful, other samples of information are not sought. No particular differences could be found between learners who used just one cue and learners who used both.

Stimulus sampling theories have almost nothing to say about which stimulus elements are sampled. The position of the theory is very similar to that of the theory of recognition known as attribute analysis, insofar as neither theory specifies the primary stimulus elements that are identified. For example, would an outlined square figure be a single element, or would it consist of a set of elements? If it consists of a set of elements, are these elements lines or angles or dots? The basic components may be different for different individuals, depending on the training to which he was exposed early in life. That some stimulus sampling occurs seems clear, but what is sampled is very obscure. Sampling theory of perception has been mainly of theoretical interest (Rozeboom, 1974), but it has potential application that needs to be explored.

Attention

Teachers have long believed that the key to learning involves gaining what is called the attention of the student. Although psychologists have been intrigued with attention as a concept in learning, they have had difficulty in coming to grips with the concept, for it does not suggest any direct means through which it can be studied. Indeed, considerable difficulty has been experienced in the identification of the events that take place when a person attends to some particular source of information. Russian psychologists have long been interested in some of the immediate reactions of the human being to stimuli that carry information of significance to him. The initial response is either one known as the *startle response* or one known as the *orienting response*. These two responses are very different in terms of the physiological reactions accompanying them. The initial stages of what is commonly referred to by American psychologists as attention can be described in terms of the orienting response—a response that is accompanied by dilation of the blood vessels in the head, the disappearance of the alpha waves in the brain, the dilation of the pupils of the eye, a temporary arrest of the breathing mechanism, and other reactions. The orientating response should be regarded as a response that prepares the individual to become the recipient of information.

The term *attention*, as it is commonly used, implies that there is a selective process of taking the information into the perceptual system. Many of the factors that result in the entry of information into the perceptual system are known and are used by teachers to ensure entry. Some of the more important ones are less well recognized. The intensity of stimulus is one factor that influences whether a stimulus is or is not received in the perceptual system as information, which is why teachers often shout in order to gain the attention of the child. Strong stimuli, whatever their content, cannot generally be blocked from entering the perceptual system. More subtle stimulus characteristics, which determine the priority of information, are those of novelty and complexity, both of which can be utilized by the teacher to gain the attention of pupils.

Attempts have been made to build theories of attention, but these have tended to be complex and beyond the scope of this book. Mackintosh (1975), who has summarized such theories, points out that all theories have to take into account that the stimulus attended to is attended to in competition with many other stimuli. Attending to a particular stimulus enhances the learning related to that stimulus and decreases learning related to other stimuli.

The basic phenomena of attention are shown even by the youngest infants. The eyes of the infant are fixated longer on what he has not seen before than on what he has. Also what attracts attention does not necessarily hold attention (Cohen, 1972). Even with the 2-day-old infant, moving objects have greater attention value than still objects, a tendency that persists throughout life (Kagan, 1972). In young preschool children there also develops a subtle distinction between what they find pleasing and what they find interesting (Aitken and Hutt, 1974). In such children there also seems to be a difference between impulsive and reflective children in their ability to attend to an object. The impulsive children tend to skip from object to object (Siegel, Kirasic, and Kilburg, 1974).

Novelty, as a factor in attention, can be regarded as having several components. A stimulus can be novel, in that it has not been presented recently. Stimuli that have not been presented for some time have priority over those that have been more recently presented. A stimulus can have novelty attributable to the fact that it appears in an unfamiliar context, that is, if there is a low probability of a stimulus being present, and the stimulus appears, the stimulus may be said to be novel. The appearance of a horse and buggy on a busy street has novelty today because there is a very low expectancy of such an event. An object can also have novelty, to the extent that it has never before been presented to the individual involved. In most of the literature on the effect of novelty on behavior, all of these meanings are used quite interchangeably.

In the case of all higher organisms, an object that has novelty attracts attention. That is it produces an orienting response followed by behavior that can be described in general terms as behavior involving watchfulness. If the novelty is not extreme, the attending response is also accompanied by approach behavior, particularly in those species that have become domesticated.

There is survival value in a tendency to give priority of attention to that which is novel. An animal that had a different assignment of priorities would not survive very long, for it is the novel that is most likely to bring disaster. The novel is always a potential threat, if not a real one. Wild animals tend to show a watchfulness of novel objects at a safe distance, but domesticated species are more likely to show cautious approach behavior.

The complexity factor as a basis for attracting attention is of both practical and theoretical significance. Travers (1970) and Aitken and Hutt (1972) have reviewed elsewhere the related research. There seems fairly clear evidence that even at the very youngest ages, babies show a preference for viewing materials that have a certain degree of complexity to them. When diagrams are displayed above the head of an infant (Thomas, 1965), the babies spend different amounts of time fixating with their eyes the different diagrams. Very simple ones are viewed the least, but there is probably an optimum amount of complexity and this optimum increases with age. A similar kind of phenomenon is also evident in studies of eye movements in which the fixation time on particular parts of a visual display can be studied. Yarbus (1967), who has brought together the numerous studies made of eye movements, finds firm evidence that when the eye scans a complex display, such as that presented by a map, the tendency is for the eye to dwell mostly on those parts that are the more complex. This finding can be interpreted in another way by saying that the eye dwells longest on those aspects of the display that present the greatest amount of information and least time on those that contain the least information. If a display consists of a map of an island, a part of which has a smooth coastline and a part of which is quite jagged, then the eye will dwell longest on the jagged coastline and least on the smooth part. If the interior of the island is represented by a blank space, with no markings, the eye will spend almost no time on the vacant area. Yarbus brings out in considering this matter that, in contemplating a human face, the viewer spends more time directing his gaze toward the eyes and the mouth than toward any other part. Oddly enough, the same is true even when an animal's face is involved. The eyes and the mouth appear to be a source of more information than is any other part. Attention, and processes related to information intake, are regulated to some degree by the amount of available information. In this kind of observing behavior, there is a very clear tendency for perception to be directed in such a way that it provides a continuous input of new information. In viewing pictures, Antes (1974) has shown a similar pattern. The individual first makes broad scanning movements of the eyes to identify the informative areas of the picture, followed by short fixations on those areas.

Studies of eye movements have produced some interesting findings related to perception. One of these is that some movement of the eye is necessary for the perception of an object. The eye does fixate objects, and, in reading, the eye will appear to stop at places along the line of print. Nevertheless, these fixations of the eye are not motionless stops, for the eye continues to make slight movements called saccadic movements. These are almost like slight vibrations and are necessary for perception. Under some experimental conditions, one can arrange conditions so that the image remains motionless on the retina. When this is done, the object producing the image disappears from view within a few seconds. The continued perception of an object requires the continued motion of the eyes. Perception is a dynamic process and the so-called fixation of the eye is only a state of relative motionlessness.

An interesting effect related to complexity has been explored by Wohlwill (1968), who prepared two sets of slides, one set showing a number of pieces of modern art and the other set showing scenes from different geographic environments. Each series of slides was scaled in terms of level of complexity. College students were given the slides and each student was allowed to view each slide as often as he chose. The study showed that the more complex the slide, the more frequently the student was likely to view it. This is what one would expect, for the more complex the presentation the more information is available and the longer time it takes-for the viewer to become saturated with that information. However, Wohlwill also found that the individual's preference for a particular slide was not related in a simple way to complexity. As the complexity increased, the preference for the slide increased up to a maximum. From that point on, an increase in complexity resulted in a decline in the expressed preference for the slide. The data suggest that individuals choose to view slides not just in terms of what they like or do not like, but in terms of the amount of information present.

Two aspects of attention of considerable practical interest are those involved in the two operations known as scanning and vigilance. These are referred to as detection tasks. In scanning tasks, an individual has to locate a particular item of information among a large quantity of irrelevant information. Such tasks in the laboratory may involve the identification of particular letters of the alphabet in long strings of random letters or in pages of meaningful printed prose. Pupils in schools are often involved in scanning tasks when they leaf through books searching for information on particular topics. Skill in scanning is, obviously, a very important one and research on scanning has considerable potential value for educational practice.

Much of the work on scanning behavior up to 1970 has been summarized by Travers (1970). The research shows that scanning is a highly trainable skill. A second important finding is that it is much more efficient to scan material searching for two or more items at the same time than it is to scan for a single item. The workers in newspaper-cutting services demonstrate this phenomenon, for they are able to scan newspapers, at high speed, searching for information on a large number of different topics simultaneously. At least one study has shown that young adults can scan for ten different items of information as rapidly as they can scan for a single item. Even among children of elementary-school age, research has shown that they can scan for two items of information as rapidly as for one, and it is possible that they might be able to scan for many more items simultaneously and with equal speed and efficiency. These findings should, perhaps, be applied with caution in that they have been derived from research using rather simple types of material. Scanning a book for information about some broad topic, such as the behavior of birds, may be a somewhat different task from that involved in scanning a page of type and identifying all the letters *e*. Indeed, the task of looking for the letter *e* in a string of random letters is different from that of looking for the same letter in prose. In the latter case, the silent *e* tends to be missed.

Scanning tasks can take place at enormous speeds. Many persons looking through printed material for particular categories of information may cover material at several thousand words per minute. How this is accomplished is far from clear, although some information is available. In order to discuss some of the explanatory concepts involved, let us introduce two technical terms used by research workers in the field. The item that is searched for during a scanning operation is referred to as the target item. The material that the target item is embedded in is referred to as consisting of nontarget items. Thus if a person is searching for references to the word *reflex*, the latter word is referred to as the target word and all other words are referred to as nontarget words. One can show that a person conducting a search has to examine, to some degree, both the target materials and the nontarget materials. This can be demonstrated by giving the individual practice in picking up certain targets. Then the nontarget materials are changed. When this is done, the task of locating the target items immediately becomes more difficult, thus providing evidence that responses to the nontarget items influence the difficulty of the task. However, a logical analysis of the task of scanning shows that this has to be the case, for how could a person ever identify target items if he were not able also to identify nontarget items? The identification of target items requires that each item be identified either as a target or a nontarget item. It is probable that the nontarget items may not be analyzed at the same level of detail as the target items.

Theories of scanning and visual search generally assume that the search is conducted in terms of particular features of the target items. There is considerable controversy concerning whether the search is conducted through all features being sought for simultaneously or whether a search for each feature is undertaken successively. The high speed at which a search can be conducted suggests that items are examined for all features at once. However, Yonas and Pittenger (1973) have evidence that such a simple model may not account for some of the facts.

Scanning tasks are commonly referred to as signal detection tasks. The targets are the signals to be detected. Another type of signal detection task, which also throws some light on the attention process, is known as a vigilance task. The latter type of activity involves the detection of rare and typically faint signals. A common laboratory task of this kind exposes the subject to a continuous tone, but from time to time the pitch of the tone is raised slightly for perhaps a quarter of a second. A corresponding visual task involves occasional slight changes in a spot of light. The number of different tasks used for the study of vigilance behavior is legion, but there are also many tasks involved in some occupations that also call for a similar ability to detect rare signals that are not readily detected.

Studies of vigilance behavior (see Sanders, 1967) demonstrate a number of significant aspects of behavior related to attention. The human being requires a continuous input of information in order for the higher levels of the nervous system to function effectively. When the input of information is reduced, as it is in the performance of vigilance tasks such as that of watching a scope to detect a faint and rare "blip" to appear on it, the individual begins to search for other sources of input. In other words, his perceptual systems are likely to become directed away from the vigilance task and toward other parts of the environment that have greater potential for providing greater inputs of information. This is why attention directed toward the vigilance task cannot be maintained for more than a short time. The evidence also shows that the level of motivation of the person engaged in vigilance behavior is highly related to his level of performance. Presumably the same would be true for most rather boring tasks. Another interesting finding is that there are great individual differences in the ability to perform vigilance tasks. Some individuals have an extraordinary ability to engage in tasks involving a very low input of information and are able to maintain their performance at quite a high level, but others cannot. Some evidence has also been found that some individuals are better on visual vigilance tasks and some on auditory tasks, though the overall performance of a group may be the same on two types of task.

Studies of vigilance bring out very clearly the fact that the maintenance of an attentive posture is highly dependent on the amount of information that is being received, the level of motivation of the person involved, and also dispositions related to the maintenance of an attending response, which are not fully understood at this time. The missing of signals that occurs in vigilance tasks with increasing frequency as time goes by is commonly explained in terms of stimulus sampling. If a signal is not included in the particular sample of stimuli taken at the instant when the signal occurs, the signal is missed. Because the sampling is least from those aspects of the environment that provide the least information, the display tends to be sampled less and less with the passage of time. Sampling theories of perception have value in explaining all kinds of perceptual failures (see the paper by Wolford, Wessel, and Estes, 1968).

Incidental Learning

The concept of attention implies that the perceptual systems can be set to take in information from a narrow region of the environment. Does this mean that no other information can be derived at the same time from other regions of the environment? This problem is known as the problem of incidental learning. The earlier writers in the field contrasted *incidental* learning with *intentional* learning. They argued that learners undertake tasks with intent to learn and, while learning what they intend to learn, they also acquire and retain other information about other aspects of the situation. This other information acquired is referred to as the material incidentally learned.

This definition turned out to be far from satisfactory. One difficulty was that of determining just what the individual originally intended to learn, for during learning his intentions may change. If the material is verbal printed material, he may begin by intending to remember the words, but then he may become bored with this task and begin to note the characteristics of the printing and typeface. When he does this, he would be considered by some psychologists as engaging in an intent to learn the characteristics of printing, but others would classify the resulting learning as incidental rather than as intentional. The word *intentional* is far from being clear and fails to provide a proper distinction between incidental and non-incidental learning.

An attempt to clarify this situation has been made by psychologists of more recent vintage who, instead of using the term intentional learning, define incidental learning as that which occurs outside the assigned task. This defines the two categories of learning in terms of the instructions given to the subjects. The procedure has a certain objectivity to it, but instructions are never entirely clear. What if a person interprets the instructions to learn a list of words as including instructions to learn about the characteristics of their printing?

Numerous different techniques have been devised for the study of incidental learning. In one technique, a person is asked to read a list of words to another individual. The assigned task for the reader is that of reading the words, but if he remembers something about the words or can remember the actual words, he has manifested incidental learning. The listener's assigned task is that of learning the words, but he may also engage in incidental learning and remember something about the characteristics of the reader, such as his accent or how the reader was dressed. However, those who participate in experiments do not always follow instructions. Indeed, some who have to read lists of words may become so bored with the task that they start learning the words to break the monotony. Postman (1964) has discussed the difficulties involved in the development of experimental techniques in this area, but an even more critical review by McLaughlin (1968) has also summarized the findings.

The main finding conforms with expectation, namely, that in the kinds of experimental tasks used more is learned by intentional learning than by incidental learning. This may be due to the nature of the tasks. Some psychologists, such as Berlyne (1960), have suggested that the latter finding is almost certainly an artifact of the experimental situation and suggest that in ordinary life the reverse may be true and more may be learned by incidental means. There seems some rather unclear evidence that most incidental learning takes place early in most tasks. Presumably, the learner begins by scanning the materials presented to him and picks up sundry pieces of incidental information. However, if the task is prolonged long enough, so that the materials have to be learned far beyond the point where they can be repeated back, substantial incidental learning also takes place in the later stages of learning. One suspects that when a learner is forced to repeat again and again a task he has mastered, he begins to explore other aspects of the material.

There are wide differences in the amount of incidental learning manifested by different subjects, an observation that ties in closely with the common observation that some individuals pick up a great amount of information about the world around them, whereas others limit their information gathering to the particular tasks that they have to undertake. These individual differences do not seem to be related to measures of intelligence. Incidental learning occurs both among the gifted and among retardates.

Some of the clearest and most consistent findings with respect to incidental learning are found in the areas of motivation. As drive level or motivation is increased, there is a tendency for the amount of incidental learning to decline. Just how this effect is produced is not clear at this time and much more experimental evidence must be collected before an acceptable explanation can be advanced. It is, of course, easy to say that under high motivation attention is restricted to the main task, but this does not mean much. A more meaningful and testable hypothesis is that the visual perceptual system naturally engages in scanning activity, but that instructions to respond to certain characteristics of whatever is presented cut down the scanning activity, and the amount that it is cut down depends on the drive level. Experiments could be undertaken to test such a hypothesis.

Perhaps one conclusion more than any other emerges from research on this problem. It is a conclusion originally reached by Postman (1964), namely, that no rigid line can be drawn between intentional and incidental learning. They are both part of a unified single process of information reception and short-term storage.

Perceptual Learning

Just as psychologists have learned that newborn infants are capable of far more instrumental learning than they had hitherto been thought capable of, so, too, have psychologists slowly learned that infants have great capacity for perceptual learning. Much of the credit for the later development must go to the invention by Fantz (1958) of an extraordinarily simple, yet powerful, technique. Fantz studied what infants looked at. He was able to show that when infants were shown a design they had seen before, side by side with a design that they had never seen, they tended to look at the design they had never seen. This meant that the infants had learned something about the design they had originally seen. This leads psychologists to the position that infants have a capability of recording the information that comes to them through their senses and that they do this completely automatically. Stone, Smith, and Murphy (1973) have made an excellent summary of the perceptual capabilities of the neonate. They conclude that newborn infants have some capacity for discriminating visual stimuli and for processing information about them. However, they do not seem to have true pattern recognition even though they concentrate their attention on contours.

Visual skills of infants are not limited to contour perception. The evidence indicates that infants are capable of responding to depth and distance by the age of 1 month and may well have that capability at birth. Infants seem capable of fixating objects shortly after birth. Neonates also show an orienting response, which can be described as a response related to attending. They also show habituation to stimuli. If whatever they attend to continues to be presented, they cease to respond to it.

Fantz's infants demonstrated what has been termed perceptual learning. A long controversy has existed among psychologists concerning whether perceptual learning could actually occur, many arguing that mere exposure was not sufficient to produce learning and that hidden reinforcements must be operating. However, evidence has slowly accumulated from many sources indicating that perceptual learning in this sense is a genuine phenomenon.

Gibson (1953) reviewed a great quantity of research that demonstrated that in many perceptual discrimination tasks improvement seemed to occur merely through the individual's attempts to make the discrimination. If a person is given pairs of objects and is asked to judge which one of each pair is heavier, he will slowly improve his performance even though he is never told whether he is right or wrong. The mere practice of an unfamiliar perceptual discrimination task results in improved performance. Similar improvements occur when other sensory systems are involved. The person who is given practice in reading letters at a greater distance than that at which they can be clearly read shows a remarkable improvement in his performance through the effect of practice alone. Many schemes for producing better vision without glasses depend on this improvement effect. One should note that although improvement in such sensory tasks takes place without any kind of feedback or reinforcement, improvement occurs more rapidly when the person knows after each trial whether he is right or wrong. The important point, however, is that even though improvement may be accelerated by feedback, feedback is not essential to learning in such tasks. This learning effect is to be contrasted with the learning of motor skills, in which some form of feedback is of more crucial significance.

A second example of perceptual learning is found in exposing subjects to particular objects and events early in life and determining the extent to which later discriminations with respect to those objects and events are facilitated by the exposure. Many psychologists have suggested that stimulation of appropriate kinds early in life results in superior cognitive development. Those who maintain this position propose that the environment of the infant in the first few months of life should contain a great variety of forms, sounds, and tactile experiences. Indeed, those who argue for such an environment have generally taken the position that the worst possible type of environment is that of foundling institutions, in which the infant sees little more than a uniform white field. The suggestion has been made that the later intellectual inadequacies of many such children may be due to their early environment.

Although the problem is one of vast significance in education, research related to it has been minimal, largely because of experimental difficulties. Experiments with human beings can be conducted with children in foundling homes, but advantage has been taken only recently of such opportunities. The earlier studies conducted on animals have been reviewed by Epstein (1967).

A distinction must be made between studies of general stimulus deprivation and studies where the effect of exposure to particular stimuli is studied. The chapter on development in the Epstein book pointed out the existence of overwhelming evidence that exposure to a bleak and uniform environment early in life generally produced an animal with extraordinary learning disabilities. The narrower question of whether exposure to *particular* stimuli produces a later facilitation in solving problems related to those stimuli is a more significant problem to investigate, and it is to that problem that our attention must now turn.

In the typical animal experiment, an experimental group of rats is raised in cages on the walls of which forms are suspended. The forms usually consist of such simple objects as equilateral triangles, circles, or squares. In a typical experiment, just two different forms are used. Half the rats from each litter used are raised in cages without such objects. Some months later, after the rats have reached an age at which they are capable of being used in form-discrimination studies, their ability to discriminate the two different shapes is tested. The studies show some consistency in findings. The evidence seems fairly clear that mere exposure to the forms results in later superior ability in discriminating between the particular shapes involved or closely related shapes. It is not clear whether there are or are not any general benefits in shape discrimination produced by exposure to particular shapes. The evidence does suggest that exposure to one particular shape alone facilitates the subsequent discrimination between that shape and other shapes to which the animal has not been exposed.

Just what is learned during the exposure to the forms is not clear at this time. It could be that the animal learns some familiarity with the shapes, but one does not have to assume that such learning takes place at all. There is a possibility that animals brought up in an environment that is visually complex learn to use vision more than rats brought up in a simpler and more barren environment. Rats do not favor the use of visual cues when other cues can be used.

The experiments reviewed by Epstein are also important for another reason. They add to the slowly accumulating body of knowledge that reinforcement is *not* an essential condition for learning. Many psychologists already make this assumption. For example, those concerned with the study of paired-associate learning commonly assume that if the two words of each pair enter the perceptual system, they will become associated. Those who take this position would view reinforcement as determining the kinds of tasks in which the person or animal engages, but would not view it as a condition of learning. Thus reinforcements may be responsible for a child's choosing to read a book, but they may not determine what he learns from the book. What he learns may be determined mainly by which material from the book enters his perceptual system.

Gibson and Gibson (1955) have formulated a definition of perceptual learning, which they define as *an increasing ability to obtain information from the environment.* This 1955 article provided an interesting demonstration of perceptual learning, in which some of the conditions favorable to such learning were identified. In this demonstation, the material used consisted of a set of visual nonsense items. Just as one can construct nonsense items out of letters of the alphabet, so, too, can one construct nonsense items out of other materials. The Gibsons used small pencil scribbles for their material. A subject was shown a small scribble printed on a card and was told that some of the items in a pack of cards had the same scribble printed on them. The standard scribble was then removed and the subject was shown the scribble on each card and had to decide whether it was the same or different from the standard one he had just inspected. After going through the pack, he was shown the standard scribble again for five seconds and then went through the pack of cards again. The procedure was continued until the individual could go through the pack, correctly identifying the standard whenever it occurred. At no time was the subject told whether he was right or wrong in his judgments, but learning took place and, after a few trials, the standard was readily identified in the pack.

Gibson and Gibson were also able to show that when the standard differed from the scribble to be judged in only one respect, differentiation was difficult to accomplish, but if the two differed in many respects, then differentiation was quite easy.

The learning that occurred cannot be understood in terms of a theory of reinforcement or feedback. The subject was able to extract slowly the information necessary for making the differentiation, and this is the core and essence of perceptual learning. In a later work (1969) Gibson explored further the nature of this process of learning to extract information from the inputs of sensory data provided by the environment.

The Gibson theory of perceptual learning is what is termed a perceptual differentiation theory. The essence of this theory is that the environment has potential for supplying a vast amount of information, and the task of the perceiver is to learn to respond to certain distinctive features of this mass of information. In the experiment in which individuals slowly came to recognize the difference between the standard scribble and other scribbles, learning involved a recognition of the distinctive features of the scribbles that made such differentiation possible. It is hardly surprising that the greater were the number of distinctive features that differentiated the standard from another scribble, the greater was the opportunity for discovering distinctive features that differentiated the two and the greater were the chances of making a successful discrimination. As the scribbles were examined on successive trials, the learner became progressively more aware of the features of the scribbles that made them different from the standard scribbles.

Gibson (1969) examines a number of other situations in which exposure results in differentiation. She points out, for example, that the basic sounds of speech, referred to as phonemes, have distinctive features that make it possible for the very young child to slowly differentiate one from another. Presumably, when the infant first hears speech, the component sounds are not at first discriminated, any more than a set of scribbles viewed by an adult are at first discriminated. Repeated exposure to the sounds of speech slowly permits the infant to make discriminations among the sounds. Ultimately, the phonemes can be sufficiently well discriminated that the child can recognize the distinctive situation in which specific combinations of them are used.

One can point to many common experiences that demonstrate the gradual recognition of distinctive features. For example, listen to a fairly complicated melody for the first time. The first time it is played, the distinctive features of the melody that give it a unique quality may not be recognized at all. The second time the melody is played, it may begin to be less a jumble of notes and more an organization of sounds. After a few repetitions, the melody is recognized as a sequence of notes completely distinctive and different from all other melodies.

Gibson offers a number of principles that account for perceptual learning. These principles have some application to the management of human learning, particularly in the case of young children, and have relevance to the task of teaching. The first three of these principles have to do with discrimination learning.

1. In the learning of perceptual discriminations, the learner discovers the differences that distinguish the sets of stimuli presented. This is a statement of the principle of differentiation already presented. A child learns to discriminate his printed name from other printed names by learning to respond to the distinguishing features. He may be able to do this long before he can learn to read the letters involved. If he goes by the name of "Lou," he may be able to learn to pick out his name from the other names merely because it is shorter than that of any of his classmates. If he is transferred to another kindergarten, in which there are other children who also have three-letter names, he may then have difficulty in picking out his name, but even though he may make mistakes, he will probably do better than he would by chance. Learning is related to the characteristics of the way his name is written. Learning related to the characteristics of an object, in contrast to learning that pertains to discriminating that object from other objects, is referred to as prototype perceptual learning. Perceptual experience results in learning dimensions of difference and also in prototype learning.

2. Discrimination learning is facilitated by emphasizing the distinctive features to be used in making the discrimination. Teachers have long used this principle. A teacher attempting to give students an understanding of what is meant by Romanesque architecture would not be content to show the students a few examples, but would almost certainly point out the distinctive features of the style. The teacher would bring to the attention of the students the round arch, the use of heavy piers, the profuse ornamentation, and so forth. By bringing these features to the attention of the students, the concept of Romanesque architecture would be developed more rapidly than if the students merely viewed many examples of it.

The students might learn to discriminate Romanesque architecture from other forms of architecture if instruction consisted only of exposure to many examples of Romanesque architecture in which the student himself could slowly identify the common features, but instruction would be much more efficient if it called the distinctive features to the attention of the student.

3. Discrimination learning is facilitated by providing first examples showing marked contrasts. Much of the research on which this principle is based comes from the study of species other than human beings. Pavlov noted long ago that in teaching an animal to respond differently to a standard note, say middle C, and other notes, training should begin with two notes that were very different from each other. After learning the coarse discrimination, training could proceed using notes that were more nearly the same. One presumes that the same principle should be applied in human learning, although evidence to support that contention could not be located. If a teacher is trying to explain what is meant by good composition in painting, he might do better to present the student with one piece showing good composition and one piece that is, beyond any question, poorly composed. The contrast should be so marked that the students can appreciate the difference and recognize that good composition has features that give a persisting unity whereas poor composition results in a disorganized appearance. The preliminary exercise in the sequence might begin with the student identifying the distinctive features that make a difference. Later, paintings can be studied in which there are finer differences and more subtle points. Discrimination learning, if well planned, should certainly begin with high-contrast situations.

Gibson also points out other techniques that may be used to facilitate discrimination learning. One of these is to exaggerate the distinctive features to be used in the discrimination. A number of experiments have been conducted that involve the use of cartoon techniques. The essential feature of a cartoon technique is that it exaggerates the distinctive features of a face or other object. The evidence suggests that the use of such techniques in teaching may have advantages. The studies in this area are somewhat remote from teaching, and one is left wondering whether children would learn to identify famous historical characters if they first viewed cartoons of them rather than lifelike portraits. The evidence suggests that the use of cartoons would facilitate the recognition of the faces, but it is quite remote evidence.

Gibson makes a distinction between learning the features of an object and learning to use the features to differentiate that object from other objects. If a discrimination task involves both learning the features and learning to use the features to discriminate it from other objects, the task is much more difficult than when the features are already known. For this reason, one may have great difficulty in discriminating between unfamiliar foreign languages. I have difficulty in discriminating between Italian, Spanish, and Portuguese, because I have no knowledge of these languages and cannot discriminate any of the words spoken. But I do know enough French and German to have no difficulty in discriminating between them, even though they are no more distinctive than Spanish and Portuguese. Once one has picked up a few of the common words in a foreign language, one has no difficulty from that point on in discriminating it from other languages.

The fact that one can point to instances of perceptual learning in which reinforcement plays no role is not a sufficient basis for denying the direct effect of reinforcement in other forms of learning. Two words may well become associated together merely because they enter the perceptual system at nearly the same time, but the events involved are very different from those involved in the acquisition of a motor skill or a problem-solving skill, in which the development of skill is highly dependent upon the consequences of performance. Indeed, even in the area of perceptual learning one can identify cases where reinforcements have an intimate relationship to learning.

The problem of the effect of reinforcement on perception is usually studied through the use of materials that can be perceptually structured in two different ways. An example of such material is shown in Figure 9-1. The two components B and C can be fitted together to form A. The two components can each be seen as a separate distinct face, but the one looks toward the left while the other looks toward the right. When A is viewed, it can be seen either as face B or face C, but it cannot be seen at the same instant as both faces. One can arrange an experiment so that whenever the one face appears, the subject who sees it is rewarded, but when the other appears there is no reward. After training by this procedure, the subject is then shown the two faces combined (A in the figure). If reward has an effect on the way in which perception is structured, then the person viewing the combined pair of faces would be expected to see the face that has been accompanied by reward rather than the nonrewarded face. Epstein (1967) has reviewed the research on this topic, noting that the results are not entirely consistent. Some studies have shown an effect of reward on the way in which the combined figure is structured, but others have not. Epstein makes out a strong case for the proposition that the differences in the results can be accounted for in terms of the value of the rewards given. Monetary rewards of a few cents in the early 1940s appear to have been effective with college students, but by the 1950s such rewards seemed to be ineffective, probably because a combination of inflation and a new affluence of students rendered such rewards trivial. If one accepts Epstein's interpretation, one would conclude that if there are alternative ways of structuring incoming information, the information is most likely to be structured in the way that has been followed by reward.

Epstein rightly points out that the results related to punshment are much less consistent, on the surface, than those related to reward. Many years earlier, however, Solley and Murphy (1960) were able to bring order into the studies that had been done up to that time and their conclusions still seem to be valid. The difficulty of interpreting the data stems from the fact that aversive events may sometimes sensitize the individual to the presence of particular stimuli and make the individual more receptive, but sometimes punishment makes him less sensitive, even to the point of ignoring the events. The crucial factor involved is whether the perception of a particular event does or does not provide a warning that the person can

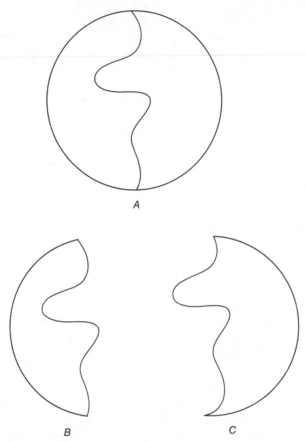

Figure 9-1. Either one of two profiles can be seen in A. The two profiles are seen separately in B and C.

use in order to turn off the source of punishment. If the experimental situation is such that the perception of a particular stimulus is a signal for punishment, a punishment that cannot be avoided, sensitivity to the particular stimulus is reduced. On the other hand, if the perception of a particular stimulus is understood to be a warning that permits the individual to take action to prevent the otherwise anticipated punishment, sensitivity for the particular stimulus is heightened. This kind of phenomenon is also seen in the two-faces experiment, in which the appearance of one face is followed by electric shock. When the combined faces are shown, the shock-related face is less likely to be seen than the other face, provided that there is no way of avoiding shock. If, on the other hand, the appearance of the one face was a warning permitting the individual to press a key to turn off the electric shock, the punished face is more likely to be seen.

PERCEPTUAL ASPECTS OF COMMON TASKS

The Perception of Pictures

A special case of visual perception that has substantial interest for educators is that of the perception of pictures. In recent times audiovisual specialists have developed the idea that there is a skill called visual literacy, which, it is believed, has to be learned. Few have asked whether there really is such a special skill that should be trained, but Kennedy (1974) has posed that question and come up with an interesting answer.

Kennedy begins his book by pointing out that patterns of light from the natural environment provide information to the perceiver. Thus when one approaches the entrance to a building one is guided by the contrast between the brightly lit frame of the door, which contrasts with the relative darkness of the interior of the building. Passage through the doorway is guided by the contrast. The boundaries of the doorway are marked by contrasts of light and shade and sometimes also by contrasts of color. Similar contrasts and patterns of light can be emitted from a flat surface. An artist is able to take a flat surface and, by placing pigments on it, arrange to produce a pattern of light closely similar to that produced by natural objects (see also Hagen, 1974). Of course, not all artists are concerned with capturing natural effects, but those that are skilled in doing so are able to produce light patterns that are informative in the same way that natural objects are informative. Audubon's painting of birds provide highly accurate information about particular birds to people who have never seen them. The pattern of light from an Audubon lithograph is a highly accurate replica of the pattern of light reflected by the bird it portrays.

Although an artist and a photographer can reproduce on a flat surface a close approximation to the patterns of light found in the natural world, Kennedy points out that there are quite obvious differences between the original and the reproduction. A flat surface reflects light in a way that makes it quite clear to the observer that the surface is flat. The individual who views a flat picture does not mistake it for a real scene, though sometimes small details may fool him. I can remember looking at a drop of water painted on a Van Gogh painting and wondering whether some three-dimensional transparency had been fixed to the painting to give it the appearance of reality. Only a very close inspection of the painting made it evident that the painted drop of water was flat. Cues of flatness tell the viewer that he is looking at a picture and not at the real world.

Kennedy reviews a number of different lines of research that have relevance to the problem of whether there is such a skill as visual literacy. For example, he asks whether animals can utilize the information from pictures. Kennedy cites the classic study of Herrnstein and Loveland (1964) showing that pigeons with minimal training can respond to the human form in pictures. The pigeons even recognized human forms when they were partly obscured by other objects. A less well-known study by Zimmerman and Hochberg (1963) showed that chimpanzees recognized three-dimensional objects in pictures even when the objects were drawn only in outline, without the use of shading. The evidence is overwhelming that higher animals see pictures in much the same way as human beings do. Viewers disregard the cues telling them that they are looking at a flat object and respond to the cues indicating that the object is three-dimensional. Kennedy argues that if animals can interpret pictures correctly, with almost no training, there is little strength to the argument that human beings have to learn visual literacy if they are to interpret pictures correctly. This latter position is substantiated by the work of Hochberg and Brooks (1962), who raised a child in an environment that contained no pictures, even eliminating opportunities for the child to see pictures on cans. Just before the child reached the age of 2 the child was shown a series of pictures, first line drawings and then photographs of common objects. The child was able to name objects without any difficulty. However, the development of the human capacity to interpret light patterns from flat surfaces is not quite that simple. Bower (1974) has shown that young infants presented with a picture react first to cues indicating flatness. Only later are they able to respond to the pictorial cues. Their difficulty seems to stem from the fact that in ordinary vision of the natural world the infant is highly dependent on binocular vision cues. He behaves as if he expected a three-dimensional world to produce different images in the two eyes. When no such difference is produced, his reaction is that the surface is flat. Perhaps not until the end of the first year of life is the infant able to override the cues of flatness and see a three-dimensional object portrayed on a flat surface.

Something must also be said about the puzzling experiences anthropologists have had in showing pictures to members of so-called primitive tribes. Early in the century some anthropologists reported that individuals in such tribes were unable to understand pictures, but later studies reported more success with the task. If animals can extract information from pictures, then surely uneducated people should be able to do the same, but what is the reason for their apparent inability to do so? Kennedy provides a convincing explanation. If a person had never seen a photograph, he would react to one by becoming interested in the photograph itself rather than in its content. He would probably examine it closely to try to find out how this reproduction had been made. If it were a black-and-white picture, such as the early anthropologists used, interest in the object might be heightened still further, for a primitive man would never have seen a colored world represented in black and white. His interest in the photograph would be much the same as mine when I first saw a three-dimensional photograph. The illusion of depth was so strong that I fingered the thickness of the photograph to convince myself that the object was not really three-dimensional. I remember even turning the card over, as if to look for the depth of the picture. Then I took a magnifying glass to examine the surface structure, to find out how the illusion of depth was created. If an anthropologist had then taken the card away and asked me what I had seen in the picture, I would not have been able to tell him. Deregowski (1968) found that children raised in a pictureless environment in Zambia had little difficulty in recognizing common objects in photographs. However, as Miller (1973) and others have pointed out, the use of depth cues given in flat pictures requires some minimal experience with pictures before the cues are used effectively. Children below age 8 have also been shown to have limited capacity to use depth and distance cues in pictures (Jahoda and McGork, 1974).

However, individual cultures do produce their stylized forms of pictorial representation, as Deregowski (1972) has pointed out, and these may not be understood outside of the culture in which they are produced. Few artists draw photographically precise pictures. In our culture, distant objects are commonly drawn disproportionately large. In addition, some conventions are introduced, as when a ball in full flight is drawn with lines behind it to form a wake, like the wake of a ship. Balls in flight do not have such a wake, but the convention helps the viewer to know the direction in which the ball is supposed to be going.

The conventions of stylized pictures are generally introduced because the conventions permit the communication of information that is not otherwise readily communicated. The Chinese artist draws his picture in layers to show scenes at different distances from the viewer, but the objects in the layers are not progressively smaller in size. Thus a picture can communicate distance without the loss of detail in relation to distance found in a photograph. The viewer has to know the convention to derive full information from such a picture, and individuals from other cultures may not understand the picture. In this sense only, is it necessary to train individuals in visual literacy.

There are a great number of quite practical issues related to the design of illustrations for textbooks that Travers and Alvarado (1970) have reviewed. For example, research indicates that young children beginning elementary school prefer highly realistic pictures and bright colors rather than soft shades; and yet school books commonly use soft shades and stylized art because it is cheap to produce and reproduce. Also, adults pick the textbooks for children and choose them in terms of adult preferences.

The Initial Perception of Speech

There is no question that speech comprehension precedes speech production in children. Young children do not learn to use words appropriately by trial and error in their use. They know how to use words before they actually use them. Thus the earliest stages in speech acquisition involve perceptual processes.

The first step in speech comprehension has to involve the identification of basic spoken structures in speech. This may not seem like a difficult task for as adults we hear speech as a set of distinct words. This is just an illusion, for when speech is recorded and the electrical record is then examined, one finds that there are no pauses between words in ordinary talk. Words come out in bursts with pauses between bursts. In short statements such as "How do you feel today?" the sound is continuous. The electrical record indicates that there is no simple way of telling where one word ends and another begins. Yet the child during his first two years of life is continuously exposed to such statements and is slowly able to extract word perceptions that are ultimately transformed into his own speech. The child has to learn the illusion that spoken language consists of separated words.

O'Neil (1973) has presented an interesting discussion of this problem and has gathered together evidence indicating that children in the preschool years are much more objective than the adult in the perception of language. Children have been studied who have invented their own writing system before going to school using the ordinary letters of the alphabet they have picked up at home. Such children do not make the distinctions between such words as *write* and *right*, but are likely to spell both as *rit*. The written representation of words invented by children are quite intelligible to adults, and perhaps far more intelligible than are ordinary written words to children. Since perception of speech by the experienced adult is far from understood, the perception of speech by the infant remains a mystery. The problem of speech perception is complicated by the fact that what we hear does not correspond very closely to the physical stimulus presented. Corcoran (1971) illustrates this by considering the perception of the sounds represented by the syllables *di* and *du*. Each consists of a vowel sound preceded by a consonant. Now we can record these sounds on tape and split off the vowel sound from the consonant sound by cutting the tape and splicing in a piece of blank tape between the two. One should now be able to play back the tape and hear first the consonant sound and then the vowel sound, but that is not what one hears at all. What one does hear is the vowel sound and the consonant sound comes out as a kind of whistle. When the two constituent sounds are separated, the syllables can no longer be identified. The sound analysis system of the brain seems to handle chunks of sound, which linguists call morphemes and which correspond roughly to syllables. The infant is presented with a flow of sounds that are not separated physically into words. Speakers run words together and place pauses between groups of words in order to take in a breath. The infant is not presented with separate word units, let alone separate sound units. Yet he does learn to discriminate words from among the flow of sounds and succeeds later in producing those words himself. Some linguists, notably Chomsky (1965), take the position that the infant functions as though he had the hypothesis that speech consists of units that have to be disentangled from a mass of sounds.

Young children not only learn to perceive in speech the structure necessary to provide meaning, but they also learn to extract information related to the speaker's identity and mood. Bartholomeus (1973) has reviewed these studies. In his own research he has also shown that nursery school children can recognize the identity of familiar individuals when a record of their voice is played backward. Bartholomeus used the technique of asking the children to match the records of the voices with pictures of the individuals involved. The child has immense capacity for analyzing voices, and much of the analysis involves incidental learning.

Perceptual Aspects of Reading

Reading is a very complex skill but it involves important perceptual components in the initial stages. Of course, reading is vastly more than being able to say the words represented by the text, for deriving meaning from the words requires that the individual understand the structure of the sentence they constitute and be able to assign functions to words within that structure. Nevertheless, the perceptual component of reading is a basic component.

Children may be taught to read by concentrating on the total characteristics of words or they may be introduced to the task by concentrating first on letter characteristics. The perceptual task is different in the two cases, but both produce some reading skill. However, until letter characteristics are recognized, each new word represents a new form. Children learning to read by the whole word method often identify words by letter characteristics, but sometimes they use general word contours. For example, a child may learn to recognize the word *children* because it is the longest word in the story. If an equally long but different word were introduced into the next story, the child would also read it as "children." Word-whole methods have the advantage of permitting the child to read a story after a relatively short learning time, but it does not provide a basis that the child may use for figuring out how to say new words he encounters. Once the child has built a sight-recognition vocabulary of about three hundred words, he has reached the limit of what he can do effectively within his system. He must then go back and master letter forms and letter discriminations that form the basis of word analysis into pronounceable components. Of course, the Chinese system of writing requires children to learn to recognize the symbol for each word, and the children taught the system learn to acquire a recognition vocabulary of thousands of words. Presumably, the establishment of such a large sight-recognition vocabulary requires an immense amount of time and effort. A written system based on a limited number of symbols should be more readily mastered as far as the perceptual component of reading skill is required. There is ample evidence that the learning of letter characteristics is crucial for learning to read efficiently (see Mason, 1975).

One basic perceptual problem encountered by the child in learning to read is that there are no simple ways of telling how the word should be divided up in terms of the sounds of which it is composed. The child's problem, as Savin (1973) points out, is to identify letter sequences that correspond to sounds. Even when such letter sequences have been identified, the child still has the problem of how to pronounce them, and the pronunciation may be specific to the word in which they are located. The phenomes *doe*, *dow*, and *dough* may all be pronounced the same or differently depending on the word in which they are located. Letters that form a syllable are either pronounced or silent according to the context. The perceptual task involved in translating printed orthography into sounds is enormously difficult, probably far more difficult than the task of identifying speech components in vocal speech. The beginning reader faced with a string of letters and struggling to structure them into components takes the easy way out. He starts at the beginning of the word and attempts to structure this first group of letters. In that task he is more likely to be successful than when he attempts to find a group of letters in the middle of the word. At least the initial letters have a clear beginning even though the reader has to decide where the group of letters ends.

At this point in the discussion one is tempted to suggest that English spelling be simplified in order to make the task of reading, writing, and spelling easier for all. Several attempts have been made and the Chicago *Tribune* for many years used a simplified system of spelling. The system did not catch on. Indeed, as a result of public pressure the Chicago *Tribune* was ultimately forced to abandon its effort. Most of the arguments used against the use of a simplified spelling system were far from rational and were based on the idea that traditional spelling has some special sanctity that should be preserved. But there are reasonable arguments in favor of retaining our present system of spelling. The English language does have the advantage that the oddities of the orthography serve a purpose: differences in spelling in words that are pronounced identically cue the reader as to their meaning. In this respect written English is a very efficient system for communicating (see, Kilma, 1973).

Consider, for example, the following two groups of words:

know	no
knowledge	nohow
knowhow	nothing
known	nowhere

They both derive from two root terms *know* and *no*. Phonetically, the left-hand column could be rewritten as:

no
nolledge
nohow
noan

By doing this, confusion has been immediately introduced. In the phonetic version one can make no distinction between *know* and *no*, and the distinction is also lost between *knowhow* and *nohow*. When the original spelling form is retained and one encounters a word beginning with the syllable *know* one is aware immediately that the word has something to do with knowing and knowledge. The syllable *no* at the beginning of a word does not give such an easy clue, though the syllable *non* with the same derivation does. Thus the differences in the spelling of the same-sounding syllable may provide important cues concerning the nature of the word of which it is a part, and this cue facilitates reading for sophisticated readers. For the beginning reader, who does not have much mastery of language, the cues merely add to the confusion. The suggestion has been made that childen may not be mature enough to use such cues until perhaps age 9 or 10 (see Llima, 1973). In other languages in which perhaps as many as twenty different words may be denoted by a single written word, the difficulties of deciphering the written language may be considerable. One does, of course, understand speech despite the fact that a single group of sounds may have several possible meanings, but the context generally provides sufficient cues to the meaning intended. Written English is an efficient medium for communication, and much might be lost by simplifying the spelling system. A part of the problem is that those who benefit most from the complicated system of English spelling are the sophisticated readers and scholars. Those who are most harmed by it are the many who have to learn to master the system and yet who derive little from it in adult life because they grow up to be neither scholars nor prolific readers. A radical revision of the spelling system might save each school child in America as much as five-hundred hours of tedious and boring study. The problems and issues related to the matter are not simple.

It is all too easy in a work such as this to overemphasize the cognitive difficulties of learning to read. Attempts to measure the effectiveness of the school curriculum are often overshadowed by the effects produced by what is sometimes termed the home curriculum. Bloom (1974) reports that in his international studies of education, the finding consistently turns up that in learning to read home background factors are more important than school factors. The three most important factors related to the acquisition of reading comprehension are (1) the reading resources in the home, (2) the socioeconomic status of the home, and (3) and the encouragment that the parents give the child to read. Other aspects of verbal ability are also related to the home curriculum.

Finally, the point must be made that the reader has to learn to adapt the perceptual processes of reading to the kind of information he wishes to extract from the text. Samuels and Dahl (1975) have shown that individuals adapt their reading rate to the nature of the information to be extracted. Skimming may be undertaken very rapidly for the purpose of obtaining superficial information, and skimming may involve no more than identifying a few key words on each page.

Self-confrontation and Self-perception Techniques and Learning in Teacher Training

The term *self-perception* has been used in the area of teaching and learning in a way that confuses the meaning of the term *perception*. In education self-perception commonly refers to the *beliefs* that a person holds about himself. Thus a person may believe that he is stupid, unsuccessful, and unattractive, and even though he may have none of these attributes, they are said to constitute his self-perception. These attributes have little to do with perception but are a set of *beliefs*, and beliefs are not perceptions. To confuse the two represents a confusion of thought. However, one can talk about self-perception when an individual hears a record of his voice or sees and hears a videotape recording of his performance. He is then engaged in a direct perceptual process that can be studied in the same way as other perceptual processes.

Over the last two decades, substantial research has been undertaken on how individuals react to their body image and how such a confrontation with themselves can be used to change behavior. Those mainly interested in such problems have been clinical psychologists, who have hoped that some behavior problems could be corrected if the individual could be brought to see himself as others see him. This research has been summarized by Fuller and Manning (1973).

Although self-confrontation techniques were at first received with enthusiasm and were widely used, they were soon found to present far more problems than they solved. Although therapists found that some patients improved through the use of the techniques, others were shown to deteriorate. The fact soon became apparent that individuals reacted to a videotape recording of themselves in an entirely different way from which they reacted to viewing the performance of another person. Indeed, the emotional reaction of an individual to his own image is typically so strong that he has difficulty in learning from what he sees and hears. A person viewing, on a television screen, a record of his teaching performance becomes preoccupied with his body image and how he appears. He is typically disturbed by the discrepancy between what he sees and what he thought he would see and this discrepancy may not be to his liking. The result of this preoccupation with the body image is that the viewer is likely to learn little about his performance as a teacher by watching himself on a television screen unless the technique is very carefully used. The only aspects of his performance that he is likely to change are those related to mannerisms that he does not like.

Fuller and Manning suggest that certain students of education and teachers can profit from the technique. Those who can are most likely to be comfortable with themselves and with their appearance. They are likely to be young rather than middle-aged or old. Such individuals are sufficiently comfortable with their appearance that they do not have to spend very much time thinking about how they appear on the television screen. Nevertheless, both with such individuals and with others, there is merit in presenting them with their telecast several times. This provides an opportunity for them to become used to the appearance of their body image and then they can become concerned with their teaching performance.

A particularly important conclusion of Fuller and Manning's review is that the use of videotape for training requires a trainer or supervisor who is fully cognizant of the problems related to the use of this technique. One of the functions of the trainer is to help the student focus on significant dimensions of his performance and avoid the trivia that are otherwise likely to preoccupy him.

SUMMARY

1. The chapter on perception treats the individual as a system that handles information. The human being lives in an information-filled environment, from which the useful information must be extracted and sometimes stored in memory.

2. Information is derived from the environment through the perceptual systems, of which there are five: the visual, the auditory, the haptic, the taste-smell, and the basic orienting. Each system includes a set of specialized receptors and a related muscular system that permits the individual to orient the perceptual system in relation to the environment.

3. Pain does not fit into the perceptual systems described here. Pain may result from an injury, either external or internal, but it may be fully experienced at high intensity without any sensory input that can be determined. Pain may be elicited through the perception of objects that have elicited pain in the past. Strong stimulation may sometimes reduce pain. Chronic pain is also associated with a condition of depression. Treatment that relieves the depression may also relieve the pain. Learning to relax may also reduce pain. A particularly interesting approach to the relief of pain is acupuncture. The phenomenon is not a result of suggestion or hypnosis, but seems to be a genuine physiological phenomenon.

4. The amount of information available to the perceptual systems is always very large, much larger, in fact, than the amount that the higher levels of the nervous

system can use. The perceptual systems are selective in the information they use and interpret.

5. A primitive type of information analysis takes place at the sense-organ level where the incoming information is first coded. Some subhuman creatures have quite complex information-analysis systems in the sense organs and peripheral nerves. Presumably, information analysis takes place at all levels of the nervous system, and each level has particular functions to perform in this respect. Information analysis at the lower levels is complicated by the fact that sensory activity can be depressed or enhanced by activity in the higher centers. Processes such as lateral inhibition also play a part.

6. The perceptual systems do not give a true-to-life picture of the world. Boundaries of objects tend to be accentuated.

7. Visual and auditory information is processed differently. The visual system has the capacity for processing large amounts of information simultaneously. Auditory information arrives in a stream, and considerable amounts have to arrive and be held in short-term memory before the information can be processed. Auditory information can be processed more rapidly than the rate presented by ordinary speech.

8. The information provided by the environment generally has some structure. The perception of an element involves the classification of the element as a member of a set. The more precise the identification, the smaller is the set to which the element is assigned. Nonspecific identification is efficient.

9. The perceptual field is structured into a figure and ground, and what becomes figure is continually changing. Structuring an element as a figure is referred to as the development of a percept. Elements can be structured in very brief exposures because the presentation of material to the perceptual systems leaves behind a trace that persists for a few seconds and can be analyzed during that time.

10. The infant probably has some capacity for structuring the information without learning, but this structuring is very primitive. The structuring process can be studied through presenting material for successive very brief exposures, which has the effect of slowing down the perceptual process. The structuring process may not result in a structure that provides correct information. Children's perceptions are particularly likely to be nonveridical. Perception is commonly followed by some kind of check on the veridicality of the perception. Expectation is an important element in determining what is perceived. Unfamiliar situations are difficult to structure perceptually. The perceptual process has the property of supplying missing details, so perception is often more complete than the data warrant. The brain has also some capacity for clarifying the data provided by the senses.

11. Psychologists have long assumed that the perceptual constancies have to be learned, but there is increasing evidence that some aspects may be innate. The visual cliff experiment indicates that the perception of depth and distance may be to some degree innate, and this is a factor in size constancy.

12. Perceptual functions are closely related to those of memory. A percept is meaningful because of previous experiences stored in memory.

13. Three kinds of theories have been proposed to account for the way in which

percepts are identified and given meaning. One of these is template matching; recognition, according to this theory, is similar to matching a particular percept with a composite photograph of related and similar previous experiences. A second theory states that recognition takes place in terms of the distinctive features or attributes. Considerable evidence supports this theory. One form of the feature analysis theory is referred to as a structural description theory. The information needed to identify a visual display may be extracted serially or through a total overall massive reception of the object as a whole. The former takes place with unfamiliar scenes, and the latter with that which is well-known to the percipient. The third theory of recognition is that known as analysis-by-synthesis, which represents more than one theory. There is some evidence that some perception may take place through an analysis-by-synthesis process.

14. Orientation is an important factor in recognition. Objects turned upside down are more difficult to recognize. In visual perception, the spatial orientation of the object may be the feature that is first identified.

15. Considerable evidence has been accumulated showing that perception involves the sampling of the information in the environment. Successive exposure to the same environment may result in different samples of information being drawn. This phenomenon can be observed when a picture is shown briefly to the same person again and again. On each exposure, he is likely to obtain new information and thus slowly build up an overall comprehension of what the picture presents.

16. The complex response known as attending has long intrigued psychologists. An important component of the attending response is the orienting response, which has been studied largely by Russian psychologists. The orienting response is a preparatory response that prepares the respondent for receiving new information. Two important environmental factors related to the attending response are those of novelty and complexity. Novel stimuli have priority over other stimuli in commanding attention. In addition, there is a certain amount of preference for inputs of information that have some degree of complexity, though there is a preferred optimum level of complexity. Studies of eye movements show that the eye also tends to be directed most toward those aspects of a visual display having the greatest complexity and containing the greatest amount of information.

17. Two signal detection tasks have been extensively studied, namely, those of scanning and vigilance. Scanning tasks are of particular interest to those involved in education, in view of the importance of scanning reference works for particular items of information. A finding of significance is that material can be scanned for more than one item of information as rapidly as for a single item. Studies of vigilance behavior show clearly how the maintenance of attention requires a continuing input of information. Tasks that provide a low input of information cannot be attended to for very long.

18. Some psychologists have suggested that more useful information may be learned by incidental learning than by intentional learning, but this would be a difficult hypothesis to test. Experimentation in the area has been difficult to pursue because of the problems involved in defining what is meant by intentional and

incidental. A significant finding in this area is that a high level of motivation to perform the central task is accompanied by a low level of incidental learning. However, no rigid line can be drawn between intentional and incidental learning.

19. Perceptual learning without the intervention of reinforcements seems to be a genuine phenomenon. Infants learn through mere exposure to objects and events in the environment. Neonates have a great capacity for processing information. Children and adults learn to improve in the visual discriminations they make, even when there is an absence of knowledge of results. For this reason, it is reasonable to assume that exposure to a rich environment early in life may give the individual intellectual advantages, since knowledge may be acquired through mere exposure. Perceptual learning is the ability to extract information from the environment. Discrimination learning may be enhanced through emphasizing the features involved in the discrimination. Examples that show marked contrasts are particularly useful for such a purpose. However, reinforcement may influence perception. Perceptions that have been rewarded are more likely to be experienced than those that have not. On the other hand, the effects of punishment on perception are more complex. If the perception of a particular stimulus enables the perceiver to escape punishment, the previous punishment has an enhancing effect on the perception. On the other hand, if the perception signals unavoidable punishment, the perception is less likely to be experienced.

20. From the point of view of education, the value of pictures lies in their ability to reproduce a pattern of light similar to that produced by a natural object. Cues to flatness tell the viewer of a picture that he is looking at a picture and not at a three-dimensional set of objects. There does not seem to be any special skill involved in the interpretation of pictures, for even many animals have this skill. Visual literacy does not seem to require special training. A child raised in an environment in which there were no pictures was able at age 2 to recognize objects shown in pictures, even when these were presented in the form of line drawings. Very young infants are not able to do this because they react first to the cues indicating flatness. Anthropologists have had difficulty in understanding the responses of primitive people to pictures, but this seems to be a result of the fact that primitive people are so curious about these extraordinary representations of objects, which they have never seen before. Most cultures have produced their stylized form of art, involving conventions peculiar to the particular culture. Young children prefer highly realistic pictures and prefer bright colors to soft shades. Pictures for children's books should be selected on the basis of children's choices, and not those of adults.

21. A special problem of perception is that of the initial perception of speech. The child first has to learn that speech consists of separately spoken words. The speech that is heard does not correspond well with the sounds that are actually produced. The infant may well have an innate capacity for making an analysis of speech sounds.

22. The perception of printed speech represents a special problem in perception. The perception of letter characteristics seems important for the acquisition of full reading skill. Word recognition, in terms of general word characteristics, has its

limitations. A central difficulty in learning to read is to identify letter sequences that correspond to sounds. The problem is complicated further by the fact that the same letter sequences correspond to different sounds in different contexts. English spelling is also a very complicated system of transmitting information that is quite beyond the comprehension of the beginning reader. A simplified spelling might help the young reader, but it would eliminate an important source of information about the meaning of words. Reading is also a group of skills and not a simple skill. The skill applied in a particular reading task should depend on the objectives of the reader.

23. An interesting aspect of perception is self-perception. The use of television recordings has made it possible to study it through easily manipulated equipment. Television recordings of one's own behavior are not materials from which one can learn easily about oneself. Individuals often respond emotionally to their own body image, and only a few can profit from such exposure.

Chapter 10
Motivation and Learning

TRADITIONAL APPROACHES TO THE PROBLEM OF MOTIVATION

Trainers of animals have long recognized that an essential condition for training is that the animal must be active or, as it is commonly said energized. Sleepy, lethargic animals are virtually untrainable until their behavior is in some way activated. The trainer will see a part of his task as that of arranging conditions so that he is working with a vigorous and energetic animal and not with a sluggish creature. This is a part of the problem of motivating the animal he wishes to train. Another aspect of motivating behavior is that of arranging conditions so that the animal's behavior becomes directed toward the performance the trainer wishes to produce. If a trainer wishes to teach a lion to climb on a stool at a given command, he must arrange conditions so that the lion moves in the direction of climbing on the stool rather than in any other direction. Thus there are two components of the problem of motivation. One involves the energizing of behavior; the other involves the direction of behavior. Let us consider first the problem of energizing behavior as it has been traditionally treated in psychological literature.

The traditional approach to the study of motivation in animals has been to assume that behavior is energized through strong stimuli that may be internal or external. The jockey applies a whip to the rear of his mount in order to provide a strong stimulus, which will, in turn, energize the horse. Such a strong stumulus that produces action is called a drive stimulus. Sometimes drive stimuli are internal and are produced by states of deprivation. Deprive an animal of food for twenty-four hours, and the body chemistry will be upset sufficiently to produce strong internal stimuli that have much the same effect on energizing behavior as does the external stimulus provided by the whip of the jockey. Hunger pangs represent a part of these strong stimuli. Any deprivation of the necessities of life, such as food, water, oxygen, or a suitable temperature, produces a bodily imbalance, which in turn activates behavior. Behavior remains active until the animal finds food or water or oxygen and the balance of chemicals in the body is restored. This is commonly referred to as a homeostatic theory of behavior. Such a theory assumes that the basic source of activity is some kind of imbalance in the chemistry of the body.

A drive state produces activity that continues until some action of the organism reduces the drive state. An example of such an action might be a thirsty and active animal drinking water. A psychologist wishing to study learning in the rat will want to experiment with an active rat, so he will probably starve the animal to be studied for twenty-four hours. Such a hungry animal is then placed in the starting box of the maze, if maze learning is the area of research. The activity of the animal takes it through the various corridors of the maze until it reaches the goal box, where it finds a small quantity of food. The amount of food provided is generally so small that it does not influence the drive level of the rat. The rat is then placed back in the starting box, and the performance is repeated.

The object in the goal box that has potential for reducing the drive is commonly referred to as the incentive, but it is also referred to as the reinforcement. The evidence is clear that the food in the goal box, like all objects related to drives, has important effects on behavior. Although it is quite obvious that there would be little learning if there were no food in the goal box, the presence of the food also has another effect, namely, on the drive itself. This is shown by the fact that relatively large amounts of food in the goal box result, for a few trials at least, in a much more vigorous performance than small amounts of food. Of course, over many trials, large amounts of food also produce a food-satiated rat likely to go to sleep in the maze. Over the short haul, however, incentive adds to the drive state produced by deprivation from food.

Although one is likely to think of deprivation from food and the resulting drive state as an example of an inborn and relatively simple drive state, quite uncontaminated by learning, such an interpretation is probably a gross oversimplification. One can show, for example, that quite young animals may have learned cravings for particular kinds of foods if they have been fed large quantities of these foods. Indeed, the craving may be such that it results in an unbalanced diet and an early death. Human behavior in relation to food in civilized countries is more like a craving than behavior that restores a chemical balance in the body, for the civilized human being eats at specified times regardless of whether he is or is not hungry. Eating behavior, and its relation to a hunger drive, is certainly a complex matter.

DIRECTIONAL PROPERTIES OF DRIVES

Although most people assume that an animal can discriminate whether it is hungry or whether it is thirsty, experimental findings do not support this common-sense belief. In one of the earlier studies of the capability of an animal to discriminate hunger from thirst, Hull (1943) had considerable difficulty in teaching animals to make such a discrimination. The animals did eventually learn, but only after a prolonged series of learning trials that must have involved both a frustrated experimenter and frustrated animal. This is hardly surprising when even the simpler sources of drive are not readily identified.

The mechanism involved in the raised level of activity that accompanies food deprivation is complex. Although the older theories took the position that the contractions of the stomach that accompany hunger were the main sources of the activity, possibly through the contractions producing pain-like sensations, Cofer and Appley (1964) cite evidence that there are at least two centers in the brain that respond to deprivation of food and satiation following feeding. The mechanism is undoubtedly complex.

The fact that animals cannot discriminate the sources of drive states, except after prolonged training, does not mean that man cannot ordinarily make the discrimination. Man has plenty of opportunity to learn to distinguish between, say, hunger and thirst and may well learn such a discrimination. However, all of us have had the experience of becoming restless during the night and of tossing and turning in a drowsy state for hours wondering what the cause may be. In such a state we may ask ourselves whether we are hungry, or perhaps not quite warm enough, or thirsty, and not be able to pinpoint what the cause of the increased level of activity may be. Indeed, we may have to experiment with pulling up another blanket, drinking some water, or eating some food, before the situation is brought under control. Under such conditions we are not able to determine the source of the drive state, perhaps because drowsiness prevents us from making fine discriminations.

Little purpose would be served by reviewing here in detail the extensive research that has been undertaken on motivation in subhuman subjects involving the deprivation of the animal from food and water. It is sufficient to have mentioned some of the important ideas that have emerged from this research. At this point, we must turn to some of the experimentation that has been undertaken on human motivation. Experimental approaches to the study of human motivation are new in that they have emerged largely since the end of World War II, but they are beginning to produce ideas of considerable importance.

HUMAN MOTIVATION

Although imbalances due to deprivation of food, water, sex, suitable temperatures in the environment, and so forth, play some small role in human behavior in a civilized society, it is also quite obvious that man's behavior is energized in other and much more important ways. Psychologists have long discussed the issue of whether man is *endowed* with sources of motivation that animals do not possess, or whether he starts life with the same basic drives as all other higher creatures and slowly builds on these a set of acquired drives or motives.

The basic concept involved in the acquisition of new drives is that a stimulus present when a drive is aroused comes to acquire drive-arousing properties of its own. If a maze is a place where a rat is placed when it is hungry and active, the maze comes to acquire, on its own, the property of producing activity in the rat even though the rat may not be hungry or thirsty. By a similar mechanism, objects that do not originally have incentive value can acquire incentive value if paired with incentives or, stated in another way, objects that do not have reinforcing value initially can acquire reinforcing value by being paired with objects that are reinforcers. Thus although a buzzer has no incentive value or reinforcing value for a rat, it can be made to acquire these properties by pairing the buzzer with the delivery of food. The theory has some experimental evidence to support it, but must nevertheless be regarded as simplistic. The fact is that even though much is known about how complex motivations are related to human behavior, psychologists cannot provide a satisfactory account of how these motives are derived.

Those who have taken the latter position consider all drives as either primary or secondary, in terms of whether they are part of the individual's native equipment or are learned. The difficulty with this position is that no agreement can be reached on what drives should be included in the list of secondary or acquired drives. For example, all higher organisms show what is termed exploratory behavior, that is, when placed in a strange environment after a period of confinement, they move around and undertake a kind of inspection of their new surroundings. They do this even though they are well fed and have had all their bodily needs taken care of. Monkeys will grasp and inspect unusual objects placed in their cages and under conditions where they are not looking for food, water, sex objects, and so forth. The question that has been asked is whether the drive underlying this behavior can can be considered to be a primary or a learned, or secondary, drive. Those who argue that the drive is learned suggest that hungry animals become active and the activity brings them into contact with new parts of their environment. In this way, the presence of novel surroundings becomes associated with a drive state and, in time, comes to trigger that drive state. Those who take the position that the drive underlying exploratory behavior is unlearned take the view that the exploration of new surroundings is so significant an activity for animals that the drive must surely be inborn. An animal that did not have a high drive to cautiously explore new surroundings would probably starve to death, and also the hazards of the new environment would never be discovered. Exploratory behavior has survival value and is as basic to the perpetuation of a species as is eating or drinking or sex behavior. The issue of whether an exploratory drive is innate cannot be settled at this time and the same is true for many other drive states, hence there is no way of drawing up an agreed-upon list of primary drives.

RELATIONSHIP OF MOTIVATION AND LEARNING

The study of simple drives in lower animals has been suggestive of what may be the relationship between motivation and learning in higher organisms, including man. There is, for example, some evidence that as drive level increases, learning also increases, until the drive reaches an optimum level. If the drive is increased further, then performance deteriorates. The evidence generally points in this direction although there is some conflicting evidence. An elaboration of this relationship between motivation and performance is found in what is known as the Yerkes–Dodson law, which states that as tasks are increased in difficulty, the optimum level of motivation declines. This means that on complex tasks the optimum level of motivation is lower than on simple tasks. As all of us well know, if we are faced with a complex task, we had better take our time. If we are highly motivated to complete it in short order, we may well make many errors. The level of motivation has to be an optimum for the task. Common experience suggests that individuals can be too highly motivated and spoil their performance because they wanted too much to succeed. The overmotivated person can be as ineffective as the undermotivated. Indeed, there does seem to be an optimum level of motivation. Also, when the problem faced is difficult, one needs to be calm and to take one's time, and this is the picture of the moderately motivated person. On the other hand, when the task is very simple, as in running a quarter of a mile, the optimum level of motivation is very high. Indeed, there is a question whether a person undertaking such an intellectually simple task *could* be overmotivated.

In addition, as the drive level is increased, there is a tendency for behavior to become more vigorous physically. This may be a great advantage in a sporting event, but of very dubious utility if the task is an intellectual one. Physical vigor may make the writer strike the keys of the typewriter harder, but it probably does little for the quality of the manuscript.

The central problem related to human motivation is the identification of the particular conditions that energize human behavior. An understanding of what these conditions are would permit the control of human motivation. A substantial beginning has been made in this respect in recent years.

GOAL OBJECTS, INCENTIVES, AND MOTIVES

Objects and events that were earlier described as reinforcers have been described by other psychologists as representing motivating conditions or incentives. The chapter on operant conditioning discussed this issue briefly, and it is appropriate to raise it once more and to point out the role of such objects and events in motivating the individual. Suppose that a 10-year-old is given a piece of paper with a problem printed on it and is asked to solve the problem. Let us also suppose that the child is not particularly intrigued by the problem for, after reading it, he says he doesn't even want to try to solve it. At this point he is told that he will be given a dollar for solving it. Immediately his behavior is energized and he begins to attack the problem with energy. Eventually he solves it. Next day he is presented with a second problem, but without being told whether or not he is going to receive a dollar, and he immediately sets about attempting to solve it. Those psychologists who talk the language of operant conditioning would say that the dollar provided a reinforcement for problem-solving behavior, for persistence in finding a solution, and for using the skills involved, and hence, although the child was reluctant to attempt to solve the first problem, the dollar reinforcement strengthened these behaviors so that they were more likely to appear on the second occasion. An alternative account of what happened is that on the first occasion the behavior of the child is energized or triggered into a drive state by the demand for the goal object and it is this same demand for the goal object that energizes behavior when the second problem is presented on the next day. The explanation is plausible, indeed, so plausible that various forms of it have been given extensive support by such notable psychologists as K. W. Spence, O. H. Mowrer, E. C. Tolman, and C. L. Hull. In addition, the area of research known as *achievement motivation*, discussed in a later section, has been powerfully influenced by the significance given to the role of what has been termed here a *demand for a goal object*, an expression originally coined by Tolman.

This account of motivation is so attractive, simple, and in keeping with personal experience that one may wonder why it has not achieved wide acceptance by psychologists. The reasons have to do with the reluctance of psychologists to build theories around terms that cannot be precisely defined. The theory of motivation being considered here involves such terms as the *anticipation* of a goal or the *expectancy* of a goal being reached, or the *demand* for a goal. These terms are rather vague and cannot be easily defined in terms of behavior that can be readily identified and observed. Some psychologists who have attempted to develop this kind of theory of motivation have suggested ways in which words such as expectancy can be tied to quite observable forms of behavior. Hull (1943) tried to do this by suggesting that the responses associated with the achievement of a goal become classically conditioned to stimuli in the situation that leads to the goal. Thus parts of a rat's eating response become classically conditioned to the stimuli provided by the maze; after a few maze running trials, when the rat is placed in the maze it immediately shows components of the eating response such as salivation and licking the lips. These, in themselves, raise the general activity level of which they are a part. In the same way, a child put in a situation that he knows can lead to his getting money shows the same kind of excitement as when he is actually confronted with money he can obtain. This kind of theorizing, involving components of the goal responses known as *fractional anticipatory goal responses*, has some plausibility to it. The chief difficulty with the theory is that it has not led to very promising lines of research and evidence that might verify it has been scarce or altogether lacking.

Despite the technical difficulties involved in defining the terms of a theory of motivation that focuses on expectancy, or anticipatory responses, or on demand for a goal, many psychologists continue to do research related to this concept.

An interesting line of research, involving numerous studies, explores issues related to the comparative effectiveness as incentives of delayed and immediate rewards. All complex cultures use systems of delayed rewards. The entire promotion system within our own society is a delayed reward system, which raises the issue of whether such delayed rewards are effective and for whom are they effective. Early research in the field established the fact (Mischel and Staub, 1965) that in order for delayed rewards to be as effective as immediate rewards, they have to be larger. Mischel (1974a, 1974b) has summarized much of the research related to the matter of the kinds of individuals who respond well to delayed rewards. He finds that the bulk of the research shows that these individuals are more likely to be future-oriented and achieve high scores on measures of ego control, achievement motivation, and intelligence. They also tend to be more mature, have a higher level of aspiration, and to be more socially responsible than those who respond best to immediate rewards. Typically they are middle class and fit the pattern of the Puritan ethic. In contrast, those who respond best to immediate rewards tend to be from the disadvantaged classes (Walls and Smith, 1970), tend to be more impulsive, have low achievement orientation and lower scores on measures of social competence. In addition, those who are classified as delinquent or psychopath are more likely to be oriented toward immediate rewards. Children who fit the immediate-reward pattern are also likely to be those who respond better to a material reward than to a situation in which the reward is some other form of reinforcement such as social approval (Benowitz and Busse, 1970). Mischel (1974) finds evidence that the ability to respond to delayed rewards depends on the individual's pattern of self-control and his belief that he can control what happens to him.

Whether a person can or cannot respond to delayed gratification depends, in some measure, on how he handles the delay. Mischel and Moore (1973) have shown that delay can be increased if the individual either calls up images of the delayed reward or sees symbolic representations of it. However, if the real object is actually present, or is imagined to be present, there is difficulty in delaying gratification. The phenomenon is a delicately balanced one, for it makes a difference whether the child views the symbolic representation as an abstract representation or a sign of what is actually present. In such experiments slight changes in the instructions to the children can reverse the results. Given the right orientation nearly all children can manage to handle delay in gratification. In order to learn to handle the frustration in delayed gratification, the child must do something other than just wait. He must not concentrate on the concrete reward itself but symbolic representations of it. He must also learn to evaluate himself positively for delaying gratification and develop a strong sense that it is he who has chosen the delay.

This type of incentive situation may be complicated, as when children accumulate tokens to obtain a reward either at the end of the particular class period, or class day, or after a longer period of time. Walls (1973) experimented with this variation and found that there was a shift from the preschool children, who wanted the immediate reward, to the sixth-graders, who preferred a deferred selection. Walls also divided the children into disadvantaged and nondisadvantaged. Although a greater proportion of the younger disadvantaged children preferred immediate reward, they did not differ with statistical significance from the nondisadvantaged children.

An important issue is whether the offering of material incentives actually improves memory. Zimmerman and Kimble (1973), who studied this problem, came to the conclusion that the enhancing effect of incentives on learning is not in an improvement of memory.

FRUSTRATIVE NONREWARD AS MOTIVATION AROUSING

Most positive reinforcers are thought of as providing incentives and, hence, as tending to energize behavior. There is a very important exception to all this, which is found in a phenomenon known as *frustrative nonreward.*

The phenomenon, like many others that are of significance to human behavior, was first established through experimentation with animals. There are many ways in which it can be demonstrated. One way is to arrange a situation in which a food-deprived rat learns to run down an alley to a goal box where it receives a pellet of food. A door then opens that gives it access to a second alley and, on running the second alley, it also receives a pellet of food. This routine can be continued as long as the rat is hungry, but an interesting variation can be introduced. Experimenters have asked the question, "What happens when, after the initial acquisition trials, no food is given after the first runway?" The answer is that the animal runs the second alley with increased vigor and increased speed. The situation is described as one of frustrative nonreward, that is to say, as one in which an anticipated reward in terms of previous experience is not received. The result is increased vigor of behavior. Nonreward functions as though it raised the level of motivation. Another technique of demonstrating the frustrative nonreward effect is the double-alley technique. Rats are run in two distinctively different alleys. In the one alley they are reinforced on 100 per cent of the trials, but in the other they are reinforced on only a proportion of the trials. The finding is that in the alley on which there is less than 100 per cent reinforcement, running is faster and more vigorous. The frustrative nonreward effect has been found in numerous experiments with animals, in which it has shown itself to be a consistent and substantial effect (see Scull, 1973).

Although the frustrative nonreward effect has long been demonstrated on animals, attempts to demonstrate it on human subjects are of much more recent vintage. Ryan and Watson (1968) have reviewed the literature covering the first ten years of research. They point out that the phenomenon was at first not readily demonstrated on young children, suggesting that it is perhaps a weaker effect in the human being than in the rat, where it is readily apparent. The technique used to demonstrate it on human beings involves a simple task of pulling one lever when one light goes on and another lever when another light is turned on. The pulling of a lever may release a marble. In order to demonstrate the nonreward frustration effect, one lever is set to provide a 100 per cent delivery of marbles (100 per cent reinforcement) while the other is set for delivery of marbles on 50 per cent or fewer occasions. What is found through the use of such equipment is that children tend to push the lever associated with occasional nonreward with greater vigor and speed than the lever associated with 100 per cent reinforcement. However, when very low rates of reinforcements are used, which approach 0 per cent, the effect is reversed and slow rates of responding occur. Thus if all levels of reinforcement are used, from 100 per cent to 0 per cent, the vigor of the response can be represented by a U-shaped curve, with the most vigorous responses in the middle range and the least vigorous at the 100 per cent and 0 per cent levels. Recent data (Schmeck and Anderson, 1974) show that although frustrative non-reward may raise motivation it may also increase errors.

In these experiments, the children involved could not regard their performance under any of the conditions as a failure, in that they must have recognized that whether they received or did not receive the reinforcement depended on the equipment and not on their own ability. A few children may have regarded the situation as one that they might be able to control if they could only find the right formula, but the research workers involved do not report such cases. The effect of frustrative nonreward occurs in situations in which the subject does not regard his performance as one of success or failure. In situations in which there is genuine failure and in which the person recognizes that because of his own inadequacies he has failed to reach a goal, the effect of failure is that of lowering motivation and reducing the vigor of response.

There is some evidence that nonreward is more frustrating for older subjects than for young preschool children. Older children have firmer expectations for reward, whereas young children often find that engaging in a task is rewarding in itself. A related kind of effect is found when the strength of the nonreward frustration effect is compared for retarded and normal children. The retarded generally show much less of the effect than do the normals (see Hayes, Siders, and Snider, 1973). The retarded do not expect reward, for their lives have not been filled with rewards, as have the lives of the normals. Middle-class children seem to show the effect less than lower-class children (see Kroes, 1973).

Nobody knows at this time whether nonreward frustration theory can be applied to the problem of raising the level of motivation in children. One can only speculate that the condition in which a child is praised for everything he does may not produce a pupil whose behavior is energized to a full degree. Appropriate withholding of praise on some occasions may be as important as providing appropriate praise.

THE GENERALIZED DRIVE CONCEPT OF MOTIVATION

One of the oldest concepts in the area of human motivation is the concept of a generalized drive. The concept derives from the fact that behavior shows variation in the level of activity both from time to time in the same individual, and also from individual to individual. Freud postulated that behavior was energized by what he termed a source of libidinal energy, and thus he identified the energizing of behavior with basic sexual functions in a doctrine that had much mysticism surrounding it. Later writers and thinkers have tended to retain the concept of a generalized drive in the development of motivation theory, but have discarded unnecessary elements of mysticism. Woodworth (1958), for example, has taken the position that it is of the nature of higher organisms to *act upon* their environments so long as they are in the waking state. Harlow has also come to a similar conclusion after observing the fact that even after the basic needs of a primate have been well satisfied, the animal continues to act on its environment by manipulating any objects it can find, engaging in climbing and swinging activity, as well as activities such as throwing and breaking small objects. Such animals are not just reacting to their environment. They are acting *on* the environment. The play of children falls into this category of activity, in that children will act on their environment through any means that they have available. Another version of this same concept is found in Skinner's concept that organisms emit behavior and do not have to wait for the appearance of particular stimuli in order for behavior to be emitted.

A very hungry animal is highly sensitive to new stimuli, but all sensory inputs have some activating properties in themselves. In the chapter on the nervous system, the point will be made that sensory inputs provide information, which goes to the sensory cortex of the brain by a quite direct route. In addition, the sensory inputs also are channeled to the reticular formation, where they produce activity that in turn, has an activating effect on the entire cortex of the brain. Generalized drive can be conceived of as the degree to which the reticular activating mechanism is producing an arousal effect in the higher centers of the nervous system. When the reticular formation is least active, as it is during sleep, behavior is least energized. A large amount of sensory input may produce a state of considerable excitement, indeed, a far higher level of excitement and arousal than is needed for effective behavior. Many primitive native dances slowly work the participants into a frenzy of excitement through a large volume of input including auditory inputs of loud music, visual inputs involving the movement of dancing figures in brightly colored costumes, and inputs from the muscles and the haptic system produced by the individual's own participation in the dance. Many nightclubs, in a similar way, try to produce high arousal in a clientele that would otherwise fall into a state of somnolence.

A difference one might expect between the quiet, subdued, and highly organized classroom and the noisier classroom of the more modern program, filled with highly interesting exhibits that are changed from day to day, is the level of arousal of the pupils. The traditional classroom probably produced conditions that did not raise the arousal level of the pupils to a sufficient extent, though some modern classrooms may do the reverse, at least for some pupils who may become overexcited.

The relationship between level of arousal and learning is almost certainly complex. Much of what is known is summarized in the famous Yerkes–Dodson law, mentioned at other points in this book. An additional word of caution must also be added here. Some research workers have pointed out that the Yerkes–Dodson law is best established in the case of aversive sources of arousal, and virtually not established in the case of arousal produced by other means (see Fantino, Kasdon, and Stringer, 1970).

Much needs to be done to identify the conditions that raise or lower the arousal level of pupils. The amount of praise and criticism offered pupils may do this, as Spear (1970) has shown. How praise or criticism is given must also determine whether it produces heightened or lowered arousal. One suspects that the teacher who automatically praises every child may not be raising the level of arousal by so doing. What is effective under one set of conditions in raising the arousal level may not be effective under other conditions (see Berlyne, 1969).

Another approach to the identification of major components of what has been termed generalized drive has been to consider it as closely akin to what is commonly called anxiety. This approach was largely developed by Janet Taylor Spence, who developed a questionnaire known as the Manifest Anxiety Scale, in order to measure this component of drive in human subjects. In terms of this scale, high anxiety would be identified as a high-drive state. Some early experiments in this area produced promising results. These experiments involved mainly simple classical conditioning tasks such as are involved in conditioning the eye-blink reflex to a sound. The eye-blink reflex is naturally triggered by a slight puff of air on the eyeball and this response can be readily conditioned to a bell, a click, or a flash of light. Those subjects who obtain high scores on the Manifest Anxiety Scale are more easily conditioned than are those who obtain low scores on the scale. However, when the task is made more complex, the reverse occurs. A slightly more complex task would be a choice-reaction task in which the subject has to learn to press a key when one of two lights goes on, but to avoid pressing the key when the other light goes on. On such tasks, the high-anxiety subjects do less well than the low-anxiety subjects. The explanation commonly given for this is that high motivation makes more responses available and these compete to take over. The competition among responses reduces the effectiveness of the subject in such a situation. The finding does fit well with other findings such as the Yerkes–Dodson law, which proposes that high motivation interferes with performance on complex tasks, except for the fact that the choice reaction task is really not a very complex task.

Although a considerable amount of data fits the Spence theory that anxiety is a generalized form of motivation, some have challenged the theory. Saltz (1970), for example, proposes that the high-anxiety individuals do more poorly on complex tasks than do the low-anxiety individuals because, he believes, they are more sensitive to the effects of failure. A high-anxiety individual may be embarrassed by the difficulty he is having with a problem task, and he may be disorganized by his concern that he may fail on it, and this may disrupt his performance. The same individual may not be concerned on a simple conditioning task that does not seem to reflect on his intelligence and, hence, he does well on that task. Saltz explains the tendency of low-anxiety individuals to do poorly on the simple eyelid-conditioning task by saying that such individuals are sensitive to punishment. Saltz views the puff of air on the eyelid as punishing, but this is a very doubtful position.

Another interpretation is offered by Wine (1971), who has summarized substantial evidence to support the position that high anxiety has the effect of distracting the attention of the learner from the task. The high-anxiety individual tends to focus his attention on himself and to become preoccupied with how he is doing, what others will think of his performance, whether he can meet his own goals, and so forth.

Despite the qualms that some psychologists feel about the interpretation of the Taylor Manifest Anxiety Scale as a measure of drive, much of the data available fits the generalized drive theory. Generally, the high-anxiety individuals do more poorly than the low-anxiety individuals on complex tasks. Most of the early studies were undertaken with college students, but rather similar findings have been reported in experiments with elementary-school children. Casteneda, McCandless, and Palermo (1956) developed a form of the Taylor Manifest Anxiety Scale for administration to children. High-anxiety and low-anxiety children were selected on the basis of the scale and then given a series of problems in which the child had to find the combination of buttons to press to turn off a particular combination of lights. They found that the high-anxiety group performed better than the low-anxiety group on the easy combinations, but that the high-anxiety group performed more poorly on the more difficult combinations.

Grimes and Allinsmith (1961) investigated the relationship of achievement to anxiety in children learning to read by two different methods. The children in twelve classrooms were taught by a phonetic method in which the teaching situation was considered to be highly structured. Children in another twelve classrooms in a different school system were taught by a look-and-say method that involved much less structured teaching and far more informal activity. They found that in the unstructured setting high anxiety was related to poor performance in reading, but that in the structured setting there was no relationship between anxiety and reading achievement.

Gaudry and Spielberger (1971) have summarized evidence relating school behavior to measures of anxiety. They find that the high-anxiety student has characteristics that distinguish him from the low-anxiety student and that some of these characteristics have a bearing on school achievement. The high-anxiety student has a poor image of himself. Such children make self-derogatory statements, blame themselves for their failures, are worriers, and have difficulties in expressing their own hostilities. Since the high-anxiety children are self-derogatory, they are particularly vulnerable to conditions that produce threats to their self-esteem, hence, failure is for them particularly demoralizing. The high-anxiety children tended to be timid in matters of exploration and could be described as low in curiosity. They also tended to be high in daydreaming, perhaps thereby compensating for failures in real life.

The high-anxiety children were generally found to be discriminated against by their classmates in the sense that these children were not popular and are not typically selected as " best friends."

In view of the fact that the high-anxiety student is penalized on examinations, it is not surprising that the same student is generally lower in academic achievement than his low-anxiety classmate (Gaudry, 1971). In the early grades anxiety is particularly evoked by the task of learning to read, but anxiety becomes displaced to arithmetic toward the end of the elementary grades. The negative relationship between anxiety and achievement holds through college, but at the college level anxiety becomes related to drop-out rates. There is also some evidence that programmed learning may help to reduce the anxiety among high-anxiety children. Of course, this does not mean that such highly structured pedagogical techniques should be used with all children.

In addition, there seems to be an interaction between how anxiety operates and the intelligence of the individual. This is to be expected. A highly anxious child may not have his behavior disrupted during the solution of a problem because for that child the problem may be very easy.

Denny (1966) undertook an experiment in which subjects were either of high or low intelligence as defined by the test given by the College Entrance Examination Board. The subjects were given a fairly complex concept-learning task. Denny found that among the most intelligent subjects, the high-anxiety subjects performed better than the low-anxiety subjects, but among the least intelligent of the subjects the reverse occurred and the least anxious subjects performed the best. The data were as if for the most intelligent students the problems were simple problems, for it is the simple problem on which the most anxious have generally been able to perform at their best. Under the right conditions anxiety has a facilitating effect, but its interaction with other variables is such that teachers probably are not in a position to predict when it will and when it will not facilitate learning.

Smith (1969) suggests that fear of failure and anxiety, as measured by tests, are both very complex variables that show some similarity, but each has some distinctive properties of its own.

The approach to the problem of anxiety and how it should be measured has changed in recent years. An important distinction that has been introduced into the field is that between *trait anxiety* and *state anxiety*. A person who scores high on trait anxiety is one whose anxiety is easily triggered. He may not be anxious at the time when his anxiety is measured or he may be. The test of trait anxiety should be so designed that the score is uninfluenced by whether the particular situation in which the test was taken was or was not anxiety-producing. The well-known Taylor Manifest Anxiety Scale and its derivatives are measures of trait anxiety. On the other hand, a test of state anxiety measures the level of anxiety in the particular situation in which the person is tested. Some devices provide measures of both trait anxiety and state anxiety.

ACHIEVEMENT MOTIVATION

One of the most significant experimental programs in the area of human motivation is that connected with the development of the concept of achievement motivation. Research related to this concept has had a long history, beginning in the mid-thirties and continuing today as a vigorous area of inquiry. The history of the development of this concept shows well the fact that useful scientific concepts in the behavioral sciences cannot be developed overnight, but are a product of long and persistent struggle. The early researches in this area were initiated by H. A. Murray and were summarized by him in a well-known book (1938). Murray proposed that human needs fall into categories, the viscerogenic and the psychogenic. The viscerogenic needs were a part of our inherited constitution and consisted of needs related to such bodily events as lack of water and food and distension of the bladder and bowel. Murray's viscerogenic needs are very similar to what other psychologists have referred to as primary drives. Psychogenic needs, on the other hand, according to Murray, are learned. His list of psychogenic needs is broad in coverage and includes such diverse needs as those to gain possession of something, to be orderly, to display oneself, to be autonomous, to show aggression, and to take care of others and help them. Some of the needs included in the list are relatively rare in occurrence, as is a need to be rejected. Few individuals manifest a need to be rejected, and a need to exhibit oneself is seen primarily in women. Murray's list includes common psychological needs as well as the rarer ones within its twenty-eight items. Not all persons are presumed to manifest all needs. Indeed, the lives of some individuals may be dominated by a high level of one particular need, and negligible influence from any of the other needs in the list.

The research of Murray stimulated research on the measurement of needs but, like all research programs, only a very small fraction of it ever bore fruit. By far the most productive line of research has been that related to the measurement and study of achievement motivation.

The work of Murray lay dormant as a scientific enterprise during the war years of the forties, although attempts were made to give it some practical applications, and it was not until peace came that further scientific initiative was shown in the development of his theory of motivation. This development was brought about first by one of Murray's original associates David McClelland, and later by a whole school of followers scattered across the world. Most of the work of this school of research workers became concentrated on the study of achievement motivation, but some of it became directed toward the investigation of affiliation motivation, the need to be accepted by others and to feel that one belongs. Of these two enterprises, the study of achievement motivation has been the most successful.

The literature in this area of motivation research is substantial. Summaries of much of the more significant earlier work is found in Cofer and Appley (1964). Somewhat later summaries of research are found in Atkinson and Feather (1966) and in Heckhausen (1967). The fact that each one of these works refers to several hundred different researches indicates the general vigor of the research enterprise involved. A volume edited by Smith (1969) is restricted to studies of achievement motivation in children.

Summaries of research in more recent years have focused on problems of current interest. Thus Maehr's article (1974) raises questions about the value of measuring achievement motivation in disadvantaged blacks with tests designed for middle-class whites, and Alper's article (1974) reviews research related to the measurement of achievement motivation in women.

Until recent times nearly all the studies of achievement motivation undertaken were directed toward the study of the phenomenon in boys and men. The main reason for this was that studies of girls and women in this area did not at first seem to provide consistent results. Perhaps there was also some cultural bias in that in the United States, in the years around midcentury, the male was seen as the hard-driving achievement-oriented individual.

The significance of the research into achievement motivation lies largely in the experimental findings, which are intertwined with theorizing that has been much less successful. Only theory at a relatively crude level is needed in order to understand the general nature of the findings. A need is a disposition that may be quiescent and latent and show no effect on behavior unless it is aroused. A person may have a high need for achievement, but if no situation arises that may challenge his need, he will not show it. Needs have to be aroused in order to be manifested. The pupils in a class may appear bored and listless, but this does not mean that they do not have potential for showing achievement motivation. Perhaps their needs are not being aroused. Attempts to measure needs under conditions under which they are not aroused produce useless measures. Needs are aroused by some stimulus related to its satisfaction. Achievement motivation is aroused by any task that challenges the individual. A listless school child, given a new and interesting problem, may suddenly become a dynamo of energy. His achievement motivation has been aroused. A motive may also be aroused by deprivation. After a prolonged and boring situation, almost any situation may arouse the achievement motivation of a person in whom this can be aroused to a high degree. Given sufficient boredom, almost anything may become a challenge and arouse achievement motivation. There are stories, for example, of Einstein sitting at tedious meetings and playing tic-tac-toe with his neighbor—perhaps not the greatest challenge for one so great, but a small avenue through which his achievement motivation could find some avenue for releasing pent-up energies.

The theory discussed here is presented at a crude level compared with the sophisticated versions found in the literature on the subject. A very sophisticated presentation of a theory of achievement motivation has been made by Atkinson and Feather (1966).

Early attempts to measure achievement motivation by means of questionnaires proved fruitless, partly because it is not sufficient just to probe for a disposition to manifest achievement need. What has to be done is to arouse that disposition, and then to determine the strength that it shows under the aroused conditions. The core of achievement motivation is that of a need to achieve some standard of excellence. A person is not showing the results of a need for achievement if he just wants to complete a particular job, for he may want to complete it to obtain money, to please a superior, or to gain status. He has to want to complete the job *well*, because it is worthwhile to do the task well, and not for other reasons. This is what distinguishes the person showing achievement motivation. How he performs makes him a success or failure in his own eyes—if he is motivated by achievement need.

The preferred method of measuring achievement motivation has become that of providing the person in whom it is to be measured with a situation in which he produces fantasies related to achievement. These fantasies are then scored. One good situation for producing fantasies is that in which the person is provided with a picture and is asked to tell a story about it. The pictures may be selected so that they arouse achievement need rather than other needs. For example, a picture of a boy poring over a book late at night is more likely to arouse achievement need than it is to arouse need for affiliation. In the typical procedure used for measuring achievement motivation, the subject is asked to organize his fantasies by answering the following questions as he looks at each of a set of pictures:

1. What is happening?
2. What has led up to the situation?
3. What are the people thinking or feeling?
4. What will be the outcome?

The fantasies reported are all recorded and are later scored. In order to accomplish this, the records are scored in each of a number of categories for what is referred to as achievement-need imagery, that is, indicating in some way a striving after a standard of excellence. The story as a whole is first scored for the extent to which it shows achievement orientation. For example, the subject who looks at the picture of the youth studying and says "The boy wants to do well in the examination tomorrow" is scored positive for achievement imagery. On the other hand, if the subject said "The boy seems to be reading a book," he would be showing an absence of achievement imagery. The statement is neutral and does not even suggest a motive for why the boy is reading at all. The technique is designed so that the subject projects his own motives into the people in the picture.

Two important categories of achievement motivation are those of expectation of success and fear of failure. Contrast the two following responses given to the same picture.

"The boy is studying because he wants to do well on the examination he has to take tomorrow."

"The boy is studying because he is afraid he might fail the examination he has to take tomorrow."

The first of these statements is success-oriented and the second is failure-oriented. The one represents the *approach* of a goal because of the intrinsic value inherent in the goal itself, but the other represents the *avoidance* of the consequences of failure rather than the pursuit of the goal of achievement for the sake of achievement. The approach response reflects, in the subject's past history, the effects of positive reinforcement, and the avoidance tendency, the effects of negative reinforcement.

In obtaining an overall score for achievement motivation, through the use of a picture interpretation test, the various component scores are added together and, from the total score, there is no way of telling whether the person is primarily motivated by an approach or an avoidance tendency or by a mixture of both. For some purposes, it is important to keep these two components separate, for they make rather different predictions concerning how behavior will occur in some situations.

Measures of achievement motivation have had some success in predicting behavior. They predict performance in tasks in which the individual is challenged and in which the level of performance is primarily a function of motivation. Give individuals a task such as that of crossing out all the *es* in a page of print, and a measure of achievement motivation is unlikely to predict performance. A slight change in the task makes performance a function of achievement motivation. This change can be brought about by telling those who are to do it that it is a task highly predictive of success in life. The task then becomes a challenge to those high in achievement motivation. The result is that performance on the task, which has now been made challenging, becomes related to measures of achievement motivation.

Measures of achievement motivation are related only very slightly to grades in most courses. A part of the reason for this is that many courses offer little challenge. An important additional point is mentioned by McKeachie and his associates (1968), who note that college students are highly motivated to obtain good grades for many reasons—some because it will lead to a good job, some because they want to please their parents, and some, perhaps, because of a generalized tendency to pour energy into whatever they do. If the students are highly motivated to work hard and do well for reasons other than that of achieving a standard of excellence, the presence or absence of achievement motivation may make little difference. Indeed, the addition of a source of motivation to a student who is already well motivated may interfere with rather than facilitate his performance.

The area in which fear of failure and expectation of success have a distinctive role is in what is called *risk-taking behavior* (see Heckhausen, 1967). In a risk-taking situation, a person is faced with a goal to be achieved that has a designated level of attractiveness. He also knows the odds that he will not be able to achieve the goal, that is, the risk of failure. Whether he will decide to go ahead and try to achieve the goal or whether he will abandon the goal in such a situation depends to a considerable extent on whether he is primarily motivated by expectation of success or fear of failure. If he is motivated primarily by fear of failure, he will accept the risk if the odds of success are either very good or very poor, but he will abandon the goal if the odds are in the moderate range. Thus the fear-of-failure-oriented student will be willing to attempt courses that are either known to be very hard or very easy, but will tend to avoid the run-of-the-mill course. The reason for this is that, for such a person the price of genuine failure is painful to pay, which is why he chooses situations in which he has a high expectation of success. The reason he also chooses the very risky situations is that he does not have to blame himself for failing in them, for he can always say to himself, "The task was so hard that anybody might have failed." In doing this he is saying that nonattainment of the goal cannot be considered as failure, for nobody could really be expected to succeed.

The success-oriented person, on the other hand, tends to choose situations in which the chances of success are in the middle range of those ordinarily encountered, and he avoids either very high-risk or very low-risk situations. The moderate-risk situation provides him with sufficient challenge to satisfy his achievement need and he also has reasonably good chances of success. The very easy, no-risk situation is avoided, for it offers little challenge, and does not arouse the achievement need. The very difficult, high-risk situation is also avoided, because it supplies only very poor opportunities for satisfying the need for achievement, which is not satisfied by failure.

The risk taking discussed here does not refer to situations involving games of chance, but risk taking where success or failure is dependent on the person's own skill and initiative. For the adult, games of chance do not arouse the achievement motive, for success or failure cannot be attributed to the individual's own capability. On the other hand, children below the age of 10 have considerable difficulty in discriminating between a situation in which they succeed because of their own skill and situations in which success is dependent on circumstances outside of their own control. When a young child wins at a game of chance, he is likely to give himself credit for winning, as if the situation were mystically under his control. The adult is more modest about his accomplishments. For this reason, the choice of risk-taking situations involving games of chance do not bear the same relationship to fear of failure and expectation of success as they do when the situations involve a genuine accomplishment.

McClelland and Watson (1973) have also explored the relationship between risk taking and the need for power. They have shown that although those high on need for achievement tend to set goals of moderate difficulty—that is, with moderate risk of failure—those with a high need for power take either very high risks or very low risks. Those high in need for power are very concerned about whether their behavior will be noticed by others when they take risky chances. They want visibility and like to be thought of as big gamblers. The low-risk situations they choose pander more to their desire to appear to be winners.

The studies that revealed the phenomena of expectation of success and fear of failure were derived almost entirely from studies of boys and men, but studies of girls and women revealed another related phenomenon. Females showed a marked tendency to manifest fear of success. Women students asked to tell a story about a girl, Anne, who was at the top of her medical class at the end of first-term finals, tended to explain her achievement as being a fluke or as having unpleasant consequences such as social rejection. The phenomenon was originally noted by Horner (1972). A study by Winchel, Fenner, and Shaver (1974) has also shown that co-education tends to enhance the effect, as also does a situation in which a woman has to perform opposite a man (Karabenick and Marshall, 1974).

A final point still has to be made about the two aspects of achievement motivation under consideration, namely, that a person can have both fear of failure and hope of success in relation to the same situation. When this happens, he may have great difficulty in deciding whether to pursue the situation through to the goal it involves or to remove himself from the situation and set himself some other goal. Fear of failure tends to make him want to withdraw, but hope of success urges him to become involved in the situation. The approach and avoidance aspects of the motivating mechanism come into conflict. When there is this kind of conflict, the person involved tends to show vacillating behavior. He first tells himself he will go ahead, but as he draws nearer to the task his fear of failure builds up and he changes his mind and withdraws. As he withdraws, the possibility of failure begins to seem more remote and he decides that perhaps he should go ahead with the task, and so he vacillates. He may resolve this conflict in many ways. One is to decide, at some point, that the task is not worth the trouble anyway. This is usually rationalization for escaping. Another is to take the position that if he fails, it is not really going to be his fault because the task is really beyond him. Thus he provides himself with a built-in excuse for failing, in the event he should fail.

Research in the area of fear of failure and hope of success is in many ways an outgrowth of an earlier series of studies on what was termed level of aspiration. This concept refers to the level of performance on a particular task that a person expects to achieve. Kurt Lewin developed this concept and many of his students went on to undertake research on it, but the research did not turn out to be productive. The level of aspiration that individuals set for themselves did not turn out to provide useful measures of motivation, perhaps because the level did not take into account whether the task involved was or was not a challenge to the person setting his level of aspiration. Success does tend to raise the level of aspiration, but the effects of failure are quite variable.

The Development of Achievement Motivation in Boys

Some important facts have slowly emerged concerning the development of this motivation, although the picture is far from clear. Though most writers take the position that achievement motivation is acquired through learning there may well be components inherent in human nature. Observers of child behavior, including Bühler and Piaget, have noted infant behaviors that have some marks of achievement-oriented behavior, and particularly the wanting-to-do-it-alone reaction that becomes particularly marked in the third year. This last response is most likely to occur in the case of newly learned skills that the child can perform with some adequacy. This response does differ from most achievement-need-motivated responses in that it occurs in the case of tasks that offer relatively little challenge, that is to say, the tasks are relatively easy and have been already quite well mastered. Heckhausen (1967) points out that in order for achievement motivation to function, the learner has to be able to perceive himself in relation to the situation and in relation to the outcomes, and that children in the first three or four years of life are not yet capable of doing this. He suggests that the wanting-to-do-it-alone reaction is a pleasure-oriented reaction of a primitive kind and has little relationship to achievement motivation.

Zigler (1970) has pointed out that achievement motivation seems to grow upon the foundation of a basic need to explore and that infants do show marked individual differences in their activity level, which must be regarded as the basis of exploratory behavior. Zigler suggests that the strong individual differences in level of activity seen from the moment a child enters the world may produce differences in achievement motivation. This problem is going to be extremely difficult to investigate, but it is a very significant one.

Heckhausen and Smith (1969) propose that the numerous studies of the development of achievement motivation collectively suggest that the motive can be first detected about the age of 5 and that it develops through the elementary-school years.

Particularly important in the development of achievement motivation are conditions in the home, and a middle-class home provides the most favorable environment in this respect. The children in whom it develops to the greatest extent are those who come from homes in which responsible freedom of action on the part of the child has been encouraged. Children who have been allowed to go downtown by themselves at an early age tend to show a higher level of achievement motivation than those whose parents are more protective. Independence is not enough, for the poor sections of our community permit their children great independence, and this does not seem to result in achievement motivation. Middle-class parents, on the other hand, combine a permissive attitude toward their children with a demand that they also achieve mastery of the skills they attack. The freedom such children have enable them to achieve competence in important areas of living. There is some conflict in the evidence of whether the relationship of children to their parents should be warm or cool, but there seems no question that it should not be hostile.

Heckhausen has summarized a great number of studies related to conditions that are favorable or unfavorable to the development of achievement motivation in men. Several studies have been made that have compared achievement motivation in different countries of the world. Heckhausen reports that Japanese mothers give their children more opportunities for independence at an earlier age than do American mothers, but this does not seem to raise achievement motivation, perhaps because it is balanced by a greater emphasis on conformity in the Japanese culture. Heckhausen suggests that lack of insistence on conformity may be of more significance than merely giving children independence. He also points out that upper-class Brazilian children show a lower level of achievement motivation than do their counterparts in the United States. He suggests that this may be because the parents express great hopes for the future of their children but nevertheless demand little of them. The result is an adult who has an excessively grandiose concept of himself, but waits for the world to bring its bounties to him. This reflects the heritage of an aristocratic culture.

There seem to be possibilities that need achievement can be trained in school, though the evidence to support this is far from substantial. Evan, Hearn, and Zwirner (1975) have summarized the evidence as a prelude to their study with ninth-grade children. In these studies a strong Hawthorne effect may be operating.

The cross-cultural studies bring out clearly the crucial role played by parent-child relationships in the development of achievement motivation, and other sources of evidence also support this. Fatherless families tend to produce children low in achievement motivation. Different religious groups also differ in the extent to which they produce achievement-oriented children. The Catholic home appears to provide a relatively unfavorable milieu for the development of this kind of motivation, perhaps because of the pressures exerted toward conformity in ideas. The latter finding is also consistent with the finding that in Western civilization Protestants have a rather better record for creative activity than do Catholics. The crucial factor, again, seems to be whether the religious training in the home involves an insistence on a broad spectrum of conformity or whether it encourages individual thinking. There are, of course, homes in all religious groups where conditions favorable to the development of achievement need occur.

Certain cultures and certain periods of history are characterized by different levels of achievement motivation. McClelland (1961) has attempted to show that one can determine the strength of achievement motivation in a society of the past by studying the documents it produced and identifying the frequency of occurrence of statements reflecting achievement need in those documents. He has also attempted to show that periods in which such statements commonly occur are followed by periods of great cultural and economic growth. The research is ingenious, but there are technical difficulties involved with its development that make it in some ways questionable. One should not jump to the conclusion that a simple way to produce progress in a society is to arrange conditions for the development of achievement motivation in the growing generation.

Alternative Interpretations of the Effect of Culture on Achievement Motivation

Until recently, the commonly held view was that a high level of achievement motivation was to be found in only certain selected cultural milieu. The male middle-class society of a modern capitalistic state and the bourgeois male community of Europe in the period of the Enlightenment provided the supreme examples of hard-driving, achievement-oriented groups. Heckhausen subscribes to this view and, hence, considers the aristocratic societies of South America as lacking in achievement motivation. Other writers have taken the position that the black community lacks achievement motivation because of the performance of blacks on tests of achievement motivation. Still other writers have concluded that women are low on achievement motivation, even though the pictures in the tests on which they were measured portrayed boys and men rather than girls and women. This thesis has been challenged by Maehr (1974).

Maehr points out that although black children may not score very high on tests of achievement need, those who have worked with such children in areas in which they can achieve success have come away with a different picture. For example, athletics is one area of achievement in which the black is no longer penalized for his blackness and can compete fairly with others. In such an area, black children show enormous drive to excel and to achieve a standard of excellence. The argument of Maehr is that if black children are studied in situations in which they have opportunities to excel, they will probably show as much achievement motivation as white children. Such areas of achievement may show only minimal overlap with the areas in which the white is free to achieve, and some areas are the specialty of blacks—for example, certain areas of music. Maehr suggests that if achievement motivation were measured in relation to areas of potential success, the black might well show the same motivation as the white.

In addition, the cultural context may, in some cultures, prohibit the child from displaying achievement motivation in certain situations. Thus the Navajo child may function badly in the kind of competitive situation in which the white child has learned to flourish. However, provide him with a cooperative work relationship and he may strive to excel. These and other facts brought out in Maehr's review raise questions about the interpretations that have commonly been made of data related to achievement motivation.

One must emphasize that the issue is not whether the underprivileged have the capability of developing achievement motivation, for all human beings have that capability. The issue is whether they have it, but do not manifest it in situations that are white middle-classed-oriented.

The Achievement Motivation of Women

A related issue concerns the achievement motivation of women. Most of the research that has been undertaken on achievement motivation has involved white middle-class men, and the thematic materials have also pertained to that same group. One cannot be surprised that women confronted with cards showing men in situations involving emotion and frustration do not respond to the cards in the same way that men do. Indeed, using such materials, achievement motivation in women turns out to be a will-o-the-wisp phenomenon. Sometimes one sees it and sometimes one doesn't. The traditional interpretation of the results has been that achievement motivation is less of a central motive for women than is affiliation motivation, the need to be accepted by others. Underlying much of the discussion of achievement motivation in women is the idea that women's constitution is such that they have built into them social motives that are more characteristic of women than men, and there is the hidden implication that perhaps such differences are inherited. Writers do not explicitly state that the inherited constitution of women produces a different motivational structure than that in men, but the implication seems there in some of the material.

Much of what is really known about this problem, in contrast to what is speculated, has come from the work of Alper (1974) on Wellesley College students. Alper recognized at an early stage in her work that the thematic materials suitable for men were probably not suitable for women and designed materials of her own. She also found that she had to score them differently from the way in which McClelland had. She scores in terms of total theme rather than on a point-by-point basis. Her early data came up with the interesting finding that although women "seemingly" (p. 195) do not want to be achievers themselves, they also want men to be less achievement-oriented than they are. However, Alper soon began to turn up evidence to show that with some materials women showed themselves to be much more achievement-oriented. As mentioned earlier, when women were presented with the story of Anne, who finds herself at the top of her medical school class, a majority are likely to respond that she will never keep up her record, that the computer made a mistake, and so forth. But if the story is changed to the nursing field, the predominant response becomes success-oriented. Alper takes the position that achievement need can function in women (and presumably in men, too) only in relation to the role they have assigned themselves in society.

Alper's data fits some previous data showing that women are afraid to reveal themselves as achievement-oriented, lest this jeopardize their chances of social success.

Alper investigated a crucial factor in determining women's responses to the test situation, namely, the way in which they conceptualized women's role. Alper developed a questionnaire to determine how women students conceptualized their role. The instrument represented a range from a very traditional role for a woman to a role that approximated that prescribed by the women's liberation movement. Those who embraced the newer role showed a high degree of success-oriented responses on a need achievement test and, in many respects, responses more comparable to those of men. Also, since the study was begun in 1964, the women at Wellesley have shown a marked tendency to embrace in progressively greater numbers the newer conception of the role of women. Alper also suggests that as women have become more achievement-oriented, men have become less so.

Just as the study of achievement motivation in men has led to studies of the child-rearing practices that produce it, so, too, have studies been developed of related aspects of development in girls and women. The history of achievement in girls is of interest in itself. Girls generally exceed boys in grades K through 12. Huston and Bailey (1973) point out that although girls set high academic standards for themselves and attempt to achieve a standard of excellence, this tendency does not seem to carry over into nonschool activities and it is not manifest in higher education. The reduced effort that takes place at increasingly higher levels of education is at least partly, if not mainly, due to the pressure to adhere to the traditional feminine role. Girls also incorporate into their own personalities the low expectation for achievement that the rest of society holds for them.

Huston and Bailey (1973) reject the notion that women are primarily motivated by a need for affiliation or external approval. Nevertheless, they do conclude that women's efforts to attain excellence are often in the area of social skills and in areas in which women can achieve success without losing status in the eyes of men.

Huston and Bailey find evidence that achievement motivation in girls is developed through a home that places pressure on the child, even sometimes through punitive means. The literature suggests that girls can be oversocialized by too much warmth and that a moderate level of warmth seems desirable. As with boys, freedom of the child is important, provided it is coupled with a demand for responsibility and achievement. Strict control of a girl is likely to produce the stereotyped, conforming adult woman. Fathers seem to be important in developing achievement motivation in their daughters. Not only can they encourage achievement behavior, but they can provide a model of achievement. A successful father is important for developing an achieving daughter.

Other Attempts to Measure Motives Within the Murray Framework

No area has been so carefully explored as has achievement motivation, but some research has also been undertaken on other motives within Murray's conceptual system. In no case has a variable with as great potential significance as achievement need been identified and measured. Measures of other needs have tended to be less reliable and have provided less consistent predictions. The concentration of research on achievement need has probably occurred because of the promise offered by the early researches. Research workers tend to migrate toward successful developments.

The area receiving the next most attention is that of affiliation need, the need to feel accepted by others and to belong to a group. This need has been measured through the same kind of exploration of the subject's fantasy, as was discussed earlier. Interest in affiliation need in relation to learning stems from the fact that it is a likely candidate as a source of motivation related to the acquisition of conforming behavior. Marlowe and Gregen (1969), who have reviewed the literature, come to the conclusion that it is those in the middle range of affiliation-need scores who are the most conforming. Studies of affiliation need bring out another interesting finding, namely, that those in whom the need is most developed show an unusually frequent use of the telephone for making local telephone calls. They also are great letter writers and visit more frequently than others do relatives and friends who are living at a distance. A number of devices designed to measure related motives have also been developed, as, for example, Crowne and Marlowe's (1964) measure of what they term the approval motive.

The terms *need for approval* and *need for affiliation* seem to be used almost interchangeably in the research literature, with one group of research workers favoring one term and another group favoring the other.

Earlier research workers had often commented on the fact that a need for approval commonly interfered with the precise measurement of personality characteristics. They noted that when subjects were given questionnaires to fill in concerning their habits, views, likes and dislikes, and so forth, answers were commonly colored by a need of the subject to present himself in a favorable light. Subjects tend to present themselves as more honest, better adjusted, socially more adept, and generally more adequate and worthy than they really are. This effect is so marked that many psychologists have been inclined to the view that the typical personality inventory may measure nothing else than the individual's need to present himself to others in a favorable light. The designers of personality measures have made considerable efforts to eliminate this contaminating effect from their measures, but even in the best designed instrument it is likely to appear.

Crowne and Marlowe developed an inventory designed specifically to measure the extent to which individuals are motivated by the need for approval. Unlike other designers of inventories they were concerned with maximizing the effect of this variable, rather than with its elimination. The questionnaire thus produced provides a measure that has been shown, in subsequent studies, to have interesting relationships to other kinds of behavior. Crowne and Marlowe went on to study differences in the behavior of persons with high and low scores on this and related devices in a number of different experimental situations. The first experiment they undertook was to expose subjects to a dull repetitive task of fitting a dozen spools into a box, then emptying the box and starting over again. Individuals with a high need for approval described the task as being more enjoyable than did subjects with a low need for approval. Presumably, the former group was afraid of offending the experimenter by making derogatory comments about the experiment and acted accordingly.

A second experiment involved typical verbal conditioning tasks. In this task subjects were required to just say words without putting them into sentences. The subject thus sat and said disconnected words one after the other. Whenever the subjects said plural nouns, they were either positively reinforced by the experimenter mumbling "Mm-hmm," or they were negatively reinforced by the experimenter saying " Uh-uh." This is a typical verbal conditioning experiment. In addition, two other verbal conditioning situations involving more common types of situations were used. One was a personal interview. In these verbal conditioning situations, the high-approval-need subjects were found to be more readily conditioned by reinforcement. Such subjects seem to be more aware of what is going on in such a social situation and more responsive to the reinforcements provided. In order to win approval, a high degree of sensitivity to what is happening in such a social situation would appear to be necessary.

Crowne and Marlowe also found evidence that individuals with high approval need tended to show more conforming behavior and, on a word association task, tended to give common associations rather than associations that might be considered to be either original or unusual.

Crowne and Marlowe also undertook a number of studies on what has been termed the defensiveness of subjects. One of their approaches was to flash on a screen for a very short time words that were either common words or words in a class that they termed taboo words. In such a task, performance depends to a marked degree on how the subject perceives the task. If he sees the task as merely a task requiring speed of perception, his need for approval will move him in the direction of performing well. However, if he perceives it as a task in which his sensitivity to dirty words is at stake, he may show delay in reporting such words if he has a high need for approval. The person with high need for approval is defensive, as is also evident in studies of high- and low-approval-need people who are undergoing therapy. The high-approval-need people are more likely to drop out of therapy than are the low-approval-need people.

Studies in this area seem to have identified a quite important variable that may significantly modify behavior as it occurs in the classroom. The course of the development of this motive still needs to be explored.

Measures of need for approval have shown themselves to be quite satisfactory predictors of behavior. For example, Morris and Coady (1974) found that elementary-school children with high scores on a need for approval scale were found to be more sensitive to social approval as an incentive than the offer of a material reward. The social incentive involved only the statement by the experimenter, " Most of your friends do very well in this game and they are liked and praised by many boys and girls when they do well." Query and Query (1973) found that urban groups showed a higher degree of affiliation motivation than the rural groups, a finding that one would anticipate.

There seems to be some tendency for achievement need, affiliation need, and the need for power to be positively correlated (about 0.3 in Bowen, 1973). The three categories of motivation are, nevertheless, sufficiently distinct for them to be referred to as separate variables. The fact that there is a mild tendency for individuals to be either high on all three or low on all three suggests that there may be an overall tendency for behavior to be more or less energized.

CURIOSITY AND EXPLORATION AS SYMPTOMATIC OF DRIVE STATES

The traditional view of the infant has been that he is a passive receptor of the impressions that the world leaves on his receptor systems. This conclusion was based largely on poor and casual observation of the developing infant, for careful observation indicates that the human infant is far from being a passive recipient of information about the world around him. The work of Gesell and Piaget, more than half a century ago began to show that the infant is a complex exploratory system. Within a few weeks after birth the infant moves his eyes from one object in the environment to the other, while his hands are beginning to explore the surface of his own body. Bower (1974) reports that infants almost from birth engage in a form of swiping movement of the arm and hand that brings them into tactile contact with objects in the environment. As this movement develops and becomes better coordinated the hand improves its ability to grasp and hold. First, the hand opens in anticipation of contact with an object, and then the degree to which the hand is opened becomes adjusted to the size of the object. The sensory systems are transported by muscular systems that permit them to make active contact with the world around them.

The infant who fixates a visually presented object may or may not habituate to the object. The term *habitutation* refers to such behaviors as moving the eyes to fixate another object, closing the eyes, or turning the head away. Whether very young infants typically do this is a matter of controversy (see Weberford and Cohen, 1973), but at least in some studies such habituation has been observed in the newborn (Friedman 1970). The inconsistency of results with babies in the first few weeks of their lives is probably a result of the difficulty of determining whether the baby is awake or asleep. A very young infant may be in a sleeplike state even though his eyes are open.

Habituation may be interpreted as a flagging state of attention. With older individuals one knows that simple stimuli produce habituation more rapidly than do complex stimuli, which suggests that habituation occurs when the viewer has taken in all of the information he can in the display. When this happens, the person turns his attention to other objects. Attention is an information-assimilating activity, but attention is maintained only so long as there is still new information to be assimilated.

Very early in the infant's life, visual attention comes to be aroused by novel objects, though there are presumably limits to the degree to which novelty can be tolerated. Babies, much like adults, like to move among familiar things and to give at least transitory attention to that which is already known to them. Considerable discussion exists in the research literature concerning the degree of novelty that is most effective in arousing attention. One view (see Friedman, 1972) has been that a mild degree of novelty is the most arousing and attention holding, with greater degrees of novelty-producing avoidance. However, Welch (1974), working with 4-month-old infants found that the greater the novelty the greater attention value the object had. The measure generally taken in such studies is the length of time of the first fixation.

The ambiguities in the data derived from young children appear to be mainly a result of the difficulties of experimenting with the very young. Observations on older children show better consistency from study to study. Some of the basic facts related to curiosity and exploratory behavior in human beings and animals have been summarized by Fowler (1965) in his well-known essay on the subject. A crucial factor in determining whether an animal will or will not show curiosity and exploratory behavior is the extent to which the object is similar or different from other objects recently examined. Basic facts related to exploratory behavior have been reviewed by Fowler (1967) and Nunnally and Lemond (1975). The greatest amount of such behavior is shown when the new object is entirely different from objects previously encountered. The behavior can also be controlled, to some degree, through deprivation procedures. Such behavior has been studied in primates through an apparatus known as a Butler box. The animal is placed in such a box and learns that by pressing a lever it can see through a window, for a short time, either a novel object or a motion picture of some novel event. The longer the animal is deprived of any novel stimuli, the more likely it is to press the lever and expose itself to the novel experience. Novel stimuli that are highly dynamic have very high incentive value for pressing the lever. In one set of experiments, the display that the primate would work hardest to see was a motion picture of a train passing by.

Animals engaged in the exploration of unfamiliar objects presented in the form of puzzles may learn to solve them even though no reinforcements are provided by the experimenter for so doing. Primates will learn quite complex disassembly tasks in which they have to take apart wire puzzles, and what is learned transfers to the solution of new problems with similar characteristics. There are also species differences and age differences in responses to novel stimuli. Harlow has pointed out important facts in this respect from observing the development of young macaque monkeys in his University of Wisconsin laboratory. When the monkey is just a few months old, it will show some approach tendencies toward novel objects, but the behavior is characterized by much conflict. This is shown in the fact that the young monkey will leave its mother to approach new objects placed in the cage, but before reaching the object it is likely to withdraw to the security of the mother. The mother provides a base from which sorties toward unusual objects are made. The older the young monkey, the more it will show approach behavior and the less there will be a tendency to retreat to the security provided by contact with the mother. The mature monkey, raised with a natural mother and provided with the security that the mother can give, ultimately learns to show positive approach tendencies toward unusual objects and events in the environment (see Schrier, Harlow, and Stollnitz, 1965).

The effect of the presence of the mother on the exploratory behavior of the infant was first observed in subhuman primates, but, of course, psychologists then became interested in whether a similar phenomenon would occur in the case of human mothers and human infants. Ainsworth and Bell (1970) studied the exploratory behavior of infants aged 49 to 51 weeks of age in the presence and absence of their mother. The main conclusion from their study was that the presence of the human mother generally increased the amount of exploratory behavior of her infant, and that the phenomenon was very similar to that observed in other primates. An additional interesting finding was that when the mother was removed from the situation for a short time and then brought back, the infant tended to show a heightened degree of attachment behavior for a short time and a depression in the amount of exploratory behavior.

Teachers and those who work with the underprivileged have long suspected that those who grow up in intellectually poor environments may show little exploratory behavior. The listless disinterestedness of Spitz's foundling home babies has been claimed to typify the lack of curiosity and exploratory behavior in neglected children. Minuchin (1971) conducted a study on eighteen 4-year-olds in a Head Start program to test this hypothesis. These children showed considerable differences in exploratory behavior. The amount of such behavior was related to the extent to which they had a definite image of themselves, the degree to which they had expectations of support in their environment, and also to a measure of intellectual development described as "concept formation." The lowest third of the children in terms of curiosity and exploratory behavior were characterized as coming from an environment where there was sustained crisis. These children saw the adults as poorly defined and had little grasp of order in the environment or of relationships between objects. The data fit with other data suggesting that curiosity and exploratory behavior are means through which children extend the order in their environment to new objects. Children whose environment is chaotic cannot be expected to go out and search for order and understanding elsewhere. Their state of bewilderment prevents this.

Devices have been developed for the study of curiosity in human beings. One such device is reported by Day (1968), who adapted it from some materials developed by Berlyne (1963). The device consisted of twenty-eight abstract designs that varied in complexity from very simple to quite elaborate. These designs were shown for five seconds each to pupils in the seventh and eighth grades, and the pupils were asked to rate each for "interestingness." A score for curiosity was derived for each pupil from the extent to which the designs were rated as interesting. A fascinating finding of this study was that this score correlated significantly with the teacher's ratings of the pupils on a curiosity scale. The study suggests that there is such a trait as general curiosity and that it can be measured through behavior in particular situations. The measure of curiosity correlated to a small and inconsistent extent with school grades. Why the highest correlation with school grades should have been in the area of spelling is something of a mystery. Could it be that the pupil who learns to spell is one who has the curiosity to look words up in the dictionary? Such speculation is fun but not very useful. More understandable are the correlations between measured curiosity and industrial arts grades and English composition. Whatever is measured by intelligence tests is a much more significant correlate of school achievement than is a measure of curiosity. This is not surprising. The mastery of most school subjects is not dependent on the pupil's curiosity, for the materials are brought to him and he does not have to seek them out. Whatever curiosity he has may actually sidetrack him from the tasks he is required to do in order to achieve the set objectives.

Finally, in accordance with expectation, Penney (1965) found a negative relationship between a measure of curiosity and the score on the Castaneda children's version of the Manifest Anxiety Scale. This fits well with what might be expected. The children filled with curiosity might be expected to display more approach behavior when confronted with the new and unusual. Anxiety would function as an inhibitor of approach behavior.

There appear to be interesting connections between exploratory behavior and the behavior involved in esthetic experience. Berlyne (1972) has long been interested in this connection and has studied the relationship between visual exploration and the physical properties of abstract designs. People explore visually those diagrams that have high relationships to "interestingness," which in turn is related to both the complexity of the design and its pleasingness. But pleasingness and complexity are also related to the esthetic properties of a design. Works of art would appear to be motivating to visual exploration.

A rather obvious application of the work on curiosity is to arouse curiosity before materials are studied. Bull and Dizney (1973) attempted to do this by using a set of suitable questions before materials were studied by students. The materials were technical articles from the fields of sociology and psychology. The use of such questions did produce improved learning. The study used an appropriate control group exposed to questions that were judged to be not curiosity-arousing.

Finally, comment must be made on a familiar way of energizing behavior in the direction of an object. Common knowledge tells us that the way to make an object attractive is to forbid people to approach it. Allen and Allen (1974) experimented with this phenomenon with fourth-graders. These research workers asked the children to rank toys in terms of attractiveness. Later, the children were told that they could not play with one of the toys and, still later, the children were asked to rank the toys again for attractiveness. The forbidden toy came out higher on the list on the second ranking. Allen and Allen suggest that children learn the association between the attractiveness of an object and it being forbidden as a part of their training in socialization. Other explanations are possible. Reactance theory proposes that any restraint on the freedom of an individual enhances the desire to engage in activities in the area in which freedom is restricted (Wicklund, 1974).

THE SELF-CONCEPT AND THE ENERGIZING OF BEHAVIOR

While some psychologists have been investigating achievement motivation, others have been following a closely allied line of research, which uses a different language for describing findings. The latter program of research is conducted by those engaged in exploring what has been termed the *self-concept*. The latter term is defined in many different ways, which often involve complicated and lengthy definitions (see Diggory, 1966). A simple form of definition is implied in most research undertaken by psychologists interested in the area, for these investigations generally use measures of the self-concept derived from the kinds of statements that the individual makes about himself. A person would be described as having a positive self-concept if he makes positive statements about himself, about what he can accomplish, about the extent to which he regards himself as a successful person, and about his expectations of being able to handle the future. A negative self-concept is indicated when a person makes statements about himself that are derogatory, that describe his performance as inadequate, and that reflect a withdrawal from challenges.

Psychologists have long believed that the self-concept is acquired through the child's listening to the statements that the adults make about him. A child hears his mother say day-in and day-out, "You're a bad little boy." The child is believed after some time to begin to make the statement about himself and to say to himself, "I'm a bad little boy." Thomas et al. (1969), in reviewing the history of the term *self-concept*, point out that psychologists and sociologists have also taken the position that the self-concept is derived in childhood not from statements of *any* adult, but from the statements of what are referred to as *significant adults*. These are adults who play a crucial role in the life of the child, such as those who provide for all of his physical needs during infancy. The evaluations of the child made by the "significant others" are listened to by the child and become his own self-evaluations.

The belief has been widely held that a positive self-concept has an energizing effect on behavior and results in a vigorous pursuit of goals that the individual believes are worthwhile. This concept is very much like the idea that a person with a high level of achievement motivation is energized by tasks that challenge him. The two concepts are closely related even though they are not quite parallel. The implication has been that a positive self-concept has energizing properties and that successful achievement is partly a result of a positive self-concept. The difficulty with this point of view is that although measures of self-concept are correlated with achievement, there is the possibility that a good positive self-concept is a product of high achievement, and not that a positive self-concept *produces* high achievement. A high level of achievement might just as plausibly produce a strongly positive self-concept as a strongly positive self-concept might lead to high achievement. Which way the relationship works is a matter that can be settled only by experimentation, but experimental attempts to change the self-concept are difficult to undertake. One such study was undertaken by Thomas et al. (1969).

In this study a systematic attempt was made to change the self-concepts of ninth-grade children by means of an intervention through their parents. The procedure involved arranging meetings between the research staff and the parents of a group of low achievers. The object of the meetings was to help the parents understand what they could do to help their children improve their schoolwork. Emphasis was placed on helping each pupil to develop a more positive concept of what he could accomplish in a school setting and to develop a recognition of the pupil's responsibility for his own accomplishments. An explanation was given of the effect of a person's self-concept on what he could accomplish. Quite specific advice was given on how the parents could help the pupil in this respect. Finally, individual conferences were held with the parents to help them work out particular problems. Two control groups were used. In one control group, called the placebo group, the parents were also invited to participate in conferences, but these were focused on the general problems faced by the adolescent. A second control group of pupils involved no parent intervention.

The attempts to work with the parents took place in November, December, and January. Measures were made on the pupils before the work of influencing the parents began in November, then again in the following June, and finally in the following January. The findings were that the group of pupils in whom an effort was made through the parents to change the self-concept showed a much more substantial improvement in grade-point average than either one of the control groups. The members of the control groups also showed an improvement, which was due to an unavoidable artifact of the experimental design. The data also provided some additional information of even greater significance.

One important fact that emerges is that the main change in the self-concept occurred during the period of November to June, but the main change in *achievement* occurred in the subsequent period of June to January. The data suggest that the change in the self-concept of the pupil had to occur first before any change could take place in his achievement. This study fits well with the results of other studies suggesting that the individual's expectations of how he will perform on a particular task are more important than his general level of optimism about how he will perform in general. A pupil's expectation of how he will succeed in mathematics seems to be much more significant for mathematics achievement than his vague expectations of how he will succeed in general.

The Thomas et al. study provides strong evidence that the self-concept does influence achievement and that parents can influence the achievement of their children through influencing the self-concept of the children. Such an influence involves changing their expectation of success in a positive direction.

The findings are not entirely consistent with what has been said about achievement motivation. The reader will recall that the person characterized by fear of failure may be one showing high achievement motivation. Yet a person who has high fear of failure would be described as a person having a negative or poor self-concept and, in terms of self-concept theory, might be expected to be poorly motivated. There is an inconsistency here that further research will have to resolve.

Although the ideal approach to the study of the relationship of the self-concept and achievement is to change the self-concept, and then to show whether there is or is not a corresponding change in achievement, another approach is also possible. The alternative is to hold constant conditions related to having a good or poor self-concept and then to relate a measure of self-concept to achievement. Cole (1974) followed the latter approach in his study of a group of third-graders who were highly homogeneous in intelligence, with IQs ranging from 93 to 103. He still found a relationship between the measure of self-concept and achievement as measured by the Metropolitan Achievement Test. It hardly seems likely that differences in achievement in such children could produce differences in self-concept. Much more likely is the possibility that each child sets for himself a level of achievement that he hopes to attain, and that level is set in terms of whether he thinks of himself as a scholar, a "regular guy," a bored participant, or whatever else.

COGNITIVE ASPECTS OF MOTIVATION

Over the last few decades psychology has become progressively more cognitively oriented, that is, oriented toward problems of knowledge, knowing, and the storage and utilization of information. Most areas in psychology have shown the impact of that trend, including the psychology of motivation. Dember (1974) and Weiner (1974) have long observed this trend and described it. They point out that the psychology of motivation was traditionally tied to simple biological concepts, such as that of physiological drive, but this concept was much too narrow to encompass numerous aspects of the energizing of behavior. The concept of motivation was then broadened by Neal Miller, who took the position that a drive was simply some strong stimulus that energized behavior, and the stronger the stimulus, the stronger its energizing properties. Dember points out that by giving motivation a sensory definition, Miller moved the concept of motivation to where it would be tied to human intellectual functions. Miller tied the motivating strength of a stimulus to its intensity, which seemed to provide a basis for its measurement. Within limits such a concept has applicability. A big explosion a block away is more likely to make us jump out of bed than the sound of a popgun, but there are obvious limitations to this approach. Words quietly said, such as "The dam has broken, run for your life," are far more energizing than a public address system that shouts "Vote for Jones." Nevertheless, the total quantity of sensory input is related to the degree to which the arousal system in the brain activates the cerebral cortex. But motivation is complex, and there is far more to it than simple quantity of stimulation.

The work on novelty and curiosity has added another chapter to the concept of motivation as a cognitive function. High novelty calls for concentrated attention and the direction of the energy of the organism toward the task of discovering the nature of the novel object that has appeared in the perceptual field. In this way, motivation became tied to the cognitive function of information processing, but it was only a beginning.

A next major step in the development of motivation as a cognitive concept came in the late 1940s and 1950s from the observations of Harlow and his staff on the animals in the Wisconsin Primate Laboratory. These workers provided dramatic evidence that primates would solve problems in almost endless succession just for the sake of solving the problems. Indeed, they worked best without any extrinsic incentive, such as the offering of food might have on a hungry animal. Later research showed that the use of such incentives had the ultimate effect of depressing the intrinsic motivation inherent in the task. Perhaps, from the layman's point of view the research provided support for what every human being knows, namely, that problem solving is fun as an end in itself. Psychologists had somehow failed to recognize the obvious, that problem solving is fun even for subhuman primates and that it requires no system of rewards or tokens to maintain it. Of course, generations of teachers had failed also to recognize this fundamental fact about human nature, depriving children the opportunity and fun of solving problems by providing them with ready-made solutions, which they turned away from in boredom.

A further development of cognitive theory of motivation appears in the works of Piaget, who takes the position that the primary energizing source in the developing child is the motive to develop. Piaget elaborates on this in his theory of equilibration. As the child develops, solutions to problems that the child has previously given with assurance are suddenly viewed by the child with uneasiness and lack of satisfaction. At that stage the child begins to look for new and adequate solutions to these same problems. When he finds a better solution he regains his equilibrium and shows satisfaction in what he has done. He then remains satisfied for a time, but, after a time, begins to feel dissatisfaction with his new solution. Thus there is an alternation of equilibrium and disequilibrium, until the child reaches the mature stage of reflective logical thought. Certainly, in transitional stages, children do make extraordinary efforts to discover new solutions to problems and they are dissatisfied with the manner in which they have solved problems in the past. In some ways, this concept of motivation has similarities to homeostatic theories. The difference lies in the fact that with homeostatic theories, when balance is restored the individual returns to his normal nonenergized state. Thus the hungry person is restless, and the ingestion of food restores the body chemistry to a normal state. In the Piaget-type of equilibration theory, the restoration of equilibrium results in establishing a balance of behavior at a higher level. The 6-year-old child who is given a set of sticks of varying lengths may be dissatisfied with the fact that the arrangement he makes doesn't really arrange them in order, as he was asked to do. He puzzles over what he had done, tries this arrangement and that, and then, after much effort, manages to arrange the sticks in order of size. He is then delighted with his new solution, which will remain with him for the rest of his life.

Related to this view of motivation is the finding of Harter (1974) that the gratification that children derive from solving a problem is positively correlated with its difficulty. The harder problems solved by the children were solved with more smiling, and a higher rating for pleasure, than were the simpler problems. When the more difficult problems were given again to the same children, there was a sharp decline in the gratification manifested by the children on solving them. The study implies that cognitive motivation is at a maximum when the individual is near the limit to what he can accomplish.

Up to this point, cognitive theory of motivation is on an experimental footing. Of course, not all the facts fit the theory but few psychological theories are supported by all the facts. As cognitive theory of motivation develops it will have to come to grips with the fact that ideas in the human brain may have enormous energizing capability. Dember points this out, commenting on the fact that the fanatic believer in some ideology may devote enormous amounts of energy to the task of bringing the ideology to others. Indeed, the ideology may dominate all of the individual's behavior. The directionality of thought may show tremendous persistence and even have a capability of overriding other aspects of personality. A revolutionary who may show much kindness to his children and friends may be capable of obliterating his political enemies with complete ruthlessness. His ideological position overrides any other responses he might have. Dember talks about ideational addiction to describe the individual captured by his own ideas and driven by them.

A particularly interesting idea, related to cognitive theory of motivation, has been introduced by Ruth Harring (personal communication) as a result of her observations on fourth- and fifth-grade children. She has noted that the intellectual life of each child tends to be dominated by a theme that may persist for months, or occasionally for years. For example, a child may become fascinated by the idea of flight and then begin to explore how all kinds of objects fly. The child may build gliders, work on balloons, study the flight of birds, visit the airport and watch airplanes, try to make objects stay suspended in the air by using a forced draft of wind produced by an electric fan, build parachutes, and so forth. The child's reading may become focused on flight, and he may begin to collect data on the flight of birds, planes, and other flying objects, thereby mastering some aspect of mathematics. The idea the child is exploring may have extraordinary driving power and may energize his entire intellectual development for a period. Harring also points out that the driving power of the idea ultimately exhausts itself, and the child then turns to some new idea that becomes the energizing force in his intellectual life. Harring views the development of themes as a characteristic of normal intellectual development and a means by which a child organizes his explorations of his environment.

LOCUS OF CONTROL AND MOTIVATION

Rotter (1966) introduced the concept that behavior is influenced by whether the individual perceives himself to be in control of the reinforcements provided by the environment or whether they are outside of his control. This has become known as the problem of *locus of control*. The problem is so stated that it avoids the philosophical issue of whether the individual does or does not have actual control of his behavior. A person may state that he believes he has control of his behavior, but this does not mean that he actually has control. Conversely, a person may believe that he is a victim of the whims of fortune, but this belief has little to do with whether he does or does not have control. Since Rotter published his original paper, a considerable amount of research has been undertaken on the effects of beliefs concerning locus of control on behavior.

Messer (1972) has reviewed some of the studies showing that belief in internal control is related to early independence training and to intellectual striving and achievement. The variable seems to share some common properties with achievement motivation. In Messer's own study, he investigated the relation of locus of control to achievement. He found that fourth-grade children who believed that their academic performance was contingent on their own effort had higher grades and higher achievement scores than those who saw themselves as externally controlled. High grades were most likely to be obtained from boys who took credit for their achievement and from girls who blamed themselves for their failures.

One might expect that an impoverished environment might have an effect on where children perceived to be the locus of control. One would expect children raised in poverty to feel that the course of life was outside of their control, but the data do not confirm this. DuCette (1972) found little difference in children's beliefs about the locus of control when he compared children in a high school serving an impoverished area with children from a suburban high school. The lack of difference is sufficiently surprising to require further study. DuCette and some earlier investigators have also found that those who believe themselves to be in control have a much more realistic view of their environment than those who believe that controls are external. Those who believe that they are in control of the situation are also motivated to a greater extent by frustration (Libb and Serum, 1974).

Related to the issue of locus of control is the matter of how the teacher functions in building in pupils either the belief that they are in control of themselves or the belief that the teacher is in control. A study by Chambers (1973) is of particular interest in this connection. He conducted a nationwide study to investigate the relationship between the facilitation of creativity in students and the behavior of college teachers. The students were doctoral students and believed that the college teachers who had had the greatest facilitating effect on their creativity were those who treated students as individuals and encouraged students to be independent. The teacher served as a model rather than a source of direction and spent considerable time with the student outside of class. The college teachers who most discouraged creativity were described as those who discouraged students, were insecure, emphasized rote learning, were dogmatic and rigid, and had narrow interests.

Notz (1975) has made an additional contribution to this area by summarizing research that compares the effect of internal incentives and motivations with external sources of motivation. He finds that the use of motivation outside the individual is likely to reduce internal motivation. Thus the person who is paid to do a task may find the task progressively more boring, but if he undertakes the same task for reasons of internal motivation, the task becomes progressively more interesting. Thus work is commonly viewed as dull as a result of the fact that the main incentive is external in the form of a pay check. Play is considered interesting because it is undertaken for reasons internal to the individual and becomes progressively more interesting as it is pursued. The latter situations are also complicated by the fact that there is often more freedom of choice in play than in work, but the experimental studies have avoided this complication.

SUMMARY

1. Much of the early experimental research undertaken on motivation was pursued in a biological tradition and with the manipulation of hunger and thirst as the main means of varying motivation. Deprivation produces an increase in activity, unless the animal is in an environment free from stray sounds and free from visual stimulation. The data suggest that deprivation produces an increase in responsiveness to stimuli.

2. In such animal experiments, the incentive provided by food or water in the goal box adds to the drive state produced through deprivation. This is evident from the fact that larger amounts of food and water may produce more vigorous behavior in running the maze.

3. Even what appear to be simple unlearned drives become at an early age interwoven with learned elements, as is shown by the fact that animals, including human beings, may develop cravings for diets and drugs that are harmful to them. Indeed, the behavior of the adult toward food is much more like that of an addict than like that of a creature consuming naturally the material that is necessary to restore homeostatic balance.

4. Although animals can be trained to discriminate between hunger and thirst, the task is difficult for rats and other species to achieve. This suggests that drive states should generally be regarded as activated states rather than as states that give direction to behavior. Human beings may well be more discriminating in this respect and the common experiences of living may provide them with the basis for discriminating the experiences associated with different drive sources.

5. Basic research with animals has provided little information about motivation that has significant implications for the control of motivation in educational situations. Such animal research has used the classification of drives into those that are native to the organism and those that are learned. The difficulty in using this classification scheme is that many drive states cannot be clearly classified in the one or the other category. Indeed, one does not know, at this time, which should be considered as mainly innate, even though there may be some learned component.

6. As motivation is increased, performance tends to show a corresponding increment in vigor until a maximum is reached. Further increments in motivation produce a decline in performance. The level of motivation that produces optimum performance varies with the nature of the task. With complex tasks, the optimum level of motivation is lower than with simple tasks. This is known as the Yerkes–Dodson law.

7. Much research related to motivation has focused on what has been called a demand for a goal object. However, research with human subjects indicates that not all individuals respond equally to an anticipated reward well in the future. Those who do respond well to delayed rewards are relatively high on measures of future orientation, maturity, level of aspiration, and other characteristics. Children can learn to respond to delayed gratification.

8. A condition related to motivation that has potential applications to teaching

is the condition known as frustrative nonreward. In this condition an expected reward is not delivered and the result is an increased vigor or response. It is a strong and well-established response in subhuman animals, which is still quite detectable in human behavior. Frustrative nonreward suggests that the withholding of rewards may be sometimes as important as the giving of a reward.

9. An important and very old concept in the area of motivation is that of a generalized drive. In the case of human motivation, one component of such a drive has been considered to be anxiety. Studies involving relationships between anxiety and performance have produced relationships that are similar to those described by the Yerkes–Dodson law.

10. Studies of anxiety as a drive have been extended to children. There are certainly very marked differences between high-anxiety and low-anxiety pupils. The general finding seems to stand up that anxiety in children interferes with work on problems that are difficult for the particular child, but may enhance his capability of undertaking problems that are familiar to him. The distinction is also now made between state anxiety and trait anxiety.

11. A human motive on which research has made some progress is that of achievement motivation or achievement need. The concept was originally derived from a theory of motivation developed by H. A. Murray, in which achievement need was one of the learned motives in the system. According to this system, needs are aroused by some stimulus related to its satisfaction. In the case of achievement need, the stimulus is a situation that provides the individual with an opportunity to achieve some standard of excellence. Just wanting to complete a task does not reflect achievement need. To reflect this need, the person must be striving to achieve some standard of excellence that he has set for himself.

12. Achievement need is measured most readily at this time through projective tests in which the person taking the test is shown a picture, selected because it has potential for arousing achievement need, and is asked to tell a story about what led up to the scene depicted, what is happening, and what is going to happen. The stories can then be scored for the extent to which they reflect achievement need.

13. Achievement motivation manifests itself in two forms. One is hope of success, and the other is fear of failure. Many individuals taking a projective test show both hope of success and fear of failure, although their behavior may show a predominance of the one or a predominance of the other. A tendency for behavior to be dominated by the one or the other influences the kind of risks that are taken. The fear-of-failure-oriented person tends to take risks that are very high or very low. If he fails at the high-risk task, he can blame the task, but if he succeeds, it is very much to his credit. The success-oriented person is, perhaps, more realistic in his choice in that he selects tasks that are both a challenge to him and on which he can succeed. Thus achievement need has a subtle relationship to what Kurt Lewin referred to as level of aspiration.

14. Straightforward relationships between measures of achievement need and performance in academic studies are not to be expected, for the student may be

motivated to do well in school for many reasons other than a need to achieve a standard of excellence. Relationships do appear between performances on tasks that the student can view as a challenge and achievement-need measures.

15. Although achievement need is discussed as though it were an acquired need, components of it may be native. The need to do it oneself may well be an inborn disposition, on the basis of which achievement need may grow. Achievement need, as it is defined here, is first detected about age 5. It is more characteristic of boys than of girls and is particularly evident in the middle class. The home conditions most likely to foster its developments are those that provide the child with independence and freedom, yet that demand that independence and freedom be enjoyed with responsibility. Independence alone is not sufficient but must be accompanied by a demand on the part of the parents that the child master skills related to his independence. Parent-child relationships are crucial for the development of achievement motivation. The religious affiliation of the parents also influences the extent to which the child develops achievement motivation.

16. Achievement need has two distinct components, *fear of failure* and *expectation of success*. Individuals high on one of these components behave somewhat differently from those higher on the other component. The difference is very apparent in risk-taking situations.

17. None of the other attempts to measure motives within the framework provided by Murray has been as successful as that involving achievement need, but some success has accompanied attempts to measure affiliation need and approval need.

18. The infant appears to be a system highly motivated to explore the environment and construct a representation of the world around him. Very early in life attention comes to be aroused by novel objects, that is, objects that have not been encountered before. In all primates, including human beings, the presence of the mother is important in giving the infant security in his explorations. Children in poor environments may be given little support for the explorations and may show little exploratory behavior. Curiosity has been measured in school children and been shown to bear little relationship to school achievement. Indeed, curiosity hardly seems to be a desirable trait from the point of view of many teachers. The arousal of curiosity about material to be studied appears to enhance learning.

19. A positive self-concept appears to have an energizing effect on behavior.

20. Cognitive aspects of motivation have recently been emphasized. Clearly, ideas can have energizing effects. Individuals can be inspired to act by great ideas and great causes. Sincere political workers are often motivated by what they see as important ideas. Children may be energized by the themes they pursue.

Chapter 11

All complex living animals show some capacity for responding adaptively to new situations by applying what they have learned previously in different situations. An organism achieves maximum efficiency as a learner to the extent that what is learned can be applied to the solution of a wide range of problems. Learning in schools would be extremely ineff.cient if children learned only to solve specific problems and were not able to apply their knowledge to the solution of a wide range of new problems. The facilitation of learning in new situations by previous learning is referred to as transfer of training. In learning a new skill, such as playing the violin, what is learned at each lesson should facilitate learning at the next lesson, and the mastery of the skill should involve an accumulation of this kind of transfer.

There may be positive transfer of training in another sense. The learning of a new skill may facilitate the retention of another previously acquired skill. For example, one may learn to skate on ice and then not skate for some years, after which one may learn roller skating. The acquisition of skill in roller skating may facilitate the retention of the related skill of skating on ice. Thus the learning of one skill may facilitate the retention of previously acquired skills and it may also facilitate the acquisition of new skills.

When the effect of transfer is on subsequent learning, the term *proaction* is often applied or one refers to *proactive transfer*. When the effect of transfer is to enhance or depress the retention of some previous learning, there is said to be *retroactive transfer*. Most of the research on transfer has to do with proactive effects. Indeed, relatively little is known about retroactive effects, though some of the research related to this problem is reviewed in the chapter on memory, in which the retroactive effect was stated to represent a major cause of forgetting.

The acquisition of a skill may sometimes have a negative effect on the retention of previously learned skills or the acquisition of new skills. I once gave French lessons to a child who had had two years of Spanish in school. A major difficulty in teaching this child French was that he persisted in reading French words with a pronunciation appropriate to Spanish. This is a case of negative transfer of training. One should note that some aspects of the skills involved in learning French transfer positively to the learning of Spanish, and that negative transfer is confined mainly to the matter of pronunciation.

The learning of a skill may also interfere with the retention of a previously acquired skill. A person who has a superficial knowledge of German spends a year in Holland, where he acquires a fluent speaking knowledge of Dutch. At the end of the year he is likely to find that when he tries to speak German, he imposes on it Dutch words and Dutch grammatical structure. The learning of Dutch has disrupted his memory of German.

Transfer is not limited to intellectual reponses alone; many emotional responses demonstrate transfer phenomena. One transferable type of response is the anxiety response. A child who is made highly anxious by the treatment accorded him by a teacher may show similar anxiety responses in the presence of other teachers. The anxiety may then spread to the entire school situation and may even transfer to the doing of homework and to all activities related to the school.

During the acquisition of a skill, some events occur that are not learning phenomena as such, but that may affect the acquisition of subsequent skills. For example, sometimes fatigue may depress the further acquisition of learning; in such a case, one would not speak of negative transfer.

Another phenomenon that resembles transfer but is not a true learning phenomenon is the " warm-up period." When a person begins a new activity, he does not function at maximum eff.ciency until some time has elapsed; this may be a matter of seconds or minutes, depending on the activity. In many activities this is a recognized phenomenon. The pitcher always goes through a warm-up workout before he is sent to the mound. The musician, even when practicing in his own home, goes through a warm-up activity such as playing scales before he undertakes more complicated exercises. The concert artist may practice behind the scenes right up to the minute of going on to the platform. The lecturer may spend some time right before his lecture reviewing ideas in his mind before he starts speaking, and he may do this even when he is to give a lecture he has given many times before. These practices have been arrived at through practical experience with the daily problems of living.

To a limited extent, one may expect that one activity may serve as a warm-up for a related activity, and there is some evidence that this is so. There also appear to be individual differences n the length of the warm-up period necessary. Some persons require little; others require an extended period. This characteristic of behavior has some implications for the planning and scheduling of the periods in the school; but not enough is known about it to be able to predict with any confidence that one arrangement of classes is better than another. Individual differences suggest that no one schedule can be arranged that will be effective for all children. Here, as elsewhere, mass education requires some compromises; and even then some children may be placed on schedules that are not the best for them.

STIMULUS GENERALIZATION, RESPONSE GENERALIZATION, AND TRANSPOSITION—SIMPLE CASES OF TRANSFER

Stimulus Generalization

Stimulus generalization was first demonstrated by Pavlov in experiments with dogs, but it has also been demonstrated with human subjects of all ages. Pavlov showed that when a dog had been trained to raise its foot to the sound of a particular note, such as middle C, the animal would almost certainly make the same response to the sound of other notes as much as an octave up and down the scale. The dog is demonstrating stimulus generalization, because it is responding to a range of stimuli other than the specific stimulus to which it was trained.

The range of stimuli to which the dog will respond by raising its foot can be reduced by providing the animal with discrimination learning training. If the animal is rewarded only when it responds to middle C and is not rewarded when it responds to other notes, it will slowly cease to respond to the other notes.

The dog in the Pavlovian experiment is demonstrating a simple form of transfer of training. It is trained to respond to a particular note, but later shows a capability of making the same response to a range of notes. What appears to be learned, in the first place, is a response to a class of notes, even though only a single note is used in training.

Much the same is true of the child who is learning to talk. He learns to call his own dog a "dog" and will not only call all other neighborhood dogs "dogs," but will use the same word to designate cats and perhaps even horses, cows, goats, and other animals. Here again generalization has occurred, and a range of stimuli are capable of eliciting the one response "dog." Here also, as in all generalization phenomena, the generalization may be limited. The child may not respond to very large animals, such as elephants, nor to very small ones, such as mice, with the word *dog*.

Objects most similar to that to which the response has been learned are more likely to elicit the response than those that are very different. A child who has learned the appropriate verbal response to the printed word *boy* may make the same response to words that have similarity of form, such as *toy*, but will not so respond to a word that is greatly different in shape and contour, such as *house*.

The concept of stimulus generalization is closely related to the concept of *equivalent stimuli*. Stimuli are said to be equivalent for an organism if they generate a similar response. In a young child all moving and living creatures encountered may arouse the response "cat." The creatures represent equivalent stimuli for him, because he has not learned to discriminate one from the other. This child's lack of discrimination is a social disadvantage in attempting to tell others about his experiences. In other situations, advantage may be gained by responding to a set of stimuli as if they were equivalent. For the child to show an avoidance response to all moving objects on the street, regardless of their shape and size, even has survival value. Learning when to generalize and when not to generalize is an important part of education.

Without stimulus generalization, the living creature would learn to respond only to the specific situations in which learning occurred. If the child learned to say " boy " when the printed word *boy* was written on the blackboard, without stimulus generalization he would not be able to make the same response if the word were written smaller or in different type. Stimulus generalization permits the learner to respond to a wide range of stimuli as though they were all the same. Thus what is learned in one situation can be applied in other situations even though they may differ.

In order that a child may learn to respond by saying " boy " only to the printed word *boy*, it is necessary that he learns to discriminate the word *boy* from other words. In this period of discrimination learning, if it is well planned, the child will first learn to make easy discriminations among words and will be exposed to successively harder discriminations. Some generalization will still occur, particularly under circumstances in which the stimulus is exposed only briefly—for example, the errors the proofreader lets by. In such cases, he responds by the correct word even though the incorrect one is printed. Years of experience in proofreading will reduce this error of stimulus generalization, but probably never to the point where it does not occur at all.

Mednick and Freedman (1960) have pointed out that the concept of stimulus generalization is an experimentally demonstrated phenomenon and one does not know, as yet, how far it can be used as a basis for understanding various aspects of behavior. A child's tendency to use a new word in a broad range of situations and not to restrict its use to the limited situation to which it can be appropriately applied may be considered to be an illustration of stimulus generalization, but what other phenomena illustrate stimulus generalization is not always entirely clear. Mednick and Freedman point out that the concept has been used to account for phenomena in psychotherapy, the behavior of brain-damaged children, the behavior of schizophrenics, psychoanalytic displacement, and numerous other events in the universe of psychology. The legitimacy of using the concept for such a variety of purposes is quite questionable.

The phenomenon of stimulus generalization is not at all a precise one, for one cannot tell just when it will take place and when it will not. If one's dog is mistreated by a neighbor whom the dog learns to avoid, will the dog generalize its avoidance response to all other strangers, to others who wear the same blue jeans, to others of similar size, to others who have the same voice, or to others who live in the same house as the neighbor, and so forth? There is no way of identifying the characteristics of the stimulus producing an avoidance response that will be reacted to in other situations. Stimulus generalization can be used to explain generalization of a response after the generalization has occurred, but cannot be used to predict when generalization will occur. A concept that explains events after they have happened, but cannot be used to predict events, is not a scientific concept.

Semantic Generalization

The early work on stimulus generalization involved quite simple stimuli. Pavlov conditioned dogs to the sound of a tuning fork of a particular pitch and determined the generalization to tones of other pitch. Other studies were conducted in other laboratories to the intensity of sound, to the size of a simple figure such as a square or a circle, and other quite uncomplicated dimensions. Later studies of generalization involved much more elaborate stimuli. An area of particular significance to human learning that has been explored through the study of stimulus generalization is that known as *semantic generalization*. The essence of semantic generalization is that a response conditioned to a particular word will generalize to words similar in meaning and, to a lesser extent, to words similar in sound. The initial work in this area was a demonstration by a Russian, Ivanov Smolensky, that a human subject conditioned to make a particular response in the presence of an object would make the same response when confronted with the word representing the object. Later, near to midcentury, Gregory Razran conducted a series of experiments in which subjects were conditioned to respond to particular words, following which the generalization to other words was studied. In most of the Razran experiments the response conditioned was that of salivation. In one early study subjects were exposed to the words *style, urn, freeze*, and *surf* while eating or chewing gum. Later, the salivary responses of the subjects were measured on exposure to other words, with interesting findings. Razran came up with the discovery that, for example, the conditioned response to the word *urn* generalized well to the word *vase* but not to the same extent to the similar sounding word *earn*. Razran concluded that subjects became conditioned more to the meaning of a word than to its visual or auditory form. There was some generalization to similar sounding and similar appearing words, but this effect was weak compared with the generalization to words similar in meaning.

A series of similar studies have been conducted over the years with similar findings. Despite the fact that many of these studies have serious experimental flaws, nobody has yet seriously disputed the general findings of Razran. Feather (1965), who reviewed the studies up to the time of his article, suggests that generalization may, perhaps, be attributed to the tendency for individuals to classify and categorize all inputs. One may take this argument one step further and propose that inputs are categorized prior to storage in memory and that perhaps the psychological location of a piece of stored information depends on how it is classified in the first place. On hearing a word such as *urn*, one may classify it as belonging in the vase class, and one might also classify it in the class of things to do with funerals. Once classified, then it would have the same response-arousing features of all other words in that class.

Gradient of Generalization

If a response has been established to a stimulus S_1, the response will occur with varying degrees of strength to stimuli S_2, S_3, S_4, and so forth, which resemble S_1 in varying degrees. The greater the degree to which the new stimulus resembles S_1, the greater is the likelihood that the response will occur or that it will occur in full strength. The relationship between the response R and the stimulus S, as S is varied from the original stimulus with which learning took place, is known as the *gradient of generalization*.

The phenomenon of the gradient of generalization was well illustrated in Pavlov's original work with salivation in dogs. A dog trained to salivate at the sound of a tone pitched at 440 vibrations per second will also salivate to a sound one octave lower (220 vibrations per second), but it will salivate to a lesser degree. Drop the pitch of the sound still lower and the dog will salivate even less. The closer the note is to the original note, the more the amount of salivation approximates that produced by the original note.

The gradient of generalization is known to occur in a great range of situations. It occurs not only in the case of positive responses that have been acquired, but also in the case of avoidance responses. A person, who through having been seriously injured by a power saw, develops a fear of power saws and withdraws from them may also show a similar but lesser withdrawal from other power tools. Although the whine of a power saw may produce in him intense fear and a need to escape from it, the noise of a power drill may merely give him the feeling that he does not want to touch the device. The drill induces an avoidance response, but it is milder than that induced by the saw.

Response Generalization

Just as a living creature is capable of responding with the same response to a range of stimuli as though they were the same, so, too, does a single stimulus have the capacity of evoking a range of responses. The fact that a stimulus may evoke not only the response with which it has been characteristically associated, but other related responses as well, is referred to as *response generalization*. This phenomenon accounts for at least some of the variability of behavior commonly observed. The note of middle C, as printed on a sheet of music, generally evokes in the piano player the response that produces on the piano the tone of middle C, but sometimes it evokes a related response, as when the notes B or D are struck instead. Another familiar example is often seen when a person encounters an old friend he has not seen for years. The friend happens to be Mr. East, but all the person can think of are such related terms as Mr. West, Mr. Coast, Mr. Orient, and so forth. The stimulus, namely, the friend, was able to evoke a range of related responses, but for some unknown reason the correct response was inhibited.

The capacity for a stimulus to evoke a range of answers is an important phenomenon that may account for some transfer of training that takes place.

When the typical response to a stimulus is blocked and the organism generally produces another response, this alternative response may also be blocked. If this happens, the organism may cease to respond, or a third response may be produced. A person writing down a telephone number may begin to write it with his pen; when the pen does not work he picks up another from the table; when the new pen does not work, he borrows a pencil. The responses thus emerge in a certain order that is sometimes referred to as the *response hierarchy*, a term originally used to describe the ordering of the clergy within a church from the highest official to the lowliest. Responses in relation to any particular stimulus can be regarded as being ordered from those most likely to occur to those least likely.

Stimulus Generalization and Transposition: Unlearned Transfer Effects

Another special case of transfer of great interest is found in what are known as *transposition phenomena*. The demonstration of this transfer phenomenon takes many forms, but in the case of young children, a common form of the demonstration is as follows:

The subject of the experiment is confronted with two upside-down dishes; one is two inches in diameter, and the other is three inches. What has to be learned is that some desired object, food or a trinket, is under the larger three-inch dish. After learning this, the task is changed so that it now involves a three-inch and a four-inch dish, and the desired object is still under the larger of the two dishes. The subject invariably goes to the larger of the two dishes. The demonstration is important in that if the subject had simply learned to respond to the three-inch dish in the first task, one would expect him to go immediately to the three-inch dish in the second task, but this is not what happens. What the subject *seems* to have learned from the first task was that the desired object was under the *larger* dish, and not that it was under the dish of a particular size. The transfer can be shown to occur in a wide range of living creatures. This transfer has long been used as a basis for arguing that animals react to relationships, in that they show a capability of learning to respond to the larger or the smaller of two objects. So long as the first task is mastered, the correct response occurs when the second task is presented, provided the experimenter has set the rule that the food is under the larger dish, or the smaller dish, and not that it is under the three-inch dish.

Transposition problems may assume various forms. Another common problem in this category is the intermediate stimulus problem. In such a problem, the subject learns that the correct choice is the middle-sized dish among three dishes that are respectively 3 inches, 4 inches, and 5 inches in diameter. Then he is presented with a new problem consisting of dishes that are 4 inches, 5 inches, and 6 inches in diameter, and chooses the 5-inch dish.

The two-stimulus problem (responding to the larger of two stimuli) is generally easier than the intermediate stimulus problem. Indeed, in the intermediate stimulus problem some learners, both animal and human, learn to respond to the particular object rather than to the middle object, and then show no transposition.

Other forms of transposition occur at more complex levels, but are so familiar that they occur daily without one's taking any notice of them. One can hear a melody played in one key and readily recognize it when it is played in another key. Without transposition, one would not be able to do this. One can recognize the plan of his city regardless of the scale to which it is drawn. One can easily identify a human figure even when it is presented in the form of a small procelain figurine. One can perform these tasks because the relations within the configuration remain the same when other characteristics are altered.

Reese (1968) has summarized hundreds of studies of transposition phenomena, but points out that no theory of transposition accounts for all the experimental results. The oldest theory was that the learner showing transposition, as in the two-stimulus problems, had learned to solve the problem by recognizing the *relationship* between the two stimuli and hence recognized the same relationship in the two new stimuli. This explanation is simple and quite plausible, but other explanations are also possible. The late Kenneth Spence was able to produce a rather complicated account of simple cases of transposition that did not require a learner to perceive relations at all. There are also some other quite simple proposed explanations that also do not assume that animals can perform the latter feat. One is that when a learner is first confronted with a three-inch and a four-inch dish and learns that a desired object is under the four-inch dish, he also learns a sense of familiarity with these two sizes of dish. When the same learner later is confronted with a 4-inch and a 5-inch dish, he is presented with a familiar dish, the 4-inch dish, and an un-familiar dish, the 5-inch dish. Now animals and human beings tend to show approach behavior toward unfamiliar objects, and for this reason the learner ap-proaches the five-inch dish rather than the familiar one. The explanation is highly plausible, but probably far from being a complete explanation of how transposition occurs. Reese takes the position that the phenomenon is probably complex and cannot be accounted for in terms of any single explanation.

Although transposition, like stimulus generalization, occurs without any identi-fiable training, numerous conditions influence the extent to which transposition is shown. The more effectively the first task is mastered, the more transposition is likely to occur on the second kind of task. Increased incentives related to the first task also seem to improve transposition, probably because they result in greater attention on the part of the learner and the better utilization of information. Prac-tice with transposition tasks also increases the amount of transposition. The fact that the phenomenon is found in subhuman animals shows that it is not dependent upon verbalization. It appears to be a quite primitive and predictable form of transfer of training.

Transfer of Training in Associative Learning

The early research on transfer of training was carried out in schoollike contexts and with schoollike materials. Such work did not yield scientific principles of the kind that researchers hoped were forthcoming, and since about midcentury there has been a tendency to study problems of transfer of training in much simpler experimental situations. One of the most productive of these situations has been that of paired-associate learning. This technique, mentioned briefly in the previous chapter, must now be discussed in greater detail in relation to transfer of training.

The general format of the paired-associated learning task requires that the subject associate the words in a set of pairs. One pair of items in the list might be the words such as *book-car*. In such a case, the task of the subject is to learn to associate the words together so that when the word *book* appears in front of him, he will either say "car" or in some way show that he knows that the correct associate is *car*. Lists commonly involve about ten pairs of words or nonsense syllables. Custom is to call the first word in a pair the *stimulus* word and the second word the *response* word. Of course, both words are, in a sense, stimuli, and the learner has to respond to each. Many different procedures are used for presenting the pairs, and the choice often depends on the purpose of the study. In what is termed the *recall procedure*, the pairs of words are presented for about two seconds for each pair. After the entire set of pairs has been run, the stimulus words alone are then presented in a scrambled order one by one and the learner must, when each is presented, either say, spell, or write the response word in each case. In the *anticipation procedure*, the stimulus word of each pair is presented first, generally for two seconds, and the learner must quickly guess the response word. Then both the stimulus word and the response word are presented together for the same length of time. On the first trial, the learner has no way of guessing the response word when he sees the stimulus word, but on the second trial and on subsequent trials he is expected to guess the response word as soon as the stimulus word appears. As soon as he has guessed, both words appear before him and he can check on the accuracy of his guess. The pairs are presented in a different order on each trial so that the learner cannot just decide to learn the list of response words, in order, and fail to associate them with the stimulus words. It is common to introduce a pause of generally about two seconds between the presentation of the stimulus word and the complete pair of words. In addition, all kinds of different time schedules have been used.

Another important variation in the paired-associate technique is that of familiarizing the learner with the separate words or syllables before beginning the learning series. If one is using nonsense syllables such as *huk*, *fov*, and *kug*, a part of the difficulty of the learner's task may be due to the fact that he has to learn the syllables themselves before he can begin to associate one syllable with the other. In order to make the task one of learning associations, and not one of learning individual syllables, a common procedure is to give the subject an initial period of familiarization training with the individual syllables. This is done by taking all the syllables and presenting them in random order. The individual is tested for his familiarity with the syllables by being given the complete list, but with one letter omitted from each. He has to fill in the missing letters. If he fails this test, he is given further familiarization training until he shows that he is thoroughly acquainted with the individual syllables. The training is then begun on learning associations between pairs.

Learning pairs of nonsense syllables may seem to be, at first sight, a long way from education, but it is not. When a child learns the names of common objects he is engaging in a task similar to the laboratory task of paired-associate learning.

When a high school student learns the vocabulary of a foreign language he learns either to associate the foreign words with objects or to associate the foreign words with the words in his native tongue. In both cases, he is engaged in paired-associate learning. Learning synonyms is also a similar task; so, too, is learning to label the parts of an animal, flower, machine, or other object. Educational activity abounds with such tasks. Maybe they are not the most crucial tasks in which the individual engages, but they are significant tasks.

The technique permits the study of a range of problems related to transfer of training. One can, for example, find the effect of transfer of training from the learning of one list to the learning of another list under a number of different conditions. One condition is the *A-B, A-C* condition. Under this condition a list is learned, and then a second list is learned in which the first word of each pair is the same as the corresponding word in the first list. One could describe the two tasks as being ones in which the stimulus element remains the same, but in which the response element is varied. Transfer under the latter condition, from the learning of the first list to the learning of the second list, can be studied. In another experiment one can study the reverse condition, in which the stimulus elements are changed but the response elements remain the same. The latter would be represented as an experiment involving *A-B* and *C-B* lists of words. In addition, there is the possibility of making two lists of words different in varying degrees. The word *house* in one list could be represented in the second list by the synonym *residence*, or by words that differed by some determined amount from the original word. Words such as *cottage, cave,* and *hat* represent a progressively more remote relationship to the original word *house*. The technique of paired-associate learning is an extraordinarily flexible one for the study of transfer of training.

The early studies in which the stimulus similarity of two tasks were varied or the response similarity was varied were summarized several decades ago by Osgood (1949), who attempted to reduce the results to the form of a graph, which has become known as the transfer surface. The graph is shown in Figure 11-1. The two dimensions of the gray plane are stimulus similarity and response similarity in the two tasks. The point in the plane farthest away from the viewer represents a case of two tasks calling for the same responses but providing different stimuli. The point nearest the viewer represents two tasks involving similar stimuli but calling for opposite responses. Paired-associate learning rarely involves learning in task 2 the opposite of the responses learned in task 1. The responses may be dissimilar, but they are not generally opposite. However, in motor-skill learning opposite responses are often introduced in task 2, as when a person learns to push a lever when a blue light goes on in task 1 and then has to pull the lever to the same stimulus in task 2.

The graph is three-dimensional. Two of the dimensions have already been discussed. One of these represents the extent to which the stimuli in two tasks resemble one another. The second dimension represents the extent to which the responses called for by the two tasks are similar or different. Thus any two tasks can be represented as a point on the gray plane shown in the figure. One such point is repre-

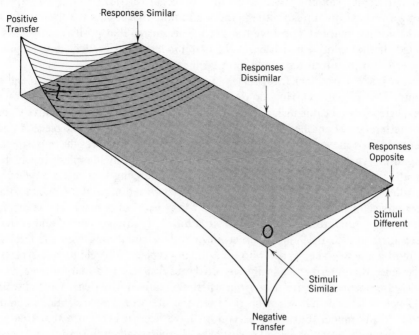

Figure 11-1. Diagram showing the relationship between response similarity and stimulus similarity of two tasks and the amount of transfer expected from one task to the other. The diagram is an attempt by Osgood (1949) to bring together the findings available at the time (*Reproduced by permission of the American Psychological Association.*)

sented by the letter X. The latter point represents two tasks that provide similar stimuli and call for similar responses. An example of two such tasks outside the field of paired-associate learning would be those of driving a small Ford with an automatic shift and driving a Cadillac also with an automatic shift. The stimuli provided by the two tasks are very similar, but not identical, and the responses are similar. As anybody knows, if one learns one of these tasks, much of what one has learned is transferred to the learning of the other task very quickly. Now if our figure correctly represents transfer, it should show that there should be positive transfer.

In order to read from the figure the amount of expected transfer, we must first note that in addition to the stimulus similarity dimension and the response similarity dimension, there is a third dimension labeled "positive transfer-negative transfer." This third dimension permits one to draw in a curved surface, indicated on the figure with ruled lines. This surface represented by the ruled lines is called the transfer surface.

Now let us go back to the two tasks represented by the point X and consider the problem of determining whether positive or negative transfer is to be expected. Draw a vertical line up from the point X and note that it cuts the transfer surface in the portion marked "positive transfer." This means that positive transfer is expected. If the point X had been in the extreme left-hand corner, an even greater degree of positive transfer would have been expected.

Now work a problem for yourself. Look at the point on the gray plane surrounded by the letter O. How do the two tasks resemble each other? What transfer is expected from the one task to the other task? There is maximum negative transfer or interference when one learns a particular set of responses on one piece of equipment and then moves to another piece of equipment that requires the opposite set of responses. An example of the latter would be learning to fly in a plane in which the throttle was opened by pulling a lever and then changing to a plane in which the throttle was opened by pushing a lever. The latter situation produces the maximum interference of the old habit with the new. Many years ago, before the controls of planes were standardized, this kind of situation fairly often occurred and accidents were attributed to the habits learned in one plane interfering with the habits required by a new plane. Those who occasionally type on a foreign-made typewriter experience this interference in the use of the backspacer and margin release keys, which are on the opposite sides from where they are in American-made machines.

Osgood claimed that when he reviewed the literature, no exceptions could be found to his model, but some exceptions have been found since that time. The figure generally provides a good means of predicting whether one can expect positive or negative transfer and how this will be changed by modifying the tasks. Although the figure is based largely on data from paired-associate learning studies, it seems to provide a sound basis for predicting transfer from one skilled performance to another in activities commonly learned in schools or pursued in daily life.

Since Osgood developed the transfer surface that carries his name, extensive additional research has been done that generally confirms his conclusions. In later reviews of the problem by Martin (1965) and by Shea (1969), the main effort of investigators has been to attempt to identify more precisely the shape of the surface, with some studies investigating the boundaries and some the interior part of the surface.

The Osgood model appears to be based partly on the mechanism of stimulus generalization that may underlie transfer phenomena. If two tasks present similar stimuli and require the same responses, what is learned in relation to the stimuli presented with one task will generalize to the related stimuli provided by the second task. Thus what is learned in relation to the one task is to some degree transferred to performance on the second task. This represents the operation of stimulus generalization. On the other hand, consider the case of two tasks that call for different responses to similar stimuli. The response learned on the first task interferes with the response to be learned on the second task, and hence negative transfer is produced.

The Osgood model takes advantage of the fact that the learning of one set of responses to stimuli can also strengthen related responses. Thus the child studying French who learns to form the association *rue-road* also learns at the same time to associate *rue-street*, even though the latter association is never deliberately practiced. The association that is directly learned, in this case the association *rue-road*. will be strengthened more than other related responses that are strengthened by generalization. Thus when a list of French words and their English equivalents have been learned, it is easy for the student to learn the same French words and the synonyms of the English words. However, the learning of the original list of French and English equivalents would not help the student to learn a new list in which the original French words had to be associated with nonsense syllables, as for example in the association *rue-tek*.

Much of the work discussed in this section has been derived from paired-associate learning. A related task, called the verbal discrimination learning task, has also been extensively used. In this task, words are also presented in pairs, but the subjects are instructed that one word is "right" in each pair and he must learn which word is right, first by guessing. This task has resulted in extensive research and much significant theorizing related to the nature of transfer (see Ekstrand et al., 1966, and Eckert and Kanak, 1974). Despite the extensiveness of the research on verbal discrimination learning, only this brief mention of it will be made here because the area of research has little practical advice to offer.

The learning and transfer that have been considered up to this point have involved quite simple processes. Such processes manifest themselves in the learning of some school subjects. For example, the learning of one foreign language may interfere with the learning of another language, but may assist the learning of still another. However, much of what is learned in school involves not the acquisition of simple habits but the acquisition of rules and strategies that have potential for subsequent problem solving, and it is the acquisition and transfer of such rules and strategies to which we must now turn.

THE TRANSFER OF RULES AND STRATEGIES

Learning How to Learn: Learning Sets

Transfer phenomena reviewed up to this point have been largely those considered to represent specific transfer. In the case of specific transfer, some quite identifiable characteristic of a situation or a response in a particular task has a subsequent effect on the acquisition or retention of another task. Not all transfer of training is of this kind, for some forms of transfer are what are called nonspecific. Postman (1969) points out that such nonspecific transfer effects do not result from simple similarities between tasks but that they involve a carry-over of skills and habits from one task to another. One of the best-explored examples of nonspecific transfer is found in the case of the phenomenon of learning how to learn.

That people can learn how to learn has long been demonstrated in experimental situations. This phenomenon has been well established in laboratory studies of the learning of meaningless nonsense syllables, chosen because such material is supposedly equally unfamiliar to all subjects. Ward (1937) showed that as subjects learned lists of syllables, their speed of learning became more and more rapid with each new list. Later, Melton and VonLackum (1941) showed that such a phenomenon could still be demonstrated after considerable amounts of practice. This learning-how-to-learn phenomenon represents a rather permanent kind of learning and is manifest for long periods after practice has stopped.

Somewhat earlier, Woodrow (1927) had demonstrated that even in such familiar classroom activities as learning poetry, facts, dates, and foreign vocabulary, pupils could be taught learning techniques that would improve their learning efficiency.

A similar phenomenon was demonstrated by Harlow (1949), who developed a program of research in this general area, first working with monkeys and later extending the studies to human subjects. In the typical Harlow type of experiment, a monkey is trained on simple discrimination problems. The monkey may be presented with two objects, a cube and a solid triangle; under one of them is a raisin. Soon, the monkey learns that the raisin is under the cube and not under the triangle. Having mastered this problem, he is presented with the next one. This time the two objects are both cubes, but one is black and one is white. He must learn a new discrimination, and it takes time to master this problem. When the monkey has mastered it, another new problem is presented, and so forth. After a long series of such problems, the monkey is able to master new problems with great speed and requires very few trials compared with the trials that were required to master the first problems. It is said that the monkey has learned how to solve problems of this kind. He has learned, so to speak, what to look for. He also has learned to switch as soon as the rules are switched. He has learned how to learn new problems. Harlow, in referring to this phenomenon, states that the monkey has acquired a *learning set* for solving the problems. A similar phenomenon has been shown to occur with young children. As problems of a particular class are solved, new problems in the same class are solved with increasing speed and facility.

A learning sequence that produces the development of a learning set generally consists of a long series of problems that are presented to the subject. It is not uncommon in this work for there to be several hundred problems in a single sequence designed to build a learning set. These problems are generally distributed over many sessions, which take place on successive days. The formation of learning sets has been demonstrated in the case of young children with materials very similar to those used in studies with subhuman primates. The same phenomenon has also been demonstrated with adults solving anagram problems in a study by Di Vesta and Walls (1968). If individuals are put through one series after another of anagram problems, they develop a great facility in looking for new rules to solve the problems and also a repertoire of rules that can be applied.

The development of learning sets would seem to involve the acquisition of at least two aspects of skill. One aspect is the learning of problem-solving strategies. Another is learning that when a strategy does not work it should be dropped quickly and another strategy should be adopted. The rules or strategies may involve verbal skills, as they do in the case of human learning, but they may be at a nonverbal level. Postman (1969) has attempted to identify through research some of the strategies involved in paired-associate learning. These strategies, which have transfer value, are very numerous and varied. Postman also points out that the learner may acquire not only rules that simplify the task of acquisition, but he may also invent ways of prompting recall. The student who has to learn a list of words, such as names of plants, may note that the first letters of the terms spell *firebol*. When this mnemonic device is memorized, it can be used to cue recall.

Internal verbalization or related thinking processes may greatly facilitate the ability to shift strategies, as is evident from a line of research involving what are called reversal shifts and nonreversal shifts.

The technique for studying reversal and nonreversal shifts, as described by Kendler and Kendler (1962), involves the presentation of pairs of stimuli such as squares and circles that may be either white or black. The subject must decide which one of the two is "right." The experimenter arranges that only one of the dimensions (either the black-white or the circle-square) is to be the relevant one in the training series, and, perhaps, he decides that a black figure is to be considered "right" and a white figure "wrong." Then, after the subject has learned to choose the black figure, the rules are changed. The change can be made in either of two ways:

1. The experimenter can reverse the rules. In this case, the white figure is now the right one and the black figure is wrong. Learning the new rule involves what is called a reversal shift.

2. The experimenter may shift to the other dimension and call the square "right" and the circle "wrong." The learning of this new rule involves a non-reversal shift. (In later studies this has been referred to as an *extradimensional* shift.)

In this technique, all of the subjects are first trained to respond to one particular characteristic, such as the black figure; that is, they learn to discriminate on the dimension of brightness. Then half of the subjects have the rule changed so as to involve a reversal shift, and the other half have the rule changed by introducing a nonreversal shift.

The Kendlers report that older children and adults perform a reversal shift more readily than a nonreversal shift, but for very young children and subhuman animals the opposite is true. This is an interesting finding, for one would expect, in terms of the Osgood transfer surface, that strong negative transfer would take place in the reversal shift situation (the stimuli are the same but the responses are opposite). The fact that with older children and adults this does not occur is inconsistent with the model and suggests that the model holds only when complex mediating responses do not occur. (The data supporting the Osgood model generally involve situations in which one does not have to assume that complex mediating responses are occurring). The Kendlers suggest that in older children and in adults a mediational mechanism is operating that permits a rapid change in response to occur in the reversal-shift situation. They propose that the mediational mechanism is a language system, for such a system distinguishes the younger children from the older.

In a later experiment, Kendler (1964) attempted to find some more direct evidence that the mediational process involved in children is verbal. She forced the children to verbalize what they were doing during the task and related this to what happened when the rules were changed. She believed that the evidence derived from the experiment supported the position that appropriate verbalization facilitated the reversal shift.

The work of the Kendlers has led to numerous related studies, but only those by Campione and his associates will be discussed here (see the review by Campione and Brown, 1974), because they have relevance to the problem of transfer. In the Campione studies simple materials are used, such as a combination of two colors and two letters of the alphabet (e.g., red T, blue T, red X, blue X). Subjects were shown pairs of these stimuli and asked to guess which one was " right." They were then given a signal indicating whether they had made a correct choice. Either the color or the form might be the relevant piece of information that they had to take into account. In addition, the problem could be presented in two different forms. In one form, the stimuli were presented simultaneously in pairs. In the other form the stimuli were presented successively in pairs, that is, first one stimulus appeared and then the other. Campione refers to the conditions of simultaneous and successive as the context factor.

An individual can learn to identify the factor that makes a stimulus a correct choice Let us suppose that the factor is color, and the individual learns that red objects are correct and blue are wrong. He can then be given a second problem, but in this second problem there are new objects, say, green and yellow Ys and Zs. In the first experiment he learned to attend to color rather than to the letters, and this tendency to attend to the color will transfer to the task in the second experiment. Attention factors seem to be quite transferable and probably are transferable in daily life. If I have had special experience in fixing carburetors, and the engine of my car stops running, I am likely to start by checking the carburetor. This is the kind of transfer that is implied.

Now let us consider what happens when the experimenter changes the form of the task in the second experiment, that is, switching either from a simultaneous presentation to a successive presentation or the reverse. When this happens, transfer of what was learned on the first task to the second task is highly disrupted. Transfer takes place best when the form of the two situations remains the same. This phenomenon is quite a familiar one in daily life. A problem about which one has knowledge but set in an unfamiliar context may appear to be baffling. One may be very familiar with house electrical circuits, but feel quite bewildered when one has to locate a bad contact in some part of the circuit of a car. Context directs one's attention toward relevant facts. Indeed, in Campione's series of experiments the effect of context overwhelms every other factor influencing transfer of training. Campione suggests that the context tells one which strategy to use. A familiar problem in a new context fails to elicit any strategy. One may have the correct strategy in one's repertoire but be unable to tap it because there is nothing in the situation that tells one how to approach the problem. The problem may even elicit incorrect strategies, as when I raise the hood of my car to solve an electrical problem, but the mass of mechanical gadgets arouse in me strategies related to mechanical problem solving that may be quite inappropriate. Finally, Campione (1973) has found these effects to occur regardless of age through the elementary-school years. Fifth-grade children are just as context-tied as are second-grade children. This suggests that when children learn useful problem solving strategies, these strategies should be used in a variety of situations, so that the strategies will not become tied to a particular context. This is not commonly done, and many children are not able to bring the strategies learned in schools to bear upon the problems encountered out of school.

Transfer in Word List Learning

Much of the research considered up to this point has involved paired-associate learning, a form of learning similar to common forms of learning in school such as learning the vocabulary of a foreign language. Other research on transfer has involved forms of learning that have no close parallel in school learning. For example, there is a large body of experimental literature involving learning to recall a list of, say, twenty words and then being confronted with a new list of twenty words to memorize, half of which were in the first list and half were new. Sternberg and Bower's review of such studies (1974) shows that this situation produces negative transfer. The second list is more difficult to learn when it includes words that were learned before than when it includes only new words. The situation does not seem to parallel any common learning situation encountered in daily life, but the research based on it has important implications for the development of a theory of learning. Sternberg and Bower (1974) take the position that when a list of familiar words is learned, some kind of marker is attached to each of the words in the memory system. The process is called tagging. Of course, there are no real tags, but information is stored with the words learned indicating that these words belong to a particular list, much as the words of a foreign language are tagged in our memory as belonging to a particular foreign language. When the words in the first list are learned they are tagged as belonging to that list, but when they are encountered in the second list, they now have to be retagged as belonging to the second list. Retagging seems to be a more difficult process than assigning a tag in the first place, so the learning of the second list is slowed down by the retagging process. Other theoretical interpretations are also possible. For example, Tulving (1966) and Tulving and Osler (1967) suggest that when the individual learns the first list, he has to organize the words in some way (such as putting all names of things made of wood together, all metal things together, etc.), but when these words are included in a second list they have to be reorganized to fit in with the new words. The old pattern of organization then interferes with the search for a new way of organizing the materials. Some evidence supports this interpretation (see the review of studies by Earhard and her own study, 1974). Nevertheless, the tagging hypothesis seems to be the stronger one at this time.

Research in this area is quite fascinating from a theoretical point of view, but the situations studied are remote from most of those encountered in daily life.

However, there is one real life situation that comes near to these experimental situations. The man who runs the parts department at your local car dealer must learn the names of the parts of the cars that are sold and serviced. Learning the names of the parts on a new model is like the part-whole list learning situation. Some of the names are new, but some are old names from the parts on previous years' models. One would expect some confusion to be produced by learning the new names among the old. For example, this year's model has a stabilizer bar with a rubber bushing, but last year's did not. The idea of a bushing has to be tagged as belonging not only to this year's model, but to the stabilizer bar. Such double tagging may be difficult to handle in the memory system.

Transfer of Organizing Skills in the Memory System

The chapter on memory and retention emphasized the point that the transfer of information from the short-term memory system to the long-term memory system takes place with the greatest efficiency if the information is organized. If disorganized material is put into the short-term memory system, it tends to be organized, as is evident from the fact that lists of words given to the individual in random order tend to be repeated back in a form that shows some degree of structure. Organizing skills are learned and, in fact, courses that claim to improve memory achieve this goal mainly by teaching the individual how to organize information in such a way that it becomes readily transferred to the long-term memory system.

Although this aspect of transfer has long been used in practical memory training courses, it can also be verified experimentally. A study by DeRosa, Doane, and Russell (1970) was able to show very clearly that by merely presenting learners with a list of words that had some organization, they were able to profit from the organization provided and apply the same system of organization to the learning of a second list. Some of the skills related to organizing materials for transfer to the long-term memory system are already taught in schools. One procedure that accomplishes that end is outlining material to be memorized. The function of outlining is that of drawing the attention of the learner to the inherent structure of what is to be learned, around which the details can be clustered.

Transfer of Principles

The studies by Kendler and Kendler drive home the importance of verbal mediating processes in the transfer of what has been learned to the solution of novel problems. Ausubel and Robinson (1969) in their review of the relevant literature come to very much the same opinion. Although they might take the position that the transfer surface developed by Osgood provides good predictions of transfer in relatively simple situations that have clearly identifiable stimuli and well-defined responses, the transfer surface cannot be applied to predicting transfer in most of the complex learning situations that occur in schools. In these situations, the crucial factor is not so much the characteristics of the stimuli and responses as it is the internal verbalizations that take place.

One of the simpler tasks in the education of the child, which has value only insofar as transfer of training results, is the concept-learning task. If a child learns the concepts of an oak, a maple, and an elm by studying the trees on the school grounds, one would hope that the same child would be able to classify other trees in other parts of town into these categories, even though these trees might be smaller or larger than the ones used for teaching. The concepts of an oak, a maple, and an elm would have been taught in the hope that transfer of training would take place. Concepts are always learned in anticipation that the classification systems they involve will be applicable to the classification of new and significantly different instances in the future. Although concepts are taught in anticipation that such transfer will take place, the conditions of transfer have not been extensively studied by research workers. A single study of this problem by Stones and Heslop (1968) throws some light on what is involved.

The Stones and Heslop study used a technique invented many years ago by a Russian named L. S. Vigotsky. The materials used in this technique involve twenty-two small wooden blocks of five different colors, six different shapes of cross section, two different heights, and two different cross-sectional areas. The problem is to classify the blocks into four groups. The four groups of blocks are named LAG, BIK, MUR, and CEV, and these names are printed underneath the block on the side on which the block rests. The LAG blocks are tall and fat, the BIK blocks are small and fat, the CEV blocks small and thin, and the MUR blocks are tall and thin. Thus, two attributes are used in the classification of the blocks. A very interesting feature of the classification task is that once the system has been learned it can be applied to the classification of other objects. In the case of the Stones and Heslop study, the children who attempted to learn the classification system eventually had to apply it to the grouping of pictures of buildings, plasticine models of men, and pictures of trees. It is fairly easy to see how the classification system could be transferred to the grouping of various objects other than the blocks on which it was learned.

The children included in the study varied in age from 6.5 years to 11.5 years. The youngest children were virtually unable to solve the concept-learning problem and, of course, had no knowledge to apply to the transfer problems. On the other hand, a considerable number of the older children were able to solve the problem, and some were able to describe what the solution involved. Between a third and a half of those children who solved the problem with the blocks were able to solve the transfer problems using different objects. A particularly striking finding is that those children who solved the block problem and those most likely to solve the transfer problems were the ones who were able to verbalize the solution. They were able to say which attributes of the blocks made them fit into one category rather than another. The data hint that a person who is able to solve the block problem at an intuitive level may not be able to transfer the solution easily to other problems. What is meant here by the solution of the problem at the intuitive level is solving the problem but being unable to state the essence of the solution. At several other places in the text the point has been made that words give man an extraordinary power over his actions, and it is hardly surprising that knowledge that is verbalized can be more extensively applied to new situations than can knowledge that is understood only at an intuitive level.

In the case of the transfer of concepts, the Osgood surface has little relevance in predicting whether transfer will or will not occur, but the presence or absence of verbal mediating responses is of great importance. The role of verbal processes becomes even more central in the learning of rules and principles for solving problems. Consider, for example, the student who learns Archimedes' principle through a demonstration involving the change in weight of a piece of lead when it is immersed in water. His understanding of the principle is then tested in a situation in which he has to explain why smoke rises in a chimney. Some students will be able to transfer the knowledge gained by studying the loss of weight of an object when immersed in water to the chimney problem. Some positive transfer will occur, but surely not because of any simple similarity between the task elements involved or the overt responses involved. What the pupil must do is recognize that a solid body immersed in water has an upward force exerted on it by the water and that a body of hot gas also has an upward force exerted on it by the surrounding air. Both situations have to be coded as situations involving an upward thrust on a body exerted by a surrounding medium. In order for the pupil to be able to do this he must have learned in the first place not just that a body immersed in water loses weight, but that this is an example of a class of situations in which a body is surrounded by gaseous or liquid substances. He has to learn to code such situations as belonging to a class. It is through learning to code situations as presenting or not presenting the essential features of Archimedes' principle that transfer becomes possible. The application of a principle to different situations demands that the situations have some similarity, but the similarity may be at an abstract level, as it was in the case just examined.

A point to be noted is that when a student learns Archimedes' principle by observing the loss of weight of a piece of lead as it is immersed in water and then applies his knowledge to understanding why smoke rises in a chimney, any positive transfer that occurs can hardly be interpreted in terms of a simple concept of stimulus similarity. A body immersed in water and smoke rising in a chimney do not have stimulus similarity in any simple sense of the term. However, the physicist who examines the two situations can *abstract* certain similarities. He sees that water provides a certain buoyancy for the lead and that the air around the chimney provides a buoyancy for the smoke in the chimney, sufficient in each case to make it rise. Transfer from the one situation to the other occurs because the individual is able to *code* the information from the two situations in the same way. If a person were not able to code the information in the two situations in the same way, involving coding categories such as *buoyancy*, transfer would probably not occur.

Two studies by Overing and Travers (1966, 1967) throw some light on some of the conditions that facilitate the transfer of knowledge of a principle to a new situation. These studies are quite complex and only their essence can be presented here. The situation used in these studies was one that has been used several times previously in related research. The situation involved the teaching of the principle of refraction and the measurement of the extent to which the learner can apply what he has learned to the solution of a novel problem. The problem to which the knowledge of refraction has to be transferred is that of shooting at a target placed under water. As most people know, if one wants to shoot at an object under water, say from the bank of a river, one must not shoot directly at where the object appears to be. Direct aim at where the object appears to be will result in a miss. This is because the light from the object is bent (refracted) as it leaves the surface of the water. In the Overing and Travers studies, the task of shooting at the object under water was simplified so that the subjects did not actually fire the gun but merely had to indicate at what spot on the surface of the water they were aiming the gun. Thus a pupil participating in the experiment might say that he was aiming the gun at the line numbered 6, or the line numbered 4.

In the first of the two experiments children in the upper elementary grades were given instruction in the principle of the refraction of light by means of one of the following four methods:

METHOD 1. The children were given a lecture through a tape recorder. The information on this tape became the basis for the information given in all other instructional procedures in which any verbal information was also transmitted through a tape.

METHOD 2. The information was given through a tape, but simple line diagrams were also used to clarify the presentation.

METHOD 3. A realistic demonstration of the refraction of light was given by showing a light beam bend as it entered the surface of the water in a fish tank. A commentary on this demonstration was also presented by means of a tape.

METHOD 4. This was the same as Method 2 except for the fact that the presentation was preceded by a brief anecdote about a hunter who was trying to shoot a crocodile from the bank of the river. The crocodile was deep in the water. The anecdote pointed out that the hunter would not hit his game if he were to shoot directly at the place where he saw the crocodile, but that he would have to aim at a point directly below the crocodile.

The interesting finding with respect to the matter of transfer is not that the realistic condition produced more effective learning and transfer to the problem than did the use of diagrams, but that almost as good results were achieved with the use of the simple line diagrams, provided that their use was accompanied by the anecdote about the hunter and the crocodile. The use of the tank along with the other features of the realistic demonstration and the use of diagrams preceded by the anecdote were about equally effective teaching procedures, and more effective than the other two teaching situations. What these two effective teaching approaches have in common appears to be that both involve linking up the knowledge to be acquired with facts and situations that are already familiar. Books on pedagogy have long suggested the importance of the latter for learning, but have failed to indicate its significance for transfer.

Another finding of the study pertains to the value of verbalizing a principle. Half of the subjects at the end of the period of instruction on the principle of refraction were required to take a written test that did not add to the information they had learned, but that required them to verbalize the information. The results of the transfer of training tests showed that the pupils who were required to verbalize their knowledge, through taking the test, performed rather better than those who were not required to verbalize the principle, although the difference is small and cannot be presented with substantial confidence.

The second study explored whether principles taught in the presence of either much or little irrelevant information could be most successfully generalized to other situations. In this experiment two training conditions were used, both involving the use of a tank of water and a beam of light. In one training condition the tank was presented in a darkened room and little could be seen except the beam of light bending as it entered the water. In the other training condition, many irrelevant cues could be seen, including the sides of the tank, the bottom of the tank, and the equipment producing the beam of light. Two testing conditions were also provided. In both testing conditions the pupils had to aim at a target under water. In one case the testing involved a very simple target, but in the other case the target was embellished with a design. The finding was that the pupils trained under conditions involving a minimum number of irrelevant cues performed well on the tests that also involved a minimum of cues, but relatively poorly on the tests that involved a considerable number of irrelevant features. On the other hand, those trained in the presence of many irrelevant cues were equally successful at the testing problems regardless of the extent to which they included irrelevant cues.

The findings of the second study suggest that one of the factors involved in learning a principle is that of learning to discriminate relevant from irrelevant features of the situation. A principle taught in a rarefied environment that eliminates all irrelevancies does not prepare the individual to handle problems in a world filled with irrelevancies.

An interesting possibility has been raised by Logan and Wodtke (1968), who suggest that the application of a principle may sometimes be interfered with because the person falls back on some rule of thumb. Teachers of technical skills have long noted this kind of phenomenon with students who have been trained in effective methods of trouble shooting, but who tend to fall back on more primitive procedures. For example, a student is confronted with an engine that does not start. Instead of undertaking a systematic diagnosis of the cause of the difficulty, he arbitrarily decides that the problem is probably in the fuel pump, which he changes. In this case, the principles involved in trouble shooting are scrapped and a rule of thumb is instituted. In the Logan and Wodtke study, students learned how to identify the number of significant figures in the product of two measurements. For example, a rectangle has sides measuring 9.53 and 8.67 centimeters; how many significant figures are there in the product that provides a measure of the area of the rectangle? The answer to this problem can be found by the application of principles that can be used to show that the answer with the correct number of significant figures is 82.6. There is also another rule-of-thumb way of arriving at the number of significant figures, which in most cases comes up with the correct answer. This simple rule is to take the same number of significant figures in the answer as there are in the factor with the fewest significant figures. Although the rule of thumb generally comes out with the right answer, it is sometimes misleading. The results of the study indicated that the giving of the rule of thumb, even with the warning that it might occasionally give incorrect results, interfered with the transfer of the principles that were also learned. It seems that problem solvers are willing to take a small risk that they may not be able to solve the problem if a simple proecdure permits obtaining an answer quickly with a fairly high chance that it will be correct.

Transfer of Logical Structures

The chapter on the work of Piaget provides some evidence that once logical structures are acquired they are then available for solving new problems. However, this conclusion has to be qualified in that logical structures are often in themselves quite specific. For example, a child learns conservation of quantity of matter by about age 7, with such tasks as a ball of clay rolled into a sausage, but this does not transfer to the conservation of weight. Conservation of weight is discovered by the child about two years later, and the conservation of volume (measured by the displacement of water when an object is immersed) appears two years later still. The conservation of energy or momentum, concepts that call for the understanding of nonobservable properties of objects, cannot be mastered until children become capable of formal operations. Logical operations of conservation appear to be learned with respect to quite specific properties of the environment. Within these properties there seems to be some generalization.

Much more needs to be learned about the extent to which formal operations can be generalized to situations other than those in which they have been mastered. Piaget and his associates write as though such generalization of formal operations to new situations were automatic, but common experience tells us that it is more than one can expect. People typically show much illogical behavior in fields outside those in which they have acquired competence.

H Theory of Transfer

Theories of how transfer occurs have been scarce in the literature. Undoubtedly there are many mechanisms involved. In the case of certain kinds of problem solving, Levine (1974) has offered a theory, which he calls H theory, of how transfer takes place. The central feature of this theory is that when an individual is confronted with a problem, he must first make a decision concerning the kind of problem that confronts him. If my car will not start in the morning, my first impression may be a simple one such as that I forget to fill up the gas tank or that a wire has come loose. If I then find that there is gas in the tank and that all wires seem to be secure, I may conclude that the problem is a different one, perhaps a fuel pump or carburetor problem. Then I begin to think about what might be wrong with fuel lines, fuel pumps, and carburetors. If everything checks out in that area, I may then begin to wonder whether there is something wrong with the ignition, and so forth. Levine would observe this sequence of behavior and say that

I attempted to solve the problem by exploring first one *domain* and then another. He would also say that I sample hypotheses from a domain that is being explored. Each question I ask myself is a hypothesis, which is why Levine calls his theory H theory, or *hypothesis theory*.

When a problem is classified as belonging to a domain, the individual samples ideas from that domain that seem to have relevance to the solution to the problem. If I decide that the problem of the car resides in the fuel system, I recall such facts as "There must be gasoline in the carburetor for the engine to start" or "Too big an intake of air through the carburetor may prevent a car from starting." These pieces of information stored in my memory constitute the essence of each hypothesis I test. I may, of course, have the correct hypothesis in my memory, but may fail to sample it. I may know vaguely that carburetors become gummy and dirty, but somehow I may never bother to rub my finger along the inside of the carburetor to see whether that is the case. The essence of H theory is that one samples from the domain within which the problem has been classified, and one's sample may or may not include the correct hypothesis.

An interesting related approach to the problem of transfer is proposed by Haselrud (1972). Haselrud takes the position that transfer is in itself learning. A person does not find a solution to a problem by searching the memory system and finding there the solution. He retrieves what he can from memory and then adapts it to the purpose in hand. Haselrud claims that the major difficulty in undertaking such a process is in retrieving potentially useful information from the memory system. This, he believes, can be overcome by memorizing information while at the same time noting the potential of the information for future use. Haselrud claims that doing this makes the information more readily retrievable. The process is like putting handles on the stored information. Information stored without thought concerning future use or anticipated uses is like a library book with no number on it that is hidden away somewhere on the shelves of a library. The chances of coming upon that book at a time when one can use the information are negligible.

Level of Learning of the First Task in Relation to the Amount of Transfer

The relationship of level of learning on one task to the amount of transfer to a second task is clearly an important and practical problem. If increased learning on the first task produces an increase in the amount of transfer, there is strong argument in favor of thorough learning of whatever is learned in school, for much of such learning is offered because of its supposed transfer value.

Underwood (1951) found that with a verbal learning task the amount of transfer depended on the degree of learning of the initial task. This is to be expected where transfer is positive and where it depends on the generalization of the response involved. Atwater (1953) found a similar effect. Another and quite complex investigation by Mandler (1954) in general confirmed these results, but also indicated that the relation between the level of learning on the first task and the amount of transfer to the second task is not a simple one.

The results of these studies generally indicate that the amount of transfer is likely to increase with increases in practice on the first task.

An outstanding fact in the whole of the literature on transfer indicates that thorough learning is a desirable condition for efficient transfer. This fits well with many common observations made on behavior. The pupil who learns to speak a halting French in the classroom becomes unable to deliver a word of the language when faced by a visitor from France. The person who has recently learned to drive a car has the greatest difficulty in switching to a new car; the driver with many years of experience has no difficulty in switching to any new model that comes off the line. The experienced musician can switch from his customary instrument to another similar one with little difficulty, but the novice is upset by any change in his equipment.

Knowledge of this aspect of transfer suggests the tremendous importance of thorough learning of whatever is learned. This in turn suggests that learning should be so planned and scheduled that overlearning is the rule. Hasty and superficial treatment of subject matter in schools would appear to be a waste of time.

Task Difficulty and Transfer

An interesting problem of some educational significance is whether transfer occurs more readily from an easy task to a complex task or from a complex task to an easy one. A few years ago psychologists were inclined to take the position that transfer would take place more readily from the complex to the simple. The argument was that the complex task would include all the elements involved in the simple task, though including also some additional elements; but when the reverse procedure was adopted the simple task would not include all the elements involved in the complex task and hence much less transfer could occur. This is a persuasive argument, and a few early studies seemed to provide supporting evidence. However, when Holding (1962) reviewed all the studies he could locate, he found as many studies reporting more transfer in the easy-to-difficult situation as those reporting more transfer in the difficult-to-easy situation.

Holding showed in a experiment of his own that with a simple task optimum transfer occurred from the easier to the more difficult problem; but with more complex tasks, optimum transfer occurred from the more difficult to the easier problems. His experiments indicate that there is a complex relationship between task difficulty and amount of transfer.

Transfer Across Sense Modality

The same information can sometimes be communicated through different sensory systems, which raises the question of whether information communicated through one system will be recognized when it is transmitted through another. One of the simplest cases of this is that of verbal communication, which can be either through the eye in the form of print or through the ear in the form of vocal communication. The adult who can read with competence can readily hear information and later recognize the same information when it appears in print, and vice versa. Verbal information seems to be coded into the same auditory form, regardless of the form in which it is received.

Some differences exist in the ability to use information from one sensory channel rather than the other. Even among children who can read well there will be some who will prefer to receive information through the auditory channel and who learn more when they do. With younger children there is a preference for auditory verbal information rather than visual verbal information because they have greater facility with hearing than with reading.

Verbal learning is a special case in which almost perfect transfer would be expected because the visual and the auditory systems feed the information into the same memory system, but what happens when somewhat different systems of memory seem to be involved? For example, suppose one is given a set of irregularly shaped objects to handle, but not to see, and told to memorize their shapes. To what extent would one recognize them visually? Von Senden (1961) long ago showed that with adults who gained vision for the first time through surgery there would be no transfer. However, with adults and children who have had long experience in relating tactile space to visual space, there is little difficulty in making the transfer. We know what a cube feels like, and we also know what a cube looks like. When we touch a cube of a particular size, we know what the cube would look like. When unfamiliar situations are used transfer may not take place. Shaffer and Howard (1974) undertook an experiment demonstrating virtually no transfer from the visual to the haptic system and from the haptic to the visual system. They trained subjects on a task involving the classification of dot patterns in one of the sensory systems, and then switched them to the same task in the other system. Training in one sensory system did not seem to help them learn the same task in the other sensory system. In another study by Mandel and Bridger (1973) transfer occurred from the visual to the auditory modality, but not the other way. The latter study involved conditioning of the galvanic skin response to verbal stimuli, presented either auditorially or visually, and results are surprising in view of the fact that most studies of verbal learning show almost perfect transfer across modalities for verbal material. The study by Mandel and Bridger suggests that the problem of cross-modality transfer is much more complex than it has been assumed to be.

An extensive study of a special aspect of cross-modality transfer was undertaken by Asher (1964), who provided different groups of undergraduates with training in vocabulary in Spanish, Japanese, Turkish, Persian, and Russian. None of the students had had any previous experience with the language in which they were given training. Asher's general procedure was to provide vocabulary training in one of these languages through one sense modality (hearing or vision), and then later he asked the same students to relearn the lists of words in the other modality. The experimenter could then determine the extent to which learning the list through one sense modality facilitated learning through the other. Because the study covered many facets of language learning, a comparison of the transfer from vision to hearing and from hearing to vision can be made only with respect to Spanish, Japanese, and Russian. In the case of Spanish and Japanese, the sequence of learning through vision and later relearning through hearing was found to be superior to the reverse; but there was no significant difference between the orders of sequences of learning for Russian. It should be noted that the Japanese was presented in the Romanized alphabet (similar to that used here), but the Russian was presented in Russian script.

Asher suggests that the problem of transfer is one of what he calls *phonetic fit*, that is, there will be good transfer of learning from hearing to seeing, or the reverse, in a language in which there is a close relationship between the spelling of words and the way they are pronounced. English is an example of a language with a poor phonetic fit. When the phonetic fit is poor, the transfer is reduced from the one modality to the other. Thus the study indicates that the extent to which there is transfer from spoken instruction in a foreign language to printed instruction, or the reverse, depends on the extent to which there is a straightforward and simple relationship between print and speech.

An interesting finding was that when intensive training in oral Russian was given first, exposure to printed Russian produced *pronunciation shock*, characterized by a decrease in the quality of spoken Russian. However, the reverse effect was found with Japanese, in which the introduction of printed material improved the quality of pronunciation.

The Asher study was concerned with the transmission of only verbal material, either through the visual or auditory modalites; but an interesting problem is given by associating an English word with a foreign word, when the learner on a later task has to name visually presented objects. One might expect that there would be less transfer across modalities when the transfer was from a task involving words to a task involving objects than when the transfer is between two verbal tasks. A direct study of this problem does not appear to have been undertaken.

A study by Kale, Grosslight, and McIntyre (1953) examined the related problem of the value of pictures, either still or in motion, in the teaching of Russian vocabulary. They found some evidence that the use of pictures, particularly motion pictures, appeared to facilitate learning. They also found that the simultaneous auditory presentation of the words displayed on the screen seemed to interfere with rather than facilitate learning.

Transfer from Simulators and Other Training Devices to Performance on the Job

The transfer of training from artificial learning situations to situations involving ordinary life situations is a matter of special importance. In a sense, the transfer of school learning to out-of-school situations is a special case of such transfer that deserves much more study than the problem has elicited. A more common form of research has been that in which an attempt is made to determine whether a training device designed to produce proficiency in a particular aspect of a job trains as effectively as on-the-job training.

The history of training devices goes back to World War I, and much of a the work has been undertaken in conjunction with the military because military organizations use extremely expensive equipment and the use of such equipment for training purposes involves an enormous capital outlay. The use of a $20 million plane for training purposes makes training an expensive enterprise, but a cheap mock-up of the plane may provide a situation in which many of the basic skills involved in operating the aircraft can be learned. Even quite expensive mock-up equipment may provide relatively cheap training. Training devices that duplicate aspects of the original equipment are referred to as simulators.

A simulator does not have to resemble the actual situation in every respect. Generally it resembles the actual situation for which training is given in certain aspects that are crucial for the training involved. A flight trainer for a jumbo jet need not provide the seat-of-the-pants experiences the pilot has related to take-off or landing in order to provide good training. However, such a flight trainer can provide realistic instrument panels and may provide realistic warning light indicators of in-flight emergencies. The flight simulator may also have built-in responses showing the pilot what happens when he handles an emergency in a particular way. He can read the gauges to tell whether the fire in the engine has been extinguished or whether it is still burning. The early flight simulators were more concerned with teaching the pilot to handle the problems of keeping a rather unstable plane in an appropriate flying posture. The famous Link Trainer, designed for this purpose, behaved like a very unstable small plane, the controls of which had to be continuously manipulated in order to keep the device from going into a nose dive or other dangerous posture. The Link Trainer, firmly fixed to the ground, provided the pilot with training in most of the skills of flying a small plane, and provided most of the experience related to the flying of such a plane short of seat-of-the-pants experiences.

Since the flight trainer was first invented, simulation as a training method has slowly been expanded to other areas too numerous to mention one by one, but a few examples will suffice. Simulators have become common in medical training. Recordings of heart beats are used for training the student in heart sounds. Computer-based problems are used for training in patient management. For example the medical student sitting at a computer terminal may be told that a patient is brought into emergency with certain symptoms and the student is asked what he would do first. The student tells the computer what he would do, and the computer types back the effect of the student's procedure. The student is asked what he would do next, and so on. The computer will indicate at each step just what happens and give such responses as "The patient has now gone into shock" or "The patient has just died."

Simulators are particularly useful for training in problem solving. The pilot and the medical student handling an emergency are examples of this type of situation that can be mimicked on a simulator. Problem-solving training, through simulators, has also been given in such fields as electronic trouble shooting and automotive trouble shooting. A mock-up of a complex piece of electronic equipment may contain only dummy components, but it may be possible for the student to apply test instruments at various points that give the same readings that would have been given by the real equipment. Then the electronics student has all the data he needs to solve the problem and determine what is wrong.

A prolific amount of research has been undertaken on the degree to which there is transfer from the trainer, or simulator, to the real situation. Most of the research shows good transfer, and also considerable savings in the cost of training. The excellent review of transfer of training with flight simulators by Blaiwes, Puig, and Regan (1973) is typical of the literature in the field. They cite studies showing substantial transfer from the flight simulator to actual flying, but they also point out that proficiency, measured by performance on the simulator, generally overestimates the level of performance in the real equipment. The decrement in performance when the learner is moved from the trainer to the real equipment is the typical decrement found when performance is measured in a situation different from that in which training occurred.

In some areas of training substantial time may be saved by using a simulated situation. For example, in electronic trouble shooting, students may solve problems without having to go through the tedious task of disassembling the equipment in order to reach particular parts. Thus a simulator may make it possible for the student to solve perhaps ten problems in a morning, whereas with the real equipment a morning would be enough to solve only one. This has been demonstrated many times in research on the military, but a study on vocational-technical high school students by Finch and O'Reilly (1974) shows the same results. One can expect excellent transfer from performance on a well-designed simulator to performance with the real equipment.

There is always a danger that simulators will become too remote from the real situation and too abstract to be useful. At least with children of elementary school age, there is evidence that concrete materials provide greater opportunity for learning than do other forms of learning aids.

OTHER IMPLICATIONS OF KNOWLEDGE OF TRANSFER FOR CLASSROOM PRACTICE

Most of the research on transfer reviewed in this chapter has been of relatively recent vintage. Research conducted by Thorndike early in the century is now so well known in education that the details were not discussed here. However, in reviewing the implications for education of the research that has been done on transfer, one cannot avoid pointing out that the studies of transfer of training undertaken nearly three quarters of a century ago probably had more impact on education than any other studies that psychologists have ever undertaken. Thorndike believed his studies and the studies of his contemporaries showed that one could not expect any broad benefits from study in a limited area, as many educators of the day believed. Thorndike emphasized that the learning of a particular skill was likely to facilitate the learning of another skill only insofar as the two skills had common elements. In contrast, educators in the early part of the century generally believed that the study of such subjects as mathematics and Latin had a general disciplining effect on the mind—a theory that took the position that the learning of a particular skill provided very broad training in a wide range of thinking skills. Thorndike's work on transfer of training provided an entirely new basis for curriculum planning. No longer could subjects be included in the curriculum because of a belief that they were generally beneficial as devices for training the mind; a school subject had to be justified because of the *specific* skills, knowledge and understanding it provided. The early research on transfer of training provided a revolutionary new basis for selecting subjects for inclusion in the curriculum.

Later research on transfer of training had other contributions to make, but none have had such sweeping effects on education as had the early research, the conclusions from which have generally proved to be valid.

The early research on transfer placed emphasis on what not to do in the field of education, such as not to teach Latin in the hope that it would generally discipline the mind. More recent research has suggested some of the things that teachers *should* do. The research suggests that a high degree of mastery is important if transfer is to occur, and hence the teacher should ensure that learning be pursued with thoroughness. This may sometimes mean that the pupil will have to develop a level of skill beyond that with which he feels satisfied.

If transfer is to take place, there is considerable data to support the point of view that the pupil should have experience with a wide range of problems that differ somewhat from one another. This provides experience in dealing with the slightly unusual and develops an expectation that each problem will have to be solved in a way that is somewhat different from that used in the solution of previous problems. In a sense, this may be called training for flexibility; but it is one of the keys to transfer of training.

The teacher should emphasize principles and their application. Many teachers make the error of citing numerous facts without indicating that each is an example of the same underlying principle. But the statement of a principle is not enough. Pupils must also have the opportunity of practicing the use of the principle in a variety of problem situations.

If a principle has been learned, the pupil should learn to apply it in situations in which there are many distracting and irrelevant elements. Unless he does this, he may have difficulty in learning to discriminate between the relevant and the irrelevant features of situations and may not see the applicability of a principle simply because he is distracted by an overwhelming mass of trivial detail. For example, applications of principles of physics in complex situations can be discussed and explored in the classroom and on excursions outside the school, and pupils can be given practice in attempting to tease out the relevant elements in complex situations. For example, what happens when a tornado forms is a problem that illustrates several different physics principles operating in a very complicated situation. Various aspects of the tornado have to be dissected intellectually in order to understand the principles that are operating. The pupil also has to be able to put aside irrelevant aspects of the tornado, such as the darkness that often accompanies it.

Another point to note is that acquired knowledge tends to be most readily available to the person who has learned it in the situation in which it was acquired. This means that opportunities should be provided for the pupil to learn and use knowledge in a variety of situations. Field trips and homework assignments can help to prevent knowledge and its uses from becoming tied to particular situations.

A final point needs to be emphasized. Teachers of today, like teachers at the start of the century, are much too optimistic in their hopes that transfer will occur. After educators ceased to believe that the difficult subjects such as Latin and mathematics had special powers for disciplining the mind, educators came up with other formulae for achieving the same goal. During the 1930s the belief was widely held that if Latin and mathematics would not do the trick, perhaps exercises in critical thinking would. Analyses were made of the nature of critical thinking, and exercises were developed that were designed to develop the component skills involved. The hope was that the skills developed through such exercises would become very general skills. The effectiveness of curricula related to critical thinking was probably never as broad as educators hoped it would be. Later research has indicated that thinking skills do not show as much generalization as most earlier educators expected. Critical thinking, learned in the context of political discussion, may not generalize to the critical thinking involved in the design of an experiment, and vice versa. The skilled politician, shrewd in the analysis of political situations, may show himself to be completely naive in the design of a simple experiment. The sophisticated physicist may think like a child in the area of political issues. Thinking skills tend to be tied to particular areas of knowledge, and especially to those in which they have been learned.

In more recent times, interest has shifted to the development of creative thinking skills. Once again the thought has been that such skills developed in a limited context will also appear in other contexts. Creative skills *may* be readily transferred to new situations, but what we know of transfer of training would lead us to expect that they would be tightly bound to the situations in which they have been learned.

The Interanimal Transfer Problem

During the last two decades, numerous studies have been undertaken in which extracts from the brains, or other organs, of trained animals have been injected into untrained animals to determine whether the untrained animals could acquire responses through these transfers. The original experiments were undertaken with planaria, free-swimming flatworms, and claims were made that pieces of the worms that learned to swim through a short T-maze transmitted this skill to planaria fed on pieces of the learners. This led to speculation that when the planaria consumed the parts of the trained worms, cells that had been involved in the original learning might have been consumed and become integrated into the body of the worm that ate them. Soon, serious criticisms of the entire enterprise were voiced. Many psychologists doubted that planaria could learn to take the correct turning on a T-maze. For a time the findings on planaria were believed to be a result of some artifact in the experiment. There was no theoretical explanation for the results, if the results were genuine at all. Indeed, most of what is known about learning would suggest that a skill could not be transmitted from one animal to another in this way. Nevertheless, other psychologists became interested in attempting to produce the phenomenon with other species.

Smith (1974) has reviewed the later attempts to transmit learning from one animal to another. Experiments have now been undertaken with goldfish, chickens, mice, hamsters, and rats. Brain extracts were used in these experiments. The brain extract from the trained, donor animal was injected into the untrained, recipient animal. In some studies, the donors and the recipients were of different species. A great variety of learning tasks were used. In one study rats learned to avoid drinking water when a light was on. In another, thirsty animals learned to avoid a saccharin solution and to drink plain water. In still another task, rats learned to balance on a wire and climb along it to obtain food.

The general trend of the studies is to show a small consistent tendency for the recipient to perform better in the task to be learned than the controls who do not receive anything from trained donors. In some studies, the controls were given extracts from untrained donors. One must emphasize the smallness of the gain in learning produced. Smith (1974) takes the position that the effect is genuine. One possible explanation is that the injections contain RNA and other proteins that might have an invigorating effect on the learning of the recipient animals. Since little is known about the brain chemistry of learning, it is useless to speculate whether skills are stored in particular protein molecules that can then be transmitted to other animals. There is also a strong possibility that the phenomenon is not genuine. If a hundred such experiments were carried out and four or five showed a weak effect of this kind, those showing a weak effect would be most likely to be accepted for publication. The 95 or 96 other studies would probably not be submitted for publication because most authors know that journals typically reject research that produces negative results. Journal policy can produce a bias in the reporting of research that tends to lead to the acceptance of positive findings that are the mere result of chance.

SUMMARY

1. Learning in one area may facilitate or interfere with subsequent learning in other areas. It may also facilitate or interfere with previous learning. These are the phenomena of transfer of training. When the acquisition of one skill facilitates the learning or retention of another skill, the term positive transfer is used. When there is interference, the term negative transfer is applied. Transfer effects may be either proactive or retroactive. Transfer is commonly distinguished from the related phenomenon of warm-up.

2. Stimulus generalization is a basic form of transfer. The essential nature of stimulus generalization is that a response that comes to be elicited by a particular stimulus can also then be elicited by a range of similar stimuli. There is a gradient of stimulus generalization in that the closer the resemblance of the new stimulus to the stimulus to which the response was originally learned, the greater is the likelihood that it will elicit the particular response.

3. Generalization takes place from learned responses to objects, to responses to the words that denote the objects. Generalization also takes place across words when responses are conditioned to words used as stimuli; in this case, generalization is to words of similar meaning rather than to words of similar sound or to words

similar in graphic form. This is referred to as semantic generalization, to indicate that generalization is along a dimension of meaning. Generalization may be due to a tendency to classify all inputs into categories, and responses are then learned to the categories and not to the specific stimuli.

4. Response generalization also constitutes another basic transfer mechanism in which the learning of a response to a particular stimulus also strengthens all related responses.

5. An additional basic transfer mechanism is that demonstrated by transposition. Although transposition has been extensively studied, the nature of the learning involved is not really understood.

6. In recent times, the study of transfer has been undertaken through research involving simple and well-defined forms of behavior. The paired-associate learning task has been found to be particularly useful for this purpose. In such tasks it is possible to find the effect of varying the stimulus element or the response element.

7. Research on transfer involving fairly simple situations using the proaction design have been quite well summarized by Osgood through a graph known as the transfer surface. This graph represents the fact that maximum positive transfer occurs when the two tasks present similar stimuli and call for similar responses, and that maximum negative transfer occurs when two tasks provide the same stimuli but call for opposite responses. The graph provides good predictions of the transfer to be expected between two tasks involving motor skills.

8. An important case of transfer related to problem solving is the acquisition of what have been termed learning sets. These are facilities in solving problems of a particular class. They appear to involve the learning of strategies and also flexibility in attempting different solutions. They do not necessarily involve the verbalization of the rules applied, as is evident from the fact that learning sets can be demonstrated in animals other than human beings. Out of this work have emerged studies of the factors that facilitate the shifting of strategies and rules for solving problems. Older children show a great capacity to make such shifts, although young children and other primates are slow. The difference between the older children and the young children and other primates is suspected to be attributable to the ability of the older children to use language in the solution of problems.

9. Although the Osgood transfer surface may provide a good description of the transfer to be expected in simple situations, it probably has little relevance when complex verbal learnings are involved. Some data suggest that being able to verbalize the solution to a concept-learning problem is important for being able to transfer the knowledge acquired to the solution of new problems. The extent to which transfer will occur in the case of human learning appears to depend much more on whether the problem is understood at a verbal level than whether it is intuitively understood, that is, understood but without the understanding being coded into words.

10. Studies of the learning of principles show that the conditions under which they are learned may facilitate or interfere with transfer. Transfer of a principle is facilitated if the situation in which it is learned involves many irrelevant cues and

if it is to be transferred to other situations involving also many, but different, irrelevant cues. The application of a principle may also be disrupted because the individual involved falls back on some rule of thumb.

11. A significant case of transfer involves the extension of a rule to produce a more comprehensive generalization. This is probably a rare form of transfer, but it does take place even with children.

12. Piaget and his associates have initiated extensive work on the transfer of logic from one situation to another. For example, much research has been undertaken related to the question of whether learning conservation in one area (such as volume) transfers to other areas (such as mass or number). Such transfer does not take place. However, there is lateral transfer within the area in which conservation has been mastered. Another theoretical area for research is the extent to which transfer involves sampling the correct set of hypotheses. When information is memorized, it should be tagged for particular uses if transfer is to occur easily.

13. The degree of learning of the first task appears to be related to the amount of transfer that occurs. The data also suggest that if there is to be expected negative transfer from task 1 to task 2, the amount of such negative transfer will decline as task 1 is more and more adequately learned.

14. The relationship of transfer to the relative difficulty of task 1 as compared to task 2 has not been clearly identified by research. The results of studies lack consistency and lead to no firm conclusion.

15. Transfer across sense modality is an important educational problem. Transfer from auditory training to visual training in a verbally taught foreign language will take place effectively if the written and spoken forms of the language display phonetic fit.

16. The use of simulators raises interesting problems in relation to transfer. Simulators provide training on equipment that is much cheaper to use than the actual equipment, or is more readily available. There is generally good transfer from a well-designed simulator to performance on the job.

17. Research on transfer of training has long had an important impact on education. The early research of Thorndike destroyed the doctrine of formal discipline and suggested that school subjects had to be justified because of their intrinsic nature. Later research has placed emphasis on the importance of the pupil's achieving thorough mastery, if transfer is to be achieved. In addition, research on the learning of principles has shown that transfer is most likely to take place if the pupil is given extensive practice in the application of the principles in a variety of situations.

18. A special case of transfer is that involved in transferring tissue from one animal to another. The meaning of the results of such studies is not clear at the present time.

Chapter 12

The Nervous System and Learning

In the last quarter of a century an intimate relationship has developed between those interested in developing a science of behavior and those concerned with the discovery of how the nervous system is built and how it controls behavior. Learning psychologists have often been able to suggest to the neurologist what he might look for in the nervous system, and the neurophysiologist has been able to suggest to the psychologist some of the factors he should take into account in attempting to identify the conditions that are related to learning. The healthy relationship between these two groups has produced many important ideas. The purpose of this chapter is to review some of these ideas, but first let us take a look at the structure of the nervous system.

The classic work on the anatomy of the nervous system is that by Ranson, which has been revised by Clark (1959). A shorter and more readily understood text is that by Gardner (1968). Several works are now available that discuss the function of the system in relation to behavior. One of the most understandable is that by Woodburne (1967). A compact summary of structure of the nervous system in relation to psychological function can be found in a work by Riklan and Levita (1969), which is mainly concerned with an evaluation of the effects of surgical treatment of Parkinson's disease. However, the book is also an excellent elementary treatise on neural functioning. Eccles' recent treatise (1973) on the brain may well become a classic.

THE MICROCOMPONENTS OF THE NERVOUS SYSTEM

Like all other tissues of the body, the nervous system is made up of cells. These cells take on many forms, but they generally have a long fiberlike structure that extends from one end, called the axon, as shown in Figure 12-1. It is mainly along this fiber, sometimes as long as several feet, that nerve impulses travel from one part of the system to another. The nerve impulse is different from a current traveling down a wire, but it is still electrical in character. The sense organs consist of specialized nerve cells that respond mainly to particular stimuli. Those in the retina of the eye, for example, respond to light, and they also respond to mechanical impact, as is evident from the experience one has when struck a blow in the eye. The nerve fibers coming from the sense organs are gathered together into white glistening bundles that enter the spinal cord, at regular intervals, through spaces between the bony vertebrae that provide a protective casing for the spinal cord. The sensory nerves come from the surface of the body and also from the interior of the body and provide a communication system through which the individual is able to know what is happening both in the outside world and in the interior of his body. The optic nerve, the auditory nerve, and the nerves associated with the sensory systems at the head end of the body enter the enlarged upper portion of the spinal cord known as the brain stem.

Nerve cells do not connect directly to other nerve cells, for each cell is completely enclosed by a membrane that separates it from all other tissues. There are places where the axon of a cell comes into close contact with either the cell body of another

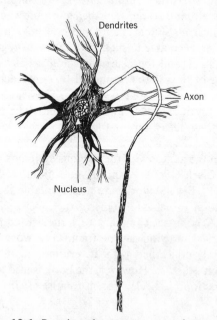

Figure 12-1. Drawing of a common type of nerve cell.

cell or with fine fiberlike structures that extend from the body of the other cell, called dendrites. A nerve impulse traveling down an axon can, at its terminal, cause chemical changes in the surrounding fluid, and these chemical changes may, in turn, initiate a response in the dendrites of a neighboring cell. In this way impulses may travel from one cell to another. The space between the termination of the axon and the dendrites or body of the other cell is referred to as the synapse, which behaves much like an on-off switch. If it is in the on position the impulse passes; if it is in the off position, then the impulse is blocked from transfer to the new cell.

Impulses in the cell body and axon are all or none phenomena, that is, the nerve cell fires an impulse or it is in a resting state. If it fires an impulse, the impulse is always of the same size. The same is true of the function of the synapse, which either passes an impulse to another nerve cell or fails to pass the impulse. It never passes an impulse in a weakened form, and it never passes a part of an impulse.

A very important fact about synapses is that they can show variation in their ability to transmit impulses across them. Impulses may be blocked at a synapse or they may be readily transmitted. If two impulses, along two different axons, arrive simultaneously at a synapse, or in rapid succession, they may be able together to initiate activity in the synapse and produce a new impulse in another nerve cell, even though either alone might not be able to do this. When two impulses, together, manage to transmit an impulse across a synapse, the impulse transmitted across the synapse is no stronger than if it were initiated by a single impulse.

Physiologists commonly assume that the synapse is the place where information is stored. If this is so, information is stored by a mechanism that involves the setting of a large number of on-off switches. It is easy to understand how all kinds of information can be represented by the setting of a series of on-off switches. For example, we can use such a set to represent the letters of the alphabet, with A represented by two switches—one set to the off position, and the other set to the on position, much as Morse code represents the letter A by the symbol - —. The letter B could be represented by four switches set in the on-off-off-off positions (— - - -). Thus a set of switches could be used to represent any written message. Somewhat more complicated is the problem of how a visual image might be represented by a set of switches, but computers are able to record information by means of what are essentially a set of on-off switches and are able to store information about visually presented diagrams, which they can later reproduce, from memory, onto a screen. There is nothing inconsistent between the idea that memory involves the storage of information through the setting of large numbers of on-off switches and that memory sometimes involves the storage of visual information in the form of images.

The number of synapses, which we have referred to here as on-off switches, is very large indeed and is in the billions. This number is far in excess of the number of corresponding on-off mechanisms found in the most advanced computer or in any computer that is contemplated.

The nervous system also contains a large number of cells of unknown function called glial cells. There are, in fact, more glial cells than there are nerve cells, and some neurophysiologists have suggested that these cells may be involved in the storage of information. Just how such a system of cells could provide an information storage system is difficult to see at this time, for they do not have any clear relationship to the input and analysis of information.

The structure of the individual cell is far more complicated than this presentation implies. The use of the electron microscope has revealed the individual nerve cell to be a structure of extraordinary complexity with specialized parts that undertake particular chemical functions. In addition, it has been shown that a single nerve cell may be "wired" to hundreds of different synapses. Eccles (1973) has summarized much of what is known about the microstructure of the nerve cell.

There is some evidence that the cells of the nervous system in higher organisms are linked together, through synapses, in an orderly and uniform manner in all members of a particular species. Horridge (1973), who has undertaken this research, has had to confine it to animals on which it is possible to trace particular nerve tracts through from one terminal to another. This tracing of the "wiring" has been undertaken on the common fly because it is easy in this creature to trace the fibers of the optic nerve. The evidence provides a picture of a very uniform wiring mechanism. When 650 fibers were traced in different flies, there were only ten cases in which there appeared to be any discrepancy in the wiring, and these discrepancies could well have been due to errors in experimenter judgments. One is tempted to generalize and conclude that a similar uniform wiring system is typical of all nervous systems and it probably is. Indeed, it would be hard to imagine how the brain could perform its computerlike functions, with uniformity from one member of the species to the next, without a high degree of uniformity in the wiring system.

THE GROSS STRUCTURE AND FUNCTION OF THE HUMAN NERVOUS SYSTEM

The human nervous system is basically a system that handles all the information provided by the sense organs, stores information, and has components that initiate and control the responses that are made. Much of it consists of bundles of nerve fibers carrying information into the system from the sense organs, called the afferent nerves, and bundles of nerve fibers through which impulses travel and initiate responses in both the muscles and glands, called the efferent nerves. The nerves from the sense organs enter the trunk line of the nervous system, the spinal cord, through bundles that join it at intervals along its length. The nerves that produce responses also have corresponding exits. The spinal cord itself is encased within the bony segments collectively called in common language the backbone. The spinal cord is thickened at its upper extremity to form what is known as the medulla. The medulla leads to a number of complex structures tucked well beneath the cerebral hemispheres, the large masses of nervous tissue that are commonly regarded as the brain.

The nervous system is immensely complicated, which is why a simple exposition of its functions is difficult to undertake. Detailed anatomical drawings and photographs are confusing except to the highly sophisticated, so let us begin with a grossly over simplified diagram of the main structures. Such a diagram is shown in Figure 12-2. In this diagram, the spinal cord is shown at the extreme right and is not represented for its entire length, and neither are the nerves entering or leaving it shown. The spinal cord as it approaches the brain itself is enlarged to form the medulla and includes a highly important structure known as the reticular activating system. There is also a thickening caused by a broad band of fibers that circle the brain stem, part way, and that have the major function of providing connections

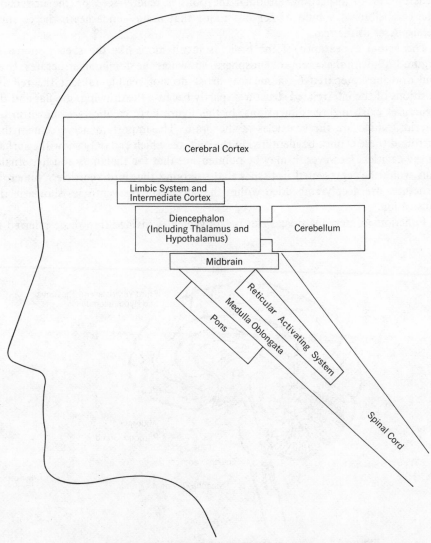

Figure 12-2. Diagramatic representation of the major structures in the nervous system.

between the two cerebral hemispheres. These fibers form what is called the pons, a word meaning a bridge, because it forms a bridge between the two sides of the brain. In ascending the system, the next massive structures are the thalamus and hypothalamus. The connection between the thalamic structures and the cerebral cortex is through the diencephalon, which also contains the important structure known as the limbic system. Then come the cerebral hemispheres, which are responsible for the most complex analyses of sensory information and produce the most complex behavior. The cerebral hemispheres hide most of the other structures from inspection, although the pons is readily seen on the underside. The cerebellum is a bulb of nervous tissue that nestles underneath the cerebral hemispheres at the rear.

The actual appearance of the brain is much more like the sketch shown in Figure 12-3, with the cerebral hemispheres shown as the dominant structures. Even fine drawings prepared by a medical artist do not readily present the relative positions of the interrelated structures, partly because the drawings are flat and the structures exist in three dimensions. In this figure large cavities are shown in the interior, which are the ventricles of the brain. The important nerve centers that surround these cannot be identified in the picture, which can only show the surface of the cavities. However, it may be pointed out that the thalamus and hypothalamus would be represented in tissues that surround the third ventricle. Numerous structures are deeply embedded within the surface of the ventricles shown in the illustration.

Functions of nervous tissues can be conveniently divided into those referred to

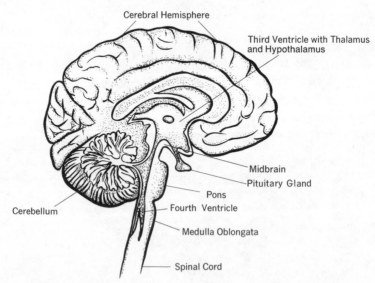

Figure 12-3. View of the brain cut through the midsection to show the main structures.

as specific and those referred to as nonspecific. Let us consider first the specific functions, that is, functions related to particular aspects of behavior. The spinal cord conducts upward impulses from the receptors associated with the sense of touch, pain, tension in the muscles, and deep pressure. The nerves from the eye, ear, taste-smell system, and sensory equipment at the head end enter the brain stem at a higher level. The spinal cord also contains major bundles of fibers that transmit impulses to the muscles and produce action. The spinal cord also includes fibers that interconnect various parts of the cord. When the cord is severed, there is complete loss of control of movement, that is, paralysis, but reflexes below the level of the cut remain and these would require the presence of many interconnecting fibers. A reflex is a simple form of behavior, but it involves complex nervous structures.

SPECIFIC AND NONSPECIFIC NEURAL SYSTEMS

The traditional approach to the study of the nervous system has been to attempt to identify the specific function of each particular anatomical component. This looks like a reasonable procedure and is feasible up to a point. This is how an engineer would go about studying a strange piece of equipment, say a piece captured from an enemy in wartime. The neurophysiologist has many techniques through which he can hope to discover whatever specific functions exist in particular locations in the nervous system, and these he has applied with some success over the last half-century.

The oldest technique for establishing the location of specific functions is that of determining the effect on behavior of damage that happens to occur to specific parts of the system. Damage caused by tumors, vascular accidents, infection, or the physical penetration of objects was used in the nineteenth century to establish relationships between location in the brain and function. This technique, first used by the famous French physician Paul Broca before the turn of the century, demonstrated that the part of the cortex of the brain centrally concerned with speech was in the left part of the frontal lobes. This led to high expectations that the entire surface of the brain, and perhaps the interior parts too, could be mapped out in terms of the functions performed, but the results of prolonged research along these lines did not justify the optimism with which the method was pursued.

The method pursued by Broca had limitations. Tumors do not always grow in places where the scientist would like to have them grow in order to see their consequences. The method soon became supplemented by the study of the effects of physical injury. However, this supplementary method, despite the fact that two world wars provided an almost inexhaustible supply of subjects, failed to provide much useful data. One problem is that the penetration of a piece of shrapnel or any fragment of metal does extensive damage through the wave produced by the impact. A bullet through the brain produces the same kind of extensive splash as would be produced by a bullet fired into a bucket of water. Few objects that have enough impact to penetrate the skull leave damage in a small, specific, and identifiable area. The damage is diffuse and typically fatal. In the case of animals, the technique can be used in a refined form by producing damage surgically. The damage can then be controlled precisely to a particular region of the brain and the precise extent of the damage can be determined later through the post-mortem study of the brain.

An additional technique involves the electrical stimulation of an exposed area of the brain. The muscular response of the person or animal stimulated can then be observed. In the case of human subjects, the experiences that accompany the stimulation can be noted. The technique can be used in the case of human subjects, because some surgical procedures require that sections of the skull be removed, exposing the brain. The removal of portions of the skull can take place with only a local anesthetic, and the actual stimulation of the surface of the brain is painless. An example of what happens is that when a certain area on the side of the cerebral hemispheres is stimulated, a person may say that he is experiencing a vivid visual memory of an event that happened many years ago. Stimulation of other areas may produce a twitch of a toe or the movement of an arm.

The technique can be further extended when subjects other than human beings are used, and electrodes can be implanted deep in the brain. The stimulation of the part of the brain in which they are implanted can be undertaken by passing a small current between the electrodes. The effect of this stimulation can then be studied.

Still another technique has evolved as biochemists have come to identify various substances used by various parts of the brain in performing their functions. For example, it is known that the part of the nervous system that has to do with reinforcement releases norepinephrine when it is active. Norepinephrine can be made to fluoresce, and thus after an animal has engaged in a particular activity and been killed, sections of the brain will show, through such fluorescence, the areas that have been active in producing norepinephrine. In addition, there are substances, such as reserpine, that deplete the brain of norepinephrine and thus permit the study of what happens when those areas that use norepinephrine are deprived of it. In addition, very small quantities of norepinephrine can be traced and followed by supplying the brain with radioactive norepinephrine, which can be then detected in minute traces.

The result of research using this diversity of techniques is to show that some systems in the nervous system have highly specific functions such as that of producing speech, transmitting information from a particular sense organ to a particular higher center, controlling movement in a particular set of muscles, controlling the temperature of the body, or controlling respiration. Other parts of the nervous system have what are called nonspecific functions, that is, they perform such tasks as keeping the higher centers in a general state of arousal or they may exercise some general control over the prevailing emotional states.

Now let us turn to a discussion of some of the discoveries made through these techniques concerning the specific functions of different components of the brain. The midbrain contains centers that control, in particular, the righting reflexes that occur when the body is thrown off balance. It is also the center that controls eye movements and the reflexes associated with the eyes. Of more extensive importance in the control of body movement and position is the cerebellum, a mass of tissue as large as a person's fist, that lies at the back of the brain stem. This important nerve center receives nerve impulses from all the sensory mechanisms involved in the adjustment of the position of the body and the orientation of the body in space. Thus it receives information from the vestibular organs of the middle ear, and also from the joints, tendons, and muscles. There are also inputs from the organs of vision, touch, and hearing, which common experience suggests play an important role in keeping a man right side up to the world. Damage to the cerebellum produces difficulties in coordinating muscular activity and problems of maintaining balance. The cerebellum also sends impulses to both sensory and motor areas of the higher centers.

The diencephalon consists largely of two major structures, the thalamus and the hypothalamus. The thalamus is most noted as a sensory relay station. In addition, the thalamus receives information from the eyes, ears, and the smell-taste system. The sensory information coming up the spinal cord is relayed at the thalamus to the higher centers of the brain. Rather than saying that the thalamus sends the information up to the specialized areas of the cortex that handle this information, the neurophysiologist says that the sensory inputs are "projected" onto the sensory areas of the cortex of the brain.

The relatively crude information coming from the lower parts of the body may well undergo analysis at the level of the thalamus, and only the analyzed information may be passed on to the higher centers. There is much speculation at this time concerning the extent to which the thalamus is an analyzer of information rather than just a relay station. Some have also suggested that the thalamus may be the center of the awareness of pain.

The hypothalamus has important functions related to hunger, thirst, and sexual excitation, and also seems to have much to do with the control of emotional states. Some have described it as the seat of the emotions. The hypothalamus contains centers that maintain a homeostatic balance, that is, a balance in the internal chemistry of the organism. If the nucleus that controls water balance is disturbed through a growth or through injury, the person excretes enormous quantities of fluid and has to take in large quantities of water to keep from becoming dehydrated. A parallel phenomenon also occurs when the working of the hunger center in the hypothalamus is upset and animals will ingest large quantities of food and become obese. The center for hunger should not be thought of as a single nucleus, for it consists of a set of separate nuclei controlling appetite, initiating feeding, and the cessation of feeding on satiation. An interesting finding is that animals that have had a part of this area destroyed not only show disturbances in their eating habits, but they also behave in a peculiarly savage way. There are also centers concerned with the maintenance of body temperature and the control of such temperature-regulating functions as those of sweating, the dilation of the blood vessels in the skin, and panting. The neural mechanisms involved in cooling oneself in a hot environment are different from those involved in raising the temperature in cool surroundings. One mechanism can go wrong while the other continues to operate. Other centers in the hypothalamus exert control over blood pressure and heart rate. The reader should take note that the description of the hypothalamus given here is a gross simplification (see Valenstein, Cox, and Kakolewski, 1970).

A generation ago Cannon discovered that the hypothalamus also has functions connected with what has been termed the rage reaction. This reaction in the cat is shown by hissing, arching of the back, the erection of hairs on the skin, the flattening of the ears, and the tightening of the muscles of the legs in a crouching position that makes it possible for the animal to rapidly attack or withdraw. Cannon showed that when connections of the hypothalamus to the cortex of the brain are severed the animal will go into the rage condition under the slightest provocation. Merely petting the animal may precipitate this response. Ordinarily, the cortex of the brain inhibits this response and prevents it from occurring, but the removal of this inhibiting influence makes the response more easily aroused.

The cortex of the brain itself shows some specialization of function in particular areas of a typical right cerebral hemisphere, as shown in Figure 12-4, but there are large areas that are quite nonspecific in what they do. A broad band down the middle is involved in muscular control and has to do with the initiation of move-

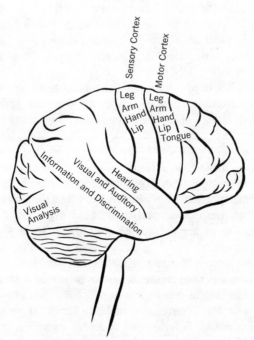

Figure 12-4. Some specialized functions located in the human right cortex.

ment. Just posterior to this region is another band of tissue, which has to do with general bodily sensibility. At the rear is an area that handles visual information analysis. An area on the right side of the brain handles auditory information analysis. The areas related to vision and hearing are not the areas in which information is stored. If these areas are stimulated electrically in a surgical patient on the operating table, the patient does not report any meaningful experience. However, there are other areas of the cortex, which do not have analysis functions, that can be stimulated electrically and that will produce vivid memories that are almost like hallucinations in the detail with which they are seen or heard. The meaning of this is probably that the specific sensory areas are involved in the analysis of information, and not the storage of information. For this reason, attempts to excite them do not arouse memories. Storage takes place in parts of the cortex other than those in which the incoming information is analyzed.

The little evidence available that comes from the study of the visual cortex of the cat is suggestive of how the specific sensory areas of the cortex handle information. Hubel (1963) has been able to show that the visual area of the cortex of the cat is arranged in a set of layers each of which identifies lines having a particular slope. This means that a visual presentation is analyzed in terms of a number of distinct attributes, each one of which is identified by a particular mechanism in the sensory cortex. The visual cortex can probably analyze many of the cues or all of the cues simultaneously. The sensory area in the cortex probably does not use all the information available in a particular display, but takes a sample of cues, which are then analyzed and provide the data necessary for identification. A small object moving rapidly across the floor is probably identified as a mouse solely on the basis of its small size and speed of movement. No other cues are necessary. An object lying on the floor can be identified as a coin merely from the size and metallic brightness. The sensory areas in the brain are probably mechanisms that pick up such relevant cues and thus permit identification of the object involved.

THE UNIQUENESS OF THE HUMAN CEREBRAL CORTEX

Scientists have long known that the two hemispheres have somewhat different functions in the human brain although they seem to have identical functions in other primates. As long ago as a hundred years Broca discovered that speech functions were controlled by the left hemisphere, but the full scope of the differences between the hemispheres was not recognized until recently. It was recognized that one hemisphere was dominant over the other and that the dominant hemisphere was generally the left one. For the purposes of this discussion we will assume that the dominant hemisphere is the left hemisphere.

In recent times our conception of the differences in function of the two cerebral hemispheres has been revolutionized by some work that was originally designed to help epileptics. This work has led to an understanding of the unique nature of the human brain and insight into our own unique properties as human beings. The work began in the early 1960s when surgeons attempted to help chronic and severe epileptics by cutting the large band of communicating nerve fibers, called the corpus callosum, that connects the two cerebral hemispheres. The theory was that by cutting this band of tissue an epileptic seizure that started in the one hemisphere would not spread to the other. Research with primates had already shown that the cutting of this band of tissue did slight damage to behavior. Indeed, the corpus callosum seemed to have little function, though we now know that it is a very important communicating system between the two cerebral hemispheres. The epileptics on whom the operation was performed showed extraordinary improvement. Apparently before the operation a seizure that would start in one hemisphere would spread to the other hemisphere, and then back again to the first; thus the patient would have one seizure after another. Cutting the corpus callosum prevented this back and forth spread of the abnormal states of excitation.

The patients did not seem to manifest any abnormal behavior as a result of the operation, but they have been changed in important but hidden ways brought out in the work of Sperry and his co-workers. Sperry knew that it was possible to feed a signal into the eye so that the message entered only one cerebral hemisphere in a patient whose corpus callosum had been severed. Sperry flashed words on a screen in such a position that the information was transmitted only to the right cerebral hemisphere. The words referred to small familiar objects and the individual was then asked to identify, by means of touch, the object to which the word referred. The subject was able to do this, which is not surprising. What is surprising is that although the person was able to pick up a nut with his left hand, after the word *nut* had been transmitted to his right brain, he was quite unaware of having seen the word and did not know what he was doing with his left hand, which he could not see since it was hidden by a screen.

When the corpus callosum is intact the individual has no difficulty in consciously recognizing the entire performance, for the corpus callosum tells the left hemisphere what is happening in the right hemisphere. A really significant point to note is that the seat of consciousness appears to be in the left hemisphere, but this form of research also leads to other important findings. One of the most important of these is that the two hemispheres have entirely different functions. Although scientists have long recognized that speech is largely a function of the left hemisphere, until the work of Sperry and his associates, the full range of differences was not appreciated. The left hemisphere is concerned with the higher-level linguistic functions of man and also with all high level analytic and logical forms of thought. It is also the primary mathematical component of the brain. The left brain is what one might term the Piaget type of brain, with its activities focused on the logical-mathematical aspects of thought. The right side of the brain has limited capacity for visual word recognition and can perform the simplest rote calculation, but it is not a brain designed for high-level problem solving. The right side of the brain, however, also has distinctive functions of its own. It seems to play a central role in the appreciation of music and art. It is sensitive to form, both in the field of space and the world of sound, and is thus said to be holistic in its approach to information. Eccles (1973), in summarizing the work, points out that the dominant hemisphere is almost illiterate with respect to pattern sense. The right hemisphere is synthetic and pattern-oriented, rather than analytic and detail-oriented.

Another interesting fact is that strong feelings stirred up in the right hemisphere are experienced in the left, even though the left hemisphere may not know the cause of the feelings. This is possible, even though the two hemispheres have been severed, because there are connections related to feelings that pass down through the midbrain and up again.

In a more recent study, Zaidel and Sperry (1973) gave a version of Raven's Progressive Matrices Test to the left or right hemispheres of patients who had had the separation operation. He found that both hemispheres had some capacity to do the test but that they solved the problems by different means, and there was left hemisphere superiority. This result is somewhat surprising in that it suggests that the right hemisphere can undertake some forms of reasoning tasks. Teng and Sperry (1973) have also found some evidence for right hemisphere verbalization. These more recent findings suggest that the division of labor between the hemispheres is much more complex and not as clear as it was originally thought to be.

NONSPECIFIC FUNCTIONS

One cannot leave the discussion of the main body of the nervous system after a brief discussion of the specific functions, for some of the nonspecific functions are at least of equal importance for the understanding of learning. Let us begin the study of these by starting at the medulla. Deeply embedded in the medulla and extending up toward the brain is a mass of cells known as the reticular formation or the reticular activating system. This mass of cells receives impulses from the sensory nerves and, in turn, sends out impulses to large areas of the cortex of the brain. The impulses that it sends to the higher centers have the ability to produce activity in them. Indeed, if the higher centers were to cease to be bombarded, the higher centers would fall into a sleeplike state. Effective action on the part of the higher centers requires that they receive this bombardment at an appropriate level. If they are not sufficiently bombarded, a state of torpor results. If they are bombarded to an excessive degree, a state of great excitement ensues. On the basis of this fact one can understand why the reticular system is also called the reticular activating system. It is sometimes referred to as a part of the arousal system. A diagram of the system is shown in Figure 12-5.

The extent to which the reticular system bombards the higher centers with impulses depends on the inputs it receives from the sensory nerves. If the input is low, the output of the reticular system is also low, and vice versa. When a person relaxes, in order to fall asleep, he begins by shutting his eyes and lying very still. As he lies there, the sense organs in his skin and muscles becomes less and less active, sending fewer and fewer impulses up the spinal cord. As the number of impulses in the main sensory tracts decrease, so, too, do the number of impulses going into the reticular system. This decreases the output to the higher centers, which slowly fall into a state of sleep. Some drugs also have the effect of reducing the activity level of the reticular system and these also produce a state of drowsiness or sleep. A crucial factor in producing sleep is the control of the inputs to the nervous system.

Certain other features of the reticular activating system need to be noted. One

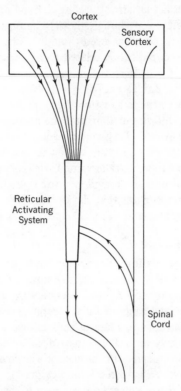

Figure 12-5. Diagram of some of the connections of the reticular activating system.

is that the higher centers also send impulses down to the reticular system and have an effect of activating it. While the reticular system excites the cortex, the cortex also excites the reticular system. In addition, the system sends impulses down the spinal cord and these also have activating functions. The effects produced by the reticular system are extensive and distributed almost over the entire central nervous system. Figure 12-5 shows some of the connections of the reticular activating system. The diagram also shows the inputs from the sensory tracts in the spinal cord, and the inputs to it from the higher centers.

The reticular activating system has no power in itself to increase wakefulness, but is dependent on inputs of impulses for it to function as the activating system. If any of the channels through which its output of impulses is distributed is destroyed, the animal is likely to fall into a drowsy state. The system also has one other function, which is far from being fully understood at this time. It is believed to exert an influence on sensory inputs and can, at times, suppress these inputs.

The reticular activating system extends upward through the midbrain into the thalamus. The part in the thalamus is referred to as the thalamic activating system and it has rather different functions from those of the reticular activating system.

The reticular system is very diffuse in its effects and activates very large areas of the cortex. In contrast, the thalamic activating system seems to activate rather more limited areas of the cortex at any one time. It probably has functions related to attention, alertness, and perhaps even to the orienting response. It also has functions in relation to the production of electrical rhythms at the level of the cortex.

An additional system that has general rather than specific functions is the limbic system, the mass of tissue that lies beneath the cortex between the thalamus and hypothalamus on the one hand and the cortex on the other. The functions of the limbic system are varied and are still far from being thoroughly explored. It probably should not be described as a single system, and it is given a single name only because it is anatomically located in one particular location in relation to the cortex and the lower part of the brain stem.

The limbic system contains three main systems that have been intensively studied. The first system is primarily connected with and serves functions related to the sense of smell. The second system is referred to anatomically as the hippocampus. The third consists of the amygdaloid nuclei.

The hippocampus is primarily a part of the arousal system. The difference between the activating function of the reticular system and the limbic system is that the reticular system is very general in the activation it produces, but the limbic activating system seems to function on more specific parts of the cortex. There is some evidence that the hippocampus has to do with the laying down of permanent memory traces. It is not the seat of memory, but the hippocampus makes it possible for the cortex to retain permanently the information that it would otherwise retain for only a matter of minutes. There is also some possibility that proper functioning of the hippocampus may be necessary for recall.

The amygdaloid nuclei, or the amygdala as they are commonly called, have been studied by observing the effects of stimulating them electrically and by damaging them through surgery. The effect of stimulation depends on where it is applied. It may produce withdrawal or flight reactions or it may produce extreme aggression. Surgical damage also produces the expected corresponding effects. A particularly interesting series of studies has been undertaken over the years, in which electrodes have been placed permanently in the septal region of the limbic system in an anaesthetized animal. The animal can then be placed in a box in which it can press a bar; when it does this, a small electric current is applied to the electrodes. This electrical stimulation of the limbic system has very strong reinforcing properties. The animal presses the lever and obtains electrical stimulation of its own brain. It will then continue to press the lever persistently and frequently. Indeed, when the animal is hungry and has a choice between pressing a lever that will deliver food and the lever that delivers stimulation to the brain, it is likely to choose stimulation to the brain. The opportunity to press the lever providing self-stimulation can be used as a reinforcement that will shape behavior in particular directions.

What this means is that direct electrical stimulation of appropriate areas of the limbic region functions in very much the same way as does positive reinforcement.

Some evidence reported by Valenstein (1966; see also Riklan and Levita, 1969) suggests that stimulation over quite a wide region produces this effect and that this is also the region that has to do with the regulation of drives. That there can be a close relationship between reinforcement and drives cannot be disputed, but just what the relationship is has not yet been adequately explored.

At the level of the cortex of the brain, some areas have specific functions, whereas others seem to be engaged in more general memory functions. Some of the large areas that remain unmapped in Figure 12–4 are those primarily concerned with retention of information. Presumably, they function both to provide a short-term memory, as when a person retains a telephone number long enough to dial it, and also long-term memory. In the case of the adult, there can be considerable damage to these nonspecific areas without any loss of particular memories. This fact suggests that particular items of remembered information are not stored in particular localities, but may be stored simultaneously in different locations. Indeed, a tumor may destroy very substantial parts of the cerebral cortex without there being a corresponding loss of memories of the past. Just what kind of a structure or structures are modified when one memorizes the name of, say, a new neighbor is not known, but it is not just the modification of a particular synapse.

THE CEREBELLUM

A beginning has been made in achieving some understanding of the large mass of nervous tissue situated to the rear of the cerebral hemispheres known as the cerebellum. Eccles, Ito, and Szentágothai (1967) have referred to this mass of tissue as being like a computer. The theme of their book is that the cerebellum receives vast amounts of data both from the higher centers of the brain and from the muscles and skin, coordinates this information, and uses it in helping to provide a smooth flow of motor behavior. The outputs of the cerebellum are all related to motor activity and the organ brings together all the information needed to ensure that the flow of motor activity will be smooth and coordinated. The cerebellum is described by Eccles et al. as always being in a state of poise with the information at its disposal always available, so that movements can be made taking into account that information. The cerebellum does not just take in and store information related to the position and state of each limb and muscle in the body; the information is stored in an organized state for immediate use. The incoming information appears to be widely distributed through the system and, like the other major brain structures, the cerebellum does not store particular pieces of information in particular locations. The physiological function of the cerebellum is such that it does not manifest sustained neural activity of the kind associated with thought. Eccles et al. point out that within 0.03 of a second after an input, activity in the cortex of the cerebellum comes to an abrupt halt and the organ is in a state of readiness to use the input and to produce the output to the motor system.

Just how the cerebellum performs its functions is far from clear. It does not initiate action, for the initiation of a sequence of movements seems to take place in the cerebral cortex. Arbib, Franklin, and Nilsson (1968) suggest that the cerebellum could perform very much like a piece of computer equipment called a compiler, which assembles a computer program. One can tell a compiler, for example, that one wants a program to calculate a square root and the compiler will list all of the detailed operations necessary for doing this. If one's cerebral cortex were to tell the cerebellum to plan a series of movements to take one to the mail box, a program of movements might be assembled such as those of getting up from the chair, going to the door, taking hold of the door knob, opening the door, going through the door, taking hold of the door knob, closing the door, and so forth. Then the program might run off fairly automatically, and one's thought processes would not have to intervene, unless something went wrong such as the door sticking and not opening. Arbib et al. point out that the decision to perform a series of actions and the execution of those actions appear to require rather different machinery, and probably quite independent machinery.

This view of the cerebellum is substantiated by the study of individuals in whom the cerebellum has been damaged. Such individuals can perform skilled acts, but they are not run off in a smooth sequence. The performance is halting. After each movement is made, the individual has to stop and think about the next component of the act, before actually performing it. The cerebellum is no longer able to assemble sequences of movements, so the person has to consciously select each component separately and perform it separately. The result is a tedious, halting, and clumsy performance.

THE BRAIN AS A COMPUTER

Since the synapses function essentially as if they were on-off switches, and since digital computers consist largely of transistors that also function as on-off switches, psychologists have long been tempted to think of the brain as though it functioned like a large digital computer. However, Powers (1973) has persuasively argued that this is a poor analogy and that the brain functions much more like an analog computer. Analog computers do not use systems of on-off switches, but they use a mechanical or electrical process to represent some aspect of the real world. A very simple example of an analog computer is an old-fashioned spring-wound clock with hands. Such a clock represents the passage of time by the degree that tension is lost on a spring. After a certain passage of time, the spring looses all tension, becomes completely unwound, and the clock stops and no longer functions as a device for computing the passage of time. The hands on the clock show the passage of time, but they also show how far the spring has lost tension. The tension in the spring is an analog for the passage of time. Powers argues that the brain is able to represent internally the ongoing events of the outside world much as the tension in the spring represents time in the universe outside the clock. Powers also proposes a system of controls that are exercised over behavior that, in turn, control the sensory inputs.

A point to note is that although the brain may well work as an analog computer in relation to what are called perceptual processes, nevertheless the brain may still work much more like a digital computer when storing items of information.

THE AUTONOMIC NERVOUS SYSTEM

An important division of the nervous system is a complex of nerves and ganglia that constitutes what is known as the *autonomic*, or *sympathetic*, nervous system. Because many significant aspects of behavior are associated with the activity of this system, some consideration of its function in relation to behavior must be given here.

The most recognizable components of this system are two cordlike structures that extend through the length of the body cavity. These are known as the sympathetic trunks. Each one of these has a number of bulges along its length consisting of masses of nerve cells. From the trunks, nerves can be seen to go to the viscera. It is also known that this system has nerves connected to all the smooth muscles of the body, which are the muscles that are both slow-acting and not under voluntary control. The system also can activate certain glands, such as the adrenal glands.

The system derives its name from the fact that most of the functions it serves are not under voluntary control, and the system gives the superficial appearance of being an independent one, functioning on its own. The appearance here is deceptive because it has been established that there are centers in the central nervous system that can induce activity in the autonomic system. The relationship to the central nervous system is highly complex.

The autonomic nervous system has built into it a complex series of reflex mechanisms. The pupil of the eye contracts automatically in the presence of bright light. Peristalsis occurs in the intestines when they are stretched by the presence of food, and by this means food is moved along the length of the tract.

The autonomic nervous system can be properly considered a part of the effector mechanism—that is, the efferent system that results in activity. That it does produce action is beyond question, but the action it produces is highly generalized and is not confined to specific muscles, as it is when an efferent nerve from the spinal cord is involved.

The autonomic nervous system also shows the effects of learning, and many visceral and other responses are acquired through a learning process that has not been clearly described as yet. The person who develops severe migraine headaches whenever he is placed in a stressful situation is manifesting an acquired response of the autonomic nervous system. The headaches are due to the activity of the small smooth muscles found in the walls of the blood vessels that supply the brain. A person's digestive system may not function properly in many situations that have been associated with stress. The blushing mechanism, in the case of a particular individual, may be triggered by numerous stimuli that do not ordinarily set it into action. Some of these learnings are relatively harmless, but others could conceivably have serious consequences and proceed to the point where the health of a person is damaged. Psychosomatic medicine is that branch of medicine that attempts to help people whose natural reflexes of the autonomic nervous system have been modified so that they are fired by inappropriate stimuli. One is tempted to suggest that the mechanism of classical conditioning might well account for disturbances of behavior occurring through the activity of the autonomic nervous system, but convincing evidence will have to be presented to prove that this is so. What can be demonstrated at the present time is that some of the reflexes associated with the autonomic nervous system can be conditioned, but there is a long step from such a demonstration to the position that psychosomatic disorders are a result of a process similar to classical conditioning.

The Location of Learning

A basic problem related to the structure of the nervous system is the matter of where learning is located in terms of gross structures. The point has already been made that the synapse is commonly suggested to be the structure in which learning is located, although this has not been definitely established. There are synapses, in billions, throughout the nervous system, so even if one were to accept the synapse as the seat of learning, it would not enable one to locate the gross structures involved mainly in learning. In addition, many synapses are involved in functions other than learning, such as the temporary holding of information, the blocking or facilitation of the transmittal of information to higher centers, and the redistribution of information.

It is quite obvious that learning is highly dependent on the functioning of the cerebral cortex, and animals that have had the cortex removed through surgery lose their capability to learn most of the complex skills they need to be capable of learning. Studies of patients who have suffered damage to various parts of the cerebral cortex show that no particular part can be associated with learning. A parallel finding is that in the adult damage to a specific area does not result in the loss of the memory for a particular piece of information. Siegel (1970) points out that the site of learning is even more elusive than this statement makes it out to be, for the complete surgical removal of the cortex does not eliminate completely the capacity to learn. At least in subhuman primates, and almost certainly in man learning can take place at the midbrain level, but here again the site of learning is elusive and different areas can be destroyed without the complete loss of learning. Because learning through midbrain functioning, in the absence of the cerebral cortex, has been quite well demonstrated at this time, one is left wondering whether learning can also take place at an even lower level, say at the level of the spinal cord. The latter has turned out to be a much more difficult problem to study than has the matter of learning at the midbrain level, despite the fact that the microanatomy of the spinal cord is much better understood than is that of the higher centers. The typical procedure involved in attempting to demonstrate learning at the spinal cord level is to work with an animal in whom the spinal cord has been severed. In such an animal a reflexive contraction of a hind limb can be produced by applying a strong electric shock to the foot. An attempt can then be made to condition this response to a stimulus provided to the other foot. The evidence suggests that conditioning does take place under these circumstances, but nobody can as yet be quite sure that it does because alternative explanations, other than conditioning, can be called upon to account for the experimental results. A best guess at this time would probably be that learning functions are very widely distributed throughout the nervous system and cannot be assumed to be the functions of only the higher centers.

Much the same controversy exists about the location of information-analysis functions. Although some areas of the cortex have been identified as specializing in the analysis of information, other areas also have information-analysis functions in addition to other functions. The cerebellum, for example, is a very complex information analysis and collating system. Some evidence suggests that the midbrain has such functions, some of which are coupled with regulatory functions related to basic body processes. There is also the possibility that even some of the masses of nerve cells that lie outside the central nervous system may be involved in information analysis.

The picture of the nervous system presented here indicates that information analysis and storage are quite different functions, dependent on different brain structures. What needs to be settled is the extent to which information from the sense organs is analyzed at successive levels of detail at the different levels of the nervous system or whether all information analysis occurs in the cortex of the brain. The very large amount of the brain that deals with the handling of the incoming information gives support to the view that learning is, to a great extent, a matter of learning to handle and utilize the incoming information. The view of learning as involving nothing more than the strengthening of a response is probably a vast oversimplification of what is known about learning and what is known about the nervous structures on which learning depends.

An additional point that emerges from the study of the nervous system is that an extraordinarily large amount of tissue is involved in what are called the activating systems. Learning is highly dependent on the extent to which these systems are or are not maintaining an appropriate level of activity in the higher centers. The data also suggest that the level of arousal can be externally controlled, because the inputs to the reticular activating system from the sensory systems are important for initiating activity in the arousal system. However, an excessive level of activity produced by the arousal system may interfere with learning.

A final very important discovery is that information is not stored in single localities. The advantages of multiple storage are many. One advantage is the physiological one, for multiple storage means that slight damage to one part of the brain does not involve the immediate loss of what might be quite crucial items of information. In terms of behavior, the storage of information in multiple localities might permit that information to be related more easily to many other different items of information. As the neurophysiologist discovers how information is stored in the central nervous system, useful suggestions will be provided concerning how man organizes the information he derives from the senses.

Brain Damage and Learning

Of great significance to the educator are the effects of brain damage on learning. Although half a century ago little recognition was given to the fact that children might suffer brain damage, the evidence is now overwhelming that a large number of children start life with some damage to the nervous system through events that happen at birth. In the early part of the present century, the lack of recognition of the effect of brain damage on development was due to the fact that the assumption was made that brain damage had to be caused either by the penetration of a sharp object or through severe impact. Neurologists have now come to recognize that a much more frequent form of brain damage results from the brain being deprived of oxygen at birth. Indeed, the evidence indicates that pressure on the brain at birth has very slight effects compared with the very damaging effects that may occur when the baby is deprived of oxygen through the umbilical cord's becoming entangled or compressed. Damage due to lack of oxygen may have devastating effects on brain tissues and produce both widespread and permanent damage.

Children who have severe brain damage are identified at a quite early age and are much more likely to have their problems appropriately managed than those who have much less damage and whose difficulties are not recognized until a teacher reports learning difficulties. A relatively common severe outcome of brain damage is cerebral palsy. The victim of such a complaint is typically characterized as having difficulties in controlling the muscles of the body. The complaint may be so severe that the child is unable to walk, feed himself, or speak, but it may also be so small that it is evident only in some slight speech impairment. Sometimes the damage is not confined to the strictly motor components of behavior, and there may also be losses in sensory functions and in thinking abilities. However, the child with cerebral palsy is recognized today to be much better off intellectually than he was previously thought to be. A child who is unable to use his muscles to express himself, through movement or speech, has difficulty in demonstrating his capacity for thought and understanding. Such children may have intellectually high potential, although they are not able to show it until they have been given special training and means are found to assist them in controlling their movements. Although it was believed at one time that most cerebral palsy cases were beyond help, today a very large percentage of them are rehabilitated to the point where they can profit from education and become to some degree self-supporting. A part of the problem of the rehabilitation of those afflicted with cerebral palsy is the bad attitude of the public toward them. Such cases are often quite unprepossessing in appearance and the public often does not understand that one cannot judge a person from his appearance.

Another dramatic form of behavior that *may* find its origins in brain injury is broadly described as the epileptic seizure. The epileptic seizure shows a quite typical pattern of electrical activity in the brain, which can be recorded through an electro-encephalograph. The record during a seizure shows a disruption of the typical electrical rhythms and very large electrical pulsations produced by many cells firing together synchronously.

Of much greater significance to the teacher are the relatively large number of cases that fall into the category of minimal brain dysfunction. The U.S. Office of Education reports on *Minimal Brain Dysfunction in Children* (1966, 1969) accept as a definition of such children (1969, p. 53) those of near average, average, or above average general intelligence with certain learning and/or behavioral disabilities ranging from mild to severe, which are associated with deviations of function of the central nervous system, These deviations may manifest themselves by various combinations of impairment in perception, conceptualization, language, memory, and control of attention, impulse, or motor function. These aberrations may arise from genetic variations, biochemical irregularities, perinatal brain insults or injuries sustained during the years which are critical for the development and maturation of the central nervous system, or from other unknown organic causes.

The definition is global and comprehensive and takes in such a wide range of cases that it does little more than alert the teacher to the fact that some children, most of whose behavior falls within the normal range, may still suffer from specific learning disabilities that are quite damaging to educational progress. For example, a child may have difficulties in the area of visual perception that make it very difficult for him to learn to read. Many of these dysfunctions may be subtle and not very evident to the teacher who has only limited contact with each child. A common characteristic of many children with minimal brain dysfunction is hyperactivity. The hyperactivity is not the typical busy goal-directed activity of normal children, but an unorganized activity characterized by an inability to stay with a task until completed and a high degree of distractibility. Such children are potentially effective learners, but the unorganized hyperactivity makes it difficult for them under ordinary classroom circumstances to stay long enough with any task to permit learning. The hyperactivity is also often accompanied by visual perceptual difficulties manifested in an inability to copy quite simple forms. Many such cases are believed to be a result of damage due to lack of oxygen at birth.

The problems of the hyperactive child have been handled in two ways. One way is to place him in an environment in which there are minimal sources of stimulation. A classroom thus designed for the hyperactive child might have a table and chair for one child, no windows, the walls a uniform neutral tone, and no equipment and materials except those with which the pupil is working. Under such circumstances, the activity of the child is greatly reduced and the conditions may favor learning. An alternative approach is to attempt to control the surplus activity by means of drugs, many of which have been used for this purpose, including phenobarbitol, reserpine, and chlorpromazine. Such agents reduce anxiety, aggressiveness, and concomitant hyperactivity. The problems related to the use of drugs for the control of behavior have been discussed earlier in the book and will not be expanded on further here.

The main bases for differentiating normal children from those with minimal brain dysfunction are the results of psychological tests, which in themselves are far from being as valid as one might wish them to be. Thorough neurological examinations are also sometimes conducted but the most developed neurological diagnostic techniques are focussed on the lower centers of the nervous system, and those directed at the higher centers are still crude and primitive. One may hope that ultimately the neurologist may develop diagnostic devices that will permit the very early identification of children who have minimal brain dysfunction so that steps can be taken at an early age to help each child.

SUMMARY

1. The nervous system consists of cells with specialized functions that transmit information into the central system and action-producing impulses to the muscles and glands. The sensitive cells in the sense organs represent nerve cells that have special functions. Nerve cells do not connect directly to other nerve cells, but are separated by gaps known as synapses. Impulses can be transmitted across the synapses through chemical changes.

2. The evidence points in the general direction of suggesting that information is stored at the synapses that function as a set of on-off switches. Storage at the synapses probably takes place through chemical changes that may well be highly stable once they have taken place.

3. That part of the nervous system that transmits information into it is called the afferent system, in constrast to the efferent system, which conducts inpulses from the centers that initiate action to the muscles and glands that produce action. Afferent nerves enter the spinal cords at various locations along its length and efferent nerves leave through nearby locations. The spinal cord represents a complex transmission system between the brain and the periphery and also provides some coordination of activity at very simple levels.

4. The structures that form what is commonly known as the brain are in origin enlargements of the upper regions of the spinal cord. In the mature nervous system the spinal cord shows some thickening as it approaches the brain. This thickening is known as the medulla. The upper part of the brain stem is also covered by the pons, a broad band of fibers that connects the two cerebral hemispheres. The largest structures in the entire system are the cerebral hemispheres, which include those structures having to do with the most detailed analysis of information, the storage of information, higher functions such as decision making, and the initiation of much action.

5. Although physiologists originally hoped that some precise function could be found for each location in the nervous system, the conception of nervous system function that this implied turned out to have only limited validity. Although some parts do have quite specific functions, much of the system involves what are called nonspecific functions. However, it is somewhat difficult to separate what is meant by a specific function from what is meant by a nonspecific function. For example, a part of the nervous system has to do with drives and the initiation of behavior through the operation of basic drives. This part is commonly said to have nonspecific functions, in that drives have a general effect on behavior. In a sense, though, this is quite a specific function and much more specific than the function of much of the cortex of the brain.

6. Brain function can be explored through a number of techniques, including those of studying the effects of lesions and mechanical injury to the brain, the effect of stimulating particular parts of the brain either through electrode implants

or through the direct stimulation of the exposed brain, or through tracing chemical substances involved in particular kinds of neural activity.

7. The cerebellum receives information from all the sensory mechanisms involved in keeping the organism right side up to the world and also controls the righting reflexes that maintain posture. The thalamus is mainly noted as a relay station and some information analysis may take place at that level. The thalamus may also be involved in awareness of pain. The hypothalamus has functions closely related to the regulation of behavior related to such basic drives as hunger, thirst, temperature regulation, and sex. The control of these functions is complex and each drive state appears to involve several different centers. The cortex of the brain shows some specialization of function. Some areas are concerned with the analysis of information coming from the senses. A large central area has to do with the initiation of movements, and an area on the left side has to do with the control of speech. One side of the cerebral cortex is the dominant side, usually the left side. The two sides have rather different functions. The dominant side engages in reasoning and in the analysis of situations. The nondominant side is more holistic in function and performs important activities related to art and music.

8. A major nonspecific function is focused on the reticular activating system in the medulla. Sensory inputs activate this body, which in turn activates widely distributed areas of the cortex. There is also a descending effect, for the cortex, in turn, sends impulses down to the activating mechanism and can increase activity in the reticular system. The extent to which a person is in a state of wakefulness or sleep depends in some degree on the state of the reticular activating mechanism. The limbic system, higher up in the nervous system, also has functions related to arousal and wakefulness and to experiencing pleasure and its opposite. The limbic system also seems to have functions related to the laying down of permanent memory traces in the cortex of the brain. The phenomenon known as self-stimulation has also been shown to occur when electrodes are placed within the amygdaloid nuclei and the animal has the opportunity of pressing a bar that will deliver a small electric current to the electrodes. The animal is likely to engage in pressing the bar under these conditions. Much of the cortex of the cerebral hemispheres has nonspecific functions. Although the cortex must be considered to be the primary seat of memory, particular pieces of information do not seem to be stored in particular places. Damage in a particular location does not generally eradicate a particular memory.

9. The nervous system obviously includes mechanisms that make it possible to hold information from the senses for short periods of time. In addition, the nervous system has mechanisms for inhibiting various responses as well as for facilitating behavior.

10. A complex network of nerves scattered through the body constitutes the autonomic nervous system. The functions it serves are not under direct voluntary control. The functions of the autonomic nervous system are closely related to behavior under stress conditions.

11. The site of learning within the nervous system is highly elusive. Some evidence

suggests that learning may take place at perhaps even all levels. Beyond any question, information analysis takes place in many different localities, from the sense-organ level to the highest levels of the entire system. Although most physiologists believe that the synapse is the place where information is stored, critical experiments to support or reject this view have not yet been designed. A few physiologists have proposed that it is the glial cells that store information through some complex chemical process.

12. The effect of brain injury on behavior is of considerable interest to the teacher, in view of the fact that many children show minimal brain dysfunction. Often these children not only present learning difficulties but are quite disruptive to the learning of others through their hyperactivity. Although this form of behavior can be controlled by drugs, the long-term results of such treatment are not known. Such children often also suffer from perceptual difficulties, which interfere with learning and particularly with the acquisition of reading skill.

PART V

**STUDIES OF SPECIALIZED
AREAS OF LEARNING**

Chapter 13

Problem Solving

For the psychologist, a human being is said to be confronted with a problem when faced with a situation in which (1) there is a goal to be achieved and (2) the individual does not have in his repertoire of behavior any readily available response that will permit him to achieve the goal. This definition can be applied to human behavior because one can identify whether the human being does or does not have a goal to achieve, for one can ask him what he is trying to accomplish. The same definition cannot be applied to animals for obvious reasons. Hence, a more widely applicable definition of a problem would state that it is a situation in which an organism is in a state of disequilibrium (hungry, thirsty, sex-deprived, etc.) and has no readily available response that will restore equilibrium. Many other variations of these definitions have been reviewed by Berlyne (1965).

After a problem has been successfully solved, one can say that a response to the situation has been learned. When the same situation is encountered the next time, the appropriate response will be produced almost immediately, or at least more rapidly than it was on the first encounter. In terms of the definition given here, the situation is no longer a problem. Let us illustrate this with a simple example.

Many children in the first grade if asked " How much is two and two and two?" will say immediately "Six." This is not problem-solving behavior because the child has been asked this question many times before and has the answer. He can produce the answer immediately after he is asked the question. This is not problem solving because he knows the answer. On the other hand, one can ask the same child, "If

I had six pieces of candy and wanted to divide them among three children, how many pieces of candy will each child get?" The child will probably have no ready-made answer to this question, which he may not have encountered before. Even if he knows what three twos make, this latter piece of knowledge may not help him, for children of that age cannot see that the new problem is the reverse of the familiar problem. When the child is asked to divide six pieces of candy among three children, without being given pieces of candy with which to do it, he is likely to make a wild guess or to say he does not know. He has no ready-made response available, even though he knows what has to be done. In such a situation he is said to be confronted with a problem.

If the child faced with the problem is given some encouragement, he may manage to concoct a solution, that is, manufacture a response that he did not have in the first place. The production of this new response is called problem solving.

Problem solving may involve behavior that can be observed by others or it may involve behavior that is internal. The child given the problem of dividing six imaginary pieces of candy among three children may attempt to find a solution by asking for six pieces of candy that he can then divide among three imaginary children. The child may even be able to find the solution through using six slips of paper that are viewed as make-believe candy. A few children in the first grade may solve the problem without manipulating any real or imaginary candy. They do this through performing internal operations commonly referred to as thinking, but which are technically referred to as mediating processes. Problems are typically solved in daily life through a combination of internal thinking operations and actual manipulations of things and objects.

After a person has solved several similar problems, he may discover general procedures for solving problems of that particular kind. These procedures for solving classes of problems are referred to as problem-solving strategies. Different individuals may acquire different strategies for solving problems as they pass through life and hence may show different approaches to solving the same problem.

THE CLASSIFICATION OF PROBLEMS

Theories of education of the last century held out the hope that education could develop general problem-solving skills through exercises involving the "hard" subjects, such as Latin and mathematics. In the present century, considerable skepticism has been expressed about the latter viewpoint and instruction in problem solving has generally been given within each subject matter area separately. Training in scientific problem solving is generally given separately from training in social studies problem solving. Psychologists have been interested in finding some more fundamental classification system in terms of which problems may be grouped and have evolved classifications of problems that do not depend on subject-matter field. One psychological system of classification that has had considerable impact on education is that advanced by Guilford (1959). Guilford takes the position that the intellect manifests itself in problem solving and that an understanding of the intellect requires an understanding of the nature of problems and a classification of problems. Guilford has a three-dimensional classification of problems. He states that problems can be classified in terms of the content of the problem, and he considers such categories of content as are involved in the use of figures, or symbols, or words and word meaning, and not subject-matter categories. He also states that problems can be classified in terms of the operations performed by the problem solver. Such operations include those of memorizing, making evaluations, recognizing, identifying, and knowing, and also what he considers convergent and divergent operations. These are not what Piaget calls operations. He also has a classification of problems in terms of their outcomes. The outcome of solving a problem may be a number, as in an arithmetical problem, or perhaps the production of a complicated system, as in designing an electronic circuit. The Guilford classification system thus involves four categories of content, five categories of operations, and six categories of products. As every problem-solving task can be classified in terms of content, operations, and product, there are altogether $4 \times 5 \times 6$ categories of problems, that is, 120 categories. A detailed discussion of Guilford's classification system and some of the implications it has for education is found in Meeker's book (1969).

The system for classifying problems has appeal, but it has not brought to problem-solving research the order that one might have hoped it would bring. There are questions of whether it has been derived on a sound basis, and many would say that not enough is yet known to produce a comprehensive set of categories. Nevertheless, the system has had impact on education at one important point by including within its scope the categories of convergent and divergent thinking Convergent thinking refers to thinking in relation to problems that have one fixed solution. Divergent thinking refers to thinking in open-ended problems, that is, problems that have no fixed solution and where many new and original solutions are possible. This classification of problems into those involving convergent thinking and those involving divergent thinking has long appealed to those engaged in problem-solving research. These categories have also appealed to the interests of educators, who have also long been interested in creative problem solving and who have taken the view that divergent problem solving is a creative activity. There is some evidence that the abilities involved in divergent thinking are different from those involved in convergent thinking and perhaps require separate training. Many educators have taken the position that problems involving convergent thinking call for noncreative thinking, but that problems in the divergent category involve creative thinking. Such a view is hardly reasonable. Consider, for example, the case of Isaac Newton pondering the problem of what kept the planets in their orbits. Eventually, Newton arrived at the principle of universal gravitation as the underlying explanation. The problem is a convergent one, in that there is only one possible solution, and yet most historians of science would view Newton's solution as highly creative. Again, if only divergent problem solving is viewed as creative, Einstein's development of the theory of relativity would have to be classified as a noncreative act, for it is a unique solution to a problem. Such a conclusion is nonsense. Convergent and divergent thinking may call for different abilities, but the categories cannot be identified with those of creative and noncreative thinking.

A few of Guilford's problem categories have been a source of considerable research, as has been the case with the convergent and divergent categories, but most research programs related to problem solving have shown little influence of his classification scheme.

Despite the interest that has been shown in measures of divergent thinking, little consistent evidence has emerged to show that the measures can make any useful predictions. Kogan and Pankove (1974), who reviewed the evidence and conducted a study in the area, have arrived at this conclusion.

Piaget, as we have already seen, has a different conception of problem solving. For him, all problem solving is creative. The very essence of problem solving is that the solver of a problem *invents* a solution. Invention is at the very core of the intellect. For Guilford, certain intellectual factors enter into creativity and others do not. Piaget views intelligence as being, in essence, an inventive capacity. Solutions, even wrong solutions, are always inventions of the intellect, but inventions may be at different levels of maturity. In the first few years of life solutions are intuitive and are tied to the perceptual aspects of the problem. For example, a child chooses to take a cookie spread out into a large, thin circle because it looks larger to him than fat, round ones, which actually contain more dough. His problem of selecting the largest cookie is solved in perceptual terms and he cannot take into account several dimensions at once. Sometimes his inventions are simple mechanical devices, as when he discovers he can use a spoon for obtaining an object beyond his reach. Such responses are viewed as accommodations to familiar objects. The child is already familiar with a spoon as a tool for bringing food to the mouth, but now he invents a new way to use a spoon and produces the accommodative response of using it as a tool for reaching an object. Such inventions are on the intuitive level. They do not involve if-this-then-that reasoning. As the child grows older, he invents logical structures through which problems can be solved. During the elementary-school years he has reached the point of being able to solve problems involving classification and certain kinds of relations, particularly those involved in seriation. He has limited capacity to reason in relation to the concrete problems that confront him, and his reasoning is characterized by reversibility. Still later he acquires the ability to undertake formal thought. Thus there are three levels of problems: those that can be solved intuitively, those that can be solved by concrete operations, and those that can be solved by formal operations.

REDUCTIONIST AND NONREDUCTIONIST APPROACHES TO THE STUDY OF PROBLEM SOLVING

The American and Russian approaches to the study of problem solving have typically followed along reductionist lines. Problem-solving research has been largely the study of certain elements of behavior in the solution of problems. The element generally considered has been the association. According to this view of problem solving, the solution to a problem is found by plugging in the right association. Consider, for example, the improvisation problem, in which one has to find an object that can be used as a screwdriver. One searches in one's mind for common objects that have an edge that can be used for turning a screw. All objects that can be associated with the property of having a metal edge are scrutinized, until one thinks of an object that has an appropriate edge. Thus the solution appears to be a matter of scanning associations between the problem situation and objects that have potential for providing a solution.

The analysis of problem solving as a process of turning up the right association is simplistic. The first step in solving the problem was not that of searching for what can be associated with having a suitable edge. The first step toward the solution of the problem was that of identifying the fact that the screw could be turned by objects other than a screwdriver but that these objects had to have an appropriate edge, small enough to fit the head of the screw yet strong enough to turn the head without buckling. The task of finding objects associated with these properties was secondary and much simpler than that of the thinking that led to it. Identifying the general nature of the problem and the solution involved reasoning, but finding an object with suitable properties involves little more than memory. Associationistic approaches to the study of problem solving emphasize the memory factor. On the other hand, approaches that involve reasoning tend to neglect associations as a component in the solution.

Guilford's approach to problem solving is an attempt to combine both approaches. He includes in his model several reasoning factors, but he also places heavy emphasis on the abilities involved in making associations. Included in the batteries of tests, from which his model is derived, are several tests that measure the ability to make associations. His so-called tests of fluency include measures of the ability to perform such tasks as thinking of as many uses as possible for a piece of broken glass, a rubber band, or a brick. Such tests measure the rate at which ideas flow, but have nothing to do with the ability to reason. Another task that appears in tests of fluency of ideas asks the individual to list the consequences of everyone in the world going blind.

Classical and operant psychologists attempt to reduce problem solving to chains of conditioned responses. The assumption is that in problem solving if the individual is capable of solving the problem, he has already in his repertoire all of the component responses and that his task is to tie them together in a way that will provide the solution to the problem. This is a form of associationistic psychology in that assocations between elements of behavior are used as the components of the problem-solving process. Although problem solving may occasionally fit this model quite well, most problem solving does not. Consider, for example, the problem of arranging a set of sticks of different lengths in order of size. A 5-year-old faced with this problem is unable to do it, but an 8-year-old can. The 5-year-old has certain essential components in his system of responses. For example, he can take two sticks and say that one is larger than the other. He cannot solve the problem because he has no broad strategy available in his repertoire of responses that will enable him to approach the problem effectively. He cannot look for the smallest, and then the next smallest, and so forth. He cannot do this partly because he cannot conceptualize the final arrangement of the sticks and partly because he has not acquired reversibility in his thinking and cannot conceive of an object being at the same time larger than a second object and smaller than a third. The strategy of serializing cannot be conceptualized in the same way as can the much simpler response of pointing to the longer or the shorter of two sticks. It is a complex internal plan for action.

Since the reductionist approach to the study of problem solving has been the dominant one in America, it is appropriate that we consider, at this point, some of the results of that research. The findings of the nonreductionist approach have already been considered in the chapter on Piaget and related topics. The reductionist has undertaken research on problems at a relatively simple level, because these problems offer the greatest possibility of having the component behaviors involved in solving them reduced to simple elements of behavior. The types of problems most often studied by American research workers are those identified as concept acquisition and the anagram problem. These do not involve the logic of problem solving, as Piaget defines logic and, therefore, may be considered to represent problem solving at a very low level. Piaget would describe the problem-solving process in concept learning and anagrams as involving either what he calls intuitive processes or perceptual processes, or even a simple search of the memory for elements that fit the solution. The findings of such research may be generalizable to problem solving at a similar level of difficulty, but probably tell little about problem solving at more complex levels.

Before plunging into a discussion of research on concept learning, one must point out that much of the research has not been tied to any particular theoretical point of view, but rather has been atheoretical. Nevertheless, concept learning has been widely cited as the main attempt of reductionists to apply their theoretical position to problem solving. One can make a strong case for the position that attempts to build a theory of problem solving in terms of simplistic concepts derived from animal studies are doomed to failure because of a fundamental difference between animal and human problem solving. Haslerud (1972) has pointed out that in all the classic studies of problem solving in subhuman primates, the animals can solve problems only with those materials that they can immediately perceive. Kohler's chimpanzees would not use a stick to retrieve a piece of banana, unless the stick was in the part of the cage that they could see. Even Sultan, Kohler's most gifted chimpanzee, would not go and search for a stick in the inner cage to use as a retrieval tool. This means that even the most intelligent primates are not able to search their memories for ideas related to tools that might be used in problem solving. In contrast, the human being has at his disposal in solving a problem his entire repertoire of skills, regardless of whether the tools related to the exercise of those skills are or are not present. A human being can look for a tool not present or adapt some material object to function as a tool in order to solve a problem. Animals are not able to recall or recreate their past in this way and are limited to living in the present and to the use of that which immediately confronts them.

Haslerud also points out that human beings have the capacity of projecting problems into the future, that is, of considering what would happen if certain changes were made or particular events happened. Subhuman forms of life are bound largely by the present, but human beings can deal with the past as if it were in the present and deal with the future as if it were already there in time. Thus the past can be retrieved, so that what was learned in the past can be projected into the future for solving problems in the future. I can say to myself "If I begin to have trouble next year with the aphids destroying my plants, I can apply the remedies I read in that book yesterday." The projection of the past into the future has given human beings an enormous advantage in coping with the environment.

CONCEPT LEARNING

A basic form of problem solving, and often one of the elements in more complex problem solving, is concept learning. In common language, the term *concept* is used to designate what is ordinarily described as an idea, but the technical use of the term requires a more precise definition.

Systematic research on concept learning has been closely tied to the observation that living creatures behave as though they classified the objects in their environment into categories. A dog behaves as though it had classified people into those toward whom it shows friendly behavior and those toward whom it barks. The same dog classifies other objects into those to be eaten and those to be avoided. It also responds to other animals either as those to be chased or those to be played with. The very complex environment is thus simplified by being treated as though it included just a few basic categories of objects and events. All other living creatures show the same tendency to categorize their encounters with their surroundings. A child learns that certain objects are all to be included in the category *dog*, other objects are all to be included in the category *flower*, and still other objects are to be included in the category of objects that are *hot*. Each category represents a concept. Learning to place objects and events in categories is sometimes referred to as categorizing behavior.

Great advantages accrue from learning to place objects in categories. Once a child has learned that certain objects fall in the category *hot*, he can learn how one behaves toward all objects that fall in that category. He learns, for example, to approach such objects with caution, to place the hand near them for a few moments before deciding to touch them, to move into their vicinity if he is cold. He learns a single set of responses to these objects that will permit him to handle effectively the entire category. He does not have to learn one set of responses to guide him in dealing with hot chocolate and another in dealing with hot porridge. A basic category of responses is learned to cope with all objects placed in the category *hot*. If the child did not place all such objects in the same category, he would have to learn a separate response to each of the objects, and life would be vastly more complex than it is. Classifying objects in the environment into categories, so that the objects in any one category are all equivalent stimuli, has the effect of simplifying transactions with a complex environment.

A concept is a category within which objects or events are treated as equivalent.

Animals develop concepts as do human beings. Pigeons can be trained to discriminate between pictures that include human figures and those that do not. In terms of the definition given here, the pigeon thus trained can be said to have a concept of a picture containing a human being in the sense that it can correctly classify such pictures. In the case of the human learner, the acquisition of a concept is closely related to the acquisition of language, although language is not necessary for concept learning.

Many words denote concepts. The word *house* does not refer to any particular instance of a house alone, but it refers to the category into which all houses are classified by the user of the term. One might say that the word *house* refers to one's idea of a house, which is another way of saying that it refers to a category. The word *move* also refers to a concept involving objects that have changes in space displacement with respect to time. However, not all words refer to concepts as they are defined here. The term *point* as it is used in Euclidean geometry refers to a position in space that has zero size and, hence, cannot be seen. One can show a person a dot but one cannot show a person a geometrical point. There is no possible physical representation of a point as defined by Euclid, and so there is nothing to place in the category of *points* that can be distinguished from *nonpoints*. Anything of visible size that can be classified is, by definition, not a point, but a dot. In a popular sense we have a concept of a point, but in terms of our present definition, we do not.

Learning a concept is a form of problem solving. A child faced with the problem of what is to be classified and what is not to be classified within the concept of a *snake* has the problem of finding out why worms are not snakes and neither are eels. Discovering the meaning of most concepts involves problem solving. At a more advanced level, a student of botany may be confronted with the problem of classifying a plant. If he has learned the concepts involved in the botanical classification system, he has the key to the solution to his problem. If he has not learned these concepts, he has to learn the concepts, and the learning of each involves learning the solution to a classification problem.

The idea of a concept considered here was originally developed by Hull as a part of his doctoral dissertation. Later, pioneer research was undertaken by Bruner that laid much of the groundwork for present research. Much of the later research, up to the mid-sixties, has been summarized by Bourne (1966). A slightly later summary is that of Byers (1967). In the last decade, there has been a declining interest in undertaking research in the area, but the general body of knowledge acquired about concept learning remains significant.

THE BASIS OF A CATEGORY

In order to experiment with concept learning, psychologists have devised simple learning tasks in which the attributes involved can be clearly identified. In one such simple task, the objects to be classified consist of triangles and squares of two sizes that are colored either red or blue. As there are two different shapes, two sizes, and two colors, the total number of objects that can be made by combining these is

$2 \times 2 \times 2 = 8$. A more complex set might involve four different shapes, three different sizes, and five different colors, providing a total number of sixty different objects. In most experiments, one of these objects is drawn on each card and the cards are shown to the learner in succession. He is told that some of the objects are "right" and some are "wrong." His task is to find out what makes a "right" object right. At first he can only guess, but he is told whether his guess is correct or incorrect. Ultimately, he will solve the problem and be able to indicate immediately whether an object belongs in the "right" or "wrong" category. He has learned, what makes an object "right."

In such an experiment, the experimenter decides on the attributes that are to make an object right. He may decide, arbitrarily, that all the objects that are blue are the "right" objects, or he may adopt a more complex rule and decide that only objects that are both blue and square are to be regarded as "right."

Two kinds of problems may be involved in such concept-learning tasks. One problem of the learner may be that of identifying the relevant attributes that have to be used in identifying a card as right or wrong. In such a task he is told, for example, that two particular attributes have to be present to make an object *right* and he must find out what they are. After several trials, he may conclude that in the particular experiment color has nothing to do with the classification, but that size and shape have and that all "right" objects involve large triangles. In another experiment he might conclude that both color and shape were the basis of classification, but that the size of the objects had nothing to do with it. In such a case, color and shape would be referred to as the *relevant* attributes, and size would be called an *irrelevant* attribute. In a second type of problem, the learner may be told what the relevant attributes are, and his task is to find out the relationship of the attributes to the designation of an object as "right" or "wrong." He may have to find out, for example, that "right" objects are either blue and triangular or red and square. When he discovers this rule, he has solved the problem, which is said to involve rule learning.

Any one of the following rules might be the key to the solution of a concept-learning problem, but his task is to find the rule that makes it possible for him to classify the objects correctly on every occasion:

All right objects and only right objects are both blue and red.

Only blue *or* red objects, or objects both blue and red, are right.

Many rules can be devised. One rule is referred to as the conjunctive rule when both attributes have to be present. The first of the rules listed above is the conjunctive rule. Another rule is referred to as the disjunctive rule and involves an *either or both* kind of statement. The second rule listed is the disjunctive rule.

Many common concepts illustrate these rules. For example, consider the concept denoted by the word *wine*. Essential attributes of wine are that it is liquid, that it is derived from fruit or plant juice, and that it contains alcohol. If any of these characteristics are not present, the substance is not wine. The attributes follow the conjunctive rule. The legal system has numerous examples of concepts that involve disjunctive rules. The concept *contempt of court* is defined by many different behaviors including that of failing to show proper respect to the judge, refusing to answer questions while under oath, and refusing to obey the court. Any one of these attributes on the part of a witness may result in his being convicted of contempt of court.

When the rule that relates attributes is the conjunctive rule, one commonly refers to the concept as a conjunctive concept. When the disjunctive rule applies, one is dealing with disjunctive concepts. The conjunctive rule and the disjunctive rule are two common rules that have to be discovered in concept learning, but there are other rules also that may have to be discovered.

In some concept-learning experiments the materials used have resembled more closely the kinds of materials used in the classroom. In one set of experiments, the materials used were cards presenting flower-like objects. The sketches of flowers were especially prepared so that the flowers were characterized by attributes such as the number and shape of the petals, the position of the flower on the stem, size of flower, and other rather obvious attributes. In the experiments, the experimenter decided, in advance, the characteristics of "right" flowers.

In the case of our experiment with sixty objects drawn on cards, in which the learner has to discover the basis for calling an object "right," all the cards in the "right" category represent what are called *positive instances* of the concept, and all cards in the "wrong" category are referred to as *negative instances*. Some writers refer to positive and negative *exemplars*, which means the same thing. In teaching a child to identify oak leaves, one might show him a number of leaves, some of which would be positive instances, that is, oak leaves, and some negative instances, that is, leaves from other trees.

Some concept-learning problems provide redundant information. If "right" instances are always both red and blue, and if neither red nor blue is found in negative instances, then these colors can be said to provide *redundant* information. If the learner notices that red is a crucial attribute, he can solve the problem even though he does not notice that blue is also a crucial attribute. The problem can be solved by noting the one attribute or the other attribute or both attributes.

Just as one can increase the number of relevant attributes, so, too, can one design problems that will increase the number of irrelevant attributes. This has the opposite effect, namely, that of making the problem potentially more difficult. One can readily understand why this is so. The more features one has to examine in order to solve a concept-learning problem, the more time it takes, and also the more information one has to remember.

It now becomes evident that, at least in real life although not always in the laboratory, concept learning involves attribute learning, and rule learning. First, the learner must identify what relevant attributes are related to the acquisition of the concept. Then he must find the rule that has to be applied in using the attributes. This is not quite the clear two-stage affair it is made out to be here, for rule learning can go along with attribute identification. In conducting experiments in the laboratory, the two kinds of learning involved are generally kept separate. At the beginning of an experiment confined to attribute learning, the experimenter may tell the learner that he has to identify the two characteristics that have to be present for an object to be classified as right, and that both characteristics have to be present. On the other hand, at the beginning of an experiment on rule learning, the person may be told that red and blue are the significant characteristics that will enable him to distinguish right instances from wrong instances, but he has to find the rule to apply so that all instances can be properly classified. The latter is a rule-learning experiment.

Concept learning is a special case of rule learning, but rule learning occurs also in numerous other situations. For example, the auto mechanic learns that a bad spark plug can cause a rough-running engine. Hence, if an engine is running roughly, a first check is to find out whether each spark plug is functioning properly. In such a case, the auto mechanic must select the right rule from many rules that might apply. There are many reasons for an engine running roughly and the faulty spark plug rule is only one of many that must be checked out. Sometimes rules interact, producing higher-order rules. Thus the auto mechanic knows the rules related to the adjustment of the ignition system and also the rules related to the adjustment of the carburetor. However, these two sets of rules interact in higher-order rules such as that "the ignition should be adjusted before the carburetor is adjusted." Scandura (1974) has pointed out that a person who knows the low-level rules may not know the higher-level rules. Knowing the higher-order rules is perhaps the sign of a higher order of competence.

When the individual attempts to solve a concept-learning problem, he tests hypotheses to find out which one is correct. Glassman and Levine (1972) have shown that such a problem solver behaves as though he had had a certain number of hypotheses at his disposal and that he sampled from his pool of hypotheses. When the pool is exhausted, he seems incapable of creating new hypotheses. If he is then required to continue to search for a solution, he is likely to resample the original pool. Resourcefulness in problem solving is partly a matter of having many hypotheses at one's disposal. Hypothesis theory has been reviewed by Brown (1974).

STRATEGIES OF LEARNING CONCEPTS AND THE LEARNING OF CONCEPTS OUTSIDE THE LABORATORY

In a classic work on the topic of concept learning, Bruner, Goodnow, and Austin (1956) proposed that individuals go about solving concept-acquisition tasks in different ways called strategies. In a laboratory situation, a learner is presented with a complicated colored geometric pattern, and he guesses that it is a "right" pattern and the experimenter confirms the correctness of his guess. The learner then says to himself, "I have a hunch that it is the presence of a large blue square that makes it right." This is a hypothesis and represents a strategy for solving the problem. His statement to himself includes three different dimensions (size, color, and shape), and he is guessing about several different things at once. He could have approached the matter more cautiously and said, "Whether a figure is right or wrong has something to do with the color blue." The latter would have been a much simpler hypothesis than the former, and he might have been content to check out this simple hypothesis and then slowly test the relevancy of other attributes one by one. These two approaches represent different strategies of solving concept-learning problems.

Two general forms of strategy have interested researchers in recent years. First, there is a *scanning strategy* in which the individual hypothesizes that a particular attribute is relevant and then tests this hypothesis on subsequent exemplars. Second, there is a *conservative focusing strategy* in which the individual focuses on a positive exemplar and then finds out what happens when first one attribute and then another is altered in subsequent exemplars. A variation of the latter strategy is the gambling focusing strategy where he watches the result of varying several characteristics at the same time.

The conservative focusing strategy can be demonstrated to be the most efficient for concept attainment (Laughlin, 1973), but there has been considerable controversy concerning how old a child has to be in order to use such a strategy effectively. McKinnery (1973) investigated this problem and found that children with mental ages of 5 and 6 were unable to profit from training in this method, but that children aged 7 to 8 were able to profit. The use of a mental age for selecting the children is controversial in this connection since mental age on the Wechsler Intelligence Scale for Children is not very closely related to level of development in terms of Piaget-type tasks. Despite this shortcoming, the data indicate that the younger children could not grasp a focusing strategy at all. They did show capacity to understand a scanning strategy, which is probably near to the kind of strategy they use, but they did not seem to profit from further training in that strategy. The older group profited from training in both strategies, but the training in a focusing strategy was the most effective.

In most research on problem solving, the learner is provided with a predetermined sequence of objects. The learner cannot vary the sequence, and he cannot decide which object he wants to look at next. Such tasks are referred to as *reception tasks*. However, in life outside the laboratory concept-learning tasks often assume a different form and the learner may be free to decide which object he is going to examine next. For example, after I had explained to a child the nature of igneous rocks, the child went out to look at different rocks and selected some to bring to me which he thought were exemplars of igneous rocks. Similar tasks may be constructed in the laboratory in which the learner is shown an array of tasks and he must decide the one which he is going to try to classify next. Such tasks are called *selection tasks*. Johnson (1971) has shown that with such tasks focusing strategies are also more efficient than scanning strategies, but a combination of both strategies may be more effective than either one alone.

APPLICATIONS OF CONCEPT-LEARNING RESEARCH

Although research on the identification of small blue squares as "right" objects may seem to be remote from anything that one recognizes a student as doing, the relationship is not as remote as first appears. In the concept-learning studies, the person involved must slowly identify the attributes that place a design in a particular class. The solution of a concept-learning problem is slow and deliberate and involves a great amount of internal activity that the learner is quite unaware of undertaking. What happens is not very different from what is believed to happen in perception when one recognizes an object, such as a leaf from a tree. In the chapter on perception, the point is made that the recognition of an object probably requires that the brain undertake a very rapid analysis of the attributes involved and then a determination of the object that could be represented by that particular combination of attributes. The latter takes place in less than a tenth of a second, but in the case of concept learning, the analysis of the attributes and a decision to classify the object as "right" or "wrong" require several seconds or even minutes. Despite the great differences in speed, the two processes have essential elements in common. They both involve the identification of attributes and a classification of whatever is being examined.

Numerous researches have been undertaken on the conditions that influence the acquisition of concepts. Many of these have been summarized by Clark (1971), Bourne (1965), and Byers (1967), who also suggest that some caution be exercised in applying the conclusions of the research in the area because it involves simplified laboratory situations and not the complex situations of daily life through which concepts are typically acquired. Nevertheless, the conclusions drawn by these reviewers from research do appear to have implications for teaching concepts to children, in view of the fact that they are highly plausible as suggestions for teaching. Some of the major conclusions are summarized as follows, after the summary provided by Clark, together with illustrations given by this writer:

1. Concepts are most easily learned when positive and negative instances are clearly distinct and where positive instances are very uniform. For example, the concept of *good taste in dress* is difficult to teach because examples of good taste in dress vary in numerous different ways and also because there is no clear demarcation between good taste and bad taste in this respect. On the other hand, the concept of a *square* is easy to teach because the attributes of objects that are square can be readily identified and precisely defined, and a square can be easily distinguished from other geometric figures.

2. Research has shown that problems in which there is redundancy of positive attributes are easier to solve than problems in which there is no redundancy. This simply means that the more cues provided for the solution of a problem, the more likely it is to be solved. However, redundant cues are generally learned one at a time (Clement and Anderson, 1975).

3. A question that has some significance for teaching is the relative extent to which the learner can be expected to benefit from positive or negative instances. Bourne has outlined the history of this problem in research involving studies of learning conjunctive rules. He concludes that learners, when first brought into the laboratory, tend to derive more information from positive instances than from negative instances, even when these are so arranged that each can provide an equal amount of information about the solution to the problem. This effect seems to be due to the fact that in daily life learning is more typically accomplished by seeing

positive instances. We learn what a French Provincial chair is like by studying a French Provincial chair and comparing it with chairs of other kinds we have seen in the past. However, although the human guinea pig tends at first to learn more from positive than negative instances, this tendency disappears after he has been trained on a large number of problems in which negative instances contribute to the solution of the problem. Bourne and Guy (1968) were able to show that on rule learning subjects performed consistently better when there was a mixture of negative and positive instances, suggesting that the best learning situation requires a judicious combination of both types of instances.

What has been said here about the relative value to the learner of positive and negative instances does not seem to apply to the learning of disjunctive concepts, in which the learner has to attend carefully to negative instances in order to identify the attributes and rules necessary for making correct classifications and hence he is forced into using positive and negative instances. Probably, any concept that is difficult to acquire forces the learner into using all the information available, and he cannot afford to concentrate solely on the positive instances. Concepts involving disjunctive rules are generally more difficult to learn than those involving conjunctive rules.

4. Most studies show that concepts are made easier to learn by reducing the number of irrelevant attributes. However, findings in this area are not as clear as one might wish. A study by Byers and Davidson (1968) compared the effect of adding relevant information and irrelevant information to a concept-learning problem. The addition of relevant information facilitated the solution of the problem, but the addition of irrelevant information had virtually no effect. Simplified drawings may help in the teaching of concepts because they cut out all the irrelevancies which may distract the student from noticing the attributes that the teacher may want him to notice. Sometimes, verbal descriptions may help in the learning of a concept because these descriptions also cut out most information except the relevant information.

5. Concept-learning skill increases with age. Young children appear to attend most readily to the physical characteristics of objects, such as form and color, and this limits the concepts they can learn, but older children attend to the functional aspects of objects, namely, what they are used for.

6. Anxiety is related to concept learning. With simple concepts, an increase in anxiety results in an increased ease with which the concept can be learned. However, if the concepts are complex, anxiety has a disruptive effect on learning. These findings are closely related to the Yerkes–Dodson law (see the chapter on motivation).

7. Concept learning is facilitated if directions are given that focus attention on the relevant attributes. Thus if a child is learning to distinguish oak trees from elms the teacher should point out the features that distinguish the two species of trees.

8. For maximum ease of concept learning, positive and negative instances should be presented side by side. An elm leaf and a maple leaf presented alongside each other are more likely to help the student distinguish between the two than is first viewing one leaf and then viewing the other.

9. Sometimes it appears to be of advantage to present several positive instances at the same time. For example, in teaching very young children the concept of a triangle, several triangles might be shown simultaneously so that the children can abstract from them the critical attributes of triangularity. Clark views the evidence as suggesting that four instances of a concept are about as many as should be presented simultaneously, because more instances may overwhelm the learner.

10. There is considerable evidence that concepts are better learned and are more readily applied to new situations if the learner verbalizes to himself the relevant attributes. He also gains by verbalizing the irrelevant attributes. For example, this suggests that he does not learn very efficiently the concept of African mahogany as a wood by merely looking at it, but he does learn effectively when he says to himself, "The wood is open-grained and a brown rust color. It is very hard and is well marked." He is also helped in remembering the concept if he says to himself the concept name "*mahogany*."

11. At least under some conditions, concept learning is enhanced if the learner can actually handle and manipulate the instances rather than if he is only allowed to view them. One would expect that this would be particularly important in teaching young children the names of classes of objects.

12. The more complete the feedback, the better the learning. A pupil gains by knowing why he is wrong as well as why he is right. Information given the pupil should be precise and complete. Any ambiguity in the information given, or any misinformation, interferes with the learning of a concept.

13. The greatest transfer to new and novel instances is most likely to occur when the original concept has been thoroughly learned through the study of many instances showing great variety.

14. Concepts should not be taught in isolation (Ausubel, 1969). The basic notion is that a pupil must be prepared for learning a new concept by providing him with a framework into which he can build it. The argument is that learning a concept in isolation limits the value of the learning.

15. Mixed methods of teaching concepts should be used. Most studies on the teaching of concepts have used highly artificial laboratory tasks, but a single study by Johnson and Stratton (1966) used methods of teaching concepts similar to those used in the classroom. The teaching methods used were (a) using a brief definition, (b) embedding the concept in a sentence, (c) showing by means of short sentences the objects or events to be included in the concept, and (d) giving synonyms for the concept. In addition, a fifth procedure involved a mixture of the four procedures, but the length of the instruction involved was the same as that in the others. Students who participated in the experiment were exposed to only one of the teaching procedures, but they took the tests designed around all five teaching procedures. The findings were that the first four teaching procedures were virtually identical in the learning produced, but the fifth mixed method showed itself to be superior. One suspects that the reason for this is that any teacher who varies the teaching procedure and who does not get stuck in a groove is going to hold the attention of students better than one who is rigid.

One of the most interesting features of the Johnson and Stratton experiment was that there was excellent transfer from one particular learning situation across all of the testing situations. For example, a student who learned a concept through a definition was as able to identify the concept when it was embedded in a sentence as when it was identified through a synonym. It seems that concepts learned in a verbal setting are readily transferred to other verbal settings.

16. In concept-learning tasks, the learner must be provided sufficient time to assimilate the information he is given. A series of studies have now well established that a critical factor in solving a concept-learning problem, under the conditions provided by most laboratory experiments, is the post-informative feedback interval. This is the time allowed after the learner has made a guess and has been told whether he is correct or incorrect. The procedure may involve the immediate presentation of the next card with the next object, or an interval may be provided during which the subject may continue to look at the card about which he has made some judgment and about which he has been provided with information by the experimenter. The length of the post-informative feedback interval was shown first by Bourne and Bunderson (1963) to be quite critical, because it is a period during which the subject has an opportunity to examine the object presented and try to find out why his guess was right or wrong. It is a period that permits the learner to make good use of the information provided. Rownton and Davis (1968) have shown that when the problem is difficult, the length of the post-informative feedback interval becomes more critical than when the problem is easy.

The research related to this particular problem shows the importance of providing sufficient time for the utilization of information in learning tasks. The findings carry with them the suggestion that learning cannot be speeded up beyond a certain point because the limiting factor is the amount of information that can be assimilated in a given time. Attempts to provide more information in a given time than the amount that can be successfully assimilated are likely to result in confusion of the learner rather than in increased efficiency.

17. Finally, something must be said about a matter that still remains controversial. Should the learner be presented with a selected series of positive and negative instances, or should he select the instances that he is to judge? One would expect that giving the learner freedom to select his own instances would facilitate learning, for the person could then select instances for checking out particular hypotheses. Although this is plausible, the single study that could be located (Huttenlocher, 1962) that throws any light on the problem came to the conclusion that in the case of the seventh-grade children studied, the learner selecting his own instances was not as efficient as the learner who was presented with a set of instances through which he had to learn the concept. This matter needs further investigation.

CONCEPTS AS ORGANIZERS OF LEARNING

Up to this point, concepts have been regarded as largely a means of reducing a complex environment to a relatively few categories. But this is a limited view of how concepts operate and influence behavior, for clearly some words refer to ideas that are very much like concepts as these have been defined here save that they are at a highly abstract level and do not represent anything that can be directly experienced. There is no way of experiencing what a physicist means by a vacuum. Such ideas are referred to as *abstract concepts*, and they play a crucial role in the sciences. They also often play a very significant role as learning organizers, a topic to which we must now return.

The notion that certain concepts may function as organizers of learning has been developed almost entirely by Ausubel. This idea is extensively discussed in Ausubel and Robinson (1969), who have summarized some of the rather sketchy research on the topic. The thesis proposed is that in order to master almost any given fragment of subject matter efficiently, the learner should first be exposed to certain anchoring ideas around which the new knowledge can be organized. The position is that unless such anchoring ideas, organizers, or advanced organizers, as they are variously called, are learned prior to particular subject-matter assignments, learning cannot be well organized.

The idea that concepts are organizers of learning is similar to the idea developed by Piaget that knowledge is organized around schemata and that knowledge cannot be assimilated in the absence of an appropriate schema. Piaget's schema is much broader in scope than Ausubel and Robinson's concept organizer, but the term schema is also applied by Piaget to concepts. The ideas of organizer and schema were developed completely independently on two different continents, but they have substantial overlap.

Organizers are concepts around which new knowledge is built. Many teachers have long used this approach to introduce new subject matter. Audiovisual specialists have also taken the position that the effective use of any instructional film requires that it be properly introduced by the teacher. The common suggestion for teaching from films is that the pupil be introduced to the topic and know in advance just what he is to look for. This is another way of saying that the teacher provides the student with a useful set of organizers so that he can learn effectively from the film presentation.

Organizers are generally at a more abstract level than the subject matter that becomes organized around them. They are also ideas representing a broader range of knowledge than the knowledge to be acquired. In introducing a new topic, the first statements presented are generally those that have to do with the general nature of the subject to be discussed. Ausubel makes the point that sometimes a a good beginning in teaching a new concept may be to explain how the concept is different from related concepts with which it may be confused. In teaching American students the nature of an Oriental religion such as Buddhism, it may be important to point out the differences that exist between Buddhism and the religions with which the student is familiar, so that he is prepared to organize his knowledge around new concepts rather than mold it in terms of his own religious concepts.

Some subject matter is extremely well structured in terms of organizing concepts. The better developed sciences such as physics and chemistry are this way. Organizers are the key terms and the powerful ideas in a discipline, and it is hardly surprising that it is in the most fully developed disciplines that there is consensus concerning what these terms are and when they should be introduced to the student. In less developed and less completely structured areas, such as the social studies, there is considerable debate concerning what the key ideas are and when the student can encounter them to greatest advantage. In the well-developed disciplines the teacher does not have to worry about when to introduce the organizing ideas, for experimentation by several generations of teachers has produced a sequence of subject matter that provides a good organization for the student and leads to the acquisition of structured knowledge in his memory system.

The chapter on memory points out that the evidence suggests that the memory system stores information in an ordered hierarchy. The theory that learning takes place best if it is planned around organizing ideas is another way of expressing the same idea. If memory is organized in a hierarchy, learning should be planned so that it permits the student to lay down in his memory a hierarchy of ideas. The difficulty of implementing this approach in practice is that one knows little about how concepts should best be organized for instructional purposes. There is not even a good system for classifying concepts to be learned.

CLASSIFICATION OF CONCEPTS

Harré has pointed out (1966) that the search for a classification of concepts is one of the oldest problems in philosophy. Aristotle was intrigued by the question and proposed a classification that included the classes of relational, substance, quantity, and quality. The latter two categories are still widely used today, and subject matter in the sciences is typically taught first by introducing qualitative concepts and then quantitative concepts. A student learns the qualitative idea of gravity before he learns how the gravitational constant is measured. He learns that the blood picks up oxygen before he measures in the laboratory how much oxygen can be carried by the blood. Harré points out that Aristotle's classification of concepts was based largely on the kinds of questions that Aristotle was interested in asking and that it is a classification of convenience rather than one based on any theory of the nature of knowledge.

Harré states that a second important approach to the classification of concepts is to order them in terms of the degree to which they have explanatory value. The concept of *universal gravitation* explains such varied phenomena as the path of a planet, the trajectory of a missile, and the behavior of a free-falling body. On the other hand, the concept of *distance*, a concept that enters into the understanding of the effects of universal gravitation, does not explain anything at all, but is one of the givens in experience. At least some concepts can thus be arranged in a hierarchy, with those concepts that explain little at the base and those that have the greatest explanatory value at the top. On the surface this sounds like a good way of arranging concepts for teaching and, in a few limited cases, it may be. In most subject-matter areas, teaching could not proceed along such lines. In the teaching of history, for instance, the concept of power and status conflict has far more explanatory value than that of the geographical circumstances of historical personages, or their hereditary standing, but one would not delay using the concept of power and status conflict until concepts with less explanatory power had been learned. The ordering of concepts in terms of explanatory power may have value in the teaching of physics, but is probably useless as a basis for teaching in most other areas.

Other approaches to the classification of concepts are illustrated in such writings as those of Gagné (1970) and Woodruff (1964), who take the firm position that concepts to be learned within formal schooling can be arranged in an optimum order. The examples commonly cited in this connection are derived from mathematics, where agreement can be reached on how concepts should be ordered.

Most of those who write in education about the ordering of concepts have not stated explicitly what the basis of the ordering should be. Some seem to believe the very unlikely proposition that the concepts in most subject-matter fields can be organized in a logical structure, much as are the concepts of mathematics. Others imply that they are following the classical tradition of ordering concepts in terms of explanatory power. Still another possibility for ordering concepts is in terms of the difficulties involved in understanding them. A concept such as the physicist's concept of mass is much more difficult to understand than the ordinary conception of weight. Any of these different attempts to arrange concepts rely heavily on intuitive judgment, and the classifications provided are of dubious validity.

RESEARCH ON THE ANAGRAM PROBLEM

One of the few partly standardized techniques that has evolved for the study of problem solving is that involving the use of anagrams. Although anagram problem solving represents a specialized activity, the study of it has yielded some results of quite broad significance. Much of the research on anagrams has been reviewed by Johnson (1966). In the typical anagram, the problem consists of several letters that have to be rearranged to form a word. The form of the problem has many advantages in that various characteristics of it can be modified and the effect of the modification on the difficulty of the problem can be studied. Some of the more obvious characteristics of the problem that might be likely to influence problem solving are the number of letters involved in the word, and the rareness or commonness of the word that constitutes the solution. In addition, the letters can be presented in different orders. Numerous different orders can be used, from those that retain some of the letters in the same order as that of the original word to orders in which the syllables are different from those that have to be produced. The letters may also be presented in an order that spells a word different from that which the problem solver has to produce. The number of anagram problems that can be produced is immensely large, because there are a great many ways in which the letters in each word can be presented. This is perhaps the reason why the anagram problem has not been completely standardized, for each investigator tends to choose words that meet his particular specifications. It is this lack of standardization that makes it difficult to compare the results of any two studies. Conflicting results of research in this area may sometimes be attributable to differences in the anagrams used. Skill in solving anagram problems is generally measured in terms of the time taken to solve the problems, but sometimes problems are given with a time limit and performance is scored on a pass-fail basis. Procedures may also involve the subject's talking aloud or working out his solution on a piece of paper. There are also an almost infinite number of different ways in which the directions may be stated.

The Johnson summary brings out very clearly that one of the most important factors in solving this kind of problem is what is termed *set*—a factor that has been well identified in many other problem-solving situations. A problem-solving set can be established by giving such instructions as that the letters spell the name of a city or the name of an animal. Similar sets can also be established by providing a long series of problems to solve in which all the solutions involve, say, names of cities. The evidence is overwhelming that the establishment of such sets facilitates the production of solutions in the case of problems in which the set is appropriate. How such sets operate is a matter of conjecture. Presumably, the task of constructing a word in a certain category involves the search of one's memory for words having the same number of letters as the number of letters presented. A set may restrict the amount of searching that has to be done. The situation is analogous to that of finding a book with certain characteristics in a library. If one knows the section of the library in which the book is to be located, the search time is much shorter than if one does not have that particular item of information to use as a guide.

Set may also operate in a different way. If a series of problems are solved by adopting a particular procedure, there is a tendency established to adopt that same procedure in the solution of future problems. This is what has been called the *einstellungen effect*, which is nothing more than the operation of the principle of reinforcement. The operation of this effect comes out quite clearly in the solution of anagrams. If the subject first solves a large number of anagram problems by starting with the last consonant given and using it as the first letter in the solution, the problem solver is likely to adopt this procedure on future problems. Such habits established through a series of successes probably influence all problem solvers. Television repairmen tend to look for bad rectifier tubes, because defective rectifier tubes are very commonly a major source of difficulty. Problem solvers appear to store large quantities of information about the probabilities of particular procedures being successful.

Many sets probably operate in any particular problem-solving situation. Complex sets can be shown to operate in the solution of anagram problems. In the solution of a particular problem, the solver may bring to the problem the set that the word to be found is the name of a bird and that it consists of two syllables. Compound sets have a stronger effect than simple sets.

Johnson also cites many studies showing that anagrams are more easily solved when the word involved is common than when the word is relatively rare. It is as if the responses that could be considered to represent a solution to the problem were arranged in a hierarchy and are produced in a particular order with the most commonly occurring words being the most available. Frequency of previous experience also has another interesting effect on procedures for solving anagram problems. When a person is given an anagram to solve, he is likely to start by arranging the letters into pairs, but he does not arrange them in pairs at random. The pairs chosen tend to be commonly occurring pairs of letters. If the given letters are G T I N H, the problem solver is likely to choose pairs such as I N and T H, which he often sees in print, and avoid a rare pair such as T G or H T. One would like to be able to generalize from these findings and state that the early stages of problem solving are characterized by familiar actions and attempts to apply commonplace solutions. However, one cannot go as far as this, for there is no substantial data derived from the study of other kinds of problems to give any support.

One of the more surprising findings of the review is that the mere performance of anagram problems, with feedback concerning the correctness of the solution, does not seem to produce any marked improvement. This suggests that the problem solver himself, when confronted with a series of anagrams, is not able to identify the elements in the situation that make for the speedy discovery of a solution. In other words, the solution of anagram problems does not help the problem solver to evolve new strategies. This finding raises the interesting question of the extent to which one can expect practice with problems to produce superior problem-solving ability. One does know that practice is effective in some cases. An example is the oddity problem, in which a person has to identify which one of three objects does not belong in the group. Both children and primates show substantial and rapid practice effects on this type of problem, but one would like to be able to formulate a general statement concerning where practice in problem solving will be effective and where it will not be effective.

The anagram problem involves the scanning of associations and memory search. Logic plays a minimum role. It is not surprising that imagery has been found to play a part in the solution of such problems, for imagery has been well established as a factor in associative learning. Dewing and Hetherington (1974) found that anagrams involving high-imagery words were more rapidly solved than those involving words with low-imagery. Imagery probably has other functions in the solution of problems because it may permit the individual to construct a representation of what the problem situation would be like if certain factors were changed (see Piaget and Inhelder, 1966).

THE ROLE OF VERBAL SSAOCIATIVE LEARNING IN PROBLEM SOLVING

Although concepts can be learned without the help of verbal processes, the labeling of the attributes by means of words can facilitate the process of concept learning. Furthermore, the utilization of concepts may be facilitated when the concept itself is given a verbal label, and thus concept learning is intimately associated with the development of language and effective thinking.

Verbal associations may sometimes show impact on problem-solving behavior. An interesting example of this is found in a study by Judson, Cofer, and Gelfand (1956). The central task for subjects that forms the focus of this study is known as the Maier two-string problem. In the original version of this problem, the subject is presented with two strings suspended from the ceiling of a room. The room is empty except for a pair of pliers, which appear to have been carelessly left on the floor. The subject is instructed that his task is to tie together the ends of the two pieces of string, a task that appears to be deceptively simple. Most subjects go about attempting to solve this problem in a direct fashion. They take hold of the end of one piece of string and then reach over to take hold of the other. They find that the two pieces of string are sufficiently far apart to make this impossible. They are long enough to be tied together, but the two ends are so far apart that it is impossible to reach one piece while holding the other. One solution to the problem is to use the pair of pliers lying on the floor. What the subject must do is to attach the pliers to one of the strings, which can then be swung as a pendulum. Once the string is swinging, it can be caught while the subject holds onto the other string, and the problem is solved. This is a rather difficult problem; not more than 50 percent of college students can be expected to solve it.

In the Judson et al. study, subjects were asked during class hours on four consecutive days to learn word lists. One of these word lists included the sequence *rope, swing, pendulum*; this word list was administered to only one group. None of the other word lists included this sequence of words. On the fifth day all groups were given the Maier string problem and asked to solve it. The important result was that the group that had learned the word list containing the "rope-swing-pendulum" sequence were significantly more successful than the other groups in solving the problem. It may be noted that in this test the Maier problem was administered in a paper-and-pencil form, with an illustration of how the strings were suspended and the sketch of a person trying to reach one while holding the other.

This study clearly illustrates the way in which past associations between words or ideas can influence and facilitate problem-solving behavior. Many times, in solving some kind of novel problem, the solution appears to come out of the blue. What probably happens in such cases is that some association built in the past suddenly influences behavior.

The research on the two-string problem brings out a very well-known problem-solving phenomenon known as *functional fixedness*. The essence of this phenomenon is that objects are not readily used for new purposes. Pliers are not used in ordinary daily life as a pendulum bob. They are used for grasping, bending, straightening, and related uses, and they are viewed as a tool for performing those activities. In order for a problem solver to use them as a pendulum bob, he must break away from the concept of how pliers should be used, which he finds difficult to do because he views pliers as having a fixed function.

Previously learned associations are not the only factor triggering novel ideas in a problem-solving situation. Glucksberg and Danks (1967) performed an ingenious experiment showing how other relationships between words may also generate solutions. Glucksberg and Danks devised an experiment in which subjects were confronted with the problem of completing a simple circuit, for which an insufficient amount of wire was provided. Subjects were provided a tool for loosening and tightening the posts to which the wires had to be attached, and the solution to the problem involved using the tool as a metallic conductor to make up for the lack of wire. For one group the tool was referred to as a *wrench*, for a second group as a *channel-lock-pliers*, and for the third group as a *pliers*. The point to note is that the terms *wires* and *pliers* rhyme. The data turned up the interesting finding that those performing best on the problem, by a considerable margin, and those who most readily used the tool as a substitute for a wire were the ones in the group for whom the tool was referred to as a pliers. The study suggests that associations along an acoustic dimension take place in such a situation and that, in the case of the study, this led to the finding of a solution. The results of this study are not quite as clear as they might be, in that the word *pliers* and the word *wires* often appear together in the same statement, as when a person says, " I cut the wires with the pliers." Such an association might account for the results of the experiment, except that it is hard to understand why, when the tool was referred to as channel-lock-pliers, the facilitating effect did not appear.

PERCEPTUAL FACTORS IN PROBLEM SOLVING

Problems differ enormously in the extent to which they involve complex perceptual processes. The anagram problem is perceptually simple, involving few elements that have to be related. In contrast, a chess board after a first few plays presents an extraordinarily complex perceptual field. The Dutch psychologist Adrian de Groot (1966) has spent almost a lifetime studying the behavior of chess players and has come away from his studies enormously impressed with the extraordinary perceptual skills of the master players. He points out that such players can glance at a game in progress and obtain an immediate impression of the skill of the two players and what the potential moves and strategies for each player might be. It now seems clear that it is not just a matter of the master player being able to recognize and remember the positions of each piece more clearly than the amateur, but that he has a complex system for coding the perceptual information that he receives. What one does not know is the kind of coding system used, the extent to which it deals with particular moves or gross strategies suggested by the particular positions of the pieces at the given time, and the degree to which it is selective in the use of information or attempts to use all the information available in the perceptual field. Our ignorance of such matters accounts for the fact that the chess programs played by computers produce a dull and unimaginative game, quite unlike that of the expert. Nobody has been able at this time to conjecture successfully the information-processing procedures that are used by the master chess players so that these can be simulated with computer programs. An understanding of what the information processing involves in the master chess player would appear to be quite essential for simulating his performance. At least, attempts to simulate his performance have been quite unsuccessful up to this time.

REASONING AND PROBLEM SOLVING

American research on problem solving has had little to say about the role of logic, which would appear to lie at the very core of the problem-solving process. This absence seems to be a result of the love affair that American psychologists have had with classical and operant conditioning and with the related associationistic psychology. Within the theories of conditioning and associationism logic finds no place, for man is conceived to be a creature controlled by the stimuli that have impact on him.

The major body of research that has been undertaken on the role of logic in problem solving is European and centers around the work of Piaget and his collaborators in his laboratory at Geneva. This work has been given a brief review in the earlier chapter of Piaget's developmental theory of learning. A few additional comments on that work seem appropriate here.

For Piaget and his associates, conditioning theories and associationistic theories of problem solving are concerned with trivial aspects of the problem-solving process. They play a central role only at the lowest level of problem solving, namely, the intuitive level. A 2-year-old finds a marble under a bush and keeps going to look under the same bush in the hope of finding more marbles. The child's problem is that of finding more marbles, and operant psychology explains his behavior by pointing out that it was reinforced on one occasion by the finding of a marble. At that level of problem solving operant psychology does quite well. When the child is a few years older, marble-finding behavior becomes much more complex and is not easily understood in terms of operant psychology. At age 6 the same child realizes that marbles do not just appear under bushes, but that they get there because they rolled there or were hidden there. The problem of finding marbles becomes one of predicting where marbles that others have lost are likely to be. The child may look down drain holes or cracks in the playground black top in order to try to find marbles. He has a concept of cause and effect that tells him that marbles are likely to be found only in certain places. He may look for marbles in a particular place not because he was once reinforced for finding a marble there, but because he has a conception of how marbles get lost and where lost marbles go. Conditioning psychologists and associationistic psychologists have little of importance to say about such matters because they have nothing to say about either logic or epistemology, that is, the nature of knowledge. A few take the position that all matters of logical behavior will one day be reduced to an understanding of the conditioned responses that they believe will ultimately be demonstrated to be the basis of such behavior, but such beliefs represent faith rather than scientific findings.

The value of training in logical reason is a matter of interest to those concerned with education. It seems fairly clear that Piaget is right in asserting that formal training in logic cannot function until the child has reached a level where he can perform formal operations. Piaget, of course, also takes the position that appropriate experiences at each age are necessary to further the development of intellectual skills. Training in the valid use of propositional logic would appear to be appropriate at the high school and college level, and some effort has been made to provide such training for adolescents and young adults. There is a need for such training, for even educated young adults can engage in much false logic. Johnson (1972) has sumarized many of the studies that have been undertaken on this matter. The data seem to lead to the conclusion that even a few hours of training can lead to substantial improvements in logical reasoning. Some individuals just do not seem to be aware of certain logical fallacies in their conclusions, but they can be made aware of these fallacies. Of course, many adults have never studied logic but have learned on their own to avoid pitfalls in reasoning.

The matter of using logic as a system for describing problem-solving behavior is not the simple matter it seems to be on the surface. Ennis (1975) has made an excellent analysis of Piaget's attempt to do this. He shows that there are no clear criteria concerning whether children are or are not engaging in formal logical thinking. There is a need for such criteria, but they have not yet been worked out in the way they need to be.

COMPUTER SIMULATION APPROACHES TO PROBLEM SOLVING

An entirely new approach to the solution of many scientific problems has been developed in recent years through the availability of high-speed computers. The chemist can now hypothesize the nature of the mechanism underlying a particular chemical process and can then set up a computer to calculate the experimental results to be expected if the mechanism actually operates. The "data" produced by the computer can then be checked against real data collected in actual experiments. The comparison permits an evaluation of the reasonableness of the hypothesized underlying mechanism. Much of the time, computers, when they are used by physical scientists, "generate" data that are later compared with actual data.

The psychologist has learned to perform similar kinds of operations with computers. Computers perform many operations that resemble thinking activities; indeed, computers are often called giant brains and the storage units they contain are called memory units. Speculative articles on building thinking machines and on using computers to perform thinking operations have been written for at least a century. It was not until an article appeared by Newell, Shaw, and Simon (1958) that any real specifications were set out concerning how this could be accomplished.

Before further discussion of this problem, the student should know that for a computer to perform the operations considered here it must be provided with (1) information to be used in solving the problems and (2) a program, or set of procedures, that tells the computer how to behave. The program may instruct the machine to look for certain elements in a problem, make comparisons, and so forth. In the study of thinking and problem-solving processes, the program includes operations that the human thinker or problem solver is believed to perform.

The basic idea presented by Newell et al. is that problem solving involves the manipulation of statements according to certain rules of logic in order to reach a particular conclusion that is sought. Consider, for example, the following very simple arithmetic problem stated in the form of two propositions that constitute the basic data and a third incomplete proposition that specifies the conclusion sought:

Board A is 6 feet long.
Board B is ⅔ the length of board A.
The length of board B is _____.

To find the solution, the problem solver must build a new statement that says, "The length of B is equal to $6 \times \frac{2}{3}$." To do this, he has to know (or be programmed in) the rules of setting up propositions from data. Just as human problem solvers can learn to make proper deductions from data and then set up new statements or propositions that represent these deductions, so, too, can computers be designed to store propositions and then derive new propositions from those stored. The computer has to be programmed so that it will perform only operations that are logically correct. An example at a more complex level would be that of starting with the axioms of Euclidean geometry and logically deducing certain conclusions, such as that two straight lines can cross at only one point. By producing new propositions on the basis of the axioms, the computer can eventually arrive at the proposition it is desired to produce as a deduction from the original axioms.

The argument of Newell and his associates was that a machine could be programmed to solve certain classes of problems and then the program could be adjusted until it solved problems in humanlike ways. The anticipation was that the research worker could produce on the computer humanlike problem solving and that in this way a model of human problem solving could be evolved.

Simulation of problem solving on the computer does require the psychologists to specify precisely the elements in a problem and exactly the operations to be performed to produce a solution. It is an excellent exercise in precise thinking about problem solving, but it can be undertaken only when one knows precisely what the problem is. Much of the time in real life our difficulties stem from the fact that we do not know exactly what the problem is that we are trying to solve.

At this time, it is difficult to evaluate just what has been accomplished by this approach to the study of problem solving. Computers have been programmed in such a way that they have undertaken quite complicated reasoning problems. The most notable demonstrations of this kind have involved utilizing computers to generate proofs of Euclidean theorems. A computer thus programmed can not only generate proofs of theorems that it has not been "taught," but it can then store the new theorems and use them in the development of subsequent proofs. In doing such work, the computer performs in quite humanlike ways as, for example, in attempting to develop a new proof by substituting terms in another theorem already stored in memory. The computer may also attempt to work backward from the proposition it is desired to prove or it may break down the problem into components, each one of which is handled separately. What this demonstrates is that computers can undertake humanlike activities, but this is a long way from demonstrating that the operations performed by a computer in solving a reasoning problem are the kinds of operations performed by the human problem solver.

Paige and Simon (1966) attempted to simulate on a computer the operations performed by children in reading arithmetic problems and then arriving at a solution. They point out that the steps involved in the solution of arithmetical problems have been outlined in books on arithmetic for generations. The first step generally involves reading the problem and finding the crucial statements in it. These statements have to be converted into numbers or symbols that are fitted into an equation. The equation is then solved and the solution is checked back against the conditions in the original statement of the problem. In solving the problem about the boards, the child would probably be faced, first, with a statement of the problem in narrative form such as the following:

> A carpenter had two boards. One was 6 feet long and the other was ⅔ of that length. How long was the second board?

In solving such a problem, the computer and the child have to recognize that the problem involves the length of two boards, one of which is specified directly, whereas the length of the other is only implied and has to be found. The one unknown quantity has to be expressed as a function of the known quantity. The basic problem is that of coding the information provided. This turns out to be one of the most difficult operations to program the computer to perform. It is also the major difficulty encountered by the child.

Up to this time, the main contribution of this approach to the study of problem solving has been to demonstrate that computers can solve certain classes of problems in much the same way that human beings are taught to solve them. The hope is that in time the method will evolve a sophisticated theory of problem solving.

A study by Hunt (1974) shows the extraordinary capability of computers to simulate not only the logic of problem solving, but also such components as perception and memory. Hunt's book also brings out the immense complexity of the problem of simulating such a common human behavior as understanding speech with its perceptual, semantic, and logical components.

The simulation of logical problem solving on a computer has had other important outcomes that must be mentioned briefly. The spark behind such research has often been the hope that the study of the problem-solving capabilities of computers will ultimately lead to the development of an artificial intelligence, that is, an intelligence nonhuman in character that might be able to solve problems far more complex than those that the human intelligence can solve. The broad goal of such work has been to produce a general problem-solving machine, perhaps even a machine that would redesign itself. Strangely enough, the work undertaken up to this point suggests that it may be used to build a device that will successfully simulate the way human intelligence works. Machines can be made to behave in strictly rational ways, but human behavior is filled with arbitrary and unexpected elements.

INTELLIGENCE AND PROBLEM SOLVING
The Nature of Intelligence

Two main theories of the nature of intelligence are represented in modern psychology. One theory derives from the work of those concerned with measurement and was founded on the work of such scientists as Binet, Burt, Spearman, and Thurstone. The other derives from a theory of child development and is almost entirely the work of Piaget. The first of these is an empirically based attempt to measure the various facets of intelligence, but it is concerned only with those that have predictive value. Thus in the measurement of intelligence in children of school age, the chief concern has been to find measures that will predict various aspects of school achievement. When Binet first became interested in the measurement of intelligence, he conceived it to be an innate ability to solve problems. With this in mind he attempted to develop problems that would not penalize the child who came from an impoverished background. His aim was to produce a test that would measure intelligence independent of background, a goal that we now know is impossible to achieve. The attempt to build tests that are as far as possible what is now termed *culture free* has persisted up to present time. Binet's test was built on the basis of a minimum of theorizing concerning the nature of intelligence. He conceived of it as being a single, comprehensive ability. A person was conceived to be more or less intelligent. He also considered it to be relatively uninfluenced by personal experience. Hence, a child who scored relatively high at age 6 might also be expected to score relatively high at age 12. Intelligence, of course, increased with age, but the child's relative standing within his age group remained unchanged.

Binet's model of intelligence soon was shown to be far too simple. The work of Thurstone in America demonstrated that the assumption that intelligence was a simple unitary trait could not be accepted, though some psychologists believed and continue to believe today that the assumption has some limited utility. These psychologists argue that although there are many components of intelligence, actual tests all show a strong component of general intelligence. At least until midcentury the belief continued to be held that measures of the general factor intelligence measured innate ability, contaminated to a minor degree by environmental effects. Although Thurstone developed tests that measured aspects of intelligence, the Binet-type test continued to be given and is still widely used in various forms. The work of Thurstone was continued and expanded by Guilford, who developed his model of intelligence, previously described, which includes a total of 120 intellectual factors. Guilford conceived of his table of 120 factors as being analogous to the periodic table used by chemists to provide an organized inventory of the elements.

Test batteries given in schools generally measure specific components of intelligence rather than a single global factor. The table shows some of the intelligence factors that are commonly measured and the kinds of test items used to measure them. An examination of the items shows that there is little pretense any longer of using only materials that are common knowledge among all children. The items appear to be highly related to what is learned in school, and it is not surprising that such tests predict school achievement rather well.

An alternative model for measuring intelligence has been described by Piaget. Various attempts have been made to develop measures of intelligence based on his model of intellectual development. Piaget himself has not been interested in the development of such a measure, although the original stimulus for his work came from the doubts he felt about the validity of Binet's concept of intelligence. Attempts to develop a measure of intellectual level of development along Piagetian lines involves listing the components of intelligence as they emerge and as they have been described in the research of Piaget and his associates. Thus the 5-year-old

SOME OF THE APTITUDE FACTORS COMMONLY MEASURED BY TESTS INCLUDED IN APTITUDE TEST BATTERIES

Illustration of Test Problem	Name Given to Factor Measured	Predictions Commonly Made with This Type of Test
What is the meaning of the word "ascend"? 1. go up 2. lift 3. elevate 4. rain	Verbal factor	Predicts grades in academic work, particularly in those fields where the content is largely verbal. Sometimes used for diagnosing difficulties in reading if the difficulty is believed to be due to a deficiency in knowledge of the meaning of words.
Multiply the numbers as indicated 46 39 × 6 × 4 ___ ___	Numerical computation	Used for the prediction in the learning of skills that require numerical operations of a simple character, as, for example, many trades and skills such as those of the machinist and the bookkeeper.
What is the next number in the series? 2 4 8 16 ———	Numerical reasoning	Used for predicting grades in academic work involving reasoning with numbers. Physics is an example of such academic work, and so, too, would be work in engineering. Tests of this kind are used for predicting success in such areas at the college level.
Which object can be made by folding the paper along the dotted lines?	Space-relations factor or perceptual factor. (There are several perceptual factors.)	Used for predicting the ability to learn engineering drawing, sheetmetal work, and other skills involving space relations.
In the following list of pairs of names, place a check in the parentheses after a pair if the two names are identical. Chamberlin Chamberlin ( ) Jeremiah Jeremiah ( ) Gleason Gleeson ( ) Learned Learned ( )	Perceptual-speed factor	Has had a long history of predicting success in simple clerical jobs.
Which jug of water is most likely to tip over?	Mechanical-aptitude factor	Predicts learning of a great range of mechanical skills.

SOME OF THE APTITUDE FACTORS COMMONLY MEASURED BY TESTS INCLUDED IN APTITUDE TEST BATTERIES (CONTINUED)

Illustration of Test Problem	Name Given to Factor Measured	Predictions Commonly Made with This Type of Test

Place a check mark in the parentheses after each word which is correctly spelled
  Perscription ( )
  Opportunity ( )
  Fundamental ( )
  Demonstrate ( )
In the following sentence choose the correct version.
  Each one of the students
  were\ allowed to
  was }correct his own
  are /examination.
	Language usage	Used for predicting performance in learning higher-level clerical tasks such as involve stenographic and secretarial skills.

may be expected to perform certain perceptual skills such as are involved in matching similar objects, the 7-year-old may have mastered conservation of volume and the reversibility of thought related to it, the 11-year-old may have mastered the concept of a null class and be able to perform certain elementary formal operations, and so forth. Inhelder (1968) has shown that such a scale could be used to diagnose various levels of mental retardation and that the tasks involved do differentiate normal children from the retarded. Piaget implies in his writings that all normal children will achieve the stage of being able to perform formal operations, provided they encounter the kinds of problems that require them to develop in themselves the necessary logical structures.

The Piaget conception of intelligence as a system of logical structures has a far more obvious relationship to problem solving than has the traditional conception of intelligence. The Piaget conception identifies particular components of the problem-solving process and shows how these fit into the total model of intelligence.

This new emerging conception of intelligence offers the possibility of identifying components of the problem-solving process and of identifying individuals who have the components necessary for solving particular classes of problems. This conception also suggests the kinds of experiences that should be provided in junior high and senior high schools in order that children may develop their maximum potentials for solving problems thoughtfully and systematically.

The Heredity-Environment Controversy

What is being written today about heredity versus environment is very little different from what was written on the subject fifty years ago. Indeed, some of the arguments presented in contemporary technical literature on the subject are based on data nearly half a century old. There is very little new in the field except controversy, although recently some have attached to tests what they call heritability ratios, which are supposed to indicate the extent to which the trait is inherited.

A good point for beginning the discussion of the problem is a brief explanation of heritability ratios. The ratio is supposed to indicate the extent to which the level shown in a trait is a product of heredity or environment. An excellent article by Anastasi (1973) on the subject brings out the misleading nature of such a ratio. For example, if a population is raised on a uniform diet, the variation in the adult height achieved by the individuals in the population cannot be accounted for in terms of diet and must probably be ascribed largely to heredity. For that population, under those particular conditions, the measure referred to as height would have a high heritability ratio, but that does not mean that diet cannot alter height. Indeed, there is substantial evidence that the increase in height of the white population over the last few centuries can be attributed largely to improvement in diet. Certainly, if the diet were cut back to the standards of the middle ages, future generations would be shorter in stature than those living at present. Anastasi stresses the point that heritability ratios have meaning only for particular populations under particular conditions. If a trait has a heritability index of 100 per cent under one set of conditions, it might have a heritability index of only 20 per cent under other conditions.

A second important point to note is that traits that may seem to be inherited to a high degree may not necessarily be inherited at all. For example, a child may be brought up in a family that fosters the belief that all males in that family are highly aggressive, particularly in their business dealings. The family imbues the boys in the family with the idea that they are to grow up to be highly aggressive. It is not surprising that the boys grow up to fulfill the expectation. Thus examination of family trees often provides superficial evidence of the inheritance of all kinds of characteristics when, in fact, only a small component of the trait or none of it reflects inherited tendencies.

A second illustration of the family tree effect brings out the fallacy of attributing the main source of traits to heredity when it is environmental. The previously cited reviews by Green *et al.* (1973) shows that underpriviliged children suffer brain damage from malnutrition even before birth. The old idea that the embryo would take from its mother whatever it needed, even at the expense of the mother's body, is not true. Malnourished mothers bear malnourished infants and the malnourishment shows up in many places in the infant including the brain. The brains of such infants are likely to be undersized and fail to fill the bony cavity as they do in well-nourished infants. Such malnourishment of the infant is likely to be continued after birth. In addition, malnourishment of the mother is likely to result in premature birth, a condition that is very unfavorable for the sound development of the nervous system and very likely to lead to mental handicap.

What is now known about the effect of malnutrition of the underprivileged and its effect on the developing nervous system leads to an important hypothesis concerning the poverty cycle. The hypothesis is that each generation of underprivileged grows up with inferior nervous systems, caused by malnutrition, and that each generation in turn raises the next generation with the same poor nutrition and with the same defects in the nervous system. Some who have noted that the underprivileged produce new generations of equally inadequate individuals have erroneously concluded that this was a clear case of the inheritance of inferior intelligence, but the fact seems to be that the main determinant has been environmental, namely, nutritional.

Another point that must be made in this connection is that even a trait that is inherited by a well-identified mechanism may be modified by the environment to a high degree. An excellent example is the inherited deformity club foot, carried by a recessive gene. Yet a surgeon can transform a club foot into a quite normal foot, despite the fact that the defect is inherited. Conversely, an acquired characteristic may represent a highly stable condition that is difficult or impossible to eradicate. Damage to the nervous system produced by poor nutrition may well represent irreversible damage. The inheritability or noninheritability of a characteristic has little to do with whether it can be modified. This is contrary to the current myth that inherited characteristics cannot be changed but that environmentally produced characteristics can.

Most important characteristics of the human race represent the result of a complex interplay of inherited characteristics and the impact of the environment on those characteristics. Piaget continually stresses this point in his writings. Intelligence develops if the child is challenged by appropriate problems at the proper level of development. The wrong challenge at the wrong time is useless. The building of the intelligent adult requires a long and complex interaction between the genetic nature of the individual and environmental impact. For Piaget, the question of whether intelligence is mainly inherited or mainly the result of environmental influences is meaningless. Most modern psychologists would agree with Piaget in this respect.

PROBLEM SOLVING AS A BASIS OF THE CURRICULUM

Those concerned with the practical business of teaching have long been intrigued with the idea that the most useful education may well be provided by problem-solving situations in which the student derives from his own experience the truths that constitute the major outcomes of his studies. This conception of education has generally been stated in the form that the student should *discover* the truths that are to be learned or that he should engage in *discovery learning*. The assumption is that he will benefit more from knowledge acquired through problem solving and discovery than from the same knowledge presented to him by the teacher through a lecture. This attractive proposition has intrigued generations of teachers. Its fascination has not waned, as is evident from the support it has received in recent years from such persons as Bruner and Piaget. The former prefers to use the term *inquiry training* rather than the more conventional *discovery learning* or *discovery teaching*. Teaching by the discovery method is contrasted with what is called *expository teaching*, which amounts to a teaching technique of presenting to the student the information he is to acquire. The issue is of particular interest in connection with the topic under discussion, in that a major claim for discovery teaching has been that it leads to greater transfer of training than teaching involving the direct memorization of subject matter.

A first point to note about problem solving as a basis for curriculum design is that problem-solving curricula generally have the merit of bringing the child into contact with real problems. Contact with the real world is an essential ingredient of a good education. Thinkers about education from Pestalozzi to Piaget have emphasized this fact. There is also evidence that merely talking about problems is a poor substitute for contact with the actual problems. Indeed, transfer from the verbal form of a problem to the concrete problem seems to be poor, even in adults (see Van Duyne, 1974). Arguments for discovery methods of learning are strong and persuasive.

In inquiry training or discovery learning the pupil is not only brought into contact with a relatively realistic problem, generally in concrete form, but he is not shown the solution and has had to find it. Although this approach to learning in schools has had a long history, it was not until after World War II that it was studied experimentally. Worthen (1968), who has reviewed many of the studies made of this problem, points out the conflicting results. Some studies purportedly gave results that supported discovery teaching, whereas others, often supposedly attacking the same problem, led to completely opposite results. Worthen concludes that the apparent conflict among the findings is due to the fact that no clear meaning has been assigned to such terms as discovery learning, guided discovery learning, and expository teaching. Indeed, the confusion is so great that what one person refers to as guided discovery learning another may label as expository teaching. Another excellent review of the problem by Wittrock (1966) emphasizes the point that one of the basic weaknesses of research in the area is that most research workers have not specified just what is to be discovered by the student.

The difficulties of deriving generalizations from research on discovery learning that can be applied to teaching can be most readily explored by considering an example. Let us suppose that the pupil is concerned with understanding the conditions under which a beam can be balanced by placing weights on it on opposite sides of the fulcrum. The student might be started on this exploration by being given two weights and a beam marked off in inches from the center. He might be given the beam balanced on a knife edge and be left to place the weights on the beam in such a way that they balanced. This would represent a very unstructured situation in which he would have few cues provided that would help him to arrive at a solution. Given the two weights, the beam, and the balancing edge, few pupils in the elementary school would be likely to discover the principle involved. Most teachers would want to provide more cues so that the pupil would have a greater chance of discovering the principle involved. One way of doing this would be to present the pupil with the balanced beam, as shown in Figure 13-1, and to ask him to state the rule of how the weights are to be placed on the beam if they are to balance. At this point he could be left to manipulate the two weights, or he could be shown other examples, such as are shown in Figure 13-1B and Figure 13-1C. He may be given unlimited

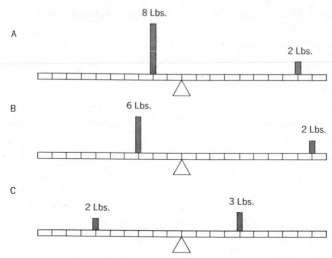

Figure 13-1. Example of task used in discovery learning procedures.

time to solve this problem or he may be given additional cues. One helpful cue that might be given might involve the statement, " Now look at A. The beam is balanced when an 8-pound weight is placed 2 inches from the balance point and when the 2-pound weight is placed 8 inches from the balance point. Write down these numbers: 8 at 2 and 2 at 8. What do you notice about them?" If the pupil still does not see the relationship, tell him to write down the corresponding numbers from **B** which would read 6 at 3 and 2 at 9. If, by that time, he has not multiplied 6 × 3 and 2 × 9, then he can be given the additional prompt of being told to multiply each weight by its distance from the point of balance. As the number of cues increases, the procedure becomes more and more closely similar to expository teaching.

In few discovery learning situations is the pupil left with almost no cues to discover a simple principle. Indeed, he would have to have the intellect of a Newton to find a principle under such circumstances. The pupil generally has to be provided with extensive cues in order to arrive at the principle he is to discover. Under such circumstances, there is likely to be very little discovery involved in the pupil work. Studies of discovery learning rarely state the degree to which cues are provided. Some of the apparent inconsistency of findings can be attributed to differences in this respect.

Another source of inconsistency across studies of discovery learning is that in some, the effect of learning is appraised through a measure of the pupil's ability to recall what has been learned, whereas others have used a measure of the ability to transfer what has been learned to the solution of new problems. The previously cited study by Worthen shows that conditions that favor the recall of what is learned may not be the most favorable for transfer. One can easily see how this might happen. If the goal is to parrot back information, rote learning may be efficient, but the acquisition of understanding may lead to effective transfer even though it may interfere with giving quick answers to short questions.

Mention must also be made of a very important condition not discussed in most studies of discovery learning. This is the matter of the amount of time spent on learning. Discovery learning procedures are generally much more time-consuming than those involving expository teaching. When more time is spent in learning, more learning is likely to take place. Indeed, learning is generally limited by the time factor rather than by any other. One suspects that in many studies that compare discovery learning with learning by expository methods, much more time is spent with the discovery methods and there should be small surprise that the additional time results in additional learning.

For reasons given here, little research support can be found at this time for using discovery methods of teaching. Although direct evidence to support the procedure is lacking, there is some indirect evidence for using discovery methods so long as they do not use much more time than expository methods. One argument is that methods of learning that require learner activity are generally superior to learning conditions that require only relatively passive reception of information. However, discovery is only one of many activities that can be introduced. The application of the knowledge that has been acquired also represents an activity that has long been used to promote learning and is probably a successful technique.

The Worthen study provides some of the better data in discovery learning. Unlike most other studies, the characteristics of expository and discovery teaching were quite well defined and the pupils were exposed to sufficiently large doses of these two kinds of pedagogy that any notable difference should have shown up. Worthen was also able to collect data on what the teachers did in the classroom and was able to provide some evidence that teachers assigned to the different methods actually did behave differently. In addition, instruction by each method involved the same amount of time. The children were tested for the knowledge and skill acquired from instruction in mathematics by expository and discovery methods at the end of the six-week period of instruction, and also five weeks and eleven weeks later. The tests involved both measures of the ability to use the knowledge directly and the ability to transfer the knowledge to the solution of novel problems. The results showed very small differences in the learning of the pupils exposed to the different teaching procedures. On the immediate measure of retention there seemed to be a very slight superiority among the pupils exposed to the expository teaching. On the delayed measures of retention there was a very slight superiority for the pupils exposed to the discovery methods. In the tests of transfer of training to new situations, differences were of negligible magnitude. The chief weakness of the study is that the account of it does not specify precisely just what the students discovered or what was presented to them in the expository teaching, perhaps because scientific accounts have to be brief and often cannot give all the details that the reader would like to know.

The results of the Worthen study follow closely a much earlier study of Wittrock (1963), in which pupils worked problems involving the deciphering of a code. In the Wittrock study the pupils could learn either by discovery or by expository teaching the rule needed to solve each problem and the answer to each problem. The only really clear results of this study were that on the test of immediate retention the expository method, which involved the giving of both the rule and the answer, produced superior results. However, when the test was delayed or when a test for transfer of training was involved, a mixture of the expository and discovery methods showed slight superiority. The mixture involved giving the rule but not giving the answer to the problem.

Mayer and Greeno (1972) and Egan and Greeno (1973) have also reported on a series of studies related to the issue of the relative effectiveness of discovery versus expository learning. These studies have been made under quite well-controlled conditions. Instruction was given through the medium of printed materials requiring virtually no teacher intervention. The learners were college students and the topic for instruction was the binomial theorem and its application to simple probability problems. A sequence of components of the binomial theorem were designed that could be taught by means of either an expository or a discovery method. The students in the study were also divided into medium, high, and low groups in terms of their scores on a mathematics aptitude test. The medium and high groups required almost identical times to master the materials in the two methods. However, the low group was much slower on the discovery method and made more errors. The data tend to support the view that in order to profit from a discovery learning procedure, the learner must have a body of related knowledge to which he can tie in the new knowledge to be acquired. Such a body of knowledge is tapped by the mathematics aptitude test, which deals with the student's broad familiarity with common mathematical concepts. The low-aptitude students did not have such a body of knowledge within themselves and had little to which they could link the new knowledge to be acquired. For them, learning by discovery was an enormously difficult task.

An interesting hypothesis has been injected into the controversy concerning the relative virtues of expository and discovery methods of learning through a study by Roughead and Scandura (1968). These research workers have taken the position that whatever is learned by a discovery method can be learned by an expository method. They argue, for example, that if the use of a discovery method teaches children how to discover principles, there must surely be rules that guide behavior in the discovery of principles and these rules can surely be learned by expository methods. One difficulty in teaching such rules by expository methods is that they have not yet been adequately identified, but there is also another difficulty involved, even when the rules are known. In expository teaching, because the children do not have to derive the rules and understand the rationale for them, there is little incentive for acquiring insight into the derivation of the rule. For this reason, they may never discover why a rule is sound. For example, the child taught the rule for multiplying simple fractions may not be interested in knowing the reason for it, for a knowledge of the rule alone enables him to get the right answers. On the other hand, the discovery method forces him to go through the procedure of inventing the rule and this he cannot do without understanding how the rule is derived.

CREATIVITY AND PROBLEM SOLVING
The Nature of Creativity

In American educational literature there is considerable contemporary emphasis on helping pupils to learn to be creative. Discussion of the subject typically implies that there is a difference between solving a problem and being creative. Whether one can or cannot make this distinction depends on how the terms are defined.

As discussed earlier, for Piaget all intellectual functioning is inventive, that is, creative as the term is used in America. If the pupil has never previously encountered the solution to a problem and after much thought arrives at a solution, one can say that he has created the solution. A child, who has never really understood why some objects sink and some float, one day arrives at the conclusion that the critical factor is whether the object weighs more or less than an equal volume of water. He has created the solution to this problem as have countless other individuals over the centuries. The solution is common knowledge and because it is some would not classify it as the result of creative acts on the part of the student. If a creative act is defined in this restricted way, as an act that produces a thought or product that has never been produced before, creative acts would be very rare events. Indeed, they would be so rare that children in school could hardly be expected to be creative. This is a very narrow conception of creativity, and of little use in an educational context. A broader definition, which defines a creative act as one that produces an adaptive response new to the individual who produces it, seems much more useful for educational purposes. However, if this definition is adopted, much of what Piaget refers to as the exercise of the intelligence is a creative performance. However, Piaget defines creativity in the narrow sense and does not consider children to be creative, only inventive.

Sometimes creativity is defined by combining the two usages we have just considered. The position is taken that all problem solving is creative, but some solutions are more creative than others. In this sense the more creative solutions are the more original. Teachers have often developed exercises for children in order to help them to be more creative. Often these exercises involve brainstorming problems, finding as many possible solutions as quickly as possible. Reese and Parnes (1970) even attempted to program such training. The overall value of such procedures is largely unknown, as is evident from the absence of any conclusions on the matter in Stein's (1974) comprehensive work. There is no doubt that creativity, as measured by tests measuring the flow of ideas, can be improved by training (Reese and Parnes, (1970), but just what that increase means is far from clear. Gerlach *et al.* (1964) long ago showed that the increase in performance on creativity tests produced by training could also be produced by giving no training, but by expanding the directions of the tests. The expanded directions encouraged the person taking the test to associate freely, without inhibitions, and with the greatest possible speed. Much of the training involving brainstorming and related activities does little more than teach the individual these things. What has *not* been demonstrated is that the person so trained also produces improved solutions on problems that call for racking one's brain for new ideas. Incidentally, Kogan and Pankove (1972) have shown that without special training scores on associative tests of creativity remain quite stable from the fifth to the tenth grade, but the fact that such measures show stability does not mean that they necessarily have any great significance or that there is a need for training.

There can be little doubt that the mere urging of subjects to produce more solutions to problems, or more associations, does increase production. Some interesting data related to this problem have been produced by Johnson, Parrott, and Stratton (1968). In their investigation, the problems used included that of writing as many titles as possible to a paragraph describing a plot, or writing titles for a table presenting agricultural data. The group *urged* to write as many solutions as possible produced more superior solutions, although the average quality was poorer. The subjects in this experiment were able to improve their judgment of the quality of the solutions they produced and hence were eventually able to exercise some control over both the quality and quantity of their solutions.

Not all the findings of research on the effect of free association training can be explained in this way. For example, Freedman (1965) found positive results of free association training, but the problem-solving test used was not one in which the subject's orientation to take it in a certain way would appear to be of any consequence. However, the research still leaves open the question of whether the ability being trained is of any consequence.

Drugs and Creativity

Stein (1974) has summarized some of the research that attempts to relate creativity to the use of drugs such as LSD, psilocybin, and mescaline, which are collectively called hallucinogens. Users have long claimed that the intake of such materials promotes creativity, but this may be an illusion much as alcohol produces the illusion in some that they are great social successes. Research to date has not provided any strong evidence that drugs can be used to enhance creative processes. However, such drugs do seem to release inhibitions that may interfere with creativity, and they may reduce anxiety in some, though the "bad trip" is commonly accompanied by enhanced anxiety to the point where it becomes almost intolerable. Solutions produced to problems by persons who have taken mind-expanding drugs may be acceptable and even commercially valuable, but that does not mean that equally good or better solutions could not have been produced without drugs.

Research on the effects of hallucinogenic drugs has been for the most part quite amateurish and is often no more than an account of personal experiences after the intake of a particular substance. The research makes no mention of the long-term effects of such intake. Only relatively recently have we come to learn that alcohol produces a slow deterioration in the brain, perhaps even when taken in such moderate amounts that intoxication is never evident. Generations of alcohol users have claimed that alcohol is harmless if taken in moderate amounts. The Indians who consumed mescaline in the form of peyote have claimed that the drug is harmless. Slow changes may be produced in the nervous system, and the individual may not be aware of what is gradually happening to him. Because foreign substances may produce slow and hidden changes in the body, physicians are becoming more and more cautious of using drugs, except where such use is imperative.

Characteristics of the Creative Problem Solver

The characteristics of the creative problem solver have long been a subject for speculation. Half a century ago the belief was commonly held that the genius was a mentally disturbed individual, otherwise incapable of looking after himself. The classic studies of Terman did much to dispose of this view and stimulated a large body of research designed to determine the combination of personal characteristics that make for effective creative effort. Stein (1974) has attempted to synthesize much of this research concluding that the creative individual can be described in the following terms:

1. He is a successful achiever and is also characterized by high achievement need.
2. He is also motivated by a need to search for order.
3. He shows high curiosity.
4. He is aggressive, assertive, and self-sufficient.
5. He is unconventional, informal, and Bohemian.
6. He is persistent and self-disciplined in his work.
7. He is independent.
8. He is critical and dissatisfied with things as they are.
9. He has a wide range of both interests and knowledge.
10. He is an enthusiastic and feeling person.
11. He values esthetic experiences.
12. He has a low interest in social relationships, but may well be socially sensitive.
13. He is intuitive.
14. He makes impact on others.

This list omits certain items that seem to be far more controversial than those listed. For example, although Stein, in contrast to Terman, finds the creative individual to be more unstable than those less creative, the evidence on which this conclusion is based is highly ambiguous. The value structure of the creative individual is also controversial.

Although the picture presented of the creative individual is that of a likable and interesting person, it does not mean that such individuals are necessarily popular among their associates. Indeed, the reverse seems to be the case. A highly creative person in industry may be seen as one who constantly wants to upset the status quo. The personnel of a company that is doing well and has a fine product may not view an inventor as anything more than a trouble maker. Despite good company profits, the inventor may develop a device that makes the company's product obsolete, causing change, upset, and upheaval. A creative person in a school system may not be popular with the administration forced to adopt his innovations and even less popular with the teachers who have to learn new ways to handle their pupils. The creative person has to learn to live with opposition to his ideas.

HOW TO BECOME AN EFFECTIVE PROBLEM SOLVER

Stein (1974) has attempted to derive from the research literature a list of actions that problem solvers may take in order to improve their ability to find a solution to a particular problem.

1. The problem solver should equip himself with a large repertoire of tools and techniques. In other words, the effective and capable problem solver is one who is very knowledgeable. This piece of advice does not help a person confronted with a particular problem because it implies that preparation for problem solving is a venture that takes effort, perhaps even over years. Thus the good auto mechanic is the experienced auto mechanic who has seen many odd things go wrong with cars and who has had a wide range or experience with mechanical objects. The effective medical diagnostician has also not only had extensive experience, but he is widely read in related fields and has an enormous knowledge of his subject. Wide experience leads to generalizable problem-solving strategies (see Boone, 1970).

2. The problem solver should back away from conventional solutions or, as psychologists say, go outside the field. A story illustrates this point. A poor, elderly woman was being treated in the outpatient department of the hospital for a crippling ailment that confined her much of the time in bed. She began to show sores on her feet that did not yield to treatment. She complained of sharp pains in her feet, particularly at night. Neither the dermatologist nor the neurologist was able to help her with her complaint, but after the experts had failed the intern, who knew something about the woman's home surroundings, came up with a brand-new hypothesis. "These are bites from rodents," he said; "the cure lies in obtaining a cat for the patient." A cat was obtained and the sores on the woman's feet were rapidly cured. The experts had failed because they had looked for solutions within their own fields. What they had to do was to go outside.

3. The problem solver may sometimes use analogies and metaphors to advantage. For example, he may gain insight into teaching and how to improve it by asking whether the teacher is like a book, a piece of scenery on the stage, a counselor, a manager, or the director of a film, and so forth.

4. The problem solver may sometimes have to take himself away from the situation in order to avoid being dazzled by its complexities. For example, when the car won't start, looking under the hood may give him a feeling of helplessness in the face of the complexities of the wiring. However, going back to his seat may lead him to recalling that the starter would not turn over, which might mean that the battery provided no electricity. That might lead to checking to see whether the car lights work. If they do, the battery is supplying electricity. If they do not, the battery might be dead or the leads to the battery might not be making a connection. Stein cites research showing that children who can do a simple arithmetical calculation may not be able to do it when the problem is perceptually complicated by placing a dollar sign before the same numbers.

5. The problem solver should recognize that his thinking is likely to become stuck in a familiar rut, a phenomenon known as functional fixedness. For example, one may need a screwdriver to tighten a screw on a car, but there is none available.

He is then likely to search for screwdriver-like objects such as knives and spoons. In the search, he may forget that objects that do not look much like screwdrivers may serve the same purpose. The dime is not considered because its function is regarded as a medium for exchange and not that of a tool. Also, if he is set on finding a screwdriver-like object, he may fail to note alternative approaches to the problem such as forgetting about turning the head of the screw and concentrating on turning the nut that holds it on the other side.

6. The problem solver should learn to operate at an optimum level of motivation. The Yerkes–Dodson law, discussed in the chapter on motivation, applies here. Difficult problems should be approached slowly and with deliberation. Excessive motivation with such problems produces ineffective results. A higher energy level is appropriate with simpler problems.

In addition there are a number of systems for systematizing efforts in solving problems, some of which have been marketed. An example of the latter is Allen's *Morphologizer* (1962), based on a conceptualization of problem solving developed by Zwicky. This writer could locate no evidence to indicate that such devices improve individuals' problem-solving capability, but they may well help the scatterbrain to work in an orderly way on problems that have to be approached systematically. However, not all problems require such an approach. The solution of a problem that calls for a leap of the imagination may well be hindered by forcing on the problem solver a high degree of systematization.

SUMMARY

1. In the case of human behavior, problem solving is defined as a situation in which there is a goal to be achieved but no previously learned response that permits the direct achievement of the goal. A broader definition is customarily used when the behavior of animals is involved. In this case, a problem is a state of disequilibrium for which there is no previously learned response for the restoration of equilibrium.

2. Problem-solving behavior often involves extensive internal activity that results in the production of a solution, if a solution is achieved. This internal behavior may be accompanied by manipulations of the environment.

3. Although many attempts have been made to find a classification of problems that would have scientific utility, no satisfactory classification has been evolved. The Guilford classification has had some small impact in encouraging research in the areas of convergent and divergent thinking, but in other areas the impact has been slight.

4. Piaget has introduced a new approach to the problem-solving field. For him, the solving of a problem is an inventive task, and invention is at the very core of the intellect. Problems may be solved by children at different levels. At the lowest level, solutions to problems are intuitively derived. Later, children invent logical structures through which problems are solved. At the highest level, problems are solved by formal operations.

5. American and Russian psychologists have usually taken a reductionist approach to the study of problem solving. The approach has generally involved an

associationistic theory, based on the belief that problem solving is largely a matter of finding the right associations. The assumption is made that the individual capable of solving a problem has in his repertoire all the component responses that are required.

6. Reductionist research on problem solving has usually been undertaken in relation to quite simple problems such as those involved in concept learning and the solving of anagrams.

7. One of the basic areas of research on problem solving has been concept learning. A concept is commonly defined as a category into which experiences may be classified. A word, such as *house*, represents a category into which certain objects in the environment may be classified and thus represents a concept in terms of this definition. This is a much narrower definition of a concept than is commonly used, and it does not include abstract concepts, which do not refer to directly observable events of the real world.

8. Objects and events are categorized on the basis of their attributes. Perception is basically a process of analyzing sensory experiences into their attributes so that objects can be identified. Attributes that define a category may be few and easily identified, or they may be many and subtle.

9. Concept-learning tasks may involve attribute identification, rule identification, or both of these. In rule-identification tasks, the learner is told what the attributes are and he must discover the rule that relates the attributes. In attribute learning he is given the rule and must identify the attributes.

10. In the experimental study of concept learning, as well as in the study of concept learning in real-life situations, positive instances and negative instances of the concept may be provided. These instances are often referred to as exemplars. Some evidence suggests that learning of concepts is best achieved through a carefully chosen combination of positive and negative instances.

11. Concept learning is a special case of rule learning. Rules are also learned in other situations. Rules may be learned in a hierarchy.

12. Problem solvers behave as though they had an inventory of hypotheses from which they could draw.

13. Concepts may be learned by several different strategies. The scanning and focusing strategies have been commonly used in research using reception tasks. These are tasks that involve a fixed sequence of presentations of exemplars.

14. Numerous conditions affect the ease with which concepts are learned. Characteristics of the objects that facilitate learning are clear distinctions between positive and negative instances, redundant relevant attributes and relatively few irrelevant attributes. Concept-learning skill increases with age. Directions that focus attention on the relevant attributes are helpful. Positive and negative instances should appear side by side. The learner should verbalize the relevant attributes. Feedback should be complete and unambiguous. Concepts should not be learned in isolation. In all concept-learning tasks the individual must be provided enough time to assimilate the information provided by feedback.

15. Concepts may function as organizers of further learning. A concept may function as an organizer of concepts at a less abstract level. Some psychologists

assume that all concepts can be ordered in a hierarchy representing the order in which they can be efficiently learned or an order in which they can be logically learned, but research on the ordering of concepts has produced little positive knowledge at this time.

16. Verbal associations play a role in some problem-solving behavior. In studies of verbal associations related to problem solving the results have clearly shown the effect of *functional fixedness*.

17. The anagram has been used extensively in problem-solving research. The results of this research emphasize the importance of *set* in arriving at a solution.

18. Some problems require the problem solver to have extraordinary perceptual skills. Chess is an example of such a complex problem. The expert chess player seems able to code the information provided by the arrangement of the pieces on the chess board. Presumably the information is coded in such a way that it can be related to possible move sequences.

19. American psychologists have not considered logic as a basis for problem solving. Research that uses logic as the model for problem solving has been mainly the enterprise of Piaget and his associates in Geneva. They view conditioning and associationism as having some relevance for understanding the problem-solving behavior of very young children, but other factors enter into the problem solving of older children. Some evidence supports the view that training in logic may help the individual avoid some of the common pitfalls.

20. A modern approach to the study of problem solving has been to attempt to simulate on a computer the behavior that human beings undertake in solving problems. The approach is interesting and novel, but it has run into many difficulties. Scientists have been able to demonstrate that computers can be programmed to perform very much like human beings, but the approach has not yet produced any fundamental new ideas in the area.

21. There have been two main foundations for building a theory of intelligence: psychometric research and logic. Binet's model of intelligence was developed in a more sophisticated form by Thurstone and Guilford, who proposed that intelligence consists of a number of components. Intelligence tests given in schools typically measure the latter. There is little pretense in most of these batteries to build tests that are culture free. Piaget's work has also been used to produce measures of intelligence, although Piaget himself has not been interested in the development of such a scale. This new conception of intelligence suggests how components of the problem-solving process may be identified.

22. The heredity-environment controversy is an old one and little new has been added to it in recent years. The introduction of heritability ratios has probably added more confusion than clarification. Data from family trees, long used to support the notion that heredity is more important than environment, probably have been largely misinterpreted. For example, the poverty cycle appears to contain successive generations of individuals whose nervous systems are damaged before birth by malnutrition. In addition, even traits that are clearly inherited may be modified by unusual environmental intervention.

23. Problem solving has been viewed as a basis for the school curriculum in

curricula that emphasize what has been termed discovery. Although there are strong arguments in favor of a discovery curriculum, there are difficulties in conducting studies to determine how components of the curriculum influence behavior. Most students of the problem have had difficulty in defining the problem with sufficient precision to make a systematic study possible.

24. Creativity can be defined in many ways. In the narrow sense creativity refers to actions producing results that have never been produced before. In the narrow sense, creativity refers to a performance that is original for the individual involved. Attempts to train for creativity, in the broader sense, have been commonly made in classrooms, but the effects are not clear. One cannot say at this time whether such training is or is not worthwhile. There is no evidence that drugs can enhance creativity, and there is always danger that drugs may do permanent harm. The creative individual has a moderately well-defined set of characteristics, which include high achievement and motivation, curiosity, assertiveness, and a Bohemian style.

25. Problem solvers can equip themselves to become better problem solvers. They should expand their repertoire of tools and techniques; they should learn to back away from conventional solutions; they should learn to use unusual metaphors and analogies. They must understand the value of sometimes withdrawing from the situation, and learn to operate at an optimum level of motivation.

Chapter 14

The Learning of Attitudes

Much of the book up to this point has been concerned with problems related to the acquisition of skills and cognitive learning, but another large class of learnings has hardly been touched upon. These learnings are related to approach and avoidance tendencies, which are first seen in early childhood when certain objects become attractive and are approached and other objects initiate withdrawal. Approach and avoidance tendencies, which are so clearly seen in the observable behavior of the child, later become a part of his internal behavior and he comes to place a positive or negative value on objects, events, and ideas. Some of these internal tendencies to accept or reject are referred to as attitudes, others as interests, and still others as values. Distinctions among these terms are not clear. Sometimes it is said that interests refer to preferences for activities; and attitudes refer to a positive approach or negative avoidance of ideas and objects. Both interest and attitude involve the concept of rejection or acceptance, and both involve some kind of affective (feeling) response to the object involved. Attitudes and interests have much more specific objects of reference than do values as they are technically defined. The latter relate to broad goals, such as the achievement of wealth or power or social status, but attitudes and interests are related to narrow channels into which activity is funneled —either toward or away from an object or idea. Interests and attitudes may determine the choice of means through which the value system and the goals implied by it may be achieved. A person's life may be dominated by religious values and religious goals, but he may have positive and negative attitudes to various religious practices and to the means of achieving religious ends.

Although the origin of attitudes is seen in simple responses of approach or withdrawal, in their more mature form attitudes represent highly complex aspects of behavior. Psychologists have slowly managed to tease out some of the components attitudes involve. Katz and Stotland (1960) suggest that attitudes include the following components:

Affective Components. Affective components consist of positive or negative affects (feelings). Attitudes may differ in the extent to which they involve such affective components. Some attitudes are quite irrational and involve little except this affective component. Political attitudes, in their most primitive form, may be primarily of this character. The person who likes one set of political ideas and dislikes another, but cannot tell why, reflects an attitude that has a major affective component but very little else. Many attitudes are of this nature.

Cognitive Components. Attitudes differ in the extent to which they involve knowledge and beliefs. Some attitudes are highly intellectualized. A person may take a particular position on a certain political issue because he has thought through the problem and, after considering all the available evidence, has decided that the position he takes is the most acceptable one. Sometimes attitudes are based on a large store of incorrect information and false beliefs. These are cognitive elements, even though they do not represent true knowledge. The cognitive basis for many attitudes may be misinformation. A person may hold an attitude and have no strong feelings about the matter—that is, the affective component may be minor. On the other hand, his attitudes may not only be highly intellectualized, but may also have a strong affective component. The intellectual component and the affective component work hand in hand, but they are still independent components. The intellectual component of attitude discussed here is somet mes referred to as the cognitive component. The word *cognitive* implies knowing. Hence, the cognitive component of an attitude is that aspect based on beliefs or knowledge.

Action Components. Every student of the psychology of attitudes is impressed with the fact that many expressed attitudes bear little relation to behavior. A person may express strong religious attitudes, and yet his membership in his church involves little more than paying a pledge. In such a case the religious attitudes lack any substantial action component. The fact that the action component can be independent of the other components is important for planning education. Much of what goes on in the name of attitude education is the education of the affective and the cognitive components of attitudes, and these components may never be carried over into action systems. Thus one finds that the American public, probably the best-informed public in the world, has a deplorably poor record at the polls; the percentage of the population voting is small compared with that of most other democratically run countries. The positive attitudes toward democratic institutions often lack appropriate action components. How relationships are established between the cognitive components of attitudes and action systems is not clear at this time. This is really a problem of transfer of training. Although there is some evidence that transfer can take place from cognitive systems to action systems, the conditions that make this possible have not yet been established. Clearly, teachers cannot remain content with educating only the cognitive aspects of attitudes, for education must involve something more than preparation for an armchair approach to life.

Although this writer finds this analysis convenient as a basis for thinking about related educational problems, the reader should not be left with the impression that psychologists are agreed on what they mean by attitudes, for obviously this is not the case. McGuire (1968), who has reviewed numerous definitions of attitudes, concludes that these definitions differ in almost every conceivable important way. Some psychologists define attitudes as inner states, but a few refer to attitudes as consisting of groups of responses. Some define attitudes as a disposition to respond but others consider the response as representing the attitude. Some regard an attitude as having a unity, but others regard it as having a set of distinct components, as do Katz and Stotland. Some distinguish between attitudes and knowledge, but others regard both as unified cognitive components. Numerous broad and important differences arise among those who use the term *attitude*. These differences reflect the fact that knowledge in the area has not yet attained a well-organized state. Despite the fact that the area has not yet reached the point where psychologists have concluded that they have identified clear and unambiguous phenomena of unquestioned importance, it is nevertheless an area of vigorous research activity and some of the findings appear to have implications for educational practice.

THE FUNCTION OF ATTITUDES

The function of skills is generally so obvious that one does not even have to discuss the matter in a chapter of a book on skill learning. One learns to type to earn a living, or to handle personal correspondence more efficiently for some other well-identified purpose, but why does one learn an attitude? The functions of attitudes are as varied as are the functions of skills, but these functions are much less easily identified. Indeed, a whole research literature has developed around the functions of attitudes. McGuire (1969) has attempted to bring together this literature and to identify a number of different categories of function. The different classes of function he proposes are the following:

Adaptive Functions. Some attitudes serve highly utilitarian purposes. Consider, for example, a withdrawal response that a child learns from touching a hot object that has burned him. The withdrawal response that occurs on subsequent occasions, whenever the object is seen, represents a primitive attitude that serves the purpose of protecting the individual from physical harm. At a more complicated and sophisticated level of attitude development, a person may develop an attitude because it enables him to become accepted by his group. A young man in business may adopt "establishment" attitudes, for he views these as aiding his advancement. The development of attitudes of convenience is a widespread phenomenon that social psychologists have studied intensively. The phenomenon can be of enormous social significance, as it was in Nazi Germany where millions adopted anti-Semitic attitudes for the purpose of surviving in a Hitlerian culture; yet when Germany was later occupied by the Allies, anti-Semitism hardly seemed to exist— or to have existed.

Cognitive Functions. Another section of McGuire's book makes the point that concepts permit the classification of the endlessly varied phenomena of the world into a limited number of categories and that in this way the environment is simplified so that interactions with it can be more readily handled. We perceive an object and classify it as a table and once we have done this, we do not have to bother about the wealth of detail that the particular table involves. Having thus classified the object as a table, we are in a position to respond to it as we respond to all objects in that particular class, by making such responses as putting things on it, eating off it, and placing chairs around it. These responses are related to the *class* of objects denoted by the word *table* rather than to particular instances of tables. Attitudes also have a similar simplifying function. They result in generalizations that are gross oversimplifications of an overwhelmingly complex universe. The Russian who takes the position that all capitalists are a menace to an egalitarian society or the American who takes the position that the only good Communist is a dead Communist are both expressing attitudes that oversimplify, to an appalling degree, the real world. Although living creatures can adapt to the world only if they are able to treat it as though it were much simpler than it actually is, sometimes oversimplification can also produce problems, as is evident in the case of the illustration just discussed.

Need Gratification Functions. The title of the category is a little confusing in that all attitudes must, in some way, serve the individual who possesses them. The functions included here are those that involve the very direct gratifications of needs. Men have positive attitudes to women and women toward men. We have positive attitudes toward good food, friendly company, and a warm and dry environment. Attitudes are also related to some of the more subtle needs.

Ego-Defense Functions. Some attitudes are held in order to bolster the individual's own evaluations of himself. An extreme example is found in the Nazi's belief that they belonged to the master race; in order to maintain this belief, they had to accept at the same time the belief that other identifiable outgroups such as Jews, Negroes, Frenchmen, Communists, and so forth, were grossly inferior to them. In the case of the Nazis, the picture is also complicated by an idealized conception of a father figure, in the form of a Führer, against whom no hostility can be felt without arousing feelings of extreme guilt. In such a situation, pent-up hostilities become directed toward outgroups against whom extreme cruelty can be exerted without arousing any feelings of guilt whatsoever. A familiar example from our own culture of an attitude functioning as an ego-defense mechanism is found in the case of political figures with a limited education who insist on referring to professors as *stupid intellectuals*. Such politicians feel enormously threatened by the academic intellectual, but the threat can be reduced by calling the intellectual stupid.

THEORIES OF ATTITUDE CHANGE

Social psychologists vigorously engaged in programs of research and producing a great harvest of experimental results have readily jumped into the task of theory building. Two large volumes have appeared summarizing, and criticizing, various theoretical positions (Abelson et al., 1968, Insko, 1967). Thus we find in the literature several reinforcement theories of attitude formation and change: classical conditioning theories, cognitive consistency theories, type theories, adaptation-level theories, and at least a dozen other theories with established names. It would be useless, even futile, to plunge the reader into this morass of theorizing.

What seems to be profitable is to consider the two main classes of theory. First, there are those theories closely tied to operant conditioning. Second, there is a category of theorizing known as cognitive dissonance theory, which, in turn, is a part of a larger family of theories known as cognitive consistency theories, which have been summarized in a massive handbook edited by Abelsen et al. (1968).

Operant Theories of Attitude Acquisition and Change

One position with respect to attitude acquisition and change comes from those interested in operant conditioning. According to this view, attitudes are groups of behaviors that can be established in the first place, or modified, through reinforcement procedures. In other words, the assumption is made that attitudes are learned in exactly the same way as are skills. This viewpoint is to be contrasted with the more conventional one that assumes that attitudes are internal conditions influencing behavior and that although attitudes may manifest themselves through behavior, they are not just groups of behaviors. Thus the psychologist who views all learning as operant conditioning considers attitudes to be observable events, whereas most psychologists would view attitudes as internal and not directly observable.

The position that attitudes change according to the principles of reinforcement has prompted a considerable body of research. The operant conditioning approach to attitude change suggests that the way to modify attitudes is to wait for some slight change in the desired direction to occur, and then reinforce the changed attitude. Thus a Republican who wishes to change the political attitudes of his Democratic friend might wait until the friend expressed some favorable opinion about the Republican party, and then he would reinforce the behavior of his friend. Another approach might be for the Republican to arrange a situation in which his friend was likely to express a favorable comment toward the Republican party and then apply reinforcement. He might do this by arranging for his friend to meet a particularly likable Republican and hope that this situation might elicit attitudes that he might want to reinforce.

Laboratory techniques have been developed for testing this theory that attitudes are learned and changed through reinforcement. These techniques have been well summarized by Insko (1967), together with the experimental results. One technique involves asking students to prepare short speeches to be presented in debating an issue. Some of the participants in the experiment are asked to support in their speeches a position opposite to or very different from their own position. This procedure requires the individuals involved to express attitudes different from those which they ordinarily express. The psychologist can then determine whether the reinforcement of these new attitudes results in their becoming established. The person who presents the speech can either win or lose the debate, and the experimenter generally rigs the experiment so that certain designated persons are declared winners, regardless of how they perform, and others are declared losers. This is one way of reinforcing the expressed attitude. An alternative is to provide cash prizes for certain performers in the debate, who are thus designated as outstanding.

Another technique for studying attitude change through reinforcement involves inducing a person to make a statement contrary to his opinion. Festinger and Carlsmith (1959) exposed subjects to a series of boring tasks and the subjects were then paid to tell other subjects that the experience had been interesting and enjoyable. Later, the participants thus paid were asked to rate truthfully how much they had enjoyed or been bored with the tasks. Still another technique requires students to write essays on an issue presenting a particular position. Students can be assigned positions to write about that differ in a specified degree from their own position. Here again, rewards may follow the performance or they may not.

In most studies, but not in all, the mere expression of an opinion different from that initially held results in a negligible amount of shift of attitude, but when these expressions of attitude are coupled with a reinforcer, such as money or praise, substantial changes in attitude occur.

It is easy to adopt a simplistic position and say that the reinforcement produces attitude change in the experiments just described, but a sufficient amount is known about the problem to be able to provide a more sophisticated explanation. In most of the studies one cannot state very clearly what is being reinforced, which is perhaps the reason that the results are not always entirely consistent from study to study. If a person is given a prize for presenting a speech that takes a position opposite to the one he holds, the prize may tell him that he has done a good job of presenting a thesis with which he does not agree. In such a case his skill in acting is what is being reinforced. On the other hand, if he is told at the time he is given the prize that his ideas were very well organized and well presented, what is reinforced is his skill in organizing ideas. Operant theory takes the position that all behaviors that precede a reinforcer are reinforced, but there is evidence that this is not necessarily so and that some of the preceding behaviors are better reinforced than others.

Closely related to the operant position is Bem's theory of attitude change, referred to as self-perception theory, which is an odd title for a theory that claims behavioristic affiliations. A consideration of Bem's theory must wait until we have considered cognitive dissonance theory, since Bem's theory is in many respects a counter position to dissonance theory.

Cognitive Dissonance Theory of Attitude Change

Let us introduce dissonance theory by considering an experiment similar to many of those that have been used to support an operant view of attitude formation and change, and in which a person is required to make statements contrary to his own attitude. Wallace conducted a study of attitude change in such a setting; he began by measuring attitudes of the subjects, and then he asked each subject to give a talk presenting a position different from that which he held. The topic was capital punishment and those not in favor of capital punishment presented speeches in favor of it. The speeches were presented in front of an audience of stooges. Although the design of the experiment was complex, the essential feature for the present discussion was that two kinds of reinforcement were given. Each member of one group at the end of the presented speech was told that the content presented was given a high rating by the audience but that the manner in which it had been presented was average. Each member of another group was told that the manner of presenting the speech was good but that the content was average. The interesting finding was that those reinforced for their ideas showed little attitude change but very substantial changes were shown by those told that their manner was excellent even though their ideas were average.

Now these results do not fit ideas commonly expressed about operant conditioning. Indeed, in terms of the latter ideas, one would have expected that those reinforced for the content of their speeches would have shown the greatest changes, but the opposite occurred. Those reinforced for their manner made the greatest changes. Wallace has an explanation.

Wallace suggests that when a subject is told that he had an excellent manner in presenting his material, it means that he has been viewed by the audience as presenting an exemplary role of one who holds the particular position given in the speech. A person who is in favor of capital punishment, when placed in such a position, would suddenly discover that he is seen by the audience as having a sincere commitment *against* capital punishment. This produces strong internal conflict, in that the subject knows himself to be in favor of capital punishment, but he also suddenly sees himself as a convincing opponent of this form of punishment. One way to resolve this conflict is to change his internal attitude; he can say to himself that he never really was completely in favor of capital punishment and that he just favored it under some circumstances. In this way he can harmonize his beliefs with his action.

The very small change in attitude that occurred when the quality of the content of the speech was rewarded also needs explanation. The simplest view in this respect would be that the subjects who were told that the content was good were not troubled in any way with the lack of harmony between what they had said in their speeches and what they believed. They recognized that there was discord, but the discord would be only temporary for they had been engaging in some kind of intellectual exercise that called for such discord. At the end of the discord they could forget about the content of the speech they had made and return to their original position. They did not have to resolve the perception of themselves as a sincere and committed believer in a new position with the position they had long previously taken on the issue. Thus the one group was highly motivated to change its attitude but the other group was not.

The data derived from the Wallace study, like that from many other studies, do not fit the reinforcement model of learning. In order to understand such data, the concept is usually introduced that human beings cannot tolerate inconsistencies that they perceive in themselves and that they will change in a direction that tends to reduce internal inconsistency. Thus a person who believes in an isolationist position on foreign policy and who feels strongly and positively about the isolationist position has almost certainly a system of beliefs consistent with the way he feels. He will tend to acquire further information consistent with the way he feels and consistent with the information previously acquired. He is likely to forget information presented to him that does not support his beliefs and feelings.

This concept of human beings that emphasizes striving toward unity has had a long history and a substantial impact on education. The great Prussian educator Froebel was one of the first to view man in this light, although he derived this conception from the theological doctrine that the soul is characterized by unity. Psychologists later came to observe that people do not really tolerate inconsistency within themselves and that many psychological mechanisms have the function of minimizing inconsistency in what the individual perceives in himself. Freud long ago observed that people commonly fail to recognize in themselves those characteristics that do not fit their own self-concept. A wealthy man who regards himself as a philanthropist may fail to recognize a streak of stinginess in his day-to-day dealings. A man of generally kindly disposition may fail to recognize the numerous small hostile acts he directs toward his mother-in-law. Later research workers noted that a reader tends to assimilate information consistent with his own personal veiwpoint much more readily than information that is inconsistent.

Such observations, backed up in recent times by a substantial body of research, have led psychologists to develop theories of cognitive consistency summarized in the handbook on the subject by Abelson et al. (1968). Such theories deal with a variety of phenomena, from an apparent tendency to remember only those facts that are consistent with previously acquired knowledge to problems related to attitude acquisition and change. One of the most influential of such theories of attitude change is that which Festinger has developed. The original theory was presented in Festinger's book (1957), but it has since received elaboration at the hands of various research workers. Festinger, unlike many other research workers in the field of attitudes, has presented a theory that emphasizes cognitive elements in attitude change, that is, elements involving knowledge. He is broad in defining what he means by these cognitive elements, in that information held that is incorrect is also thought of as a cognitive element. These elements are called cognitions. Festinger does not make a distinction in formulating his theory between knowledges, beliefs, and opinions, because so long as they are a part of the individual's psychological make-up, they function in a very similar way.

Although the theme of Festinger's book is that human beings strive to remove inconsistency, he prefers to use the term *dissonance* rather than *inconsistency*. The entire book is concerned with four propositions. First, the presence of dissonance is "psychologically uncomfortable" (p. 3), hence, dissonance motivates the person to reduce it. Second, the person actively avoids situations likely to increase any dissonance already present. Third, an inconsistent environment tends to continuously produce dissonance within the individual. Fourth, individuals differ in the extent to which they will tolerate dissonance within themselves. Festinger also suggests a number of mechanisms that commonly come into play when dissonance occurs. Some of these can be illustrated by an example. Suppose that a person strongly opposed to the United States' program of foreign aid were exposed to a lecture in which the arguments in favor of foreign aid were clearly presented and evidence was given to support the arguments. Such a lecture presents a situation producing dissonance in our listener. He may reduce this dissonance in a number of different ways. First, he may pass off the arguments and evidence as "nonsense" and forget about the whole affair, Second, he may retain the information provided in the lecture but take the stand that it involves assumptions he does not accept. Third, he may change his attitude toward the foreign aid issue. He is most likely to do this when the arguments are only moderately different from his present position. If the arguments are highly inconsistent with his present position, he is more likely to behave in terms of the first two alternatives.

Festinger describes four conditions to which dissonance may be attributed. These four conditions bring out quite clearly the role that cognitions, that is, beliefs about the world, play in his theory. The first source of dissonance is logical inconsistency. Consider the following two statements:

1. Cigarette smoke damages the lungs.
2. Cigarette smoking will not hurt me.

If a smoker, like many smokers, makes both statements to himself he will be in a state of dissonance. The one is logically inconsistent with the other.

A second source of dissonance is inconsistency with cultural mores. This writer can remember in 1965, when there were still few anti-Vietnam demonstrations, joining a small band of people protesting the war. The group of about thirty individuals marched through town under the eyes of a hostile police force, and a mob of swearing and unruly citizens. Such a situation produces dissonance, for the behavior involved was highly inconsistent with the need to be accepted by others. The dissonance provides a situation highly favorable for attitude change, but in the case of the situation described the high morale and the mutually supportive behavior of the members of the small group of marchers probably counteracted the dissonance effect.

A third source of dissonance is where there is inconsistency between a particular behavior and the general trend in behavior, or, as Festinger says, between one cognition and a more general cognitive state. A cautious and well-trained automobile driver who takes liberties with the speed limits because he is in a hurry experiences such dissonance.

A fourth source is probably the most common. Whenever an event does not fit our past experience, dissonance is produced. If an old friend is suddenly rude to us, or if the car that has always started does not start, or if the voice we expect to greet us at the door is not heard: in all of these situations dissonance occurs.

Another important aspect of Festinger's theory is that he deals with situations in which decisions have to be made. It is in such situations that dissonance is most likely to occur and attitudes are most likely to be changed. Because in the making of decisions rewards are generally at stake, the magnitude of the reward is also a factor in determining the degree of dissonance that the decision and the resulting state of affairs produces. Suppose that an honest politician has to choose between (1) backing a corrupt candidate he does not like, but with the understanding that if he does so he will receive a large party contribution toward his own election, or (2) choosing somebody he likes and not obtaining party funds. Under such conditions, if he backs the corrupt candidate, his action is dissonant with his own standard of ethics, but the extent he experiences dissonance will depend upon the size of the party's reward in contributing campaign funds. If the reward is small, the resulting dissonance will be large, but if the financial contribution is large, the amount of dissonance will be relatively low. The dissonance is small when the reward is large because, under that set of circumstances, he can say to himself that the large sum of money makes it all worthwhile and that the money will support a good cause, and that the good accomplished outweighs the bad. Under such circumstances dissonance is resolved.

The presence of dissonance is believed to be necessary for attitude change. Consider the case of the person who chooses to attend a lecture presenting an opinion with which he disagrees. If he finds the speaker extremely likable, even though the views of the speaker are different from his own, he will experience little dissonance in the situation. He will say to himself that he is willing to listen to views he rejects because the speaker is such a likable fellow. He can justify his presence by saying to himself that he is there because he likes the speaker, and what the speaker has to say is not a reason for being there and so it does not change his attitude. However, if the speaker is disagreeable, much more dissonance will be produced and more attitude change may be produced. Under these circumstances, the listener cannot find in the speaker reason for being there. He can resolve the dissonance produced by his presence in a disagreeable situation by telling himself that perhaps the speech is important and worth listening to. His improved evaluation of what the speaker has to say increases the likelihood that the speech will have impact on him. Dissonance theory has produced some predictions such as this one that have been verified experimentally. They are not the predictions that most people would make, but they are the predictions that derive from dissonance theory. Incidentally, the disagreeable speaker produces more attitude change than the pleasant speaker only when the listener is not forced to listen to a presentation and when attendance is voluntary (see Jones and Brehm, 1967).

A different approach to the study of the effect of dissonance on attitude is found in a series of studies reviewed by Aronson (1968). These studies go back to the often cited classic one by Festinger and Carlsmith (1959) in which individuals were paid either $1 or $20 for making statements contrary to their beliefs. In such experiments the individuals are asked to undertake a dull repetitive task and are then asked to tell another individual, described as a future subject, that the task was quite interesting. Later, attitudes toward the task are again determined to find out whether the attitude has shifted. Such studies are designed to determine the extent to which requiring the individual to say that the task was interesting improves attitude toward the task.

The conclusions from such experiments are surprisingly consistent, namely, that when the reward offered for the presentation of the counterattitude is small, the change in attitude is larger than when the reward offered is greater. The proponents of dissonance theory interpret this by saying that when the reward is small, subjects have to find a reason for saying the things they are saying. The easiest reason to find is that what they are saying really has some truth to it. On the other hand, when the reward is large, the person admits to himself that he is being bribed, and this is justification for expressing beliefs with which he does not agree. Aronson also points out that there are a few studies in which this effect was not found, but they are all studies in which the subjects did not have to face an audience when they were presenting ideas inconsistent with their own beliefs. In this situation they typically wrote essays. In such situations there is an entirely different relationship between reward and change than there is in the face-to-face situations. While in the public situations the greatest change occurs when the reward is smallest, in those situations that do not involve face-to-face relationships the largest reward produces the greatest change. There is apparently a real and important difference between facing an audience and presenting ideas in which one does not believe and doing this in a more secluded situation. Aronson suggests that the psychological difference between these two situations is a difference in what he calls the commitment involved.

Some more recent results summarized by Gerard, Conolley, and Wilhemly (1974) indicate that the phenomenon is more complex than it had first seemed to be, a not unusual turn of events in psychological research. When the range of rewards is extended, an additional effect is found. The data presented by Gerard et al. confirm the findings that small rewards are associated with the greatest attitude change and that a larger reward produces less attitude change, but when the reward is increased still further the amount of attitude change begins to rise again. This implies a U-shaped curve relating amount of reward to attitude change. Rewards that appear ridiculous in size seem to have effects not included in dissonance theory.

The relationship of reward to attitude change in the class of experiment just discussed is different from what one would expect in terms of reinforcement theory. In these experiments, increasing the size of the reward has a negative effect on the learning one is interested in bringing about. Dissonance theory, in this situation, makes better predictions than those made from reinforcement concepts. However, it must be noted that dissonance theory makes good predictions only when there is commitment on the part of the subject, in the sense in which the term commitment is used by Aronson.

One of the very interesting events predicted by dissonance theory is that a mild threat is more likely to make a person desist from an activity he likes to engage in than a strong threat. Aronson (1968) has been largely responsible for developing and testing this hypothesis and has reviewed the early studies related to it. Later studies have been reviewed by Bem (1974). Aronson originally argued that if a child is threatened with severe punishment for performing an activity that he likes to perform, he will continue to like the activity but perhaps temporarily stop performing it. The threat is sufficient justification for not performing it but he will return to the activity later if the threat is removed. However, if the threat is mild, the threat and the activity are dissonant, and dissonance can be reduced by the child's telling himself that he really does not like the activity. As a result, his tendency to perform the activity is reduced. Aronson reports a series of experiments in which children were threatened with either mild or severe punishment for playing with a desired toy. Those threatened with mild punishment showed a reduced liking for the toy, but those threatened with severe punishment continued to show a liking for the toy at the same level as previously.

Another prediction made also by Aronson and his associates (1968) was that individuals who went through a disagreeable initiation ceremony in order to enter a group would be more likely to value highly the activities of the group than those who went through a bland and innocuous initiation. In this experiment, women students in a psychology class were divided into three groups. In order to become a member of a discussion group on the psychology of sex, the members of one group were each required to read aloud, to a male instructor, a list of taboo words, that is, words not ordinarily used in social life. Another group had a mild initiation involving no socially prohibited words, and the third group had no initiation ceremony. All groups then heard a recording of a discussion of the psychology of sex. They did not know that it was a taped recording but believed that what they heard through the earphones was an ongoing, live discussion. The discussion had been made deliberately boring. At the end of the session the subjects had to make an evaluation of the discussion. Those who had been subjected to the severe initiation evaluated the discussion with more praise than those who had had either a mild initiation or who had had no initiation. The dissonance produced by reciting the list of taboo words was reduced by taking the position that it was a price worth paying for gaining access to an interesting discussion.

The findings of the initiation-ceremony experiment have been confirmed rather strikingly in studies in which the severe initiation was replaced by a series of electric shocks (Gerard and Mathewson, 1966). Once again it was found that following electric shock, the discussion that subjects listened to was rated higher.

Cognitive dissonance theory in its various forms has been immensely successful as a stimulus for research, as is evident from the large number of studies produced that are related to the ideas that flow from it. Some of these experiments have also had considerable significance to the whole field of psychology, in that they have pointed out some of the limitations of the predictions that can be made from a simple reinforcement theory. The reader should not think there is an issue of whether cognitive consistency theories are nearer or farther from the truth than reinforcement theories, for this is not a real issue. In some situations cognitive dissonance theories provide the best predictions, but there are other situations in which reinforcement concepts are the most serviceable. The immediate scientific problem is to identify the conditions under which each can be most effectively applied, much as physicists have discovered the conditions under which the wave theory of light and quantum theory can each be most effectively applied to the making of predictions. Whether the wave theory of light and quantum theory can be fully resolved still remains to be seen. Reinforcement and dissonance theory may also have a long history of mutual coexistence.

The chief limitation on dissonance theory, for which it has been widely criticized, is the vagueness of the term dissonance. Festinger originally described two elements as being dissonant if the "obverse of one element would follow from the other" (1967, p. 13). The word *obverse* is highly ambiguous and is used by Festinger as a synonym for opposite, but this is not really what obverse means in logic, where it is widely used. Perhaps the word *opposite* would have been a more appropriate one to use, but even that is not a very clear term. The term *inconsistency* is also widely used as a synonym for dissonance. Aronson (1968) suggests that when it is said that two cognitions are dissonant it means that given the one cognition the expectancy of the other cognition is very low. If I buy a car for £8000 and it refuses to start, there is dissonance for, having paid a high price for a car, I expect it to go. If I believe in capital punishment and find myself in a situation in which I am arguing against capital punishment, there is dissonance because given the fact that I believe in capital punishment, I do not expect to find myself advocating its abolition. Dissonance seems to be quite well defined in terms of conflicts between cognitions and expectancies, but the measurement of expectancies is not always easily undertaken.

Katz (1958) points out that another source of evidence that runs against dissonance theory is the very evident fact that people do not resolve many, or perhaps even most, of the dissonances within themselves. If they did, each would end up with nice tidy views of the world devoid of any inconsistencies. Many individuals are not at all concerned about the fact that the views they proclaim on Sunday about brotherly love are quite inconsistent with the ways in which they behave during the rest of the week. They also make no attempt to resolve these inconsistencies and, indeed, commonly do not even recognize them in their behavior. Such observations suggest that one aspect of dissonance theory that has to be developed is the identification of the conditions under which inconsistency becomes a motivating force that energizes behavior in the direction of resolving the inconsistency.

Despite these limitations, dissonance theory has proven itself to be one of the most stimulating innovative ideas in social psychology and has been the initiator of research in a whole area of learning where straightforward reinforcement concepts have had only the most limited value. The theory has also done more than stimulate research, for it has also been effective in making predictions in situations in which predictions have not been effectively made from alternative formulations. This does not mean that dissonance theory can be viewed as a general substitute for reinforcement concepts. Both systems provide limited capabilities for predicting behavior in limited situations.

Finally, the point must be made that the results of the classical experiments on dissonance are reproducible, but the dissonance explanation has been challenged by a number of sources. Perhaps the most impressive challenge comes from Nuttin (1975), whose studies are unusual in that the individuals he studied were not aware of the fact that they were the objects of study. Also, Nuttin measured attitudes under conditions that would lead the subjects to believe that the measure had nothing to do with the part of the experiment that involved the expression of attitude. The attitude measures were completed as a favor to a graduate student to fill in a few minutes' time while waiting for the professor. Through a series of ingenious experiments under these conditions, Nuttin accumulated evidence to show that the main effect of a large reward is that of providing "a strange, embarrassing, novel . . . stimulus which simply disturbs, and/or arouses the subject" (p. 129). The large reward is dissonant only in that it seems to disrupt any change in attitude that might occur.

Another interesting interpretation of dissonant effects comes from Insko et al. (1975). They suggest that the crucial factor in the effect of large or small rewards on attitude change is whether the individual takes responsibility for his actions. If the reward is large, the subject may say to himself, "The experimenter is making me do this by giving me a large sum of money, so whatever happens is his responsibility." Under such conditions the individual washes his hands of any responsibility and his attitude remains uninfluenced by the experimental procedure. On the other hand, when the reward is small, the individual takes the position that it is he, and not the reward, that makes him do what he is doing. He is then responsible for his actions and feels compelled to bring his attitudes into line with what he is required to do.

Self-perception Theory of Attitude Formation and Change

Bem (1972) has developed an ingenious alternative to dissonance theory that attempts to account for the experiments that have been claimed to support dissonance theory. Bem claims that individuals know their own emotions and attitudes by inferring them from observations of their own overt behavior. Thus the individual functions toward himself in much the same way as others function toward him. Bem refers to this theory of attitude as self-perception theory. He points out that in certain areas of behavior this conception of self-understanding is accepted. A person who becomes restless in the late morning concludes that he is hungry, but another person who observes his restlessness may say to him, "You seem hungry!" The position of Bem differs from that of behaviorism in that it includes a "self" that does the observing. Nevertheless, despite this departure, Bem refers to his position as being close to the radical behaviorism of Skinner.

As an example of how the Bem theory works, consider again the Festinger and Carlsmith experiment in which individuals were paid either $1 or $20 for making statements contrary to their beliefs. Bem asks how an observer would respond if he saw an individual perform a dull task and then for $1 (or $20) told another individual that the task was enjoyable and interesting. Bem argues that if the observer heard the person say that the task was enjoyable and interesting when only $1 was offered, there must be something about the task that is actually interesting. On the other hand, the observer who saw the same performance for a $20 reward would conclude that it was the money that made him make the statement. Bem argues that the subjects paid $1 or $20 observe themselves in exactly the same way and come to the same conclusions as the independent observer would.

On the surface, the interpretation that Bem gives to the Festinger and Carlsmith experiment, and to similar experiments, is not only ingenious but also quite convincing. Nevertheless, the simple explanation is far from satisfactory. The subject in the experiment paid $1 to make a statement contrary to his beliefs also knows that he is under pressure to do what the experimenter asks of him and that if the experimenter asks him to do something that seems quite silly, he will cooperate and do it because he wants to help the experimenter. If such is the case, it becomes quite difficult to account for the attitude change in the subjects paid $1. One answer might be that the subject later remembers the situation as being so bizarre that in its totality it seems interesting.

Bem has undertaken a number of experiments designed to support his position. The difficulty with all of them is that they are complicated by social and other factors that open them to alternative explanations. Bem found, for example, that shocks of short duration that were terminated by the experimental subject himself were rated as more severe than shocks of the same intensity that were of longer duration. Bem argues that an observer who saw a person terminating a shock would judge the shock to be more disagreeable than when the shock was tolerated for longer periods. The difficulty with the latter explanation is that individuals adapt rapidly to electric shock, and a longer duration of shock may result in some adaptation; the shock may thus be more tolerable than when it is of a shorter duration.

In addition, information that plays an essential role in the formation of attitudes is stored and does not manifest itself directly in behavior. When a person assesses his attitude with respect to some important issue, his assessment of his attitude may involve a review of the information he has stored. It does not involve a review of any observable behavior. It may also involve a review of how he has acted in various situations. One might expect the Bem model to describe well the way an individual assesses his attitude in areas in which he does not have much stored information that has attitudinal implications but in which he has engaged in action. This view is substantiated by a study of Taylor (1975), who found that a group of college students assessed their attitudes from their behavior when a snap judgment with no remote consequences was required. However, if the situation carried the implication that there might be long-term consequences, the students consumed much time in thinking through their position. Taylor concludes that Bem's description of the process of assessing one's attitude is most likely to operate when unimportant and inconsequential issues are involved. The Bem model is enormously attractive because of its simplicity, but it has not so far demonstrated itself to be a strong model that produces research in significant attitudinal areas.

Information and Attitude Change

Some attempt has been made to develop a theory of how information has an impact on attitude. We do constantly acquire new pieces of information related to our attitudes. Some of the information strengthens positions we already accept and some runs counter to our positions and endorses alternative positions. Considerable work has been undertaken on the impact of information on attitude change. This body of knowledge is known as *information integration theory*. It proposes that a piece of information received by a person is assigned both a weight and a position on a scale with respect to a particular attitude. Suppose that I have an extremely conservative attitude with respect to the death penalty and consider it a necessary evil to deter people from committing crimes of violence. Then I read an article presenting data showing that states that have had the death penalty for many years do not have fewer crimes of violence than those that long ago abolished it. When I receive this piece of information I behave as though I did two things to it: I decide the weight that I am going to give it in my thinking and the place to assign it on a scale covering the range of attitudes from pro-death penalty to anti-death penalty. I might decide to give this item little weight because it represents propaganda from those against the death penalty, or I might decide to give it much weight because it comes from an authoritative source. I would probably assign the piece of information a scale value near to the end of the scale representing opposition to the death penalty. The weight and scale value I give to the piece of information is claimed by information integration theorists to reflect the impact the information will have on my attitude. The theory is quite simple and testable and has accumulated around it some scientific evidence giving it support (see Anderson, 1971). The reader has to be warned not to take the theory literally. The individual behaves *as if* he assigned a scale value and weight to each item of information. It is strictly an *as if* theory and does not mean that the individual deliberately and consciously behaves in this way. The Anderson theory maintains that a person's attitude represents an average of all the attitudinal values assigned to the different items of information related to the attitude object. In this respect, the brain functions much like a computer, automatically producing average values. Anderson has attempted to demonstrate this in a later paper (1973). In the 1973 study, Anderson experimented with the problem by providing his subjects with items of information concerning particular Presidents of the United States. The data provided evidence of the averaging hypothesis.

A point to note about the Anderson theory of the use of information in the formation of attitudes is that as each piece of information is received, it has an attitude value assigned to it and this attitude value becomes integrated immediately into the attitude. The information may then be forgotten, but it has already had its impact on attitude. The attitude is not dependent on verbal memory. Anderson also stresses that the information integration theory of attitude deemphasizes reinforcement concepts that he believes have little to do with the formation of attitudes. Learning and the formation of attitudes are for him cognitive processes.

A rather similar model of attitude formation has been advanced by Fishbein and Coombs (1974) to account for voting behavior. According to this theory, the voter acquires beliefs about a candidate, and each belief has an attitudinal component. These attitudinal components, collectively, constitute the attitude toward the candidate and determine voting behavior. Evidence from a local survey of voting behavior provided some support for this position.

Predictive Value of Measures of Attitude

The main concentration of research on attitudes has focussed on the problem of the development of attitudes and the conditions that produce attitude change. This focus of interest probably came about because early investigators typically failed to find a relationship between some measure of expressed attitude and other forms of behavior that one might expect to be related to the expressed attitude. Particularly influential were three studies. In the first, LaPiere (1934), an Oriental, visited 251 eating and lodging places where he was refused service only once. Later, these places of business were sent a questionnaire asking them whether they would serve Oriental customers, and of the half that responded more than 90 per cent said they would not. Second, in the Kutner, Wilkins, and Yarrow study (1952) a similar plan was adopted, with two whites and a black visiting eating places, but the subsequent contact with the restaurants was made by phone. A majority of the restaurants said they would not serve blacks. In the third study, by Minard (1952) the attitude of white miners toward blacks was studied in three different situations described as the work situation, the work-related situation such as the union hall, and the residential setting. The actions of the miners were compared with statements, made by the miners, concerning how they thought they would act toward blacks. Again there was little correspondence between the actions and the statements. The attitudes measured in terms of behavior in these three situations showed little relationship to what the individuals said they would do. Textbooks on social psychology have typically cited these studies as demonstrating that attitudes do not predict behavior and, as a result, graduate students have been reluctant to pursue such studies for a thesis or dissertation. Although these studies have been cited in textbooks on social psychology for a generation, they have now come under considerable attack.

Recent criticisms are found in the articles by Dillehay (1973) and Kelman (1974). The tone of such articles is found in the title of the Kelman article, "Attitudes are alive and well and gainfully employed in the sphere of action." In both articles, the criticisms are essentially the same. The vital criticism of the LaPiere article is that the personnel in the restaurants and lodging houses who provided services to the Oriental were different from those who answered the questionnaire. Thus a manager might set general policies in terms of his attitudes, but his subordinates might or might not be aware of the policies and might or might not carry them out. Thus one would expect little relationship between the responses to the questionnaire and the service actually provided to the Oriental. (These studies were carried out before the public accommodations act became law.) The criticism that can be leveled at the LaPiere study can also be directed toward the Kutner et al. study. Again, the people contacted to assess attitudes were other than those who showed no discrimination in the real situation. The Minard study is in a rather different category in that there was no attempt made to assess attitudes except through inferences from behavior in the actual situations. The miners may not have formed attitudes with any stability and, hence, may have showed fluctuating standards of behavior.

Kelman also points out that in order to predict action toward a specific object in a particular situation one should assess all the relevant attitudinal components of the behavior involved. Thus a person might have negative attitudes toward Italians in general, but that attitude would not predict his actions toward a particular Italian with whom he had had favorable personal experiences. The person's attitude toward that particular Italian would be a vital element in predicting his action toward him. Fishbein (1974) has proposed that attitude scales might be expected to predict the general trend of a sequence of acts, but not single acts. Conversely, in predicting a single act, a multiplicity of attitudes should be taken into account. In predicting how a person will act toward another of a different race, one should take into account not only racial attitudes but also the relationship of this individual to this other person. If it is a relationship of work supervision, attitude toward authority should be taken into account. If the other person is an employee, the attitude toward employees is a factor. If the other person is simply a fellow guinea pig in the experiment, the relationship to that other person may be so inconsequential that attitudes can hardly be expected to operate. The evidence available suggests that the more specific the attitude to the action involved, the better is the prediction from the attitude. Weigel, Vernon, and Tognacci (1974) found this to be so in a study of attitudes related to ecology, which were later correlated with willingness to cooperate with the Sierra Club.

There are, of course, areas in which there is a clear relationship between attitudes and behavior. Voting behavior is the most notable and best-studied illustration. Individuals do vote in terms of their attitudes and successful studies have been undertaken concerning the way in which voter attitudes are built and have impact on voting behavior (Fishbein and Coombs, 1974).

Kelman concludes that the present analysis of the relationship of attitudes to action leads to the expectation that there will be quite small relationships between attitudes and behavior, unless there is a highly refined analysis of attitudes that makes it possible to take into account the many components that are operating.

An attempt to identify a central difficulty in predicting behavior from attitudes has been made by Rokeach (1967), who suggests that individuals maintain attitudes to both situations and objects. Since objects always exist in situations, any attempt to predict behavior toward the object must take into account the behavior to be expected toward that particular situation. For example, a person may not like a particular President but, may behave cordially toward him if invited to the White House because he believes that such behavior is called for by any visitor to the White House. A visit to the White House involves an attitude to the presidency in general, symbolized by the White House. Under such circumstances, the individual's attitude toward the presidency takes precedence over his attitude toward the particular President. The reverse is also conceivable in which the attitude toward this particular president overrides the attitude toward the situation.

Noll and Shupe (1975) conducted a study related to this problem in which they assessed the attitudes of Caucasians. The objects evaluated were racial categories: Caucasian, Negro, and Oriental. The three situations evaluated were (1) "in a classroom I attend," (2) "at a party I attend," and (3) "my marriage to." The data supported the position that attitudes toward the situations function independently of attitudes toward the objects. Noll and Shupe also found that the two components of attitude do not function additively, but that one may overwhelm the other.

Finally, the reader should recognize that there are a few sociologists and psychologists who believe that attitudes may not prove to be good predictors of behavior. Stewart (1975), for example, takes the position, originally attributed to George Mead, that attitudes are not so much forces underlying behavior, but components of behavior.

Communications That Change Attitudes

Up to this point in the chapter we have undertaken a rather brief exploration of major positions that have been used to account for attitude change. This review has highlighted the difficulty of making predictions of the conditions under which attitude change can be most readily produced. In educational settings, the setting most likely to be used to bring about attitude change involves written or spoken communication. A considerable amount is known at this time about the particular conditions occurring during a communication that make for effective attitude changes, and it is to these conditions that consideration must now be given.

Many hundreds of studies on the effectiveness of communications in producing attitude changes have been reviewed by Berscheid and Walster (1969). This excellent review divides the problem into three components: (1) the characteristics of an effective communicator, (2) the characteristics of an effective communication, and (3) the characteristics of the receivers of communications, for some receivers are much more likely than others to react to a communication. This section of the chapter is addressed to the the problem of attitude changes and is not concerned with the problem of the effectiveness of communications for imparting information. Following the structure provided by Berscheid and Walster, let us consider each one of these aspects of communciation separately.

The Characteristics of the Effective Communicator. The best explored of these characteristics are expertness and trustworthiness. The sources of some communications represent a higher level of expertness than do others and the assumption has long been made that the more expert the source, the greater will be the influence on attitudes. Research on this issue is complicated by the fact that the immediate effect is often different from the long-term effect. The more expert or credible the source of a communication, the greater is the immediate effect on attitudes. However, when the effect of a highly expert source was compared with a less expert source, the difference in the change in attitudes produced declines with time. Berscheid and Walster suggest that memory for the characteristics of a communicator fades much more rapidly than does the content of the message itself. Thus any influence that the communicator may have on the attitudes of the person receiving the message also declines rapidly with the passage of time.

The relationship of the person who hears a communication to the source of the communication can vary in so many different ways that the effect of each one of these relationships on attitude change has not yet been fully investigated. Most studies have varied simultaneously several of the factors involved without making it possible to separate in the data the effects involved. The listener may be a part of a captive audience, just as most children in school are captive audiences and cannot walk out on the source of communications. The listener may be noncaptive and happen to overhear a communication. The communicator may hold a very different opinion from that of the listener or his opinion may be rather close to that of the listener. The communicator may announce that his intention is to change the attitude of the listener or he may blandly declare that he is not interested in changing anybody's beliefs but is merely engaged in passing on information. The effect of each of these variables cannot be clearly and concisely determined at this time from the research findings to date.

There is some trend in the findings of studies to suggest that communications overheard as if by accident produce greater attitude change than those directed to the listener. Much seems to depend on whether the overheard communication has or does not have relevance for the listener. If I am overweight and eavesdrop on a discussion of the importance of weight reduction, the discussion is likely to have no influence on my attitude toward the problem unless I want to reduce, even though I have not found a way to do it.

The effect of the size of the discrepancy between the communicator's attitude and that of the listener has been studied and with some suggestion that the greater the discrepancy between the listener and the speaker, the greater will be the attitude change. If such a finding can be solidly established, it will strike a strong blow in favor of dissonance theory. The larger the discrepancy the greater is the dissonance, and the greater the dissonance the greater is the need to resolve it.

Communicator characteristics that have little relevance to the communication may have an influence as well as relevant characteristics on the degree to which a particular communication influences a listener's attitudes. Indeed, these so-called irrelevant characteristics may often have more influence than relevant characteristics. The attractiveness of the speaker has long been a subject for research, but the results are not as clear-cut as one would like them to be. Earlier, mention was made of the fact that when a person voluntarily listens to a presentation, a speaker rated as somewhat disagreeable may produce greater attitude change than a speaker who is personally more attractive. An example of an effect of this kind was obtained by Zimbardo et al. (1965) in a study in which an effort was made to persuade Army recruits and students to eat a highly objectionable food, namely, fried grasshoppers. The audience for this experiment was a captive audience, but each was free to decide whether he would or would not choose to taste fried grasshoppers. An important feature of this experiment appears to be freedom of choice. Some of the subjects were exposed to a communicator who was considerate, pleasant, and calm, and who was described as the positive communicator. Other subjects were exposed to a negative communicator, who was disagreeable, irritable, and cantankerous. Both communicators were well organized and credible in their presentations. Before and after the experimental procedure, the attitude of subjects toward eating grasshoppers was measured by a paper-and-pencil device prepared for the purpose. The interesting finding of this study was that those who were confronted with the negative communicator and who tasted the grasshoppers showed a more favorable change in attitude than those who tasted them and who were exposed to a positive communicator. Those who did not taste the grasshoppers showed a boomerang effect regardless of the communicator and ended up with an even greater aversion for fried grasshoppers than that with which they started.

Such findings give support for dissonance theory. There is dissonance between the action of eating grasshoppers and the initial attitude toward doing it. This dissonance is increased by the presence of a disagreeable communicator and, it is presumed, increases the tendency for attitudes to change. A positive communicator, on the other hand, reduces the dissonance, for the listeners justify listening to the speech by saying to themselves that he is a nice fellow and that one should treat him courteously.

The relationships that have been discussed between the attractiveness of the speaker and change in attitude are found only under certain conditions, namely, those under which the listener chooses to listen or chooses whether or not to engage in certain activities. In the typical research in which the subjects are captive and are required to listen to a speech on some topic, the opposite findings are more typical. Under the latter conditions, the attractiveness of a speaker is positively related to the extent to which attitudes are changed as a result of the presentation.

Finally, a review by Simons, Berkowitz, and Moyer (1970) brings out some other characteristics that generally make for a more persuasive communicator; he is generally more competent than the other members of his peer group, better informed, gregarious, and tends to belong to the top crust of the social class with which he is identified. He is also, in a peculiar way, what is called super-representative of his group: that is, although he stands apart, he embodies in a vivid way the group characteristics. He is also viewed as an instrument for achieving goals important to the group members.

The Characteristics of the Communication. It is quite evident that the characteristics of the communication influence its persuasive properties, and some of these characteristics are so obvious that nobody has even bothered to study them. One such characteristic is whether the ideas are clearly presented. In many areas, a clear presentation of the facts appears to be important for changing attitudes, particularly when the attitudes to be changed are founded on misinformation. For example, many individuals on the American continent have long held that the mixing of the blood of different racial groups has disastrous biological effects on the offspring. This belief has led to the adoption in many states of laws that forbid the intermarriage of different racial groups. A change in the attitudes related to such a belief has been highly dependent on presenting facts to show that the alleged biological disasters do not occur when members of different races intermarry.

Differences among communications in the information or misinformation they present are easily recognized and can be directly measured. Communications may also differ with respect to much more subtle characteristics. One such property of communications is the emotional tone they convey. Some communications are coldly intellectual, some humorous and charming, some are hostile or threatening, and some attempt to coax the reader into new ways of thinking. There is also an additional vast range of different overtones that may be carried by the main theme of a communication. Educators need to know much more about the significance of these intangible aspects of the communicator's skill, but little is known as yet about their effect on the receiver of a message. Most research up to this time has been involved with much more tangible aspects of persuasive communications.

One of the oldest controversies in the field of attitude change is whether a communication designed for such a purpose should be one-sided or two-sided. Although these terms have long been used, there is considerable ambiguity concerning what really constitutes a one-sided argument, which is generally defined as one in which only positive support is given for the position the writer or speaker wants to sustain. One could conceivably design a one-sided argument in which only a particular view was presented, along with a rebuttal for all the opposing arguments. Equally, two-sided arguments that have been used for study in research are not really two-sided. Such arguments provide positive support for the position it is desired to support but they also give opposing arguments, along with a rebuttal of each of these arguments. In a sense, the arguments are really still one-sided, even though they mention both sides of the issue. Other variations are also possible. The positive side may be presented either first or last. Arguments may be presented so that they draw a firm conclusion or they may be presented in such a way that the listener or reader has to draw his own conclusions. So many different variations are possible that a generation of graduate students looking for problems for master's theses will not exhaust all the possibilities.

Numerous pieces of research have appeared since the reviews on which this summary is based were published, but they do not change the general picture to any extent. Subsequent research contains many odd and interesting items of information. For example, Giles (1973) found that the dialect of a communicator influenced the amount of attitude change produced by his speech. The greatest change in attitude occurred when the dialect of the speaker was the same as that of the listeners. The same talk delivered in the prestige dialect of so-called standard English produced no attitude change. However, when the talk was given in standard English, it was rated as being higher in quality in the arguments it used than when it was given in local dialects. Another odd and interesting piece of information comes from a study by Sloan, Love, and Ostram (1974), who showed that heckling a speaker has the tendency to neutralize any attitude change he might produce. Numerous other studies might be cited, each of which turned up some interesting pieces of information. However, such studies need to be repeated before they can be taken seriously and, at this time, they do not contribute to the broad picture of how attitudes are developed.

Berscheid and Walster (1969) have attempted to fit together the results of research on this problem, as has McGuire (1969), Both of these reviewers agree that when the overall effects of a one-sided argument are compared with the results of a two-sided argument (as a two-sided argument is defined here), there is very little difference in the amount of attitude change produced, but much depends on the circumstances of the experiment. If the subjects are relatively intelligent, they are more likely to be influenced by a two-sided argument than a one-sided argument, but the reverse seems to be true if the subjects are relatively dull. The research suggests that the relatively dull subjects are confused by the two-sided argument.

The Characteristics of Receivers of Communications and Attitude Change. Inquiries into the ability and personality traits that characterize persuadable people have long been investigated, but the problem has shown itself to be much more complex than any of the early research workers had expected it to be.

The nature of a message is highly important in determining whether it does or does not attract attention and hence permit the possibility of having impact. Psychologists have always been attracted to the hypothesis that individuals will readily listen to messages with which they agree, but may turn away to other things when confronted with a message with which they do not agree. This has sometimes been termed a cognitive consistency theory of selective attention, and the evidence for it has been summarized in the sourcebook on the subject edited by Abelson et al. (1968). A briefer summary has been provided by Berscheid and Walster (1969) in an article that brings together some of the more important research findings. Berscheid and Walster point out there is quite substantial evidence showing that in daily life people do actually listen to and read a preponderance of messages with which they agree and fail to attend to the majority of available messages in their environment with which they disagree. The evidence shows, for example, that Republicans tend to listen to talks by Republican candidates, and Democrats listen to Democrats. Such a trend is found not only with respect to the major issues of life, but also with respect to the lesser issues. For example, those who have given blood through the Red Cross are more likely to attend a film urging people to donate blood than are nondonors. The evidence seems to be incontrovertible that when audiences consist of members who choose to attend a speech, most speakers find themselves addressing people with whose opinions they already agree.

The basis for this trend in behavior is still not properly understood. One simple plausible explanation runs along these lines. A Republican is a Republican because he has been reinforced throughout his childhood for listening to Republican points of view. Such reinforcements would have led to a habit of attending to Republican messages, which manifests itself in the studies undertaken. Also, because a Republican has not developed a habit of attending to Democrat messages, he is unlikely to attend to such messages. Such habits undoubtedly play a part in these attention phenomena, but they are probably not the entire story. An alternative explanation is found in cognitive consistency theory, which, in its simplest form, states that individuals will assimilate information consistent with the information they have already stored and will tend to reject information that is inconsistent.

Psychologists have attempted to design experiments to tease out the different factors involved. In the kind of research we have just been considering, clear tendencies were shown for people to go to certain sources of information rather than to others. Similar kinds of studies can be undertaken under laboratory conditions, where, for example, one can measure the attitude of individuals toward established religions and then offer them the titles of various articles, one or more of which they must choose to read. The titles show clearly that some of the articles are favorable toward established religions and others are unfavorable. The researcher can then test the hypothesis of whether individuals tend to choose articles supportive of their own particular position. Sears (1968) has reviewed the numerous laboratory studies conducted in this area and finds that unlike studies based on everyday behavior, there is no clear-cut tendency for people to seek supportive information and avoid nonsupportive information. The discrepancy between laboratory studies and the common life situations needs to be explained. One reason may well be that many of the subjects for the laboratory studies were college students who have been trained to seek out information that conflicts with their opinion. This explanation is plausible, but one may well doubt whether education is as successful as this theory suggests it to be. The conclusion of Berscheid and Walster is that when individuals have confidence in their knowledge and their positions with respect to particular issues that they are more likely and willing to read communications with which they almost certainly differ. Unwillingness to do this reflects insecurity.

Not all individuals can have their attitudes changed with equal readiness. Most experiments in this area show very large individual differences in this respect and some individuals are highly resistant to all efforts to change their attitudes. McGuire summarizes the findings on the influenceability of attitudes by pointing out that one of the most significant variables is age. He concludes that suggestibility increases through early childhood until about age 9. From that age on, there is a decline in suggestibility until adolescence, and then this tendency levels off. The picture is complicated by the fact that this age effect is not the same for all techniques of attitude change. For example, the effect of prestige on attitude change is different from the effect of suggestions at different age levels.

Berscheid and Walster (1969) point out that enough is now known to say that no simple relationship can be expected between intelligence, or educational level achieved, and persuasibility. They go on to note that if a complex argument is presented to promote a point of view, the less intelligent may not be moved by it because they do not understand it. The intelligent may be persuaded because they see points they had not seen before. But this does not mean that the more intelligent are always the more persuasible, for they are not. The less intelligent are often more readily persuaded to change their attitudes by a quite naive argument, which may antagonize those who are able to see through it. Thus sometimes the more intelligent and sometimes the less intelligent are the more persuasible, depending on the nature of the communication.

One of the more influential sources of individual differences in influenceability is sex. A long history of research in this area comes up with the unassailable conclusion that women's attitudes are more readily influenced than are those of men. An explanation of this is much more difficult to deliver than the fact itself. On the surface this seems to suggest that women are just more suggestible than are men, but McGuire comes up with an alternative explanation, probably closer to the facts and one that is much less insulting to women and less flattering to men. McGuire musters evidence to support the proposition that the effect is largely due to the fact that women are better listeners than men and that in almost any teaching situation women learn rather more than do men. Certainly among youth of school age this is true, and the girls tend to be a little ahead of boys in what they learn. The essence of the theory of the greater influenceability of women is that because women are likely to absorb more of messages designed to influence their attitudes than are men, they are also more likely to have their attitudes influenced. The relative lack of influence on men is attributable to their inability to listen.

There are also greater individual differences in men than in women in influenceability. This is hardly surprising in that men show greater differences among themselves than do women in practically all abilities and this effect is particularly marked in the case of personality traits and measures of interests. The source of this greater uniformity among women than among men is usually attributed to the fact that girls are expected to conform more than are boys. Also, boys are given much more freedom than are girls and are therefore able to expose themselves to a greater variety of experiences.

Another variable that offers some promise as a correlate of persuasibility is vaguely defined as self-esteem. Although research workers generally shy away from such concepts because of the difficulty of defining them, this one can be defined in quite specific terms. This has been done in experiments in which a deliberate effort has been made to lower or raise self-esteem by administering a test to the subjects and then telling some subjects, regardless of how they performed, that they did very poorly and telling others, also regardless of how they performed, that they had done well. Such an experience of being told that one has done poorly, or well, does have the effect of changing a person's behavior during at least the few hours that follow the experience. Whatever is changed by such a procedure is referred to as self-esteem.

Another technique is to administer a questionnaire that attempts to measure self-esteem. This technique could be regarded as one that attempts to explore the individual's self-concept by finding out what the individual says to himself about himself.

The findings derived from the study of this problem seem to be somewhat inconsistent and difficult to fit together. Berscheid and Walster (1969) conclude that attempts to raise or lower self-esteem indicate that when it is lowered, there tends to be increased influenceability, but when self-esteem is directly measured by means of a questionnaire, no such simple effect is found. McGuire (1968) suggests that a high degree of modifiability of attitudes is associated with either a very high or a very low level of self-esteem. Those who are in the middle range on this variable are the most unchangeable.

An entirely different but insightful approach to the problem comes from research on the characteristics of so-called dogmatic or authoritarian people. This research came into the limelight with the development of a number of testing devices, produced for the purpose of measuring personal dogmatism. The best known of these devices are the California F Scale and the Rokeach Dogmatism Scale, which have had some success in identifying persons who are commonly described as dogmatic, closed-minded, closed to new ideas, authoritarian, and inflexible. There seems clear evidence that the dogmatic style of personality exists and can be identified, as is evident in a review of the related research by Vacchiano, Strauss, and Hochman (1969). The latter reviewers find the high-dogmatism individual to be psychologically immature in addition to being stereotyped in his thinking and defensive. In addition, such an individual has been shown to be intolerant, impulsive, and poorly adjusted. On the other hand, the low-dogmatism individual has been found to be enterprising, calm, mature, forceful, and efficient. One is tempted to speculate that high-dogmatism individuals would also be those whose attitudes would be most difficult to change. One can certainly say that such a hypothesis is attractive. Miller and Rokeach (1968) have reviewed research related to these problems and have come up with the answer that here, just as in other areas of attitude research, simple hypotheses are attractive but misleading. The early research in this area produced the finding in some studies that the highly rigid person, thus defined, was not one whose attitudes and beliefs were readily changed, but in a few studies such individuals were shown to be highly susceptible to being changed. Some insight has now been achieved with respect to these inconsistent findings, which are not really inconsistent at all. Miller and Rokeach point out, as a basis for understanding the early findings, that the person who scores high on dogmatism scales is a person who prevents himself from being exposed to views inconsistent with those that he holds. He also avoids information inconsistent with his views and, when he encounters it, is more likely than the nondogmatic person to forget it. Thus he protects himself from any external influence that might produce change in him. He cannot tolerate information or beliefs that are inconsistent with his own. On the other hand, the person who scores at the other end of the dogmatism scale has less difficulty memorizing inconsistent information and is much less bothered by expressed beliefs different from his own. The difficulty encountered by the highly dogmatic or authoritarian personality is that he cannot tolerate inconsistency or, in terms of theory of attitudes, he has a very low tolerance for dissonance and therefore avoids encounters that might produce dissonance.

But what happens to the high-dogmatism individuals when they cannot avoid being exposed to information inconsistent with their beliefs? This condition can occur in experiments in which students are required to participate in order to fulfill course requirements, and it can also occur in daily life. One interesting situation of the latter kind identified by Miller and Rokeach was derived from a study, undertaken for another purpose, in relation to the Eisenhower-Stevenson presidential contest. This study by Paul (1956) involved identifying a group of voters as either authoritarian or equalitarian. Some people in each one of these categories voted for Eisenhower and some voted for Stevenson. Eisenhower, of course, won the election and hence those who voted for Stevenson would have experienced dissonance through their nonfavorite candidate winning the election. The dissonance thus produced could be reduced by taking a more favorable view of Eisenhower. However, the authoritarian individuals should experience more dissonance because of their inability to tolerate any inconsistency. If they experienced more dissonance, there should be greater incentive for them to change their view of Eisenhower. This Paul actually found. When the highly dogmatic group was appraised later of their view of Eisenhower, they were found to have changed more in a favorable direction than the equalitarian group.

Miller and Rokeach also cite a number of convincing experimental studies to show that the same kind of phenomenon revealed in connection with the study of the Eisenhower-Stevenson election can be produced in the laboratory. Perhaps the most impressive of these is an unpublished study by Hunt and Miller, for which quite complete data are given by Miller and Rokeach. In the latter study, the technique was adopted of requiring subjects to write statements of belief related to the topic of disarmament. One group wrote statements that they believed, a second group wrote irrelevant statements, and a third group wrote statements contrary to their beliefs. The subjects were also so selected for the experiment that they were either high-dogmatic or low-dogmatic. The attitudes of the subjects toward disarmament were measured before the experimental procedure was undertaken, and also afterward. One group that showed a substantial change in attitude was the high-dogmatic group that wrote statements at odds with their own belief. This is the group that could tolerate least the inconsistency between their own belief and what they were writing.

The overall evidence from such studies shows that whatever is measured by scales of dogmatism and authoritarianism is a powerful variable related to the individual's ability to tolerate that which is inconsistent with his own characteristics. The same individual may respond to such inconsistencies either by ignoring the incompatible element or by making changes in himself that will tend to remove the inconsistency. Which one he will do will depend on the particular circumstances involved. One suspects that the first response is that of ignoring the newly presented inconsistent element. Only when this action is not possible will the individual make changes in himself to reduce the inconsistency.

The results of research on the relationship between measures of dogmatism and persuasibility should not lead the reader to assume that the high-dogmatism person is any less likely to benefit from traditional schooling than is the low-dogmatism individual. Ehrlich and Lee (1969) have reviewed studies relating dogmatism scores to school performance and found that most of these studies showed no relationship between these variables. They did manage to uncover some interesting evidence of a case (Costin, 1968) in which students were learning to discard their misconceptions about behavior in a basic course in psychology. The high-dogmatism students had a significantly greater difficulty in discarding their misconceptions than did the low-dogmatism students. This is an example of the way in which this characteristic, dogmatism, may interfere with becoming educated.

Delayed Effects of Conditions That Produce Attitude Change

Capon and Hulbert (1973) have summarized studies on delayed effects of attempts to produce attitude change. If an experiment is designed to produce attitude change, and if the attitude is measured after various different times have elapsed, there may be for some time after exposure to the experimental materials designed to change attitudes a steady change in attitude. This phenomenon is quite marked and sometimes may cover a period as long as several months. In a World War II study cited by McGuire (1969), troops were exposed to a film on the Battle of Britain, which was designed to develop in them highly positive attitudes toward the cause for which they were fighting. Eleven weeks after the showing, the impact of the film was still continuing to have an effect. This so-called *sleeper effect* is not understood at this time, although there are a number of theories concerning how it might operate. One difficulty in arriving at an explanation is that one cannot control what happens to the subjects after the end of the main experimental procedures, and what happens may account for at least some of the subsequent attitude change. The men in the World War II study may have discussed the film among themselves during the eleven-week period, and the discussion may have been instrumental in producing further changes in viewpoint. There is also evidence from a number of sources that psychological processes related to beliefs and knowledge, that is, cognitive processes, may undergo a very slow organizing and consolidating process during the time that follows an experience that introduces new cognitive elements into the picture. This slow consolidation may well be the cause of the sleeper effect. Presumably, this consolidation effect may sometimes involve verbal processes, as when a person thinks through what he has recently heard and draws conclusions that he did not draw at the time when he first encountered the particular communication.

The slow increased change that may follow an attempt to change attitudes ultimately levels off. There then follows a change in the reverse direction and the position of the attitude tends to slip slowly back to the position taken before the attempt to change it was made. The slippage of the attitude back to its previous position is very much like forgetting. Attitude tends to slip back because the individual tends to forget slowly those arguments and points that originally resulted in opinion change. McGuire has been able to demonstrate, by measuring both attitude and knowledge retained of the message that produced an initial attitude change, that as the memory for the message declines so does the attitude tend to slip back.

Strengthening Attitudinal Positions So That They Are Resistant to Attack

Most teachers, and particularly religious teachers, have long been interested in whether attitudes can be bolstered by defenses in such a way that they become highly resistant to change. Many of the ways in which this has been done in our society have not represented techniques with which experiments can be readily undertaken. One social technique is that of associating deep guilt feelings with deviant opinions. Most religions do this by developing in the young the belief that any deviation from the teachings of the particular religious institution is grievously sinful or will lead to eternal damnation. The technique seems to be moderately successful, although some individuals do grow up to master their guilt feelings and do change their attitudes, beliefs, and opinions. A second technique, widely used by religious groups, is that of denying the individual access to either printed material or discourse that might produce a change. Some religious groups place on a censored list certain books to which the faithful are prohibited from having access, and some adopt the related technique of prohibiting their members from mixing with or attending meetings of other religious groups. I once lived in a neighborhood where the predominant religion was X, and the children, the little xs, were forbidden to play with the little ys. The technique of denying access to other ideas is obviously successful as long as it lasts, but children cannot be kept forever from mixing with those of other faiths and, when they do, a boomerang effect may well occur.

A third technique of making attitudes resistant to change is what has been termed the anchoring technique. A prejudice may be given stability by tying it to strongly held beliefs. The traditional prejudice of the Anglo-Saxon toward those with darker skins has been anchored to a set of beliefs such as that those with other shades of skin are stupid, unmotivated, and immoral. Such beliefs, accepted as if they represented knowledge, keep the prejudice from being shaken.

A fourth technique involves producing in the individual what is termed commitment, which is a difficult term to pin down but generally means a commitment to some form of action. A young man who decides to become a priest has a commitment in life, and this commitment in itself is likely to prevent the related attitudes and beliefs from being changed. The mere making public of one's position on an issue results in a commitment that makes the underlying attitudes extremely resistant to change. For this reason, many religious groups encourage the public pronouncement of their beliefs by the faithful. Public testimony seems to be an effective way of fixing beliefs.

Experiments in strengthening attitudes to make them resistant to change have generally taken an intellectual approach to the problem. There are several quite obvious ways of attempting to bolster a person's attitudinal structure against attack. One of these is to warn him that his attitude will be attacked. It seems reasonable to assume that in the psychological field, as in the physical, to be forewarned is to be forearmed. Another technique is to provide him with supportive arguments for his point of view. If he is raised to believe in marriage as an institution, he may learn to argue that the institution protects children, that it provides some order and stability on a society, and so forth. A third approach involves learning how to rebut arguments presented to change the person's attitudes. The religious person learns many such arguments during his upbringing and thus when he is told that there is no visible evidence for the existence of a God he can make the comeback that many realities, such as subatomic particles, also cannot be observed directly.

The problem considered here has been commonly described as that of *psychological immunization*. Common observation and excellent experimentation support one another in the conclusion that such immunization is possible and probably generally effective. Indeed, the extraordinary stability of beliefs of individuals during early adult life reflects to some extent the effectiveness of the immunization that takes place during childhood and adolescence. Such a conclusion is, of course, speculative in that one does not know the extent to which individuals are exposed to propaganda designed to change their attitudes. Only experimentation can provide direct evidence of the effectiveness of immunization procedures. Such evidence has found clear-cut results indicating that immunization procedures are effective in producing stability of attitudes (see McGuire 1968). Even the simple technique of forewarning a person that one of his cherished beliefs is going to be attacked may increase his resistance to changing his attitudes. Just why forewarning has this effect is not clear. The evidence seems to suggest that forewarning, particularly when it provides some information concerning the nature of the attack to be encountered, activates appropriate defense mechanisms that require a warm-up before they can operate effectively.

Evidence from experimentation also supports the conclusion that the learning of either supporting or rebutting arguments protects attitudes from being changed, but that the rebutting arguments are more effective in this respect than are the supporting arguments. This is not surprising. Suppose that I am a firm believer in a free enterprise system and have to debate with a socialist. All the arguments I can muster to support free enterprise may not dispose of my opponent's arguments, for perhaps I am not as smart as he is. My supportive arguments may make me feel better under attack, but my opponent's counterarguments still lurk in the background of my mind because they have not been disposed of. On the other hand, if I were able to provide a complete rebuttal of my opponent's arguments, I could dispose of them and they would not haunt me as threats to my position.

The most substantial work in this area is found in a series of studies by McGuire and his associates carried out over almost a decade. These studies and their conclusions have been summarized by Kiesler, Collins, and Miller (1969) in their book on attitude change. The findings of this series of studies may be summarized as follows:

1. The most effective immunization of a belief against attack is to provide both supportive arguments for the belief and exercises involving the presentation of arguments against the belief followed by counterarguments.

2. The immunization produced by the presentation of arguments against the belief, followed by refutations of those arguments, derives its effect from giving the person practice in mustering his defenses. This is shown by the fact that after

such immunization, he also shows an improved capability of refuting novel arguments against his beliefs that he has not heard before.

3. A condition of threat, introduced by telling the subject that the experiment is a test of their persuasibility, enhances the effect of immunization. A related finding is that telling the subjects that others accept the particular beliefs as true beyond question reduced the effect of immunization. It would seem that in the latter case the subjects were lulled into a state of apathy where they were not willing to muster counterarguments when faced with an attack on their beliefs.

4. The effect of immunization first increases for a short period at the end of the immunization training period, and then declines. The decline is to be expected in view of the fact that memory is involved and the information contained in the counterarguments will slowly become less and less readily available.

Finally, a limitation is placed on the generality of the conclusions that can be drawn from most immunization studies, in that they have typically used a single category of belief for study. Most of the studies have focused on the stability of common beliefs when these come under attack. Examples of such beliefs are represented by such statements as that one should brush one's teeth after every meal or that mental illness is not contagious. The results of such studies need to be confirmed with a range of materials before they can be considered to have general application.

In addition to the studies designed to investigate the intellectual manipulation of beliefs, McGuire (1969) has located a number of studies that collectively support the thesis that commitment provides stability for attitudes. The typical study in the latter connection is one in which the stability of attitudes are compared for individuals who have publicly proclaimed their attitudes and those whose attitudes remain private. Such studies provide a rather frightening view of the politician who, because he has publicly committed himself to a certain position, may be locked into a position from which he cannot readily escape. Even more frightening are the results of unpublished studies also cited by McGuire indicating that those who have to publicly defend their opinions show even more resistance to change than those who simply proclaim their attitudes.

VALUES

Sociologists and psychologists have long made a distinction between attitudes and values. The main distinction made in the past is that values are broad and encompassing, but attitudes pertain to specific objects. Thus a value statement is exemplified by " I believe in equality for all men," but a statement reflecting an attitude in the same area might be "I believe that blacks and whites should be treated in every way equal." In this case the attitude is a specific example of the value to which it is related, but numerous other attitudes reflect the same value. Rokeach (1973), who has written extensively on this matter, points out that a value represents a single broadly encompassing belief, but an attitude reflects a belief or a group of beliefs all focused on a particular object. Thus an attitude transcends objects or situations whereas attitudes are object- or event-tied. In addition, Rokeach points out that a value is a standard but an attitude is not a standard. In a sense, a value represents a standard by which an attitude is viewed as good or bad. I view an attitude favoring white-black equality as good because I have an underlying value that favors all kinds of equalities in our society. For similar reasons I condemn an attitude that denies white-black equality. The value is the standard by which attitudes are judged. Values and value systems are rather few in number, but attitudes are extremely numerous and sometimes even inconsistent. Finally, Rokeach points out that values occupy a much more central and pervasive position in personality than do attitudes. For this reason values tend to be more closely related to motivation and the kinds of direction that the life of the individual may take.

It would seem that values are of far greater significance than attitude, yet research has concentrated on the study of attitudes, perhaps because these are components of the personality that are far easier to measure. The superficial is typically easier to study than the deeper but more obscure.

Rokeach goes on to make the point that values are the translation of needs into cognitive elements, that is, beliefs, and only human beings are capable of such cognitive elements. He also points out that they are also the translation of society's needs and social expectations. For example, the values of the liberal in our society are characterized by the values described by the words equality and freedom. Society and institutions socialize the individual and succeed to some extent in building these values into him.

Values are also related to interests in that interests may reflect the value system of the individual, though often in a loose way. Stamp collecting may appeal to the individual's esthetic value, but it may be far more firmly rooted in an individual's possessiveness and perhaps even his compulsive tendency to arrange, order, and produce closure by completing a system.

Rokeach suggests that values or beliefs may have direct relationships either to "modes of conduct or end-states of existence" (p. 7). Values related to modes of conduct are referred to as instrumental values and those that pertain to end-states are referred to as terminal values. For example, equality of individuals in a political sense is a terminal value. It is a state that one may work toward, hoping that it will be ultimately achieved, though probably not in one's lifetime. On the other hand, *honesty*, an instrumental value, represents a state of affairs that one may hope to achieve in each of one's transactions with others. Thus terminal values are related to idealized end-states and instrumental values refer to idealized modes of behavior. Nevertheless, this distinction is not as clear as one might like it to be, for terminal values can function as instrumental values. Although I may hope that the United States may achieve true equality among its citizens, I may also believe that the way to achieve this end is to treat all those I come into contact with as equals. When I behave in this way, then equality as a value in my personality would seem to be functioning as an instrumental value.

Rokeach lists eighteen terminal values including those described as a comfortable life, a world at peace, equality, family security, freedom, salvation, self-respect, and wisdom. His list of eighteen instrumental values includes ambition, broadmindedness, courage, honesty, logicalness, lovingness, and self-control. The list is, of course, not comprehensive but claims to include most of the values that are of prime importance in the lives of most adults in the American culture. Rokeach devised a simple means of assessing the strength of each value in an individual by asking him to rank the eighteen values in each list (for which definitions are provided) in order of importance. The rankings do have some stability over a year or more. Whatever is ranked high on one occasion tends to be ranked high on future occasions. However, some individuals seem to be much more stable than others in the values that are important to them.

Rokeach has shown that values vary among different sections of American society. For example, when blacks and whites are compared on the terminal value dimensions, the most striking difference is in the category of *equality*. For the blacks this is a much more significant value than it is for the whites. The category " comfortable life " is also more important for blacks than for whites. Whites rate a comfortable life low in their priorities because they have already achieved that state of being. Blacks also place a higher value on being clean and obedient, and whites a higher value on a world of beauty, family security, and being loved.

There are also striking differences between the values of men and women. Men place a much higher value than women on a comfortable life, an exciting life, a sense of accomplishment, freedom, pleasure, and social recognition. Women value significantly more than men a world at peace, happiness, inner harmony, salvation, self-respect, and wisdom.

The theory in this area of research has been that attitudes underlie values and that attitudes reflect specific aspects of particular values or combinations of values. Rokeach has attempted to determine the extent to which this theory accounts for the facts. For the most part he finds a certain consistency between values and attitudes. For example, he found that the value most closely associated with attitude toward blacks, the poor, church activism, and student protest is equality. The importance that individuals give to religion is closely related to the way they view salvation as a value. Those who have authoritarian personalities in terms of the California F scale are those who score high on the values of salvation and obedience. Nevertheless, not all the findings are as consistent with stereotyped expectation, which may often be no more than just prejudice. For example, the value of a *world at peace* scores as high for hawks as for doves. Racists score higher on the value *family security* than do those who are less racist.

Rokeach has also explored the relations of values to behavior through the study of the values of individuals who engage in such activities as joining the NAACP, engaging in eye contact with members of other racial groups, participating in civil rights activities, attending church, engaging in partisan politics, or returning pencils they have borrowed. The value equality predicts joining the NAACP, participating in a civil rights demonstration and eye contact between blacks and whites. The value *salvation* predicts church-going and the value *world of beauty* is characteristic of artists. An interesting point to note is that while measures of attitudes have not predicted very well such behaviors, the measures of attitudes do seem related to common forms of behavior.

An interesting application of Rokeach's system of values is found in his work on the relation of the system to political ideology. He finds that two main values dominate political thought and action: *equality* and *freedom*. His thesis is that the main political ideologies of the world are differentiated in terms of these values. Thus communism is a system that stresses equality as a positive value but places no worth at all on freedom. In contrast, a capitalist society has the reverse set of values, stressing the worth of freedom but having little use for equality. Fascism has no value either for freedom or equality, but socialism, in theory, emphasizes both freedom and equality. In order to test this theory an analysis was made of the writings of proponents of each of these four systems. The writings of Lenin were taken to represent communism, those of Hitler fascism, those of Goldwater capitalism, and those of Norman Thomas and others to represent socialism. The analysis of these data provided results that fitted perfectly the differentiation expected in terms of the emphasis placed on freedom and equality. Fascism was shown to have values that are the complete opposite of socialism and, communism and capitalism also showed complete opposition.

Rokeach argues that the strength of a person's values for freedom and for equality determine the kind of political position that he is most likely to accept. He suggests that those who value equality highly and discount freedom would be prone to accept communism. In a survey undertaken he found that only 2.4 per cent of adult Americans fell into this category and only 1.8 per cent of students. Of course, these percentages are not the percentage of those embracing a communist philosophy but only those that would be prone to do so because of their value structure. The data are like data from a test identifying those likely to get cancer. The data only indicate a certain proneness and perhaps even a majority of those who are shown to be cancer prone will never actually contract it. Only a small part of an already very small communism-prone group is likely to embrace a communist philosophy. The survey also showed that the majority of Americans, both students and nonstudents had a value orientation that would lead them to a middle of the road position, with positive feelings for both freedom and equality, but not of overwhelming strength.

In addition there is evidence that political activism is related to holding one or both of the values of freedom and equality to either a very high or very low degree. For example, peace marchers were found to value more highly both freedom and equality than downtown pedestrians in the same city.

Of particular importance to the theme of Rokeach's book is a set of studies that attempted to produce change in the value system of individuals and in which the effects of subsequent behavior were studied. Rokeach takes the position that behavioral change is best brought about by identifying the values that support present behavior and changing those values, with the result that the individual becomes dissatisfied with his own behavior and is thereby motivated to change it.

The basic plan of Rokeach's studies of value change was to identify a group that was high on the freedom dimension and relatively low on the equality dimension. Then an effort was made to make the individuals in the group feel a dissatisfaction with this discrepancy. They were told that their low evaluation of equality meant that they wanted freedom for themselves but did not want freedom for others. An attempt was made to show that their position was contradictory and that it would become consistent only if they learned to evaluate equality higher. Data were presented showing that a lack of emphasis on equality would place them among those who were against civil rights, and so forth. Long-term follow-up of these individuals provided data showing that changes were produced in their values and also that these changes were evident fifteen to seventeen months after the attempt had been made to produce change.

In the follow-up studies the strength of the value *equality* was measured, as was the specific attitude of whites toward blacks. The data from the study provided evidence that both the value and its related attitude underwent change. The data also suggest, but do not demonstrate very conclusively, that value change tends to precede attitude change, but there is also the possibility that in some individuals the attitude might first change and then the value might be changed to conform to the attitude. Nevertheless, values seem to be more fundamental than attitudes and probably a more effective place in which to initiate change. The individuals involved in the experiment were tested on several occasions later (3 weeks, 3–5 months, and 15–17 months). The data tended to show that attitude change occurred later than value change, suggesting that the change in attitude followed a change in value.

As a part of this same experiment, Rokeach tried to determine whether the attempt to change attitudes would change behavior other than verbal behavior. A discussion of equality might well influence how a person talked about equality, how he talked about equality for blacks, and how he might answer a questionnaire on the subject, but his relationships to blacks in a face-to-face situation might remain unchanged. The technique adopted by Rokeach was to have the NAACP send each person in the experimental group and control group an invitation to join. This was done first 3 to 5 months after the experiment began and again 15 to 17 months after the start. As a result of the first mailing far more of the experimental than control subjects joined the organization. The effect was highly significant statistically. A considerably less significant effect was found the second time the invitation was mailed.

The experimental group showed also another effect. The members tended to take more courses related to ethnic problems and to shift to a social science curriculum.

Rokeach has reviewed the various possible explanations for his findings. He comes to the conclusion that the essential factor in producing a change in values is the arousal of dissatisfaction of the individual with his present position. In other words, the explanation fits cognitive consistency theory rather than any other theory. An interesting feature of the data was the slow change in attitude that followed the training session in which an attempt was made to change value. Apparently the effects of such a session are not immediate but represent a long-term development that continues to take effect long after the training session comes to an end. This impact on values and the chain effect it seems to have on attitude is to be contrasted with the rather transitory effects of attempts to change attitudes. The latter effects are not only short term but tend to wear off rather quickly. Perhaps Rokeach has discovered a key to the development of desirable social attitudes.

SUMMARY

1. Attitudes emerge in a primitive form in the early years of life, manifesting themselves as tendencies to approach or withdraw from particular classes of objects. The terms attitude, interest, values, and approach and withdrawal tendencies cannot be clearly differentiated. The term interest is used to refer to the person's relationship to particular activities, and the term attitude refers to behavioral tendencies related to particular objects and ideas. The term value generally refers to a broad goal.

2. Attitudes are generally considered to be complex and such a view has led to productive research. The view that attitudes are simply particular responses has been held by psychologists interested in operant conditioning, and although it has stimulated some research, it has not represented an especially productive approach to problems of attitude learning and change.

3. Those who view attitudes as complex have commonly taken the position that all attitudes have a number of components. A major component is the cognitive component, that is, the mass of beliefs, some true and some false, on which an attitude is based. A second component is the affective component, that is, the tendency of the attitude to be represented by positive and negative feelings. This is the component of attitude commonly measured by attitude scales. Why this component has become the focus of attitude research is hard to say, but the main reason may well be that devices for measuring this component have been readily available. Most psychologists deplore the lack of research in the third component of attitudes, namely, the action component, but such research has not been extensively undertaken largely because it is difficult to carry out. Attitude research has been largely limited to studies of what people say about themselves.

4. Attempts have been made to identify the functions of attitudes, but these functions are numerous, and perhaps not very well identified. Attitudes may serve highly utilitarian purposes, as when a person adopts the attitudes of a particular political group because he belongs to that group's constituency. More subtle are the cognitive functions of attitudes. Attitudes function very much like concepts, in that they help to simplify transactions with a very complex world. Attitudes may also provide a very direct gratification of needs. In addition, attitudes may bolster the individual's conception of himself and may help to defend him against psychological attack.

5. Research on attitude acquisition and attitude change has been rich in the production of theory. Although some of the theorizing has been closely linked to traditional theories of learning, such as operant and classical conditioning, some of the newer developments represent new departures in theory construction. Dissonance theory of attitude acquisition and change has played a very important role in the development of social psychology and is probably the newest and most vigorous of the three theoretical positions considered.

6. Considerable research has been undertaken on the basis of the belief that

attitudes are particular categories of behavior and that reinforcement procedures, such as those advocated in operant conditioning, are the key to attitude acquisition and change. Some of the experiments on attitude change, undertaken near to mid-century, appeared to give support to this position. Later work has thrown considerable doubt on the usefulness of operant conditioning for understanding the mechanism involved in attitude change.

7. Another major theoretical position is that of dissonance theory, a branch of cognitive consistency theory. Cognitive dissonance theory takes the position that individuals cannot easily tolerate inconsistent elements in their cognitive system, that is, the system that includes knowledge, beliefs, opinions, images, and so forth. Much of the development of dissonance theory owes its origins to the appearance of a work by Festinger (1957). The central thesis of dissonance theory of attitude change is that dissonance is a condition that individuals seek either to avoid or remove. A person who encounters new information inconsistent with his attitudes may reduce the dissonance involved by ignoring the new information, or by taking the position that it really is not relevant or that it involves assumptions he does not accept, or he may change his attitude to make it consistent with the new information. Dissonance may be derived from logical inconsistency, inconsistency with cultural mores, inconsistency with the general trend in behavior, or inconsistency with past experience.

8. Dissonance theory has much to say about decision situations because it is often through such situations that attitudes are changed. It also incorporates statements about the effect of rewards. The effects of rewards predicted by dissonance theory are different from those predicted on the basis of operant conditioning theory, and the former theory has provided more accurate predictions in some situations. A finding of considerable significance derived from dissonance studies is that mild threats are more likely to exert a lasting effect on the behavior of children than are severe threats.

9. The major limitation placed on dissonance theory comes from the fact that the terms used to state the theory lack precision. Clarification of these terms will be achieved ultimately and some progress has already been made. The proposal that dissonance can be defined in terms of conflicting expectancies is one suggested improvement that may help to clarify some of the issues.

10. Dissonance theory has stimulated a large number of studies related to communication and how to make communication effective in changing opinion. The most intensively studied characteristics of the communicator are those of trustworthiness and expertness. These characteristics have immediate impact in producing attitude change, but they do not seem to have a lasting effect. Those who are exposed to a communication by an expert are influenced by the fact that he is an expert. A communication overheard is more likely to be of influence than a communication known to be directed toward the communicator. However, an overheard communication is likely to have little influence unless the hearer has some intent to change. Sometimes irrelevant characteristics of the communicator, that is, characteristics that have no bearing on the worth of a communication, may have

considerable impact on the effect of a communication. At least under some conditions, a negative communicator may have more impact than a positive communicator.

11. Dissonance theory has been challenged from a number of sources. The large reward situation may simply be disruptive. Another suggestion is that the crucial factor may be whether the individual does or does not take responsibility for his actions.

12. A new approach to the interpretation of attitude change is found in self-perception theory. This position assumes that the individual infers his own attitudes from his own behavior. If a person observes himself undertaking what looks like a dull task for only a dollar, he must assume that there is something of inherent interest in the task. When he is forced to say that the task is interesting, he finds reasons to justify what he has said.

13. Attempts have been made to relate the properties of information to attitude change. Theories relating information to attitude change assume that there is a cumulative effect, depending on the value given each piece of information. Each piece of information is assumed to be assigned both a position on a scale and a value. The weighting given each new piece of information is integrated into the total body of information already available in relation to the particular attitude.

14. In recent years, assessments of the value of measures of attitude for predicting behavior have become more favorable. Classic experiments that tended to show that measures of attitude had little predictive value have been shown to contain basic weaknesses. There are also clear areas, such as voting behavior, in which measured attitudes have been shown to have high predictive value.

15. The characteristics of communications that are persuasive have been intensively studied, but much of the research has been directed toward the study of the rather unclear issue of whether one-sided or two-sided arguments are the more persuasive. Such studies, considered collectively, show little difference between these two approaches. Much depends on the ability of the individuals involved. Two-sided arguments may confuse relatively dull listeners or readers. Relatively bright listeners are more receptive to the so-called two-sided argument than to the one-sided.

16. Individuals differ in persuasibility. The persuasibility of children seems to increase to a maximum at about age of 9. The relationship of intelligence to persuasibility is obviously complex. A communication that is highly persuasible for one level of intelligence may be quite ineffective for other levels. Women's attitudes are more readily influenced than those of men, perhaps because men are poorer listeners. Self-esteem is also another characteristic that appears to have some effect on whether subjects are readily influenced.

17. One of the most productive approaches to the problem of identifying the characteristics of the persuasible individual comes from research on the dogmatic or authoritarian personality. The dogmatic individual tends to avoid information inconsistent with that which he possesses, but when exposed, he is more readily changed in attitude than is the less dogmatic individual.

18. Changes produced in attitudes tend to disappear as time goes by, partly because there is some forgetting of the factual information involved. In addition, there is a tendency for a change produced in attitudes to be enhanced for a short period after the impact of some event that produces change. It takes time for the event to have full impact.

19. Several techniques designed for preventing attitudes from being changed have been studied. The most effective of these is to arm the individual with arguments that are supportive of his beliefs and arguments that could be used against any counterarguments that the individual might encounter. Mere security in knowing that one's beliefs are shared by others has little effect except that of lulling the individual into a state of false security. An important condition that produces stability of attitudes is what is referred to as commitment.

20. Since values are the coordinators of attitudes, they would seem to have broad significance. In addition, values also represent society's needs and social expectations. Rokeach believes that values may be expected to have direct relationships to action. Rokeach views values as either terminal or instrumental, and he has attempted to list the most important ones in our society. Measured values differ for different groups. The attitudes of individuals tend to be consistent with their values. Values are related to political ideology, particularly those values described by the words *equality* and *freedom*. Political activism is also related to the degree to which one or both of these values are held to a high degree. Rokeach has undertaken studies showing that changes in attitudes may result in related changes in behavior.

Chapter 15

Some Social Factors in Learning

A chapter on social factors related to learning cannot cover a topic that is commonly discussed in book-sized treatises. The wealth of material is evident when one contemplates the fact that the current edition of *The Handbook of Social Psychology* includes five massive volumes. Although it is true that not all of social psychology is involved with conditions related to learning, much of it is, and one could make out a strong case for the proposition that teachers should receive far more training in that field than they now receive.

In this chapter an attempt has been made to select a very few topics from the field of social psychology that appear to have particularly significant implications for the teacher. Most learning still takes place in a social setting and social factors play an important role in determining what is learned and how efficiently it is learned. The social setting of learning is there because society has decreed that one or more adults and a large number of children shall occupy the same area of a school. Some attempts have been made by educational technologists to reduce or eliminate much of the social context of learning by proposing, and sometimes introducing, teaching machines at which the pupil may work in an isolated booth, but the effect of social isolation produced by such an instructional setting is not known at this time.

SOCIAL FACTORS IN INFANT LEARNING

Studies of learning in infancy commonly fail to recognize the social context in which such learning occurs. Every psychologist who has ever experimented with infants knows that he must conduct his experiments with the mother near at hand. Indeed, the mother, or mother figure, is an essential feature of the infant's learning environment. The human being, like other primates, learns to cope with his environment in a social context.

Stone, Smith, and Murphy (1973) have reviewed much of the literature related to mother-infant relationships among primates. Throughout this literature are found descriptions of the extreme distress manifested by infants separated from their natural mothers: whimpering, crying, and much behavior described as "depressive." This behavior occurred even when the infants could see their mothers though separated from them by a partition. When the infants were returned to their mothers there was typically prolonged clinging to them and disturbances of behavior that lasted for days. The separation effect is limited not only to separation from the mother, but separation from peers produces a comparable effect. The responses observed seem to take place in many species when there is separation from an object to which the young animal has acquired an attachment. An interesting point to note is that in most primates, other than human beings, the crucial factor in the early social relationship is in physical contact, which is why only being able to see the mother is not enough. However, in the human infant, eye contact seems to be the crucial element. The 3-month-old child remains quiet and happy while he can see his mother, but as soon as the mother leaves the room he begins to whimper, kick, and show signs of distress.

The human being has been described as being "socially hooked" by the age of 3 months. By that time, he does not tolerate being alone, but requires the constant presence of another person. There seem to be some advantages in the human presence being represented by a single person for, as Rabin (1965) has shown in his study of child-rearing in the kibbutzim, many adults may collectively take the place of the mother, but the group does not seem to fully satisfy the needs of the infant. The infants raised by many caretakers, including the mother, in the kibbutzim show greater emotionality during the early years of life than do children raised in the typical nuclear family. The kibbutzim infants may have difficulties in handling relationships with several adults because this places greater strain on their intellects than would a relationship with a single mothering figure. A fundamental learning undertaken by the infant in relationship to his mother is that of anticipating what the mother will do and how the mother will react. To learn this in relation to several adults may be highly taxing on the infant's capabilities. However, the kibbutz-raised infant does not seem to suffer permanent damage from the multiple mothering situation.

The mother of the infant provides the infant with the basic experience of living in an orderly world. The mother, unlike other parts of the environment, can be relied on more than any unfamiliar person. If the infant emits a signal of distress, he knows that the mother will come to his help. The mother provides him with his first experience of the predictability of events.

As was pointed out in the chapter on motivation, the mother also becomes the base of security from which the world is explored. Without such a secure base the infant might be expected to engage in little exploratory activity, a characteristic seen in foundling home children who have lacked a proper mothering relationship.

In addition, the mother's face becomes one of the objects that the infant learns to discriminate from other similar objects. This requires that the infant learn to make difficult visual discriminations. The mother's voice also provides him with exercise in learning to discriminate one vocal sound from another. Even by the age of 4 weeks, it seems, the infant has learned to make eye-to-eye contact with the mother. The data suggest that the infant has learned that the eyes indicate what the mother is going to do next.

A particularly important contribution of the mother in facilitating learning in the infant results from the fact that the mother holds the infant in an upright position. The early studies of infant behavior demonstrated very little learning because the infant was lying on his back. In such a position the infant tends to be in a semiawake condition and has only the most limited capacity to either learn or perform. On the other hand, if the head and shoulders are raised, alertness is increased and the infant learns. An important part of mothering is to change the posture of the infant through being picked up and thus increasing his opportunity to learn. Another important, but indirect, contribution of the mother is that of providing the infant with movement and stimulation, which appears to be important for development. The stillness of the crib is a poor environment for development, physical or psychological. One wonders what happened to all the children raised in Skinner-box-type cribs during the 1940s and 1950s when it was fashionable to raise infants in sterile, warm, and clothing-free environments, where they would remain in a horizontal position.

Smiling is known to be an innate response. Although it can be elicited by a great range of stimuli, it becomes attached early in infancy to human stimuli such as the face and the voice. Whether the focus of smiling on stimuli derived from human sources is innate in origin still remains to be demonstrated.

The interaction of the mother with her baby is a two-way interaction. Some babies are easier than others to interact with, and some mothers are much more understanding of their infants than are others. However, a baby with an easy disposition, who does not fuss much, produces in turn a less anxious and happier mother. Success in the mother role requires that the mother be able to understand the infant's needs.

An interesting point related to the social context of intellectual development is that the infant's first understandings related to the permanency of objects develop in relation to his mother (see Bell, 1970). The evidence indicates that the infant shows an understanding of the permanency of his mother and her continued existence even when he cannot see her considerably before he shows an understanding that objects in general continue to exist even when he cannot see them. This seems particularly true of infants who have a strong maternal attachment.

At more advanced levels of child development the phenomenon of imitation is generally referred as *modeling*, an aspect of learning to which we must now turn.

MODELING IN CHILDHOOD

Flanders (1968) has reviewed research showing that animals far down the evolutionary scale can be taught to imitate models through reinforcement. This does not rule out an innate tendency to imitate in other species that have stronger social tendencies. It is not surprising that rats, which pay no attention to other rats except for mating purposes, have to be shaped through reinforcement to imitate the behavior of a member of their own species. However, nobody has yet shown that the young of highly social species, such as primates, have to be reinforced in order to imitate members of their own species.

The vocabularly that has evolved in this area uses the term *model* to refer to any behavior performed in the presence of a member of the same species. If the behavior presented by the model is copied by the other species member, it is said to be modeled, and the entire process is referred to as modeling. The expression *a behavior model* does not imply that the behavior presented is useful, or good, or adaptive, but only that a distinct sequence of behavior is presented. The classic work on modeling in children was conducted by Bandura and Walters (1963); their well-known studies of aggression will be discussed later in the chapter. Although the early work suggested that a model would be imitated if the model's behavior were reinforced, more recent results (see Kaplan, 1972) seem to indicate that children tend to imitate models regardless of whether the model's behavior is or is not reinforced. Operant psychologists interpret this as indicating that the children have learned that behavior they model is likely to be reinforced, regardless of whether it is or is not reinforced in the model.

The role of modeling in intellectual development has been studied only relatively recently in the United States, perhaps because little thought has been given to the role of the teacher as an intellectual model in the classroom. The teacher is expected to be a good model of the sexual and political codes of the community in which he works, but there is little pressure on him to provide in the classroom either a model of good interpersonal relations or a model of intellectual competence.

A study of particular interest was conducted by Murray (1974) on the effect of the performance of a model on the development of conservation concepts in children. The children were divided into those who conserved volume, those who were in a transitional state related to conservation of volume, and those who did not yet conserve. Equal numbers of children in each of these three groups were exposed to adult models who were conservers, transitional, and nonconservers. A matter of particular interest is that the conservers who observed a nonconserving model did not regress or become confused. They still continued to be conservers. Presumably, once conservation is learned, a model who does not conserve merely looks stupid. On the other hand, the nonconservers and those in a transitional state who observed a conserving model made some progress toward giving conservation responses. They did not become instant conservers, and progress was quite small, but there appeared to be progress. One suspects that children have to be ready to make some progress in this respect before the model can have any effect. One would like to know what would be the effect of continued exposure to models who conserved and how much facilitation would be produced in developing conservation structures of thought.

Intellectual modeling is not always as simple a matter as the Murray study might indicate. Zimmerman and Dialessi (1973) undertook a study that had some surprising results. They were interested in the development of what have been termed *fluency* and *flexibility*, which some psychologists believe to be related to creativity. An example of behaviors related to these two factors is seen when children are presented with the task of describing unusual uses of a cardboard box. Fluency is measured by the number of unusual uses they come up with in a given period of time. Flexibility is measured by the number of times they change to new areas of application. For example, a child who proposed using the box (1) for grass clippings, (2) for trash, and (3) to store old clothes would have selected all the uses from the same general area, namely, that of storage. The flexibility score would be zero. In contrast, the child who proposed using the box (1) for storing old clothes, (2) as a container for raising tomato plants, (3) as an umbrella, and (4) as a source of cardboard for making Xmas decorations would have switched fields of application three times and would have a flexibility score of three.

Zimmerman and Dialessi found that exposure to a fluent model performing such a task increased children's fluency, but exposure to a flexible model actually decreased their flexibility. The results are quite puzzling. The increase in fluency is probably just a recognition by the children of the kind of performance required of them.

We need to know much more about how the intellectual behavior of the teacher influences the intellectual behavior of the child. We also need to know much more about how the style of interaction that the teacher has with the children rubs off on the children. The problem is complex, for it has even been shown that the amount of modeling depends on the pupil's self-esteem. A review by Bourdon (1970) brings together some scattered research on this matter. Various scales have been developed that measure self-esteem, which can be described in broad terms as the extent to which the individual thinks well of himself. Such measures of self-esteem are related to the tendency to imitate or to match the behavior of another. Those whose self-esteem is highest show least tendency to imitate. One presumes that individuals who feel adequate have a repertoire of behaviors of their own to call upon to handle situations that arise, but those who feel less adequate perhaps have a lesser repertoire and have a greater need to borrow behaviors from others.

SOCIAL FACILITATION AND INHIBITION OF LEARNING

Some learning in natural settings occurs in group structures and some occurs in isolation. In many of the early experimental studies in the area of social psychology, the results showed that performance in group settings was superior to that in the isolated situation. Similar results were found when the individual involved was asked to learn some task rather than to perform a familiar task. Another aspect of the social setting has been studied in situations in which the individual has learned either in the presence of an observer or alone. These studies are generally referred to as studies of the effect of an audience. Ganzer (1968) has reviewed previous audience studies and has conducted a study of his own for the purpose of accounting for some of the inconsistencies in findings. He points out that many of the inconsistencies can be explained if one distinguishes between the performance of a well-practiced act and the acquisition of a new act. The presence of an audience appears to facilitate the performance of a well-practiced act but is detrimental to the learning of new skills. This does not account for all of the apparent inconsistencies, but the study of Ganzer makes a further contribution.

Ganzer selected the subjects for his study from the upper, middle, and lower thirds on the Taylor Manifest Anxiety Scale. They were given the task of learning a set of nonsense syllables either after being told that there was an observer behind a one-way glass screen or with the one-way screen covered and no mention being made of an observer. When the learning of the observed and the nonobserved groups were compared, the observed group did less well. However, when the groups were also divided into high-, middle-, and low-anxious, the finding was that the high- and middle-anxious did less well under the observed condition, but that the low-anxious group was unaffected by the announcement that an observer would be present.

The effect of an observer wears off rapidly. Indeed, in most studies in social psychology involving an observer, effects are found to disappear rather rapidly as the subject of the experiment becomes used to his or her presence (see Mills, 1969). In the case of the Ganzer study, the effect was no longer observable when a second session of the experiment was conducted a day later.

Zajonc (1966) suggested that the presence or absence of the facilitating effect depended on the task undertaken. Zajonc theorized that the effect of the presence of others was to raise the level of arousal of the individual. The effect of raising the level of arousal was to facilitate performance on simple tasks, but the raised level of arousal might interfere with performance on more complex tasks. The Yerkes–Dodson law states that at the optimum level of arousal there might be a positive facilitating effect with simple tasks and a negative interfering effect with complex tasks. This theory enables one to make predictions in many cases concerning the effect of the presence of others on work performance, but Steiner (1972) points out that more recent research indicates that the facilitating or interfering effect occurs mainly when the other individuals are in a position to affect the outcomes of the performer. Thus children in a class may influence the performance of each pupil by their presence because they set a standard by which each pupil may judge his performance and by which he will be judged.

Psychologists have long suggested that some types of teachers are more effective with some kinds of some types of students, although research workers have been at a loss to suggest what these types might be. Cunningham (1975) has reviewed some of the research related to this problem and has concluded that there is no consistent picture of favorable social interactions. In his own study he classified students in terms of their attitudes toward different aspects of teaching, and their racial and social backgrounds. Students were classified in terms of both background and test scores. He did find significant relationships between teacher background and pupil background in terms of learning. The kindergarten pupils seemed to learn most when they worked with teachers most like themselves.

AGGRESSION AND HARM DOING TO OTHERS: ACQUISITION AND CONTROL

This topic has been included in this chapter for a number of reasons. First, much disruptive behavior that occurs in school falls into this general category. Second, America is a country in which the control of violence presents special problems. Third, schools are beginning to introduce materials into their classrooms related to the control of international violence. Fourth, there is considerable pressure from schools to take some kind of action to help children learn nonviolent methods of handling problems.

The word *aggression* is applied by psychologists and laymen alike to a wide range of behaviors. It is not a precisely defined term, but its usage continues because it includes within its scope many forms of behavior that have grave consequences for human happiness and even for human survival. Different studies define the term in different ways, and the multiplicity of definitions used has led to a body of research literature in which there is little coherence. Many psychologists are disturbed by the fact that research in the area has proceeded without an adequate and well-accepted definition of the term, but such a state of affairs should disturb nobody. Many scientific terms have slowly evolved their meaning as research has proceeded, and research has been necessary in order to evolve a satisfactory definition. The lack of an adequate definition of aggressive behavior does not invalidate particular studies directed toward the investigation of particular forms of aggression. The difficulty comes when one tries to fit together the knowledge derived from a diversity of studies, for then one has to decide whether there is any relationship between aggression manifested in one form and aggression manifested in another.

Although this writer believes that the clarification of the term will come as research proceeds, some of the theoretical attempts to introduce clarification seem useful and worth mentioning. Buss (1966) and Rule (1974) find it convenient to distinguish between instrumental aggression and hostile or angry aggression. The former is a means of achieving a particular goal, as when one person robs another. The latter is illustrated by the person who makes a sarcastic or cutting remark. Buss has also suggested three other ways of classifying aggressive behavior. These involve the categories of (1) the active versus the passive, contrasting the person who engages in direct violence with the person who refuses to help another who needs help; (2) the physical versus the verbal, contrasting the person who strikes another with the person who engages in verbal abuse; (3) the direct versus the indirect, contrasting the person who confronts his victim with the person who damages the victim's car.

Tedeschi, Smith, and Brown (1974) have provided an excellent review of the difficulties associated with the various definitions of human aggression. They seem to reject definitions that encompass both animal and human behavior, but definitions related to human behavior generally involve the concept of *intent* to do harm, and they find the concept of *intent* too vague to handle effectively. They propose that the term aggression be limited with reference to human behavior to those behaviors that involve the exercise of coercive power. They make some effort to define the attributes of behaviors that show coercive power. Other definitions attempt to define aggression in terms of the vocabulary of operant psychology. Cahoon (1972) attempts to do this, but comes up with a very restricted definition that seems to fit only the few operant studies that have been undertaken in the area. The problem of definition remains one that is not likely to be handled satisfactorily until far more knowledge has been accumulated.

LEARNING AND AGGRESSION IN OTHER THAN HUMAN SPECIES

Although human aggression is often subtle, involving only the words of one person directed against another, species further down the evolutionary scale engage in numerous and less subtle forms of attack behavior. Numerous studies of the attack of one animal on another have been made, and Johnson (1972) has provided a readable and thoughtful analysis of the literature that forms the basis of the present discussion. Johnson points out that the aggressive behavior of animals other than human beings always must have had a function in the preservation and evolution of the species involved, but its function is often difficult to determine at this time, millions of years after the behavior evolved. Many species of animals set up territories that they defend against intrusion by other members of their species. The defense of the territory has the effect of preserving their food supplies and also the spacing out of the species over a wide area. The overall effect of such territorial defense has been to develop a condition under which the species can flourish and multiply. The defense of a life space is usually only against the same species. This is adaptive in that other species that infringe on the territory probably consume different foods and are not a threat. Lorenz (1963), who first worked extensively on this problem, concluded that human beings behave much like territorial animals. Lorenz assumes that human beings have inherited this adaptive response and behave like territorial animals not only in international political situations but also when they build a fence around their yard: the response persists even though it is no longer a suitable adaptive response.

Territorial behavior has the typical effect of distributing animals over the available food supply. This is true even in human beings. When the land in the eastern seaboard areas had been fully settled and claimed, new generations had to move out into Ohio and Kentucky and Indiana to find new land. Immigration to the West was behavior typical of territorial animals. But what happens when all the land available is occupied and there is an increase in population? Something is known about this in subhuman species forced to live under crowded conditions. Studies have been undertaken in which rats have been free to multiply in areas of 10,000 square feet. In these experiments food has not been evenly distributed over the entire living space area but has been available at certain points. Under such conditions territorial behavior of some of the stronger rats takes over the areas that include the sources of food. The rats with territories remote from the sources of food have a high mortality rate, as do their offspring. The result is that the colony never reached the full size that the space could support and, as a matter of fact, reached only 30 per cent of that size. On the other hand, in studies in which food has been readily accessible to all, animal populations have grown to a size far beyond that which the space can support. Under these conditions enormous amounts of fighting behavior occur and mortality is high.

Although one is tempted to generalize from these studies of crowding to the probable effect of crowding on human behavior, many psychologists urge caution. Schaar (1975) goes as far as to suggest that some degree of crowding may even be a good condition for human beings. Lawrence (1974) believes there may be a relationship between crowding and human behavior but concedes that the relationship is probably very complex. A part of the problem of generalizing from animal data is that in the crowding studies the animals lived in crowded conditions with population densities that far exceed those found even in the worst slums. What might be considered to be a normal population density for monkeys might exceed the density of slum populations. The term crowding has been used quite loosely and with resulting confusion.

No simple generalization can be made from such studies to predict what will happen to human populations as a result of crowding. As far as crime rates are concerned, population density seems to be less important than the nature of living conditions. For example, high-rise low-cost housing projects have produced much violent behavior and crime, but the same density of population housed in two- and three-storey apartments, with less recreation space and more time spent on the street, reduces most of these problems. Again, with easy access to the streets, the street areas around each group of apartments is treated by the inhabitants as their territory in which they maintain control and some degree of order.

There has been an increasing interest in work on territoriality, which has now been extended to human behavior. Edney (1974) has reviewed these studies, which are difficult to put together into a unified picture because they involve such diverse definitions of the phenomenon. Examples include research on the areas of mental hospitals preempted by mental patients, the taking over of areas of the library by specific college students, and the territories claimed by youthful offenders in juvenile homes. Edney points out a wide range of problems that still need to be explored, including the matter of whether the taking over of a territory by a human being satisfies his need or merely whets his appetite. In addition, there is a need for research on the effects of upbringing on territoriality, and there is also the fascinating issue of whether there is a territoriality in the world of ideas. Does a profession such as medicine invent its own unnecessarily complex vocabulary in order to ensure that others will not intrude on this domain of ideas?

Some aggressive behavior has evolved around mating behavior. A species can benefit in some respects if the males compete for the right of relating sexually to the females because the strongest males will then produce the offspring. Thus some features of physical strength become preserved, if not enhanced. On the other hand, the survival of a species may be jeopardized if such fighting for the right to reproduce results in a high casualty rate among the males. The latter problem has been taken care of in many species through the evolution of ritualized fighting behavior. When this evolves, the competing males may fight, but when a point is reached at which one has a strong advantage, the other gives up. In some species, such as elk and moose, the weapons used for fighting, namely, the antlers, are so cumbersome that little damage is likely to be inflicted on the opponent. Despite the protections that have evolved that prevent animals from killing a member of its own species some fatalities do occur from intra-species conflict in almost every case that has been systematically studied. Johnson cites studies involving intra-species killing for such varied species as lions, baboons, zebras, bees, chimpanzees, lizards, elephants, rodents, and termites. These conflicts took place in various situations including issues of territory, disputes over ownership of prey, conflicts related to sex, and an accidental wounding of a member of a species resulting in the others turning on the one that was injured.

Many animals have specific inhibitions built into them that prevent them from killing their own species. Poisonous snakes do not use their fangs against their own species. In some species there is a signal honored by all members that indicates that an animal will give up and fight no more. The signal often involves exposing a vulnerable part of the body. Thus a dog may indicate that it gives up in a fight by rolling on its back and exposing the soft and vulnerable underbelly. Some biologists, impressed with these forms of behavior, have suggested that one of the great problems of human beings is that they have not evolved such inhibitions that would prevent them from destroying members of their own species. This is an attractive argument, but the fact is that there is no evidence that human beings destroy a greater proportion of their species than do other species. Richardson (1960), who has attempted to estimate the total number of deaths from violence in the world from 1820 to 1949, has estimated that deaths from wars and war-related causes amounted to about 1.28 per cent and that murders amounted to 0.27 per cent. During the period studied, deaths from wars were estimated to be 46.8 millions and from murders 9.7 millions. These proportions of deaths due to violence are probably not very different from those found in many other species, a fact that runs against the theory that human beings have no built-in inhibitions that prevent them from killing members of their own species.

Aggression is only one of the forms of behavior that evolved to preserve a species and was not necessarily the most successful one. Other species, for example many herd animals, have developed highly cooperative behavior, through which they can ward off attack. The musk oxen, faced with a predatory enemy, arrange themselves in a circle with the bulls on the outside and offer a formidable defense. Not all animals can evolve such passive systems of defense, particularly if their food supply is very scattered and animals cannot afford to forage near to one another. The survival mechanisms that evolve are always closely tied to the nutritional requirements of the creature and the nature of the habitat in which it lives.

There are many oddities of attack behavior. One that has been widely discussed in recent times because of the extensive experimental program related to it is that of pain-elicited aggression. An animal exposed to a sudden painful stimulus, such as a shock in the laboratory, tends to attack any object that happens to be present at the same time. The nature of the object is quite unimportant. If the animal is a rat and the only other object present is another rat, the painful stimulus results in an attack on the other rat. The behavior is much more like a reflex than anything else and probably has little relation to any other form of aggressive behavior. A few have made the unconvincing claim that it is a basic form of aggression that can become conditioned to other stimuli. If the rat given the shock were exposed to a bright light on each occasion of the shock, the bright light would elicit the aggressive response. Through this kind of mechanism, it is claimed, an animal can learn to aggress in a wide variety of situations. Although pain-elicited aggression can be nicely and easily demonstrated to undergraduate classes and is easily filmed, it is probably of only trivial importance in understanding other forms of aggression. The response does have survival value. If an animal experiences sudden pain, the chances are that it is being attacked and the best life-preserving procedure for that animal is counterattack. It is a life-preserving response that has evolved in every species so far studied, but it is a narrow and limited response that does little to account for other forms of aggression.

Various attempts have been made to state generalizations about the conditions under which aggression will occur. The most famous of these is the frustration-aggression hypothesis first discussed by Freud, later stated by a group of Yale psychologists (Dollard et al., 1939), and still later reformulated by many psychologists, including Miller (1941). This hypothesis states that aggression is a response to situations characterized by frustration, but the difficulty has been to define what is meant by frustration. The common definition states that frustration is a situation in which a goal is to be reached and in which some barrier exists in front of the goal. Some experiments have been set up to copy such situations, as when children are shown a room full of toys but a glass wall prevents them from reaching the toys. Other experiments using this concept have used more symbolic barriers, as when a person is given a problem that looks easy to solve but that is actually insoluble. To enhance the frustration the person may be told that most third-graders solve the problem in five minutes. The barrier here is psychological rather than physical. Another version of this hypothesis is to conceive of frustration as a situation in which an expected reward does not occur or as one in which there is an unexpected punishment (see Cole and Jensen, 1972). An implausible suggestion is that the termination of a pleasurable stimulus produces frustration and hence aggression, which would lead one to expect a child to strike out on finishing a lollipop. The many attempts to redefine the characteristics of frustrating situations have brought little clarity to the hypothesis, but experiments have shown that children do generally, though not invariably, show forms of aggression when exposed to frustrating situations defined in one or another of these ways. Also, the aggression thus produced often amounts to no more than an increased vigor of response. The frustration-aggression hypothesis is a vague, but not entirely useless, generality.

The frustration-aggression hypothesis also leads to the suggestion that aggression can be conditioned to take place in the presence of certain stimuli. This leads to the idea that if a child is constantly thwarted and frustrated by adults in reaching goals, adults, in general, may come to elicit aggressive responses from him. The classical conditioning theory of aggression in this context is attractive, but experiments designed to find support for it have generally been sufficiently remote from real life to raise questions concerning their validity for explaining common forms of human aggression.

Most work on animal aggression leads to the conclusion that it has instrumental value in preserving the species in whom it has evolved. Under natural conditions it preserves rather than endangers the species. However, under abnormal conditions, such as are found in zoos and laboratories, animals that naturally may show little aggression toward their own kind, may manifest extraordinary cruelty. Under natural conditions animals limit their aggression to a few situations, and extensive learning and generalization does not take place to new situations.

HUMAN AGGRESSION—ORIGIN

Two million or more years ago there came into being a primitive creature, a hominid, who showed strikingly different characteristics from those of his tree-loving ancestors. Freeman (1966), an anthropologist, has discussed the characteristics of this new Australopithecene hominid in relation to the problem of the development of an aggressive primate species. He points out that this new primate lived on grassy plains and had become a carnivore. Although he had a small brain, about a third the size of the modern human brain, he had invented lethal weapons for use in preying on other living creatures, which he was poorly adapted for killing with his own hands and jaws. Unlike any other primate, he became a hunter. He was no longer the timid animal, although he could retreat to the tree tops when endangered. He was now the attacker. Man did not long remain merely content to kill and devour other species, for the evidence seems clear that Pithecanthropus man, who lived slightly later, devoured the brains of his fellows, for this seems to be the only explanation of the peculiar holes cut in the backs of so many of the skulls found. Cannibalism came quite early in human history and was probably a common form of behavior. But there was probably no organized warfare until much later—perhaps as late as the Neolithic period of only ten thousand years ago.

The early hominid was not an aggressive, attacking creature merely because he was carnivorous, for there are many carnivorous animals that kill only for food. Unlike other carnivorous animals he was a weapon maker, which gave him unlimited power over other living creatures. Perhaps because he was so dependent on killing for survival, and because he had the specialized tools for destroying other forms of life, he became nature's prime killer. The tools were his own creation, but the invention of the tools did not carry with them any inborn inhibitions about the tools of destruction being used only to satisfy nutritional needs. Other carnivorous animals have a built-in mechanism that limits the utilization of their killing power, but human beings do not.

Wars probably came into being after human beings had developed agriculture. Prior to that time, the nomadic roving groups would hardly have come into conflict with one another, but once agriculture had been developed it became possible for them to accumulate wealth. Those that had better soil, or who were more frugal in their habits, were able to accumulate and store some of the products of the soil. They were also able to pay for the services of others and to accumulate still more wealth. It then became a temptation for groups that had poor crops to raid those that had stored past harvests. There must also have been a temptation for groups having poor land to attempt to take by force the land that seemed to produce better harvests. In some tribes these early wars became ritualized, with conflict being engaged in every so many moons or at certain seasons; but such ritualized conflicts tended to be deadly, as the ritualized conflicts of other animals did not.

AGGRESSION IN CHILDHOOD: DEVELOPMENTAL ASPECTS

Although many psychologists have taken the position that the aggressiveness observed in the play of boys is a result of the reinforcement of such behavior by adults, the evidence on this point is far from clear. McGrew (1972) made a study of naturally occurring social interactions in 4-year-olds and classified such behavior as agonistic, quasiagonistic, and nonagonistic. The term agonistic means, generally, *struggling*, but in psychological literature the term has acquired the meaning of inflicting harm on another. Agonistic behavior of a 4-year-old toward another is behavior that inflicts harm on another; quasiagonistic behavior is rough-and-tumble behavior; nonagonistic behavior is a more subdued type of social interaction. McGrew found in a nursery school setting that girls interacted most frequently on a nonagonistic basis, but most of the interactions between boys were either agonistic or quasiagonistic. McGrew points out that the data on the children correspond quite closely to that collected on subhuman primates in natural settings. Infant males of both rhesus macaques and crab-eating macaques show much more rough-and-tumble behavior than do the females, and this is unlikely to be a result of parental encouragement. Primate parents are typically quite permissive in this respect but typically do not permit one of the young to hurt another. A cry of pain from one of the young brings instant intervention of an adult.

This kind of evidence suggests that there is an inherent boisterousness in the interaction of the young males in human beings and other primates and that this boisterousness is not a result of encouragement by the adult. Boisterousness may well turn to deliberate aggression when the young creature acquires a glimmering of understanding of the gains to be achieved by dominating another.

Hartup (1974) has also studied the developmental pattern of aggression. He suggests that children learn initially about the efficacy of aggressive action through tantrums, though there is no evidence that the adult's reaction to tantrums influences the course of development. Hartup's own study was of children aged 4 to 7 in an educational program. The older children showed fewer aggressive incidents per unit of time, but the aggression of these older children tended to be hostile rather than instrumental. A 4-year-old might push aside another child in order to take a toy from that child. In that case the aggressive act is instrumental in obtaining the toy. The 7-year-old is more likely to make a hostile remark to another child because he does not like that child. Among the younger children, derogation tends to produce the reaction of hitting, but the older child responds with derogation. Boys and girls did not differ with respect to instrumental aggression at any age, but the boys showed a higher incidence of hostile aggression at the upper age levels.

A point of considerable interest brought out by Perry and Perry (1974) is that children who engage in physical aggression expect their victims to manifest symptoms of pain. If the victims do not, the level of aggression is increased. Such studies of the development of aggression fail to bring out the conditions that result in a reduction or increase in aggressive behavior. The little that is known about this problem will be discussed in the next few pages.

Some Conditions Related to Aggressive Behavior

Aggression in modern society derives from many sources, some of which involve learning. Let us consider some of these sources.

1. *Chromosome Abnormalities.* In much of what has been said, the assumption has been made that the major sources of human aggression are learned. Human beings do not innately behave in such a way as to endanger the lives of members of their own species and there is no such unfortunate characteristic in their genetic constitution. Nevertheless, there is some evidence that impulsive violence in a small section of the population may be due to some inherent defect in their physiological structures.

There is evidence, for example, that departures from the normal gene structure, as when an individual may have an extra Y chromosome, may result in the development of an individual who is easily triggered to violence. Mark and Ervin (1970) and Jarvik *et al.* (1973) point out that only a small percentage of prison inmates involved in crimes of violence have such extra Y chromosomes. Mark and Ervin also point out that the mere presence of the extra chromosome or chromosomes cannot directly influence behavior. Presumably the presence of these bodies influences development in some way so as to produce structures that influence behavior. One possibility is that the chromosome may result in some abnormal balance of the hormones. Another is that it may result in abnormal development in the brain. There is also the puzzling fact that some individuals with extra Y chromosomes have been identified who have no record of violence.

2. *Brain Damage.* Another source of violent behavior is brain damage, which can be produced by many causes. One cause is oxygen deficiency at birth. The result of such damage may be hyperactivity, impulsive violence, and an aimless striking out

against people and objects. Although these defects may be produced by lack of oxygen at birth, similar effects may be produced in the newborn by infection, Rh factor incompatibility, and actual physical damage to the brain at birth. Some of these children are helped by drugs, but for those in whom the damage to the brain is very extensive the main source of help is surgery designed to destroy a part of the limbic system known as the amygdala. In such cases of brain damage, the difficulty seems to arise through an imbalance between the limbic system and the higher centers that ordinarily control limbic activity. Surgery attempts to restore this balance, presumably at a price, but the side effects of the surgical procedure are not known at this time.

Another source of violent behavior is temporal lobe epilepsy. The vast majority of epileptics do not show violent behavior and live normal lives, and this is true even of those who have temporal lobe seizures. Such individuals may run wild and such abnormalities of behavior may occur between seizures. Often the violent aspects of behavior slowly grow over a period of many years, and a person whose seizures are followed early in adult life by surliness and depression may slowly emerge into a person who becomes extremely dangerous after a seizure. Some control can be exercised by the use of drugs. Considerable success has been achieved in the control of this condition by means of surgery designed to restore balance between the limbic system and higher centers.

In most of the cases discussed by Mark and Ervin, behavior therapy had failed, suggesting that serious brain dysfunction cannot be handled by psychotherapy. Also, it may be noted that drugs seem to have limited capability of providing temporary relief of the condition.

3. *Emotional Characteristics of the Human Species.* Aggression appears to be related to a problem raised by Hebb and Thompson (1968), who suggest that primates are basically more emotional than simpler creatures in the evolutionary scale. Dogs may show sulking behavior and the baring of teeth and raising of hair when they are attacking or are attacked, but these are transitory states. In contrast, human beings may show prolonged anger, during which they may attack all kinds of objects, either living or inanimate. Nobody ever saw a dog bite a tree in anger, but it is common to see a man strike the top of a desk with his fist when some subordinate has transgressed. Anger behavior and other forms of extreme emotionality appear to be related to what we term aggressive acts. However, this is obviously not the only condition that triggers aggressive acts. Some of the most appalling acts of cruelty in history have been committed, in cold blood, by men who showed no observable signs of emotion.

4. *Modeling.* Studies of modeling aggressive behavior have used numerous different situations. Preference has been to show the behavior to be modeled on film, for the identical behavior can then be shown to different children at different times, and considerable evidence is available to support the contention that film performance and live performance have almost identical results on the observer children. In some studies of aggression, the model is shown as handling roughly, or even

hitting, a doll. In other studies one adult is shown taking over the possessions of another adult either forcibly or accompanied by aggressive verbal behavior. Sometimes the models manifest very mild aggressive behavior, as when they rebuke or insult another person for no good reason. There is almost no limit to the variation in the aggressive behavior that has been used in studies of the effect of models on behavior. In addition, studies vary enormously in what happens after the model behaves aggressively. The model may be punished or rewarded. The model may reprimand himself or show that he is pleased with what he has done. The situations in which the observer may be placed following his observation of the model are many and diverse. An observer who has seen a doll abused, may be given an identical doll and the experimenter may record how he behaves toward it. On the other hand, the child who watches the model behave aggressively toward the doll may be observed in a situation in which his interactions with another child become the focus of interest.

The early research on the effect of observing an aggressive model on subsequent aggressive behavior was summarized by Bandura and Walters (1963), who were largely responsible for the development of research in the area. Later reviews of research are provided by Bandura (1969) and also Aronfreed (1968), as well as several articles, notably that of Hartup and Coates (1967). The results are difficult to interpret. The observation of a model that is either rewarded for showing aggressive behavior or not rewarded produces more aggressive behavior in an observer than does the observation of a model punished for manifesting such behavior. The important point to note is that aggressive behavior tends to be imitated whether it is or is not rewarded. On the other hand, the observation of an aggressor who is punished has a definite inhibiting effect on aggressive behavior. In some studies the rewarding of a model seems to play a crucial role, but sometimes imitation seems to have little to do with whether the model's behavior is or is not rewarded (provided it is not punished). Aronfreed (p. 135) suggests that the difference among these studies may lie in whether the act of aggression is or is not one that the observer enjoys performing. If a child enjoys hitting a rag doll with a stick, this behavior can be easily initiated by observing a model, and whether the model is or is not rewarded is inconsequential. On the other hand, if a child does not really like taking things away from other children, this behavior is not triggered easily by observing another perform it; but if the model is highly rewarded for such a transgression of custom, the reward provided can make the activity attractive to perform.

In the context of a social situation, the effects of a model on behavior are enormously complicated by many factors. It may make a difference, for example, whether the model is liked or rejected by the observer. A related factor that has been extensively studied is whether the model has been previously involved in the distribution of rewards to the observer (see Hartup and Coates, 1967). The weight of the evidence shows that models that have been identified as the source of reinforcements generally evoke more imitative behavior than those that are not so identified. Caution must be exercised in the interpretation of the latter finding because other sources of data show that if the relationship of the model to the observer has been one of punishment, more imitation is also to be expected. The crucial factor would appear to be not reinforcement as such, but the fact that the model was capable of attracting the attention of the observer through having been either rewarded or punished.

Although the results reported here are both dramatic and interesting, there are certain differences between the laboratory situations and situations that occur in daily life. For this reason, one should exercise some caution in generalizing from the laboratory to events in the real world. Laboratory situations are typically brief and often the behavior of the model may involve only a few seconds of action followed by a few words of praise or criticism representing reward or punishment. Life situations that are commonly believed to provide models of influence may present sequences of action lasting for hours, as they do in full-length movies, and the reinforcement for the actions observed in the movies may involve a brief terminal event such as winning a bride or exoneration for wrong-doing. Rosenkrans (1967) used a film showing how to play a particular game. Although the length of the film is not specified in the paper, the indications are that it lasted several minutes. Under such conditions the rewarding or the punishment of the model presented in the movie made relatively little difference in the amount of imitation. The latter situation is an artificial one only remotely related to events in real life such as those of seeing a full length movie or a 1-hour television thriller which produces very unexpected audience responses. Perhaps the child who watches the lengthy transgressions of the crook, sees him eventually give himself up and confess and then sees him shot by a trigger-happy sheriff, is likely to learn only that *confession* results in punishment.

A superficial view of the studies of the effect of the behavior of a model on the behavior of an observer child might take the line that these studies demonstrate that aggression may be learned by example. However, the meaning of the studies is much less clear, as is shown in an excellent analysis of them by Aronfreed (1969), who points out that most studies of modeling behavior do not demonstrate learning at all. Consider the case of a child who views a movie of an adult hitting an inflated plastic doll and who shortly thereafter spends time himself hitting a similar doll. Did the model induce the observer to perform a new form of behavior? Almost certainly not! The child probably had already indulged in a similar behavior on previous occasions, and the effect of the model was to release this behavior. Nothing new was probably learned. Most studies of modeling behavior have not included an attempt to determine the extent to which the behavior manifested by the model is already a part of the repertoire of the observer, so the extent to which learning of aggressive behavior occurred is not known. Aronfreed also points out that in most studies involving the modeling of aggressive behavior, the observer children show little precise imitation of the model and very often there is a very general display of aggression toward a wide array of objects. The data suggest that exposure to the model results in the release of a general aggressive tendency.

The failure of children to reproduce with any precision the behavior of a model is not necessarily accounted for in terms of a lack of incentive to do so. Some light is thrown on this matter by the finding that the verbal behavior of the model is more likely to be imitated than the gross actions in which the model is engaged. The general activity of the model may be observed but, because the behavior is not readily coded into words, perhaps cannot be easily retained. The verbal behavior of the model, on the other hand, is readily retained, for the memory system seems highly capable of retaining large quantities of verbal information at a high level of precision. The imitation of action may be limited because the memory system of the observer does not permit him to retain the information needed for precise reproduction of the activity.

Knowledge derived from the study of modeling suggests not only that society should refrain from exposing children to models that show aggressive behavior, and particularly aggressive behavior that is rewarded; it also suggests that the teaching of history should avoid stressing reinforced aggressive models. Because most nations teach their children that the wars in which their nation has engaged were just wars and that the leaders of those wars were good leaders, history is to some extent taught as a sequence of aggressive, reinforced models. History will have to be interpreted differently if it is to function in some way other than as a releaser of aggressive behavior. Education will also have to work systematically on the problem of developing in children mechanisms that will actively inhibit aggressive behavior. Deep convictions that such behavior is wrong will have to be developed. Another approach, which needs further study, is that of converting human-against-human aggression into ritualized forms, much as animals have done. The Olympic Games represent one step in that direction.

A word must be said about the possibility of controlling aggression through punishment, that is, controlling aggression through aggression. The effect of punishment on a response, under these conditions, is somewhat different from the effect of punishment in most simple laboratory situations. Parke (1970) has conducted studies in this area and comes to the conclusion that punishment may increase the response that it has been introduced to block. Punishment designed to reduce aggressive behavior, in fact, may actually increase it.

The relationship of modeling to subsequent aggressive behavior is complicated by the fact that the effect of a model on a child depends on the aggressiveness of the child. Singer (1971) points out that aggressive children probably do not become more aggressive after viewing a model, but the unaggressive child does. One can, of course, argue that the unaggressive child may be helped by learning to show more positive behavior in a society that demands it for success.

A few studies of modeling have supported what is called the catharsis hypothesis, which is that aggressive tendencies in the individual can be dissipated by viewing an aggressive performance. Both Singer (1971) and Johnson (1973) have reviewed these studies in detail and find they are not strong enough to support the idea that aggression can be eliminated by exercising it against a harmless object. The mass of the evidence points in the opposite direction. Of course, there may be occasions on which the viewing of aggression on the part of another may become a substitute for the individual's own aggression, but the general trend of the evidence is that models release rather than reduce aggressive behavior (see Konečni, 1975).

Finally, it must be pointed out that most of the research has had to do with very limited exposures to aggressive behavior, and the effect of aggression has been studied mainly through a play situation. The nature of play is such that it encourages the pursuit of fantasies derived from other sources. Singer (1971) points out that although the viewing of a model may increase the amount of aggression toward a toy, it may not increase it toward a real person. The conclusions that can be drawn from such studies is extremely limited.

5. *Exposure to Media.* Political debate has long been pursued on the issue of the effect of television on the amount of violence expressed in our society. Many people take the position that the viewing of violence on television particularly enhances the amount of violence manifested by individuals in our society. The assumption is also made that this enhancement effect is particularly marked in the young. The evidence previously cited in relation to modeling is commonly voiced as support for this position, but modeling is commonly assumed to be only one part of the problem. The claim is also made that the media teach young people techniques through which violence may be committed.

It must be quite evident that children cannot be protected indefinitely from learning that they are growing up in a violent society. Hiding the nature of society from them cannot achieve any useful objective, for their ultimate discovery might have serious emotional consequences. Children cannot be protected from seeing the nature of human violence, both past and present, for to do this one would have to withhold from them most of history, including such documents as the Bible, which includes a vast amount of violence. Also, children soon learn that much of the entertainment that adults enjoy involves the theme of death by violence. Children recognize early that many of the great dramas of life involve death and killing for base motives. The issue is how to introduce children to violence without having them accept it as inevitable and how to make them recognize it and yet, in a sense, keep apart from it. Murray (1973) takes the position that television violence does not mirror societal violence but presents a stereotyped television version. The area is filled with controversy. The only aspect in which there is agreement is that televised violence may influence some children, at least in the way they play after being exposed to such programs. The report by Liebert, Neale, and Davidson (1973) takes a rather more positive stand after reviewing a number of studies, many of which are very much open to criticism. In the experimental studies the effect of exposure was typically measured in a play situation immediately after the exposure. Studies that related the amount of viewing performance to the aggressive behavior of children in school situations do not take into account the fact that it is the more aggressive children who choose to watch television violence. With this kind of self-selection the correlation between viewing and behaving is not surprising. This lack of solid data makes such people as Singer (1971) and Feshbach and Singer (1971) skeptical about the conclusions that can be drawn concerning the effect of the media on violence in our society.

On the other hand, other reviewers, such as Murray (1974), come out quite strongly with the conclusion that viewing television *causes* children to become more aggressive. Murray was impressed with the fact that children exposed to segments from "The Untouchables" were more willing to hurt other children than those exposed to blander programs. Murray also brings out the important point that research has also shown that viewing violence on television sensitizes children to seeing violence in their surroundings and also increases their acceptance of violence as a means of resolving conflicts.

None of the data are helpful in solving the problem of how to introduce children to the fact that human society is violent. One type of observation does suggest how this needs to be done. Young children typically watch television programs by themselves. When they do this they are free to draw their own conclusions, which may be far different from those that the adult who developed the program had in mind or what an adult viewer would derive from the program. Children probably need to watch programs involving violence with an adult who can interpret the values involved and who can be on guard lest the child simply concludes that violence pays. Buss (1971), for example, points out that children who are really up on the news might well conclude that violence pays. The heads of organized crime live in comfort, and mass killers in time of war, such as Sergeant York, are made into national heroes. History also tells children that aggressive acts such as the seizure of land from Mexico in the last century had magnificent payoffs. These examples make the effect of television seem quite pale in contrast.

6. *The Effect of Hormones.* Biologists have long speculated that an important factor in the development of aggressive behavior is the amount of the male sex hormone, testosterone, that is present. The theory is that boys are more aggressive than girls because of the effect of the male hormone. An alternative explanation is that boys are raised to be rough whereas girls are trained to be demure. Slowly evidence is beginning to throw some light on this problem, though as the problem is studied it is seen as much more complex than it was first thought to be. Rose (1974) has summarized some of the evidence, which suggests a relationship between aggressive behavior and the action of the hormone. There is even one study, which needs to be replicated, showing that an excess of testosterone during the fetal life of girls resulted in an increased amount of tomboy behavior in later years. Firm conclusions in this area will have to wait further research.

MORAL DEVELOPMENT

Two main lines of thought have guided research on moral development over the last few decades. One of these places strong emphasis on factors related to socialization and has been quite characteristic of the approach taken by sociologists, social psychologists, anthropologists, and to some extent clinical psychologists. The second of these approaches derives from the work of those interested primarily in child development and owes its impetus to the work of Piaget.

Work on the first of these two approaches has been summarized by Hogan (1973). He points out that the traditional approaches assume that all social behavior occurs within a rule system and that social behavior is basically a rule-regulated system of behavior. Second, it assumes that human rule systems have associated with them ethical standards of fairness, or of what is right. Third, although individual behavior is accounted for in terms of the application of the rule systems, individual differences are a result of differences in the way in which rule systems are applied. Presumably, rule systems have evolved as a result of biological pressures. For example, the ethic of sharing may well have arisen in the family group in relation to the distribution of food because when one member killed game he had more food on his hands than he could use. Distributing food among family members would contribute to the survival of the entire group. All of this is very speculative, but not unreasonable. Morality, at least at the lower levels, involves a set of rules that define the reciprocal rights of individuals toward each other in a group. Sometimes these reciprocal rights may have an innate basis as when, in some species, the territorial rights of one animal are respected by other animals of the same species, but not necessarily by animals of other species. Hogan takes the position that the acquisition of moral behavior is dependent on the following five conditions:

Moral Knowledge. Common sense takes the position that moral behavior cannot occur unless the individual has acquired knowledge about the moral rules of the community in which he lives. Psychologists have generally taken the position that moral knowledge is acquired through learning. Most religious institutions take the position that the acquisition of moral knowledge is necessary for living a good life and, hence, have taken steps to institutionalize the acquisition of such moral knowledge. However, although such a position has a commonsensical approach, many great thinkers have had doubts concerning its validity. Great philosophers, including Kant and Bergson, have questioned the validity of the notion and have proposed an inherent moral principle in life itself. The latter does not exclude the possibility that the moral principle has evolved. Experimental research has also provided little support for the idea that moral knowledge is an important foundation of moral behavior. The studies reviewed by Hogan show virtually no relationship between what children know about right and wrong and how they act.

Socialization. Although many psychologists have taken the position that human beings are innately antisocial and have to be trained to meet the demands of society, the evidence today generally indicates that human beings, like all other primates, belong to a highly social species. Certainly primates are harmed intellectually when they are raised in an environment devoid of appropriate social contacts. The problem is not so much how to socialize the child as how to prevent him from becoming antagonized toward society. The natural, warm, nurturant relationships to parents seem to be desirable, but these should be coupled with consistent and reasonable systems of control. The process of socialization, as it is considered here, seems to be completed by the time the child enters school and leaves the child with a tendency to conform rigidly to convention and to the rules established by authority. There is some correlation between socialization and moral development. For example, delinquents show, on the average, lower levels of social development than nondelinquents. Nevertheless, many delinquents may show adequate socialization.

Empathy. Much moral behavior depends on the ability to see things from the other person's point of view. Hogan refers to some of his own research, in which he developed devices for measuring the ability of the individual to empathize with another, and was able to show that the scores were related to delinquency, and in the expected direction. However, empathy is a complex phenomenon. It has long been thought that empathy requires taking the other person's role, and to do that requires effective intellectual functioning. A person may not be able to empathize with another because the intellectual task is beyond his ability. The over-indulged child may never have the need to assume the role of the other and thus may not learn empathy, even though capable of doing so.

Autonomy. The dimensions discussed to this point do not explain much except a tendency to follow rules rigidly. They do not cover the individual who insists on behaving ethically because it would be beneath his dignity to behave otherwise. Various attempts have been made to measure the degree to which individuals can be considered to be autonomous in their behavior. These measures generally indicate that the so-called autonomous individual is a strong and forceful character, and gives a good impression of himself; little is known about the relation of this variable to moral behavior. Autonomy is introduced into the system to help account for the fact that the highly developed moral character is not rigidly rule-bound but can formulate its own rules and ethical principles.

Moral Judgment Factor. The moral judgment factor is the most obscure of Hogan's five factors. He implies that there is an ethic of conscience and of responsibility, the source of which is as yet not explained. Individuals who have this characteristic in a high degree are said to be "thoughtful." They do the ethical thing because they understand that it will result in a better world, not because they want to help some other individual or because it involves some rule learned during the period of socialization.

Hogan has attempted to bring together many sources of information about this problem, but the assembly of his ideas represents a quite traditional approach. He has some interesting conclusions about the nature of moral behavior, but they are not likely to be given the attention they deserve because at the present time interest is in stage theory. Hogan gives virtually no recognition to research that contributes to the development of a stage theory of morality.

Stage theory of morality originated in the work of Piaget in the early 1930s. Piaget had been exposed to the philosophical work of Immanuel Kant during his high school days and had been impressed with Kant's work as a basis for understanding human behavior. Kant postulated an inherent moral factor in human behavior and Piaget set out to study the nature of this factor. Through his research he came to the conclusion that moral development showed a series of well-defined stages. In the preschool years Piaget found that the child's morality could be described as a one-way relationship to authority. Respect for the adult was the basic source of moral obligation. The obligations to tell the truth and to refrain from stealing come from the adult to the child; they are adult commands that the child accepts. This led Piaget to take his famous stance that the child understands an act is right because it is sanctioned by the adult or wrong because it is a consequence of his own will. Within the framework of this morality there is no place for an act being inherently good or inherently bad. It is good or bad only in terms of who sanctions it.

In the second stage of moral development Piaget sees the child developing broad rules of right and wrong that can be generalized to new situations. The rules are no longer just a part of external authority, but are within the child himself. They may be applied with extreme rigidity by the child, as is evident from the rigid and definite pronouncements made by the 6-year-old concerning what is right and what is wrong.

In the third stage, autonomy proper is achieved by the child in the making of moral judgments. The achievement of this autonomy takes place through the child learning to understand cooperative relationships. Piaget held that reciprocity of social relationships was the foundation for moral autonomy that requires mutual respect, which calls for the individual to treat others as he would like to be treated. Thus moral development moves from authoritarian relationships to cooperative relationships.

Although Piaget's work on moral development was undertaken in the late 1920s, little was done to develop it further until after midcentury. The significance of Piaget's work was finally recognized by a doctoral student, Lawrence Kohlberg, who attempted to develop it further in a doctoral dissertation (1958). Kohlberg follows closely the Piagetian position that development occurs in stages and that developments at one stage are a necessary foundation for moving to the next stage. Within the framework of such a theory, there can be no skipping of stages. Kohlberg's basic work has been reprinted in many sources, and a convenient source for those in education is Kohlberg and Turiel (1971), which also summarizes much of the more recent work in the field.

Kohlberg postulates a premoral stage of development, which presumably includes the early months of life. These are followed by three broad stages of moral development referred to as the preconventional, the conventional, and the postconventional. Each of these is further divided into two substages. Let us consider them separately.

At the first part of the preconventional stage, the infant is punishment-oriented. There is deference to the power of the adult. Behavior does not involve moral concepts but is practically oriented toward the avoidance of punishment. There is no respect for authority, as such, merely deference to it. Performance is not very different from that of a puppy that learns there are certain things it can do without being punished and certain things it cannot do.

In the second part of the preconventional stage, right action is interpreted as meaning that which satisfies one's own needs, though sometimes it may also satisfy the needs of others. There is a beginning of reciprocity as the basis for action and the notion, "You do something for me and I will do something for you." This is a strictly practical matter, and not a matter of responsibility of one individual toward another. The second part of the preconventional stage involves a move from deference to authority, as described by Piaget, to a relationship of cooperation with others. Piaget views the latter as occurring at a more advanced stage than does Kohlberg. Studies of the development of cooperative behavior are surprisingly lacking (see Cook and Stingle, 1974).

The conventional stage involves the acceptance of the values of the group. In the first part of the conventional stage, the child, generally of elementary-school age or in the early teens, accepts the peer group standards as those to be followed. At this stage a child conforms to the morality of the peer group, which may often be in contrast to the morality of the adult world. The concept of intention becomes introduced into morality at this stage and a child begins to take the position that inappropriate behavior can be considered moral because the individual means well.

In the second part of the conventional stage the basis of morality is expanded from the peer group to the broader community. This is the stage of rigid loyalty to authority represented by the community, state, or nation. An act is right because it is in conformity with the laws. The person has a moral obligation to do his duty in a very traditional sense. This stage of morality is the law-and-order stage, which often leads to the position that national policy should be supported regardless of whether it is right or wrong. This is the stage achieved by most individuals in our society and leads to the rigid enforcement of rules and the suppression of individualism in the exercise of moral judgment.

The postconventional stage involves the development of stages of morality higher than those ordinarily achieved. As with the preconventional and the conventional stages, this stage is also divided into two substages. The first is referred to as the social-contract legalistic orientation. The previous stage involves a morality based on quite specific rules such as those of avoiding direct theft, saluting the flag, and exchanging socially sanctioned courtesies. In this stage the rules of morality are at a more general level and involve the notion of individual rights. Right and wrong have to be judged in terms of general principles. There is some recognition that individuals differ in their values and have a right to differ, but there is also recognition that there has to be an orderly way of reaching consensus on what society is going to permit. Honorable relationships between people is the essence of morality at this stage, and this is the morality sanctioned by the Constitution.

In the second stage of the postconventional level, achieved by only a few, right and wrong are defined by decisions of conscience. Conscience is guided by abstract ethical principles that are believed to have universality and that form a logically consistent system. These universal principles of justice imply the equality of rights of all individuals and the dignity of the person. Perhaps some of those who framed the Constitution would be considered to represent this level of morality.

The concept of a stage, and the process through which a child moves his thinking from one stage to a higher stage, is essentially the same as that described by Piaget. In order to produce moral development, according to this theory, a determination must first be made of the stage at which the individual is operating. Once this has been done, problems are presented that arouse moral conflict and uncertainty, and the child is urged to seek new and alternative solutions. This procedure is to be contrasted with that found in traditional moral training, in which the child is told the solution at the higher level and rewarded for applying that type of solution and perhaps even punished for applying lower level solutions. Kohlberg and Turiel's summary of evidence (1971) indicates that the procedure for producing moral development based on stage theory seems to be considerably more effective than that of traditional procedures. It also seems to be superior to that based on operant conditioning procedures. They point out that the stage theory procedures for producing moral development have implications for the teaching of social studies where much of the material has important moral implications.

Kohlberg and Turiel take the position that moral values represent a legitimate field of education in the public schools. They point out that the study of the Constitution cannot be undertaken without considering moral issues because the Constitution has implicit in it a code of morality. Teachers often try to avoid moral issues in relation to their teaching but moral issues are inescapable. Even the organization of the classroom involves a code of morality that generally implies a respect for the rights of others and sometimes the assumption of the basic dignity of each individual. Of course, it is not hard to find classrooms, and even entire school systems, in which such values are sorely neglected.

Kohlberg and Turiel summarize evidence that children pass through similar stages of moral development regardless of the culture in which they are raised, but most individuals never achieve the highest levels of moral development. In American society, the typical stage of moral development achieved by the adult is the higher level of the conventional stage. This is often described as the hard-hat morality, or the law-and-order stage, with its emphasis on blind obedience to authority and to the letter of the law. In some simple communities, in which there is little education, moral development may not reach much beyond the preconventional stage. Although moral development may be arrested at different levels in different cultures and different communities, the order in which the stages appear is invariant.

In addition, the same stages appear in the development of children raised in different religions. Moral beliefs have far more to do with stage of development than with religious affiliation.

The attainment of higher stages is dependent on the individual being stimulated in a way that will raise doubts in his mind about the wisdom and worth of traditional solutions to moral problems.

Although Kohlberg's contribution to research on morality has stimulated considerable quantities of research, his position on the matter remains controversial. Two of his harsher critics, Kurtines and Grief (1974), have reviewed the evidence for the existence of stages of morality and for the validity of Kohlberg's measuring technique and have come to the conclusion that moral development probably does not have to follow the rigid course that Kohlberg implies. They also find the evidence for the validity of the moral behavior scale very weak. This writer prefers to take the position that at the lower levels of the moral scale there is evidence that development follows a single and rigid order. At the higher levels this may also be true, but too little work has been undertaken to come to any firm conclusions.

This writer also finds some of the evidence quite persuasive that the scale of morality has validity. At least nondelinquents score higher than delinquents, and activists on the campus score higher than nonactivists, on the average.

Altruistic and Helping Behavior

An aspect of behavior of great significance related to moral development and conduct is that referred to as altruistic or helping behavior. Although this area has long been of interest to psychologists, research on problems related to it has suddenly mushroomed during the last decade, perhaps because of the wide recognition for developing a society in which such behaviors are more common. The reviews of research by Bryan and London (1970) and Krebs (1970) together list several hundred references. In addition, a symposium on the subject, edited by Macaulay and Berkowitz (1970), presents many interesting lines along which research is developing. Rubin and Schneider (1973) have also reviewed research in the area.

Altruistic behavior has been difficult to define, but recent attempts to define it have begun to sharpen the concept. The person who behaves altruistically performs in a way that has high cost to him and *apparently* low immediate payoff. The word *apparently* is used advisedly because there are payoffs to altruistic acts that are not all evident to observers. A person who gives away a fortune may later confide to another that he felt good about the act of giving. The statement suggests that his act of generosity resulted in some kind of internal payoff. Philosophers have long been interested in internal payoffs labeled by such words as pleasure, happiness, and satisfaction, and a school of philosophers, the hedonists, have argued that these payoffs determine much, if not all, of human behavior. The role of such internal payoffs has been difficult to study. Aronfreed (1969) has argued that young children are first reinforced by adults telling them that they are good, or kind, or in some way virtuous, and that children learn to make these same utterances to themselves and, in this way, provide events that have reinforcing properties. The latter position is really no stronger than that of the philosophers, for it is based mainly on speculation.

Because the identification of the payoff of altruistic or helping behavior has so far been a quite fruitless pursuit, research workers have become more concerned with the conditions in the social milieu that lead to altruistic or helping behavior. Bryan and London present evidence to show that altruistic behavior is most likely to be observed in children who come from homes where such behavior is common. Altruistic behavior is least likely to be seen in children who come from homes where a competitive spirit is encouraged, as it is among some of the well-to-do, or from homes where poverty virtually excludes generosity. A family that stresses status needs also provides a poor environment for the development of generosity. The learning of this behavior in the home appears to occur in the first decade of life, for altruistic behavior reaches its peak toward the end of that decade. Krebs (1970) adds to this conclusion by saying that research also demonstrates that people give to those who are similar to themselves, and also to those whom they consider prestigious or from whom they stand to gain.

The phenomenon of altruistic behavior is obviously extremely complex, as both the Krebs and the Bryan and London reviews bring out. One factor that complicates research on the problem is that altruistic behavior or helping behavior is elicited much more in some situations than in others. Dependency is an important condition eliciting such behavior, especially in females. Males often feel threatened when another person becomes highly dependent on them, and the threat tends to suppress altruistic behavior that might otherwise occur. After reviewing such facts, Krebs points out that although a person may appear to act altruistically, he may not be genuinely altruistic by nature, that is, he may not be acting out of genuine concern for the other person.

This area of knowledge, like all rapidly developing areas, yields endless interesting facts that do not fit together very well. For this reason let us cite here just a few of such facts provided by the Macaulay and Berkowitz symposium (1970). The symposium has an interesting paper on why bystanders in crowds do not intervene and offer helping behavior in emergencies. The suggestion is that each bystander looks at the other bystanders and tends to interpret lack of action as lack of feeling. The person who interprets the behavior of others as not indicating real feeling for the emergency is likely to respond by suppressing his own feelings and doing nothing. The bystander's interpretation of the lack of feeling on the part of others is probably wrong, but it leads to inactivity. Another series of studies reported in the symposium provide evidence that merely observing the behavior of a model engaged in altruistic behavior does not necessarily produce altruism, for the consequences of altruism are important, including the extent to which the altruistic person seems to experience pleasure from the act. Mere talk on the part of a model about being generous has little effect on the behavior of children who are listening. The actions of models are of far greater influence than anything the models may say. A special case of altruistic behavior is found in those who give body organs, such as one of their kidneys, to help another. In such a case of altruism, the act itself may have dramatic effects on the future behavior of the donor. Significant acts of self-sacrifice may be landmarks in life that lead to periods of great change. The early findings from research on altruistic behavior are so fascinating that they are likely to attract able research workers to make further explorations, and the time may not be distant when the environment of the child can be planned to produce a more altruistic generation. Not enough is known as yet to be able to do this with any confidence.

Rubin and Schneider (1973) have reviewed an extensive body of knowledge showing that helping and sharing behavior increases, at least until age 10. Rubin and Schneider accept Piaget's explanation, namely, that the younger children are highly egocentric and unable to understand a reciprocal relationship. An understanding of the viewpoint of another requires a cognitive development that younger children do not have. Rubin and Schneider in their own research found a relationship between the amount of helping behavior shown and a measure that they called communicative egocentrism presumed to be related to Piaget's concept of egocentrism. However, one cannot really conclude from the study that a decline of egocentrism produces an increase in helping behavior, for there is the possibility that the two functions may develop along parallel paths, and that the one may not cause the other.

Many educators have long commented on the competitive atmosphere of American education. One of the more recent essays on this theme is that of Clevenger (1973), who points out that schools systematically teach competitiveness rather than cooperativeness or helping behavior. Clevenger claims that before such teaching occurs children do not respond positively to situations in which rewards are tied to competitiveness. Our schools, like the schools of all other countries, reflect the values of the culture, and in our culture competitiveness is considered a virtue. In the schools in the Israeli kibbutzim competitiveness plays no role, except in athletics in which some degree of competitiveness is acceptable. The children in the kibbutzim, according to Rabin's excellent study (1965), grow up to fit into a highly cooperative society. However, the lack of competition among the adults seems to produce a society in which there is little striving for achievement and a highly static structure.

The Soviet educational system combines cooperativeness and competitiveness in an interesting way, though little is known about the effect of this system on the drive and initiative of the adult who emerges from it. Children are encouraged to excel, in that such excellence contributes to the classroom collective or the component of that collective of which the child is a part. The child is not praised for his outstanding performance, but the group to which he belongs is. A competitive element is introduced through the introduction of nation-wide examinations, used for selecting children for the higher levels of education. Clevenger points out that although these examinations are an inconsistency in their system, the Russians do not see them in such a light.

The British Infant School is also often cited as an institution in which competition is reduced to a minimum. The quality of the human relationships in the classroom is considered to be of the greatest importance.

Clevenger (1973) cites some research to suggest that competition may not always have deleterious effects, but that it seems to serve a useful function only when the children are equally matched and the rewards are equally distributed. Athletic coaches have long recognized the value of applying such principles in training for athletic events. In such training the athletes compete against others of equal talent, knowing that they have a chance to win. Unequally matched athletes are not paired in competition.

How cooperative behavior is learned is far from clear, although extensive research has been done on this topic. Cook and Stingle (1974), who have reviewed the research, do not come out with a clear answer. They point out that on the surface operant research seems to suggest that one only has to reinforce cooperative behavior in order to produce cooperative individuals. However, they also point out that despite the fact that the reinforcement of cooperative behavior produces an increase in its incidence, there is an accompanying increase in noncooperative behavior. What is reinforced is highly specific and does not generalize. Also, in the area of the use of models for increasing the incidence of cooperative behavior, they found that a model rewarded for cooperative behavior did not produce greater effect than a model that was not rewarded. The development of cooperative behavior is much more complex than can be accounted for in simple operant terms.

In order to increase the incidence of cooperative behavior, the classroom has to be restructured from the way in which it is commonly organized in American schools. One suggestion is to use games in which teams can compete against each other. DeVries and Edwards (1973), for example, used the learning game Equations and found that it increased the amount that students helped one another. They also found, as others have found, that a cooperative enterprise increases the student's liking for the subject matter. Wheeler and Ryan (1973) found the same effects with a social studies curriculum.

SOME RESEARCH ON CONTROL AND LEADERSHIP WITH IMPLICATIONS FOR TEACHING

A central issue in the conflict among the advocates of different teaching methods is the matter of the leadership pattern considered to be most effective in promoting learning. Some laboratory research has been undertaken in this area and includes a study that has probably had more widespread influence on educational thought than any other experimental study ever undertaken. For this reason, it has to be mentioned in a chapter on social factors in learning, even though it leaves much to be desired by modern research standards. The reference here is to the study by Lewin, Lippitt, and White (1939), entitled "Patterns of Aggressive Behavior in Experimentally Created 'Social Climates.'" As the title indicates, the focus of the study was not on leadership in relation to learning, but leadership in relation to the incidence of aggressive behavior; the implications drawn are generally related to learning.

In the study of Lewin, Lippitt, and White, boys of 10 and 11 were assigned to three types of groups, each type having a characteristic leadership that distinguished it from the other types. The three leadership patterns were (1) an authoritarian leader who directed the group in what to do, (2) a democratic leader who encouraged group-decision processes and who functioned as a member of the group, and (3) laissez-faire leadership that left the children to their own devices. The activities involved were those that would be considered hobbies: the building of model boats and planes, painting, and other manual arts and crafts. The incidence of aggressive behavior showed marked differences in relation to the three types of leadership involved. Laissez-faire leadership was accompanied by the highest incidence of aggressive behavior, and somewhat lower was the democratically led group. The groups with the authoritarian leaders showed either a very high incidence of aggressive behavior or a very low one. Although these results are of interest in connection with problems of discipline, so many of which are problems of aggression, they do not throw any direct light on problems of learning except insofar as aggressive behavior may interfere with learning. However the research workers involved in this study also collected some additional data concerning the amount of time spent in work under the three leadership situations, and these results have more direct bearing on the problem of learning. Output of work was related to type of leadership. As long as the authoritarian leader was present, there tended to be a high output of work; but the output declined rapidly when this type of leader left the room. In the groups exposed to democratic leadership, there was less output in the presence of the democratic leader, but the output of work continued in the absence of the leader. Under laissez-faire leadership, the presence of the leader seemed to be a disadvantage to the work of the group.

The results of this study have been widely applied to the planning of leadership roles for teachers, but many psychologists doubt whether such application is justified. Rarely are the results of a single psychological experiment so sound and so secure that one can be certain they would be reproduced in other experiments. As far as this writer can determine, there has been no real attempt in America to replicate the experiment, a step that should be taken before any extensive applications of the results are made. Similar experiments have been conducted by Japanese psychologists working with Japanese children. White and Lippitt (1960) report two studies conducted by Misumi and his colleagues and cite the following conclusions:

> The group morale was higher in the democratic groups than in the other two. They frequently exchanged friendly remarks and showed more concern and satisfaction with the work and more willingness to continue it....As to the quantity of work, the democratic groups obtained the highest rating; the autocratic groups the next, and the laissez-faire groups last. As to the quality, the autocratic groups did the best work, the democratic groups were next, and the laissez-faire groups last.

In a second experiment by Misumi and his colleagues (see White and Lippitt, (1960) some complicating results were found. On the more interesting of two tasks, the work done in the democratic group was superior; in the less interesting task, the autocratic groups performed best.

Anyone tempted to apply the results of the studies of Lippitt, White, Lewin, and others to a classroom situation should also read a study by Guetzkow et al. (1954) that virtually tried to apply the findings at the college level. The latter investigators were in charge of a seminar for graduate teaching assistants, the members of which decided to study the effects of different teaching methods in a course in general psychology. The teaching methods involved (a) a *recitation-drill* method, which was run on strictly authoritarian lines, with the instructor each day giving a short lecture and asking the class prepared questions; (b) a *group-discussion* method, in which interactions with the instructor at meetings of the class were initiated largely by the students themselves and where the instructor played the role of chairman of the session; and (c) a *tutorial-study* method, in which the instructor was available for helping the students find answers to the questions that came up in their independent study. These methods were selected because they represent different degrees of self-directed versus teacher-directed work, and because they also permitted a contrast between an emphasis on group work and an emphasis on individual work. The learning of the students was evaluated on the basis of a number of tests and other devices at the end of the course. The performance of the three groups in terms of measures in the course was strikingly similar; the only significant differences were on those measures on which the recitation-drill group did best—namely, the final examination and the choice to go on and take more work in psychology. In terms of the usual measures of academic success, the classes run along authoritarian lines appeared to be the most successful.

Some of the data more recently published about the original experiment by Lewin, Lippitt and White suggest that the autocratic leadership may have been so contaminated by an unpleasant social atmosphere that the results produced were quite inevitable. White and Lippitt (1960) state that the autocratic leaders gave disrupting commands in 11 per cent of their verbal behavior; that of the democratic leader was only 1 per cent. Twenty-four per cent of the verbal behavior of the democratic leaders represented guiding suggestions; but only 6 per cent of that of the autocratic leaders did. Little praise was given in any of the leader roles; but the autocratic leaders devoted 5 per cent of their remarks to praise and the democratic leaders 2 per cent, a slight margin in favor of the practices of the autocratic leaders. The general trend of the evidence indicates to this writer that autocratic leadership was accompanied by certain irrelevant and unpleasant elements that may have seriously stacked the deck. An experimenter who had read Machiavelli's *The Prince* might have designed a style of autocratic leadership that produced quite different outcomes. This writer is not arguing in favor of autocratic leadership in education; he is merely curious about the relationships that really exist between leadership and the performance of those led.

One is tempted to speculate at this point that the main difference between judicious autocratic leadership and judicious democratic leadership in a classroom may not be found in the quality or the quantity of learning produced, but in other factors. Learning under democratic conditions may be more pleasant. In addition, democratic practices may encourage decision making and other activities that can have important later consequences. Futhermore, of course, democratic practices in teaching may well contribute to the development of democratic values.

Further light on the relationship between classroom leadership and productivity and morale has been shed through a study by Meade (1967) undertaken in a Hindu culture in India. The plan of the study was very much like that of the original study in this area, but included only the so-called democratic and authoritarian leaders. In this study both morale and productivity were found to be superior under the authoritarian leader. Morale was measured in terms of the amount of absenteeism, the wish to continue the activities, and the expressed desire to remain under the particular leader. Meade suggests that the Hindu children had been raised in an authoritarian culture, which includes living in a communal family ruled over in an autocratic style by the senior woman in the group. With such a background, adaptation to a group run by a democratic leader is difficult, and the situation is sufficiently strange to interfere with effective work. Meade states, but without supporting data, that the Hindu children showed a greater number of acts of aggression under the democratic than under authoritarian leadership.

An overall view of the data suggests that the responses of children to different types of leadership in learning situations depends more on their cultural background than on the leadership as such. In both the United States and Japan, children are raised in a quite permissive environment in which the parents give guidance rather than orders. Such children adapt well to similar conditions in the classroom. Hindu children, raised in a highly authoritarian society, also adapt best to school conditions similar to those in which they have been raised, namely, authoritarian conditions.

The problem discussed here is a part of the general problem of what constitutes effective human leadership. Perhaps one of the reasons why research on styles of leadership in teaching situations has not flourished is that it is generally considered to be a special case of leadership that has not been attractive to research workers. Research on leadership in other situations has flourished, but it has tended to avoid such broad categories as the democratic and the authoritarian. Indeed, the trend in research has been to analyze leadership into more basic components of behavior in particular situations. The studies cited elsewhere in this chapter on the conditions under which a leader can be effective in helping a group to solve a problem reflect the trend in research. The result has been the identification of some specific activities in which leaders can be trained. A review of leadership research by Hollander and Julian (1969) also brings out the fact that there has been a declining interest in the personal qualities of leaders and a tendency to focus on the situations in which leadership can make a contribution and the nature of the contribution that can be made. The evidence seems clear that there is little meaning in talking of individuals as leaders, as if they were a special group of individuals capable of exercising leadership in all situations.

Fiedler (1971, 1973) has brought together information to support such a model, which he refers to as the contingency model of leadership. He postulates that task-oriented leaders function best in situations that are either very favorable or very unfavorable. Intermediate situations seem to be better handled by leaders who are oriented not so much to the task to be accomplished but to the human-relationship aspects of group functioning. *Favorableness* is defined as the extent to which the situation provides the leader with "potential power and influence over the group's behavior" (1971, p. 129). The classroom would appear to be at an intermediate level for the exercise of leadership. On this basis the role of the teacher would be viewed as one in which a high degree of task orientation would be important for producing achievement, and the human-relationship aspect of teaching, though not considered unimportant, would be viewed as secondary.

SUMMARY

1. Only a limited number of aspects of the effect of the social environment on learning can be considered in this chapter. The earliest impact is that of the mother. The human infant needs eye contact with the mother as a reassuring element in his exploration of the environment. Groups of caretakers may fill the role of the mother, but the results are not as satisfactory as those of a single caretaker. Infants learn to anticipate the behavior of the mother and thus acquire a basic social skill;

the mother becomes the base from which the world is explored. The mother also holds the infant in the upright position, which is a position in which the infant is alert. Smiling is an innate response, which comes to be elicited by the human face and voice. The mother is probably the first object which the infant comes to regard as having permanency. Imitation is a social form of learning, although the infant does not produce any new responses through imitation.

2. Animals far down the evolutionary scale can be taught to model their behavior after other members of their own species through reinforcement procedures. Primates appear to imitate members of their own species without reinforcement. This is also true of children. Teachers should be intellectual models for children, and also models of ethical behavior, but little has been done to study this phenomenon. Transitional conservers, on the verge of discovering conservation, benefited by watching a model able to conserve in solving a particular problem. It seems that children have to be able to recognize and understand the behavior that is being presented by the model for it to have impact. Thus children may model for fluency, which they recognize, but not flexibility, which they do not recognize.

3. The tendency to imitate seems to be related to a person's self-esteem. Presumably, the person with high self-esteem finds no need to borrow behaviors from another.

4. Substantial evidence has now been provided that in many species the exposure of a member of the species to another already trained to perform a task results in a facilitation in the performance of the observer on the same task. The underlying mechanism is not understood, but those who have studied such phenomena generally assume that the effect of the model is to draw the observer's attention to elements in the task. The modeling effect is most likely to take place when the model has some influence over the individual doing the modeling.

5. The term *aggression* refers to a broad category of behavior. A useful distinction seems to be between instrumental aggression and angry aggression. Aggression can also be classified in terms of the dichotomies of active versus passive, physical versus verbal, and direct versus indirect. Aggressive behavior, in species other than human, must serve in some way to preserve the species. For example, the defense of a territory serves to defend a feeding ground. Human immigration is a typical form of territorial behavior resulting from those already occupying land defending it against use by others. In studies of overcrowding with animals, the animals do not produce a maximum density for the area involved, since a few stronger animals take over the sources of food. There are dangers in generalizing from such studies to man. The conditions under which human beings live seem to be more important than the density of the population.

6. The concept of territoriality has been explored in relation to human behavior. Students may claim territories in libraries, people build fences around their yards, and professionals build language territories.

7. Ritualized fighting behavior among the males of a species results in the stronger males reproducing, without a loss of species members through injury. Animal conflicts do, nevertheless, produce some loss through death. Most species have evolved a signal to indicate when conflict is to end, thus protecting the life

of the weaker member. Man has evolved no such signal. Despite this, there is no reason for believing that man destroys more of his species than other animals do.

8. Although aggression may preserve or improve a species, cooperative behaviors may also serve the same purpose.

9. Pain-elicited aggression has been proposed as a basic form of aggression. However, it seems to be little more than a basic defensive response, almost reflex in character, which does little to account for other forms of aggression.

10. The frustration-aggression hypothesis has been advanced in various forms, but has not been a satisfactory starting point for producing knowledge.

11. The early hominids made weapons, which they used for hunting. The invention of weapons did not result in the evolution of any inhibitions related to their use against other human beings. Other carnivorous animals with natural weapons such as claws do not use them against their own species to any extent. Wars came into existence after human beings had learned the art of agriculture and had learned to accumulate excess crops. Some early wars became ritualized, but the ritualization of war did not become general. Lorenz has suggested that man should make an effort to ritualize conflict.

12. Data on the development of aggressive behavior is closely similar for different primates. The young males show more agonistic behavior than the females, and also more rough-and-tumble behavior. The behavior of the young males is inherently more boisterous. The aggressive behavior of the 4-year-old tends to be instrumental in character, and that of the 7-year-old hostile. Children who engage in physical aggression expect their victims to show pain.

13. The causes of excessive aggression are not clear. Those who have an extra Y chromosome appear to show a higher incidence of aggression for unknown reasons. Brain damage at birth may produce impulsive violence, and some success has been achieved in helping such individuals with brain surgery designed to restore balance in the brain between the limbic system and the higher centers. Temporal lobe epilepsy may also produce acts of violence, though the epileptic does not typically show violence. Behavior therapy is ineffective for such individuals, and drugs have only temporary value in producing relief.

14. Modeling has been considered a major cause of aggressive behavior in our society. However, the effect of a model seems to be to release aggression rather than to teach aggression. The release of aggression may give the behavior practice and strengthen it. Most psychologists reject the catharsis hypothesis and believe that aggression has to be controlled. The effect of media on the production of aggressive behavior appears to be well established. Children play differently after viewing television violence and may be more willing to hurt other children.

15. There seems to be a relationship between the amount of the male hormone testosterone and the amount of aggressive behavior. The effect seems to be particularly marked if girls are exposed to increased amounts of testosterone during fetal life.

16. The traditional view of moral behavior has been that it represents the acquisition of a set of rules. According to this view, a first step is in knowing the rules. There is virtually no evidence to support this position. Socialization has been held to be an important factor in moral development. Certainly the human

being is a highly social creature. Moral behavior would also seem to require that the individual be able to decenter his behavior and to see it from the other's point of view. The autonomous individual is commonly regarded as being highly moral, though not bound by the rules of the society in which he lives. The so-called autonomous individual has been shown to be a strong, forceful character, but how this is related to morality is still not known. The moral judgment factor has also been cited as a contributor. The enumeration of such factors has not been a particularly useful enterprise in understanding the learning of moral behavior.

17. Piaget introduced stage theory of moral development over half a century ago. Piaget sees three stages of moral development. The first stage shows the child involved in respect for authority and an obligation to follow rules established by the adult. An act is right because it is sanctioned by the adult. In the second stage, the child begins to construct a morality of his own. The child develops rules of conduct that enable him to say that certain acts are right and others are wrong. In the third stage full autonomy is achieved but the child understands the reciprocity of all social relationships. The early work of Kohlberg has now been extended and further developed. Kohlberg postulates three stages of moral development: preconventional, conventional, and postconventional. In the preconventional stage there is at first deference for authority and an orientation toward the avoidance of punishment. In the later part of this stage there is the beginning of reciprocity and cooperation. The conventional stage involves an acceptance of the values of the group. First, the values of the peer group are accepted. Later, the conventional values of the larger society become the basis of the moral code. The postconventional stage involves the construction of conceptions of morality beyond those ordinarily encountered. The rules of morality constructed at this highest stage are more general than those at lower stages. Conscience becomes guided by abstract ethical principles.

18. Moral training, in terms of the Piaget or Kohlberg positions, involves presenting moral dilemmas at a time when the individual is ready to make a transition to a higher level of morality. The evidence indicates that such training does have value. There is also evidence that all children throughout the world pass through a similar set of stages of moral development.

19. Helping or altruistic behavior has been difficult for psychologists to understand. One view is that it involves internal reinforcements, such as the individual telling himself how virtuous he is. However, the existence of such internal reinforcements has not been established. Altruistic behavior requires that the child have developed beyond the stage of egocentrism and that he understand the importance of reciprocity. Sharing behavior is not encouraged by the American school system in that the system has made a virtue out of competitiveness. There is little evidence that cooperative behavior can be usefully reinforced, because what is learned seems to be quite specific and does not generalize to other situations.

20. The classic work on leadership related to teaching is that by Lewin, Lippitt, and White. Further research has indicated that the effects of democratic or authoritarian roles on the part of teachers depends on the cultural setting.

REFERENCES

Abelson, R. P., *et al.* (Eds.). *Theories of cognitive consistency: A sourcebook.* Chicago: Rand McNally, 1968.

Abelson, W. D., & Zigler, E. Effects of a four-year follow-through program on economically disadvantaged children. *Journal of Educational Psychology*, 1974, *66*, 756–771.

Abramov, I., & Gordon, J. Seeing. Ch. 17, pp. 359–406, in E. L. Carterette and M. P. Friedman (Eds.), *Handbook of perception* (Vol. 3). New York: Academic Press, 1973.

Acken, L. R. Language factors in learning mathematics. *Review of Educational Research*, 1972, *42*, 359–385.

Adams, J. A. *Human memory.* New York: McGraw-Hill, 1967.

Adams, J. A., Goete, E. T., & Marshall, P. H. Response feedback and motor learning. *Journal of Experimental Psychology*, 1972, *92*, 391–397.

Ainsworth, M. D. S., & Bell, S. M. Attachment, exploration and separation: Illustrated by the behavior of one-year-olds in a strange situation. *Child Development*, 1970, *41*, 45–67.

Aitken, P. O., & Hutt, C. Do children find complex patterns interesting or pleasing? *Child Development*, 1974, *45*, 425–431.

Allen, M. S. *The Allen morphologizer.* Englewood Cliffs, N.J.: Prentice-Hall, 1962.

Allen, V. L., & Allen, P. S. On the attractiveness of forbidden objects. *Developmental Psychology*, 1974, *10*, 871–873.

Alper, T. G. Achievement motivation in college women. *American Psychologist*, 1974, *29*, 194–203.

Allport, F. H. *Theories of perception and the concept of structures.* New York: Wiley, 1955.

Ammons, H., & Irion, A. L. A note on the Ballard reminiscence phenomenon. *Journal of Experimental Psychology*, 1954, *48*, 184–186.

Ammons, R. B., Farr, R. G., Neumann, E., Dey, M., Marion, R., & Ammons, C. H. Long-term retention of perceptual-motor skills. *Journal of Experimental Psychology*, 1958, *55*, 318–328.

Anastasi, A. Common fallacies about heredity, environment and human behavior. *ACT Research Report*, No. 58. Iowa City: American College Testing Program, 1973.

Anderson, D. G., Jameson, J. L., & Man, S. C. Analgesic effects of acupuncture on the pain of ice water. *Canadian Journal of Psychology*, 1974, *28*, 239–244.

Anderson, J. R., & Bower, G. H. Recognition and retrieval processes in free recall. *Psychological Review*, 1972, *79*, 97–123.

Anderson, N. H. Integration theory and attitude change. *Psychological Review*, 1971, *78*, 171–206.

Anderson, N. H. Information integration theory applied to attitudes about U.S. presidents. *Journal of Educational Psychology*, 1973, *64*, 1–8.

Antes, J. R. The time course of picture viewing. *Journal of Experimental Psychology*, 1974, *103*, 62–70.

Arbib, M. A., Franklin, G. F., & Nilsson, N. Some ideas on information processing in the cerebellum. Pp. 43-58 in C. E. Caianiello (Ed.), *Neural networks.* New York: Springer, 1968.

Aronfreed, J. The problem of imitation. Pp. 209–319 in L. P. Lipsitt and H. W. Reese (Eds.), *Advances in child development and behavior* (Vol. 4). New York: Academic Press, 1969.

Aronson, E. Dissonance theory: Progress and problems. Pp. 5–27 in R. P. Abelson *et al.* (Eds.), *Theories of cognitive consistency: A sourcebook.* Chicago: Rand McNally, 1968.

Ash, P., & Jaspen, N. The effects and interpretation of rate of development, repetition, participation, and room illumination on learning from a rear-projected film. *Technical Report*, Special Devices Center, Office of Naval Research, 269 7–39, 1953.

Asher, J. J. Vision and audition in language learning. *Perceptual and Motor Skills*, 1964, *19* (Monograph Supplement No. 1), 255–300.

Atkinson, J. W., & Feather, N. T. (Eds.) *A theory of achievement motivation.* New York: Wiley, 1966.

Atkinson, R. C., & Wickens, T. D. Human memory and the concept of reinforcement. Ch. 4, pp. 66–120, in R. Glaser (Ed.), *The nature of reinforcement.* New York: Academic Press, 1971.

Atwater, S. K. Proactive inhibition and facilitation as affected by degree of prior learning. *Journal of Experimental Psychology*, 1953, *46*, 400–404.

Ausubel, D. P., & Robinson, F. G. *School learning: An introduction to educational psychology.* New York: Holt, Rinehart & Winston, 1969.

Ayllon, T., & Azrin, N. H. *The token economy.* New York: Appleton-Century-Crofts, 1968.

Bahrick, H. P., Bahrick, P. O., & Whittlinger, R. P. Fifty years of memory for names, and faces: A cross-sectional approach. *Journal of Experimental Psychology*, 1974, *104*, 54–75.

Baldwin, T. L., McFarlane, P. T., & Garvey, C. J. Children's communication accuracy related to race and socioeconomic status. *Child Development*, 1971, *42*, 345–357.

Ballard, P. B. Obliviscence and reminiscence. *British Journal of Psychology, Monograph Supplement*, 1913, *1* (No. 2).

Bandura, A. *Principles of behavior modification.* New York: Holt, Rinehart & Winston, 1969.

Bandura, A. Behaviour theory and the models of man. *American Psychologist*, 1974, *29*, 859–869.

Bandura, A., Grusec, J. E., & Menlove, F. L. Vicarious extinction of avoidance behavior. *Journal of Personality and Social Psychology*, 1967, *5*, 16–23.

Bandura, A., & Walters, R. *Social learning and personality development.* New York: Holt, Rinehart & Winston, 1963.

Barber, T. X., Suggested ("hypnotic") behavior: Trance paradigm versus an alternative paradigm. Ch. 30, pp. 386–411, in D. Shapiro *et al.* (Ed.), *Biofeedback and self-control 1972.* Chicago: Aldine, 1973.

Barber, T. X., & DeMoor, W. D. A theory of hypnotic induction procedures. *American Journal of Clinical Hypnosis*, 1972, *15*, 112–135.

Bartholomeus, B. Voice identification by nursery school children. *Canadian Journal of Psychology*, 1973, *27*, 464–472.

Bartlett, F. C. *Remembering: An experimental and social study.* Cambridge: University Press, 1932.

Baumrind, D., & Black, A. E. Socialization practices associated with dimensions of competence in preschool boys and girls. *Child Development*, 1967, *38*, 291–327.

Becker, W. C., Thomas, D. R., & Carnine, D. *Reducing behavior problems: An operant conditioning guide for teachers.* Washington, D.C.: U.S. Department of Health, Education and Welfare, 1969. (ERIC Document Reproduction Service No. Ed 034 570, PS 002 300.)

Bell, S. M. The development of the concept of object as related to infant-mother attachment. *Child Development*, 1970, *41*, 291–311.

Bell, S. M., & Salter, M. D. Infant crying and maternal responsiveness. *Child Development*, 1972, *43*, 1171–1190.

Beller, K. B. Research on organized programs of early education. Ch. 18, pp. 530–600, in R. M. W. Travers (Ed.), *Second handbook of research on teaching.* Chicago: Rand McNally, 1972.

Bem, D. J. Self-perception theory. Pp. 1–62 in L. Berkowitz (Ed.), *Advances in experimental social psychology* (Vol. 6). New York: Academic Press, 1972.

Benowitz, M. L., & Busse, T. V. Material incentives and the learning of spelling words in a typical school situation. *Journal of Educational Psychology*, 1970, *61*, 24–26.

Berlyne, D. E. *Conflict, arousal, and curiosity*. New York: McGraw-Hill, 1960.

Berlyne, D. E. Complexity and incongruity variables as determinants of exploratory choice and evaluative ratings. *Canadian Journal of Psychology*, 1963, *17*, 274–290.

Berlyne, D. E. *Structure and direction in thinking*. New York: Wiley, 1965.

Berlyne, D. E. The reward value of light increment under supranormal and subnormal arousal. *Canadian Journal of Psychology*, 1969, *23*, 11–16.

Berlyne, D. E. Ends and means of experimental aesthetics. *Canadian Journal of Psychology*, 1972, *26*, 303–325.

Bernstein, A. *The coordination and regulation of movements*. New York: Pergamon Press, 1967.

Berscheid, E., & Walster, E. Attitude change, part II. Pp. 121–231 in J. Mills (Ed.), *Experimental social psychology*. New York: Macmillan, 1969.

Bertalanffi, L. von *Organismic psychology and systems theory*. Barre, Me.: Barre Publishing, 1968.

Bindra, D. A motivational view of learning. *Psychological Review*, 1974, *81*, 199–213.

Bjork, R. A. Positive forgetting: The noninterference of items intentionally forgotten. *Journal of Verbal Learning and Verbal Behavior*, 1970, *9*, 255–268.

Bjork, R. A., & Woodward, A. E. Directed forgetting of individual words in free recall. *Journal of Experimental Psychology*, 1973, *99*, 22–27.

Black, R. W. Shifts in magnitude of reward and contrast effects in instrumental and selective learning. *Psychological Review*, 1968, *75*, 114–126.

Blaiwes, A. S., Puig, J. A., & Regan, J. J. Transfer of training and the measurement of training effectiveness. *Human Factors*, 1973, *15*, 523–533.

Blanchard, E. B., & Young, L. D. Self-control of cardiac functioning: A promise as yet unfulfilled. *Psychological Bulletin*, 1973, *79*, 145–163.

Bloom, B. S. Implications of the I.E.A. studies for curriculum and instruction. *School Review*, 1974, *82*, 413–435.

Bolles, R. C Reinforcement, expectancy, and learning. *Psychological Review*, 1972, *79*, 394–409.

Bornstein, H., & Roy, H. L. Comment on "Linguistic deficiency and thinking: Research with deaf subjects 1964–1968." *Psychological Bulletin*, 1973, *79*, 211–214.

Bosco, J. J. *Social class and the processing of visual information* (First Report, Project No. 9-E-041). Washington, D.C.: U.S. Department of Health, Education and Welfare, Office of Education, 1970.

Bosco, J. The visual information processing speed of lower and middle class children. *Child Development*, 1972, *43*, 1418–1422.

Bosco, J. *Behavior modification drugs and the schools*. Grand Rapids Public Schools, Center for Educational Studies, 1973.

Boswell, J. J., & Spatz, K. C. Reminiscence: A rich source of individual differences. *Journal of Motor Behavior*, 1975, *7*, 1–7.

Bourne, L. E. *Human conceptual behavior*. Boston: Allyn & Bacon, 1966.

Bourne, L. E. Knowing and using concepts. *Psychological Review*, 1970, *77*, 546–556.

Bourne, L. E., Jr., & Archer, E. J. Time continuously on target as a function of distribution of practice. *Journal of Experimental Psychology*, 1956, *51*, 25–33.

Bourne, L. E., Jr., & Bunderson, C. V. Effects of delay of informative feedback and length of postfeedback interval on concept identification. *Journal of Experimental Psychology*, 1963, *65*, 1–5.

Bourne, L. E., Jr., & Guy, D. E. Learning conceptual rules. II: The role of positive and negative instances. *Journal of Experimental Psychology*, 1968, *77*, 488–494.

Bowen, D. D. Reported patterns in TAT measures of needs for achievement, affiliation and power. *Journal of Personality Assessment*, 1973, *37*, 424–430.

Bower, G. H. Chunks as interference units in free recall. *Journal of Verbal Learning and Verbal Behavior*, 1969, *8*, 610–613.

Bower, G. H., Clark, M. C., Lesgold, A. M., & Winzenz, D. Hierarchical retrieval schemes in recall of categorized word lists. *Journal of Verbal Learning and Verbal Behavior*, 1969, *8*, 323–343.

Bower, T. G. R. The object in the world of the infant. *Scientific American*, 1971, *225*, 30–38.

Bower, T. G. R. *Development in infancy*. San Francisco: Freeman, 1974.

Bowlby, J. *Maternal care and mental health*, Geneva: World Health Organization, 1951.

Bowlby, J. *Attachment and loss: I. Attachment*. Honolulu: Hogarth Press, 1969.

Brady, J. V. Ulcers in "executive" monkeys. *Scientific American*, October 1958, *199*, 95–103.

Brainerd, C. J. Training and transfer of transitivity, conservation, and class inclusion of length. *Child Development*, 1974, *45*, 324–334.

Brainerd, C. J., & Allen, T. W. Experimental induction of the conversation of "first order" quantitative variants. *Psychological Bulletin*, 1971, *75*, 128–144.

Bringle, R., Lehtinen, S., & Steiner, I. D. The impact of the message content of rewards and punishments on the attribution of freedom. *Journal of Personality*, 1973, *41*, 272–286.

Broadbent, D. E. *Perception and communication*. New York: Pergamon Press, 1958.

Brody, A. L. Statistical learning theory applied to an instrumental avoidance situation. *Journal of Experimental Psychology*, 1957, *54*, 240–245.

Brown, A. L., Campione, J. L., Bray, N. W., & Wilcox, B. L. Keeping track of changing variables: Effects of rehearsal training and rehearsal prevention in normal and retarded adolescents. *Journal of Experimental Psychology*, 1973, *101*, 123–131.

Brown, A. S. Examination of hypothesis sampling theory. *Psychological Bulletin*, 1974, *81*, 773–790.

Brown, D. (Ed.) *Behavior modification in child and school mental health: An annotated bibliography on application with parents and teachers* (Publication No. HSM 71–9043). Rockville, Md. : Department of Health, Education and Welfare, National Institute for Mental Health, 1971.

Brown, P. L., & Jenkins, H. M. Auto-shaping of the pigeon's key peck. *Journal of the Experimental Analysis of Behavior*, 1968, *11*, 1–8.

Brown, P. L., & Presbie, R. J. *Behavior modification skills*. Hicksville, N.Y.: Research Media, 1974.

Brown, R. *A first language*. Cambridge, Mass.: Harvard University Press, 1973.

Brown, R. Development of the first language in the human species. *American Psychologist*, 1973, *28*, 97–106.

Brown, R., & McNeill, D. The "tip of the tongue" phenomenon. *Journal of Verbal Learning and Verbal Behavior*, 1966, *5*, 325–337.

Bruner, J. S. Processes of growth in infancy, Pp. 205–228 in A. Ambrose (Ed.) *Stimulation in early infancy*. New York: Academic Press, 1969.

Bruner, J. S. Nature and uses of immaturity. *American Psychologist*, 1972, *27*, 687–708.

Bruner, J. S. Organization of early skilled action. *Child Development*, 1973, *44*, 1–11.

Bruner, J. S. Volition, skill and tools. Sect. 98, pp. 577–583, in L. J. Stone, H. T. Smith, & L. B. Murphy (Eds.), *The competent infant*. New York: Basic Books, 1973.

Bruner, J. S., Goodnow, J. J., & Austin, G. A. *A study of thinking*. New York: Wiley, 1956.

Brush, F. R. (*Ed.*) *Aversive conditioning and learning*. New York: Academic Press, 1971.

Bryan, J. H., & London, P. Altruistic behavior by children. *Psychological Bulletin*, 1970, *73*, 200–211.

Bryan, W. L., & Harter, N. Studies in the physiology and psychology of the telegraphic language. *Psychological Review*,, 1897, *4*, 27–53.

Bucher, B., & Lovaas, O. I. Use of aversive stimulation in behavior modification. Pp. 77–145 in M. R. Jones (Ed.), *Miami symposium on the prediction of behavior, 1967: Aversive stimulation*. Coral Gables, Fl.: University of Miami Press, 1968.

Bugelski, B. R. Presentation time, total time, and mediation in paired associate learning. *Journal of Experimental Psychology*, 1962, *63*, 409–412.

Bugelski, B. R. The image as mediator in one-trial paired-associate learning. III. Sequential functions in serial lists. *Journal of Experimental Psychology*, 1974, *103*, 298–303.

Bugelski, B. R., & McMahon, M. L. The total time hypothesis: A reply to Stubin, Heurer, and Tatz. *Journal of Experimental Psychology*, 1971, *90*, 165–166.

Bull, S. G., & Dizney, H. F. Epistemic-curiosity-arousing questions: Their effect on long-term retention. *Journal of Educational Psychology*, 1973, *65*, 45–49.

Buss, A. H. Instrumentality of aggression, feedback, and frustration as determinants of physical aggression. *Journal of Personality and Social Psychology*, 1966, *3*, 153–162.

Buss, A. H. Aggression pays. Ch. 1, pp. 7–18, in J. L. Singer (Ed.), *The control of aggression and violence*. New York: Academic Press, 1971.

Butterfield, E. C., Wambold, C., & Belmont, J. M. On the theory and practice of improving short-term memory. *American Journal of Mental Deficiency*, 1973, *77*, 654–669.

Byalic, R., & Bersoff, D. N. Reinforcement practices of black and white teachers in integrated classrooms. *Journal of Edcuational Psychology*, 1974, *66*, 473–480.

Byers, J. L. Verbal and concept learning. *Review of Educational Research*, 1967, *37*, 494–513.

Byon, S. W. Development in the preschool years. *American Psychologist*, 1975, *30*, 824–835.

Cahoon, D. D. A behavioristic analysis of aggression. *Psychological Record*, 1972, *22*, 463–476.

Cain, L. F., & De V. Willey, R. The effect of spaced learning on the curve of retention. *Journal of Experimental Psychology*, 1939, *25*, 209–214.

Campione, J. C. The generality of transfer: Effects of age and similarity of training and transfer tasks. *Journal of Experimental Child Psychology*, 1973, *15*, 407–418.

Campione, J. C., & Brown, A. L. The effects of contextual changes and degree of component mastery on transfer of training. Pp. 70–114 in H. W. Reese (Ed.), *Advances in child development and behavior* (Vol. 9). New York: Academic Press, 1974.

Capon, N., & Hulbert, J. The sleeper effect—an awakening. *Public Opinion Quarterly*, 1973, *37*, 333–358.

Castaneda, A., McCandless, B. R., & Palermo, D. S. The children's form of the Manifest Anxiety Scale. *Child Development*, 1956, *27*, 317–326.

Chambers, J. A. College teachers: Their effect on creativity of students. *Journal of Educational Psychology*, 1973, *65*, 326–334.

Chomsky, N. Review of *Verbal Behavior* by B. F. Skiiner. *Language*, 1959, *35*, 26–58.

Chomsky, N. Language and the mind. *Psychology Today*, 1968, *1*, 8–51; 66–68.

Chomsky, N. *Language and mind*. New York: Harcourt, Brace & World, 1969.

Clark, D. C. Teaching concepts in the classroom: A set of teaching prescriptions derived from experimental research. *Journal of Educational Psychology* (in press).

Clement, M. A., & Anderson, D. R. Strategies in learning redundant cues in concept identification. *Journal of Experimental Psychology: Human Learning and Memory*, 1975, *1*, 209–214.

Clevenger, D. J. Competition and the culture. *Educational Leadership*, 1973, *30*, 555–559.

Cofer, C. N., & Appley, M. H. *Motivation: Theory and research*. New York: Wiley, 1964.

Cohen, L. B. Attention getting and attention holding processes of infant visual preferences. *Child Development*, 1972, *43*, 869–879.

Cohen, L. B., & Salaptakek, P. *Infant perception: From sensation to cognition* (Vols. 1 and 2). New York: Academic Press, 1975.

Cole, J. K., & Jensen, D. D. (Eds.) *Nebraska symposium on motivation, 1972.* Lincoln: University of Nebraska Press, 1972.

Cole, J. L. The relationship of selected personality variables to academic achievement of average aptitude third graders. *Journal of Educational Research,* 1974, *67,* 329–333.

Cole, M., & Maltzman, I. (Eds.) *A handbook of contemporary Soviet psychology.* New York: Basic Books, 1969.

Cook, H., & Stingle, S. Cooperative behavior in children. *Psychological Bulletin,* 1974, *81,* 918–933.

Cook, T. W. Distribution of practice and size of maze pattern. *British Journal of Psychology,* 1937, *27,* 303–312.

Corcoran, D. W. J. Acoustic factors in proofreading. *Nature,* 1967, *214,* 851–852.

Corcoran, D. W. J. *Pattern recognition.* London: Penguin Books, 1971.

Costin, F. Dogmatism and learning: A follow-up of contradictory findings. *Journal of Educational Research,* 1965, *59,* 186–188.

Coughlin, R. C. The aversive properties of withdrawing positive reinforcement: A review of recent literature. *Psychological Record,* 1972, *22,* 333–354.

Crossman, E. R. F. W. A theory of the acquisition of speed-skill. *Ergonomics,* 1959, *153–166.*

Cunningham, W. G. The impact of student-teacher pairing's on teacher effectiveness. *American Educational Research Journal,* 1975, *12,* 169–189.

Dale, P. S. Language learning, early. In L. C. Deighton (Ed.), *The encyclopedia of education* (Vol. 5). New York: Macmillan, 1971.

Dale, P. S. *Language development: Structure and function.* Hillsdale, Ill.: Dryden, 1972.

Das, J. P., & Molloy, G. N. Varieties of simultaneous and successive processing in children. *Journal of Educational Psychology,* 1975, *67,* 213–220.

Davison, G. C., & Wilson, G. T. Critique of desensitization: Social and cognitive factors underlying the effectiveness of Wolpe's procedure. *Psychological Bulletin,* 1972, *78,* 28–31.

Day, H. Role of specific curiosity in school achievement. *Journal of Educational Psychology,* 1968, *59,* 37–43.

Deese, J. *Psycholinguistics.* Boston: Allyn & Bacon, 1970.

de Groot, A. Perception and memory vs. thought. Ch. 3, pp. 19–50, in B. Kleinmuntz (Ed.), *Problem solving.* New York: Wiley, 1966.

Dember, W. N. Motivation and the cognitive revolution. *American Psychologist,* 1974, *29,* 161–168.

Denenberg, V. H. *Education of the infant and young child.* New York: Academic Press, 1970.

Deregowski, J. B. Pictorial recognition in subjects from a relatively pictureless environment. *African Social Research,* 1968, *5,* 356–364.

Deregowski, J. B. Pictorial perception and culture. *Scientific American,* 1972, *227,* 82–88.

DeRosa, D. V., Doane, D. S., & Russell, B. The influence of first-list organization upon second-list free-recall learning. *Journal of Verbal Learning and Verbal Behavior*, 1970, *9*, 269–273.

Deutsch, C. P. Education for disadvantaged groups. *Review of Educational Research*, 1965, *35*, 140–146.

DeVries, D., & Edwards, K. J. Learning games and student teams: Their effects on classroom process. *American Educational Research Association*, 1973, *10*, 307–318.

Dewing, K., & Hetherington, P. Anagram solving as a function of word imagery. *Journal of Experimental Psychology*, 1974, *102*, 764–767.

DiCara, L. V. Learning in the autonomic nervous system. *Scientific American*, 1970, *222*, 30–39.

DiCara, L. V. Learning mechanisms. Ch. 7, pp. 81–89, in D. Shapiro *et al.* (Eds.), *Biofeedback and self-control 1972*. Chicago: Aldine, 1973.

Dick, A. O., & Dick, S. O. An analysis of hierarchical processing in visual perception. *Canadian Journal of Psychology*, *1969*, *23*, 203–211.

Diggory, J. C. *Self-evaluation: Concepts and studies*. New York: Wiley, 1966.

Dillehay, R. C. On the irrelevance of the classical negative evidence concerning the effect of attitudes on behavior. *American Psychologist*, 1973, *28*, 887–891.

Dinsmoor, J. A. Escape from shock as a conditioning technique. Pp. 33–75 in M. R. Jones (Ed.), *Miami symposium on the prediction of behavior, 1967: Aversive stimulation*. Coral Gables, Fl.: University of Miami Press, 1968.

Di Vesta, F. J., & Walls, R. T. Multiple-versus single-problem training and variations of solution rules in the formation of learning sets. *Journal of Educational Psychology*, 1968, *59*, 191–196.

Dollard, J., Doob, L. W., Miller, N. E., Mowrer, O. H., & Sears, R. R. *Frustration and aggression*. New Haven: Yale University Press, 1939.

Drachman, D. A. Memory impairment in the aged: Storage versus retrieval deficit. *Journal of Experimental Psychology*, 1972, *93*, 302–308.

DuCette, J. Locus of control and levels of aspiration in black and white children. *Review of Educational Research*, 1972, *42*, 493–504.

Duker, S. (Ed.) *Time compressed speech* (3 vols.). Metuchen, N.J.: Scarecrow Press, 1974.

Dunham, P. J. Punishment: Method and theory. *Psychological Review*, 1971, *78*, 58–70.

Earhard, M. Free-recall transfer and individual differences in subjective organization. *Journal of Experimental Psychology*, 1974, *103*, 1169–1174.

Ebbinghaus, H. *Über das Gedächtnis*. Leipzig: Duncker & Humblot, 1885.

Eccles, J. C., Ito, M., & Szentagothai, J. *The cerebellum as a neuronal machine*. New York: Springer-Verlag, 1967.

Eccles, J. C. *The understanding of the brain*. New York: McGraw-Hill, 1973.

Eckert, E., & Kanak, N. J. Verbal discrimination learning: A review of the acquisition, transfer and retention literature through 1972. *Psychological Bulletin*, 1974, *81*, 582–607.

Edney, J. J. Human territoriality. *Psychological Bulletin*, 1974, *81*, 959–975.

Egan, D. E., & Greeno, J. G. Acquiring cognitive structure by discovery and rule learning. *Journal of Educational Psychology*, 1973, *64*, 85–97.

Egeland, B. Training impulsive children in the use of more efficient scanning techniques. *Child Development*, 1974, *45*, 165–171.

Ehrlich, H. J., & Lee, D. Dogmatism, learning, and resistance to change. *Psychological Bulletin*, 1969, *71*, 249–260.

Eichorn, D. H. The Berkeley longitudinal studies: Continuities and correlates of behavior. *Canadian Journal of the Behavioral Sciences*, 1973, *5*, 297–320.

Ekstrand, B. R., Wallace, W. P., & Underwood, B. J. A frequency theory of verbal discrimination learning. *Psychological Bulletin*, 1966, *73*, 566–578.

Ellis, H.C., & Daniel, T.C. Verbal processes in long-term stimulus recognition memory. *Journal of Experimental Psychology*. 1971, *90*, 18–26.

Ellis, H. C., Parente, F. J., & Walker, C. W. Coding and varied input versus repetition in human memory. *Journal of Experimental Psychology*, 1974, *102*, 284–290.

Ennis, R. H. Children's ability to handle Piaget's propositional logic: A conceptual critique. *Review of Educational Research*, 1975, *45*, 1–41.

Entwisle, D. R., & Huggins, W. H. Iconic memory in children. *Child Development*, 1973, *44*, 392–394.

Epley, S. W. Reduction of the behaviorist effects of aversive stimulation by the presence of companions. *Psychological Bulletin*, 1974, *81*, 271–293.

Epstein, W. *Varities of perceptual learning*. New York: McGraw-Hill, 1967.

Epstein, W., Wilder, L., & Robertson, L. The effect of directed forgetting on the time to remember. *Memory and Cognition*, 1975, *3*, 401–404.

Estes, W. K. An experimental study of punishment. *Psychological Monographs*, 1944, 57 (No. 263).

Evans, D. R., Hearn, M. T., and Zwirner, W. W. Need achievement training with grade nine students. *Canadian Journal of Behavioral Sciences*, 1975, 7, 54–59.

Eysenck, H. J. Reminiscence, drive, and personality theory. *Journal of Aboral and Social Psychology*, 1956, *53*, 328–333.

Fantino, E., Kasdon, D., & Stringer, N. The Yerkes–Dodson Law and alimentary motivation. *Canadian Journal of Psychology*, 1970, *24*, 77–84.

Fantz, R. L. Pattern vision in young infants. *Psychological Record*, 1958, *8*, 43–47.

Fantz, R. L. Visual pattern at birth as shown by patterns of selectivity. *Annals of the New York Academy of Sciencies*, 1965, *118*, 831–859.

Feather, B. W. Semantic generalization of classically conditioned responses. *Psychological Bulletin*, 1965, *63*, 425–441.

Feldman, C. F., Lee, B., McLean, J. D., Pillemer, D. B., & Murray, J. R. *The development of adaptive intelligence*. New York: Jossey-Bass, 1974.

Ferster, C. B. A functional analysis of depression. *American Psychologist*, 1973, *28*, 857–870.

Feschback, S., & Singer, R. D. *Television and aggression*. San Francisco: Jossey-Bass, 1971.

Festinger, L. *A theory of cognitive dissonance*. Evanston, Ill.: Row, Peterson, 1957.

Festinger, L., & Carlsmith, J. M. Cognitive consequences of forced compliance. *Journal of Abnormal and Social Psychology*, 1959, *58*, 203–210.

Fiedler, F. E. Validation and extension of the contingency model of leadership effectiveness: A review of empirical findings. *Psychological Bulletin*, 1971, *76*, 128–148.

Fiedler, F. E. The contingency model: A reply. *Organizational Behavior and Human Performance*, 1973, *9*, 356–368.

Finch, C. R., & O'Reilly, P. A. The effects of simulation on problem solving development. *Simulation and Games*, 1974, *5*, 47–71.

Fishbein, M., & Ajzen, I. Attitudes towards objects as predictors of single and multiple behavioral criteria. *Psychological Review*, 1974, *81*, 59–74.

Fishbein, M., & Coombs, F. S. Basis of decision: An attitudinal analysis of voting behavior. *Journal of Applied Social Psychology*, 1974, *4*, 95–124.

Fitts, P. M., & Posner, M. I. *Human Performance*. Belmont, Calif.: Brooks Cole, 1967.

Flavell, J. H. *The developmental psychology of Jean Piaget*. Princeton, N.J.: Van Nostrand, 1963.

Fleishman, E. A., & Hempel, W. Factorial analysis of complex psychomotor performance and related skills. *Journal of Applied Psychology*, 1956, *40*, 96–104.

Fleishman, E. A., & Parker, Jr., J. F. Factors in the retention and relearning of perceptual-motor skill. *Journal of Experimental Psychology*, 1962, *64*, 215–226.

Foster, H. L., & Newman, A. P. Language problems of inner-city children. Pp. 334–338 in L. C. Deighton (Ed.), *The encyclopedia of education* (Vol. 5). New York: Macmillan, 1971.

Fowler, H. *Curiosity and exploratory behavior*. New York: Macmillan, 1965.

Fowler, H. Satiation and curiosity: Constructs for a drive and incentive-motivation theory of exploration. In K. W. Spence and J. T. Spence (Eds) *The psychology of learning and motivation:* 1. New York: Academic Press, 1967.

Franks, C. M., & Wilson, G. T. (Eds.) *Annual review of behavior therapy 1973*. New York: Bruner/Mazel, 1973.

Freeberg, N. E., & Payne, D. T. Parental influence on cognitive development in early childhood: A review. *Child Development*, 1967, *38*, 65–87.

Fitts, P. M., & Peterson, J. R. Information capacity of discrete motor responses. *Journal of Experimental Psychology*, 1964, *67*, 103–112.

Freeman, D. Human aggression in anthropological perspective. Pp. 109–119 in J. D. Carthy and F. J. Ebling (Eds.), *The natural history of aggression*. New York: Academic Press, 1966.

Friedes, D. Human information processing and sensory modality. *Psychological Bulletin*, 1974, *81*, 284–310.

Friedman, P. Relationship of teacher performance to spontaneous student verbalization within the classroom. *Journal of Educational Psychology*, 1973, *65*, 59–64.

Friedman, S. Newborn visual attention to repeated exposure of redundant vs. novel targets. *Perception and Psychophysics*, 1972, *12*, 291–294.

Friedman, S., Nagy, A. N., & Carpenter, G. C. Newborn attention: Differential response decrement to visual stimuli. *Journal of Experimental Child Psychology*, 1970, *10*, 44–51.

Fuller, F. F., & Manning, B. A. Self-confrontation reviewed: A conceptualization for video playback in teacher education. *Review of Educational Research*, 1973, *43*, 469–528.

Furth, H. G. Linguistic deficiency and thinking: Research with deaf subjects 1964–1969. *Psychological Bulletin*, 1971, *76*, 58–72.

Furth, H. G. Further thoughts on thinking and language. *Psychological Bulletin*, 1973, *79*, 215–216.

Gaardner, K. Control of states of consciousness: II. Attainment through external feedback augmenting control of psychophysiological variables. Ch. 3, pp. 49–73, in J. Stoyva *et al.* (Eds.), *Biofeedback and self-control 1971*. Chicago: Aldine-Atherton, 1972.

Gagné, R. M. *The conditions of learning*. New York: Holt, Rinehart & Winston, 1965.

Gagné, R. M. *The conditions of learning* (2nd ed.). New York: Holt, Rinehart & Winston, 1970.

Galbraith, K. J. Evaluation of a token economy in the treatment of a chronic psychiatric population. *Canadian Journal of Behavior Science*, 1972, *4*, 91–100.

Gaudry, E., & Spielberger, C. D. *Anxiety and educational achievement*. New York: Wiley, 1971.

Ganzer, V. J. Effects of audience presence and test anxiety on learning and retention in a serial learning situation. *Journal of Personality and Social Psychology*, 1968, *8*, 194–199.

Gardner, E. *Fundamentals of neurology*. Philadelphia: Saunders, 1968.

Garner, W. R. *The processing of information and structure*. New York: Wiley, 1974.

Geller, A., Jarvik, M. E., & Robustelli, F. Incubation and the Kamin effect. *Journal of Experimental Psychology*, 1970, *85*, 61–65.

Gelman, R. Logical capacity of very young children: Number invariance rules. *Child Development*, 1972 *43*, 75–90.

Gerard, H. B., Conolley, E. S., & Wilhelmy, R. A. Compliance justification and cognitive change. Pp. 217–247 in L. Berkowitz (Ed.). *Advances in experimental social psychology* (No. 7). New York: Academic Press, 1974.

Gerard, H. B., & Mathewson, G. C. The effects of severity of initiation on liking for a group: A replication. *Journal of Experimental Social Psychology*, 1966, *2*, 278–287.

Gerlach, V. S., Schutz, R. E. Baker, R. L., & Mazer, G. E. Effects of variations in test directions on originality test response. *Journal of Educational Psychology* 1964, *55*, 79–83.

Gibson, E. J. Improvement in perceptual judgments as a function of controlled practice or training. *Psychological Bulletin*, 1953, *50*, 401–431.

Gibson, E. J. *Principles of perceptual development and learning*. New York, Appleton-Century-Crofts, 1969.·

Gibson, E. J. Progressive training of human infants: Specific augmentation. Sect. 106, pp. 615–617, in L. J. Stone, H. T. Smith, and L. B. Murphy (Eds.), *The competent infant*. New York: Basic Books, 1973.

Gibson, J. J. *The senses considered as perceptual systems*. Boston: Houghton Mifflin. 1966.

Gibson, J. J., & Gibson, E. J. Perceptual learning: Differentiation or enrichment? *Psychological Review*, 1955, *62*, 32–41.

Giles, H. Communicative effectiveness as a function of accented speech. *Speech Monographs*, 1973, *40*, 330–331.

Glaser, R. Educational psychology and education. *American Psychologist*, 1973, *28*, 557–566.

Glassman, W. E., & Levine, M. Unsolved and unsoluble problem behavior. *Journal of Experimental Psychology*, 1972, *92*, 146–148.

Glucksberg, S., & Danks, J. H. Functional fixedness: Stimulus equivalence mediated by semantic-acoustic similarity. *Journal of Experimental Psychology*, 1967, *74*, 400–405.

Goldstein, S. B., & Slegel, A. W. Facilitation of discrimination learning with delayed reinforcement. *Child Development*, 1972, *43*, 1004–1011.

Gordon, I. J. *Early childhood stimulation through parent education*. Final report to Children's Bureau, Department of Health Education and Welfare. Mimeographed. Gainesville: University of Florida Institute for Development of Human Resources, 1969. (ERIC-ECE, Urbana, Ill., No. ED 038 166.)

Gordon, I. J. *Baby learning through play*. New York: St. Martin's Press, 1970.

Gordon, I. J. *An early intervention program: A longitudinal look*. Gainsville: University of Florida, Institute for Development of Human Resources, 1973.

Goulet, L. R., Kerry, G. W., & Hay, C. M. Longitudinal changes in intellectual functioning in preschool children. *Journal of Educational Psychology*, 1974, *66*, 657–662.

Gray, S. W. & Klaus, R. A. The early training project: A seventh year report. *Child Development*, 1970, *41*, 909–924.

Green, R. L., Bakan, R. F., McMillan, J. H., & Lezotte, L. W. Research and the urban school: Implications for educational improvement. Ch. 19 in R. Travers (Ed.), *Second handbook of research on teaching*. Chicago: Rand McNally, 1973.

Green, R. L., Hofman, L. J., Hayes, M. E., & Morgan, R. F. *The educational status of children in a district without public schools*. U.S. Office of Education, Cooperative Research Project No. 2321, 1964.

Greeno, J. G. Acquisition of a simple cognitive structure. Ch. 9, pp. 353–377, in E. Tulving & W. Donaldson (Eds.), *Organization and memory*. New York: Academic Press, 1972.

Grimes, J. W., & Allinsmith, W. Compulsivity, anxiety, and school achievement. *Merrill-Palmer Quarterly*, 1961, *7*, 247–271.

Guetzkow, H., Kelly, E. L., & McKeachie, W. J. An experimental comparison of recitation, discussion, and tutorial methods in college teaching. *Journal of Educational Psychology*, 1954, *45*, 193–207.

Guilford, J. P. Three faces of intellect. *American Psychologist*, 1959, *14*, 469–479.

Haber, R. N. Repetition, visual persistance, visual noise and information processing. Pp. 121–140 in K. N. Leibovic (Ed.), *Information processing in the nervous system*. New York: Springer-Verlag, 1969.

Hagen, M. A. Picture perception: Towards a theoretical model. *Psychological Bulletin*, 1974, *81*, 471–497.

Hahn, W. W., & Slaughter, J. Heart rate responses of the curarized rat. Ch. 21, pp. 308–314, in J. Stoyva *et al.* (Eds.), *Biofeedback and self-control 1971*. Chicago: Aldine-Atherton, 1972.

Halford, G. S. A theory of the acquisition of conservation. *Psychological Review*. 1970, *77*, 302–316.

Halle, M., & Stevens, K. Speech recognition: A model and a program for research. *IRE Transactions*, 1962, IT-8, 155–159.

Hamilton, J., & Standahl, J. Suppression of stereotyped screaming behavior in a profoundly retarded institutionalized female. *Journal of Experimental Child Psychology*, 1969, 7, 114–121.

Hammer, G. J., & Natale, G. M. Initial learning of a motor skill without motor involvement. *Journal of Business Education*, 1964, *39*, 282–283.

Harby, S. F. Comparison of mental practice and physical practice in the learning of physical skills. *Technical Report*, Special Devices Center, Office of Naval Research, 269-8-27, 1952.

Harlow, H. F. The formation of learning sets. *Psychological Review*, 1949, *56*, 51–65.

Harlow, H. F. Learning set and error factor theory. In S. Koch (Ed.), *Psychology: A study of a science* (Vol. 2). New York: McGraw-Hill, 1959.

Harner, M. S. Towards an understanding of achievement related conflicts in women. *Journal of Social Issues*, 1972, *28*, 157–175.

Harré, R. The formal analysis of concepts. Pp. 3–18 in H. J. Klausmeier & C. W. Harris (Eds.), *Analyses of concept learning*. New York: Academic Press, 1966.

Harter, S. Pleasure derived by children from cognitive challenge and mastery. *Child Development*, 1974, *45*, 661–669.

Hartley, J. *Research report*. New Education, 1966, *2*, 29–35.

Hartup, W. W. Aggression in childhood. *American Psychologist*, 1974, *29*, 336–341.

Hartup, W. W., & Coates, B. Imitation of a peer as a function of reinforcement from the peer group and rewardingness of the model. *Child Development*, 1967, *38*, 1003–1016.

Haslerud, G. M. *Transfer, memory, and creativity*. Minneapolis: University of Minnesota Press, 1972.

Hayes, C. S., Siders, C., & Snider, B. Effects of partial reward on lever pulling and activity of retarded youth. *Perceptual and Motor Skills*, 1973, *37*, 669–670.

Head, H. *Studies in neurology*. Oxford: Oxford University Press, 1920.

Hebb, D. O. *A textbook of psychology*. Philadelphia: Saunders, 1958.

Hebb, D. O. *A textbook of psychology* (2nd ed.). Philadelphia: Saunders, 1966.

Hebb, D. O. *A textbook of psychology* (3rd ed.). Philadelphia: Saunders, 1972.

Hebb, D. O., & Thompson, W. R. The social significance of animal studies. Pp. 729–774 in G. Lindzey and E. Aronson (Eds.), *The handbook of social psychology* (2nd ed.; Vol. 2) Reading, Mass.: Addison-Wesley, 1968.

Heckhausen, H. *The anatomy of achievement motivation.* New York: Academic Press, 1967.

Herrnstein, R. J., & Loveland, D. H. Complex visual concept in the pigeon. *Science,* 1964, *146,* 549–551.

Hilgard, E. R., & Marquis, D. G. Conditioned eyelid responses in monkeys, with a comparison of dog, monkey, and man. *Psychological Monographs,* 1936, *47* *47* (No. 212), 186–198.

Hogan, R. Moral conduct and moral character. *Psychological Bulletin,* 1973, *79,* 217–232.

Holding, D. H. Transfer between difficult and easy tasks. *British Journal of Psychology,* 1962, *53,* 397–407.

Holding, D. H. *Principles of training.* New York: Pergamon Press, 1965.

Holding, D. H. Sensory storage reconsidered. *Memory and Cognition,* 1975, *3,* 31–41.

Hollander, E. P., & Julian, J. W. Contemporary trends in the analysis of leadership processes. *Psychological Bulletin,* 1969, *71,* 387–397.

Honzik, M. P. Environmental correlates of mental growth: Prediction from the family setting at 21 months. *Child Development,* 1967, *38,* 337–364.

Horridge, G. A. Integration in the nervous system. Ch. 3, pp. 39–87, in E. C. Carterette and M. P. Friedman (Eds.), *Handbook of perception* (Vol. 3). New York: Academic Press, 1973.

Howe, M. J. A. *Introduction to human memory.* New York: Harper & Row, 1970.

Huang, K. L., & Payne, R. B. Individual and sex differences in reminiscence. *Memory and Cognition,* 1975, *3,* 252–256.

Hubel, D. H. The visual cortex of the brain. *Scientific American,* November 1963, *209,* 54–62.

Hull, C. L. *Principles of behavior.* New York: Appleton-Century-Crofts, 1943.

Hull, C. L. *A behavior system.* New Haven, Conn.: Yale University Press, 1952.

Hunt, D. E. Adolescence: Cultural deprivation, poverty, and the dropout. *Review of Educational Research,* 1966, *36,* 463–473.

Hunt, E. *Artificial intelligence.* New York: Academic Press, 1974.

Hunt, J. M. *Intelligence and experience.* New York: Ronald, 1961.

Ingling, N. W. Categorization: A mechanism for rapid information processing. *Journal of Experimental Psychology,* 1972, *94,* 239–243.

Inhelder, B. (tr. W. B. Stephens). *The diagnosis of reasoning in the mentally retarded.* New York: Chandler, 1968.

Inhelder, B., & Piaget, J. *The growth of logical thinking from childhood to adolescence.* New York: Basic Books, 1958.

Inhelder, B., & Piaget, J. *The early growth of logic in the child.* New York: Humanities Press, 1964.

Inhelder, B., Sinclair, H., & Bovet, M. *Learning and the development of cognition.*

Cambridge: Harvard University Press, 1974.

Insko, C. A. *Theories of attitude change.* New York: Appleton-Century-Crofts, 1967.

Insko, C. A., Worchel, S., Folger, R., & Kutkus, A. A balance theory interpretation of dissonance. *Psychological Review,* 1975, *82,* 169–183.

Irion, A. L. A brief history of research on the acquisition of skill. Ch. 1 in E. A. Bilodeau (Ed.), *Acquisition of skill.* New York: Academic Press, 1966.

Jacobson, E. *Progressive relaxation.* Chicago: University of Chicago Press, 1938.

Jacobson, L. I., & Greeson, L. E. Effects of systematic conceptual learning on the intellectual development of preschool children from poverty backgrounds: A follow-up study. *Child Development,* 1972, *43,* 1111–1115.

Jahoda, G., & McGurk, H. Pictorial depth perception: A developmental study. *British Journal of Psychology,* 1974, *65,* 141–149.

Jarvik, L. F., Klodin, V., & Matsuyama, S. S. Human aggression and the extra Y chromosome. *American Psychologist,* 1973, *28,* 674–681.

Jaspen, N. Effect on training of experimental film variables: Audience participation. *Technical Report,* Special Devices Center, Office of Naval Research, 269-7-11, 1950.

Jenkins, H. M., & Moore, B. R. The form of the autoshaped response with food or water reinforcers. *Journal of the Experimental Analysis of Behavior,* 1973, *20,* 163–181.

Jenkins, J. G., & Dallenbach, K. M. Oblivescence during sleep and waking. *American Journal of Psychology.* 1924, *35,* 605–612.

Jenkins, W. O., & Stanley, J. C., Jr. Partial reinforcement: A review and critique. *Psychological Bulletin,* 1950, *47,* 193–234.

Johnson, D. M. Solution of anagrams. *Psychological Bulletin,* 1966, *66,* 371–384.

Johnson, D. M. *Systematic introduction to the psychology of thinking.* New York: Harper & Row, 1972.

Johnson, D. M., Parrott, G. L., & Stratton, R. P. Production and judgment of solutions to five problems. *Journal of Educational Psychology, Monograph Supplement,* 1968, *59* (6, Pt. 2), 1–21.

Johnson, D. M., & Stratton, R. P. Evaluation of five methods of teaching concepts. *Journal of Educational Psychology.* 1966, *57,* 48–53.

Johnson, E. S. Objective identification of a strategy on a selection concept learning task. *Journal of Experimental Psychology,* 1971, *90,* 167–196.

Johnson, R. N. *Aggression in man and animals.* Philadelphia: Saunders, 1972.

Johnston, J. M. Punishment of human behavior. *American Psychologist,* 1972, *27,* 1033–1054.

Jones, J. G. Motor learning without demonstration of physical practice. *Research Quarterly,* 1965, *36,* 270–276.

Jones, R. A., & Brehm, J. W. Attitudinal effects of communicator attractiveness when one chooses to listen. *Journal of Personality and Social Psychology,* 1967, *6,* 64–70.

Judson, A. J., Cofer, C. N., & Gelfand, S. Reasoning as an associative process:

II. "Direction" in problem solving as a function of prior reinforcement of relevant responses. *Psychological Reports*, 1956, *2*, 501–507.

Kagan, J. Do infants think? *Scientific American*, 1972, *227*, 76–82.

Kale, S. V., Grosslight, J. H., & McIntrye, L. J. Exploratory studies in the use of pictures and sound for teaching foreign languages. *Technical Report*, Special Devices Center, U.S. Navy SPECDEVCEN, 269-7-53.

Kaplan, B. J. Malnutrition and mental deficiency. *Psychological Bulletin*, 1972, *78*, 321–324.

Kaplan, K. J. Vicarious reinforcement and model's behavior in verbal learning and imitation. *Journal of Experimental Psychology*, 1972, *95*, 448–450.

Karabenick, S. A., & Marshall, J. M. Performance of females as a function of fear of success, fear of failure, type of opponent, and performance-contingent function. *Journal of Personality*, 1974, *42*, 220–237.

Karnes, M. B., Teska, J. A., Hodgins, A. S., & Badger, E. D. Educational intervention at home by mothers of disadvantaged infants. *Child Development* 1970, *41*, 925–935.

Katz, D. Consistency for what? The functional approach. Ch. 8, pp. 179–191, in R. P. Abelson *et al.* (Eds.), *Theories of Cognitive consistency: A sourcebook*. Chicago: Rand McNally, 1968.

Katz, D., & Stotland, E. A preliminary statement to a theory of attitude structure and change. Pp. 423–475 in S. Koch (Ed.), *Psychology: A study of a science* (Vol. 3). New York: McGraw-Hill, 1959.

Kaufman, A. S., & Kaufman, N. L. Tests built from Piaget's and Gesell's tasks as predictors of first grade achievement. *Child Development*, 1972, *43*, 521–535.

Kavanau, J. L. Behavior: Confinement, adaptation, and compulsory regimes in laboratory studies. *Science*, 1964, *143*, 490.

Kazdin, A. E. Role of instructions and reinforcements in behavior changes in token reinforcement programs. *Journal of Educational Psychology*, 1973, *64*, 63–71.

Kazdin, A. E. Time out for some considerations on punishment. *American Psychologist*, 1973, *28*, 939–941.

Keele, S. W. Movement control in skilled motor performance. *Psychological Bulletin*, 1968, *70*, 387–403.

Kelman, H. C. Attitudes are alive and well and gainfully employed in the sphere of action. *American Psychologist*, 1974, *29*, 310–324.

Kendler, H. H., & Kendler, T. S. Vertical and horizontal processes in problem solving. *Psychological Review*, 1962, *69*, 1–16.

Kendler, T. S. Verbalization and optional reversal shifts among kindergarten children. *Journal of Verbal Learning and Verbal Behavior*, 1964, *3*, 248–436.

Kennedy, J. M. *A psychology of picture perception*. Washington, D.C.: Jossey-Bass, 1974.

Kiesler, C. A., Collins, B. E., & Miller, N. *Attitude change*. New York: Wiley, 1969.

Kimmel, H. D. Instrumental conditioning of autonomically mediated responses in human beings. *American Psychologist*, 1974, *29*, 325–335.

King, D. J. Total presentation time and total learning time in connected discourse learning. *Journal of Experimental Psychology*, 1974, *103*, 586–589.

Kintsch, W. *Memory for prose*. Paper presented by the American Association for the Advancement of Science, New York, 1975.

Kintsch, W. *Memory representations of text*. Paper presented at the Loyola Symposium, 1975.

Kintsch, W., & Keenan, J. Reading rate and retention as a function of the number of prepositions in the base structure of the sentence. *Cognitive Psychology*, 1973, *5*, 257–274.

Kleinsmith, L. J., & Kaplan, S. Paired-associate learning as a function of arousal and interpolated interval. *Journal of Experimental Psychology*, 1963, *65*, 190–193.

Klema, E. S. How alphabets might reflect language. Pp. 57–58 in J. F. Kavanagh and I. G. Mattingley (Eds.), *Language by eye and ear*. Cambridge, Mass.: MIT Press, 1973.

Koffman, E. C., & Weinstock, R. B. Total time hypothesis in low meaningful serial learning: Task, age, and verbalization instruction. *Journal of Experimental Psychology*, 1974, *103*, 1210–1213.

Kogan, N., & Pankove, E. Creative ability over a five-year span. *Child Development*, 1972, *43*, 427–442.

Kogan, N., & Pankove, E. Long-term predictive validity of divergent thinking tests: Some negative evidence. *Journal of Educational Psychology*, 1974, *66*, 802–810.

Kohlberg, L. *The development of modes of moral thinking and choice in years ten to sixteen*. Unpublished doctoral dissertation, University of Chicago, 1958.

Kohlberg, L., & Turiel, E. Moral development and moral education. Ch. 15 in C. S. Lesser (Ed.), *Psychology and educational practice*. Glenview, Ill.: Scott, Foresman, 1971.

Konecni, V. J. Annoyance, type and duration of postannoyance activity, and aggression: The "Cathartic effect." *Journal of Experimental Psychology: General*, 1975, *104*, 76–102.

Kounin, J. S. *Discipline and group management in classrooms*. New York: Holt, Rinehart & Winston, 1970.

Krebs, D. L. Altruism—An examination of the concept and a review of the literature. *Psychological Bulletin*, 1970, *73*, 258–302.

Kroes, W. H. Study of frustrative nonreward in children. *Journal of Genetic Psychology*, 1973, *122*, 89–92.

Kuhfittig, P. K. F. Learning aids in the classroom: Experimental evidence of their effectiveness. *Education*, 1973, *94*, 135–136.

Kurtines, W., & Grief, E. B. The development of moral thought: Review and evaluation of Kohlberg's approach. *Psychological Bulletin*, 1974, *81*, 453–470.

Kutner, B., Wilkins, C., & Yarrow, P. R. Verbal attitudes and overt behavior involving racial prejudice. *Journal of Abnormal and Social Psychology*, 1952, *47*, 647–652.

LaPiere, R. T. Attitudes vs. actions. *Social Forces*, 1934, *13*, 230–237.

Laughlin, P. R. Focusing strategy in concept attainment as a function of intructions and task complexity. *Journal of Experimental Psychology*, 1973, *98*, 320–327.

Lawrence, J. E. S. Science and sentiment: Overview of research on crowding and human behavior. *Psychological Bulletin*, 1974, *81*, 712–720.

Lazarus, R. S. A cognitively oriented psychologist looks at biofeedback. *American Psychologist*, 1975, *30*, 553–561.

Lebo, D., & Lebo, E. Aggression and age in relation to verbal expression in nondirective play therapy. *Psychological Monographs*, 1957, *71* (No. 449).

Leith, G. O., Biran, L. A., & Opollot, J. A. The place of review in meaningful verbal learning. *Canadian Journal of the Behavioral Sciences*, 1969, *1*, 113–118.

Lenneberg, E. H. On explaining language. *Science*, 1969, *164*, 635–643.

Leventhal, G. S. Reward magnitude, task attractiveness, and liking for instrumental activity. *Journal of Abnormal Psychology*, 1964, *68*, 460–463.

Levine, F. M., & Fasnacht, G. Token rewards may lead to token learning. *American Psychologist*, 1974, *29*, 816–820.

Levine, M. A transfer hypothesis whereby learning-to-learn, einstellung, the PREE, reversal/nonreversal shifts, and other curiosities are elucidated. Ch. 4, pp. 289–303, in R. L. Solso (Ed.), *Theories in cognitive psychology: The Loyola Symposium*. Potomac, Md.: Lawrence Erlbaum Associates, 1974.

Levine, S. Stress and behavior. *Scientific American*, 1971, *224*, 26–31.

Lewin, K., Lippitt, R., & White, R. K. Patterns of aggressive behavior in experimentally created social climates. *Journal of Social Psychology*, 1939, *10*, 271–299.

Lewis, D. J. Partial reinforcement: A selective review of the literature since 1950. *Psychological Bulletin*, 1960, *57*, 1–28.

Libb, J. W., & Serum, C. Reaction to frustrative nonreward as a function of perceived locus of control of reinforcement. *Journal of Experimental Psychology*, 1974, *102*, 494–497.

Liebert, R. M., Neale, J. M., & Davidson, E. S. *The early window*. New York: Pergamon Press, 1971.

Light, L. L., Kimble, G. A., & Pellegrino, J. W. Comments on episodic memory: When recognition fails, by Watkins and Tulving. *Journal of Experimental Psychology: General*, 1975, *104*, 30–36.

Lintz, L. M. The delay-retention effect with auditory presentations. *Child Development*, 1968, *39*, 933–943.

Liu, I. M. A theory of classical conditioning. *Psychological Review*, 1964, *71*, 408–411.

Logan, T. H., & Wodtke, K. H. Effects of rules of thumb on transfer of training. *Journal of Educational Psychology*, 1968, *59*, 147–153.

London, P. The end of ideology in behavior modification. *American Psychologist*, 1972, *27*, 913–920.

Longstreth, L. E. Tests of the law of effect using open and closed tasks. *Journal of Experimental Psychology*, 1970, *84*, 53–57.

Lorenz, K. (tr. M. K. Wilson). *On aggression*. New York: Harcourt Brace & World, 1963.

Lorge, I. L. *The influence of regularly interpolated time intervals upon subsequent learning*. New York: Columbia University, Teachers College Contributions to Education, 1930 (No. 438).

Luborsky, L., Auerbach, A. H., Chandler, M., Cohen, J., & Bachrach, H. M. Factors influencing the outcome of psychotheraphy: A review of quantitative research. *Psychological Bulletin*, 1971, *75*, 145–185.

Luria, A. R., & Yudovich, F. la. *Speech and the development of mental processes in the child*. Baltimore: Penguin Books, 1971.

Luthe, W. Autogenic therapy: Excerpts on applications to cardiovascular disorders and hypercholesteremia. Ch. 33 in J. Stoyva *et al.* (Eds.), *Biofeedback and self-control 1971*. Chicago: Aldine-Atherton, 1972.

Luthe, W., & Schultz, J. H. *Autogenic therapy*. New York: Grune & Stratton, 1970.

Macaulay, J., & Berkowitz, L. (Eds.) *Altruism and helping behavior*. New York: Academic Press, 1970.

Mackintosh, N. J. A theory of attention: Variations in the associability of stimuli with reinforcement. *Psychological Review*, 1975, *82*, 276–298.

MacLeod, C. M. Long-term recognition and recall following directed forgetting. *Journal of Experimental Psychology: Human Learning and Memory*, 1975, *104*, 271–279.

MacNamara, J. Cognitive basis of language learning in infants. *Psychological Review*, 1972, *79*, 1–13.

Macready, C.. & Macready, G. B. Conservation of weight in self, others, and objects. *Journal of Experimental Psychology*. 1974, *103*. 372–374.

Maehr, M. L. Culture and achievement motivation. *American Psychologist*, 1974, *29*, 887–896.

Maier, N. R. F. *Frustration: The study of behavior without a goal*. New York: McGraw-Hill, 1949.

Mandel, I. J., & Bridges, W. H. Cross modality transfer of differential galvanic skin response conditioning to word stimuli. *Journal of Experimental Psychology*, 1973, *99*, 157–161.

Mandler, G. Transfer of training as a function of degree of response overlearning. *Journal of Experimental Psychology*, 1954, *47*, 411–417.

Mandler, G., & Anderson, R. E. Temporal and spatial cues in seriation. *Journal of Experimental Psychology*, 1971, *90*, 128–135.

Mark, V. H., & Ervin, F. R. *Violence and the brain*. New York: Harper & Row, 1970.

Markowitz, N., & Renner, K. E. Feedback and the delay-retention effect. *Journal of Experimental Psychology*, 1966, *72*, 452–455.

Marlowe, D., & Gregen, K. J. Personality and social interaction. Ch. 25, pp. 590–665, in G. Lindzey and E. Aronson (Eds.), *Handbook of social psychology* (Vol. (Vol. 3). Reading, Mass.: Addison-Wesley, 1969.

Martin, D. W., and Kelley, R. T. Secondary task performance during directed forgetting. *Journal of Experimental Psychology*, 1974, *103*, 1074–1079.

Martin, E. Transfer of verbal paired associates. *Psychological Review*, 1965, *72*, 327–343.

Maslach, G., Marshall, G., & Zimbardo, P. Hypnotic control of peripheral skin temperature. *Psychophysiology*, 1972, *9*, 600–605.

Mason, M. Reading ability and letter search time: Effects of orthographic structure defined by single letter positional frequency. *Journal of Experimental Psychology: General*, 1975, *104*, 146–166.

Massaro, D. W. Perceptual images, processing time, and perceptual units in auditory perception. *Psychological Review*, 1972, *79*, 124–179.

Mayer, R., & Greeno, J. G. Structural differences between learning outcomes produced by different instructional methods. *Journal of Educational Psychology*, 1972, *63*, 165–173.

McCarthy, D. Language development. In L. Carmichael (Ed.), *Manual of child psychology*. New York: Wiley, 1954.

McClelland, D. C. *The achieving society*. Princeton, N.J.: Van Nostrand, 1961.

McClelland, D. C., & Watson, R. I. Power motivation and risk taking behavior. *Journal of Personality*, 1973, *41*, 121–139.

McClure, C. M. Cardiac arrest through volition. Ch. 5, pp. 49–50, in D. Shapiro *et al.* (Eds.), *Biofeedback and self-control 1972*. Chicago: Aldine, 1973.

McCormack, P. D. Recognition memory: How complex a retrieval system. *Canadian Journal of Psychology*, 1972, *26*, 19–41.

McGrew, W. C. *An ethological study of children's behavior*. New York: Academic Press, 1972.

McGuire, W. J. The nature of attitudes and attitude change. Ch. 21, pp. 136–314, in G. Lindzey and E. Aronson (Eds.), *The handbook of social psychology* (2nd ed.; Vol. 3). Reading, Mass.; Addison-Wesley, 1969.

McKinney, J. D. Developmental study of the acquisition and utilization of conceptual strategies. *Journal of Educational Psychology*, 1972, *63*, 22–31.

McKinney, J. D., Mason, J., Perkerson, K., & Clifford, M. Relationship between classroom behavior and academic achievement. *Journal of Educational Psychology*, 1975, *67*, 198–203.

McLaughlin, B. "Intentional" and "incidental" learning in human subjects. *Psychological Bulletin*, 1965, *63*, 359–376.

McNeill, D. *The acquisition of language*. New York: Harper and Row, 1970.

Mednick, S. A., & Freedman, J. L. Stimulus generalization. *Psychological Bulletin*, 1960, *57*, 169–200.

Meeker, M. N. *The structure of the intellect*. Columbus, Ohio: Merrill, 1969.

Melnick, G. I. A mechanism of transition of concrete to abstract cognitive processes. *Child Development*, 1973, *44*, 599–605.

Melnick, M. J., Lersten, K. C., & Lockhart, A. S. Retention of fast and slow learners following overlearning of a gross motor skill. *Journal of Motor Behavior*, 1972, *4*, 187–193.

Melton, A. W., & Von Lackum, W. J. Retroactive and proactive inhibition in retention: Evidence for a two-factor theory of retroactive inhibition. *American Journal of Psychology*, 1941, *54*, 157–173.

Messer, S. B. The relation of internal-external control to academic performance. *Child Development*, 1972, *43*, 1456–1462.

Miller, G. R., & Rokeach, M. Individual differences and tolerance for inconsistency. Ch. 60, pp. 624–632, in R. D. Abelson *et al.* (Eds.), *Theories of cognitive consistency: A sourcebook*. Chicago: Rand McNally, 1968.

Miller, N. E. Frustration aggression hypothesis. *Psychological Review*, 1941, *48*, 337–342.

Miller, N. E. Learning of visceral and glandular responses. *Science*, 1969, *163*, 434–443.

Miller, N. E. Interaction between learner and physical factors in mental illness. Ch. 34, pp. 460–476, in D. Shapiro *et al.* (Eds.), *Biofeedback and self-control 1972*. Chicago: Aldine, 1973.

Miller, N. E., & DiCara, L. V. Instrumental learning of heart rate changes in curarized rats: Shaping, and specificity to discriminative stimulus. *Journal of Comparative Physiological Psychology*, 1967, *63*, 12–19.

Miller, R. J. Cross-cultural research in the perception of pictorial materials. *Psychological Bulletin*, 1973, *80*, 135–150.

Mills, J. *Experimental social psychology*. New York: Macmillan, 1969.

Minard, R. D. Race relationships in the Pocahontas coal field. *Journal of Social Issues*, 1952, *8*, 29–44.

Minuchin, P. Correlates of curiosity and exploratory behavior in preschool children. *Child Development*, 1971, *42*, 939–950.

Mischel, W. Process in delay in gratification. Pp. 249–292 in L. Berkowitz (Ed.), *Advances in experimental social psychology*. New York: Academic Press, 1974.

Mischel, W. Cognitive appraisals and transformation in self-control. Pp. 33–50 in B. Weiner (Ed.), *Cognitive views of human motivation*. New York: Academic Press, 1974b.

Mischel, W., & Moore, B. Effects of attention to symbolically-presented rewards upon self-control. *Journal of Personality and Social Psychology*, 1973, 28, 172–179.

Mischel, W., & Staub, E. Effects of expectancy on working and waiting for larger rewards. *Journal of Personality and Social Psychology*, 1965, *2*, 625–633.

Montague, W. E., Adams, J. A., & Kiess, H. O. Forgetting and natural language mediation. *Journal of Experimental Psychology*, 1966, *72*, 829–833.

Montague, W. E., & Carter, J. E. Vividness of imagery in recalling connected discourse. *Journal of Educational Psychology*, 1973, *64*, 72–75.

Morganstern, K. P. Implosive therapy and flooding: A critical review. *Psychological Bulletin*, 1973, *79*, 318–334.

Morris, P., & Coady, H. The effect of need for approval and incentives upon children's probability learning responses. *Child Development*, 1974, *45*, 862–865.

Mowrer, O. H. *Learning theory and behavior*. New York: Wiley, 1960.

Murdock, B. B. *Human memory: Theory and data*. New York: Wiley, 1974.

Murray, H. A. *Explorations in personality*. New York: Oxford University Press, 1938.

Murray, J. P. Television and violence: Implication of the surgeon general's research program. *American Psychologist*, 1973, *28*, 472–478.

Murray, J. P. Social learning and cognitive development: Modeling effects on children's understanding of conservation. *British Journal of Psychology*, 1974, *65*, 151–160.

Myer, J. S. Associative and temporal determinants of facilitation and inhibition of attack by pain. *Journal of Comparative and Physiological Psychology*, 1968, *66*, 17–21.

Nachman, M., & Jones, D. R. Learned taste aversion over long delays in rats: The role of learned safety. *Journal of Comparative and Physiological Psychology*, 1974, *86*, 949–956.

Nakamura, C. Y., & Boroczi, G. Effect of relative incentive value on persistence and response speed. *Child Development*, 1965, 547–557.

National Institute of Education. Performance in school linked to birth weight. *Quarterly Newsletter of the National Institute of Education*, 1974, *1* (1, No. 2).

Neimark, E. D., & Estes, W. K. *Stimulus sampling theory.* San Francisco: Holden-Day, 1967.

Neisser, U. *Cognitive psychology.* New York: Appleton-Century-Crofts, 1967.

Nelson, D. L., Brooks, D. H., & Fosselman, J. R. Words as sets of features: Processing phonological cues. *Journal of Experimental Psychology*, 1972, *92*, 312.

Nelson, T. O., & Smith, E. E. Acquisition and forgetting of hierachically organized information in long-term memory. *Journal of Experimental Psychology*, 1972, *95*, 388–396.

Newell, A., Shaw, J. C., & Simon, H. A. Elements of a theory of human problem solving. *Psychological Review*, 1958, *65*, 151–166.

Newman, H. H., Freeman, F. N., & Holzinger, K. J. *Twins: A study of heredity and environment.* Chicago: University of Chicago Press, 1937.

Noll, V. L. Contextual dimensions in attitudes as a function of group-originating identities. *Sociological Focus*, 1975, *8*, 66–77.

Notz, W. W. Work motivation and the negative effects of extrinsic rewards. *American Psychologist*, 1975, *30*, 884–891.

Nunnally, J. C. & Lemond, L. C. Exploratory behavior and human development. Pp. 59–109 in *Advances in Child Development and Behavior.* Reese, H. W. (Ed.). New York: Academic Press, 1973, (Vol. 8).

Nuttin, J. M., Jr. *The illusion of attitude change.* New York: Academic Press, 1975.

Nuttin, J., & Greenwald, A. G. *Reward and punishment in human learning.* New York: Academic Press, 1968.

O'Dell, S. Training parents in behavior modification: A review. *Psychological Bulletin*, 1974, *81*, 418–433.

Office of Economic Opportunity. *An experiment in performance contracting: Summary of preliminary results.* Washington, D.C.: 1972a.

Office of Economic Opportunity. *A demonstration of incentives in education.* OEO Pamphlet 3400–7. Washington, D.C.: Author, 1972b.

Office of Economic Opportunity. *A demonstration of incentives in education.* OEO Pamphlet 3400–7. Washington, D.C.: 1972c.

O'Leary, K. D. Behavior modification in the classroom: A rejoinder to Winett and Winkler. Ch. 30 in C. M. Franks & G. T. Wilson (Eds.), *Annual review of behavior therapy*. New York: Bruner/Mazel, 1974.

O'Leary, K. D., & Drabman, R. Token reinforcement program in the classroom: A review. *Psychological Bulletin*, 1971, *75*, 379–398.

O'Neil, W. Our collective phonological illusions: Young and old. Pp. 111–116 in J. F. Kavanagh and I. G. Mattingley (Eds.), *Language by eye and ear*. Cambridge, Mass.: MIT Press, 1973.

Orme-Johnson, D. W. Autonomic stability and transcendental meditation. In N. E. Miller *et al.* (Eds.), *Biofeedback and self-control 1973*. New York: Aldine-Atherton, 1974.

Osgood, C. E. The similarity paradox in human learning: A resolution. *Psychological Review*, 1949, *56*, 132–143.

Overing, R. L. R., & Travers, R. M. W. Effect upon transfer of variations in training conditions. *Journal of Educational Psychology*, 1966, *57*, 179–188.

Overing, R. L. R., & Travers, R. M. W. Variation in the amount of irrelevant cues in training and test conditions and the effect upon transfer. *Journal of Educational Psychology*, 1967, *58*, 62–68.

Paige, J. M., & Simon, H. A. Cognitive processes in solving algebra word problems. Pp. 51–118 in B. Kleinmuntz (Ed.), *Problem solving*. New York: Wiley, 1966.

Paivio, A. Mental imagery in associative learning and memory. *Psychological Review*, 1969, *76*, 241–263.

Paivio, A., & Bleasdale, F. Short-term memory: A methodological caveat. *Canadian Journal of Psychology*, 1974, *28*, 24–31.

Paivio, A., & Rowe, E. J. Noun imagery, frequency, and meaningfulness in verbal discrimination. *Journal of Experimental Psychology*, 1970. *85*, 264–269.

Palermo, D. S., & Molfese, D. L. Language acquisition from age five onward. *Psychological Bulletin*, 1972, *78*, 409–428.

Palermo, D. S. Imagery in children's learning: Discussion. *Psychological Bulletin*, 1970, *73*, 415–421.

Parke, R. D. The role of punishment in the socialization process. Ch. 5, pp. 81–108, in R. A. Hoppe, G. A. Milton, and E. C. Simmel (Eds.), *Early experiences and the process of socialization*. New York: Academic Press, 1970.

Paul, G. L. *Insight vs. desensitization in psychotherapy*. Stanford, Calif.: Stanford University Press, 1966.

Paul, I. H. Impressions of personality, authoritarianism, and the *fait-accompli* effect. *Journal of Abnormal and Social Psychology*, 1956, *53*, 338–344.

Peeck, J. Retention of pictorial and verbal content of a text with illustrations. *Journal of Educational Psychology*, 1974, *66*, 880–888.

Penfield, W. Memory mechanisms. *Transactions of the American Neurological Association*, 1951, *76*, 15–31.

Penney, R. K. Reactive curiosity and manifest anxiety in children. *Child Development*, 1965, *36*, 697–702.

Perry, D. G., & Perry, L. C. Stimulus to violence in aggressive boys. *Child Development*, 1974, *45*, 55–62.

Peters, E. N. Nonexistent individual differences in reminiscence. *Psychological Bulletin*, 1973, *78*, 375–378.

Piaget, J. (tr. M. Gabain). *The moral judgment of the child*. Glencoe, Ill.: Free Press, 1932.

Piaget, J. (tr. M. Cook). *The origins of intelligence in infants*. New York: Norton, 1952.

Piaget, J. (tr. G. Gattegno and F. M. Hodgson). *The child's conception of number*. London: Routledge & Kegan Paul, 1952.

Piaget, J. (tr. M. Cook). *Construction of reality in the child*. New York: Basic Books, 1954.

Piaget, J. (tr. G. Gattegno and F. M. Hodgson). *Play, dreams, and imitation in childhood*. New York: Norton, 1962.

Piaget, J. (tr. M. Cook). *The origins of intelligence in children*. New York: Norton, 1963.

Piaget, J. (tr. Marjorie Gabain). *The child's conception of physical causality*. Totowa, N.J.: Littlefield, Adams, 1969.

Piaget, J. (tr. B. Walsh). *Biology and knowledge*. Chicago: University of Chicago Press, 1971.

Piaget, J., & Inhelder, B. (tr. P. A. Chilton). *Mental imagery in the child*. New York: Basic Books, 1971.

Piaget, J., & Inhelder B. (tr. A. J. Pomeraus). *Memory and intelligence*. New York: Basic Books, 1973.

Pihl, R. O., & Greenspoon, J. The effect of the amount of reinforcement on the formation of the reinforcing value of a verbal stimulus. *Canadian Journal of Psychology*, 1969, *23*, 219–226.

Pines, M. Cracking the mystery of memory: The race is on. *APA Monitor*, 1974, *5*, 8.

Pitts, C. E. (Ed.) *Operant conditioning in the classroom*. New York: Crowell, 1971.

Postman, L. Short-term memory and incidental learning. Pp. 145–201 in A. W. Melton (Ed.), *Categories of human learning*. New York: Academic Press, 1964.

Postman, L. Experimental analysis of learning to learn. *Psychology of Learning and Motivation*, 1969, *3*, 241–297.

Poulton, E. C. Tracking behavior. Ch. 8 in E. A. Bilodeau (Ed.), *Acquisition of skill*. New York: Academic Press, 1966.

Powers, W. T. *Behavior: The control of perception*. Chicago: Aldine, 1973.

Pubols, B. H. Incentive magnitude, learning and performance in animals. *Psychological Bulletin*, 1960, *57*, 89–115.

Pylyshyn, Z. W. What the mind's eye tells the mind's eye tells the mind's brain: A critique of mental imagery. *Psychological Bulletin*, 1973, *80*, 1-24.

Quay, L. C. Negro dialect and Binet performance in severely disadvantaged black four-year-olds. *Child Development*, 1972, *43*, 245–250.

Query, W. T., & Query, Joy M. Birth order: Urban-rural effects on need affiliation and school activity participation among male high school students. *Journal of Social Psychology*, 1973, *90*, 317–320.

Rabin, A. I. *Growing up in the kibbutz*. New York: Springer, 1965.

Rachman, S. Systematic desensitization. *Psychological Bulletin*, 1967, *67*, 93–103.

Ranson, S. W., & Clark, S. L. *Anatomy of the nervous system*. Philadelphia: Saunders, 1959.

Ray, O. S. Personality factors in motor learning and reminiscence. *Journal of Abnormal and Social Psychology*, 1959, *59*, 199–203.

Reese, H. W., & Parnes, S. J. Programming creative behavior. *Child Development*, 1970, *41*, 414–423.

Reppucci, N. D., & Saunders, J. T. Social psychology of behavior modification. *American Psychologist*, 1974, *29*, 649–660.

Richardson, A. Mental practice: A review and discussion. II. *Research Quarterly*, 1967, *38*, 263–273.

Richardson, L. F. *Statistics of deadly quarrels*. Pittsburgh: Boxwood Press, 1960.

Rieber, M. Delay of reward and discrimination learning in children. *Child Development*, 1964, *35*, 559–568.

Riklan, M., & Levita, E. *Subcortical correlates of human behavior*. Baltimore: Williams & Wilkins, 1969.

Rimland, B. Effectiveness of several methods of repetition of films. *Technical Report*, Special Devices Center, Office of Naval Research, 269–7–45, 1955.

Robbins, D., Bray, J. F., Irvin, J. R., & Wise, P. S. Memorial strategy and imagery: An interaction between instructions and rated imagery. *Journal of Experimental Psychology*, 1974, *102*, 706–709.

Robin, S. S., & Bosco, J. J. Ritalin for school children: The teachers' perspective. *Journal of School Health*, 1973, *43*, 624–628.

Rock, I. *Orientation and form*. New York: Academic Press, 1972.

Rokeach, M. Attitude change and behavioral change. *Public Opinion Quarterly*, 1967, *30*, 529–550.

Rokeach, M. *The nature of human values*. New York: Free Press, 1973.

Roschal, S. M. Effects of learner representations in film-mediated perceptual-motor learning. *Technical Report*, Special Devices Center, Office of Naval Research, 269–7–5, 1949.

Rose, R. M. Editorial: Testosterone and aggression in man. *Psychosomatic Medicine*, 1974, *36*, 467–468.

Rosekrans, M. A. Imitation in children as a function of perceived similarity to a social model and vicarious reinforcement. *Journal of Personality and Social Psychology*, 1967, *7*, 307–315.

Rosenfeld, H. M., & Baer, D. M. Unnoticed verbal conditioning of an aware experimenter by a more aware subject. *Psychological Review*, 1969, *76*, 435–432.

Rosenshine, B., & Furst, N. The use of direct observation to study teaching. Ch. 5 in R. M. W. Travers (Ed.), *Second handbook of research on teaching*. Chicago: Rand McNally, 1973.

Rosenzweig, M. R., Bennett, E. L., & Diamond, M. C. Brain changes in response to experience. *Scientific American*, 1972, *26*, 23–29.

Rotter, J. B. Generalized expectancies for internal versus external control of reinforcement. *Psychological Monographs*, 1966, *80* (Whole No. 609).

Roughead, W. G., & Scandura, J. M. What is ' learned' in mathematical discovery. *Journal of Educational Psychology*, 1968, *59*, 283–289.

Rozeboom, W. W. The learning tradition. Ch. 11 in E. C. Carterette and M. P. Friedman (Eds.), *Handbook of perception* (Vol. 1). New York: Academic Press, 1974.

Rubin, K. H., & Schneider, F. W. Egocentricism and altruistic behavior. *Child Development*, 1973, *44*, 661–665.

Rule, B. G. The hostile and instrumental functions of human aggression. In W. W. Hartup and J. de Wit (Eds.), *Determinants and origins of aggressive behavior*. The Hague: Mouton, 1974.

Rutter, Michael. *Maternal deprivation reassessed*. Baltimore: Penguin Books, 1972.

Ryan, T. J., & Watson, P. Frustrative nonreward theory applied to children's behavior. *Psychological Bulletin*, 1968, *69*, 111–125.

Rylyshyn, Z. W. What the mind's eye tells the mind's brain: A critique of mental imagery. *Psychological Bulletin*, 1973, *80*, 1–24.

Salama, A. A., & Hunt, J. McV. Fixation in the rat as a function of infantile shocking, handling and gentling. *Journal of Genetic Psychology*, 1964, *105*, 131–162.

Saltz, E. Manifest anxiety: Have we misread the data. *Psychological Review*, 1970, *77*, 568–573.

Sameroff, A. J. Learning and adaptation in infancy. Pp. 169–214 in H. W. Reese (Ed.), *Advances in child development and behavior*. New York: Academic Press, 1972.

Samuels, S. J., & Dahl, P. R. Establishing appropriate purpose for reading and its effect on reading rate. *Journal of Educational Psychology*, 1975, *67*, 38–43.

Sanders, A. F. *Attention and performance*. Proceedings of a Symposium held at Driebergen, August 17–20, 1966, under the auspices of the Institute for Perception RVO-TNO, Svesterberg, The Netherlands. Amsterdam: North Holland, 1967.

Sasson, R. Y., & Fraisse, P. Images in memory for concrete and abstract sentences. *Journal of Experimental Psychology*, 1972, *94*, 149–155.

Savin, H. B. What the child knows about speech when he starts to learn to read. Pp. 319–326 in J. H. Kavanagh and I. G. Mattingley (Eds.), *Language by ear and eye*. Cambridge, Mass.: MIT Press, 1973.

Scandara, J. M. Role of higher order rules in problem solving. *Journal of Experimental Psychology*, 1974, *102*, 984–991.

Schaar, K. Crowding: What's bad for rats may be OK for humans. *APA Monitor*, 1975, *6*, 7.

Schmeck, R. R., & Anderson, V. Error produced frustration: Additional data. *Perceptual and Motor Skills*, 1974, *38*, 1012.

Schrier, A. M., Harlow, H. F., & Stollnitz, F. *Behavior of nonhuman primates: Modern research trends.* New York: Academic Press, 1965.

Schwartz, G. E. Biofeedback as therapy: Some theoretical and practical issues. *American Psychologist,* 1973, *28,* 666–682.

Scott, J. P. *Early experience and the organization of behavior.* Belmont, Calif.: Brooks/Cole, 1968.

Scull, J. W. The Amsel frustration effect: Interpretation and research. *Psychological Bulletin,* 1973, *79,* 352–361.

Sears, R. R. Relation of early socialization experiences to self-concepts and gender role in middle childhood. *Child Development,* 1970, *41,* 267–289.

Sears, R. R., Maccoby, E. E., & Levin, H. *Patterns of child rearing.* New York: Harper & Row, 1957.

Shaffer, R. W., & Howard, J. The transfer of information across sensory modality. *Perception and Psychophysics,* 1974, *15,* 344–348.

Shapiro, D., & Schwartz, G. E. Biofeedback and visceral learning: Clinical application. Ch. 35, pp. 477–491, in D. Shapiro *et al.* (Eds.), *Biofeedback and self-control 1972.* Chicago: Aldine, 1973.

Shea, M. Formulation of a generalization surface for the simultaneous variation of stimulus and response similarity. *Journal of Experimental Psychology,* 1969, *80,* 353–358.

Shephard, R. N. Recognition memory for words, sentences, and pictures. *Journal of Verbal Learning and Verbal Behavior,* 1967, *6,* 156–163.

Shuell, T. J. Clustering and organization in free recall. *Psychological Bulletin,* 1969, *72,* 353–374.

Shuell, T. J., & Keppel, G. Learning ability and retention. *Journal of Educational Psychology,* 1970, *61,* 59–65.

Siegel, S. The physiology of conditioning. Pt. VI, pp. 367–415, in M. H. Marx (Ed.), *Learning interaction.* New York: Macmillan, 1970.

Simons, H. W., Berkowitz, N. N., & Moyer, R. J. Similarity, credibility, and attitude change. *Psychological Bulletin,* 1970, *73,* 1–16.

Singer, J. L. (Ed.) *The control of aggression and violence.* New York: Academic Press, 1971.

Skinner, B. F. *The behavior of organisms.* New York; Appleton-Century-Crofts, 1938.

Skinner, B. F. *Science and human behavior.* New York: Macmillan, 1953.

Skinner, B. F. *Verbal behavior.* New York: Appleton-Century-Crofts, 1957.

Skinner, B. F. The steep and thorny way to a science of behavior. *American Psychologist,* 1975, *30,* 42–59.

Sloan, L. R., Love, R. F., & Ostram, T. M. Political heckling: Who really loses. *Journal of Personality and Social Psychology.* 1974, *30,* 518–525.

Smith, C. P. (Ed.) *Achievement-related motives in children.* New York: Russell Sage Foundation, 1969.

Smith, J. C. Meditation as psychotherapy: A review of the literature. *Psychological Bulletin,* 1975, *82,* 558–564.

Smith, L. T. The interanimal transfer phenomenon. *Psychological Bulletin*, 1974, *81*, 1078–1095.

Smith, M. E. An investigation of the study of the development of the sentence and the extent of the vocabulary in young children, *University of Iowa Studies of Child Welfare*, 1926, *3* (No. 5).

Smith, S. G., & Smith, W. M. Auto-shaping: A three-manipulanda technique for dogs. *Psychological Record*, 1972, *22*, 377–380.

Snodgrass, J. G., & Antone, G. Parallel versus sequential processing of pictures and words. *Journal of Experimental Psychology*, 1974, *103*, 139–144.

Snow, C. E. Mother's speech to children learning language. *Child Development*, 1972, *43*, 549–565.

Solley, C. M., & Murphy, G. *Development of the perceptual world.* New York: Basic Books, 1960.

Solomon, R. L. Punishment. *American Psychologist*, 1964, *19*, 239–253.

Solomon, R. L., & Wynne, L. S. Traumatic avoidance learning: Acquisition in normal dogs. *Psychological Monographs*, 1953, *67* (No. 354), 1–19.

Spear, P. S. Motivational effects of praise and criticism on children's learning. *Developmental Psychology*, 1970, *3*, 124–132.

Spector, A., Laughery, K. R., & Finkelman, D. G. Rehearsal and organization in intentional forgetting. *Journal of Experimental Psychology*, 1973, *98*, 169–174.

Spence, K. W. *Behavior theory and conditioning.* New Haven: Yale University Press, 1956.

Sperling, G. The information available in brief visual presentations. *Psychological Monographs*, 1960, *74* (No. 498).

Spitz, R. A. Hospitalism: An inquiry into the genesis of psychiatric conditions in early childhood. *Psychoanalytic Study of the Child*, 1945, *1*, 53–74.

Staats, A. W. *Learning, language, and cognition.* New York: Holt, Rinehart & Winston, 1968.

Start, K. B. Kinaesthesis and mental practice. *Research Quarterly*, 1964b, *35*, 316–320.

Stein, A. H., & Bailey, M. M. The socialization of achievement orientation in females. *Psychological Bulletin*, 1973, *80*, 345–367.

Stein, M. I. *Stimulating creativity.* New York: Academic Press, 1974.

Stein, Z., & Susser, M. Mutability of intelligence and epidemiology of mild mental retardation. *Review of Educational Research*, 1970, *40*, 29–85.

Steiner, I. D. *Group process and productivity.* New York: Academic Press, 1972.

Sternbach, R. A. *Pain: A psychophysiological analysis.* New York: Academic Press, 1968.

Sternberg, R. J., & Bower, G. H. Transfer in part-whole and whole-part free recall: A comparative evaluation of theories. *Journal of Verbal Learning and Verbal Behavior*, 1974, *13*, 1–26.

Stewart, K. L. On "socializing attitudes". A symbolic interactionist view. *Sociological Focus*, 1975, *8*, 37–45.

Stewart, M. L. *The process of motor coordination in the human infant.* Kalamazoo,

Michigan: Western Michigan University, College of Education, 1974.

Stone, L. J., Smith, H. T., & Murphy, L. Editor's introduction. The capabilities of the newborn. Pp. 239–256 in *The competent infant*. New York. Basic Books, 1973.

Stone, L. J., Smith, H. T., & Murphy, L. Editor's introduction: Early experience, deprivation and enrichment. Pp. 753–774 in *The competent infant*. New York: Basic Books, 1973.

Stone, L. J., Smith, H. T., & Murphy, L. Editor's introduction. The social infant. Pp. 983–1014 in *The competent infant*. New York: Basic Books, 1973.

Stones, E., & Heslop, J. R. The formation and extension of class concepts in primary school children. *British Journal of Educational Psychology*, 1968, *38*, 261–271.

Strike, K. A. Behavioristic language. *American Educational Research Journal*, 1974, *11*, 103–120.

Stunkard, A. New therapies for eating disorders. Ch. 36, pp. 391–412, in N. E. Miller *et al.* (Eds.), *Biofeedback and self-control*. Chicago: Aldine-Atherton, 1974.

Sturges, P. T. Information delay and retention: Effect of information in feedback and tests. *Journal of Educational Psychology*, 1972, *63*, 32–43.

Surgeon General's Scientific Advisory Committee on Television in Social Behavior. *Televison and growing up: The impact of televised violence*. Washington, D.C.: U.S. Public Health Service, 1972.

Sutherland, N. S. Object recognition. Ch. 8, pp. 157–185, in E. C. Carterette and M. P. Friedman (Eds.), *Handbook of perception* (Vol. 3). New York: Academic Press, 1973.

Swift, M. S., & Spivach, G. *Alternative teaching strategies*. Champaign, Ill.: Research Press, 1974.

Tarpy, R. M., & Sawabini, F. L. Reinforcement delay: A selective review of the last decade. *Psychological Bulletin*, 1974, *81*, 984–997.

Taylor, S. E. On inferring one's attitudes from one's behavior: Some delimiting conditions. *Journal of Personality and Social Psychology*, 1975, *31*, 126–131.

Tedeschi, T. T., Smith, R. B., & Brown, R. C. The reinterpretation of research on aggression. *Psychological Bulletin*, 1974, *81*, 540–562.

Teng, E. L., & Sperry, R. W. Interhemispheric interaction during simultaneous bilateral presentation of letters or digits in comisuratomized patients. *Neuropsychologia*, 1973, *11*, 131–140.

Thomas, H. Visual-fixation responses of infants to stimuli of varying complexity. *Child Development*, 1965, *36*, 629–638.

Thomas, S., Brookover, W. B., Lapere, J. M., Hamacheck, D. E., & Erickson, E. L. An experiment to modify self-concept and school performance. *Sociological Focus on Education*, 1969, *3*, 55–67.

Thorndike, E. L. *Fundamentals of learning*. New York: Teachers College, Columbia University, 1932.

Thorndike, E. L. *The psychology of wants, interests, and attitudes*. New York: Appleton-Century-Crofts, 1935.

Thornton, J. W., & Jacobs, P. D. Learned helplessness and human subjects. *Journal of Experimental Psychology*, 1971, *87*, 367–372.

Toppen, J. T. Money reinforcement and human operant (work) behavior: II. Within-subject comparisons. *Perceptual and Motor Skills*, 1965, *20*, 1193–1199.

Trabasso, T., & Bower, G. H. *Attention in learning.* New York: Wiley, 1968.

Travers, R. M. W. *A study of the advantages and disadvantages of using simplified visual presentations in instructional materials.* Final Report on Grant No. OEG-1-7-070144-5235, U.S. Office of Education, 1969.

Travers, R. M. W. *Man's information system.* San Francisco: Chandler, 1970.

Travers, R. M. W., & Alvarado, V. The design of pictures for children in elementary school. *AV Communication Review*, 1970, *18*, 47–64.

Travers, R. M. W. Age and levels of picture interpretation. *Perceptual and Motor Skills*, 1973, *36*, 210.

Trotter, S. Patuxent: 'Therapeutic' prison faces test. *APA Monitor*, 1975, *6*, 1, 5, 11.

Tulving, E. Subjective organization and effect on repetition in multitrial free-recall learning. *Journal of Verbal Learning and Verbal Behavior*, 1966, *5*, 193–197.

Tulving, E. The effects of presentation and recall of material in free-recall learning. *Journal of Verbal Learning and Verbal Behavior*, 1967, *6*, 175–184.

Tulving, E. Theoretical issues in free recall. In T. R. Dixon and D. L. Horton (Eds.), *Verbal behavior and general behavior theory.* Englewood Cliffs, N.J.: Prentice-Hall, 1968.

Tulving, E. Episodic and semantic memory. In E. Tulving and W. Donaldson (Eds.) *Organization and memory.* New York: Academic Press, 1972.

Tulving, E., & Osler, S. Transfer effects in whole-part free-recall learning. *Canadian Journal of Psychology*, 1967, *21*, 253–262.

Tulving, E., & Thomason, D. M. Encoding specifity and retrieval processes in episodic memory. *Psychological Review*, 1973, *80*, 352–373.

Tulving, E., & Watkins, M. J. Structure of memory traces. *Psychological Review*, 1975, *82*, 261–275.

Turner, L. H., & Solomon, R. L. Human traumatic avoidance learning, *Psychological Monographs*, 1962, *76* (No. 559), 1–32.

Tversky, B., & Sherman, T. Picture memory improves with longer on time and off time. *Journal of Experimental Psychology: Human Learning and Memory*, 1975, *104*, 114–118.

Tyler, L. A. Design for a hopeful psychology. *American Psychologist*, 1973, *28*, 1021–1029.

Ulrich, R. E. A behavioral view of Sesame Street. *Educational Broadcasting Review*, 1970, *4*, 17–22.

Ulrich, R. E., Hutchinson, R. R., & Azrin, N. H. Pain-elicited aggression. *Psychological Record*, 1965, *15*, 111–126.

Underwood, B. J. Associative transfer in verbal learning as a function of response similarity and degree of first-list learning. *Journal of Experimental Psychology*, 1951, *42*, 44–53.

Underwood, B. J. Attributes of memory. *Psychological Review*, 1969, *76*, 559–573.

U.S. Department of Health, Education and Welfare. *Minimal brain dysfunction in children*. Public Health Service Publication No. 1415, 1966.

U.S. Department of Health, Education and Welfare. *Minimal brain dysfunction in children*. Public Health Service Publication No. 2015, Washington, D.C., 1969.

Vacchiano, R. B., Strauss, P. S., & Hochman, L. The open and closed mind. *Psychological Bulletin*, 1969, *71*, 261–273.

Valenstein, E. S. The anatomical locus of reinforcement. Pp. 149–190 in E. Stellar and J. M. Sprague (Eds.), *Progress in physiological psychology* (Vol. 1). New York: Academic Press, 1966.

Valenstein, E. S., Cox, V. C., & Kalolewski, J. W. Reexamination of the role of the hypothalamus in motivation. *Psychological Review*, 1970, *77*, 16–31.

Van Duyne, P. C. Realism and linguistic complexity in reasoning. *British Journal of Psychology*, 1974, *65*, 59–67.

Van Wagenen, R. K., & Murdock, E. E. A transistorized single-package for toilet training of infants. *Journal of Experimental Child Psychology*, 1966, *3*, 312–314.

Von Senden, M. (tr. Peter Heath) *Space and sight*. Glencoe, Illinois: Free Press, 1961.

Wallace, R. K., & Benson, H. The physiology of meditation. Ch. 28, pp. 353–364, in D. Shapiro *et al.* (Eds.), *Biofeedback and self-control 1972*. Chicago: Aldine, 1973.

Wallen, N. R., & Travers, R. M. W. Analysis and investigation of teaching methods. Ch. 10 in N. L. Gage (Ed.), *Handbook of research on teaching*. Chicago: Rand McNally, 1963.

Walls, R. T. Delay of reinforcement development. *Child Development*, 1973, *44*, 689–692.

Walls, R. T., & Smith, T. S. Development of preference for delayed reinforcement in disadvantaged children. *Journal of Educational Psychology*, 1970, *61*, 118–123.

Ward, L. B. Reminiscence and rote learning. *Psychological Monographs*, 1937, *49* (No. 220).

Warden, C. J. The distribution of practice in animal learning. *Comparative Psychological Monographs*, 1923, *1* (No. 3).

Warren, N. African infant precocity. *Psychological Bulletin*, 1972, *78*, 353–367.

Warren, N. Malnutrition and mental development. *Psychological Bulletin*, 1973, *80*, 324–328.

Warren, R. M. Verbal transformation effect and auditory perceptual mechanisms. *Psychological Bulletin*, 1968, *70*, 261–270.

Watkins, M. J. Concept and measurement of primary memory. *Psychological Bulletin*, 1974, *81*, 695–711.

Watkins, M. J., & Tulving, E. Episodic memory: When recognition fails. *Journal of Experimental Psychology: General*, 1975, *104*, 5–29.

Watkins, M. J., & Tulving, E. Recall and recognition: A reply to Light, Kimble, and Pellegrino. *Journal of Experimental Psychology: General*, 1975, *104*, 37–39.

Watson, J. B. *Behaviorism*. New York: People's Institute, 1924.

Webb, R. A., Massar, B., & Nadolny, T. Information and strategy in the young child's search for hidden objects. *Child Development*, 1972, *43*, 91–104.

Weberford, M. J., & Cohen, L. B. Developmental changes in infant visual preferences for novelty and familiarity. *Child Development*, 1973, *44*, 416–424.

Wei, T. T. D., Lavatelli, C. B., & Jones, R. S. Piaget's concept of classification: A comparative study of socially disadvantaged and middle class young children. *Child Development*, 1971, *42*, 919–927.

Weigel, R. H., Vernon, D. T. A., & Tognacci, L. N. Specificity of the attitude as a determinant of attitude—behavior congruence. *Journal of Personality and Social Psychology*, 1974, *30*, 724–728.

Weinberg, M. *Desegregation research: An appraisal.* Bloomington, Ind.: Phi Delta Kappa, 1970.

Weiner, B. (Ed.) *Cognitive views of human motivation.* New York: Academic Press, 1974.

Weininger, D. Mortality of albino rats under stress as a function of early handling. *Canadian Journal of Psychology*, 1953, *7*, 111–114.

Weininger, O. Effects of parental deprivation: An overview of literature and report on some current research. *Psychological Reports*, 1972, *30*, 591–612.

Weiss, R. F., Boyer, J. L., Colwick, J. T., & Moran, D. J. A delay of reinforcement gradient and correlated reinforcement in the instrumental conditioning of conversational behavior. *Journal of Experimental Psychology*, 1971, *90*, 33–38.

Welch, M. J. Infants visual attention to varying degrees of novelty. *Child Development*, 1974, *45*, 344–350.

Werner, H. The concept of development from a comparative and organismic point of view. In D. B. Harris (Ed.), *The concept of development.* Minneapolis: University of Minnesota Press, 1957.

West, L. J. Vision and kinesthesis in the acquisition of typewriting skill. *Journal of Applied Psychology*, 1967, *51*, 161–166.

West, L. J. *Acquisition of Typewriting Skills.* New York: Pitman, 1969.

West, L. J. Implications of research for teaching typewriting. *Delta Pi Epsilon Bulletin*, No. 4. St. Peter, Minn.: Gustavus Adolphus College, 1974.

Wexler, D. B. Token and taboo: Behavior modification, token economies and law. Ch. 13 in C. M. Franks & G. T. Wilson (Eds.), *Annual review of behavior therapy* (Vol. 2). New York: Bruner/Mazel 1974.

Wheeler, R., & Ryan, F. L. Effects of cooperative and competitive classroom environments on the attitudes and achievement of elementary school students engaged in social studies inquiry activities. *Journal of Educational Psychology*, 1973, *65*, 402–407.

White, R. K., & Lippitt, R. *Autocracy and democracy.* New York: Harper & Row, 1960.

Wickelgren, W. A. The long and short of memory. *Psychological Bulletin*, 1973, *80*, 425–437.

Wickens, C. D. Temporal limits of human information processing: A developmental study. *Psychological Bulletin*, 1974, *81*, 739–755.

Wicklund, R. A. *Freedom and reactance.* New York: Wiley, 1974.

Wilkins, W. Desensitization: Social and cognitive factors underlying the effectiveness of Wolpe's procedure. *Psychological Bulletin*, 1971, *76*, 311–317.

Wilkins, W. Desensitization: Getting it together with Davison and Wilson. *Psychological Bulletin*, 1972, *78*, 32–36.

Wilson, G. T., & Davison, G. C. Process of fear reduction in systematic desensitization: Animal studies. *Psychological Bulletin*, 1971, *76*, 1–14.

Winchel, R., Fenner, D., & Shaver, P. Impact of coeducation on "fear of success" imagery expressed by male and female high school students. *Journal of Educational Psychology*, 1974, *66*, 726–730.

Wine, J. Test anxiety and direction of attention. *Psychological Bulletin*, 1971, *76*, 92–105.

Winer, G. A. Conservation of different quantities among preschool children. *Child Development*, 1974, *45*, 839–842.

Winett, R. A., & Winkler, R. C. Current behavior modification in the classroom: Be still, be quiet, be docile. Ch. 29 in C. M. Franks & G. T. Wilson (Eds.), *Annual review of behavior therapy*. New York: Bruner/Mazel, 1974.

Wittrock, M. C. Verbal stimuli in concept formation: Learning by discovery. *Journal of Educational Psychology*, 1963, *54*, 183–190.

Wittrock, M. C. The learning by discovery hypothesis. Pp. 33–75 in L. S. Shulman & E. R. Keislar (Eds.), *Learning by discovery*, Chicago: Rand McNally, 1966.

Wohlwill, J. F. Amount of stimulus exploration and preference as differential functions of stimulus complexity. *Perception and Psychophysics*, 1968, *4*, 307–312.

Wolfe, J. B. Effectiveness of token rewards for chimpanzees. *Comparative Psychological Monographs*, 1936, *12* (Serial No. 60), 72.

Wolford, G. L., Wessel, D. L., & Estes, W. K. Further evidence concerning scanning and sampling assumptions of visual detection models. *Perception and Psychophysics*, 1968, *3*, 439–44.

Wolpe, J. *Psychotherapy by reciprocal inhibition*. Stanford, Calif.: Stanford University Press, 1958.

Woodburne, L. S. *The neural basis of behavior*. Columbus, Ohio: Merrill, 1967.

Woodrow, H. The effect of type of training upon transference. *Journal of Educational Psychology*, 1927, *18*, 159–172.

Woodruff, A. D. The use of concepts in teaching and learning. *Journal of Teacher Education*, 1964, *15*, 81–99.

Woods, P. J. A taxonomy of instrumental conditioning. *American Psychologist*, 1974, *29*, 584–597.

Woodworth, R. S. *Dynamics of behavior*. New York: Holt, Rinehart & Winston, 1958.

Worthen, B. R. Discovery and expository task presentation in elementary mathematics. *Journal of Educational Psychology, Monograph Supplement*, 1968, *59* (1, Pt. 2), 1–13.

Yarbus, A. L. *Eye movements and vision*. New York: Plenum Press, 1967.

Yaroush, R., Sullivan, M. T., & Ekstrand, B. R. Effect of sleep on memory. II. Differential effect of the first and second half of the night. *Journal of Experimental Psychology*, 1971, *88*, 361–366.

Yonas, A., & Pittenger, J. Searching for many targets: An analysis of speed and accuracy. *Perception and Psychophysics*, 1973, *13*, 513–516.

Zaidel, E., & Sperry, R. W. Performance on the Raven's Colored Progressive Matrices Test by subjects with commisurotomy. *Cortex*, 1973, *9*, 34–39.

Zajonc, R. B. *Social psychology: An experimental approach*. Belmont, Calif.: Brooks/Cole, 1966.

Zigler, E. Learning, development, and social class in the socialization process. Pp. 193–287 in M. H. Marx (Ed.), *Learning interactions*. New York: Macmillan, 1970.

Zimbardo, P. G., Weisenberg, M., & Firestone, I. Communicator effectiveness in producing public conformity and private attitude change. *Journal of Personality*, 1965, *33*, 233–256.

Zimmerman, B. J., & Dialessi, F. Modeling influences on children's creative behavior. *Journal of Educational Psychology*, 1973, *65*, 127–134.

Zimmerman, J., & Kimble, G. A. Effects of incentive and false recognition. *Journal of Experimental Psychology*, 1973, *97*, 264–266.

Zimmerman, M., & Hockberg, J. E. Pictorial recognition in the infant monkey. Cited in J. M. Kennedy, *A psychology of picture perception*. Washington, D.C.: Jossey-Bass, 1974.

Zoll, E. J. Research in programmed instruction in mathematics. *Mathematics Teacher*, 1969, *62*, 103–110.

Zubek, J. P. *Sensory deprivation*. New York: Appleton-Century-Crofts, 1969.

INDEX OF NAMES

McClelland, D. C., 360, 364, 367, 368, 585
McClure, C. M., 139, 585
McCormack, P. D., 279, 585
McFarlane, J., 220, 221
McFarlane, P. T., 567
McGrew, W. C., 542, 585
McGuire, W. J., 493, 494, 513, 515, 516, 518, 520, 521, 585
McGurk, H., 337, 580
McIntyre, L. J., 411, 581
McKeachie, W. J., 363, 559, 577
McKinney, J. D., 81, 585
McLaughlin, B., 326, 585
McLean, J. D., 574
McMahon, M. L., 289, 570
McMillan, J. H., 477, 577
McNeill, D., 208, 269, 570, 585
Mednick, S. A., 388, 585
Meeker, M. N., 449, 585
Melnick, G. I., 117, 186, 585
Melnick, M. J., 585
Melton, A. W., 398, 585
Menlove, F. L., 53, 567
Messer, S. B., 381, 585
Miller, G. R., 516, 517, 585
Miller, N., 374, 520, 581
Miller, N. E., 18, 131, 136, 540, 573, 586
Miller, R. J., 336, 586
Mills, J., 535, 586
Minard, R. D., 507, 586
Minuchin, P., 374, 586
Mischel, W., 352, 353, 586
Molfese, D. L., 215, 588
Molloy, G. N., 316, 572
Montague, W. E., 284, 586
Moore, B., 353, 586
Moore, B. R., 580
Moran, D. J., 597
Morgan, R. F., 577
Morganstern, K. P., 99, 586
Morris, P., 371, 586
Mowrer, O. H., 57, 59, 352, 540, 573, 586
Moyer, R. J., 511, 592
Murdock, B. B., 268, 270, 280, 586
Murdock, E. E., 48, 596
Murphy, G., 309, 333, 593
Murphy, L., 26, 228, 327, 531, 570, 594
Murray, H. A., 359, 360, 368, 383, 384, 586
Murray, J. P., 533, 534, 548, 549, 586, 587

Murray, J. R., 574
Myer, J. S., 87, 587

N

Nachman, M., 87, 587
Nadolny, T., 169, 596
Nagy, A. N., 576
Nakamura, C. Y., 90, 587
Natale, G. M., 120, 578
Neale, J. M., 548, 583
Neimark, E. D., 318, 587
Neisser, U., 314, 317, 587
Nelson, D. L., 270, 587
Nelson, T. O., 274, 587
Neumann, E., 566
Newell, A., 471, 472, 587
Newman, A. P., 217, 575
Newman, H. H., 234, 587
Newton, I., 5
Nilsson, N., 434, 435, 566
Noll, V. L., 509, 587
Notz, W. W., 381, 587
Nunnally, J. C., 373, 587
Nuttin, J. M., Jr., 504, 587
Nuttin, J., 48, 587

O

O'Dell, S., 85, 587
Office of Economic Opportunity, 83, 587
O'Leary, K. D., 77, 78, 80, 588
O'Neil, W., 338, 588
Opollot, J. A., 289, 583
O'Reilly, P. A., 413, 575
Orme-Johnson, D. W., 588
Osgood, C. E., 394, 395, 396, 399, 402, 404, 417, 588
Osler, S., 401, 595
Ostram, T. M., 512, 592
Overing, R. L. R., 404, 405, 588

P

Paige, J. M., 472, 588
Paivio, A., 271, 291, 588
Palermo, D. S., 215, 291, 357, 571, 588
Pankove, E., 450, 483, 582
Parente, F. J., 281, 574
Parke, R. D., 547, 588
Parker, J. F. Jr., 114, 115, 575
Parnes, S. J., 483, 590
Parrott, G. L., 484, 580